OLE DB and ODBC
Developer's Guide

OLE DB and ODBC
Developer's Guide

Chuck Wood

M&T Books
An imprint of IDG Books Worldwide, Inc.

Foster City, CA ◆ Chicago, IL ◆ Indianapolis, IN ◆ New York, NY

OLE DB and ODBC Developer's Guide

M&T Books
An imprint of IDG Books Worldwide, Inc.
919 E. Hillsdale Blvd., Suite 400
Foster City, CA 94404
www.idgbooks.com (IDG Books Worldwide Web site)

ISBN: 0-7645-3308-8

Printed in the United States of America

10 9 8 7 6 5 4 3 2 1

1B/QZ/QZ/ZZ/FC

Distributed in the United States by IDG Books Worldwide, Inc.

Distributed by Macmillan Canada for Canada; by Transworld Publishers Limited in the United Kingdom; by IDG Norge Books for Norway; by IDG Sweden Books for Sweden; by Woodslane Pty. Ltd. for Australia; by Woodslane (NZ) Ltd. for New Zealand; by Addison Wesley Longman Singapore Pte Ltd. for Singapore, Malaysia, Thailand, and Indonesia; by Norma Comunicaciones S.A. for Colombia; by Intersoft for South Africa; by International Thomson Publishing for Germany, Austria and Switzerland; by Distribuidora Cuspide for Argentina; by LR International for Brazil; by Galileo Libros for Chile; by Ediciencia S.A. for Ecuador; by Ediciones ZETA S.C.R. Ltda. for Peru; by WS Computer Publishing Corporation, Inc., for the Philippines; by Contemporanea de Ediciones for Venezuela; by Express Computer Distributors for the Caribbean and West Indies; by Micronesia Media Distributor, Inc. for Micronesia; by Grupo Editorial Norma S.A. for Guatemala; by Chips Computadoras S.A. de C.V. for Mexico; by Editorial Norma de Panama S.A. for Panama; by Wouters Import for Belgium; by American Bookshops for Finland. Authorized Sales Agent: Anthony Rudkin Associates for the Middle East and North Africa.

For general information on IDG Books Worldwide's books in the U.S., please call our Consumer Customer Service department at 800-762-2974. For reseller information, including discounts and premium sales, please call our Reseller Customer Service department at 800-434-3422.

For information on where to purchase IDG Books Worldwide's books outside the U.S., please contact our International Sales department at 317-596-5530 or fax 317-596-5692.

For consumer information on foreign language translations, please contact our Customer Service department at 800-434-3422, fax 317-596-5692, or e-mail rights@idgbooks.com.

For information on licensing foreign or domestic rights, please phone +1-650-655-3109.

For sales inquiries and special prices for bulk quantities, please contact our Sales department at 650-655-3200 or write to the address above.

For information on using IDG Books Worldwide's books in the classroom or for ordering examination copies, please contact our Educational Sales department at 800-434-2086 or fax 317-596-5499.

For press review copies, author interviews, or other publicity information, please contact our Public Relations department at 650-655-3000 or fax 650-655-3299.

For authorization to photocopy items for corporate, personal, or educational use, please contact Copyright Clearance Center, 222 Rosewood Drive, Danvers, MA 01923, or fax 978-750-4470.

Library of Congress Cataloging-in-Publication Data

Wood, Chuck, 1963-

OLE DB and ODBC Developer's Guide / Chuck Wood.

    p.   cm.

ISBN 0-7645-3308-8 (alk. paper)

1. C++ (Computer program language)
2. Database design.   3. Microsoft Visual C++.
I. Title

QA76.73.C153W65   1999

005.26'8--DC21   99-16045
                                                  CIP

 is a registered trademark under exclusive license to IDG Books Worldwide, Inc., from International Data Group, Inc.

ABOUT IDG BOOKS WORLDWIDE

Welcome to the world of IDG Books Worldwide.

IDG Books Worldwide, Inc., is a subsidiary of International Data Group, the world's largest publisher of computer-related information and the leading global provider of information services on information technology. IDG was founded more than 30 years ago by Patrick J. McGovern and now employs more than 9,000 people worldwide. IDG publishes more than 290 computer publications in over 75 countries. More than 90 million people read one or more IDG publications each month.

Launched in 1990, IDG Books Worldwide is today the #1 publisher of best-selling computer books in the United States. We are proud to have received eight awards from the Computer Press Association in recognition of editorial excellence and three from Computer Currents' First Annual Readers' Choice Awards. Our best-selling ...*For Dummies*® series has more than 50 million copies in print with translations in 31 languages. IDG Books Worldwide, through a joint venture with IDG's Hi-Tech Beijing, became the first U.S. publisher to publish a computer book in the People's Republic of China. In record time, IDG Books Worldwide has become the first choice for millions of readers around the world who want to learn how to better manage their businesses.

Our mission is simple: Every one of our books is designed to bring extra value and skill-building instructions to the reader. Our books are written by experts who understand and care about our readers. The knowledge base of our editorial staff comes from years of experience in publishing, education, and journalism — experience we use to produce books to carry us into the new millennium. In short, we care about books, so we attract the best people. We devote special attention to details such as audience, interior design, use of icons, and illustrations. And because we use an efficient process of authoring, editing, and desktop publishing our books electronically, we can spend more time ensuring superior content and less time on the technicalities of making books.

You can count on our commitment to deliver high-quality books at competitive prices on topics you want to read about. At IDG Books Worldwide, we continue in the IDG tradition of delivering quality for more than 30 years. You'll find no better book on a subject than one from IDG Books Worldwide.

John Kilcullen
Chairman and CEO
IDG Books Worldwide, Inc.

Steven Berkowitz
President and Publisher
IDG Books Worldwide, Inc.

Eighth Annual
Computer Press
Awards ≥1992

Ninth Annual
Computer Press
Awards ≥1993

Tenth Annual
Computer Press
Awards ≥1994

Eleventh Annual
Computer Press
Awards ≥1995

IDG is the world's leading IT media, research and exposition company. Founded in 1964, IDG had 1997 revenues of $2.05 billion and has more than 9,000 employees worldwide. IDG offers the widest range of media options that reach IT buyers in 75 countries representing 95% of worldwide IT spending. IDG's diverse product and services portfolio spans six key areas including print publishing, online publishing, expositions and conferences, market research, education and training, and global marketing services. More than 90 million people read one or more of IDG's 290 magazines and newspapers, including IDG's leading global brands — Computerworld, PC World, Network World, Macworld and the Channel World family of publications. IDG Books Worldwide is one of the fastest-growing computer book publishers in the world, with more than 700 titles in 36 languages. The "...For Dummies®" series alone has more than 50 million copies in print. IDG offers online users the largest network of technology-specific Web sites around the world through IDG.net (http://www.idg.net), which comprises more than 225 targeted Web sites in 55 countries worldwide. International Data Corporation (IDC) is the world's largest provider of information technology data, analysis and consulting, with research centers in over 41 countries and more than 400 research analysts worldwide. IDG World Expo is a leading producer of more than 168 globally branded conferences and expositions in 35 countries including E3 (Electronic Entertainment Expo), Macworld Expo, ComNet, Windows World Expo, ICE (Internet Commerce Expo), Agenda, DEMO, and Spotlight. IDG's training subsidiary, ExecuTrain, is the world's largest computer training company, with more than 230 locations worldwide and 785 training courses. IDG Marketing Services helps industry-leading IT companies build international brand recognition by developing global integrated marketing programs via IDG's print, online and exposition products worldwide. Further information about the company can be found at www.idg.com.   1/24/99

Credits

ACQUISITIONS EDITOR
John Osborn

DEVELOPMENT EDITORS
Matthew E. Lusher
Eric Newman

TECHNICAL EDITOR
Jonathan Mark

COPY EDITORS
Nancy Crumpton
Amy Joy Eoff
Victoria Lee

COVER DESIGN
©mike parsons design

COVER IMAGE
©Michael Simpson/FPG
INternational LLC

PRODUCTION
IDG Books Worldwide Production

PROOFREADING AND INDEXING
York Publication Services

About the Author

Chuck Wood is a systems consultant, instructor, and author with more than 10 years' experience in developing software in Java, PowerBuilder, C++, Visual Basic, and other languages.

OLE DB and ODBC Developer's Guide is Chuck's most ambitious work to date. In addition to this book, Chuck is also the author of *Visual J++ Secrets* (IDG Books Worldwide), *Visual J++, Special Edition Using PowerBuilder,* and *Special Edition Using Watcom SQL.* He contributed to *PowerBuilder 4, Client/Server Unleashed,* and *Special Edition Using Turbo C++ for Windows.*

Chuck has also spoken internationally on database design, object-oriented design, and Windows development and has taught classes in Advanced System Development in Java and Web Database Development at the University of Minnesota and C and C++ at Indiana Vocational Technical College. He has a bachelor's degree in corporate finance and computer science and a master's degree in business administration. He is currently pursuing a Ph.D. in information and decision sciences at the University of Minnesota.

I dedicate this book to the three girls in my life:
Lyn, Kailyn, and Kelly.
Thanks for putting up with me as I write yet another book.
Every guy should be so lucky.

Preface

Visual C++ is a very complex development environment. So many Visual C++ books give you an introduction to Visual C++ by discussing the Visual Studio environment like the AppWizards, toolbars, and menus. Database development is often relegated to a single chapter or part of a chapter, if it is covered at all.

Some database books do focus on Visual C++, but these books often leave you, the reader, in somewhat of a quandary. Some books cover databases extremely lightly without taking time to delve into what you, the developer, need to know most. Topics such as OLE DB providers, special rowsets, and COM are often barely covered. Worse, some C++ database books don't use the Windows graphical user interface (GUI). Such books make some database calls, and then use `printf` statements to show the output in a DOS screen. These books do little to show how databases can enhance the Windows development effort.

It is my contention that database development is the most important part of 99 percent of all development efforts. This book answers the obvious need for better database coverage inside Visual C++ books. Here's what this book offers:

◆ Source code examples that you can use to illustrate a technique

◆ Descriptions of OLE DB database development, including provider development and special OLE DB consumers

◆ ODBC development and a description of ODBC

◆ Special topics, such as OLAP, SQL, and Visual Studio database administration tools

◆ Database development inside working Visual C++ Windows applications

Whom This Book Is For

This book is not for everyone. It targets the advanced Visual C++ user.

◆ This book is *not* for new programmers. This book is *not* for those first starting to learn C++. Topics in this book relate to database applications. You should find another book for Visual C++ introduction, and *then buy and read this book!* This book covers database development in a way that introductory books simply can't because of space limitations.

◆ This book *might* be good for existing C++ programmers who have never delved into Visual C++, although I suggest they find a Visual C++ introductory book as well that concentrates on the Visual C++ environment rather than on the C++ language.

◆ This book *is definitely* for Visual C++ programmers who want to hone their database skills or who want to develop using the new OLE DB tools. The coverage you find in this book about database development can't be found in *any other book*.

OLE DB and ODBC Developer's Guide took the Visual C++ 6.0 environment and *ripped it apart* to find out how to write sophisticated Visual C++ database applications. This book starts where most other Visual C++ books end. It covers areas that other books don't (unless the authors of those other books read this one first!). Instead of repeating documentation, I delved into the entire ODBC and OLE DB packages and picked apart, tested, reviewed, and documented with source code examples. *OLE DB and ODBC Developer's Guide* is more than just a reprint of tools used in Visual C++ 4.0 with a couple of added features (as many other Visual C++ books are). Visual C++ 6.0 is *vastly different* in terms of database access from earlier versions of Visual C++. OLE DB is entirely new to Visual C++ 6.0 and appears to be the tool Microsoft is positioning as the new database access tool. Those that don't learn it and don't know it will be left behind.

Although this book is advanced it's not hard to read. This book has *tons of code* inside, often as many as *four fully functional, fully commented Visual C++ applications per chapter!* That's more than any other Visual C++ book. Included are:

◆ AppWizard instruction that goes beyond how to paint a window

◆ Dynamic HTML that can use OLE DB consumers to give database capabilities to your Web applications using Visual C++ programs

◆ OLE DB provider instruction so you can write providers for your nondatabase data sources, such as text files, directory structures, or EMAIL

◆ ODBC topics that show the inside of ODBC, and how to make ODBC work for you

You also get to see how ADO and DAO applications work inside Visual C++, and you get examples, step-by-step instructions, screen shots, and Tips, Cautions, Cross-References, and Notes about database development.

The Importance of OLE DB

Visual C++ 6.0 introduced tools that enable you to quickly build OLE DB consumers that access OLE DB provider data. Before Visual C++ 6.0, most OLE DB database access was done through ADO. While in other languages ADO is still the premier tool for OLE DB access, in Visual C++ 6.0, OLE DB consumers have replaced ADO as the premier database development tool. OLE DB consumers can be developed that use Active Template Libraries (ATL) to easily develop fast Visual C++ applications. OLE DB consumers allow faster access to OLE DB provider data with greater control.

This book delves into OLE DB as no other book does. Here, you will find numerous ATL examples (as well as MFC examples), examples of how to write an OLE DB provider, and examples of special rowsets and special processing within OLE DB.

How to Use This Book

OLE DB and ODBC Developer's Guide is divided into five parts.

Part I: Introduction to Visual C++ Databases

In Part I, database fundamentals and the Visual Studio tools are discussed. Also included in this part is coverage of Microsoft's Universal Data Access (UDA) paradigm, SQL, and database administration of database projects. Database stored procedures, triggers, views, diagrams, and the New Database Wizard are also discussed.

Part II: ODBC Programming

In Part II, the entire ODBC package is picked apart. Here, the ODBC API is discussed, as well as ODBC registry entries; ODBC Windows applications and reports; putting add, change, and delete capabilities inside your ODBC applications; transaction support; table joins; and multiple ODBC recordsets.

Part III: OLE DB Programming

Part III dives into a component technology overview, the OLE DB Consumer structure, lots of MFC OLE DB consumer applications, and even more ATL OLE DB consumer applications. The OLE DB error-handling chapter is extremely useful in that it shows you how to find out exactly what went wrong with your database application. Command rowsets, table rowsets, bookmarks, and BLOBs are also covered. Special rowsets, such as bulk rowsets, array rowsets, multiple result rowsets, and enumerator rowsets, are also discussed. Finally, OLE DB providers are introduced in this part.

Part IV: Special Database Topics

In Part IV, you get to develop Web applications using Visual C++ COM objects with Dynamic HTML. More OLE DB providers are developed in this part to show you how to access text and EMAIL using OLE DB consumers. OLAP is also introduced as a coming trend that has the capability of replacing the way databases are stored. Application deployment, ADO, and DAO are also discussed in this part.

Part V: Appendixes

Some topics are important but just don't seem to fit with the rest of the book. That's why there's an Appendix section to cover these important topics:

♦ There's no easy way to show the error codes inside text. Instead, Appendix A shows HRESULT codes, SQL State codes, and ADO error codes.

♦ The MFC AppWizard allows you to create ODBC applications by using classes that "wrap around" the ODBC API. However, you may need to access the ODBC API directly, as shown by Part II in this book. Appendix B gives some needed documentation on the ODBC API functions, return codes, and deprecated (obsolete) functions.

♦ OLE DB properties allow the OLE DB consumer to control OLE DB provider functionality. These properties are listed in Appendix C.

♦ A list of what is included on the book's CD-ROM can be found in Appendix D.

In addition to the normal text and explanations, this book contains many features, such as Notes, Tips, Cautions, sidebars, and code. Within code listings, shading indicates code that has been generated or code that has already been discussed; new code is left unshaded. For example:

```
//This is code generated by the compiler
//This is code added by Chuck Wood in a previous section
//This is new code added by Chuck Wood
//
//*******************************
//This is code generated by the compiler
```

This presentation will enable you to tell what code was added and its position in relation to code that already exists in the project.

Some of the icons used for the special features are shown below.

You may be able to find references or needed explanations to the current topic in the book. This icon is used to direct you to other explanations of topics in this book.

If you can find something on the CD-ROM, like source code, this icon tells you where it is.

A Caution tells you of some possible problem that many developers encounter. This feature warns you so that you can avoid the mistakes made by others.

A Tip describes some technique that you should be aware of to help your development effort or improve the quality of your program.

A Note expands upon some topic that is mentioned in the text. Notes are not really part of the text but can help the reader understand the text more completely.

What's a Sidebar?

This is a sidebar. If a secret is outside the normal scope of the book and is pretty lengthy, it may be included in a sidebar. Sidebars separate out the lengthy information so that the reader is not distracted when trying to learn Visual C++ advanced database development.

A Few Final Words

Microsoft's Visual C++ has become the standard to which other compilers are compared. Visual C++ enjoys more market share, and has a more robust environment, than any other C++ compiler.

This book will help you on your journey to becoming a world-class Windows and Internet database developer. This book is the result of many Herculean efforts not only of the author but also its publisher. The result is a fantastic book that can really help you become a better Visual C++ database developer. I hope you enjoy this book

Acknowledgments

Authors never write books by themselves. Any book is impossible without the combined efforts of several underpaid, unacknowledged, and under-appreciated hardworking individuals. I want to take a moment to acknowledge them.

Very special thanks goes to Jonathan Mark, who reviewed this work cover to cover and made suggestions and comments on my programs and code. I have never worked with a more capable and hardworking technical editor. (He didn't let me get away with *anything*!) More kudos to Eric Newman, Matt Lusher, and John Osborn of IDG Books. Their tireless efforts, reviews, comments, and encouragement made this book possible. A special thanks goes out to Chris "Deal Maker" Vanburen of Waterside, Inc., for putting me in contact with the wonderful people at IDG Books. I'd also like to thank the following people at IDG Books who helped get this book out: Nancy Crumpton, Amy Eoff, Victoria Lee, and Linda Marousek. Finally, a special thanks to my wife, Lyn, and my daughters, Kelly and Kailyn, who have to put up with me while I exist on a diet of coffee and no sleep while I write.

Contents at a Glance

Table of Contents

Part II   ODBC Programming

Part II   OLE DB Programming

Part I

Introduction to Visual C++ Databases

Chapter 1

Databases and Visual C++

IN THIS CHAPTER

- ◆ Understanding the importance of client/server, SQL, and Universal Data Access
- ◆ Understanding the position of OLE DB, ODBC, and ADO in the Universal Data Access plan
- ◆ Understanding the issues of application design when developing database applications
- ◆ Understanding how OLE DB, ADO, and ODBC relate to each other, and how each is structured

IT SEEMS THAT MANY Visual C++ books often cover database development as an afterthought, if at all. This book is different in that database development inside Visual Studio using Visual C++ is the *only* topic of this book. This chapter not only goes over some of the basic concepts that are included with Visual C++ but also serves as a road map for the rest of this book.

The Importance of Client/Server

When computers first started being employed in business in the 1960s and into the late 1970s, they were much too expensive for most individuals to purchase. Mainframes were the only computers in existence. In a major corporation, mainframes did all the processing, file sharing, and database management, and information was disseminated to "dumb" terminals whose sole function was to communicate with the mainframe computer. This is shown graphically in Figure 1-1.

In the early 1980s, PCs were introduced. These machines enabled stand-alone processing, especially for spreadsheet analysis, but were almost never hooked up to a mainframe or central storage area. However, as PCs became more cost-effective, complex, and capable, industries started to see PC networks as a way to allow some computing to occur at each workstation, thereby taking the burden off of the central mainframe computer. As time went on, networks started replacing the mainframe in many industries. (See Figure 1-2.)

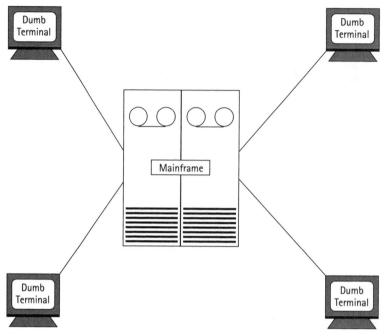

Figure 1-1: Mainframe computing forced all processing and storage to occur at a centralized location.

Networks gave rise to client/server computing. In client/server computing, some of the processing or storage occurs on a centralized server (or servers), and some of the processing or storage occurs at the client level. By distributing the work to where it's most appropriate, client/server computing reduces network traffic and enables faster, more flexible, and more sophisticated programming (such as Windows applications), even though the centralized computer may not be as powerful as the mainframe it replaced.

By considering database capabilities at the server level as well as processing capabilities at the client level, developers were able to provide users access to advanced programs to do their own work as well as access to centralized data that could be shared with everyone. When employing a database server, the database engine runs at the server to provide data to other client machines that request this data. Several advancements came out of this configuration, including SQL, which was a common language that enabled developers to use the same techniques for querying and updating a database; ODBC, which enabled standard routines for access to any database; and, more recently, OLE DB and ADO, which enable standardized access to any data source, not just those data sources that exist on a centralized database.

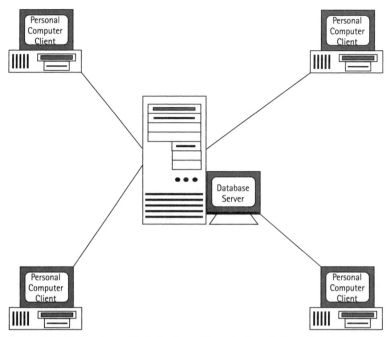

Figure 1-2: Networks enabled client machines to share information with servers, giving rise to client/server computing.

This section discusses three areas that are particular to modern client/server technology. These issues are SQL, application design issues, and Web issues.

Standard Query Language (SQL)

SQL was developed in the 1970s, and still exists today as the *de facto* standard language of all databases. SQL served two functions:

◆ SQL provided a common language for database access so that developers trained in one database would be able to apply their same techniques to another database.

◆ SQL was designed for relational database access. Unlike their approach to traditional process-driven languages, the developers of SQL considered only database access when they developed this language.

Before SQL, developers who wanted to access file or database information had to go through some complicated code. For instance, say you wanted to set a date column in a table or file to today's date if the date on the table or file is more than a year old. Without SQL, you would need to perform a routine similar to the following pseudocode:

```
open file or table
do
 do while next record is locked by another user
  wait
 loop
 lock record
 read record into data structure
 if not EOF
  if date is over 1 year old
   set date in data structure to today's date
   update date with data in data structure
  end if
 end if
 unlock record
loop until EOF
close file or table
```

Even this pseudocode is pretty complicated. Actually implementing it may be quite difficult. Now consider the SQL alternative:

```
Update MyTable set MyTable.date = today()
 where MyTable.date - today() > 365
```

This SQL assumes the existence of a date function that returns a date, and that the date can be subtracted from another date to return the number of days. Although functions and storage differ from database to database, there should be some functions and operations in any SQL-enabled database that can achieve the goal in this SQL with a similarly minimal amount of coding.

As you can see, the SQL UPDATE statement takes advantage of the relational structure of the database to change data with a minimal amount of effort.

Chapter 2 discusses SQL in detail.

Application Design Issues

Application design has never been easy. However, with modern development techniques, a poor application design can negatively affect your software sales or productivity. You should consider many application design issues when developing your application:

♦ What about the Web? With the Web, database issues have never been more complicated. Instead of having a "captive" machine that runs your application and terminates it normally, now you may have hundreds of people hitting your Web site each day. Each person may be running a different browser and can't be relied upon to hit an Exit button before leaving the page. With Microsoft's Internet Information Server (IIS), you can use a C++ program to use Dynamic HTML to deliver an Active Server Page that will be readable from *any* browser in *any* operating system. This may be more suitable for you than traditional Java development or client-side scripting.

For more on Web-based database development using Visual C++, see Chapter 14.

♦ What platform is your client running on? This question is important. In many systems and even in current database books and programming books, many authors assume that text-based DOS or UNIX environments are still in use, and their code reflects this. (For example, some books use `printf` extensively to print to a command prompt.) This book assumes that, because you're writing in a Visual Studio environment, you'll want to take full advantage of all the graphical features that Visual C++ can deliver through Windows 9x. There is no text-based output in this book. This way, graphical developers don't need to struggle with converting text-based examples into graphically based applications.

♦ What tools are available to you? The team at IDG Books and I went through great pains to discover the new techniques that can be used for database development, especially through the ATL (Active Template Library). You'll find that these routines are often sparsely documented, but are *much* simpler to use than OLE DB/ADO development in previous versions of Visual C++. This book also concentrates on the MFC (Microsoft Foundation Classes). If you still like pure ODBC (non-OLE DB) development, the MFC is the best way to go. You can even write OLE DB applications through MFC, although I recommend you use ATL instead.

This book goes by the premise that most of you want development to be as simple as possible but want your applications to be robust and of commercial-grade quality. With this in mind, this book often takes wizard output and customizes it to fit the chapter's needs, much as you would do in your corporate environment.

◆ What technology do you need to support? While this book shows how to easily develop database applications for the traditional corporate world, it also delves into areas that no other book tries — areas such as ATL development, Web database applications written in Visual C++, OLAP databases, and OLE DB provider development, just to name a few.

With all the issues facing a developer, application design is most important. These questions should be asked before developing any project, and the application should take advantage of as much technology as possible to ensure that programs don't become obsolete too quickly.

Understanding Universal Data Access (UDA)

When programming languages first were developed, storage was done through files that existed on tape and then later on a hard drive. These files contained only raw data records with no indexing, and data access was slow and tedious. In the late 1960s and the 1970s, databases were developed that enabled you to store data in an easily retrievable format. Databases advanced so that access was easier and data protection was built in. Today, business can't function without a database to keep track of corporate data. Every application from games to corporate Web sites requires some sort of database to enable users to view, update, or remove data from the database.

Microsoft started its database support with Open Database Connectivity (ODBC) standards, Remote Data Objects (RDO), and Database Access Objects (DAO). ODBC is a set of standard functions that enable developers to connect and manipulate any database. Database access has increased exponentially, usually attributed to the tools and interoperability that ODBC delivered. RDO typically used ODBC data sources to access data on a remote server. DAO was for use, mainly, with databases that used the Jet database engine used in Microsoft Access, although later versions of DAO also enabled ODBC access.

A problem exists that accompanied the use of personal computers. Whereas there used to be a push to centralize all data, now there is a need for every member in an organization to keep data in whatever format is most suitable to the individual. There is data in spreadsheets, data in text documents, data coming over the

Internet through a socket/modem connection, and data in e-mail files, just to name a few sources of nonrelational data (see Figure 1-3). Rather than a push to standardize relational databases, Microsoft saw a need to standardize *all* data access, whether or not it was from a database. To answer this need, Microsoft developed Universal Data Access.

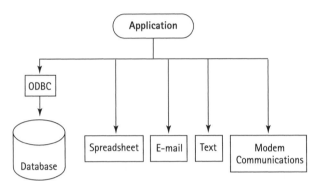

Figure 1-3: Data access was different for every data source using traditional data access techniques

Universal Data Access is the strategy employed by Microsoft to provide common routines to access all types of relational *and* nonrelational information. Universal Data Access enables all Visual Studio tools to access any data source on any platform, as long as an OLE DB provider exists for that data source. The Universal Data Access protocol enables applications to use one set of API-class library calls to access myriad data sources. Universal Data Access consists of three core technologies:

◆ Object Linking and Embedding Databases (OLE DB) is the protocol used to communicate with any data source.

◆ ActiveX Data Objects (ADO) is the technique used by all non-Visual C++ programs that enable access to OLE DB data.

◆ Open Database Connectivity (ODBC) is still used to connect to any database. Microsoft includes an OLE DB provider that accesses any ODBC data source.

The end result of this protocol is a layer between all data sources that can be accessed by any program. This is shown graphically in Figure 1-4.

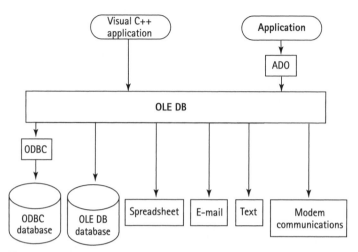

Figure 1–4: UDA uses OLE DB technology to access any data source.

The following sections describe the UDA components and discuss their implications for Visual C++ developers.

Object Linking and Embedding Databases (OLE DB)

OLE DB is Microsoft's newest standard for database connectivity. OLE DB consists of a set of COM interfaces that provide several database management services. OLE DB is designed to access several different kinds of data sources. Many database vendors (such as Oracle, Informix, and Microsoft) provide OLE DB drivers or have OLE DB providers available, as well as ODBC drivers, to access their databases.

The two basic constructs of OLE DB are the *OLE DB provider* and the *OLE DB consumer*. The provider is written to provide access to a particular data source. This data source is often a database but also could be any other data source, such as a modem transmission, a spreadsheet, a Word document, or a text file. You can capture any data stream inside a provider. This data stream can then be used, with some exceptions, in an OLE DB consumer just as a database table would be used, with complete scrolling backward and forward, and even updates if your provider has enabled that capability. Figure 1-5 shows the basic structure of OLE DB.

As shown in Figure 1-5, each data source available to an application can have a single OLE DB provider that is written to access this data source. Several different OLE DB consumers can use this OLE DB provider. These consumers can all be identical, or a specialized consumer can be written to take advantage of any specialized processing enabled by the provider. In this way, OLE DB is not only powerful in that OLE DB allows simplified data access to every data source, but it is also flexible in that consumers can be written which take advantage of different aspects of the provider.

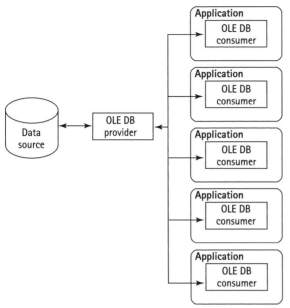

Figure 1-5: OLE DB relies on the interaction between OLE DB providers and OLE DB consumers.

Part III of this book goes over OLE DB and discusses much of the functionality that OLE DB can deliver.

ActiveX Data Objects (ADO)

ADO is a layer of classes that provide quick and easy access to OLE DB, as shown earlier in Figure 1-4. In actuality, ADO is a generic OLE DB consumer that is designed to access any OLE DB provider. ADO was designed to be similar to ODBC, DAO, and RDO coding so that those who wish to move to OLE DB can do so easily. ADO was also designed so that ADO duplicates the interfaces supported by earlier database techniques. ADO also made some improvements to these previous interfaces by simplifying awkward tasks and increasing performance. The main goal of ADO is to make it easy to do the common operations supported by OLE DB providers. Because ADO uses OLE DB, you'll notice many similarities between the objects, interfaces, and overall functionality of both technologies. ADO also hides many incompatibilities between various OLE DB providers and makes up for missing functionality in some providers.

ADO is used across platforms, enabling developers of any language, including Visual J++, to access data seamlessly. All of the Visual Studio tools can use ADO to access data. ADO drastically reduces the amount of time needed to write complex client/server and ActiveX code. ADO and Visual J++'s visual database tools are discussed later in this chapter. Calls you can make with ADO are addressed later in the book.

Chapter 18 goes into ADO development.

Open Database Connectivity (ODBC)

ODBC is the most open and currently the most successful standard used to connect to a relational database. Most databases include ODBC drivers, in addition to native drivers, to access their database. Some databases have even given up on native drivers and use ODBC exclusively. Figure 1-6 shows how ODBC is configured.

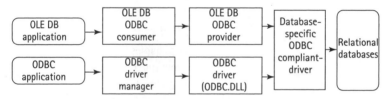

Figure 1-6: ODBC is designed to connect to a wide variety of relational databases.

In Figure 1-6, you can see that all a database vendor needs to do is write a database-specific ODBC-compliant driver. Then the ODBC driver can be used to access that database and deliver database data to ODBC and OLE DB applications.

ODBC databases also enable easy migration from different databases. If you change your database engine, you simply need to configure the ODBC interface to point to the new database rather than replace all the old proprietary database calls in your application with new proprietary database calls.

OLE DB does not use the ODBC Driver Manager, but rather, for efficiency, uses its own ODBC provider to enable quick access to ODBC data. In this sense, you can still use OLE DB to access ODBC data with OLE DB's efficiency without losing the ODBC benefit of multiple database support.

OLE DB versus ODBC

OLE DB is not yet widely supported by all major database vendors and as yet has had little acceptance in the Visual C++ market. ODBC, on the other hand, is still more widely used than any other database platform in Visual C++. However, it seems that ODBC and OLE DB are somewhat duplicative. The rumor mill has it that Microsoft plans to phase ODBC out of the picture when OLE DB is fully functional.

One might understand why a new OLE DB standard, with roots going back to Windows 3.0 and even before, is in order. However, lot of tools still require ODBC to function. Java's JDBC, PowerBuilder, several CASE tools, and even certain aspects of Visual Studio (such as database projects) still require ODBC as a database front-end. Still, if I had to pick a current technology to develop new applications with, I would choose OLE DB and leave ODBC behind. OLE DB will soon enjoy the same level of support that ODBC currently enjoys, and you wouldn't want all your applications to be written using a soon-to-be obsolete technology.

Part II of this book goes over ODBC and discusses much of the functionality that ODBC can deliver.

The Application Wizards

Visual C++ uses application wizards to quickly develop Visual C++ database applications or to add database functionality to an existing application. The following wizards are discussed in detail in this book to show how they relate to database development:

◆ The MFC AppWizard is used to develop Microsoft Foundation Class (MFC) programs using either OLE DB, ODBC, or DAO.

◆ The ATL AppWizard is used to develop quick, small, and efficient programs using Microsoft's Active Template Library (ATL). Templates enable easy development when one is writing OLE DB applications.

◆ The ATL Object Wizard enables you to quickly add ATL objects, such as OLE DB providers or consumers or ATL dialog boxes, to your existing ATL or MFC application.

As you continue through this book, you'll find that these wizards enable a much easier database development process.

Summary

Visual C++ offers a variety of tools for easy database development. The application wizards, database projects, and MFC tools make Visual C++ an extremely powerful tool for client/server, database development. To recap:

◆ Client/server technology enables some processing and storage to occur at both the client and the server machines. Database development takes advantage of client/server architecture.

◆ SQL is the standard language used by most databases. SQL is a huge aid in database application development because SQL enables relational commands whereas traditional process-oriented languages do not.

◆ Application design can be extremely complicated. This chapter includes some of the questions you'll need to ask before developing a database application.

◆ UDA is Microsoft's vision of having one interface for all data sources.

◆ UDA consists of OLE DB, ADO, and ODBC.

◆ OLE DB is the Microsoft database development tool of choice. OLE DB makes use of data providers and data consumers to enable a flexible method of accessing any data source.

◆ Microsoft Visual Studio includes visual database development tools that enable the developer to paint OLE DB, ODBC, and DAO functionality on the window.

◆ DAO and RDO can still be used to connect to a database; however, new Visual C++ development should be done using ODBC or OLE DB.

◆ Wizards are included with Visual C++ that enable easy database development. Database application development with these wizards is discussed throughout this book.

Chapter 2

Understanding Structured Query Language (SQL)

IN THIS CHAPTER

- ◆ Mastering the fundamentals of SQL
- ◆ Examining SQL SELECT statements
- ◆ Implementing INSERT, UPDATE, and DELETE statements

SQL (STRUCTURED QUERY LANGUAGE) IS A language used by most databases. Using SQL, you can manipulate data no matter what the database source. This chapter delves into how to use SQL and the ways you use SQL in a C++ program.

Some database interfaces require a semicolon (;) at the end of each SQL statement, whereas some do not. You cannot use the semicolon when programming inside Visual C++. This chapter does not add semicolons to the SQL examples, but you should do so if the database interface you're using to test SQL requires it.

Using the SELECT Statement

The SELECT statement is used to pull information from the database. The format for the simplest SELECT statement is as follows:

```
SELECT column1, column2,...
FROM table1, table2
```

For instance, if you have a Microsoft Access database table with the format shown in Figure 2-1, you can SELECT all the rows (or records) from the Student table by using the following SQL:

```
SELECT StudentID,
       FirstName,
       MidName,
       LastName,
       Address,
       City,
       StateOrProvince,
       PostalCode,
       PhoneNumber,
       EMAIL,
       Major,
       StudentSSN
FROM Student
```

The preceding SQL statement retrieves all the rows in the Student table.

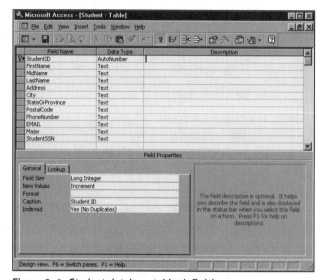

Figure 2-1: Student database table definition

Understanding the * Operative

You can retrieve all the columns from a table using an SQL * operative. The following statement selects all the rows and all the columns from the Student table:

```
SELECT * FROM Student
```

TIP The * operative has caused some concern in developer circles. If a database table changes, then every program that relies on the current table configuration becomes invalid. The general rule is to use the * operative only when writing a class library.

Using the WHERE Clause

Sometimes you don't want all the rows from a table, but rather you need a subset of all the rows. To combine criteria with a SELECT statement, you need to add a WHERE clause. A SELECT statement using a WHERE clause has the following format:

```
SELECT column1, column2,...
   FROM table1, table2
WHERE column1 = 'value'
```

Consider the following SQL:

```
SELECT StudentID,
       FirstName,
       MidName,
       LastName,
       Address,
       City,
       StateOrProvince,
       PostalCode,
       PhoneNumber,
       EMAIL,
       Major,
       StudentSSN
FROM Student
WHERE FirstName = 'Chuck' AND LastName = 'Wood'
```

This SQL statement retrieves all the rows in the Student table where "Chuck" is stored in the FirstName field and "Wood" is stored in the LastName field.

Using the ORDER BY Clause

When SELECTing multiple rows, the order in which the rows are retrieved is often important. SQL standards claim that all returning rows can be in a random order unless specified by an ORDER BY clause. Consider the following statement:

```
SELECT StudentID,
       FirstName,
       MidName,
       LastName,
       Address,
       City,
       StateOrProvince,
       PostalCode,
       PhoneNumber,
       EMAIL,
       Major,
       StudentSSN
FROM Student
ORDER BY StudentID
```

Now, instead of retrieving Students at random, the student records are sorted in StudentID order by the database engine before being retrieved by the program.

How to Use WHERE and ORDER BY

Using WHERE and ORDER BY clauses give you several development and performance benefits when developing a database program:

◆ The WHERE clause can limit the number of records you retrieve. This makes database access quicker and reduces network traffic in a client/server environment.

◆ The ORDER BY clause can handle complex sorting for you so you don't have to worry about it inside a program. Properly done, this speeds up not only development but also program execution.

◆ Indexes are important when using WHERE and ORDER BY clauses. Indexes provide a quick search of certain fields within tables. When a field is specified in a WHERE or ORDER BY clause, the database engine first checks to see if the columns specified are indexed. If so, the index is used to make searches quicker. If you are using WHERE or ORDER BY clauses, be sure to see if you can establish an index on the fields that you are using.

Instead of using a column name in an ORDER BY clause, you can also use a column number. Because StudentID is the first column retrieved by the SELECT statement, you can sort by StudentID using either the following ORDER BY clause:

```
ORDER BY StudentID
```

or by using the sequential number of the StudentID. Because StudentID is
the first column, its column number is 1, so the following ORDER BY clause
also sorts by Student ID:

```
ORDER BY 1
```

Understanding SQL Expressions

In addition to SELECTing fields from a table, you can also SELECT expressions that
perform functions or operations on a field or set of fields. There are three building
blocks for creating SQL expressions:

♦ *Granular* functions, which consider only one row at a time

♦ *Aggregate* functions, which work on a group of rows at a time

♦ *Operations*, which enable you to combine column information and/or
function results

UNDERSTANDING SQL GRANULAR FUNCTIONS

Databases can perform operations with SELECT statements:

```
SELECT purchase_price * (1 + tax_rate) AS total_due
FROM purchases
```

The preceding code formats a column called total_due that is equal to the purchase price plus the tax. In addition to straight arithmetic, most databases come
with a large set of granular functions that affect the value of a row. For instance,
the ABS function is often used to take the absolute value of a number:

```
SELECT ABS(day_due - day_delivered) AS days_off
FROM purchases
```

The preceding SQL SELECT statement subtracts the day an item is delivered from
the day it is due and takes the absolute value.

Most databases have hundreds of granular functions. Check your database documentation to see which granular functions you have.

UNDERSTANDING SQL AGGREGATE FUNCTIONS

In addition to the granular functions supported in a database, databases also have
a few aggregate functions that consider all the rows or a group of the rows
SELECTed. Table 2-1 shows the common SQL aggregate functions.

TABLE 2-1 SQL AGGREGATE FUNCTIONS

SQL Aggregate Function	Description
AVG(columnName)	Returns the average of the column specified.
COUNT (*)	Returns the number of rows retrieved.
MAX(columnName)	Returns the maximum value of a column.
MIN(columnName)	Returns the minimum value of a column.
SUM(columnName)	Returns the sum of a column.

For instance, the following SQL returns a count of the number of students who have either a computer science or MIS major:

```
SELECT  COUNT(*)
FROM    Student
WHERE   Major = 'Computer Science' OR Major = 'MIS'
```

UNDERSTANDING SQL OPERATIONS

You should avoid thinking of the SELECT statement as a tool for retrieving only column information. SELECT statements can retrieve *expressions*. An SQL expression can be one of the following:

◆ A column

◆ A function (either granular or aggregate)

◆ An operation

For instance, you can retrieve information for a mailing label for students in the Student table by using the following SELECT:

```
SELECT [FirstName] + ' ' + [LastName] AS name,
       Address,
       City,
       StateOrProvince,
       PostalCode,
```

```
        RIGHT(PhoneNumber, 8) AS LocalPhone
FROM Student
WHERE LEFT(PhoneNumber, 5) = '(514)'
```

As you can see by the preceding SQL, in addition to querying columns, a string operation ([FirstName]+' '+[LastName]) and an SQL function (RIGHT (PhoneNumber, 8)) are added to the SQL. In addition, the WHERE clause tests against a function rather than a column.

Operations and SQL functions add power to SQL to make your coding much easier. By using expressions in the SQL queries used by your Visual C++ programs, you can reduce the size and complexity of your C++ code.

Using the GROUP BY Clause

You often don't want an aggregation of every row in a SELECT statement, but rather you want to group the rows that are returned by the SELECT statement in some order. This is done using the GROUP BY clause. The GROUP BY clause enables aggregate functions to be performed on a series of rows within a group returned by a SELECT statement. The following statement lists all the majors and how many students are enrolled in each major:

```
SELECT  Major,
        COUNT(*)
FROM    Student
GROUP BY Major
ORDER BY 2 DESC, 1 ASC
```

In the preceding statement, each major has its students counted separately from every other department. Then the rows that are retrieved are returned in descending order of the number of students enrolled in the majors, with the greatest number of students appearing at the top of the list, and the ascending order by name. Ascending (ASC) is the default and is never required except for clarity, such as when you mix ascending and descending order, as shown by the preceding example.

As you can see by the preceding statement, ORDER BY and GROUP BY statements work well together. As mentioned previously, the ORDER BY clause can use either the column name *or* the column order in a SELECT statement. Because the COUNT(*) is the second column selected, and Major is the first column selected, the preceding ORDER BY sorts by COUNT(*) and then by Major name.

Using the HAVING Clause

One problem with the WHERE clause is that you cannot use aggregate functions inside it. For instance, you *cannot* use WHERE AVG(score) > 90 in a SELECT statement. Consider the Grades table in Figure 2-2.

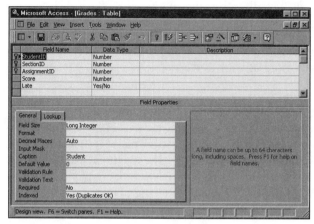

Figure 2-2: Grades database table definition

To select aggregate conditions, you need to use the HAVING clause in conjunction with the GROUP BY clause. The following code selects those StudentIDs whose average score is greater than 90:

```
SELECT StudentID,
       Avg(Score) AS AverageScore
FROM Grades
GROUP BY StudentID,
HAVING Avg(Score) > 90
ORDER BY 2 DESC, 1
```

Using Join Operations

So far, all of our SQL examples involve SELECT statements from one table. A developer often wants to SELECT from several tables at once. To do so, a join is usually used. A join uses more than one table in a SELECT statement. Consider the three tables in Figure 2-3.

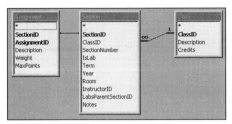

Figure 2-3: The Assignment, Section, and Class table definitions

In Figure 2-3, each class can have several sections, and each section can have several assignments. If you want to list all the assignments by class, you need to join these three tables. The following SQL can be used to link the three tables so that you can see the class description along with all the assignments associated with each section of the class:

```
SELECT Class.Description,
       SectionNumber,
       Assignment.Description
  FROM Class,
       Assignment,
       Section
WHERE Assignment.SectionID = Section.SectionID
  AND Class.ClassID = Section.ClassID
ORDER BY Class.Description
```

In the preceding SQL:

◆ The Assignment and Section tables were joined by their respective
  SectionID fields.

◆ The Section and Class tables were joined by their respective ClassID fields.

◆ The results were sorted by the Description column in the Class table.

◆ Because both the Class and Assignment tables have a Description
  column, the name had to be fully qualified with a *tablename.column*
  notation rather than using the field as was done before.

Notice how the table name is used to qualify the field name in the preceding SQL. With large SQL statements, this can be quite cumbersome. SQL enables you to assign aliases to tables in a SELECT statement to make the chore of writing SQL statements easier:

```
SELECT c.Description,
       s.SectionNumber,
       a.Description
  FROM Class c,
       Assignment a,
       Section s
WHERE a.SectionID = s.SectionID
  AND c.ClassID = s.ClassID
```

As shown by the preceding code, you can assign table name aliases in the FROM clause by placing the alias name right after the table name but before the comma. In the preceding example, the Class table is given an alias of c, the Assignment table an alias of a, and the Section table an alias of s. The resulting SQL statement was shorter and easier to read.

Using Inner Joins

Until recently, all joins were done in the WHERE clause. ANSI Standard SQL '92 defined the use of joins inside the FROM clause rather than the WHERE clause. The format for joins when using the FROM clause is as follows:

```
FROM table1 [[AS] alias] JoinType table2 [[AS] alias]   [ON
condition]
```

Often, *inner joins* are used in place of WHERE clauses. Inner joins are a way of combining two tables and can be more efficient than using WHERE clauses (depending on the database). The following is an example of an inner join:

```
SELECT c.Description,
       s.SectionNumber,
       a.Description
FROM (Class c INNER JOIN Section s ON c.ClassID = s.ClassID)
INNER JOIN Assignment a ON s.SectionID = a.SectionID
```

Although vendors have embraced the new join standard, many databases (especially older ones) still require that joins be done in the WHERE clause. WHERE clauses are often converted by the database engine into inner joins whenever possible, so usually there is no performance benefit when using inner joins. In addition, inner join syntax can be different from database to database.

Using Outer Joins

Inner joins and joins done using a WHERE clause return only those rows that have matches in the corresponding table. *Outer joins* are done if you want all the entries of a table and the matching entries of another table.

Say you wanted to return a list of all students in a class. However, if the class has no students assigned, you still want it listed. Possible SQL syntax for this outer join might be as follows:

```
SELECT Class.Description,
       Section.SectionNumber,
       [FirstName]+' '+[LastName] AS Name
FROM   ((Class INNER JOIN Section ON Class.ClassID =
Section.ClassID)
LEFT OUTER JOIN StudentClass
ON Section.SectionID = StudentClass.SectionID)
LEFT OUTER JOIN Student
ON StudentClass.StudentID = Student.StudentID
```

The results from this SQL can be seen in Table 2-2.

___

TABLE **2-2 OUTER JOIN RESULTS**

Description	Section Number	Name
Macro Economic Theory	1	Margaret Peacock
Macro Economic Theory	1	Tim Smith
Macro Economic Theory	1	Brandon Coake
Macro Economic Theory	1	Nancy Davolio
Macro Economic Theory	1	Helvetius Nagy
Macro Economic Theory	1	Matthew Dunn
Macro Economic Theory	1	Deborah Peterson
Introduction to Management Information Systems	2	Nancy Davolio

Continued

TABLE **2-2 OUTER JOIN RESULTS** *(Continued)*

Introduction to Management Information Systems	2	Margaret Peacock
Introduction to Management Information Systems	2	Matthew Dunn
Introduction to Management Information Systems	2	Helvetius Nagy
Introduction to Management Information Systems	2	Deborah Peterson
Introduction to Management Information Systems	2	Tim Smith
Introduction to Management Information Systems	2	Brandon Coake
Relational Database Design	1	Tim Smith
Relational Database Design	1	Margaret Peacock
Relational Database Design	1	Helvetius Nagy
Relational Database Design	1	Nancy Davolio
Relational Database Design	1	Matthew Dunn
Relational Database Design	1	Brandon Coake
Relational Database Design	1	Deborah Peterson

As you can see by the results in Table 2-2, all classes were listed with the enrolled students, and classes with no students were also listed with a blank name.

TIP Along with column information, you can also display computed columns. In the SQL shown immediately before Table 2-2, FirstName, a space, and LastName are concatenated and given an alias of Name. You can do other mathematical or string functions inside a SELECT statement. Check your database help manual for operators, functions, or expressions that can be used inside a SELECT statement.

In the FROM clause (in the SQL shown immediately before Table 2-2), the following steps are written:

1. Join the Class table with the Section table with a normal inner join. This selects only those classes with a valid section:

```
Class INNER JOIN Section ON Class.ClassID = Section.ClassID
```

2. Place the INNER JOIN clause written in step 1 in parentheses, and do an outer join to the StudentClass table from the Section table. This lists *all* the Class table/Section table combinations and joins the matching records from the StudentClass table. If there is no StudentClass record match, the Class table/Section table combinations are still listed with no relating StudentClass information:

```
(Class INNER JOIN Section ON Class.ClassID = Section.ClassID)
LEFT OUTER JOIN StudentClass
ON Section.SectionID = StudentClass.SectionID
```

3. Place the INNER JOIN/LEFT OUTER JOIN clause written in step 2 in parentheses and LEFT OUTER JOIN the results with the Student table. This joins *all* the records from step 2 to related records from the Student table. If there is no Student record match, the step 2 combinations are still listed with no relating Student information:

```
((Class INNER JOIN Section ON Class.ClassID =
Section.ClassID)
LEFT OUTER JOIN StudentClass
ON Section.SectionID = StudentClass.SectionID)
LEFT OUTER JOIN Student
ON StudentClass.StudentID = Student.StudentID
```

The result is a list of all students enrolled in a class along with class/section combinations that have no students enrolled. (In this case, the name column is NULL, which means that the name cannot be determined.)

There are usually several ways to write an inner/outer join combination. The preceding SQL SELECT statement can also be written as follows:

```
SELECT Class.Description,
          Section.SectionNumber,
          [FirstName]+' '+[LastName] AS name
FROM (Class INNER JOIN Section
          ON Class.ClassID = Section.ClassID)
     LEFT OUTER JOIN
```

```
          (StudentClass LEFT OUTER JOIN Student
              ON StudentClass.StudentID = Student.StudentID)
    ON Section.SectionID = StudentClass.SectionID
```

The logical steps that went into this SQL statement are as follows:

1. This step is the same as the preceding step 1. Join the Class table with the Section table with a normal inner join. This selects only those classes with a valid section:

```
FROM Class INNER JOIN Section
ON Class.ClassID = Section.ClassID
```

2. Write a left outer join to join *all* StudentClass records with matching Student records:

```
FROM Student Class LEFT OUTER JOIN Student
ON StudentClass.StudentID = Student.StudentID
```

3. Write another left outer join to join *all* records from step 1 with matching records from step 2:

```
FROM (Class INNER JOIN Section
    ON Class.ClassID = Section.ClassID)
LEFT OUTER JOIN
    (StudentClass LEFT OUTER JOIN Student
    ON StudentClass.StudentID = Student.StudentID)
ON Section.SectionID = StudentClass.SectionID
```

As you can see, two different logical thought processes went into creating the same results. Just as with all coding, complex SQL coding can often be accomplished using different SQL syntax.

Oracle, Sybase, and Microsoft SQL Server Joins

Oracle does not use joins in the same way as Microsoft Access. With Oracle, the LEFT OUTER JOIN clause is not supported, so WHERE clauses must be used for all INNER joins. Outer joins are supported by using the (+) on the table where you want to enable NULLs. The preceding FROM clause in step 3 would look like the following:

```
FROM Class,
    Section
    StudentClass,
```

```
        Student
WHERE Class.ClassID = Section.ClassID
   AND Section.SectionID = StudentClass.SectionID (+)
   AND StudentClass.StudentID = Student.StudentID (+)
```

Sybase SQL Server and Microsoft SQL Server both support the *= operator for outer joins:

```
FROM Class,
     Section
     StudentClass,
     Student
WHERE Class.ClassID = Section.ClassID
   AND Section.SectionID *= StudentClass.SectionID
   AND StudentClass.StudentID *= Student.StudentID
```

The reason for this confusion is that ANSI did not define outer join syntax until database vendors already were placing such syntax features in their databases. Also, because both the Sybase/Microsoft method and the Oracle method seem easier to use and understand than the INNER JOIN/OUTER JOIN clauses, there is little reason to change. It would be a good idea to check to see what outer join syntax is supported by your database.

Using UNION Clauses

Rather than joining tables together, you may want to combine *all* similar records from two different tables, which is done using a UNION clause. UNION clauses are used simply to combine the results of two SELECT statements.

Say you wanted the names, e-mail, and a flag for all instructors and students. This can be done by using the following UNION:

```
   SELECT [FirstName]+' '+[LastName] AS Name,
          EMAIL,
          'Student' as 'Student Or Instructor'
   FROM   Student
UNION
   SELECT Name,
          EMAIL,
          'Instructor' as 'Student Or Instructor'
   FROM   Instructor
ORDER BY 1, 2, 3
```

As you can see by the preceding code, two select statements are performed. For all UNION clauses, the following two conditions must apply to each SELECT statement inside the UNION:

◆ Each SELECT statement must contain the same number of columns.

◆ Every column in each SELECT statement must return the same data type. In other words, you cannot combine number and string columns. (However, you *can* use an SQL function to convert a number to a string.)

Using SubSELECT Operations

SubSELECTs (also called *subqueries*) are used when one SELECT statement is embedded in another. SubSELECTs are used inside a WHERE clause to compare information from a column with the results from another query. The following SQL uses a subSELECT to retrieve the name of the students with the highest scores on each assignment:

```
SELECT  stu.FirstName + ' ' + stu.LastName AS Name,
        stu.Major,
        c.Description,
        sec.SectionNumber,
        g1.Score
FROM    ((Student stu
        INNER JOIN Grades g1 ON g1.StudentID = stu.StudentID)
        INNER JOIN Section sec ON sec.SectionID = g1.SectionID)
        INNER JOIN Class c ON c.ClassID = sec.ClassID
WHERE   g1.Score = (SELECT MAX(g2.score)
                    FROM Grades g2
                    WHERE g2.AssignmentID = g1.AssignmentID
                    AND g2.SectionID = g1.SectionID)
```

In the preceding code, the student's score for a particular section and assignment is compared with the maximum score for that section and assignment.

TIP Notice that although the same table was used, two different aliases enable you to specify two fields from different declarations of the same table.

The Problems with subSELECTs

When you use subSELECTs, you are actually doing another query for each row returned on the master SELECT. In the preceding example, say that you averaged a class size of 50 students. For each assignment, you would have to go through each record to reselect the maximum score for the assignment. If you had 300 assignments, the result would be 15,000 (300 × 50) SELECTs to return results for these 300 assignments.

For bigger tables, the results are even worse. Say you had a table with 100,000 records and used a subSELECT that queried 10,000 records. The result would be *one billion* queries against the database. (Most database engines would have trouble finishing this request *this week*, let alone immediately.)

If possible, it's usually better to perform two queries within your Visual C++ program and store the results in memory. In the preceding example, you would form a 300-row table in memory and 50 SELECT statements to compare against the 300-row memory table. The result would be 350 (300 + 50) queries rather than 15,000 queries, or roughly an amazing 98 percent decrease in database traffic plus some extra CPU processing at the local machine.

Using the DELETE Statement

A DELETE statement removes one or more rows from a database table. The syntax for the DELETE statement is:

```
DELETE FROM tablename
WHERE condition
```

For example, to DELETE all rows from the Student table with the FirstName of "Chuck" and the LastName of "Wood," use the following SQL:

```
DELETE FROM Student
WHERE FirstName = 'Chuck' AND LastName = 'Wood'
```

Using the UPDATE Command

The UPDATE command changes the values in the columns of the database. The SQL syntax for the UPDATE command is as follows:

```
UPDATE tablename
SET column1 = value1, column2 = value2...
WHERE condition
```

For example, if you want to change the address of the "Chuck Wood" record, you use the following UPDATE command:

```
UPDATE Student
SET    Address = '123 4th St.',
       City = 'Nowhere',
       StateOrProvince = 'NY',
       PostalCode = '00000'
WHERE FirstName = 'Chuck' AND LastName = 'Wood'
```

Using the INSERT Command

The INSERT command adds a new record to a table in the database. There are two ways to INSERT a record into a database table. For single-row entries, a simple INSERT statement is required. For multiple-row entries, an INSERT statement combined with a subSELECT statement is required.

Inserting a Row

The basic SQL syntax for the INSERT command is as follows:

```
INSERT INTO tablename
    (column1, column2, ...)
VALUES
    (value1, 'value2', ...)
```

To INSERT a new row into the Instructor table, use the following SQL syntax:

```
INSERT INTO Instructor
            (Name,
            DepartmentCode,
            EMAIL,
            Notes)
    VALUES
            ('Chuck Wood',
            'MIS',
```

```
'chuckw@theu.edu',
'')
```

 TIP If a field is defined as autoincrement or a counter, the database engine figures out the proper value for the field. It also means that you *cannot* specify its value in an INSERT or UPDATE. Consequently, the InstructorID, which is autoincrement, is not specified in the INSERT.

Inserting Multiple Rows Using Nested SELECT Statements

SQL can often be used for bulk operations. For instance, you would probably want to back up your grades on occasion in case your computer failed or someone found a way to unethically change their grades.

You can INSERT several rows at a time into a table by using nested SELECT statements inside an INSERT statement:

```
INSERT INTO GradesBackup
           (StudentID,
            SectionID,
            AssignmentID,
            Score,
            Late)
    SELECT StudentID,
           SectionID,
           AssignmentID,
           Score,
           Late
      FROM Grades;
```

 TIP Nested SELECT statements are often used in conjunction with the * operative to archive information. The following statement copies all grades into a GradesBackup table:

```
INSERT INTO GradesBackup
      SELECT * FROM GRADES
```

> **TIP**
>
> In addition, many databases enable the use of the SELECT INTO clause to create a new table or add to an existing table. The following SQL also backs up the Grades table:
>
> SELECT * INTO GradesBackup

Summary

This chapter gives C++ developers an overview of SQL. To recap:

- ◆ SELECT statements receive information from the database in a number of formats and configurations by using SQL expressions, WHERE clauses, ORDER BY clauses, and other SELECT syntax.

- ◆ INSERT, UPDATE, and DELETE statements change existing data on a database table.

- ◆ The INSERT statement enables you to use a subSELECT to insert many records with one SQL command.

- ◆ The SELECT INTO clause can act as a bulk insert.

- ◆ SELECT statements can be used to group several rows together using aggregate functions.

Chapter 3

Using Database Projects with ODBC

IN THIS CHAPTER

- ◆ Creating ODBC database projects
- ◆ Creating a SQL Server database using Visual Studio
- ◆ Administering a database by creating tables and views and executing SQL inside Visual Studio
- ◆ Understanding database administration for advanced databases such as Microsoft SQL Server and Oracle, using triggers, stored procedures, and diagrams inside Visual Studio

IN THIS CHAPTER, YOU LEARN how you can take advantage of Visual Studio's database projects to manage your ODBC or Microsoft SQL Server database.

Understanding Database Projects

Visual Studio enables you to define database projects. Database projects contain no code but enable you to manipulate databases that you may be using in your programs.

 TIP You can have standalone database project workspaces. However, developers usually add database projects to existing workspaces. That way, the developer can access existing databases and the code that accompanies them at the same time.

To create a new database project, follow two simple steps:

1. Choose File → New from the Visual Studio menu. Then click the Projects tab, and choose the Database Project icon. If you are adding a database

35

project to an existing workspace, click the Add to current workspace radio button, as shown in Figure 3-1. Otherwise, click the Create new workspace radio button. Type in your project name, and click OK.

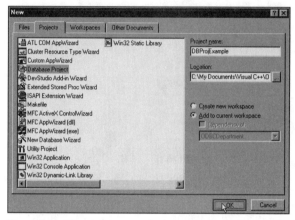

Figure 3-1: New database projects can be created using the Database Project choice in the New dialog box.

2. Visual Studio then creates your database project. Before creation of the project is finished, the Select Data Source dialog box opens. Here, you must choose an ODBC data source that will be used for the database project, as shown in Figure 3-2.

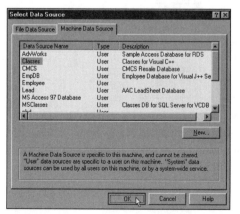

Figure 3-2: You can choose an ODBC machine data source or an ODBC file data source to serve as your database project data source.

Now you can see the database project, and if you select the Data View tab in the workspace pane, you see the contents of the database you chose. I chose an Access database, so I can only add, view, and edit tables and views, because those are the only choices in Access (Figure 3-3). However, if you instead choose another more fully featured database, such as Oracle or Microsoft SQL Server, you may see other types of items in your database project, such as diagrams or stored procedures (Figure 3-4).

In Access, a query is similar to a view in other database packages. In fact, many database packages such as CASE (Computer Aided Software Engineering) tools used for database administration regard Access queries identically to views.

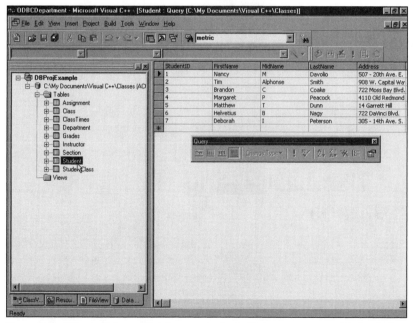

Figure 3-3: Microsoft Access database projects enable you to access tables and views.

Using a database project, you can enhance database administration. All ODBC databases can be accessed from database projects, and database projects enable you to easily administer several different types of databases with one common user interface.

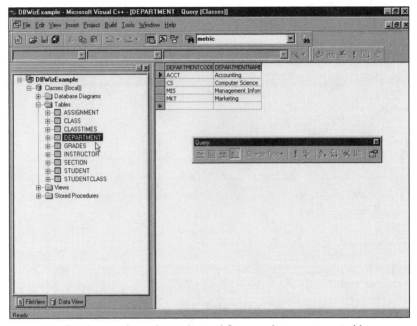

Figure 3-4: Database projects show advanced features that are supported by some databases. This Microsoft SQL Server database enables database diagrams and stored procedures as well.

Creating a New MS SQL Server Database Using the New Database Wizard

You can create a new Microsoft SQL Server database by choosing File → New, clicking the Projects tab, and choosing the New Database Wizard for the project type, as shown in Figure 3-5. The New Database Wizard can create a new Microsoft SQL database and connect to it through a database project. You can also connect to an existing Microsoft SQL Server database without going through ODBC by using the New Database Wizard.

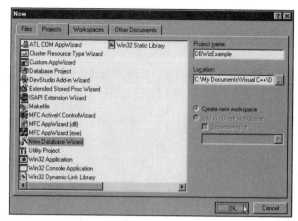

Figure 3-5: New Database Wizard projects enable you to
create new Microsoft SQL Server databases.

The New Database Wizard - Step 1 of 4 dialog box then opens, as shown in
Figure 3-6. Here, you indicate what SQL Server database you want to use for this
project.

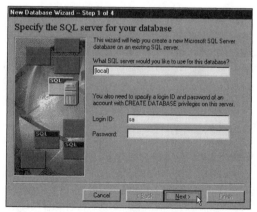

Figure 3-6: In the New Database Wizard - Step 1 of 4,
you declare which MS SQL server you plan to use.

The Bug with Local Databases

Local databases are new to Microsoft SQL Server 7.0. Visual Studio, which was released before Microsoft SQL Server 7.0, does not support local databases very well. However, you can access local databases by following these tedious steps.

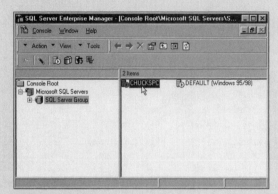

To connect to a local MS SQL Server database server inside Visual Studio, you must first create a "bogus" server using Enterprise Manager.

1. In the New Database Wizard - Step 1 of 4, declare that data source where you wish to connect. You need to enter "(local)" for the database server, but you cannot enter (local) into this field. The accompanying figure shows how CHUCKSPC, which is not a valid server, is entered. Because the New Database Wizard won't accept (local), you can just type anything in the SQL Server field — the idea is to get a login failure and get to the SQL login dialog, which does accept (local).

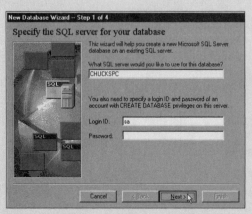

Enter the invalid server inside the New Database Wizard - Step 1 of 4.

2. Next, the connection fails. A SQL Server Login dialog box appears that is populated with a drop-down box of all the available servers. Choose (local) to access your local database, and click OK, as shown in the accompanying figure. You are then connected to your local server.

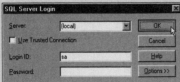

The SQL Server Login dialog box then enables you to choose a local database.

These steps are necessary to connect to a local database using Microsoft SQL Server.

After you declare which database server you plan to use, the New Database Wizard - Step 2 of 4 dialog box opens. Here, you define the database device and the log file device you are using. In Figure 3-7, I create a new database device for my new database.

Figure 3-7: You can create new database devices using the New Database Wizard.

When you create a new device, you are asked for the device name and the size. In Figure 3-8, I define a Classes device and assign it 4MB. I also create a ClassesLog device that can be used for disaster recovery.

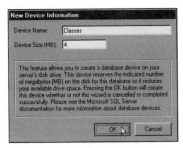

Figure 3-8: Visual Studio prompts you for any new device using the New Device Information dialog box.

When you're finished, you should see the database devices you've chosen in the New Database Wizard - Step 2 of 4 dialog box (Figure 3-9).

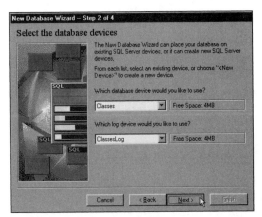

Figure 3-9: After you create the devices, the New Database Wizard - Step 2 of 4 is populated with the new device names.

Next, in the New Database Wizard - Step 3 of 4 dialog box, you need to name your new database. In Figure 3-10, "Classes" was chosen for the database name, and an appropriate amount of disk space was reserved for the database and log file.

From here, you can click Finish or click Next and Finish on the next step. Your new database is created. In addition, a new database project is created that accesses your new database *directly* rather than going through ODBC.

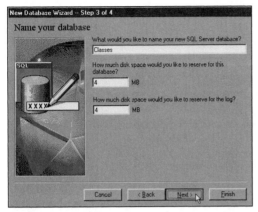

Figure 3-10: You can name your new database in the New Database Wizard - Step 3 of 4 dialog box.

Upsizing Your Database

This section is designed to show you how to create a new database using Visual Studio. However, if you are just following examples in this book, you could convert Classes.mdb into other databases by using tools that come with the database. Many major database vendors and CASE products have tools that can convert tools from one database to another.

For example, you can convert an Access database to an SQL Server database by performing the following steps:

1. In Access go to Help → Microsoft on the Web → Free Stuff.

2. Choose Microsoft SQL Server Upsizing Tool.

3. Download and install it.

4. Open your Access database (Classes.mdb on this book's CD-ROM), and choose Tools → Add-ins → Upsize to SQL Server.

5. Follow the instructions to create a Classes database on the server.

Note that it's simplest to turn off validation rules and triggers when converting an Access database to another database because Access does not support these advanced features.

Understanding Common Database Administration

All databases use tables to hold information. In addition, most use some type of view (also known as a *query* in some databases) that can be used to combine information from different tables and store that information in a tablelike structure. This section shows how you can administer your tables and views using database projects inside your Visual Studio environment.

Administering Tables

To access table information inside a database project, double-click the Tables older in the Data View tab of your Workspace window. From here, you can create new tables, view column information, modify table design, or enter information into a table.

VIEWING TABLES AND ENTERING INFORMATION

To see the columns inside a table, click the + sign next to the table whose columns you want to view. In Figure 3-11, the tables of Classes database are displayed, and the Assignment and Department tables are shown.

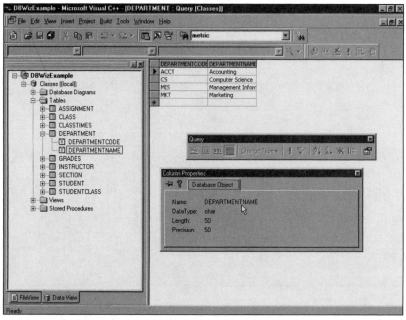

Figure 3-11: Using database projects, you can view the columns and data types inside a table or enter information into that table.

In addition to viewing table structure, database projects enable you to view table contents and enter or change records in a table. By double-clicking the table name, you open up a *query* (also shown in Figure 3-11). Queries are used for viewing and entering information inside a database. When the query opens, simply type information into the rows shown in the query. New records can be added at the bottom of the query.

CREATING AND CHANGING TABLES

In addition to adding or changing records inside a database project, you can also change table design or create new tables. To change table design, right-click any table, and choose design. In Figure 3-12, I right-clicked the Instructor table and chose design from the pop-up menu. The instructor table is then shown inside the Table Design window. You can manipulate table design many ways inside the Table Design window:

- ◆ You can change column names.

- ◆ You can add new columns by typing them in the bottom of the list.

- ◆ You can change the data types of the columns.

- ◆ You can change the length, or precision, of numeric fields.

- ◆ You can declare that a column can or cannot contain NULL values.

- ◆ You can set a default value for a column.

- ◆ You can make a column a primary key by clicking the Identity checkbox.

- ◆ You can make a column an autoincrement (also known as a *counter*) field by choosing the identity seed where you want to start counting and choosing the identity increment.

- ◆ Finally, you can declare a field to be an OLE field by clicking the IsRowGuid field.

To create a new table, right-click the Tables folder, and choose New Table from the pop-up menu. You are asked for the new table name. Type in the new table name. The Table Design window then opens, enabling you to type the columns and choose their attributes.

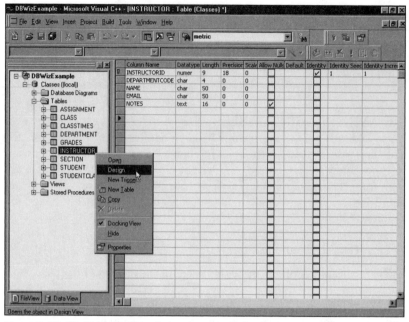

Figure 3-12: The Table Design window is opened whenever you modify a table design or create a new table.

Administering Views

Tables are defined using database design concepts brought up in Chapter 2. However, data from a database is usually stored with efficiency, not ease of retrieval, in mind. It can sometimes be quite difficult to retrieve the information you want in the format you want it. *Views* were created to meet this need. A view combines data from several tables based on given criteria. Each view then can be accessed identically to a table. Some views can even be updated if the database is set up to enable updateable views, and the view is set up correctly to enable some or all of its fields to be updated.

This section delves into views and shows how to create, edit, and use views in database projects.

TIP   In Microsoft Access, a view is called a *query*.

VIEWING VIEWS

To run a view and look at the results, simply double-click that view in the Data View tab of the Workspace window. In Figure 3-13, the Microsoft SQL Server Columns view (defined by SQL Server when the database is created) is run to show all the columns in the local Classes database.

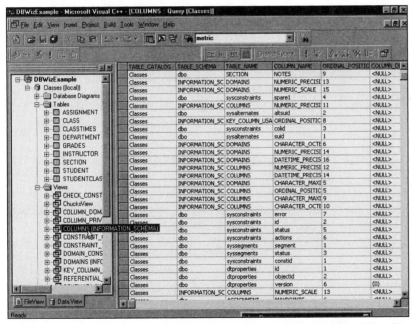

Figure 3-13: You can run a view in a database project simply by double-clicking it.

CREATING AND EDITING VIEWS

Just as with tables, you can create a new view by right-clicking the Views folder in the Workspace window and choosing New View from the pop-up menu, as shown in Figure 3-14. You can also right-click a view and choose Design, just as you did with tables, to edit a view.

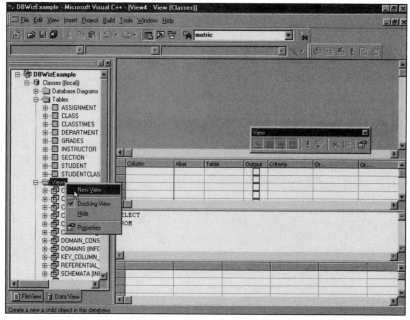

Figure 3-14: Create a new view by right-clicking Views and choosing New View.

When you create or edit a view, four windowpanes open:

◆ The Diagram pane is used to "paint" your view by enabling you to choose
   tables and columns that make up your view. If you type in SQL in the SQL
   pane, this SQL is parsed and reflected in the Diagram pane.

◆ The Grid pane shows the columns that you have chosen, their table,
   whether or not you want them displayed, and the criteria (if any) used for
   selection inside a WHERE clause.

◆ The SQL pane shows the SQL that is generated when you paint your view
   in the Diagram pane and when you add criteria, aliases, or output inside
   your Grid pane. You can also type in SQL directly at this point.

◆ The Results pane shows the results of the view when it is executed.

To create your view, simply use the following steps:

1. Drag the tables over from the Tables tab in the Workspace window to the
   Diagram pane. Notice that the relationships are automatically formed, and
   the SQL in the SQL pane changes to reflect which tables you dragged over.

2. Choose any columns you want to be in your view by clicking the checkbox next to each column. As with the tables, the columns are reflected in the SQL pane.

3. Choose any column aliases or criteria for selection. These, too, are reflected in the SQL pane in the column list and the WHERE clause.

4. Click the run icon (the one on the Query toolbar that looks like an exclamation point) to execute your view. The results are shown in the Results pane.

Figure 3-15 shows how a newly created view looks when it is formed and executed. Now the view can be used just as a table inside a SELECT statement.

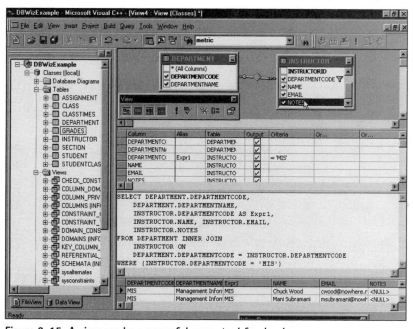

Figure 3-15: A view can be a powerful query tool for developers.

 In a view, you can't have two columns with the same name. Notice in Figure 3-15 that I had two DepartmentCode columns. One had to be given an alias ("Expr1") so that the view could differentiate between the two columns.

Views can be notoriously inefficient, especially when joined together in a SELECT statement. Inside a multitable join, you may get better results by avoiding views and using only tables.

EXECUTING SQL USING VIEWS

You can also use the SQL pane inside the View Design window to execute SQL statements. In Figure 3-16, a DELETE command is typed and executed from the SQL pane.

See the section "Using the DELETE Statement" in Chapter 2.

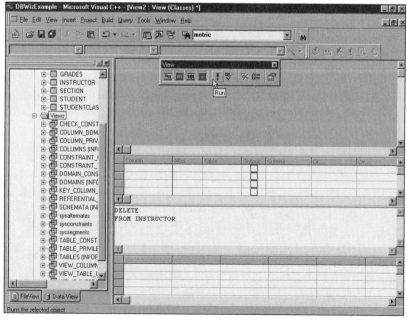

Figure 3-16: You can also use the SQL pane for non–SELECT statements, such as DELETE, UPDATE, INSERT, or CREATE.

Advanced Database Administration

Much of a database administrator's (DBA's) role can be accomplished with SQL execution, table administration, and view creation and modification. However, some databases, such as Oracle or SQL Server, have advanced capabilities that a DBA can use to make life easier. These capabilities include stored procedures, triggers, and database diagrams, which are stored at the database level.

Creating and Editing Stored Procedures

A stored procedure (also known as a *database procedure* or simply *procedure*) is a routine that is stored at the database level. Programs, other stored procedures, or triggers can call these routines.

The following is an example of a Microsoft SQL Server stored procedure:

```
CREATE PROC dept_instructors @dept varchar(4)
AS
SELECT  Department.DepartmentCode,
        Department.DepartmentName,
        Instructor.Name,
        Instructor.EMail,
        Instructor.Notes
FROM    Department
        INNER JOIN Instructor ON
            Department. DepartmentCode = Instructor. DepartmentCode
WHERE   (Department.DepartmentCode = @dept)
```

TIP   Most Microsoft SQL Server procedures also work with Sybase SQL Server.

In the preceding stored procedure, all the instructors are selected from a given department. This stored procedure can then be called whenever you call a SELECT statement (for example, to form a recordset) or inside another procedure.

In addition to normal SQL, most stored procedure syntax enables looping constructs (such as WHILE, FOR, and DO), decision support constructs (for example, IF and CASE), and variable declaration. Stored procedures offer the following two *enormous* benefits:

◆ Any program that is accessing your database can call a stored procedure. Therefore, stored procedures offer amazing modularity and control. A DBA or developer can write, optimize, and test a store procedure once to be used by all the developers in a company, even if the developers are using different languages.

♦ Stored procedures are faster than traditional SQL commands, especially with Microsoft SQL Server. Stored procedures are preparsed and stored, ready to immediately execute. By contrast, any SQL you pass to the server via a database program needs to be parsed and checked for syntax errors before it can be executed. This gives stored procedures a huge performance benefit over traditional SQL inside a program.

 Although stored procedures should be used when possible when developing a database, this book does not discuss them further. This is because stored procedure syntax differs from database to database, and Microsoft Access does not support stored procedures. Because most developers seem to have a copy of Microsoft Access, the database examples in this book tend to center on Microsoft Access. However, when you see a recordset being formed in the examples in this book, you could also ask yourself if you could perform the same solution by coding stored procedure instead of coding a SELECT statement.

Check your database documentation or your DBA to see what you can accomplish with stored procedures.

Creating and Editing Triggers

Say you tell a programmer that every time a change is made to the Grades table, an insert must be made to an Audit table. That programmer then has to make sure that no mistake ever occurs on any program that the programmer ever writes. In addition, that programmer had better make sure that no other programmer ever makes writes to the Grades table without also writing to the Audit table. Finally, that programmer had better make sure that all future developers also know the situation.

In this situation, an accident *will* happen someday when a programmer doesn't know or forgets to write an audit trail record when the Grades table is changed. Instead of forcing programmers to always remember a rule, you could use database triggers instead.

Whereas stored procedures are not tied to a table and are executed explicitly by a program or another procedure, triggers are executed automatically if an event occurs to a specific table. Because they occur automatically, there is no need to remember or communicate the need for special circumstances when changes are made to a table. In the previously described example, instead of having to instruct the programmer, you can simply set up a trigger to automatically insert a record into the Audit table whenever a change is made to the Grades table. This section goes through the process of using Visual Studio to develop a trigger for your database.

Say you created a new table called Audit, shown in Figure 3-17. This table is identical to the Grades table except for two features:

♦ There are two new columns called TypeChange (which holds a "DELETE", "INSERT", "UPDATE old", or "UPDATE new" depending on the change to the Grades table) and TimeChange (which defaults to the current date and time).

♦ The two new columns, TypeChange and TimeChange, can serve as the primary key.

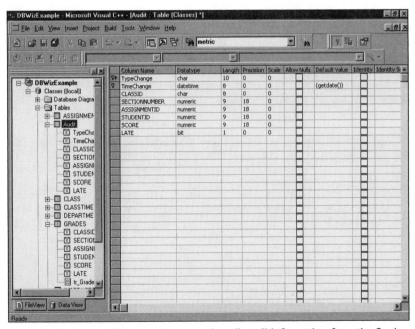

Figure 3-17: A new table is needed to track audit trail information from the Grades table.

You would want a trigger to automatically fill the Audit table with the appropriate record rather than rely on another programmer (or yourself) to remember to update the table every time a change is made to the Grades table. To create a new trigger, right-click a table name under the Tables folder in the Workspace window, and choose New Trigger. This creates a blank trigger template, as shown in Figure 3-18.

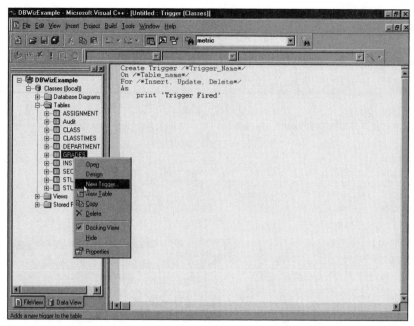

Figure 3-18: Triggers can be easily created using the Visual Studio environment.

Now you can write your own trigger. Consider the following trigger that updates the dbo.Grades table for every DELETE, INSERT, or UPDATE that is issued against the table:

```
Create Trigger tr_GradesChanged
On dbo.GRADES
For Delete, Insert, Update
As

/* Define  variables */
    declare @insertedCount int /* Number of records inserted */
    declare @deletedCount int /* Number of records deleted */
    declare @typeChange char(6)  /* INSERT, UPDATE, or DELETE */
    declare @updateType char(4)  /* old or new update */

/* Get number of inserted records */
    SELECT @insertedCount = COUNT(*) FROM inserted
/* Get number of deleted records */
    SELECT @deletedCount = COUNT(*) FROM deleted
/* Initialize @updateType */
    SELECT @updateType = ''
/* Determine what kind of change this is */
```

```
    SELECT @typeChange =
    CASE
        WHEN @insertedCount > 0 AND @deletedCount > 0
            THEN 'UPDATE'
        WHEN @insertedCount = 0 AND @deletedCount > 0
            THEN 'DELETE'
        ELSE 'INSERT'
    END
/* Insert Old records into the audit table from the deleted temp
table*/
/* set the updatetype variable to differentiate
old records from updates, if applicable */
    IF @typeChange = 'UPDATE' SELECT @updateType = ' old'
    INSERT into Audit
        (TypeChange,
        ClassID,
        SectionNumber,
        AssignmentID,
        StudentID,
        Score,
        Late)
    SELECT @typeChange + @updateType,
        ClassID,
        SectionNumber,
        AssignmentID,
        StudentID,
        Score,
        Late
    FROM deleted
/* Next insert an audit row from the inserted temp table */
/* set the updatedtype variable to indiciate
new records from updates, if applicable */
    IF @typeChange = 'UPDATE' SELECT @updateType = ' new'
    INSERT into Audit
        (TypeChange,
        ClassID,
        SectionNumber,
        AssignmentID,
        StudentID,
        Score,
        Late)
    SELECT @typeChange + @updateType,
        ClassID,
        SectionNumber,
        AssignmentID,
```

```
      StudentID,
      Score,
      Late
FROM inserted
```

In the preceding trigger, the following steps were coded:

1. The trigger is named, the table that it applies to is chosen, and the function (DELETE, INSERT, UPDATE or, in this case, a combination of all three) is chosen at the beginning of the Create Trigger command:

```
Create Trigger tr_GradesChanged
On dbo.GRADES
For Delete, Insert, Update
As
```

2. Declare any variables you need. You need to specify their length and type:

```
/* Define  variables */
 declare @insertedCount int /* Number of records inserted */
 declare @deletedCount int /* Number of records deleted */
 declare @typeChange char(6)  /* INSERT, UPDATE, or DELETE */
 declare @updateType char(4)  /* old or new update */
```

3. Variables are initialized or set to the number of inserted or deleted records. In the example, two integers are set to the number of inserted or deleted records, and the @typeChange string is set to "INSERT", "DELETE", or "UPDATE" depending on the type of change:

```
/* Get number of inserted records */
   SELECT @insertedCount = COUNT(*) FROM inserted
/* Get number of deleted records */
   SELECT @deletedCount = COUNT(*) FROM deleted
/* Initialize @updateType */
   SELECT @updateType = ''
/* Determine what kind of change this is */
   SELECT @typeChange =
   CASE
      WHEN @insertedCount > 0 AND @deletedCount > 0
         THEN 'UPDATE'
      WHEN @insertedCount = 0 AND @deletedCount > 0
         THEN 'DELETE'
      ELSE 'INSERT'
   END
```

> In MS SQL Server and Sybase SQL Server, two temporary tables hold deleted and inserted records. The name of the temporary table that holds the deleted records is called `deleted`, while the name of the temporary table that holds the inserted records is called `inserted`. All databases that support triggers have some means to inspect the record before the change as well as after the change.

4. Use the temporary deleted table to insert records into the Audit table that have been deleted:

```
IF @typeChange = 'UPDATE' SELECT @updateType = ' old'
INSERT into Audit
    (TypeChange,
    ClassID,
    SectionNumber,
    AssignmentID,
    StudentID,
    Score,
    Late)
SELECT @typeChange + @updateType,
    ClassID,
    SectionNumber,
    AssignmentID,
    StudentID,
    Score,
    Late
FROM deleted
```

5. Use the temporary inserted table to insert records into the Audit table that have been inserted:

```
IF @typeChange = 'UPDATE' SELECT @updateType = ' new'
INSERT into Audit
    (TypeChange,
    ClassID,
    SectionNumber,
    AssignmentID,
    StudentID,
    Score,
    Late)
SELECT @typeChange + @updateType,
    ClassID,
    SectionNumber,
    AssignmentID,
```

```
            StudentID,
            Score,
            Late
    FROM inserted
```

You need to write a trigger only once to handle *any* update from *any* tool or program. In an audit trail, this can give your database program security that ensures that no unwarranted changes remain undetected.

 This code writes all changes to an audit trail table, but be sure to establish proper security for that table. Otherwise, people could change their grades and thus change the Audit table.

Consider the following SQL to be executed:

```
/* Clear out the tables for this test */
DELETE FROM Grades
DELETE FROM Audit
/* OK, now begin the test */
/* Do an INSERT into the Grades table */
INSERT INTO Grades
            (ClassID, SectionNumber, AssignmentID,
            StudentID, Score, Late)
    VALUES ('MIS3030', 2, 1, 1, 90, 0)
/* Do an UPDATE to the Grades table */
UPDATE Grades
    SET Score = 100
    WHERE StudentID = 1
/* DELETE a record from the Grades table */
DELETE FROM Grades
    WHERE StudentID = 1
```

In the preceding SQL, A DELETE is issued to clear out the Grades and Audit tables. Then a new record is inserted into the table. That record is then updated with a new score. Finally, that record is deleted from the Grades table. Although the Audit table wasn't ever directly accessed (beyond the initial cleaning of all records off the Audit table), the trigger used the Audit table to automatically keep track of the changes made to the Grades table, as shown in Table 3-1, without any interventio from the programmer.

TABLE 3-1 AUDIT TABLE RECORDS

TypeChange	TimeChange	ClassID	Section Number	Assignment ID	Student ID	Score	Late
INSERT	7/9/99 9:04:02 PM	MIS3030	2	1	1	90	0
UPDATE old	7/9/99 9:04:02 PM	MIS3030	2	1	1	90	0
UPDATE new	7/9/99 9:04:02 PM	MIS3030	2	1	1	100	0
DELETE	7/9/99 9:04:02 PM	MIS3030	2	1	1	100	0

As you can see, triggers can be invaluable in ensuring the data integrity of a database and in keeping track of valuable information just in case that information is inadvertently deleted or, even worse, deliberately and maliciously altered or destroyed.

TIP   Most Microsoft SQL Server triggers also can function as Sybase SQL Server triggers.

Viewing Diagrams

Some databases, such as Microsoft SQL Server, actually store data diagrams on their database. Visual Studio also enables you to view or update diagrams of databases that are stored at the database level. Using the Microsoft SQL Server Enterprise Manager, the database model diagram shown in Figure 3-19 was created. In Figure 3-19, the diagram that was created can be manipulated inside Visual Studio.

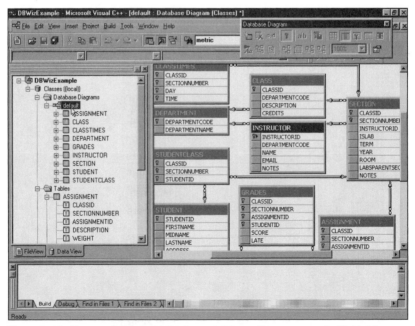

Figure 3-19: If supported by the database, database diagrams can clarify database development, especially if the developer is not familiar with the database.

Diagrams that already exist on the database can be changed in one of the following ways:

◆ You can change the position of the tables on a diagram.

◆ You can change what is shown on a table. The tables in Figure 3-19 show the column names, but you can show column names and column descriptions, or no column names at all and only table names.

◆ You can add new tables to your diagram.

You can also create a new diagram to be stored on your database or delete existing diagrams from your database.

As with stored procedures, Microsoft Access does not support triggers.

Database diagrams are a neat feature of a database and should be used if they can be easily developed so that those who use your database can easily see the database layout. However, there's no substitute for a CASE (Computer Aided Software Engineering) tool. Not only are CASE tools usually easier to use than coding SQL to accomplish the same task, but they also enable you to convert database diagrams from one database to another in case migration is necessary.

Summary

This chapter shows you how you can administer your database using Visual Studio. Although no C++ code is found in this chapter, this chapter can be a valuable resource for C++ database developers who want to fully access Visual Studio's database management tools. To recap:

◆ Database projects enable you to create new tables and views for your ODBC database. You can also execute SQL using a database project view.

◆ Some databases provide advanced features, such as diagrams and stored procedures. Visual Studio is a good tool for developing and maintaining these constructs.

◆ Triggers are available for some databases. Triggers are procedures that are tied to a table and are automatically executed when some action has been taken.

◆ Using the New Database Wizard, you can create a new Microsoft SQL Server database and establish a database project that points to the new database without going through ODBC.

Part II

ODBC Programming

Chapter 4

Understanding the ODBC API

ODBC IS THE MOST POPULAR database connection tool. This chapter describes ODBC, shows how to configure an ODBC database, and then shows how to use ODBC databases via the Microsoft Foundation Class (MFC). This chapter is a good background builder for the next two chapters, in which you'll be developing ODBC applications using the Visual C++'s Application wizards and Class wizards to help you quickly develop ODBC applications.

Understanding ODBC

Microsoft developed ODBC to become a standard way for accessing data in a client/server environment. ODBC is based on the Call Level Interfaces specification put forth by the SQL Access Group. ODBC is an open, vendor-neutral way of accessing data from any database. The following benefits exist when using ODBC:

◆ **ODBC is vendor-neutral.** If you are using an ODBC interface for your database, the program calls are the same regardless of which database is used. Furthermore, you can migrate from one database to another, but little or no modification may be needed in your ODBC program.

◆ **ODBC is open and well supported.** Every major database has developed an ODBC driver to enable access to the data through ODBC. Development tools, such as Visual C++, Visual Basic, PowerBuilder, and others, can access ODBC-supported databases without additional enhancements to the development environment.

◆ **ODBC is powerful.** It enables sophisticated access to databases often with little coding from the developer. ODBC insulates the developer from each database's idiosyncrasies and from any modifications made to the DBMS. You can even access data from several different ODBC data sources from within the same application.

ODBC is achieved through the use of a Driver Manager, combined with database-specific drivers. The application uses ODBC calls that access the ODBC Driver Manager. The ODBC Driver Manager then calls the specific ODBC driver that was written for the database. Then the database-specific ODBC driver accesses the data on the database. This is shown graphically in Figure 4-1.

Figure 4-1: The 32-bit ODBC framework

The result of the ODBC interface is that each ODBC application can access a wide variety of databases using the exact same database calls, as shown in Figure 4-2.

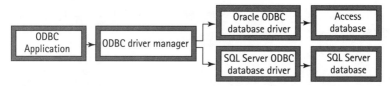

Figure 4-2: Multidatabase access with ODBC

Using the ODBC Data Source Administrator

Every ODBC data source must be defined by the ODBC Data Source Administrator before it can be used inside an ODBC application. To get into the ODBC Data Source Administrator, click the ODBC icon in your control panel. You get to the control panel by clicking Settings → Control Panel on your Windows taskbar Start button. The ODBC Data Source Administrator opens with the User DSN tab, which lists all databases currently using ODBC (Figure 4-3).

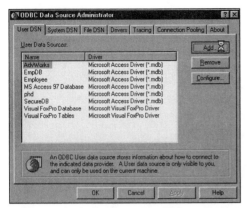

Figure 4-3: The ODBC Data Source Administrator

The User DSN tab lists the databases currently assigned to your user. If there are multiple *logged on* users in your Windows 9x system, your databases are accessible by you and no other users unless they configure them. System DSN and File DSN tabs enable you to add databases at a system-wide level.

If you click the ODBC Drivers tab, you see all the ODBC database drivers currently installed on your system, as seen in Figure 4-4. You cannot delete these drivers or add new drivers through the ODBC Data Source Administrator. This must be done using your installation disk or by directly accessing the Registry. (Directly accessing the Registry is pretty risky and is discussed later in this chapter.)

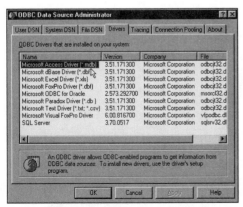

Figure 4-4: The Drivers tab of the ODBC Data Source Administrator lists all database drivers installed on your system.

Create a new ODBC data source by clicking the Add button in the User DSN tab (shown in Figure 4-3) to open the Create New Data Source dialog box, as shown in Figure 4-5. Choose the type of database you want to create, and then click Finish. For this example, I used the Microsoft Access driver to access the Access Classes database created for this book (and included on the CD-ROM that accompanies this book).

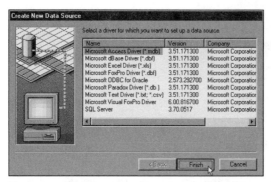

Figure 4-5: The Create New Data Source dialog box enables you to create a new database or assign an existing database to an ODBC DSN name.

If you picked Microsoft Access as your driver, the ODBC Microsoft Access 97 Setup dialog box opens, as shown in Figure 4-6. Click Select to assign an ODBC DSN name to an existing Access database. Using the Select Database dialog box, find the database you want to set up for ODBC. In Figure 4-6, I attached to the Access Classes database that I have created for this book. When you return to the ODBC Microsoft Access 97 Setup dialog box, you see the selected database placed in the Data Source Name textbox shown in Figure 4-6. Enter a data source name, enter a description of the database, and click OK.

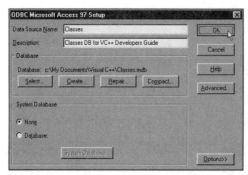

Figure 4-6: You can select an existing database to set up for ODBC. The database name appears in the ODBC Microsoft Access 97 Setup dialog box.

When you return to the ODBC Data Source Administrator, the database you configured is shown in the User DSN tab (Figure 4-7).

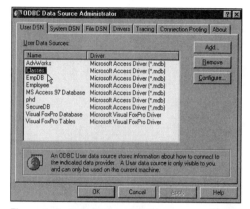

Figure 4-7: All additional databases are added to the list of databases on the User DSN tab of the ODBC Data Source Administrator.

Mastering the Registry

The Registry is a database used in Windows NT and Windows 9.*x* to store configuration information about the programs currently installed on your system. When you run the ODBC Administrator, the ODBC Administrator updates the Registry.

You can modify the Registry to configure your ODBC database. Although this is not as easy as using the ODBC Data Source Administrator, the Registry enables you to remove database engines from your system. You can also view how ODBC is set up, from a system standpoint, by viewing the Registry.

TIP Editing the Registry to alter your system can be dangerous. If you have never modified the Registry, you may want to pick up a Windows 95 or Windows NT book and read about it. Check out *Optimizing the Windows Registry*, by Kathy Ivens, published by IDG Books Worldwide.

To open the Registry Editor, run `Regedit.exe` choosing Run from the Start button on the taskbar. The ODBC databases installed are listed in `HKEY_LOCAL_MACHINE\SOFTWARE\ODBC\ODBCINST.INI\ODBC DRIVERS`, as shown in Figure 4-8. There, you can see all the ODBC drivers that various packages have installed.

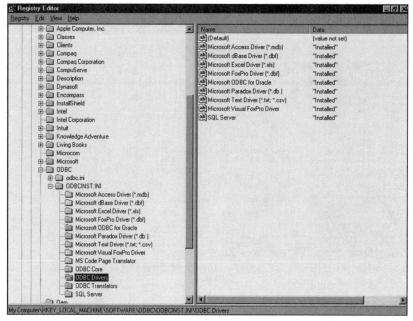

Figure 4-8: The ODBCINST.INI key contains a list of all ODBC drivers.

If you click a specific driver inside the ODBCINST.INI key, you see the drivers needed to run the database and set up a new database entry, as shown in Figure 4-9.

To remove a database driver by manually editing the Registry:

1. *Make a backup!* This enables you to undo your changes.

2. Delete all relevant drivers from your hard drive. These include the files listed in the Driver and Setup areas, as well as any files in the FileList. Note that some drivers can call other executables, ActiveX modules, or dynamic link libraries (DLLs); so you may want to research which files are included with your driver.

3. Remove the key folder from the ODBCINST.INI key by clicking the folder you want to remove and pressing Delete.

4. Remove the name of the database driver from the ODBC DRIVERS key by highlighting the name of the driver and pressing Delete.

5. Search the Registry for any references to the deleted ODBC driver, and either delete them or change them to an appropriate driver.

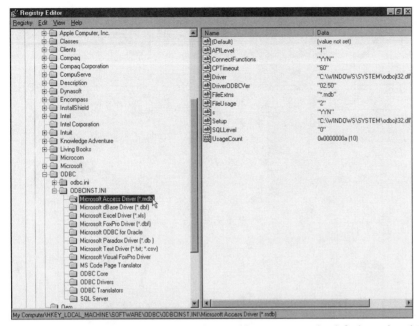

Figure 4-9: The Microsoft Access Driver key enables you to see the defaults assigned to all new Access databases.

All user database information is found in the HKEY_CURRENT_USER\Software \ODBC\ODBC.INI key. Here you see a list of all databases currently configured in ODBC. To see all the databases configured on your system and their database type, click ODBC Data Sources, as shown in Figure 4-10.

By clicking a database in the ODBC.INI folder, you see which drivers, directories, and files are used for that particular database, as shown in Figure 4-11.

The ODBC Registry is how programs, including the ODBC Data Source Administrator, access your ODBC database information.

It's important to understand how ODBC stores its ODBC data in case you need to view or modify it. However, try to avoid modifying an ODBC data source or database driver using the Registry. Instead, use the ODBC Data Source Administrator to remove a data source or a developer tool's setup program to remove a driver. It is safer and easier, and you have a lot better chance of clearing out all related files from your system.

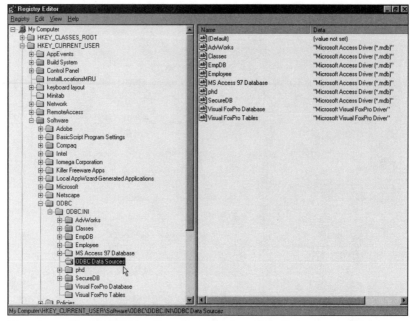

Figure 4-10: The ODBC.INI key lists all the databases installed on your system.

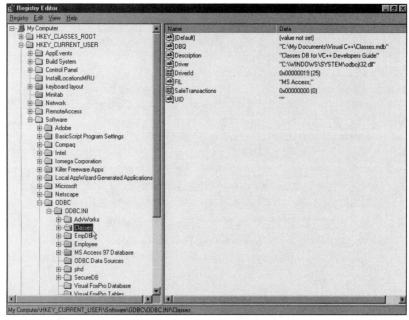

Figure 4-11: Each ODBC database has a key that describes files and drivers associated with that database.

The Perils of Modifying the Registry

Whenever you modify the Registry, you run the risk of making one or more programs completely inoperable or causing your Windows environment to lock up. When this happens, there is little you can do to fix your problems. You'll need to run Windows Setup again, specifying a different Windows directory. Then when it is done, remove the old Windows directory, and run Setup again on all your applications.

If messing around with the Windows Registry is new to you, you should pick up a copy of *Optimizing the Windows Registry* (by Kathy Ivens and published by IDG Books Worldwide). In this book, you can find out ways you can back up your Registry, restore an old Registry if the changes you made have caused a mess, or even to discover the bad things that can happen to you if you make a mistake while updating your Registry.

Accessing ODBC through the MFC

Most ODBC access in Visual C++ is done through Microsoft Foundation Class (MFC) functions. There are two MFC classes used to access ODBC data: CDatabase and CRecordset. These two classes are inherited from the CObject MFC class, as shown in Figure 4-12.

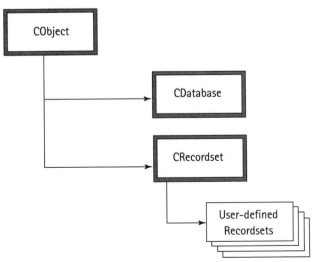

Figure 4-12: CRecordset and CDatabase inside the MFC hierarchy

ODBC programs usually have a class that is inherited from the CRecordset class, as seen by the following class definition:

```
class CODBCProgramSet : public CRecordset
```

By inheriting from CRecordset, your application has access to all the CRecordset functionality. In addition, the CRecordset class is designed to work well with the CDatabase class. This section goes over each of these classes and describes how they are used to access ODBC databases.

Understanding the CDatabase Class

The CDatabase class contains database-specific functions. These are functions that connect to a database, control transactions, and can execute command SQL (for example, INSERT, UPDATE, and DELETE).

CONNECTING TO A DATABASE
Every database application needs to connected to a database before that database can be used. The CDatabase::Open function is used to connect, and the CDatabase::Close function is used to close a connection. However, the CRecordset class (from which you should inherit your main recordset class) contains the functionality to handle the database connection so that you don't have to worry about it.

CRecordset contains the GetDefaultConnect function that you should override to return an ODBC connect string to the database:

```
CString CODBCDepartmentSet::GetDefaultConnect()
{
    return _T("ODBC;DSN=Classes");
}
```

As you can see by the preceding code, not much is required to connect to an ODBC database. If more information is required to attach to the database (for example, user ID and password), the user is prompted for all missing information. You can also add to the connect string by separating fields with semicolons:

```
CString CODBCDepartmentSet::GetDefaultConnect()
{
    return _T("ODBC;DSN=Classes;UID=cwood;PWD=myPassWord");
}
```

In the preceding command, a user ID of "cwood" and a password of "myPassWord" is added to the connect string.

EXECUTING SQL USING THE CDATABASE CLASS

After connecting to a database, you can execute SQL by using the `Execute` function. Adding the following line executes a copy of all the records in the Grade table to an archive grade table:

```
m_pDatabase->ExecuteSQL("SELECT * INTO GradeArchive FROM Grades");
```

In the preceding code, `m_pDatabase` is a public member variable in `CRecordset`, used by all `CRecordset` descendants to store the `CDatabase` object. The `CDatabase` class contains the `ExecuteSQL` function that enables you to execute SQL directly on the database where you are connected.

You cannot use the `ExecuteSQL` function to execute any `SELECT` command except for a `SELECT  INTO` command. You need to use the `CRecordset` `::Open` method to retrieve information from the database using a table name or a `SELECT` command. This is covered later in this chapter.

USING ODBC TRANSACTIONS

Transactions are a way to group changes together and keep database operations temporary and easily reversible. Using transactions, a developer can group several different operations into a logical work set. Transactions are often used to ensure database integrity (avoiding situations where half of an operation gets done and half does not) and to enable the confirmation of saves (so the user can erase all the changes made to the database if so desired).

Transactions usually correspond to the following steps:

1. Begin a transaction.

2. Do database changes.

3. If the database changes in step 2 are acceptable, *commit* those changes. Committing a transaction makes the database changes in step 2 permanent.

4. If the database changes in step 2 are not acceptable, *roll back* those changes. Rolling a transaction back erases the changes made in step 2.

SETTING UP ODBC TRANSACTIONS   To start a database transaction, you need to call the `CDatabase::BeginTrans` function, as follows:

```
m_pDatabase->BeginTrans();
```

Some ODBC data sources, such as Excel spreadsheets and text, do not support transactions. To test for transaction support, you can use the `CDatabase::CanTransact` function. This can be combined with the `BeginTrans` as follows:

```
if (m_pDatabase->CanTransact() ) {
    m_pDatabase->BeginTrans();
}
```

COMMITTING ODBC TRANSACTIONS   To make changes to a transaction permanent, you must commit the transaction. When you commit the transaction, the transaction ends, and the changes made to the database since the last commit or the last `BeginTrans` function call are made permanent. To commit a transaction using ODBC, use the `CommitTrans` function:

`m_pDatabase-> CommitTrans();`

ROLLING ODBC TRANSACTIONS BACK   To erase changes made to a database since the last `BeginTrans` function was called, use the `CDatabase.Rollback` method. When you roll back the transaction, the transaction ends, and the changes made to the database since the last `BeginTrans` function call are erased. To roll back a transaction using ODBC, use the `Rollback` function:

`m_pDatabase->Rollback();`

In the next chapter, you see some transaction processing inside an application. Some of the code samples here may make more sense when viewed in context with an application.

USING CDATABASE FUNCTIONS

Table 4-1 lists all the function prototypes of all `CDatabase` functions in alphabetical order and gives a short description of each function.

TABLE 4-1 CDatabase FUNCTIONS

CDatabase Function Prototype	Description
`BOOL BeginTrans( );`	Starts a transaction which enables later committing or rolling back of all `UPDATE`, `INSERT`, `DELETE`, or `CRecordset` updates to the database. The data source must support transactions for `BeginTrans` to have any effect. A `FALSE` is returned if the `BeginTrans` function fails. Note that transactions do not nest. After calling `BeginTrans`, you must call `CommitTrans` or `Rollback` before calling `BeginTrans` again.
`void BindParameters (HSTMT hstmt)`	You override this method to enable you to bind parameters before calling `CDatabase ::ExecuteSQL` to immediately execute your SQL.
`void Cancel( );`	Cancels this database's current asynchronous operation or a process from a second thread. This is not often used because the MFC ODBC classes no longer support asynchronous operations.
`BOOL CanTransact( ) const;`	Returns `FALSE` if the database that is referenced by the `CDatabase` object does not enable transactions.
`BOOL CanUpdate( ) const;`	Returns `FALSE` if the database referenced by the `CDatabase` object is read only and is not updateable.
`virtual void Close();`	Closes the ODBC data source connection. Usually the MFC library handles this so you don't have to worry about it.
`BOOL CommitTrans( );`	Makes all `UPDATE`, `INSERT`, `DELETE`, and `CRecordset` updates made to the database permanent since the last `BeginTrans` function call. A `FALSE` is returned if the function fails.

Continued

TABLE **4-1** CDatabase FUNCTIONS *(Continued)*

CDatabase Function Prototype	Description
void ExecuteSQL(LPCSTR lpszSQL);	Executes an SQL statement where no data records are returned. The ExecuteSQL function can be used to execute an UPDATE, INSERT, DELETE, or SELECT INTO command. This function can throw a CDBException.
DWORD GetBookmarkPersis tence( ) const;	Identifies the operations through which bookmarks persist on CRecordset objects. Bookmarks are covered later in this chapter.
const CString& GetConnect ( ) const;	Returns the ODBC connect string used to connect the CDatabase object to a data source in an Open or OpenEx function call. If no Open call has been attempted, an empty string is returned.
int GetCursorCommit Behavior( ) const;	Identifies the effect of committing a transaction on an open recordset object. Cursor behavior with recordsets is covered later in this chapter.
int GetCursorRollback Behavior( ) const;	Identifies the effect of rolling back a transaction on an open recordset object. Cursor behavior with recordsets is covered later in this chapter.
CString GetDatabaseName ( ) const;	Returns the name of the database currently in use. If no database is currently in use, an empty CString is returned.
BOOL IsOpen( ) const;	Returns FALSE if the CDatabase object is not currently connected to a data source. This is not used that often because MFC can control database connections. However, if you are constantly opening and closing databases, the IsOpen function could become quite useful.
virtual void OnSetOptions (HSTMT hstmt);	This function is called by the MFC to set standard ODBC connection options. This is not often used and was of more use to set the query timeout value before Visual C++ 4.2. (To set the default query timeout value, call the SetQueryTimeout function.)

CDatabase Function Prototype	Description
`virtual BOOL Open ( LPCTSTR lpszDSN, BOOL bExclusive = FALSE, BOOL bReadOnly = FALSE, LPCTSTR lpszConnect = "ODBC;", BOOL bUseCursorLib = TRUE );`	Establishes a connection to a data source (through an ODBC driver). Returns a FALSE if the user presses Cancel on the ODBC login dialog. This function can throw a CDBException or a CMemoryException.
`virtual BOOL OpenEx( LPCTSTR lpszConnectString, DWORD dwOptions = 0 );`	Establishes a connection to a data source (through an ODBC driver). Returns a FALSE if the user presses Cancel on the ODBC login dialog. Usually the MFC library handles this so you don't have to worry about it. This function can throw a CDBException or a CMemoryException.
`BOOL Rollback( );`	Erases all UPDATE, INSERT, DELETE, and CRecordset updates made to the database since the last BeginTrans function call. A FALSE is returned if the function fails.
`void SetLoginTimeout ( DWORD dwSeconds );`	Sets the number of seconds to enable a database connection. The attempt to connect times out after the allotted number of seconds expires.
`void SetQueryTimeout ( DWORD dwSeconds );`	Sets the number of seconds to enable a database query. The query times out after the allotted number of seconds expires. SetQueryTimeout affects all subsequent recordset Open, AddNew, Edit, and Delete function calls.

Understanding the CRecordset Class

The `CDatabase::ExecuteSQL` function is used to execute most SQL commands. However, when the SQL commands return a series of rows, as with an SQL SELECT statement, then a recordset needs to be formed. A *recordset* is an internal table in memory that contains the results of a database query. The MFC uses the `CRecordset` class to form and manipulate recordsets. Inside each recordset, fields are declared. The recordset object's field data members, taken together, constitute a display and edit buffer that holds the selected columns of one record.

EXECUTING SQL TO FORM A CRecordset CLASS

Just as you use an Open function to form a database connection and a Close function to close a database connection, you could also use an Open function to form a recordset and a Close function to close a recordset. However, the CRecordView class, which is generated from the MFC AppWizard and used extensively in this book, contains the functionality to automatically form a recordset as soon as the connection is made to the database. The GetDefaultSQL function is used to pass either SQL or the table name used in the query:

```
CString CODBCDepartmentSet::GetDefaultSQL()
{
    return _T("Department");
}
```

The _T macro converts a string to either an ASCII or Unicode string. By defining _UNICODE with a #define directive, you can use _T to return a Unicode string. ASCII is the default. Unicode can be used to write programs in other languages, even character-based languages such as Chinese, Japanese, or Korean. All programs in this book use ASCII.

As you can see by the preceding code, the name of the Department table is returned, implying that this code wants all the columns returned from the department table. You can also use SQL instead of a table name:

```
CString CODBCDepartmentSet::GetDefaultSQL()
{
    return _T("SELECT * FROM Department");
}
```

The CRecordset class enables direct updates to the database if a table name is used for the query in the GetDefaultSQL function. However, using a SELECT statement to form a recordset may not enable any updates to the recordset if you are joining multiple tables in the SELECT statement. So if you use a SELECT statement with a join to form a query, you must form an ExecuteSQL statement to perform any inserts, updates, or deletes to your database tables. When possible, use a table name or an updatable view name.

A CRecordset descendent is created when you use the MFC AppWizard to create an ODBC program (described in the next chapter) or when you use the New Class dialog box (by clicking Insert → New Class) and choosing CRecordset as that base class. Inside the CRecordset descendent class constructor, you probably need to perform three tasks:

1. Initialize the database variables that you are going to use to store your recordset information.

2. Set the m_nFields class variable to indicate the number of fields you are retrieving.

3. Set the m_nDefaultType to dynaset or snapshot. A dynaset type forces changes made by other users to be reflected in your recordset as you scroll through the records. A snapshot type is useful for reports, and quickly retrieves all records in a database without constantly checking to see if the records have been updated.

An example of these steps is reflected in the following code:

```
CODBCDepartmentSet::CODBCDepartmentSet(CDatabase* pdb)
    : CRecordset(pdb)
{
    m_DepartmentCode = _T("");
    m_DepartmentName = _T("");
    m_nFields = 2;
    m_nDefaultType = dynaset;
}
```

SORTING

Sorting records in a recordset can be done one of two ways. When using SQL, you can specify a sort using an ORDER BY clause in a SELECT statement in the CODBCDepartmentSet::GetDefaultSQL function:

```
CString CODBCDepartmentSet::GetDefaultSQL ()
{
    return _T("SELECT * FROM Department \
ORDER BY 1");
}
```

In the preceding SELECT statement, the recordset is sorted by the first column.

The `CRecordset::m_strSort` variable can be used to issue an `ORDER BY` clause (without the `ORDER BY`) to a recordset:

```
CString CODBCDepartmentSet::GetDefaultSQL()
{
    m_strSort = "DepartmentCode ASC";
    return _T("Department");
}
```

In the preceding code, the records are selected from the Department table and sorted in ascending order by DepartmentCode.

USING FILTERS

Especially with large datasets, it becomes important to reduce the number of returned rows. This is done through a process called *filtering*. Filtering records reduces the records based on some criteria.

With SQL, filtering is done through the `WHERE` clause, as seen by the following code:

```
CString CODBCDepartmentSet::GetDefaultSQL()
{
    return _T("SELECT * FROM Department \
WHERE DepartmentCode = 'CS' \
OR DepartmentCode = 'MIS'");
}
```

This can also be accomplished inside SQL by using CString variables and the + operator:

```
CString CODBCDepartmentSet::GetDefaultSQL()
{
CString CSDept = "CS";
CString MISDept = "MIS";
    return _T("SELECT * FROM Department " +
"WHERE DepartmentCode = '"
+ CSDept +
"' OR DepartmentCode = '"
+ MISDept +
"'");
}
```

You can accomplish the same task by using the `CRecordset::m_strFilter` class variable and returning a table name from the `CODBCDepartmentSet::GetDefaultSQL` function. The `CRecordset::m_strFilter` class variable is identical to a `WHERE` clause (without the `WHERE`).

```
CString CODBCDepartmentSet::GetDefaultSQL()
{
CString CSDept = "CS";
CString MISDept = "MIS";
//Set the CRecordset::m_strFilter variable
m_strFilter = "DepartmentCode = '"
+ CSDept +
"' OR DepartmentCode = '"
+ MISDept +
"'";
//Now return the table name
return _T("Department");
}
```

UNDERSTANDING FIELD EXCHANGE

Older ODBC interfaces forced the developer to constantly poll the database and the screen to make sure that the two were in sync. In other words, the developer had to ensure that the database reflected the user's changes and that the user saw the data from the database. This task was usually quite time consuming.

The MFC supports *binding* a database column to a program variable. Binding means that changes made to a variable are reflected in a database table, while changes made to a database table are reflected in the variable.

When the recordset is first opened and is about to read the first record, *record field exchange* (*RFX*) can bind each selected column to the address of the appropriate field data member. When the recordset updates a record, RFX calls ODBC API functions to send an SQL UPDATE or INSERT statement to the driver. All this is done with very little work from the developer.

 The ClassWizard or the AppWizard generates the code in the following sections for you. The following sections describe the code that is generated by these wizards.

USING THE DoFieldExchange FUNCTION   To accomplish a record field exchange, you must override the CRecordset::DoFieldExchange function. Then the CRecordset parent class calls your DoFieldExchange function to set up a field exchange. Consider the following DoFieldExchange function:

```
void CODBCDepartmentSet::DoFieldExchange(CFieldExchange* pFX)
{
    pFX->SetFieldType(CFieldExchange::outputColumn);
    RFX_Text(pFX, _T("[DepartmentCode]"), m_DepartmentCode);
    RFX_Text(pFX, _T("[DepartmentName]"), m_DepartmentName);
}
```

In the preceding function, `CODBCDepartmentSet` is inherited from `CRecordset`. The `SetFieldType` function is called using the `CFieldExchange::outputColumn` enum to indicate that you are binding output columns. Then, the `RFX_Text` function is called to indicate that column variables (that is, `DepartementCode`) are to be bound to class variables (`m_DepartmentCode`).

The parameter to the `DoFieldExchange` is a **CFieldExchange** object. The **CFieldExchange** class has only two functions that are accessible to you. The **CFieldExchange** function that you'll use most is the `CFieldExchange::SetFieldType` function. This function enables you to tell what *field type*, or kind of columns, you are binding to your objects. (Binding parameters is discussed next.) In the previous code example, we say that any RFX functions that occur are output columns. The other function, the `CFieldExchange::IsFieldType` function, is hardly ever used. The `CFieldExchange::IsFieldType` enables you to test what field type the current field exchange is currently accepting.

BINDING PARAMETERS Simple queries, as described earlier in this chapter, use static filters where the filter information does not change. However, often a more complex filter is needed where you need to be able to bind *parameter* information (rather than *column* information as done before). Besides exchanging data between the data source and the recordset's field data members, RFX also manages binding parameters. This can be accomplished through a series of steps:

1. Define any parameter variables in your `CRecordset` descendent:

   ```
   CString m_CSDepartment;
   CString m_MISDepartment;
   ```

2. Set the `CRecordset::m_nParams` variable to the number of parameters in your `CRecordset` descendent constructor:

   ```
   m_nParams = 2;
   ```

   I also originally set the `m_CSDepartment` and the `m_MISDepartment` variables in the `CRecordset` descendent constructor, although you could set them or reset them anywhere in your program:

   ```
   m_CSDepartment = "CS";
   m_MISDepartment = "MIS";
   ```

3. Set the `CRecordset::m_strFilter` class variable in the `CODBCDepartmentSet::GetDefaultSQL` function. Use ? for each parameter:

   ```
   CString CODBCDepartmentSet::GetDefaultSQL()
   {
       m_strFilter = "DepartmentCode = ? OR DepartmentCode = ?";
       return _T("Department");
   }
   ```

4. Modify the `CODBCDepartmentSet::DoFieldExchange` function. After you bind output columns, use the `CFieldExchange::SetFieldType` function to change the RFX field type to parameters. Then bind the parameters indicated in the `m_strFilter` variable in step 3 to the new class variables defined in step 1:

```
void CODBCDepartmentSet::DoFieldExchange(CFieldExchange* pFX)
{
    pFX->SetFieldType(CFieldExchange::outputColumn);
    RFX_Text(pFX, _T("DepartmentCode"), m_DepartmentCode);
    RFX_Text(pFX, _T("DepartmentName"), m_DepartmentName);
    pFX->SetFieldType(CFieldExchange::param);
    //Parameter names are not important
    RFX_Text(pFX, _T("Param1"), m_CSDepartment);
    RFX_Text(pFX, _T("Parm2"), m_MISDepartment);
}
```

 TIP If you need to pass a NULL to a parameter, you must use the `SetParamNull` function, passing the parameter number (starting with zero). To set the first parameter to NULL, you use the following syntax:

```
SetParamNull(0);   //"0" is the first parameter
```

Now every time your bound parameter variables (in this case, `m_CSDepartment` and `m_MISDepartment`) change, you must *requery* your recordset using the `CRecordset::Requery` function for the new parameters to take effect:

```
if (CanRestart()) {
    Requery();
}
else {     //Database does not support requeries
    Close();
    Open();
    MoveFirst();
}
```

> **TIP** Although not shown here, you can also use `CFieldExchange::input`
> `Param`, `CFieldExchange::outputParam`, and `CFieldExchange::`
> `inoutParam` to make calls to stored procedures in a recordset. Check out
> your database documentation to see how your particular database supports
> stored procedures. (If you can't find information on "stored procedures," look
> under "procedures".)

BINDING BLOBS Most people associate "blob" with a scary sci-fi movie. However, databases use the term *BLOB* to stand for binary large object. (While not as scary as the movie, BLOBs can be every bit as ugly.) BLOBs are used to store information that is too big to be stored in a single field. Examples of BLOBs are pictures or large volumes of text. Because BLOBs cannot be stored in any standard field, they need a special class that enables you to deal with them. The MFC has two different classes that can be used for BLOB storage: the `CByteArray` class and the `CLongBinary` class.

The `CByteArray` class is the preferred way for dealing with BLOBs. The `CByteArray` class treats a BLOB as a series of bytes and enables a lot of control over the BLOB at the byte level. The `CByteArray` contains many functions that can be used to manipulate bytes. In addition, RFX can be used to bind a `CByteArray` to a field:

```
RFX_Binary(pFX, _T("Picture"), m_Picture, PictureByteSize);
```

The `CLongBinary` class was used in 16-bit MFC when `CByteArray` objects were limited to a size of 32K. With 32-bit addressing, `CLongBinary` variables are no longer needed. However, you'll still find people using the `CLongBinary` class, both in older programs, and with programmers who are used to using `CLongBinary` fields to store BLOBs.

- ◆ `CLongBinary::m_dwDataLength` is the number of bytes contained in the BLOB.

- ◆ `CLongBinary::m_hData` contains a Windows HGLOBAL handle to the BLOB image object so you can pass the BLOB to Windows functions. This is often used for drawing the picture.

As with `CByteArray`, the `CLongBinary` class can be used with RFX:

```
void RFX_LongBinary(pFX, _T("Picture"), m_Picture);
```

As you can see, `CLongBinary` can be used instead of `CByteArray`, but `CByteArray` adds more functionality than `CLongBinary`, which is why it's the preferred method for retrieving BLOBs. In addition, the RFX_LongBinary function has no bulk equivalent, whereas the RFX_Binary_Bulk function transfers BLOB queries and updates just as the RFX_Binary function does for nonbulk functions. Bulk operations are discussed later in this section.

RFX FUNCTIONS   You can transfer many different data types. Table 4-2 lists all the nonbulk RFX function prototypes and a short description of each. (Bulk functions are discussed later in this section.)

TABLE 4-2 RFX FUNCTIONS

RFX Function Prototype	Description
void RFX_Binary(CFieldExchange * pFX, const char* szName , CByteArray& value , int nMaxLength = 255);	Transfers arrays of bytes of type CByteArray. This can be used for BLOBs.
void RFX_Bool(CFieldExchange* pFX , const char* szName, BOOL& value);	Transfers Boolean data.
void RFX_Byte(CFieldExchange* pFX , const char* szName, BYTE& value);	Transfers a single byte of data.
void RFX_Date(CFieldExchange* pFX , const char* szName, CTime & value);	Transfers time and date data using CTime or TIMESTAMP_STRUCT.
void RFX_Double(CFieldExchange * pFX, const char* szName , double& value);	Transfers double-precision floating-point data.
void RFX_Int(CFieldExchange* pFX , const char* szName, int& value);	Transfers integer data.
void RFX_Long(CFieldExchange* pFX , const char* szName, LONG& value);	Transfers long integer data.
void RFX_LongBinary(CFieldExchange * pFX, const char* szName , CLongBinary& value);	Transfers BLOBs of type CLongBinary. The CLongBinary class is simple to use but does not have as much functionality as the class used in the function. In addition, RFX_LongBinary has no bulk equivalent.

Continued

TABLE **4–2** **RFX FUNCTIONS** *(Continued)*

RFX Function Prototype	Description
```void RFX_Single(CFieldExchange * pFX, const char* szName , float& value);```	Transfers single-precision floating-point data.
```void RFX_Text(CFieldExchange* pFX , const char* szName, CString & value, int nMaxLength = 255 , int nColumnType = SQL_VARCHAR , short nScale = 0);```	Transfers string data.

BULK OPERATIONS MFC supports *bulk database operations*. Bulk operations involve retrieving many rows at once from a database, rather than one row at a time. To fetch bulk records and bind them to C++ class variables, you need to perform the following steps:

1. Declare your field data *as pointers* rather than primitive data types. Pointers enable C++ to store your information in an array:

```
class CODBCDepartmentSet : public CRecordset
{
public:
    LPSTR m_DepartmentCode;
    LPSTR m_DepartmentName;
// . . .
```

2. Declare long pointer for field size in your CRecordset descendent so you know how long each field is:

```
// pointers for the lengths of the field data
long* m_rgCodeLength;
long* m_rgNameLength;
```

3. Initialize all your field data and field data lengths to NULL:

```
CODBCDepartmentSet::CODBCDepartmentSet(CDatabase* pdb)
    : CRecordset(pdb)
{
  m_DepartmentCode = NULL;
  m_DepartmentName = NULL;
  m_rgCodeLength = NULL;
```

```
m_rgNameLength = NULL;
m_nFields = 2;
}
```

4. Override the CRecordset::DoBulkFieldExchange function just as you would the CRecordset::DoFieldExchange function for nonbulk updates:

```
void CODBCDepartmentSet::DoBulkFieldExchange(CFieldExchange*
pFX)
{
pFX->SetFieldType( CFieldExchange::outputColumn );
RFX_Text_Bulk( pFX, _T( "DepartmentCode" ),
& m_DepartmentCode, & m_rgCodeLength, 5);
RFX_Text_Bulk( pFX, _T( "DepartmentName" ),
& m_DepartmentName, & m_rgNameLength, 51 );
}
```

TIP

You'll notice that the field length in the RFX_Text_Bulk macros in the preceding code is one character more than is present in the database. This is because you need one extra byte to hold the null terminator for the string field.

5. Next, in your CRecordset descendent class, override the Open function to ensure that bulk mode is implemented. This can be done by logically ANDing the useMiltirowFetch enum with the current database options and then letting the Open continue:

```
BOOL CODBCDepartmentSet::Open(UINT nOpenType, LPCTSTR
lpszSql, DWORD dwOptions)
{
    //Use a logical or to make sure
    //that bulk mode is implemented
    dwOptions |= useMultiRowFetch;
    return CRecordset::Open(nOpenType, lpszSql, dwOptions);
}
```

There are several considerations you should review before implementing bulk mode:

◆ It's faster than single-record mode. Bulk mode enables more data to be transferred at once.

◆ It is not as safe as single-record mode. Data that has been updated since the last Move function is not flagged in a bulk mode program.

◆ Bulk mode is for queries only. The AddNew, Edit, Delete, and Update functions fail if attempted in bulk mode. Similarly, the IsDeleted, IsFieldDirty, IsFieldNull, IsFieldNullable, SetFieldDirty, and SetFieldNull functions cannot be used on recordsets that implement bulk row fetching. This makes bulk mode good for batch reporting, but lousy for user windows.

◆ The Move functions perform differently in bulk mode. The MoveNext function retrieves the next *block* of records, or rowset, not the next record. Similarly, the MovePrev function retrieves the previous rowset, not the previous record. The default rowset size for bulk mode is 25, but you can change it using the SetRowSize function.

◆ The class wizard, discussed in the next chapter, can be used for single-record manipulation. However, the Class Wizard is not equipped to deal with bulk mode.

◆ Finally, bulk mode uses the CRecordset::DoBulkFieldExchange function, not the CRecordset::DoFieldExchange function used by single-record functions.

Table 4-3 lists all the bulk RFX function prototypes and gives a short description of each.

TABLE 4-3 RFX BULK MODE FUNCTIONS

RFX Bulk Mode Function Prototype	Description
RFX_Binary_Bulk	Transfers arrays of bytes of type CByteArray. This can be used for BLOBs.
RFX_Bool_Bulk	Transfers arrays of Boolean data.
RFX_Byte_Bulk	Transfers arrays of single bytes.
RFX_Date_Bulk	Transfers arrays of data of type TIMESTAMP_STRUCT. Note the CTime is not supported in bulk mode, unlike in single-record mode.
RFX_Double_Bulk	Transfers arrays of double-precision floating-point data.
RFX_Int_Bulk	Transfers arrays of integer data.

RFX Bulk Mode Function Prototype	Description
RFX_Long_Bulk	Transfers arrays of long integer data.
RFX_Single_Bulk	Transfers arrays of single-precision floating-point data.
RFX_Text_Bulk	Transfers arrays of data of type LPSTR. The strings are stored in a two-dimensional char array. For example, with the previous code that retrieves the DepartmentName, the first string starts at m_DepartmentName, and the second string starts at m_DepartmentName + 51.

CRECORDSET FUNCTIONS

Table 4-4 lists all the CRecordset function prototypes in alphabetical order and gives a short description of each function.

TABLE 4-4 CRecordset FUNCTIONS

CRecordset Function Prototype	Description
virtual void AddNew( );	Prepares for adding a new record. You need to call Update to complete the addition. A CDBException is thrown if an error occurs during the AddNew function.
BOOL CanAppend( ) const;	Returns FALSE if new records cannot be added to the recordset via the AddNew member function.
BOOL CanBookmark( ) const;	Returns FALSE if the recordset does not support bookmarks.
void Cancel( );	Cancels this recordset's current asynchronous operation or a process from a second thread. This is not often used because the MFC ODBC classes no longer support asynchronous operations.
void CancelUpdate( );	Cancels any pending updates due to an AddNew or Edit operation.

Continued

TABLE **4-4** **CRecordset FUNCTIONS** *(Continued)*

CRecordset Function Prototype	Description
BOOL CanRestart( ) const;	Returns FALSE if the Requery function cannot be called to run the recordset's query again. If you cannot restart, you can achieve the same results by closing the recordset using the Close method and then opening it again using the Open method.
BOOL CanScroll( ) const;	Returns FALSE if you cannot scroll through the records.
BOOL CanTransact( ) const;	Returns FALSE if the data source does not support transactions.
BOOL CanUpdate( ) const;	Returns FALSE if the recordset cannot be updated. This function tests if you can add, update, or delete rows using your recordset.
virtual BOOL Check (RETCODE nRetCode) const;	Overridable CRecordset function used to intercept ODBC return codes and test them. Check returns a FALSE if there was an error.
virtual void CheckRowset Error(RETCODE nRetCode);	Overridable CRecordset function called to handle errors generated during record fetching. You may want to consider overriding CheckRowsetError in order to implement your own error handling during bulk row fetching. A CDBException can be thrown during this function.
virtual void Close( );	Closes the recordset. This function deallocates CRecordset memory and the ODBC HSTMT associated with the CRecordset.
virtual void Delete( );	Deletes the current record from the recordset. After calling this function, you must explicitly scroll to another record after the deletion. A CDBException is thrown if an error occurs during this function.

CRecordset Function Prototype	Description
`virtual void DoBulkField Exchange( CFieldExchange * pFX );`	This function is overridden and called to exchange bulk rows of data from the data source to the recordset. Implements bulk record field exchange (Bulk RFX). A `CDBException` can be thrown if this function fails.
`virtual void DoField Exchange( CFieldExchange * pFX );`	This function is overridden to exchange data between the field data members of the recordset and the corresponding record on the data source. Implements record field exchange (RFX). A `CDBException` can be thrown if this function fails.
`virtual void Edit( );`	Prepares for changes to the current record. You need to call the `Update` function to complete the edit. This function can throw a `CDBException` or a `CMemoryException` if an error occurs.
`BOOL FlushResultSet ( ) const;`	Retrieves the next result set of a stored procedure that returns multiple result sets. This function returns a `FALSE` if there is not another result set to be retrieved. This function can throw a `CDBException` if an error occurs
`void GetBookmark( CDB Variant& varBookmark );`	Assigns the bookmark to the current row of the recordset. The bookmark is stored in a CDBVariant variable. A `CDBException` or `CMemoryException` is thrown if an error occurs.
`virtual CString GetDefault Connect( );`	This function is overridden to return the default connect string.
`virtual CString GetDefault SQL( );`	This function is overridden to return the default SQL string to execute or table name to query.

Continued

TABLE **4-4 CRecordset FUNCTIONS** (Continued)

CRecordset Function Prototype	Description

void GetFieldValue(LPCT STR lpszName, CDBVariant & varValue, short nFieldTy pe = DEFAULT_FIELD_TYPE);
 	
void GetFieldValue(short nIndex, CDBVariant& var Value, short nFieldType = DEFAULT_FIELD_TYPE);
 	
void GetFieldValue(LPCT STR lpszName, CString& str Value);
 	
void GetFieldValue(short nIndex, CString& str Value);
	Sets the value of a Variant or CString parameter to the value of a field in a recordset either by using a column name or a column number as the first parameter. This function can throw a CDBException or a CMemoryException if an error occurs.

short GetODBCFieldCount ( ) const;	Returns the number of columns in the recordset.
void GetODBCFieldInfo (LPCTSTR lpszName, CODBC FieldInfo& fieldinfo); void GetODBCFieldInfo (short nIndex, CODBCField Info& fieldinfo);	Sets a CODBCFieldInfo structure with specific kinds of information about a field in a recordset identified by a column name or column number. A CDBException can be thrown if an error occurs during this function.
long GetRecordCount ( ) const;	Returns the number of records in the recordset. If there are no records, a zero is returned. If the number of records cannot be determined, a -1 is returned.
DWORD GetRowsetSize ( ) const;	Returns the number of records you wish to retrieve during a single fetch. This is useful only when bulk row fetching.

CRecordset Function Prototype	Description
DWORD GetRowsFetched ( ) const;	Returns the actual number of rows retrieved during a fetch. This is useful only when bulk row fetching.
WORD GetRowStatus(WORD wRow) const;	Returns the status of a row identified by a 1-based row number (so row 1 is the first row). This can be used to determine whether the row has been updated or deleted since the recordset was opened..
const CString& GetSQL ( ) const;	Returns the SQL string that was formatted to select records for the recordset.
void GetStatus(CRecordset Status& rStatus) const;	Sets a CRecordsetStatus instance, which contains the index of the current record and whether a final count of the records has been obtained.
const CString& GetTable Name( ) const;	Gets the name of the table on which the recordset is based. This is only valid if table name is returned from the GetDefaultSQL function is a single table, not an SQL statement or a table join.
BOOL IsBOF( ) const;	Returns FALSE if the recordset has not been positioned before the first record and there is no current record.
BOOL IsDeleted( ) const;	Returns FALSE if the recordset is not positioned on a deleted record.
BOOL IsEOF( ) const;	Returns FALSE if the recordset has not been positioned after the last record and there is no current record.
BOOL IsFieldDirty (void* pv);	Returns FALSE if the specified field in the current record has not been changed. The pv parameter is a pointer to the member variable of the CRecordset class, or a NULL if all fields are to be checked. A CMemoryException can be thrown if an error occurs during this function.

Continued

TABLE **4–4** **CRecordset FUNCTIONS** *(Continued)*

CRecordset Function Prototype	Description
BOOL IsFieldNull (void* pv);	Returns FALSE if the specified field in the current record is not NULL. The pv parameter is a pointer to the member variable of the CRecordset class to be checked, or a NULL if all fields are to be checked for any NULL in any field. A CMemoryException is thrown if this function fails.
BOOL IsFieldNullable (void* pv);	Returns FALSE if the specified field in the current record cannot be set to NULL. The pv parameter is a pointer to the CRecordset variable to be checked, or a NULL if all fields are to be checked for the allowance of NULL in any field. A is thrown if this function fails. This function cannot be used in bulk mode, and you must instead use the function.
IsOpen BOOL IsOpen ( ) const;	Returns FALSE if a recordset is not open. This usually is not necessary when using CRecordView because MFC classes usually handle the opening and closing of all recordsets.
virtual void Move(long nR ows, WORD wFetchType = SQL _FETCH_RELATIVE);	Positions the recordset to a specified number of records from the current record in either direction if the wFetchType parameter is set to the default SQL_FETCH_RELATIVE. All other uses of the Move function have been replaced by other CRecordset functions. A CDBException or CMemoryException is thrown if an error occurs.
void MoveFirst( );	Positions the current record on the first row of a recordset. A CDBException or CMemoryException is thrown if an error occurs.
void MoveLast( );	Positions the current record on the last row of a recordset. A CDBException or CMemoryException is thrown if an error occurs.

CRecordset Function Prototype	Description
`void MoveNext( );`	Positions the current record on the next row of a recordset. After this function, you should test using the `IsEOF` function. A `CDBException` or `CMemoryException` is thrown if an error occurs.
`void MovePrev( );`	Positions the current record on the previous row of a recordset. After this function, you should test using the `IsBOF` function. A `CDBException` or `CMemoryException` is thrown if an error occurs.
`virtual void OnSetOptions ( HSTMT hstmt );`	This function can be overridden to set options for the specified ODBC statement.
`virtual BOOL Open( UINT nO penType = AFX_DB_USE_DEFAU LT_TYPE, LPCTSTR lpszSQL = NULL, DWORD dwOptions = none );`	Opens the recordset by retrieving the table or performing the query that the recordset represents. A `CDBException` or `CMemoryException` can be thrown if there is an error. Usually, the `lpszSQL` parameter is set to `NULL`, which forces the `Open` method to use the SQL query returned by the recordset's GetDefaultSQL method.
`void RefreshRowset( WORD wRow, WORD wLockType = SQL_LOCK_NO_CHANGE );`	In bulk mode, this function refreshes the data and status of the specified row. If the row specified is zero, every row is refreshed.
`virtual BOOL Requery( );`	Runs the recordset's query again to refresh the selected records. A `FALSE` is returned if the recordset is not successfully rebuilt. In addtion, a `CDBException` or `CMemoryException` can be thrown if the function fails.
`void SetAbsolutePosition ( long nRows );`	Positions the recordset on a specific row. A `CDBException` or `CMemoryException` is thrown if an error occurs.
`void SetBookmark( const CD BVariant& varBookmark );`	Positions the recordset on bookmark that has been previously set using the `GetBookmark` function. A `CDBException` or `CMemoryException` is thrown if an error occurs.

Continued

TABLE **4-4** CRecordset FUNCTIONS *(Continued)*

CRecordset Function Prototype	Description
void SetFieldDirty(void * pv, BOOL bDirty = TRUE);	Marks the specified field in the current record as updated. The pv parameter is a pointer to the CRecordset variable to be marked as updated, or a NULL if all fields are to be marked. By using a second parameter of FALSE, you can also set any or all fields to nonupdated.
void SetFieldNull(void * pv, BOOL bNull = TRUE);	Sets the value of the specified field in the current record to NULL. The pv parameter is a pointer to the variable to be set to NULL. If the pv parameter is NULL, all fields are set to NULL.
void SetLockingMode (UINT nMode);	Sets the locking mode to determine how records are locked for updates. The nMode parameter can be set to optimistic (default) or pessimistic. to "optimistic" locking (the default) or "pessimistic" locking.
void SetParamNull(int nIndex, BOOL bNull = TRUE);	Sets the specified parameter to NULL (having no value).
void SetRowsetCursorPosition(WORD wRow, WORD wLockType = SQL_LOCK_NO_CHANGE);	Positions the cursor on the specified row within the rowset when using bulk row fetching.
virtual void SetRowsetSize (DWORD dwNewRowsetSize);	Specifies the number of records you wish to retrieve during a fetch when using bulk row fetching.
virtual BOOL Update( );	Completes an AddNew or Edit operation by saving the new or edited data to the data source. A CDBException is thrown if this function fails.

CRecordset CLASS VARIABLES
Table 4-5 lists all CRecordset class variables in alphabetical order and gives a short description of each variable.

TABLE 4-5 CRecordset CLASS VARIABLES

CRecordset Class Variable	Description
HSTMT m_hstmt	This handle contains the ODBC statement handle for a recordset. m_hstmt is used when calling the ODBC API directly, instead of through the MFC.
UINT m_nFields	This number needs to be set to indicate the number of field data members in a recordset.
UINT m_nParams	This number needs to be set to indicate the number of parameter data members in a recordset.
CDatabase* m_pDatabase	Contains a pointer to the Cdatabase object through which a recordset is connected to a data source.
CString m_strFilter	Contains a CString that specifies a WHERE clause (excluding the word "WHERE"). The WHERE clause in a SELECT statement is used for filtering records from a recordset.
CString m_strSort	Contains a CString that specifies an ORDER BY clause (excluding the words "ORDER BY"). The ORDER BY clause in a SELECT statement is used for sorting records in a recordset.

Understanding the CRecordView Class

The CRecordView class displays database records in window controls. The CRecordView class always works in close conjunction with the CRecordset class by displaying and updating recordsets directly using dialog data exchange (DDX) in conjunction with record field exchange (RFX) to automatically track changes in a recordset. A pointer to a CRecordset descendent class is defined in the CRecordView descendent header. This pointer is usually called m_pSet because that's how the Class Wizard (discussed in the next chapter) defines it. In the following code, CODBCDepartmentView is inherited from CRecordView, and a CODBCDepartmentSet pointer (m_pSet) is defined:

```
class CODBCDepartmentView : public CRecordView
{
public:
    CODBCDepartmentSet* m_pSet;
//. . .
```

The m_pSet variable is set to null in the CRecordView descendent constructor. However, your MFC document contains a CRecordset descendent instance:

```
CODBCDepartmentSet m_oDBCDepartmentSet;
```

This CRecordset descendent is assigned to the m_pSet pointer during the OnInitialUpdate function:

```
void CODBCDepartmentView::OnInitialUpdate()
{
    m_pSet = &GetDocument()->m_oDBCDepartmentSet;
    CRecordView::OnInitialUpdate();
//. . .
```

> **TIP**　The MFC document / view relationship is beyond the scope of this book. If the MFC document / view relationship seems confusing to you, you should pick up a book on programming for the MFC.

This section delves into displaying data from a recordset, updating a recordset, and transaction processing using the CRecordView class.

UNDERSTANDING THE DIALOG DATA EXCHANGE (DDX)

Just as MFC binds a database column to a program variable, MFC also enables binding a variable to a window control, such as an edit box. This means that changes made to a class variable are reflected in an edit box, while changes made to an edit box are reflected in a class variable.

Dialog data exchange (*DDX*) can bind selected window controls to the address of the appropriate class variable. When the user updates a window control (for example, by typing into an edit box), DDX automatically stores the value of the window control into the class variable. Similarly, when a class variable is updated, DDX automatically updates the bound window control with the new display value.

DDX and RFX are used in conjunction with each other to bind a table column to a window control. This is done by first using RFX to bind a table column to a class variable and then using DDX to bind that same class variable to a window control, as shown in Figure 4-13.

In Figure 4-13, the CRecordView descendent contains a pointer to an instance of a CRecordSet descendent (usually called m_pSet). The CRecordSet descendent uses the RFX to transfer table information to recordset class variables. Then the CRecordView descendent takes the recordset class variables and binds them to window controls using DDX.

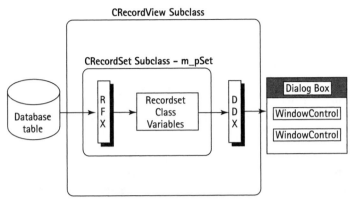

CRecordView Subclass

CRecordSet Subclass - m_pSet

Database table

R F X

Recordset Class Variables

D D X

Dialog Box

WindowControl

WindowControl

Figure 4-13: Table information is transferred to a Windows dialog box through RFX and DDX.

USING THE DoDataExchange FUNCTION   Inside your view class inherited from the CRecordView class inside your MFC application, you override the CRecordView::DoDataExchange function to indicate how the recordset variables also exchange with the window controls, such as edit boxes. Consider the following DoDataExchange function:

```
void CODBCDepartmentView::DoDataExchange(CDataExchange* pDX)
{
    CRecordView::DoDataExchange(pDX);
    DDX_FieldText(pDX, IDC_DEPARTMENTCODE, m_pSet->m_DepartmentCode,
m_pSet);
    DDX_FieldText(pDX, IDC_DEPARTMENTNAME, m_pSet->m_DepartmentName,
m_pSet);
}
```

In the preceding code, the ancestor CRecordView::DoDataExchange function is called. Then two edit fields, IDC_DEPARTMENTCODE and IDC_DEPARTMENTNAME are set to exchange with m_pSet->m_DepartmentCode and m_pSet->m_Department Name, which are the two CRecordset variables shown in the DoFieldExchange function discussed earlier.

By combining the DoDataExchange function with the DoFieldExchange function, you can easily link database table values with Windows controls without much work. Now any changes made to the IDC_DEPARTMENTCODE edit box are automatically reflected in the DepartmentCode field of the recordset. This is discussed more in the next chapter. Table 4-6 lists all the DDX_field function prototypes and gives a brief description of each.

TABLE 4-6 DDX_FIELD FUNCTIONS

DDX Function Prototype	Description
void AFXAPI DDX_FieldCBIndex (CDataExchange* pDX, int nIDC , int& index, CRecordset * pRecordset);	Transfers data between an integer field and a combo box. The integer is the index of the entry in the combo box list.
void AFXAPI DDX_FieldCBString (CDataExchange* pDX, int nIDC , CString& value, CRecordset * pRecordset);	Transfers data between a CString field and a combo box. This function sets the combo box to the first entry that *begins with* the same characters as the CString parameter.
void AFXAPI DDX_FieldCBString Exact(CDataExchange* pDX , int nIDC, CString& value , CRecordset* pRecordset);	Transfers data between a CString field and a combo box. This function sets the combo box to the first entry that *exactly matches* the same characters as the CString parameter.
void AFXAPI DDX_FieldCheck (CDataExchange* pDX, int nIDC , int& value, CRecordset * pRecordset);	Transfers Boolean data between an integer (usually BOOL) data type and a checkbox.
void AFXAPI DDX_FieldLBIndex (CDataExchange* pDX, int nIDC , int& index, CRecordset * pRecordset);	Transfers data between an integer field and a listbox. The integer is the index of the entry in the list.
void AFXAPI DDX_FieldLBString (CDataExchange* pDX, int nIDC , CString& value, CRecordset * pRecordset);	Transfers data between CString field and a listbox. This function sets the listbox to the first entry that *begins with* the same characters as the CString parameter.
void AFXAPI DDX_FieldLBString Exact(CDataExchange* pDX, int nIDC, CString& value, CRecord set* pRecordset);	Transfers data between CString field and a listbox. This function sets the listbox to the first entry that *exactly matches* the same characters as the CString parameter.

DDX Function Prototype	Description
```void AFXAPI DDX_FieldRadio (CDataExchange* pDX, int nIDC , int& value, CRecordset * pRecordset);```	Clicks on or retrieves the *nth* radio button based on the `value` integer.
```void AFXAPI DDX_FieldScroll (CDataExchange* pDX, int nIDC , int& value, CRecordset * pRecordset);```	Sets or gets the scroll position of a scrollbar control in a `CRecordView` based on the `value` integer.
```void AFXAPI DDX_FieldText (CDataExchange* pDX, int nIDC , BYTE& value, CRecordset * pRecordset);```	The `DDX_FieldText` function is the most used `DDX_Field` function. Overloaded versions of the `DDX_FieldText` function enable transferring int, UINT, long, DWORD, CString, float, double, short, COleDateTime, and COleCurrency data between a field and an edit box.
```void AFXAPI DDX_FieldText (CDataExchange* pDX, int nIDC , int& value, CRecordset * pRecordset);```	
```void AFXAPI DDX_FieldText (CDataExchange* pDX, int nIDC , UINT& value, CRecordset * pRecordset);```	
```void AFXAPI DDX_FieldText (CDataExchange* pDX, int nIDC , long& value, CRecordset * pRecordset);```	
```void AFXAPI DDX_FieldText (CDataExchange* pDX, int nIDC , DWORD& value, CRecordset * pRecordset);```	
```void AFXAPI DDX_FieldText (CDataExchange* pDX , int nIDC, CString& value , CRecordset* pRecordset);```	

Continued

TABLE **4-6** DDX_FIELD FUNCTIONS *(Continued)*

DDX Function Prototype

```
void AFXAPI DDX_FieldText
( CDataExchange* pDX, int nIDC
, float& value, CRecordset
* pRecordset );

void AFXAPI DDX_FieldText
( CDataExchange* pDX, int nIDC
, double& value, CRecordset
* pRecordset );
```

There are other DDX transfer functions. The functions described in Table 4-6 are those that transfer only database data. For other nondatabase DDX functions, consult the online help or get a Visual C++ book that covers the topic.

UNDERSTANDING DYNAMIC DATA VALIDATION (DDV) Along with exchanging data, you can also validate data upon entry. Using DDV functions in conjunction with DDX functions enables you to set a maximum number of characters per field, or to set a minimum and maximum for numeric values. DDV functions are added to the CRecordView::DoDataExchange function:

```
void CODBCDepartmentView::DoDataExchange(CDataExchange* pDX)
{
    CRecordView::DoDataExchange(pDX);
    DDX_FieldText(pDX, IDC_DEPARTMENTCODE, m_pSet->m_DepartmentCode,
m_pSet);
    DDX_FieldText(pDX, IDC_DEPARTMENTNAME, m_pSet->m_DepartmentName,
m_pSet);
    DDV_MaxChars(pDX, m_pSet->m_DepartmentCode, 4);
    DDV_MaxChars(pDX, m_pSet->m_DepartmentName, 50);
}
```

In the preceding code, the m_DepartmentCode and the m_DepartmentName variables are limited as to how many characters can be entered for each. Now when you type in values in the IDC_DEPARTMENTCODE and the IDC_DEPARTMENTNAME edit boxes, the edit box does not enable you to type anymore when it has reached its maximum length. Other DDV functions display an error message if the validation fails.

Table 4-7 shows all the DDV function prototypes and a description of each.

TABLE **4-7 DDV FUNCTIONS**

DDV Function Prototype	Description
void AFXAPI DDV_MaxChars(CData Exchange* pDX, CString const & value, int nChars);	Limits the number of characters that can be typed into an edit box.
void AFXAPI DDV_MinMaxByte(C DataExchange* pDX, BYTE value , BYTE minVal, BYTE maxVal);	Sets the minimum and maximum values for a byte.
void AFXAPI DDV_MinMaxDateTime (CDataExchange* pDX, COleDate Time& refValue, const COleDate Time* refMinRange, const COle DateTime* refMaxRange); void AFXAPI DDV_MinMaxDateTime(CDataExchange* pDX, CTime& ref Value, const CTime* refMinRange , const CTime* refMaxRange);	Sets the minimum and maximum date and time in a date and time picker control. This can be used with the COleDateTime class or the CTime class.
void AFXAPI DDV_MinMaxDouble(C DataExchange* pDX, double const & value, double minVal , double maxVal);	Establishes a minimum and a maximum for a double-precision floating-point.
void AFXAPI DDV_MinMaxDWord(C DataExchange* pDX, DWORD value , DWORD minVal, DWORD maxVal);	Establishes the minimum and maximum for a DWORD. A DWORD is a 32-bit unsigned long integer usually used for addressing.
void AFXAPI DDV_MinMaxFloat(C DataExchange* pDX, float const & value, float minVal , float maxVal);	Establishes a minimum and a maximum for a single-precision floating-point.
void AFXAPI DDV_MinMaxInt(CData Exchange* pDX, int value, int minVal, int maxVal);	Establishes a minimum and a maximum for an integer.

Continued

TABLE 4-7 DDV FUNCTIONS (Continued)

DDV Function Prototype	Description
void AFXAPI DDV_MinMaxLong(C DataExchange* pDX, long value , long minVal, long maxVal);	Establishes a minimum and a maximum for a long integer.
void AFXAPI DDV_MinMaxMonth(C DataExchange* pDX, CTime& ref Value, const CTime* pMinRange , const CTime* pMaxRange);	
void AFXAPI DDV_MinMaxMonth(C DataExchange* pDX, COleDateTime & refValue, const COleDateTime * refMinRange, const COleDate Time* refMaxRange);	Sets the minimum and maximum date and time in a date and month calendar control. This can be used with the COleDateTime class or the CTime class.
void AFXAPI DDV_MinMaxShort(C DataExchange* pDX, short value , short minVal, short maxVal);	Establishes a minimum and a maximum for a short integer.
void AFXAPI DDV_MinMaxSlider(C DataExchange* pDX, DWORD value , DWORD minVal, DWORD maxVal);	Establishes the minimum and maximum values for a CSliderCtrl control.
void AFXAPI DDV_MinMaxUInt(C DataExchange* pDX, UINT value , UINT minVal, UINT maxVal);	Establishes a minimum and a maximum for a unsigned integer (UINT) data type.

NAVIGATING THROUGH A RECORDSET

A recordset holds only one database row at a time. However, the CRecordset class has many functions that enable you to load different rows into your CRecordset class. To load the first row of a recordset into a CRecordset variable, you can use the MoveFirst function:

```
m_pSet->MoveFirst();
```

To move to the next row, use the MoveNext function:

```
m_pSet->MoveNext();
```

To move to the previous row, use the `MovePrev` function:

```
m_pSet->MovePrev();
```

To move to the last row in a recordset, use the `MoveLast` function:

```
m_pSet->MoveLast();
```

> The `MoveFirst` and `MovePrev` functions require that your database support backward scrolling through cursors. Check with your DBA or your database documentation to see if backward scrolling through cursors is supported.

To move to a specific row in a recordset, use the `SetAbsolutePosition` function. The following function positions the recordset cursor to the fifth row in the recordset.

```
m_pSet->SetAbsolutePosition(5);
```

> Unlike most things in C++, the record position starts from one, not zero. In other words, by using `m_pSet->SetAbsolutePosition(5);`, you really are positioning the cursor at the fifth record, and not at the sixth record.

You can also use negative parameters to use the `SetAbsolutePosition` function to position records at an absolute position from the *end* (rather than the beginning) of a recordset. The following line positions the recordset at the last record:

```
m_pSet->SetAbsolutePosition(-1);
```

You can also skip over to any row in a recordset. To skip five rows from your current record position, you can use the `Move` function:

```
m_pSet->Move(+5); //The plus sign is not required
```

You can also move backward by using a negative number inside your `Move` parameter. The following line moves five rows previous from your current position:

```
m_pSet->Move(-5);
```

Many move operations can move you *before* the first record or *after* the last record. In ODBC, recordsets have beginning of file (BOF) and end of file (EOF) record markers, as shown in Figure 4-14.

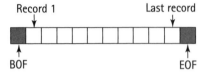

Figure 4–14: BOF is before record 1, and EOF is after the last record.

When using the MovePrev function, you need to test if you are at the BOF. This can be done with the IsBOF function and the following syntax:

```
m_pSet->MovePrev();
if (m_pSet->IsBOF()) {
 m_pSet->MoveFirst();
}
```

Similarly, when using the MoveNext function, you need to test if you are at the EOF. This can be done with the IsEOF function and the following syntax:

```
m_pSet->MoveNext();
if (m_pSet->IsEOF()) {
 m_pSet->MoveLast();
}
```

GETTING RECORDSET INFORMATION

So far, you've seen how you can use binding to retrieve variables without much programming. However, MFC enables you to retrieve information without binding, if you wish. This is especially important if you're not sure about the results of a query.

GETTING FIELD INFORMATION FROM A RECORDSET   The MFC's CRecordset class enables you to retrieve information about the recordset. The GetODBCFieldCount function returns the total number of fields that were found when the query was returned:

```
short numfields = m_pSet->GetODBCFieldCount();
```

The `GetODBCFieldInfo` function can be used to get information about each field. If you know the field name, you can use the name in the `GetODBCFieldInfo` function call:

```
CODBCFieldInfo info;
//I know the column names
m_pSet->GetODBCFieldInfo("DepartmentCode", info);
```

If you don't know the name of the columns in your recordset, you can also use the column number:

```
CODBCFieldInfo info;
//I don't know the column names
m_pSet->GetODBCFieldInfo((short)0, info); //Get first field (Field
0).
```

The `CODBCFieldInfo` structure variables are defined in Table 4-8.

TABLE 4-8 CODBCFieldInfo STRUCTURE VARIABLES

Structure Variable	Description
`CString m_strName;`	Contains the name of the string.
`SWORD m_nSQLType;`	Contains the ODBC SQL data type of the field. This can be `SQL_BIT`, `SQL_TINYINT`, `SQL_SMALLINT`, `SQL_INTEGER`, `SQL_REAL`, `SQL_FLOAT`, `SQL_DOUBLE`, `SQL_DATE`, `SQL_TIME`, `SQL_TIMESTAMP`, `SQL_NUMERIC`, `SQL_DECIMAL`, `SQL_BIGINT`, `SQL_CHAR`, `SQL_VARCHAR`, `SQL_BINARY`, `SQL_VARBINARY`, or `SQL_LONGVARBINARY`. These values can be found in the sqlext.h header file.
`UDWORD m_nPrecision`	Gives the precision, or number of digits, in a number, if ;applicable.
`SWORD m_nScale`	Gives the number of decimals to the right of the ;decimal point.
`SWORD m_nNullability;`	Can either be `SQL_NULLABLE` or `SQL_NO_NULLS` depending on whether or not the field is enabled to be nulls.

Finally, the GetFieldValue function can retrieve the value of a variable. If you know the field name, you can retrieve the value and store it in a CString variable:

```
CString deptcode;
//Get the DepartmentCode column and store it.
m_pSet->GetFieldValue("DepartmentCode", deptcode);
```

The preceding code automatically converts the column into a string if needed. If you don't know the field name, you can also retrieve the value by number and store it into a CDBVariant field:

```
CDBVariant var;
//Get the first column and store it.
m_pSet->GetFieldValue(0, var);
```

The following function can scroll through your fields in a recordset and determine the name and type of each column:

```
void CODBCDepartmentView::ScrollThroughFields()
{
    CODBCFieldInfo info;
    short numfields = m_pSet->GetODBCFieldCount();
    for (int loop=0; loop < numfields; loop++) {
        m_pSet->GetODBCFieldInfo(loop, info);
        CString name = info.m_strName;
        CString type = "";
        switch (info.m_nSQLType) { // Be sure to #include <sqlext.h>
        case SQL_BIT :
            type = "Bit";
            break;
        case SQL_TINYINT :
            type = "Tiny";
            break;
        case SQL_SMALLINT :
            type = "Small";
            break;
        case SQL_INTEGER :
            type = "int";
            break;
        case SQL_REAL :
            type = "float";
            break;
        case SQL_FLOAT :
            type = "float";
```

```
        break;
    case SQL_DOUBLE :
        type = "double";
        break;
    case SQL_DATE :
        type = "date";
        break;
    case SQL_TIME :
        type = "time";
        break;
    case SQL_TIMESTAMP :
        type = "timestamp";
        break;
    case SQL_NUMERIC :
        type = "float";
        break;
    case SQL_DECIMAL :
        type = "float";
        break;
    case SQL_BIGINT :
        type = "long";
        break;
    case SQL_CHAR :
        type = "string";
        break;
    case SQL_VARCHAR :
        type = "string";
        break;
    case SQL_BINARY :
        type = "Binary";
        break;
    case SQL_VARBINARY :
        type = "var binary";
        break;
    case SQL_LONGVARBINARY :
        type = "long var binary";
        break;
    default :
        type = "unknown type";
    }
    }
}
```

COUNTING THE NUMBER OF RECORDS IN A RECORDSET You can use the
GetRecordCount function to retrieve the number of records in a recordset.
However, the number of records is always unknown until you have scrolled
through each record using the MoveNext function and have reached EOF.

To determine if counters have been resolved, you can use the CRecordset::
GetStatus function to return information about your database table. The GetStatus
function accepts a CRecordsetStatus structure as its parameter:

```
CRecordsetStatus rStatus;
m_pSet->GetStatus(rStatus);
```

The CRecordsetStatus structure has two variables:

♦ CRecordsetStatus::m_lCurrentRecord is a long integer that contains
  the zero-based index of the current record in the recordset, if known. If
  the index cannot be determined, this member contains
  AFX_CURRENT_RECORD_UNDEFINED. If the recordset is at BOF, then
  m_lCurrentRecord is set to AFX_CURRENT_RECORD_BOF. (Both these
  error conditions are negative numbers.) If at the first record, then it is set
  to 0; second record, 1; and so on.

♦ CRecordsetStatus::m_bRecordCountFinal is a BOOL. It is set to FALSE
  if the total number of records in the recordset has not been determined. To
  set this value to TRUE, you must start at the beginning of the recordset
  and call the MoveNext function until the IsEOF does not return FALSE. If
  this member is zero, the record count as returned by GetRecordCount
  returns an invalid number.

To display the current record number in a MFC program, try these steps:

1. The CMainFrame class is built by the MFC Application Wizard (discussed
   in the next chapter). The status bar of the current frame is accessed by the
   m_wndStatusBar protected variable inside the CFrameWnd class, which is
   the ancestor class of CMainFrame. Include the following code in your
   MainFrm.h header file so you can access the status bar:

```
public:
    inline CStatusBar* GetStatusBar() {
        return &m_wndStatusBar;
    }
```

2. Add a DisplayRecordPosition function prototype to the CRecordView
   descendent header file (that is, CODBCDepartmentView.h) and override the
   CRecordView::OnMove function:

```
class CODBCDepartmentView : public CRecordView {
public:
    void DisplayRecordPosition();
    virtual BOOL OnMove(UINT nIDMoveCommand);
```

3. **Now code the** DisplayRecordPosition **and** CRecordset::OnMove
functions:

```
BOOL CODBCDepartmentView::OnMove(UINT nIDMoveCommand)
{
    BOOL returnCode = CRecordView::OnMove(nIDMoveCommand);
    DisplayRecordPosition();
    return returnCode;
}

void CODBCDepartmentView::DisplayRecordPosition() {
    long currentRec;
    long totalRec;
    CString str;
    CRecordsetStatus rStatus;
    CMainFrame* pFrame=(CMainFrame*) AfxGetApp()->m_pMainWnd;
    CStatusBar* pStatus = pFrame->GetStatusBar();
    m_pSet->GetStatus(rStatus);              //Get Status
    currentRec = rStatus.m_lCurrentRecord;   //Get current
record
    if (!rStatus.m_bRecordCountFinal) {        //See if the
final record has been determined
        UpdateData(FALSE);              //Don't update
        //Record count is unknown
        m_pSet->MoveFirst();            //Start at the beginning
        while (!m_pSet->IsEOF()) {           //Go until EOF
            m_pSet->MoveNext();     //Get next record
        }
        //Restore previous record position
//First place cursor before current record
        m_pSet->SetAbsolutePosition(currentRec);
        //Now move next to capture current record
        m_pSet->MoveNext();
        UpdateData(TRUE);
    }
    currentRec++;                        //Current record is zero
based
    totalRec = m_pSet->GetRecordCount();   //Get total count
    str.Format("Record %ld of %ld", currentRec, totalRec);
//Format display string
```

```
        pStatus->SetPaneText(0, str);              //Display the
string
    }
```

By looking at the preceding code, you can see how the rStatus.m_bRecord Count Final variable is checked to see if a record count can be retrieved. If not, you must scroll through each record using the MoveNext function until you hit EOF. After the recordset reaches EOF, the position is restored to the current record again. Finally, a CString variable is formatted and displayed.

USING BOOKMARKS

In addition to standard navigation functions such as MoveNext, you can also use *bookmarks* to set your position in a cursor on a database. To mark the current row with a bookmark, you need to call the GetBookmark function:

```
CDBVariant cdbv;
m_pSet->GetBookmark(cdbv);
```

Bookmarks are then stored in a CDBVariant field. To set the recordset to the bookmarked position, you need to use the SetBookmark function:

```
m_pSet->SetBookmark(cdbv);
```

TIP Not all databases support bookmarks. To see if your database supports bookmarks, you need to use the CanBookmark function in code similar to the following:
```
CDBVariant cdbv;
if (CanBookmark()) {
    m_pSet->GetBookmark(cdbv);
}
```

UPDATING A RECORDSET

There are two ways to update a database using MFC and ODBC. The first is by using the ExecuteSQL function that was discussed earlier in this chapter. The second is to use CRecordset functions that enable updates directly from the recordset.

If you use SQL join in the GetDefaultSQL function, you won't be able to update your recordset. Recordsets can be updated only if they are derived from a table or SQL query from a single, unjoined table.

To delete a row from a table on the database, you can use the Delete function. The following line of code deletes the current recordset row from the database:

```
m_pSet->Delete();
```

To update the current row, you need to throw the recordset into *edit mode* using the Edit function and then issue an Update function:

```
m_pSet->Edit();
//update member variables here
m_pSet->Update();
```

Similarly, to add a new row to a table, you need to place the recordset into *add new mode* using the AddNew function and then issue an Update function:

```
m_pSet->AddNew();
//update member variables here
m_pSet->Update();
```

If you call the AddNew function or the Edit function but decide that you don't want to call the Update function, you can abort the operation by calling the CancelUpdate function:

```
m_pSet->CancelUpdate();
```

TESTING CURSOR BEHAVIOR WITH TRANSACTIONS

Some databases corrupt a recordset sequence after a commit. Other databases completely corrupt cursors after commits, and the recordset that uses the cursor needs to be closed. To test for your particular database's behavior after a commit, be sure to #include <SQL.h> in your header. Then you can use the GetCursorCommit Behavior or the GetCursorRollbackBehavior functions following test after a commit.

Internally, the MFC uses a database construct called a *cursor* to form recordsets. Cursors are used to form a table in memory and populate the table with the results of a SELECT statement. With most databases, transactions simply make changes to a database permanent. However, certain databases have detrimental effects on open cursors when a transaction is committed or rolled back. If you have an open CRecordset object when calling a CommitTrans or Rollback function, you may need some additional processing.

The following code shows how to use the CommitTrans and GetCursor CommitBehavior functions:

```
if (m_pDatabase->CanTransact()) {
//CommitTrans or Rollback function
m_pDatabase->CommitTrans();
//Test using GetCursorCommitBehavior
//or GetCursorRollbackBehavior
switch(m_pDatabase-> GetCursorCommitBehavior()) {
    case SQL_CB_CLOSE :
// Call CRecordset::Requery immediately
// following the transaction commit.
        if (CanRestart()) {
            Requery();
        }
        else {
            Close();
            Open();
            MoveFirst();
        }
        break;
    case SQL_CB_DELETE:
// Call CRecordset::Close immediately
// following the transaction commit.
        Close();
        Open();
        MoveFirst();
        break;
    case SQL_CB_PRESERVE :
    default:
//Business as usual
        break;
    }
}
```

Some databases do not support requeries. If your database does not support requeries, or if you're not sure, you must use the CanRestart function to test for requery capability, and, if not, use an Open/Close combination to requery.

CRecordView FUNCTIONS

Table 4-9 shows the `CRecordView` functions.

TABLE 4-9 CRecordView FUNCTIONS

CRecordView Function Prototype	Description
`virtual CRecordset * OnGetRecordset ( ) = 0;`	Returns a pointer to the `CRecordset` object associated with the `CRecordView`. This is usually not needed because the ClassWizard overrides this function for you and creates the recordset if necessary. If you used the MFC Application Wizard (discussed in the next chapter) to generate your Visual C++ code, use `CrecordView ::m_pSet` instead of this function.
`BOOL IsOnFirst Record( );`	Returns `FALSE` if the current record is not the first record in the associated recordset.
`BOOL IsOnLast Record( );`	Returns `FALSE` if the current record is not the last record in the associated recordset.
`virtual BOOL OnMove ( UINT nIDMove Command );`	If the current record has changed, the `OnMove` function updates the data source (if needed), then moves to the specified record (next, previous, first, or last). The nIDMoveCommand parameter can be `ID_RECORD_FIRST`, `ID_RECORD_LAST`, `ID_RECORD_NEXT`, or `ID_RECORD_PREV`, depending on the move command issued by the program. Override this function to control movement and updating yourself. The `OnMove` function throws the CDBException when an error occurs.

CRecordView is inherited from CFormView (which is inherited from CScrollView, which is inherited from CView, and so on). As such, CRecordView has nondatabase functionality built into it. This section describes only functionality needed for database access. More functionality can be reviewed from a good MFC or Visual C++ book.

Implementing Table Joins

Joining tables enables you to correlate related rows from two different tables. For instance, you may want to retrieve all the instructor names from the Instructor table along with their corresponding department names from the Department table. To do this for a read-only recordset, you could use SQL:

```
CString CODBCDepartmentSet::GetDefaultSQL()
{
    return _T("SELECT DepartmentName,
                      Name \
              FROM    Instructor i, \
                      Department d \
              WHERE d.DepartmentCode = i.DepartmentCode");
}
```

 With MFC, using a table join prevents you from updating the database using Edit() or AddNew().

A more versatile (but complicated) way to join two tables is by returning both table names from the GetDefaultSQL function. This involves several steps.

1. Put the where clause in the m_strFilter class variable and return both table names separated by commas in the GetDefaultSQL function. Notice that if you are joining two columns from two tables that have the same names, you must fully qualify those column names with the table name in the filter:

```
CString CODBCDepartmentSet::GetDefaultSQL()
{
    m_strFilter =
"Department.DepartmentCode = Instructor.DepartmentCode";
    return _T("Department, Instructor ");
}
```

2. Be sure to initialize your field variables inside your recordset constructor and increase the m_nFields variable to indicate the new number of fields you have:

```
CODBCDepartmentSet::CODBCDepartmentSet(CDatabase* pdb)
    : CRecordset(pdb)
{
    m_DepartmentCode = _T("");
```

```
    m_DepartmentName = _T("");
    m_EMAIL = _T("");
    m_InstructorID = 0;
    m_Name = _T("");
    m_Notes = _T("");
    m_nFields = 6;
    m_nDefaultType = dynaset;
}
```

3. Incorporate the new fields you are using in the `DoFieldExchange` function in your recordset module. Notice that if there are any duplicate column names inside the two tables, you must also specifically qualify each one. In the following code, DepartmentCode is qualified with the Department table (`"Department.DepartmentCode"`) to indicate that we want to retrieve the DepartmentCode from the Department table, not the DepartmentCode from the Instructor table.

```
void CODBCDepartmentSet::DoFieldExchange(CFieldExchange* pFX)
{
    pFX->SetFieldType(CFieldExchange::outputColumn);
    RFX_Text(pFX, _T("Department.DepartmentCode "),
m_DepartmentCode);
    RFX_Text(pFX, _T("DepartmentName"), m_DepartmentName);
    RFX_Text(pFX, _T("EMAIL"), m_EMAIL);
    RFX_Long(pFX, _T("InstructorID"), m_InstructorID);
    RFX_Text(pFX, _T("Name"), m_Name);
    RFX_Text(pFX, _T("Notes"), m_Notes);
}
```

4. Now you can use the new columns from the recordset. For example, in the MFC view program in the `DoDataExchange` function, you can add the fields to a data exchange so that the fields are bound to edit boxes and are updated by the user when a dialog box is displayed:

```
void CODBCDepartmentView::DoDataExchange(CDataExchange* pDX)
{
    CRecordView::DoDataExchange(pDX);
    DDX_FieldText(pDX, IDC_DEPARTMENTCODE, m_pSet-
>m_DepartmentCode, m_pSet);
    DDX_FieldText(pDX, IDC_DEPARTMENTNAME, m_pSet-
>m_DepartmentName, m_pSet);
    DDX_FieldText(pDX, IDC_EMAIL, m_pSet->m_EMAIL, m_pSet);
    DDX_FieldText(pDX, IDC_INSTRUCTORID, m_pSet-
>m_InstructorID, m_pSet);
    DDX_FieldText(pDX, IDC_NAME, m_pSet->m_Name, m_pSet);
    DDX_FieldText(pDX, IDC_NOTES, m_pSet->m_Notes, m_pSet);
}
```

Using ODBC API Functions

If you wish, you can avoid the use of the MFC and call ODBC functions directly using the ODBC API. This is not recommended for two reasons:

◆ The ODBC API is C-based, not C++-based. As a result, it is not object-oriented. The main result to you, the developer, is that ODBC API functions cannot preserve class variables and thus require that you do it yourself. In addition, you usually must pass many parameters to these functions. By contrast, the MFC ODBC interface keeps track of class variables (such as connections and recordsets) that have been used before and that require less effort to use.

◆ The MFC is supported by the Class Wizard and the Application Wizard. The ODBC API is not. As a result, the MFC ODBC interface is extremely easy to use, often requiring little effort from the developer to write fully functional applications. By contrast, the ODBC API requires a lot more development time.

That being said, you still may need to understand the ODBC API because of older applications or C++ applications written in another language, or because you need asynchronous processing, which is not supported by the MFC ODBC interface. Also, the MFC greatly simplifies ODBC access, and you may need more complex access for certain applications.

To call an ODBC API function directly, you must perform the following steps:

1. Allocate storage for any results the call returns.

2. Pass an ODBC HDBC or HSTMT handle, depending on the parameter signature of the function. If you like to use MFC, but need to make an ODBC API database call, the CDatabase::m_hdbc and CRecordset::m_hstmt variables can be used so that you do not need to allocate and initialize these yourself.

3. Call any needed additional ODBC functions to prepare for or follow up the main call.

4. Deallocate storage when you finish.

 A list of all ODBC API functions can be found in Appendix B.

USING ASYNCHRONOUS DATABASE CALLS

One of the only times you'll want to use the ODBC API is to handle asynchronous database operations. Asynchronous operations are operations that run "in the background" of a machine and enable other statements to continue processing while they complete. For instance, say you wanted to issue the following SQL command:

```
DELETE FROM Student WHERE RIGHT(LastName, 4) = 'mith'
```

With an extremely large student table, this call would take an extraordinarily long time. Because the database engine would not be able to use any index, the database engine would need to examine every record in the student table. While this is occurring, you may wish to run other functions or continue the program, but asynchronous operations were disabled from MFC. The only way to execute an asynchronous ODBC operation is to use the ODBC API. However, you *can* use both in conjunction with each other. The following code shows how to execute an asynchronous ODBC call inside an MFC class:

```
void CODBCDepartmentView::AsynchronousExample()
{
    //Instead of SQLAllocHandle, try the m_pSet handle
    SQLHSTMT hstmt;
    //Allocate the SQL statement handle hstmt
    SQLAllocHandle(SQL_HANDLE_STMT,
        m_pSet->m_pDatabase->m_hdbc,
        &hstmt);
    // Specify that hstmt is to be executed asynchronously.
    SQLSetStmtAttr(hstmt,
        SQL_ATTR_ASYNC_ENABLE,
        (SQLPOINTER) SQL_ASYNC_ENABLE_ON,
        0);
    //Execute the command using SQLExecDirect
    SQLExecDirect(hstmt, (unsigned char *)
        "DELETE FROM Student WHERE RIGHT(LastName, 4) = 'mith'",
        SQL_NTS);
    /*
Now do the rest of your program. When you're done, call
AFX_ODBC_CALL to continue processing until the SQL statement is
finished.
    */
    //Now use AFX_ODBC_CALL to deallocate when done
    RETCODE nRetCode;    //Needed for the AFX_ODBC_CALL macro
    AFX_ODBC_CALL(SQLFreeHandle(SQL_HANDLE_STMT, hstmt));
}
```

In the preceding code, the following steps are executed:

1. The MFC database handle m_pSet->m_pDatabase->m_hdbc is used to allocate a new SQLHSTMT handle (hstmt).

2. The SQLSetStmtAttr function is called to turn on the asynchronous attribute for the statement.

3. The SQL statement is executed using the ODBC API SQLExecDirect function. Note that instead of passing the length of the SQL command, SQL_NTS is used to indicate to the SQLExecDirect function that a NULL-terminated string is being passed.

4. Now the SQL statement is executing while your program does other things.

5. Before you can leave your function, you must deallocate your statement handle. This can be done using the SQLFreeHandle function in conjunction with the AFX_ODBC_CALL function, which executes an ODBC API function repeatedly until the SQL_STILL_EXECUTING error no longer is flagged.

As you can see, it's not that difficult to still execute an asynchronous statement using a combination of MFC and ODBC API calls.

 If connection-level asynchronous processing is not supported, the SQL_ATTR_ASYNC_ENABLE statement attribute is read-only. Attempting to set it returns SQL_ERROR and SQLSTATE HYC00 (optional feature not implemented).

CALLING THE Check FUNCTIONF
The MFC also enables you to intercept ODBC API error codes that are returned to Check function. Whenever you want to incorporate special error handling, you can call the Check function to process your ODBC API errors.

```
//Now use AFX_ODBC_CALL to deallocate when done
RETCODE nRetCode;      //Needed for the AFX_ODBC_CALL macro
AFX_ODBC_CALL(SQLFreeHandle(SQL_HANDLE_STMT, hstmt));
//*****
//Now call the Check function
//*****
if ( !m_pSet->Check( nRetCode ) ){
    AfxThrowDBException( nRetCode,
```

```
    m_pSet->m_pDatabase,
    hstmt);
}
```

In the preceding code, the Check function is called after the AFX_ODBC_CALL macro call. If the Check function returns a FALSE, an exception is thrown. You can also override the Check function if you wish certain return codes to get special handling.

 A list of all ODBC API return codes can be found in Appendix B.

Understanding ODBC Exceptions

Of course, every database needs to handle database exceptions. The MFC does a good job with default error handling, but there are times when you'll want to override error processing with your own error logic. You can use the C++ try...catch block to handle errors:

```
try {
    m_pSet->MoveNext( );
}
catch(CDBException* e1) {
    CString error = "Database exception in MoveNext: " + e1->m_strError
    AfxMessageBox(error, MB_ICONEXCLAMATION );
}
catch(CMemoryException * e2) {
    char *error = new char[254];
    char *message = new char[254];
    strcpy(error, "Memory exception in MoveNext: ");
    e2->GetErrorMessage(message,1);
    strcat(error, (const char *) message);
    AfxMessageBox(error, MB_ICONEXCLAMATION );
}
```

In the preceding block, any errors were trapped. A message box then was called to show the error message and where the error occurred. As you can see, CDBException includes a m_strError variable that is really handy for error processing, whereas CMemoryException does not and requires some more code.

As seen by the code in the previous section "Calling the Check Function," you can use the `AfxThrowDBException` function to throw a CDBException:

```
RETCODE nRetCode;
AfxThrowDBException( nRetCode,
    m_pSet->m_pDatabase,
    hstmt);
```

Throwing exceptions is a good way to avoid immediately handling an error, and enabling the calling module to handle it instead.

Summary

In this chapter, ODBC programming with Visual C++ was explored. To recap:

- ◆ The MFC has much functionality that makes it easy to program ODBC applications. In the following two chapters, you'll see how ODBC/MFC programming can be made even easier by taking advantage of the MFC Application Wizard.

- ◆ The MFC has three main classes that handle ODBC support: `CDatabase`, `CRecordset`, and `CRecordView`.

- ◆ You can access the ODBC API directly from Visual C++, but it's much more cumbersome than the MFC. Still, the ODBC API is the only way to access some advanced functionality, such as asynchronous processing.

Chapter 5

Developing ODBC Projects

IN THIS CHAPTER

- ◆ Easily developing a database application by using the MFC Application Wizard

- ◆ Adding, deleting, and querying records in an MFC Application Wizard application

- ◆ Processing transactions inside an MFC/ODBC application

- ◆ Easily joining tables with the MFC Application Wizard

- ◆ Opening multiple recordsets within a single application

DATABASE DEVELOPMENT can be extremely complicated. You need to know not only the programming language (Visual C++) but also the database language (SQL), the database setup, and the database API. Visual C++ simplifies this process by making database development somewhat easier.

 TIP Some of the function calls may seem cryptic, especially if you don't read this book sequentially. The preceding chapter contained an overview of ODBC with MFC and Visual C++ and showed what several of the functions can do.

Easy Development with an ODBC Application

It really is easy to develop a fully functional Visual C++ database application. To develop an application that scrolls through a table and enables you to update any record takes only ten easy steps:

1. Click File → New to open the New dialog box as seen in Figure 5-1. Click the Projects tab, then choose MFC AppWizard (exe). Type in a project name (**ODBCDepartment** for this example), and click OK.

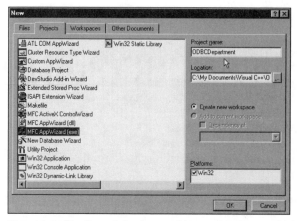

Figure 5-1: The New dialog box enables you to choose which kind of project you wish to create. Here, an MFC Application Wizard executable is chosen.

2. The MFC App Wizard - Step 1 of 6 dialog box now opens. Click Single Document and Document/View architecture support. Then click Next.

3. In the MFC App Wizard - Step 2 of 6 dialog box, choose Database view without file support. Then click the Data Source button as shown in Figure 5-2.

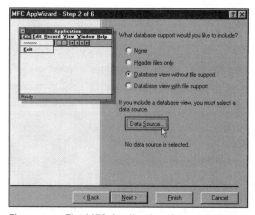

Figure 5-2: The MFC Application Wizard enables you to assign a data source to your MFC application.

4. In the Database Options dialog box, choose ODBC and Dynaset. Then choose your ODBC data source. In Figure 5-3, the Classes ODBC data source was chosen.

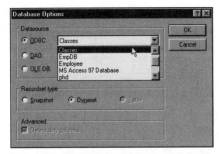

Figure 5-3: The Database Options dialog box enables you to choose a database to associate with your MFC application.

5. Next, the Select Database Tables dialog box opens (Figure 5-4). After you have chosen your data source, you now must pick the table or tables that you want to include inside your MFC application. In Figure 5-4, the Department table is chosen. After you click OK, the MFC App Wizard - Step 2 of 6 dialog box reappears. You should see your database and table listed below the Data Source button. Click Next.

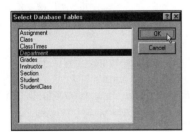

Figure 5-4: The Select Database Tables dialog box enables you to choose tables from your database to be used inside your MFC application.

6. The MFC App Wizard - Step 3 of 6 dialog box opens. Accept all the defaults, and click Next. The MFC App Wizard - Step 4 of 6 dialog box then opens. Deselect (turn off) Printing and print preview, and click Next. The MFC App Wizard - Step 5 of 6 dialog box then opens. Accept all the defaults, and click Next.

7. The MFC App Wizard - Step 6 of 6 dialog box opens. Here, you can change the program names of the C++ classes that will be generated for you. Usually you accept all the defaults, and click Finish.

Here, you should see the New Project Information message box appear. If you scroll down in the box a little, your options should look like the options in Figure 5-5. After you click OK, your project is created, and a dialog box is opened. You can use the painting tools to paint your dialog box.

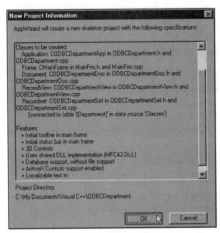

Figure 5-5: The New Project Information message box describes all the options that you've chosen for your MFC application.

8. On the dialog box that opens, delete the TODO label. Then add any fields you need to contain your database fields. In Figure 5-6, two edit boxes were added to contain the two columns in the department table. Then the properties were opened, and the edit box names were changed to IDC _DEPARTMENTCODE and IDC_DEPARTMENTNAME.

Be sure you rename all your window controls to names that correspond to your database column names. Development is easier when you know which controls need to be tied to which field.

9. Pull up the MFC Class Wizard by clicking View → Class Wizard. Click the Member Variables tab. In Figure 5-7, you can see the names of the control IDs that you just added to your dialog box.

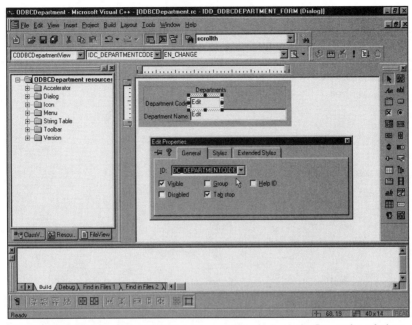

Figure 5-6: Add controls for each database column, and use the Properties window to rename each control to a more appropriate name.

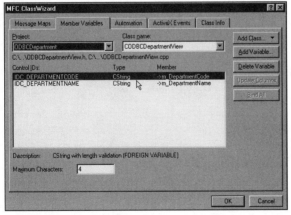

Figure 5-7: The Member Variables tab of the MFC Class Wizard lists all the window controls that you've added to your MFC application.

10. Double-click each control listed in the Member Variables tab of the MFC Class Wizard. This enables you to pull up the Add Member Variable dialog box. Here, you can choose which database column is to be bound to which window control. In Figure 5-8, the m_DepartmentCode variable contained in the m_pSet CRecordset variable is joined to the IDC _DEPARTMENTCODE window control.

Figure 5-8: The Add Member Variable dialog box enables you to easily bind the variables of your CRecordset class to your window controls.

When you're finished, you should see your CRecordset variables listed next to the appropriate window control. Click OK.

11. Choose Build → Execute from the menu, or click Ctrl+F5. This builds and runs your program.

As you can see in Figure 5-9, it really is easy to develop a fully functional MFC database application using the MFC Application Wizard.

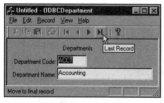

Figure 5-9: Using the 11 steps in this section, you are only minutes away from an MFC/ODBC database application.

The code for the version of ODBCDepartment can be found in the
ODBCDepartmentA directory on the CD-ROM accompanying this book.

Using Adds, Deletes, and Queries

The ODBCDepartment example in the previous section enabled scrolling through records as well as updates. In this section, you'll learn how to easily create add, delete, and query functionality inside an MFC ODBC application. Adding add, delete, and query functionality to an existing MFC/ODBC application such as the ODBCDepartment application requires the following six steps:

1. Pull up the menu from the Resources tab. Add the menu items in Table 5-1 to the Record menu item.

TABLE **5-1** ODBCDepartment MENU ITEMS

Text	ID	Prompt
&Add Record	ID_RECORD_ADDRECORD	Insert a new record.
&Delete Record	ID_RECORD_DELETERECORD	Delete this record.
&Query Record	ID_RECORD_QUERYRECORD	Find a department code.

Figure 5-10 shows how the menu should look when you're finished.

2. Edit your dialog box to include an edit box used for querying. The query box in Figure 5-11 includes an edit box named IDC_FINDCODE to contain the new department number that is used to query the database.

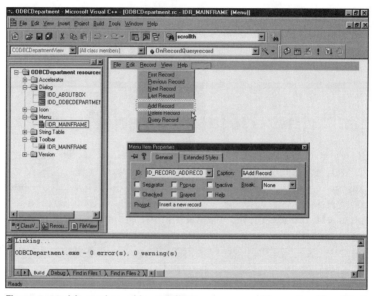

Figure 5-10: It's good to add menu items when you add new functionality to a program.

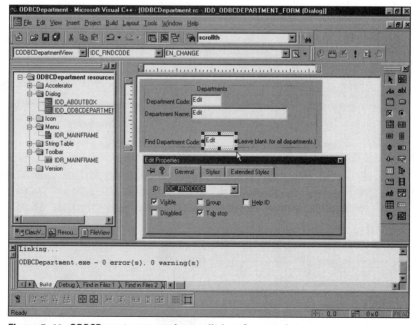

Figure 5-11: ODBCDepartment needs an edit box for querying.

3. If you wish, make new toolbar buttons to tie to your new menu items. As you can see in Figure 5-12, three new toolbar items where added for adding, deleting, and querying.

 You can open your Resources tab to find your toolbar. Not only can you paint new toolbar icons, but you can also cut and paste icons from existing toolbars into your toolbar.

After you're done painting the toolbars, give them the same control name as your corresponding menu items. That way, you need to write only one set of code to handle both the menu and toolbar functions.

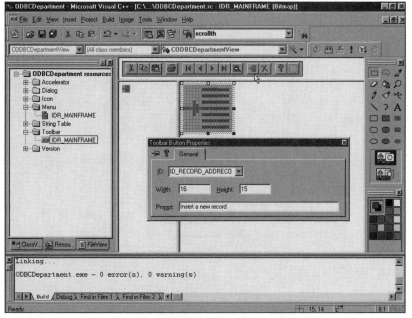

Figure 5-12: Toolbars can make running your program much easier.

4. Now use the Class Wizard to bind a new variable (m_FindDeptCode) to your new control (IDC_FINDCODE). Next, enter 4 in the Maximum Characters box (because department codes are limited to four characters). When you're done, your member variables should look like those in Figure 5-13.

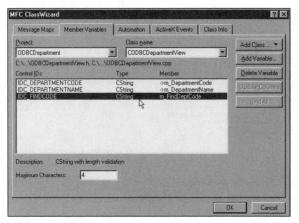

Figure 5-13: You need to bind a variable to an edit box for your query.

5. Click the Message Maps tab, and add an OnMove function to the
   CODBCDepartmentView class. Also add COMMAND functions for ID_RECORD
   _ADDRECORD, ID_RECORD_DELETERECORD, and ID_RECORD _QUERYRECORD.
   Also add an UPDATE_COMMAND_UI function for ID_RECORD _DELETERECORD
   so that you can disable delete functionality if you don't have a record.
   Figure 5-14 shows how your Class Wizard should look after you complete
   this step.

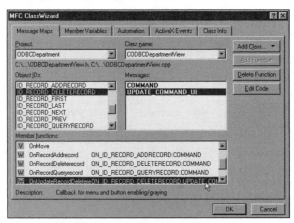

Figure 5-14: Use the Class Wizard to add functions to your classes for overriding
parent classes or controlling windows.

6. At this point, we've come a long way *without writing any Visual C++ code* but rather using Visual C++ to generate code for us. However, to complete this program, you need to write five functions defined in step 5: `OnRecordAddrecord`, `OnMove`, `OnRecordDeleterecord`, `OnUpdateRecordDeleterecord`, and `OnRecordQueryrecord`.

Writing OnRecordAddrecord and OnMove

Writing the `OnRecordAddrecord` function is not difficult but requires the most knowledge of ODBC and the `CRecordset` class of any of the other functions. To add a record, you need to put the recordset into AddNew mode. Furthermore, you need a flag to indicate what mode you're currently in so that other functions know that you're currently trying to add a record. To incorporate add record functionality into your Visual C++ application, perform the following steps:

1. First, add the following BOOL flag to your `CRecordView` descendent class's header file. (In this case, it is the `CODBCDepartmentView` class in the ODBCDepartmentView.h header file):

```
public:
    BOOL m_bAddingRecord;
```

2. Initialize the `m_bAddingRecord` in your `CRecordView` descendent constructor:

```
CODBCDepartmentView::CODBCDepartmentView()
    : CRecordView(CODBCDepartmentView::IDD)
{
    //{{AFX_DATA_INIT(CODBCDepartmentView)
    m_pSet = NULL;
    m_FindDeptCode = _T("");
    //}}AFX_DATA_INIT
    m_bAddingRecord = FALSE;
}
```

3. In the `OnRecordAddrecord` function in your `CRecordView` descendent class, you need to do the following:

a. Update any program variables that currently need updating from the dialog box by using the `UpdateData` function, setting Edit mode if needed, and issuing an Update command:

```
UpdateData(TRUE);      //Get data from dialog box
if (!m_bAddingRecord) {      //Currently adding?
    //If not, set CRecordset in edit mode for updating
```

```
        m_pSet->Edit();
    }
    m_pSet->Update();      //Update data if needed
```

b. Move to the last field using the MoveLast function. This ensures that you're not on the first record when you add:

```
m_pSet->MoveLast();      //Get off record 1
```

c. Set your add flag to TRUE:

```
m_bAddingRecord = TRUE;      //Set flag
```

d. Clear the fields in the dialog window by setting them to NULL:

```
m_pSet->SetFieldNull(NULL);      //Clear all fields
```

e. Place the recordset in AddNew mode:

```
m_pSet->AddNew();      //Set database in AddNew mode
```

f. Use the UpdateData function to display the cleared fields in the dialog box:

```
UpdateData(FALSE);      //Update dialog box fields
```

These steps can be seen in the following OnRecordAddrecord function:

```
void CODBCDepartmentView::OnRecordAddrecord()
{
    CRecordsetStatus rStatus;          //Status variable
    m_pSet->GetStatus(rStatus);          //Get CRecordset
status
    if (rStatus.m_lCurrentRecord >= 0) {      //Records Exist?
        UpdateData(TRUE);              //Get data from dialog box
        if (!m_bAddingRecord) {      //Currently adding?
//If not, set CRecordset in edit mode for updating
            m_pSet->Edit();
        }
        m_pSet->Update();          //Update data if needed
        m_pSet->MoveLast();          //Get off record 1
    }
    m_bAddingRecord = TRUE;      //Set flag
    m_pSet->SetFieldNull(NULL); //Clear all fields
    m_pSet->AddNew();          //Set database in AddNew mode
```

```
            UpdateData(FALSE);     //Update dialog box fields
        }
```

4. By default, the OnMove function updates the existing record before completing its move by placing the recordset in Edit mode and calling the Update function. However, because you are now enabling adds to the recordset, you need to override this action so you can add any new records that must be added. This can be done by the following additions to the OnMove function:

```
BOOL CODBCDepartmentView::OnMove(UINT nIDMoveCommand)
{
    if (m_bAddingRecord) {      //Currently adding?
        //If so, Update the record before the move
        UpdateData(TRUE);      //Get data from dialog box
        m_pSet->Update();      //Update data if needed
        m_pSet->MoveLast();    //Go to the added record
        m_bAddingRecord = FALSE;    //Reset flag
    }
    //Continue with normal processing
    return CRecordView::OnMove(nIDMoveCommand);
}
```

Adding a new record is probably the most complicated database feature to understand. However, once you grasp how the MFC handles updates and how ODBC recordsets are placed in AddNew mode, the coding is not that difficult.

Writing OnRecordDeleterecord

While adding a record takes the greatest understanding of MFC and ODBC, deleting a record requires the most handling and error checking. While the Delete function itself is relatively straightforward, there are other considerations whenever a record is deleted:

◆ You need to make sure that the user really wants to delete the record. You can do so with a message box asking if the user really wants the record deleted:

```
if (AfxMessageBox(     //Be sure to verify your deletes
        "Are you sure you want to delete?",
        MB_YESNO)
    != IDYES) {
    return;
}
```

♦ You have to make sure that the record really exists. If the user tries to delete a new record before adding it, then you merely cancel the add rather than delete a record:

```
if (m_bAddingRecord) {     //Currently adding?
    //Don't delete, just cancel add.
    m_pSet->CancelUpdate();
    m_bAddingRecord = FALSE;
    m_pSet->MovePrev();
    return;
}
```

♦ You have to catch any errors that may occur during a delete. The CRecordset::Delete function throws a CDBException if there is a database error during the delete:

```
try {
    m_pSet->Delete();     //Delete record
}
catch(CDBException* e1) {     //Failed
    AfxMessageBox("Delete Failed:\n" +
        e1->m_strError,
        MB_ICONEXCLAMATION);
    m_pSet->MoveFirst();     //We lost our place.
    e1->Delete();            //Delete Error Message
    UpdateData(FALSE);       //Update dialog box fields
    return;
}
```

Error Trapping and try . . . catch Blocks

C++ functions often return a code indicating an error, which is accomplished by a series of return codes that link several functions together. This is shown graphically in the following figure.

Traditional error processing required error chaining.

The figure includes three functions: f1, f2, and f3. The f1 function calls the f2 function, which calls the f3 function. The f3 function returns an error that is captured by the f2 function and passed back to the f1 function. This technique is sometimes called *error chaining*.

Although error chaining is most often used in C++ programs for error handing, error chaining requires all linking functions to return the error code. If some function was not in a position to return an error, then valuable error information was lost.

try ... catch blocks (or just try blocks) are a later addition to the C++ standard. try ... catch blocks enable functions to "throw" errors that can be "caught" at any phase of the error chain. The following figure shows how try ... catch blocks change the error chain structure.

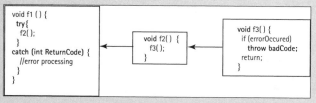

```
void f1 ( ) {
    try{
        f2( );
    }
    catch (int ReturnCode) {
        //error processing
    }
}
```

```
void f2( ) {
    f3( );
}
```

```
void f3( ) {
    if (errorOccured)
        throw badCode;
    return;
}
```

try ... catch blocks enable functions to "catch" any error that is "thrown."

As you can see by the second figure, instead of returning a value through a series of functions, the later function simply throws an error. Any previous function in the error chain can catch this error and process it without the need for a return code.

You can catch as many errors as are thrown by placing multiple catch blocks after your try block. You can also throw an error within a try block, and it will be caught by the catch block immediately following the try block. try ... catch blocks simplify multiple error processing in complex situations.

♦ After a successful delete, you need to reposition the recordset so the user can still view records. If the last record is deleted, you should probably go to either the previous record or the first record. Otherwise, you should probably reposition the recordset to the next record:

```
m_pSet->MoveNext();              //Go to next record
if (m_pSet->IsDeleted()) {       //Was there a next record?
    m_pSet->MoveFirst();         //Deleted last record
}
```

◆ Next, if you have deleted the last record, you probably need to set the fields up to add a new record because there are no records to display. This involves closing and opening the recordset to position the pointer off the deleted record and then calling the `OnRecordAddrecord` function written in the previous section to set up a new record:

```
try {
    if (m_pSet->IsDeleted()) {      //Can't find a record
        AfxThrowDBException(SQL_ERROR,
            m_pSet->m_pDatabase,
                m_pSet->m_hstmt);
    }
}
// catch the error that was thrown
catch(CDBException* e2) {      //No records exist
    AfxMessageBox("No more records",
        MB_ICONEXCLAMATION);
    e2->Delete();            //Delete Error Message
    //Close and Open to get rid of the Deleted record
    m_pSet->Close();
    m_pSet->Open();
    //No records, so set up an add record
    OnRecordAddrecord();
}
```

◆ Finally, add an `UpdateData(FALSE)` statement to your function so that the dialog box is updated with the new values.

The code you need to add to the `CODBCDepartmentView ::OnRecordDelete record` function is as follows:

```
void CODBCDepartmentView::OnRecordDeleterecord()
{
    if (AfxMessageBox(      //Be sure to verify your deletes
            "Are you sure you want to delete?",
            MB_YESNO)
        != IDYES) {
        return;
    }
    if (m_bAddingRecord) {      //Currently adding?
        //Don't delete, just cancel add.
        m_pSet->CancelUpdate();
        m_bAddingRecord = FALSE;
        m_pSet->MovePrev();
        return;
```

```
    }
    try {
        m_pSet->Delete();      //Delete record
    }
    catch(CDBException* e1) {      //Failed
        AfxMessageBox("Delete Failed:\n" +
            e1->m_strError,
            MB_ICONEXCLAMATION);
        m_pSet->MoveFirst();       //We lost our place.
        e1->Delete();              //Delete Error Message
        UpdateData(FALSE);         //Update dialog box fields
        return;
    }
    try {
        m_pSet->MoveNext();                //Go to next record
        if (m_pSet->IsDeleted()) {     //Was there a next record?
            m_pSet->MoveFirst();       //Deleted last record
        }
        if (m_pSet->IsDeleted()) {     //Can't find a record
            AfxThrowDBException(SQL_ERROR,
                m_pSet->m_pDatabase,
                m_pSet->m_hstmt);
        }
        UpdateData(FALSE);       //Update dialog box fields
    }
    catch(CDBException* e2) {     //No records exist
        AfxMessageBox("No more records",
            MB_ICONEXCLAMATION);
        e2->Delete();              //Delete Error Message
        //Close and Open to get rid of the Deleted record
        m_pSet->Close();
        m_pSet->Open();
        //No records, so set up an add record
        OnRecordAddrecord();
    }
}
```

Writing OnUpdateRecordDeleterecord

The OnUpdateRecordDeleterecord function is used to disable ("gray out") the Delete Record menu item and the corresponding toolbar item if a delete does not make sense. Here, you test using the IsBOF, IsEOF, and IsDeleted functions to see if there's a current record. If so, you enable the delete functionality. Adding an Enable function call to the OnUpdateRecordDeleterecord function can do this:

```
void CODBCDepartmentView::OnUpdateRecordDeleterecord(CCmdUI* pCmdUI)
{
    //Disable delete functionality if no record is found
    pCmdUI->Enable(            //Enable delete if there's a record
        !m_pSet->IsBOF() &&
        !m_pSet->IsDeleted() &&
        !m_pSet->IsEOF());
}
```

Writing OnRecordQueryrecord

To add a query, you need to assign a value to the CRecordset::m_pSet->m _strFilter variable. The can be done with the following steps:

1. If you are in the middle of updating or adding a new record, you need to issue an Edit (unless you are adding a record and have already issued an AddNew):

```
UpdateData(TRUE);     //Get data from dialog box
if (!m_bAddingRecord) {    //Currently adding?
    //Set to update
    m_pSet->Edit();
}
m_pSet->Update();     //Update data if needed
m_bAddingRecord = FALSE;    //Reset flag
```

2. Check the bound filter variable (m_FindDeptCode) that was defined in step 4 at the beginning of this section, and if a value is in the field, form an SQL WHERE clause (without the WHERE) and assign it to a string variable:

```
CString newFilter = "";    //Default is no filter
if (m_FindDeptCode != "") {
    //Setup new filter
    newFilter = "DepartmentCode = '" + m_FindDeptCode + "'";
}
```

3. Check to see if you need to apply the new filter. You need to apply the filter if it is different from the last filter used to perform the recordset query. The last filter is stored in the CRecordset::m_strFilter variable. If you reassign the filter, you must call the Requery function to apply the new filter:

```
if (newFilter != m_pSet->m_strFilter) { //Filter has changed
    m_pSet->m_strFilter = newFilter;    //Assign new filter
    if (!m_pSet->Requery()) {        //Requery
//Error occurred
        AfxMessageBox("Requery has failed");
```

```
            m_pSet->m_strFilter = "";      //Try to get back
            m_pSet->Requery();             //Requery again
        }
    //Continue processing
    }
```

4. Next, test to see if the new recordset has any records, and move to the first record, if possible. If not, display a message saying there are no records, and issue an Add by calling the OnRecordAddrecord function to clear the fields:

```
try {
    //Go to the first record of the new filtered recordset
    m_pSet->MoveFirst();
}
catch(CDBException* e)     {
    //Move failed because there are no records
    AfxMessageBox("No records were found", MB_ICONEXCLAMATION
);
    e->Delete();          //Delete Error Message
    //No records, so set up an add record
    OnRecordAddrecord();
}
```

5. Finally, add an UpdateData(FALSE) statement to your function so that the dialog box is updated with the new values.

Put the code in the OnRecordQueryrecord function. The following code can be written to accomplish the tasks described in the preceding steps:

```
void CODBCDepartmentView::OnRecordQueryrecord()
{
    CString newFilter = "";     //Default is no filter
    UpdateData(TRUE);     //Get data from dialog box
    if (!m_bAddingRecord) {     //Currently adding?
        //Set to update
        m_pSet->Edit();
    }
    m_pSet->Update();     //Update data if needed
    m_bAddingRecord = FALSE;     //Reset flag
    if (m_FindDeptCode != "") {
        //Setup new filter
        newFilter = "DepartmentCode = '" + m_FindDeptCode + "'";
    }
    if (newFilter != m_pSet->m_strFilter) {
        //Filter has changed
```

```
            m_pSet->m_strFilter = newFilter; //Assign new filter
            if (!m_pSet->Requery()) {         //Requery
                //Error occurred
                AfxMessageBox("Requery has failed");
                m_pSet->m_strFilter = "";     //Try to get back
                m_pSet->Requery();            //Requery again
            }
            try {
            //Go to the first record of the new filtered recordset
                m_pSet->MoveFirst();
            }
            catch(CDBException* e)    {
                //Move failed because there are no records
                AfxMessageBox("No records were found",
    MB_ICONEXCLAMATION );
                e->Delete();            //Delete Error Message
                //No records, so set up an add record
                OnRecordAddrecord();
            }
        }
        UpdateData(FALSE);     //Update dialog box fields
    }
```

When you're finished, your application should look similar to the application shown in Figure 5-15.

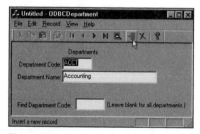

Figure 5-15: An example of an MFC ODBC program that supports adding, deleting, and querying

The code for the version of ODBCDepartment can be found in the ODBCDepartmentB directory on the CD-ROM that accompanies this book.

Saving and Transactions

Many modern commercial packages give the user the option to save or reject changes. This can be easily accomplished using database transactions. Transactions enable a developer to group together a series of database updates, and then either *commit* (make permanent) those changes to the database or *roll back* (erase) those changes from the database.

Access, Transactions, and CRecordset

Some databases act strangely with transactions. For instance, if you set up a transaction in Microsoft Access, you cannot have a cursor open. With traditional database programming techniques, it is not a problem, but with the MFC, it becomes a big problem.

With the MFC, you almost always have a CRecordset object open at all times. Behind this CRecordset object is a database cursor. As a result, you must *close the CRecordset* before opening a transaction:

```
CRecordsetStatus rStatus;            //Status variable
m_pSet->GetStatus(rStatus);          //Get CRecordset status
m_pSet->Close();                     //Close recordset and
cursor to start transaction
m_pSet->m_pDatabase->BeginTrans(); //Begin transaction
m_pSet->Open();                            //Reopen the
recordset and cursor
//Restore record position
if (rStatus.m_lCurrentRecord >= 0) {
    m_pSet->SetAbsolutePosition(rStatus.m_lCurrentRecord+1);
}
```

Of course, the preceding technique doesn't work very well if you don't know the current record number. ODBC does not count records and keeps track of records only if you scroll through them from beginning to end. However, you could code an application-specific routine that searched for a given key.

If your transaction processing does not appear to be working, be sure to check with your DBA or your database documentation to examine cursor behavior.

When the user indicates that the changes are to be saved, a `CommitTrans` function is called. When the user decides to discard the changes, a `Rollback` function is called. This can be accomplished using the following steps:

1. You need a Save menu function. You can add this function yourself, or you can generate a new project using the techniques discussed earlier in this chapter and choose the Database view with file support option in Step 2 of 6 in the MFC App Wizard (Figure 5-16). Then generate this project with the same options you used at the beginning of this chapter.

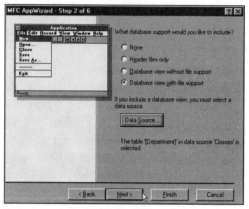

Figure 5-16: The Database view with a file support option adds file functionality to your MFC window.

2. If you choose to generate a new project, you may need to delete some generated File options (such as Open) that make little sense with your application. You may also want to use the New menu option to add a record rather than the Add Record menu option used earlier in this chapter. In Figure 5-17, you can see that the File menu option has only three choices: New, Save, and Exit.

   Because the New menu choice is now being used for new records, the Add Record menu choice is no longer needed. As you can see in Figure 5-18, only the Delete Record and Query Record choices remain.

3. Edit your toolbar to include any additional functionality (Figure 5-19).

4. Use the Class Wizard to add the following functionality to your `CRecordView` descendent (`CODBCDepartmentView`). You should use the Add Function button to create the functions listed in Table 5-2.

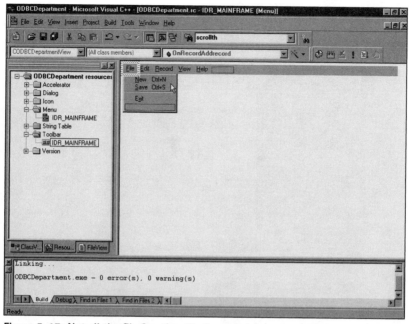

Figure 5-17: Not all the file functionality is needed for every project.

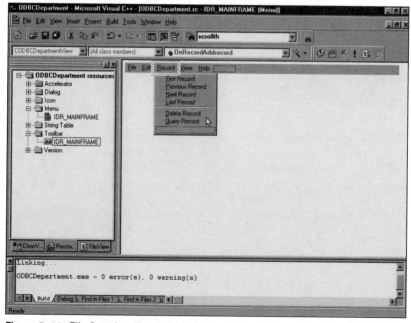

Figure 5-18: File functionality should not be duplicated; therefore, the Add Record choice is no longer needed.

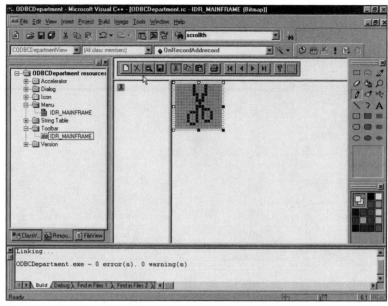

Figure 5-19: Toolbars need to be adjusted to show additional functionality.

TABLE 5-2 ODBCDepartmentView CLASS WIZARD EVENTS

Function Name	Object ID	Message
OnRecordDeleterecord	ID_RECORD_DELETERECORD	COMMAND
OnUpdateRecordDelete record	ID_RECORD_DELETERECORD	UPDATE_COMMAND_UI
OnRecordQueryrecord	ID_RECORD_QUERYRECORD	COMMAND
OnMove	CODBCDepartmentView	
OnFileNew	ID_FILE_NEW	COMMAND
OnFileSave	ID_FILE_SAVE	COMMAND
OnUpdateFileSave	ID_FI:LE_SAVE	UPDATE_COMMAND_UI
OnDestroy	CODBCDepartmentView	ON_WM_DESTROY
OnChangeDepartment code	IDC_DEPARTMENTCODE	EN_CHANGE
OnChangeDepartment name	IDC_DEPARTMENTNAME	EN_CHANGE

5. Code the events you described in step 4. The `OnMove`, `OnRecordDelete` record, `OnUpdateRecordDeleterecord`, and `OnRecordQueryrecord` functions are identical to the functions with the same names listed in Table 5-2, with one exception: instead of calling an `OnRecordAddrecord` as before, now you call the `OnFileNew` function. Code for the `OnFileNew` function is identical to the code for the previously described `OnAddRecord` function.

6. You need to flag when you are in the middle of an add, as before. You also need to flag when a change is made. This can be done by defining public class variables in the `CODBCDepartmentView` class:

```
public:
    BOOL m_bAddingRecord;
    BOOL m_bFieldsChanged;
```

7. Initialize your Boolean variables to `FALSE` in the `CODBCDepartment` constructor:

```
CODBCDepartmentView::CODBCDepartmentView()
    : CRecordView(CODBCDepartmentView::IDD)
{
    //{{AFX_DATA_INIT(CODBCDepartmentView)
    m_pSet = NULL;
    m_FindDeptCode = _T("");
    //}}AFX_DATA_INIT
    m_bAddingRecord = FALSE;
    m_bFieldsChanged = FALSE;
}
```

8. Next, add code to the `OnChangeDepartmentcode` and `OnChangeDepartmentname` functions to set the `m_bFieldsChanged` to `TRUE` in the `CODBCDepartmentView` class:

```
void CODBCDepartmentView::OnChangeDepartmentcode()
{
    m_bFieldsChanged = TRUE;
}
void CODBCDepartmentView::OnChangeDepartmentname()
{
    m_bFieldsChanged = TRUE;
}
```

9. Use the `OnUpdateFileSave` function to disable the Save button and Save menu choice if no changes have been made.

```
void CODBCDepartmentView::OnUpdateFileSave(CCmdUI* pCmdUI)
{
//Enable save functionality if a record has changed
```

```
        pCmdUI->Enable(m_bFieldsChanged);
    }
```

10. Open your transaction before processing in the OnInitialUpdate function inside the CODBCDepartmentView class:

```
void CODBCDepartmentView::OnInitialUpdate()
{
    m_pSet = &GetDocument()->m_oDBCDepartmentSet;
    CRecordView::OnInitialUpdate();
    GetParentFrame()->RecalcLayout();
    ResizeParentToFit();
    m_pSet->Close();      //Close to start transaction
    if (m_pSet->m_pDatabase->CanTransact()) {
        m_pSet->m_pDatabase->BeginTrans();
    }
    m_pSet->Open();       //Open after starting transaction
}
```

11. Write the OnFileSave function. This consists of the following steps:

    a. Make sure transactions are enabled and that fields have changed:

    ```
    if (m_bFieldsChanged && m_pSet->CanTransact()) {
    ```

    b. Issue an update to update the current record, if needed. Make sure the recordset is in either Edit mode or AddNew mode first:

    ```
    if (!m_bAddingRecord) {    //Currently adding?
        m_pSet->Edit();        //If not, set edit mode
    }
    UpdateData(TRUE);          //Get data from dialog box
    m_bAddingRecord = FALSE;   //Reset flag
    m_pSet->Update();          //Update data if needed
    ```

    c. Commit the transaction to permanently save any changes made:

    ```
    m_pSet->m_pDatabase->CommitTrans();    //Commit changes
    ```

    d. After you issue a CommitTrans or a Rollback function, the transaction ends. You need to restart the transaction again by using a BeginTrans:

    ```
    m_pSet->m_pDatabase->BeginTrans();    //Start Transaction
    m_bFieldsChanged = FALSE;   //Reset flag
    ```

    e. The code to do this for a Microsoft Access database (which includes the closing of the CRecordset before beginning a transaction) is as follows:

    ```
    void CODBCDepartmentView::OnFileSave()
    {
    ```

```
        if (m_bFieldsChanged && m_pSet->CanTransact()) {
            if (!m_bAddingRecord) {     //Currently adding?
                m_pSet->Edit();      //If not, set edit mode
            }
            UpdateData(TRUE);     //Get data from dialog box
            m_bAddingRecord = FALSE;     //Reset flag
            m_pSet->Update();     //Update data if needed
        //Commit changes
            m_pSet->m_pDatabase->CommitTrans();
            CRecordsetStatus rStatus;     //Status variable
            m_pSet->GetStatus(rStatus);     //Get CRecordset
    status
            m_pSet->Close();     //Close to start transaction
        //Start Transaction
            m_pSet->m_pDatabase->BeginTrans();
            m_pSet->Open();             //Reopen CRecordset
            //Restore record position
            if (rStatus.m_lCurrentRecord >= 0) {
                m_pSet ->
    SetAbsolutePosition(rStatus.m_lCurrentRecord+1);
            }
            m_bFieldsChanged = FALSE;     //Reset flag
            UpdateData(FALSE);     //Update dialog box fields
        }
    }
```

12. With certain databases, uncommitted changes are erased when the connection terminates. Other databases default to automatically committing those changes when the transaction terminates. To ensure that neither behavior occurs, when a user terminates your program, you need to check to see if there are uncommitted changes, which can be done in the OnDestroy function using the following steps:

a. Check if transactions are supported and if the fields have changed:

```
if (m_pSet->CanTransact()) {
    if (m_bFieldsChanged) {
        //Handle changes
    }
    else {
    //No changes, but close the transaction with a commit.
        m_pSet->m_pDatabase->CommitTrans();
    }
}
```

b. Where the //Handle changes comment is in the preceding code, you know that changes have been made. You must check to see if the user wants these changes saved and, if not, roll back your changes:

```
if (AfxMessageBox (
    "Records have been changed.  Do you want to save?",
        MB_YESNO) == IDNO) {
    m_pSet->m_pDatabase->Rollback();
}
```

c. If the user clicks Yes in response to the message box in the preceding code, you must accept any current changes. As with the OnFileSave function, this entails making sure the recordset is in AddNew or Edit mode, accepting any changes, updating the database, and committing the transaction:

```
if (!m_bAddingRecord) {     //Currently adding?
    m_pSet->Edit();        //If not, set edit mode
}
UpdateData(TRUE);          //Get data from dialog box
m_pSet->Update();          //Update data if needed
// Now Commit the changes to the database
m_pSet->m_pDatabase->CommitTrans();
```

These changes should be added to the OnDestroy function in the CODBC DepartmentView class:

```
void CODBCDepartmentView::OnDestroy()
{

//Check for changed fields and transaciton ability
    if (m_pSet->CanTransact()) {
        if (m_bFieldsChanged) {
            if (AfxMessageBox (
              "Records have been changed.  Do you want to save?",
                MB_YESNO) == IDNO) {
                m_pSet->m_pDatabase->Rollback();
            }
            else {
              if (!m_bAddingRecord) {     //Currently adding?
              //If not, set edit mode
                  m_pSet->Edit();
              }
              UpdateData(TRUE);    //Get data from dialog box
              m_pSet->Update();    //Update data if needed
              m_pSet->m_pDatabase->CommitTrans();
```

```
            }
        }
        else {
        //No changes, but close the transaction with a commit.
            m_pSet->m_pDatabase->CommitTrans();
        }
    }
    CRecordView::OnDestroy();
}
```

When you're finished, your program should look similar to the one shown in Figure 5-20.

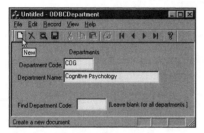

Figure 5-20: The ODBCDepartment application now uses transactions to support saving the data.

When you leave the ODBCDepartment application after making changes, the program prompts you with a message box such as the one shown in Figure 5-21 to see if you want to save your changes.

Figure 5-21: It's good to prompt users to see if they want to save their changes.

Certain databases, such as Microsoft SQL Server, limit the size of their transaction log. A transaction log often fills up if too many database updates are done without committing or rolling back. Be sure to check your database documentation to see your transaction limits, and don't enable numerous database updates over an extended period of time without committing those changes.

The code for the version of ODBCDepartment can be found in the ODBCDepartmentC directory on the CD-ROM.

Using Joins

You often need to bring in more than one table for display. For instance, say you wanted to see and update Instructor records as you scrolled through each department. The simplest way to achieve this is through a table join.

Development using table joins with the MFC Application Wizard is almost identical to development with a single table. Perform the following steps:

1. Use the MFC Application Wizard. In the Step 2 of 6 dialog box, choose Database view without file support. Then click the Data Source button.

2. In the Database Options dialog box, choose ODBC and Dynaset. Then choose your ODBC data source. When the Select Database Tables dialog box opens, choose two or more tables to be joined together. In Figure 5-22, the Department table and the Instructor table are chosen for the join.

3. In the Step 4 of 6 dialog box, deselect (turn off) printing and print preview. Accept the rest of the defaults.

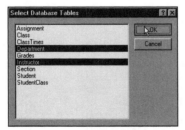

Figure 5-22: When generating an MFC ODBC application, you can pick more than one table.

4. Paint your screen. Don't forget to rename your edit boxes to something more readable. Figure 5-23 shows the dialog box designed for this table inquiry.

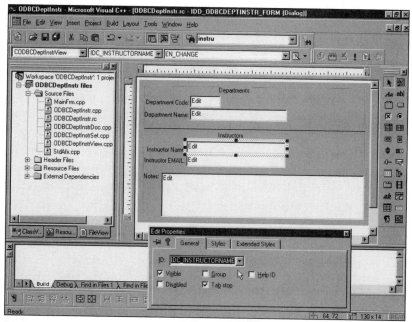

Figure 5-23: In the dialog box, add all the fields needed for all the tables in your join.

5. Use the Class Wizard to bind database fields to your edit boxes, as shown in Figure 5-24.

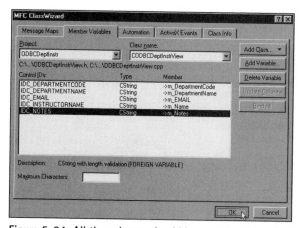

Figure 5-24: All the columns should be available for selecting.

TIP Notice that, when you have duplicate column names, such as DepartmentCode, that you have two variables that correspond to these columns (m_pSet->DepartmentCode and m_pSet->Department Code2). If you are joining on the field with the same name, then simply picking one of the columns to bind is fine because both columns, in a join, should contain the same value. However, if you use columns that have the same name ("Name", "Type", and so on) that are not part of a join, you have to be careful which field is bound to which table. The DoFieldExchange function that is overridden in your CRecordset descendent should show you fully qualified column names (when needed) and the variable where the column name is bound.

6. Next, add the join criteria using the m_strFilter string in the CRecordset descendent constructor. In the following code, you can see that the CODBCDeptInstrSet constructor contains a line that tells ODBC how to join the two related tables.

```
CODBCDeptInstrSet::CODBCDeptInstrSet(CDatabase* pdb)
    : CRecordset(pdb)
{
    //{{AFX_FIELD_INIT(CODBCDeptInstrSet)
    m_DepartmentCode = _T("");
    m_DepartmentName = _T("");
    m_InstructorID = 0;
    m_Name = _T("");
    m_DepartmentCode2 = _T("");
    m_EMAIL = _T("");
    m_Notes = _T("");
    m_nFields = 7;
    //}}AFX_FIELD_INIT
    m_nDefaultType = dynaset;
    m_strFilter =
"Instructor.DepartmentCode = Department.DepartmentCode";
}
```

When you're done, compile your program. As Figure 5-25 shows, when you scroll through your record, you can see values from both tables.

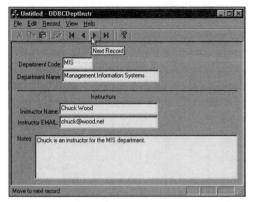

Figure 5-25: Joined tables can give you information from several tables at one time.

Using Multiple ODBC Recordsets

It's much simpler to use a single recordset for every dialog box than to use multiple recordsets in a dialog box. In the last example, you could create a joined recordset in mere minutes. However, there are some problems with this approach:

◆ You cannot, by default, update your recordset. With a joined recordset in ODBC, the columns are not updateable. This also makes adding or deleting records somewhat problematic because the recordset won't know which table to add to or delete from.

◆ Depending on your join, your results may contain duplicate values (for example, many of the same department codes and names for each instructor).

To get around this restriction, you may want to open more than one related CRecordset classes at the same time: each containing only one table. In Figure 5-26, you can see that there are two CRecordset classes open at once; one CRecordset for the Department table, and then a related CRecordset that opens all the related instructors for that department.

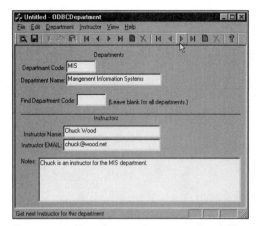

Figure 5-26: You often need to open related CRecordset classes at the same time.

The layout for Figure 5-26 is shown in Figure 5-27. Figure 5-27 contains one independent CRecordset object that uses the Department table. Further below are all the related instructors (if any) for that department. Whenever the department record changes, the related CRecordset must be immediately requeried to be populated with corresponding Instructor records.

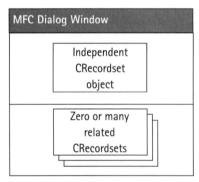

Figure 5-27: The formats of a one-to-many display, also called a "drill down" format, are common in many custom and commercial applications.

The following sections show how to code for multiple related CRecordset objects. In this part of the chapter, we take the ODBCDepartment project and add code for a second Instructor table recordset.

Creating a Second CRecordset Class

When using multiple CRecordset classes, the first task to complete is to create a second CRecordset object. This can be done using the Class Wizard and the following steps:

1. Click View → ClassWizard, and click the Add Class button. Choose New from the pop-up menu.

2. In the New Class dialog box, enter the name of your new class (CODBCInstructorSet), then choose CRecordset as the Base class, and click OK, as shown in Figure 5-28.

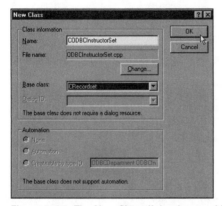

Figure 5-28: The New Class dialog box enables you to create a new class from an existing base class and add it to your project.

3. Because you chose a base class of CRecordset, the Database Options dialog box then opens, as shown in Figure 5-29. Choose ODBC, and pick the ODBC database you want to use. This database should be the same as the database you picked before for your primary CRecordset class.

4. Next, you should pick your table (Instructor) from your database using the Select Database Tables dialog box shown in Figure 5-30. This should be a table that relates to the primary table somehow. After you choose this table , you should return to the Class Wizard main window. Click OK to return to your Visual C++ environment. Your new class is now added to your source files.

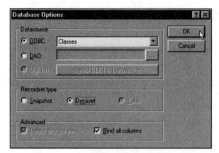

Figure 5-29: You should pick the same database that you chose earlier, when creating your MFC application.

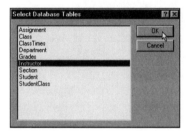

Figure 5-30: You then pick a related table using the Select Database Tables dialog box.

5. The only change you need to make to your second CRecordset class is to add a parameter. This is a pointer that will, eventually, point to the related field in the other CRecordset object. First, declare your pointer in the header file of your new class (CODBCInstructor.h):

```
//Parameters
public:
    CString *m_pDepartmentCode;
```

Next, indicate the number of parameters in the constructor of your new class (CODBCInstructor.cpp) by assigning the number of related columns (usually 1) to the m_nParams class variable:

```
CODBCInstructorSet::CODBCInstructorSet(CDatabase* pdb)
    : CRecordset(pdb)
{
    //{{AFX_FIELD_INIT(CODBCInstructorSet)
    m_InstructorID = 0;
    m_Name = _T("");
    m_DepartmentCode = _T("");
    m_EMAIL = _T("");
    m_Notes = _T("");
```

```
        m_nFields = 5;
        //}}AFX_FIELD_INIT
        m_nParams = 1;
        m_nDefaultType = dynaset;
    }
```

Finally, assign the parameter in the DoFieldExchange class
(CODBCInstructor.cpp). Assign a WHERE clause string to the m_strFilter
filter, use the SetFieldType function to indicate the field exchange that
you are going to use to bind a parameter, and then use the appropriate
RFX function to bind your pointer as a parameter.

```
void CODBCInstructorSet::DoFieldExchange(CFieldExchange* pFX)
{
    //{{AFX_FIELD_MAP(CODBCInstructorSet)
    pFX->SetFieldType(CFieldExchange::outputColumn);
    RFX_Long(pFX, _T("[InstructorID]"), m_InstructorID);
    RFX_Text(pFX, _T("[Name]"), m_Name);
    RFX_Text(pFX, _T("[DepartmentCode]"), m_DepartmentCode);
    RFX_Text(pFX, _T("[EMAIL]"), m_EMAIL);
    RFX_Text(pFX, _T("[Notes]"), m_Notes);
    //}}AFX_FIELD_MAP
    m_strFilter = "DepartmentCode = ?";    //Assign a filter
    //Indicate that you're binding parameters
    pFX->SetFieldType(CFieldExchange::param);
//Now bind the paramter to the m_pDepartmentCode pointer
//Filter parameter names (i.e. "Parm1") aren't important
    RFX_Text(pFX, _T("Parm1"), *m_pDepartmentCode);
}
```

Implementing Changes to CRecordView Class

Your record view requires the most changes when you add a second recordset to
your record view. Not only do you need to make changes to the dialog, menu, and
toolbar resources, but you also need to instantiate and deallocate your new recordset and program all the additional functionality yourself.

IMPLEMENTING CHANGES TO RESOURCES WITH THE CLASS WIZARD

Although resources are not technically part of the CRecordView class, the CRecord
View class interacts with resources more than any other MFC class in your application. When adding any fields to a database, you need to change your dialog boxes
and menu items to accommodate the new changes.

The Instructor table has five columns: InstructorID, Name, EMAIL, Notes, and DepartmentCode. Because the Instructor table is being joined to the Department table through the DepartmentCode column, there is no need to redisplay it. Also, because InstructorID is an autoincrement field used to create a primary key, there is no need to show that either. The other fields (Name, EMAIL, and Notes) should be added to your dialog box, as shown in Figure 5-31.

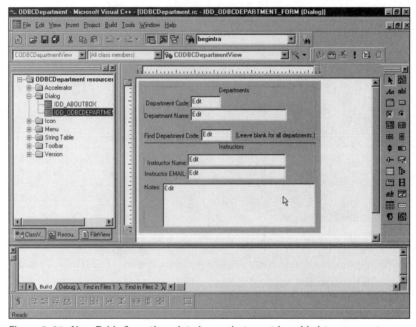

Figure 5-31: New fields from the related recordset must be added to your system.

Next, you need to add menu functionality. Earlier, you used the default Records menu choice because you had only one set of records. Now, with both Department records and Instructor records, you probably want to differentiate. However, rename only the menu options, and don't rename their control ID, because it is used to call functions that are already written. Figure 5-32 shows how Record was renamed to Department and an Instructor menu option was added with all the appropriate adding, deleting, and scrolling functionality.

Finally, your toolbar should also have some functionality dedicated to the new recordset. As you can see in Figure 5-33, two sets of database options (one color-coded green, and one color-coded purple when you run the executable) are added to the toolbar. This way, one can be used for Department recordset functionality while the other can be used for Instructor recordset functionality.

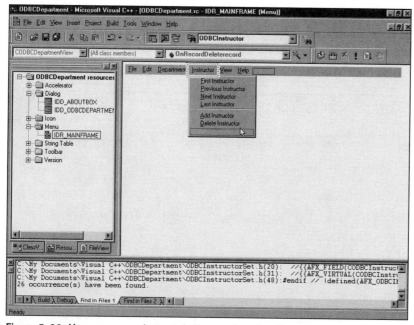

Figure 5-32: Your new recordset needs its own functionality.

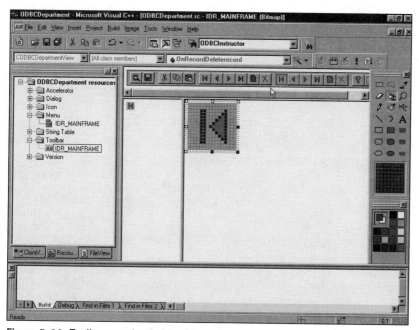

Figure 5-33: Toolbars can be tied to the new menu options for toolbar support of your new recordset.

Table 5-3 shows the functions you'll need to define for the new menu structure, and which ones are new to this multi-record example. You should use the class wizard to generate these commands for you so you don't need to mess with the definitions.

TABLE 5-3 MENU FUNCTIONS FOR ODBCDepartmentView

Menu Item	New	Function	Object ID
File			
New	No	OnFileNew	ID_FILE_NEW
Save	No	OnFileSave	ID_FILE_SAVE
Save	No	OnUpdateFileSave	ID_FILE_SAVE
Department			
Delete Record	No	OnRecordDeleterecord	ID_RECORD _DELETERECORD
Delete Record	No	OnUpdateRecordDelete record	ID_RECORD _DELETERECORD
Query Record	No	OnRecordQueryrecord	ID_RECORD _QUERYRECORD
Instructor			
First Instructor	Yes	OnInstructorFirstrecord	ID_INSTRUCTOR _FIRSTRECORD
First Instructor	Yes	OnUpdateInstructorFirst record	ID_INSTRUCTOR _FIRSTRECORD
Previous Instructor	Yes	OnInstructorPrevious record	ID_INSTRUCTOR _PREVIOUSRECORD
Previous Instructor	Yes	OnUpdateInstructor Previousrecord	ID_INSTRUCTOR _PREVIOUSRECORD
Next Instructor	Yes	OnInstructorNextrecord	ID_INSTRUCTOR _NEXTRECORD
Next Instructor	Yes	OnUpdateInstructor	ID_INSTRUCTOR _NEXTRECORD

Menu Item	New	Function	Object ID
Last Instructor	Yes	OnInstructorLastrecord	ID_INSTRUCTOR _LASTRECORD
Last Instructor	Yes	OnUpdateInstructorLast record	ID_INSTRUCTOR _LASTRECORD
Add Instructor	Yes	OnInstructorAdd instructor	ID_INSTRUCTOR _ADDINSTRUCTOR
Delete Instructor	Yes	OnInstructorDelete instructor	ID_INSTRUCTOR _DELETE INSTRUCTOR
Delete Instructor	Yes	OnUpdateInstructor Deleteinstructor	ID_INSTRUCTOR _DELETE INSTRUCTOR

In addition to the menu options defined by the Class Wizard, the control event handlers in Table 5-4 should also be created in order to trap for transactions.

TABLE 5-4 CONTROL EVENTS USED FOR TRANSACTIONS

New	Function	Object ID	Message
No	OnDestroy	CODBCDepartmentView	WM_DESTROY
No	OnChangeDepartmentcode	IDC_DEPARTMENTCODE	EN_CHANGE
No	OnChangeDepartmentname	IDC_DEPARTMENTNAME	EN_CHANGE
Yes	OnChangeEmail	IDC_EMAIL	EN_CHANGE
Yes	OnChangeInstructorname	IDC_INSTRUCTORNAME	EN_CHANGE
Yes	OnChangeNotes	IDC_NOTES	EN_CHANGE

NEW FUNCTIONS NEEDED FOR THE CrecordView.h HEADER FILE

After you use the Class Wizard to add functions to your project, your CrecordView .h header file (CODBCDepartmentView.h) should have many functions added to it. However, you still need to add the following:

◆ You need to add an include statement to the header file you just created:

```
#include "ODBCInstructorSet.h"
```

◆ You need to add a Boolean variable to indicate if you are currently adding a record to your new recordset:

```
public:
    BOOL m_bAddingInstructor;
```

◆ You need to add function prototypes to the following functions:

```
public
    void OpenInstructorRecordset(long nRows = 0);
    void UpdateInstructor();
    void AddInstructor();
```

◆ You need to create a pointer to the new recordset. This should be done after the //{{AFX_DATA(CODBCDepartmentView) comment so that the Class Wizard still functions after you bind your variables.

```
public:
    //{{AFX_DATA(CODBCDepartmentView)
    enum { IDD = IDD_ODBCDEPARTMENT_FORM };
    CODBCDepartmentSet* m_pSet;
    CString     m_FindDeptCode;
    //}}AFX_DATA
    CODBCInstructorSet* m_pInstructorSet;
```

NEW FUNCTIONS NEEDED FOR THE CRecordView

Several functions have to be written or modified to handle the second recordset. In addition, you must code those functions that you generated from the Class Wizard, which can be done using the following steps:

1. Just as with the primary recordset, you need a function to place the second recordset into AddNew mode and to set up the display to add a new record. The following AddInstructor function sets the add flag, clears out the instructor fields, and places the InstructorSet CRecordset in AddNew mode:

```
void CODBCDepartmentView::AddInstructor()
{
    m_bAddingInstructor = TRUE;    //Set flag
    m_pInstructorSet->SetFieldNull(NULL);    //Clear fields
//Set database in AddNew mode
    m_pInstructorSet->AddNew();
    UpdateData(FALSE);    //Update dialog box fields
}
```

The AddInstructor function is called in three situations:

- The user requests to add an instructor through the menu or a toolbar button.

- The user requests to add a new department.

- The user scrolls through a department, but there are no related Instructor records. In this case, the dialog box is set up to add an instructor. If no changes are made, the CRecordset::Update function won't write the new record to the database.

2. You need a function to open your recordset both initially and after each transaction BeginTrans call. The OpenInstructorRecordset is used to initially open the InstructorSet recordset and to reopen the recordset after a transaction begins:

```
void CODBCDepartmentView::OpenInstructorRecordset(long nRows)
{
    m_pInstructorSet->Open();
    m_pInstructorSet->Requery();
    CRecordsetStatus rStatus;            //Status variable
//Get CRecordset status
    m_pInstructorSet->GetStatus(rStatus);
    //no records Exist?
    if (rStatus.m_lCurrentRecord < 0) {
        //No isntructor records, so add one.
        AddInstructor();
    }
    else {
        this -> m_pInstructorSet ->
SetAbsolutePosition(nRows+1);
    }
}
```

3. You need a function to handle your updates. The following UpdateInstructor function shows how an update should be written for your second recordset:

```
void CODBCDepartmentView::UpdateInstructor()
{
    if (!m_bAddingInstructor) {
        if (m_pInstructorSet->IsBOF() ||
            m_pInstructorSet->IsEOF() ||
            m_pInstructorSet->IsDeleted()) {
            return;
        }
```

```
        m_pInstructorSet->Edit();
    }
    m_bAddingInstructor = FALSE;
    UpdateData(TRUE);    //Get data from dialog box
    m_pInstructorSet->m_DepartmentCode
        = *m_pInstructorSet->m_pDepartmentCode;
    m_pInstructorSet->Update();
}
```

4. With the Class Wizard, you should have indicated that you wanted to trap certain OnChange functions. That way, you can set a flag to indicate that changes have been made and that you need to ask if the user wants to save their changes. In the following three functions, the m_bFields Changed flag is set when changes are made in any of the edit boxes:

```
void CODBCDepartmentView::OnChangeEmail()
{
    m_bFieldsChanged = TRUE;
}
void CODBCDepartmentView::OnChangeInstructorname()
{
    m_bFieldsChanged = TRUE;
}
void CODBCDepartmentView::OnChangeNotes()
{
    m_bFieldsChanged = TRUE;
}
```

5. Add code for the Add Instructor menu choice. When the user wishes to add an instructor, first call a function to update the instructor in case some changes were made to the existing window. Then call a function to add an instructor:

```
void CODBCDepartmentView::OnInstructorAddinstructor()
{
    UpdateInstructor();
    AddInstructor();
}
```

6. Add code for the Delete Instructor menu choice using the same technique you used when coding the Delete Department menu choice:

```
void CODBCDepartmentView::OnInstructorDeleteinstructor()
{
    if (AfxMessageBox(     //Be sure to verify your deletes
    "Are you sure you want to delete this instructor?",
            MB_YESNO)
        != IDYES) {
```

```
            return;
    }
    if (m_bAddingInstructor) {      //Currently adding?
        //Don't delete, just cancel add.
        m_pInstructorSet->CancelUpdate();
        m_bAddingInstructor = FALSE;
        OnInstructorPreviousrecord();
        return;
    }
    try {
        m_pInstructorSet->Delete();      //Delete record
    }
    catch(CDBException* e1) {      //Failed
        AfxMessageBox("Delete Failed:\n" +
            e1->m_strError,
            MB_ICONEXCLAMATION);
        e1->Delete();            //Delete Error Message
        OnInstructorFirstrecord();      //Recapture place
        return;
    }
    try {
        OnInstructorNextrecord();      //Go to the next record
        if (m_pSet->IsDeleted()) {      //Next record exists?
//Deleted last record
            OnInstructorFirstrecord();
        }
        if (m_pSet->IsDeleted()) {      //Can't find a record
            AfxThrowDBException(SQL_ERROR,
                m_pInstructorSet->m_pDatabase,
                m_pInstructorSet->m_hstmt);
        }
        UpdateData(FALSE);      //Update dialog box fields
    }
    catch(CDBException* e2) {      //No records exist
        AfxMessageBox(
            "No more Instructors for this department",
            MB_ICONEXCLAMATION);
        e2->Delete();            //Delete Error Message
        //Close and Open to get rid of the Deleted record
        m_pInstructorSet->Close();
        m_pInstructorSet->Open();
        //No records, so set up an add record
        OnInstructorAddinstructor();
    }
}
```

7. You need to code for the CRecordset record movement menu choices (that is, First Instructor, Previous Instructor, Next Instructor, and Last Instructor). This entails first updating the instructor, then moving the CRecordset to the appropriate position in the recordset, and then updating the dialog box from CRecordset. The following four functions do this:

```
void CODBCDepartmentView::OnInstructorFirstrecord()
{
    UpdateInstructor();
    m_pInstructorSet->MoveFirst();
    UpdateData(FALSE);      //Update dialog from database
}
void CODBCDepartmentView::OnInstructorLastrecord()
{
    UpdateInstructor();
    m_pInstructorSet->MoveLast();
    UpdateData(FALSE);      //Update dialog from database
}
void CODBCDepartmentView::OnInstructorNextrecord()
{
    UpdateInstructor();
    m_pInstructorSet->MoveNext();
    if (m_pInstructorSet->IsEOF()) {
        m_pInstructorSet->MoveLast();
    }
    UpdateData(FALSE);      //Update dialog from database
}
void CODBCDepartmentView::OnInstructorPreviousrecord()
{
    UpdateInstructor();
    m_pInstructorSet->MovePrev();
    if (m_pInstructorSet->IsBOF()) {
        m_pInstructorSet->MoveFirst();
    }
    UpdateData(FALSE);      //Update dialog from database
}
```

8. You need to gray out menu and toolbar choices when they do not apply:

- You cannot delete a record when you are not positioned on a record or there is no current record:

```
void
CODBCDepartmentView::OnUpdateInstructorDeleteinstructor(
CCmdUI* pCmdUI)
{
```

```
                //Disable delete functionality if no record is found
        pCmdUI->Enable(        //Enable delete if there's a
record
                !m_pInstructorSet->IsBOF() &&
                !m_pInstructorSet->IsDeleted() &&
                !m_pInstructorSet->IsEOF());
}
```

■ You cannot go to the first record or the previous record if you are already at the first record:

```
void
CODBCDepartmentView::OnUpdateInstructorFirstrecord(CCmdUI*
pCmdUI)
{
        CRecordsetStatus rStatus;          //Status variable
//Get CRecordset status
        m_pInstructorSet->GetStatus(rStatus);
        pCmdUI->Enable(                //Disable at first record
                rStatus.m_lCurrentRecord > 0);
}

void
CODBCDepartmentView::OnUpdateInstructorPreviousrecord(CCmdU
I* pCmdUI)
{
        CRecordsetStatus rStatus;          //Status variable
        m_pInstructorSet->GetStatus(rStatus);
//Get CRecordset status
        pCmdUI->Enable(                //Disable at first record
                rStatus.m_lCurrentRecord > 0);
}
        *       You cannot go to the last record or the next
record if you are already at the last record:
void
CODBCDepartmentView::OnUpdateInstructorLastrecord(CCmdUI*
pCmdUI)
{
        CRecordsetStatus rStatus;          //Status variable
        m_pInstructorSet->GetStatus(rStatus);
//Get CRecordset status
        if (rStatus.m_bRecordCountFinal) {
                long recs = m_pInstructorSet->GetRecordCount()
- 1;
                pCmdUI->Enable(                //Disable at last
record
```

```
                              rStatus.m_lCurrentRecord < recs);
          }
          else { //Can't tell if we're at the end
                 pCmdUI->Enable(TRUE);
          }
     }


     void
     CODBCDepartmentView::OnUpdateInstructorNextrecord(CCmdUI*
     pCmdUI)
     {
          CRecordsetStatus rStatus;              //Status variable
          //Get CRecordset status
          m_pInstructorSet->GetStatus(rStatus);
          if (rStatus.m_bRecordCountFinal) {
           long recs = m_pInstructorSet->GetRecordCount() - 1;
           pCmdUI->Enable(            //Disable at last record
                 rStatus.m_lCurrentRecord < recs);
           }
           else {//Can't tell if we're at the end
                 pCmdUI->Enable(TRUE);
           }
          }
     }
```

CHANGES NEEDED TO EXISTING CRecordView FUNCTIONS

Finally, you must update existing functions that you've already used for your single recordset. Do this with the following steps:

1. Update the CRecordView constructor to set your new recordset to NULL and to initialize your Boolean adding variable:

```
CODBCDepartmentView::CODBCDepartmentView()
    : CRecordView(CODBCDepartmentView::IDD)
{
    //{{AFX_DATA_INIT(CODBCDepartmentView)
    m_pSet = NULL;
    m_FindDeptCode = _T("");
    //}}AFX_DATA_INIT
    m_bAddingRecord = FALSE;
    //Next two lines added by Chuck Wood for
    //instructor table support
    m_pInstructorSet = NULL;
    m_bAddingInstructor = FALSE;
```

```
        m_bFieldsChanged = FALSE;
}
```

2. Edit the `DoDataExchange` function to bind records to the new recordset. Note that, while you can use the Class Wizard to do this, the new recordset variables won't appear on your drop-down list of choices. It may be easier to type them in yourself:

```
void CODBCDepartmentView::DoDataExchange(CDataExchange* pDX)
{
    CRecordView::DoDataExchange(pDX);
    //{{AFX_DATA_MAP(CODBCDepartmentView)
    DDX_Text(pDX, IDC_FINDCODE, m_FindDeptCode);
    DDV_MaxChars(pDX, m_FindDeptCode, 4);
    DDX_FieldText(pDX, IDC_DEPARTMENTCODE, m_pSet ->
m_DepartmentCode, m_pSet);
    DDV_MaxChars(pDX, m_pSet->m_DepartmentCode, 4);
    DDX_FieldText(pDX, IDC_DEPARTMENTNAME, m_pSet ->
m_DepartmentName, m_pSet);
    DDV_MaxChars(pDX, m_pSet->m_DepartmentName, 50);
//}}AFX_DATA_MAP
    DDX_Text(pDX, IDC_EMAIL, m_pInstructorSet->m_EMAIL);
    DDV_MaxChars(pDX, m_pInstructorSet->m_EMAIL, 50);
    DDX_Text(pDX, IDC_INSTRUCTORNAME, m_pInstructorSet ->
m_Name);
    DDV_MaxChars(pDX, m_pInstructorSet->m_Name, 50);
    DDX_Text(pDX, IDC_NOTES, m_pInstructorSet->m_Notes);
}
```

3. You need to do three tasks in the `OnInitialUpdate` function:

   a. Construct your new recordset.

   b. Set the joined variable pointer that is used as a parameter in the second recordset to the address of the joined variable in the first recordset.

   c. Call the function to open your recordset after the primary recordset has been opened.

   These three steps can be seen in the nonshaded lines that follow:

```
void CODBCDepartmentView::OnInitialUpdate()
{
    m_pSet = &GetDocument()->m_oDBCDepartmentSet;
//Step 1: Construct a new CODBCInstroctorSet
    m_pInstructorSet = new CODBCInstructorSet(m_pSet ->
m_pDatabase);
    /*
```

```
Step 2: Set the m_pDepartmentCode CODBCInstroctorSet pointer
in the m_pInstructorSet class to address the m_DepartmentCode
variable in the m_oDBCDepartmentSet class
*/
    m_pInstructorSet->m_pDepartmentCode =
        &GetDocument() ->
m_oDBCDepartmentSet.m_DepartmentCode;
      CRecordView::OnInitialUpdate();
      GetParentFrame()->RecalcLayout();
      ResizeParentToFit();
      m_pSet->Close();      //Close to start transaction
      if (m_pSet->m_pDatabase->CanTransact()) {
          m_pSet->m_pDatabase->BeginTrans();
      }
      m_pSet->Open();      //Open after starting transaction
      m_pSet->MoveFirst();
/* Step 3: Open the Instructor recordset after the joined
Department record set has been opened so you can display
related instructors
*/
      OpenInstructorRecordset();
      UpdateData(FALSE);      //Update dialog box fields
}
```

4. Whenever you change records on the primary recordset, you need to do the following:

   a. Update any related records on the secondary dataset before the move takes place.

   b. Requery and display the first record on the second recordset after the move takes place.

   c. If there are no related records after the move, throw the second recordset in AddNew mode to see if the user wants to add a record.

   This functionality can be placed inside the OnMove function:

```
BOOL CODBCDepartmentView::OnMove(UINT nIDMoveCommand)
{
    if (m_bAddingRecord) {      //Currently adding?
        //If so, Update the record before the move
        UpdateData(TRUE);      //Get data from dialog box
        m_pSet->Update();      //Update data if needed
        m_pSet->MoveLast();      //Go to the added record
        m_bAddingRecord = FALSE;      //Reset flag
    }
```

```
    UpdateData(FALSE);      //Update dialog box fields
    UpdateInstructor();
    BOOL returnCode = CRecordView::OnMove(nIDMoveCommand);
    m_pInstructorSet->Requery();
    CRecordsetStatus rStatus;      //Status variable
    //Get CRecordset status
    m_pInstructorSet->GetStatus(rStatus);
    if (rStatus.m_lCurrentRecord < 0) {      //Records Exist?
        //No isntructor records, so add one.
        AddInstructor();
    }
    return returnCode;
}
```

5. At the end of the OnFileNew function, add a record to the primary recordset using the add function you defined earlier:

```
void CODBCDepartmentView::OnFileNew()
{
//. . .
//Previous OnFileNew code goes here
//. . .
    //No isntructor records, so add one.
    AddInstructor();
}
```

6. Don't forget that during transaction processing, you need to:

   a. Update your second recordset.

   b. Get the position of your second recordset.

   c. Close your second recordset.

   d. Open the new transaction with a BeginTrans function, as before.

   e. Position the new transaction to the appropriate record in the recordset, if possible.

   These steps are done in the OnFileSave function. Note that the OpenInstructorRecordset function (written earlier in this section) is used to both open the recordset and position it to the appropriate record:

```
void CODBCDepartmentView::OnFileSave()
{
    if (m_bFieldsChanged && m_pSet->CanTransact()) {
        if (!m_bAddingRecord) {      //Currently adding?
            m_pSet->Edit();      //If not, set edit mode
        }
        UpdateInstructor();      //Update Instructor too
```

```
        UpdateData(TRUE);      //Get data from dialog box
        m_pSet->Update();      //Update data if needed
        m_bAddingRecord = FALSE;      //Reset flag
    //Commit changes
        m_pSet->m_pDatabase->CommitTrans();
        CRecordsetStatus rStatus;            //Status variable
    //Get CRecordset status
        m_pSet->GetStatus(rStatus);
        m_pSet->Close();      //Close to start transaction
        CRecordsetStatus rStatus2;            //Status variable
    //Get CRecordset status
        m_pInstructorSet->GetStatus(rStatus2);
    //Close second transaction
        m_pInstructorSet->Close();
    //Start Transaction
        m_pSet->m_pDatabase->BeginTrans();
        m_pSet->Open();      //Reopen CRecordset
    //Restore record position
        if (rStatus.m_lCurrentRecord >= 0) {
            m_pSet ->
    SetAbsolutePosition(rStatus.m_lCurrentRecord+1);
        }
        m_bFieldsChanged = FALSE;      //Reset flag
        OpenInstructorRecordset(
            //Reopen second instructor
            rStatus2.m_lCurrentRecord);
        UpdateData(FALSE);      //Update dialog box fields
    }
}
```

7. The CRecordset class automatically detects changes made after an Edit or AddNew function call. These changes are written to the database by using the Update function. When using multiple CRecordset classes, you must make sure that *all* AddNew and Edit function calls are made before *any* UpdateData(TRUE) calls are made. UpdateData(TRUE) takes data from the dialog box and places it in the bound CRecordset variables. However, any changes that may trigger a database update are not detected until after an AddNew or Edit function is called.

Be sure to use the following steps to update your database from two CRecordset classes:

a. Place the first recordset into Edit or AddNew mode:

```
if (!m_bAddingRecord) {      //Currently adding?
    m_pSet->Edit();      //If not, set edit mode
}
```

b. Place the second recordset into Edit or AddNew mode.

c. Call the `UpdateData(TRUE)` function:

```
UpdateData(TRUE);   //Get data from dialog box
```

d. Call the `Update` function for both `CRecordset` classes:

```
m_pInstructorSet->Update();
```

If you use the `UpdateData(TRUE)` function before both `CRecordset` classes are in either Edit or AddNew mode, the `CRecordset` won't be able to detect your changes and therefore won't update the database when the `Update` function is called.

8. When you exit your program, you may need to update your recordset, and you need to deallocate your new recordset. This can be done in the OnDestroy function, which is triggered when the window is destroyed:

```
void CODBCDepartmentView::OnDestroy()
{
//Check for changed fields and transaction ability
    if (m_pSet->CanTransact()) {
        if (m_bFieldsChanged) {
           if (AfxMessageBox (
    "Records have been changed.  Do you want to save?",
            MB_YESNO) == IDNO) {
            m_pSet->m_pDatabase->Rollback();
          }
          else {
            if (!m_bAddingRecord) { //Currently adding?
            //If not, set edit mode
                m_pSet->Edit();
            }
            UpdateInstructor();
            UpdateData(TRUE); //Get data from dialog box
            m_pSet->Update(); //Update data if needed
            m_pSet->m_pDatabase->CommitTrans();
          }
        }
        else {
          m_pSet->m_pDatabase->CommitTrans();
        }
```

```
    }
    if (m_pInstructorSet != NULL) {
        m_pInstructorSet->Close();
        delete m_pInstructorSet;
    }
    CRecordView::OnDestroy();
}
```

 The code for the version of ODBCDepartment can be found in the ODBCDepartmentD directory on the CD-ROM accompanying this book.

Summary

This chapter showed how easy ODBC development can be using Visual C++ and the MFC Application Wizard. To recap:

- ◆ You can quickly generate a scrolling or updateable application with little or no code using the MFC Application Wizard.

- ◆ With a little code you can add insert and update capability and transaction support to your MFC application.

- ◆ Transactions are a little tricky, and you should check with your DBA or database documentation for any transaction restrictions on your database.

- ◆ Joins are almost as easy as single table applications when using the MFC Application Wizard.

- ◆ Sometimes, your application may require multiple CRecordset objects. The easiest way to do this is to start with an MFC application and add additional functionality.

Chapter 6

Developing ODBC Reports

IN THIS CHAPTER

- ◆ Creating a print-ready MFC program
- ◆ Making a WYSIWYG database report program
- ◆ Using the OnDraw function for reports
- ◆ Separating the screen drawing from the printing using the OnPrint function

MANY DATABASE PROGRAMS consist of making reports. Reporting capabilities enable your database program to summarize database information. Database reports are often the cornerstone of important managerial decisions. This chapter gives step-by-step instructions and shows how you can quickly and easily make a database report using MFC and ODBC.

 TIP Some of the function calls may seem cryptic, especially if you don't read the book sequentially. The preceding two chapters contain an overview of ODBC with MFC and Visual C++ and show what several of the functions can do.

Understanding MFC Reporting

To understand graphical reports, you need to understand, at the least, device contexts, fonts, and painting functions. This section introduces MFC reporting concepts.

TIP This section delves into topics that are needed for graphical database reports in Windows, but a host of other graphical capabilities can be accessed in Visual C++ and in the MFC, including bitmaps, palettes, drawing shapes, and regions. If you want to read more about this material, check out the help file or find a book that delves into Visual C++ graphics programming.

Using Device Contexts

Device contexts are a link between a Windows application and a device driver (Figure 6-1). In short, device contexts are how a Windows program "talks" to a hardware device, such as a monitor or a printer. Device contexts are always used for graphical images and to track permission to use a device.

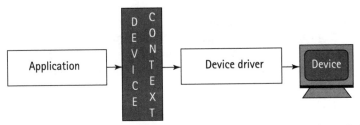

Figure 6-1: The device context is the bridge between the application and the device driver.

When Windows was first introduced, device contexts were difficult to use and keep track of, but the MFC enables you to easily manipulate device contexts by using the CDC class. (Examples of CDC class usage can be seen later in this chapter.) Over 100 CDC functions can be used to manipulate a device context, most of which handle some sort of graphical operation or graphical support. However, for reporting purposes in this chapter, you need concern yourself with only five. For fonts, you need the SelectObject function and the GetTextMetrics function, and for writing graphical text to a device, you need the TextOut and the TabbedTextOut functions. The SetMapMode function can control the interpretation of positions on the window.

MAPPING MODE

When you pass values to the CDC class, you often specify a location using (x, y) coordinates. These (x, y) coordinates represent a logical unit of measurement (for example, inches, pixels, millimeters, and so on). CDC then changes these logical units into device units.

The mapping mode defines the logical unit of measurement. Mapping mode is used to determine how the numbers you pass the CDC class are to be interpreted. Mapping mode can be set using the `CDC::SetMapMode` function or the `CScrollView::SetScrollSizes` function. Table 6-1 lists the valid mapping modes.

TABLE 6-1 MAPPING MODES

Mapping Mode	Description
MM_HIENGLISH	Each logical unit is converted to 0.001 inch. The y position must be negative.
MM_HIMETRIC	Each logical unit is converted to 0.01 millimeter. The y position must be negative.
MM_ISOTROPIC	Logical units are converted to arbitrary units with equally scaled axes; that is, 1 unit along the x axis is equal to 1 unit along the y axis.
MM_LOENGLISH	Each logical unit is converted to 0.01 inch. The y position must be negative.
MM_LOMETRIC	Each logical unit is converted to 0.1 millimeter. The y position must be negative.
MM_TEXT	Each logical unit is converted to 1 pixel. The y position must be positive.
MM_TWIPS	Each logical unit is converted to 1/20 of a point, or 1/1440 of an inch. The y position must be negative.

The `CDC::SetMapMode` function can be used as follows:

```
pDC->SetMapMode(MM_LOENGLISH);     // x, y are in 1/100 of an inch
```

The following is an example of the `CScrollView::SetScrollSizes` function that would appear in a CScrollView dependent class:

```
//Limit size to 8" x 20"
CSize sizeTotal(800, 2000);
SetScrollSizes(MM_LOENGLISH, sizeTotal);
```

GRAPHICAL TEXT OUTPUT FUNCTIONS

Two major CDC functions can be used to print text output to a device context. These two functions are TextOut and TabbedTextOut. The function prototype for TextOut is:

```
BOOL TextOut( int x, int y, const CString& str );
```

In the preceding TextOut function call, x and y represent the position of the text on the screen. Note that, depending on your map mode, y can be positive or negative. The CString you pass to the TextOut function is the output you wish to display. The following line is an example of the CDC::TextOut function:

```
pDC->TextOut(200, 0, "ODBC Student Report");
```

Although initially more complicated, the CDC::TabbedTextOut function can be used to quickly format and print columns of data. The following is a function prototype for the TabbedTextOut function:

```
CSize TabbedTextOut( int x, int y, const CString& str, int
nNumberTabs, LPINT tabArray, int nTabOrigin );
```

In the preceding function prototype, a string (str) is printed at a given (x, y) coordinate that specifies the location of the top-left corner of the rectangle containing the first character. The line contains an nNumberTabs of tabs stored in the tabArray integer array. Tabs are to be measured from nTabOrigin, which is usually set to zero. One way to use the TabbedTextOut function is to follow these steps:

1. Initialize the tab stops with an integer array. Assuming a MM_LOENGLISH mapping mode was defined, the following line of code sets tab stops at 1 inch, 2.75 inches, and 6.5 inches:

   ```
   int TabStops[] = {100, 275, 650};
   ```

2. Define a CString variable, and use the CString::Format function to format a variable using printf command codes \t (TAB) and %s (string):

   ```
   CString line;    //This is the print line
   //Format the detail line
   line.Format("%s\t%s\t%s\t%s %s",
       m_pSet->m_DepartmentCode,
       m_pSet->m_Name,
       m_pSet->m_Description,
       m_pSet->m_FirstName,
       m_pSet->m_LastName);
   ```

3. Use the CDC::TabbedTextOut function to print the line.

```
//Output the print line at (0, 0) using 3 tabs
pDC->TabbedTextOut(0, 0, line, 3, TabStops, 0);
```

FONTS

When PCs first became popular, the printer controlled fonts using buttons or switches. Most programs printed only text, and only the most advanced printed graphics, on only a limited number of printers. In Windows, fonts are graphical and no longer pure text. Fonts can be measured using width, height, and external leading space, as shown in Figure 6-2.

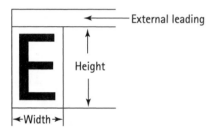

Figure 6-2: Font dimensions are a combination of width, height, and external leading space.

When you use text output functions, you need to keep track of the (x, y) coordinates. You do so through the TEXTMETRIC structure and the following steps:

1. Declare a TEXTMETRIC structure:

```
TEXTMETRIC metrics;    //Font measurements
```

2. Initialize the y coordinate variable to zero:

```
int y = 0;        //Current y position on report
```

3. Use the CDC::GetTextMetrics function to retrieve the text metrics structures:

```
pDC->GetTextMetrics(&metrics);
```

4. Compute the line height using the TEXTMETRIC.tmHeight and the TEXTMETRIC.tmExternalLeading variables:

```
int LineHeight = metrics.tmHeight +
metrics.tmExternalLeading;
```

LineHeight must be recalculated every time the font changes.

5. Now, every time you output a line, you must also increment the y coordinate:

```
//Output the line at (0, y) using 3 tabs
pDC->TabbedTextOut(0, y, line, 3, TabStops, 0);
y -= LineHeight;     //Adjust y position
```

Actual font appearance is controlled using the CFont::CreateFont function. The following is the function prototype for the CFont::CreateFont function:

```
BOOL CFont::CreateFont(int nHeight, int nWidth, int nEscapement, int
nOrientation, int nWeight, BYTE bItalic, BYTE bUnderline, BYTE
bStrikeOut, BYTE nCharSet, BYTE nOutPrecision, BYTE nClipPrecision,
BYTE nQuality, BYTE nPitchAndFamily, LPCTSTR lpszFacename );
```

The CreateFont function parameters are explained in Table 6-2.

TABLE 6-2 CREATEFONT FUNCTION PARAMETERS

Parameter	Description
nHeight	This parameter describes the height of the font in some measurement unit. Measurement units are dependent on the mapping mode set by either the CDC::SetMapMode function or the CScrollView::SetScrollSizes function. If this parameter is set to zero, a reasonable size is used.
nWidth	This parameter sets the average width of the font. If this is set to zero, a reasonable width is used.
nEscapement	This specifies the angle to print in .1-degree units. Using this parameter, you can write at an angle (for example, 450 is a 45-degree angle) or backwards (for example, 1800 writes backwards). Usually this is zero for normal placement of text.
nOrientation	This parameter specifies the angle (in 0.1-degree units) between the baseline of a character and the x axis.
nWeight	This parameter is used to create the "boldness" of a font. Usual values are FW_DONTCARE (use the default), FW_NORMAL (for normal text), and FW_BOLD for bolded text. Check the MSDN for all values if these values don't meet your needs.
bItalic	This parameter contains a TRUE or FALSE indicating if this font is in italics.

Parameter	Description
bUnderline	This parameter contains a TRUE or FALSE indicating if this font is underlined.
bStrikeOut	This parameter contains a TRUE or FALSE indicating if this font uses a strike out.
nCharSet	This parameter specifies the character set. Usually, ANSI_CHARSET or DEFAULT_CHARSET is used, although some internationally sold products may require a different character set.
nOutPrecision	This parameter specifies the output precision, which defines how closely the output must match the requested font's height, width, character orientation, escapement, and pitch. Usually, OUT_DEFAULT_PRECIS is used.
nClipPrecision	This parameter specifies the clipping precision, which defines how to clip characters that are partially outside the clipping region. It is usually set to CLIP_DEFAULT_PRECIS.
nQuality	This parameter defines the quality of the font. Possible values are DEFAULT_QUALITY, DRAFT_QUALITY, and PROOF_QUALITY.
nPitchAndFamily	Pitch can be either fixed (where all the characters are the same width) or variable (where characters vary in width depending on each letter.) Pitch has three variables: DEFAULT_PITCH, VARIABLE_PITCH, and FIXED_PITCH.
	Family is available if you are using a TrueType font. The "family" gives Windows a hint for choosing a font when the exact font desired is not loaded on the user's system. Any Family variable must be logically ORed with the Pitch variable. Possible values for Family are: FF_DECORATIVE for novelty fonts; FF_DONTCARE if you don't care what family; FF_MODERN for fixed pitch fonts such as Courier New, Pica, or Elite; FF_ROMAN for variable pitch and with serifs such as Times New Roman; FF_SCRIPT for fonts designed to look like handwriting such as Script; and FF_SWISS for variable pitch and without serifs, such as Arial and MS Sans Serif.
	To use this parameter, you need to logically OR the pitch with the family (for example, VARIABLE_PITCH | FF_SWISS for Arial font).
lpszFacename	The name of the font (for example, Times New Roman, Arial, Courier New, and so on); try to use True Type fonts for the best appearance and WYSIWYG conversion from monitor to printer.

You can also OR in TMPF_TRUETYPE in the nPitchAndFamily variable (for example, `VARIABLE_PITCH | FF_SWISS|TMPF_TRUETYPE`) if you want to force Windows to choose a TrueType font.

To change the font of a device context, you must use the `CDC::SelectObject` function. The `SelectObject` function is used to set graphical properties of a device context. When setting a font, the format for the `SelectObject` function is:

```
CFont* SelectObject(CFont pFont);
```

The `SelectObject` function sets a new font and returns the old font. That way, you can restore the original font of the device context before your function changes it. The following code shows how the `CreateFont` and `SelectObject` functions work together to change the font of a device context:

```
CFont HeadingFont;    //Font for headings
//Bold and underlined font for headings
HeadingFont.CreateFont(36, 0, 0, 0, FW_BOLD, FALSE, TRUE, 0,
    ANSI_CHARSET, OUT_DEFAULT_PRECIS, CLIP_DEFAULT_PRECIS,
    DEFAULT_QUALITY, DEFAULT_PITCH | FF_ROMAN,
    "Times New Roman");
//Capture default settings when setting the title font
CFont* OldFont = pDC->SelectObject(&HeadingFont);
```

Generating Reports

The previous section gave some needed background to understand reports. This section describes the step-by-step procedures required to quickly generate an ODBC report using the MFC AppWizard. Printing in Microsoft Windows has always been somewhat difficult, but the MFC encapsulates much of the functionality and makes it a little easier. This section gives two examples of reports: one that displays exactly what is on the report, and one that changes the report somewhat.

Reports Using the OnDraw Function

MFC Reports use a combination of the `CRecordView::OnDraw` and `CRecordView::OnPrint` functions. The `OnDraw` function is called by the CRecordView ancestor and is passed a pointer to the device context of the monitor. As a default, the `OnPrint` function immediately calls the `OnDraw` function and passes it the device context of the printer so that what is displayed on the window is also what is printed. By overriding the `OnDraw` function, you can graphically control the output that goes to the monitor as well as the output that goes to the printer.

You can quickly generate an ODBC report by using the following steps:

1. Create a new project using the MFC Application Wizard as shown in the previous chapter. Choose Single Document in Step 1 of 6. In Step 2 of 6, select Header files only (Figure 6-3) for your database support. This enables you to easily incorporate recordsets into your application but does not set up the update dialog boxes shown in the previous chapter.

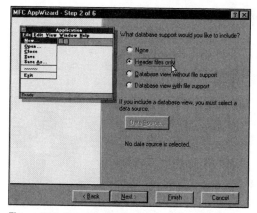

Figure 6-3: You need only database header file support inside an MFC ODBC database when generating reports.

In Step 6 of 6, change the base class to CScrollView (Figure 6-4). This enables reports that scroll off the window.

When you're finished, you should see the options in the New Project Information message box shown in Figure 6-5.

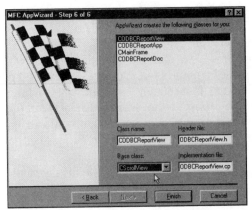

Figure 6-4: The CScrollView class should be used for most WYSIWYG reports.

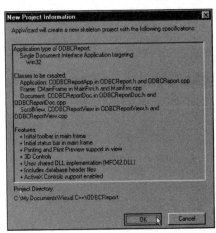

Figure 6-5: The New Project Information message box shows the options
you have chosen when creating your project.

2. After you have generated your application, select View → ClassWizard to
   go into the MFC Class Wizard. Click on the Add Class button, and choose
   New from the pop-up menu. You should then see the New Class dialog
   box shown in Figure 6-6. Name your new class (CODBCReportSet in
   Figure 6-6), and choose CRecordset as the base class. Click OK.

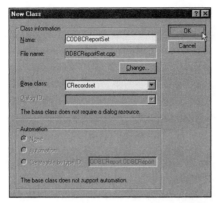

Figure 6-6: You need to add a CRecordset descendent to your ODBC report.

3. You should now see the Database Options dialog box (Figure 6-7). Choose the database that you'll be drawing the report from.

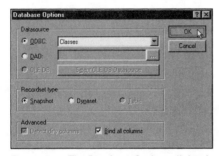

Figure 6-7: The Database Options dialog box enables you to choose which database you want to use for your CRecordset descendent class.

4. Next, you should see the Select Database Tables dialog box. Here, choose one or more tables that you need for your report. In Figure 6-8, six tables are chosen.

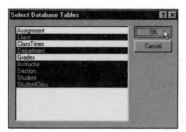

Figure 6-8: The Select Database Tables dialog box enables you to select
the tables that you wish to use for your report recordset.

5. You need to add a database to your document header file. In our example,
open the ODBCReportDoc.h source file, and add the following nonshaded
lines:

```
// ODBCReportDoc.h : interface of the CODBCReportDoc class
//
/////////////////////////////////////////////////////////////////

#if
!defined(AFX_ODBCREPORTDOC_H__FA789B99_4121_11D2_9949_B575777
8F646__INCLUDED_)
#define
AFX_ODBCREPORTDOC_H__FA789B99_4121_11D2_9949_B5757778F646__IN
CLUDED_

#if _MSC_VER > 1000
#pragma once
#endif // _MSC_VER > 1000
#include "ODBCReportSet.h"

class CODBCReportDoc : public CDocument
{
protected: // create from serialization only
    CODBCReportDoc();
    DECLARE_DYNCREATE(CODBCReportDoc)

// Attributes
public:
    CODBCReportSet m_dbSet;
```

6. Place your join and sort information inside your CRecordset constructor.
In our example, the following lines were added to the CODBCReportSet
constructor:

```
CODBCReportSet::CODBCReportSet(CDatabase* pdb)
    : CRecordset(pdb)
{
    //{{AFX_FIELD_INIT(CODBCReportSet)
    m_ClassID = _T("");
    m_Description = _T("");
    m_Credits = 0;
    m_DepartmentCode = _T("");
    m_DepartmentName = _T("");
    m_InstructorID = 0;
    m_Name = _T("");
    m_DepartmentCode2 = _T("");
    m_EMAIL = _T("");
    m_Notes = _T("");
    m_SectionID = 0;
    m_ClassID2 = _T("");
    m_SectionNumber = 0;
    m_IsLab = FALSE;
    m_Term = _T("");
    m_Year = 0;
    m_Room = _T("");
    m_InstructorID2 = 0;
    m_LabsParentSectionID = 0;
    m_Notes2 = _T("");
    m_StudentID = 0;
    m_FirstName = _T("");
    m_MidName = _T("");
    m_LastName = _T("");
    m_Address = _T("");
    m_City = _T("");
    m_StateOrProvince = _T("");
    m_PostalCode = _T("");
    m_PhoneNumber = _T("");
    m_EMAIL2 = _T("");
    m_Major = _T("");
    m_StudentSSN = _T("");
    m_StudentID2 = 0;
    m_SectionID2 = 0;
    m_nFields = 34;
    //}}AFX_FIELD_INIT
    m_nDefaultType = snapshot;
    m_strSort = "Department.DepartmentCode, \
                Instructor.Name, \
                Student.LastName";
    m_strFilter = "Instructor.DepartmentCode \
```

```
            = Department.DepartmentCode \
    AND Section.InstructorID \
            = Instructor.InstructorID \
    AND Section.ClassID \
            = Class.ClassID \
    AND StudentClass.StudentID \
            = Student.StudentID \
    AND StudentClass.SectionID \
            = Section.SectionID";
}
```

The preceding lines join together the six tables and sort the results.

7. Add the following lines to the CRecordView header file
   (ODBCReportView.h) to enable database support:

```
// ODBCReportView.h : interface of the CODBCReportView class
//
//////////////////////////////////////////////////////////////////
////////////////
#if
!defined(AFX_ODBCREPORTVIEW_H__FA789B9B_4121_11D2_9949_B57577
78F646__INCLUDED_)
#define
AFX_ODBCREPORTVIEW_H__FA789B9B_4121_11D2_9949_B5757778F646__I
NCLUDED_

#if _MSC_VER > 1000
#pragma once
#endif // _MSC_VER > 1000
#include "ODBCReportSet.h"

class CODBCReportView : public CScrollView
{
protected: // create from serialization only
    CODBCReportView();
    DECLARE_DYNCREATE(CODBCReportView)

// Attributes
public:
    CODBCReportDoc* GetDocument();
    CODBCReportSet* m_pSet;
```

8. Add the following lines to the OnInitialUpdate function in the
   ODBCReportView.cpp. The following lines give a title to the window, make
   an 8 × 20-inch window, set sizes to be reported in 1/100 inch increments,
   set up the database, and open the database recordset.

```
void CODBCReportView::OnInitialUpdate()
{
    CScrollView::OnInitialUpdate();
    //Limit size to 8" x 20"
    CSize sizeTotal(800, 2000);
    //Because of MM_LOENGLISH, Sizes are in .01 of an inch
    SetScrollSizes(MM_LOENGLISH, sizeTotal);
    //Retrieve the document
    CODBCReportDoc* pDoc = GetDocument();
    ASSERT_VALID(pDoc);     //Make sure it's valid
    //Set the window title
    pDoc->SetTitle("ODBC Student Report");
    //Set the m_pSet pointer to the m_dbSet recordset
    m_pSet = &pDoc->m_dbSet;
    //Open the recordset
    m_pSet->Open();
}
```

9. Don't forget to close your recordset in the destructor so the system can reclaim your resources:

```
CODBCReportView::~CODBCReportView()
{
    m_pSet->Close();     //Close the recordset
}
```

10. All that remains is to write the OnDraw function. The OnDraw function is passed a pointer to both the monitor and printer device contexts. These device contexts will be used when printing or displaying.

```
void CODBCReportView::OnDraw(CDC* pDC)
{
    CString line;       //This is the print line
    TEXTMETRIC metrics;     //Font measurements
    int y = 0;          //Current y position on report
    CFont TitleFont;        //Font for Title
    CFont HeadingFont;      //Font for headings
    CFont DetailFont;       //Font for detail lines
    //Tab stops at 1 inch, 2.5 inches, and 6.5 inches
    int TabStops[] = {100, 275, 650};

    //Set the recordset at the beginning
    m_pSet->Requery();
    //Bold font for Title
    TitleFont.CreateFont(44, 0, 0, 0, FW_BOLD, FALSE, FALSE, 0,
        ANSI_CHARSET, OUT_DEFAULT_PRECIS, CLIP_DEFAULT_PRECIS,
```

```
            DEFAULT_QUALITY, DEFAULT_PITCH | FF_ROMAN,
            "Times New Roman");
        //Bold and underlined font for headings
    HeadingFont.CreateFont(36, 0, 0, 0, FW_BOLD, FALSE, TRUE, 0,
            ANSI_CHARSET, OUT_DEFAULT_PRECIS, CLIP_DEFAULT_PRECIS,
            DEFAULT_QUALITY, DEFAULT_PITCH | FF_ROMAN,
            "Times New Roman");
        //Normal font for detail
    DetailFont.CreateFont(18, 0, 0, 0, FW_NORMAL, FALSE, FALSE,
            0,ANSI_CHARSET, OUT_DEFAULT_PRECIS,
            CLIP_DEFAULT_PRECIS, DEFAULT_QUALITY,
            DEFAULT_PITCH | FF_ROMAN, "Times New Roman");
        //Capture default settings when setting the title font
        CFont* OldFont = (CFont*) pDC->SelectObject(&TitleFont);
        //Retrieve the heading font measurements
        pDC->GetTextMetrics(&metrics);
        //Compute the heading line height
        int LineHeight = metrics.tmHeight +
    metrics.tmExternalLeading;
        //Set Y to the line height.
        y -= LineHeight;
        pDC->TextOut(200, 0, "ODBC Student Report");
    /*
    Y must be set to negative numbers because MM_LOENGLISH was
    used in the CODBCReportView::OnInitialUpdate function.
    */
        //Set the Heading font
        pDC->SelectObject(&HeadingFont);
        //Format the heading
        line.Format("%s\t%s\t%s\t%s", "Dept", "Instructor",
    "Class", "Student");
        //Output the heading using tabs
        pDC->TabbedTextOut(0, y, line, 3, TabStops, 0);
        //Detect empty recordset
        if (m_pSet->IsBOF()) {
            return;
        }
        //Compute the detail line height
        LineHeight = metrics.tmHeight +
    metrics.tmExternalLeading;
```

```
    y -= LineHeight;     //Adjust y position
    //Set the detail font
    pDC->SelectObject(&DetailFont);
    //Retrieve detail font measurements
    pDC->GetTextMetrics(&metrics);
    //Compute the detail line height
    LineHeight = metrics.tmHeight +
metrics.tmExternalLeading;
    //Scroll through the recordset
    while (!m_pSet->IsEOF()) {
        //Format the detail line
        line.Format("%s\t%s\t%s\t%s %s",
            m_pSet->m_DepartmentCode,
            m_pSet->m_Name,
            m_pSet->m_Description,
            m_pSet->m_FirstName,
            m_pSet->m_LastName);
        //Output the detail line using tabs
        pDC->TabbedTextOut(0, y, line, 3, TabStops, 0);
        //Get the next recordset number
        y -= LineHeight;     //Adjust y position
        m_pSet->MoveNext();
    }
    //Restore default settings
    pDC->SelectObject(OldFont);
}
```

When you're finished, your window should display all the records from the recordset, as shown in Figure 6-9.

Because the printer device context is also passed to the OnDraw function, your printed report will be almost identical to the report that is being displayed. Because the MFC Application Wizard automatically generates print preview and print functionality, you can use File→Print Preview to view the printout, as shown in Figure 6-10.

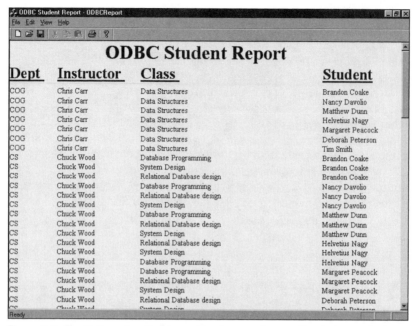

Figure 6-9: The OnDraw function is used to draw on the monitor device context.

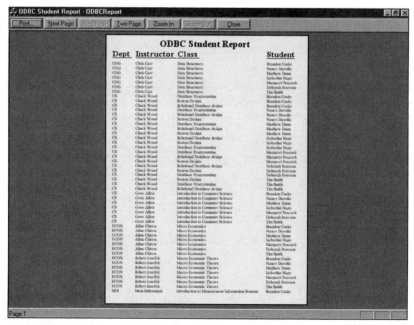

Figure 6-10: Printing and Print Preview functionality is automatically taken care of by the MFC AppWizard.

Building Reports Using the OnPrint Function

The report in Figure 6-10 looks almost identical to the report being displayed in Figure 6-9, but not all records were printed. When the page ran out, no more records were displayed. Furthermore, if there were more than one page, you'd want a heading for each page and a footer displayed as well. In other words, you hardly ever have a case where you can use the *exact same* functionality for both the printed report and the screen report. However, that doesn't mean you can't use much of the same functionality.

By default, the OnPrint function calls the OnDraw function and uses the same code for the printout as it does for the screen. If you want to separate the printed report from the screen report, you need to override the OnPrint function by using the MFC Class Wizard. Choose the OnPrint message for the CODBCReportView object ID, and click the Add Class button, as shown in Figure 6-11.

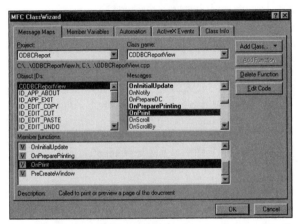

Figure 6-11: Most MFC reports override the OnPrint function by using the MFC Class Wizard.

You now see the following OnPrint function added to the bottom of your ODBCReportView.cpp source file:

```
void CODBCReportView::OnPrint(CDC* pDC, CPrintInfo* pInfo)
{
    // TODO: Add your specialized code here and/or call the base class
    CScrollView::OnPrint(pDC, pInfo);
}
```

Notice that you not only have a CDC device context pointer for the printer, as with the OnDraw function, but you also have a CPrintInfo class pointer as a parameter. CPrintInfo contains information about a print or print-preview request. The MFC creates an instance of the CPrintInfo class each time the Print or Print Preview command is chosen and destroys it when the command is completed. Table 6-3 lists the class variables of the CPrintInfo class, and Table 6-4 lists the functions.

TABLE 6-3 CPRINTINFO CLASS VARIABLES

CPrintInfo Class Variable	Description
BOOL m_bContinuePrinting	TRUE or FALSE indicating whether the framework should continue the print loop. Your print code can use this flag to signal when the last page of the document has been reached.
BOOL m_bDirect	TRUE or FALSE indicating whether the document is being printed directly (without displaying the Print dialog box).
BOOL m_bDocObject	TRUE or FALSE indicating whether the document being printed is a DocObject. TRUE indicates that the document being printed is part of a container document that defines the page numbering when the application acts as a server of OLE document objects.
BOOL m_bPreview	TRUE or FALSE indicating whether the document is being previewed.
CPrintDialog* m_pPD	Contains a pointer to the CPrintDialog object used for the Print dialog box.
CRect m_rectDraw	Specifies a rectangle defining the current usable page area.
CString m_strPageDesc	Contains a format string for page-number display to be displayed in print preview on the status bar. Default is "Page %u\nPages %u-%u\n" indicating that "Page x" should be displayed in a single page preview and that "Pages x-y" should be displayed in two-page preview.

CPrintInfo Class Variable	Description
`int m_dwFlags`	Contains DocObject printing operations; the flags contain ANDed values of one or more of the following variables: `PRINTFLAG_MAYBOTHERUSER`, `PRINTFLAG_PROMPTUSER`, `PRINTFLAG_USERMAYCHANGEPRINTER`, `PRINTFLAG_RECOMPOSETODEVICE`, `PRINTFLAG_DONTACTUALLYPRINT`, `PRINTFLAG_FORCEPROPERTIES`, or `PRINTFLAG_PRINTTOFILE`. This flag has no effect unless `m_bDocObject` is TRUE.
`LPVOID m_lpUserData`	Contains a LPVOID pointer to a user-created structure, which is not often used, and only when you want to store printing-specific data that you do not want to store in your view class.
`UINT m_nCurPage`	Contains the current page number.
`UINT m_nNumPreviewPages`	1 or 2 indicating the number of pages displayed in the preview window.
`UINT m_nOffsetPage`	Contains the number of pages preceding the first page of a particular DocObject in a combined DocObject print job.

TABLE 6-4 CPRINTINFO CLASS FUNCTIONS

CPrintInfo Class Function	Description
`UINT GetFromPage() const;`	Returns the number of the first page being printed.
`UINT GetMaxPage() const;`	Returns the number of the last page of the document.
`UINT GetMinPage() const;`	Returns the number of the first page of the document.
`UINT GetOffsetPage() const;`	Returns the value of the `CPrintInfo::m_nOffsetPage` variable.

Continued

TABLE **6-4** CPRINTINFO CLASS FUNCTIONS *(Continued)*

CPrintInfo Class Function	Description
`UINT GetToPage() const;`	Returns the number of the last page being printed.
`SetMaxPage(UINT page);`	Sets the number of the last page of the document. The default maximum pages for any document is 1.
`SetMinPage(UINT page);`	Sets the number of the first page of the document. The default for the first page is 1.

The `OnPrint` function is called *at the beginning of each page* rather than at the beginning of a report (Figure 6-12). As a result, you need to keep track of your place in the report from page to page.

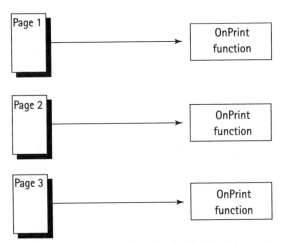

Figure 6-12: Remember that the OnPrint function gets called for every page, not just once per report.

To enable multipage reports and footer records from a single device context, perform the following steps:

1. Add the `OnPrint` function to your CODBCReportView class as shown previously.

2. Next, edit the ODBCReportView.h to add the `OutputReport` function prototype after the implementation public declaration. The `OutputReport`

function will be called by both the OnDraw function and the OnPrint function to handle both device contexts.

```
// Implementation
public:
    virtual ~CODBCReportView();
    void OutputReport(CDC* pDC, CPrintInfo* pInfo = NULL);
```

3. Change the OnDraw function to call the new OutputReport function. Notice that the pInfo variable in the OutputReport function prototype defaults to NULL. Because the OnDraw function contains no CPrintInfo parameter, you can test pInfo == NULL in the OutputReport function to determine if the device context is the display or a printer:

```
void CODBCReportView::OnDraw(CDC* pDC)
{
    OutputReport(pDC);     //Display contents
}
```

4. Call the OutputReport function in the OnPrint function:

```
void CODBCReportView::OnPrint(CDC* pDC, CPrintInfo* pInfo)
{
    OutputReport(pDC, pInfo);     //Display contents
}
```

5. Write the OutputReport function. It is similar to the OnDraw function shown in the last section, except with the following changes:

   - The query at the beginning only queries the first page in the printed output. This is done by first testing pinfo to see if the device context is a printer or print preview. Then it continues to requery and test for records as was done in the OnDraw function shown in the last section:

     ```
     if (!pInfo || pInfo->m_nCurPage == 1) {
         //Set the recordset at the beginning
         m_pSet->Requery();
     }
     ```

   - Create a footer font:

     ```
     //Small font for footer
     FooterFont.CreateFont(12, 0, 0, 0, FW_NORMAL, FALSE, FALSE,
     0,ANSI_CHARSET, OUT_DEFAULT_PRECIS,
     CLIP_DEFAULT_PRECIS,DEFAULT_QUALITY, DEFAULT_PITCH |
     FF_ROMAN, "Times New Roman");
     ```

   - While scrolling through your recordset, stop printing records when you've run out of paper. Because there are still more records at this time, use the `CPrintInfo::SetMaxPage` function to increment the total pages by one.

```
while (!m_pSet->IsEOF()) {
    if (pInfo && abs(y) > 1000) {
        pInfo->SetMaxPage(pInfo->m_nCurPage + 1);
        break;
    }
```

- Finally, at the end of the loop that scrolls through your recordset, print a footer:

```
if (pInfo) {
    //Set the footer font
    pDC->SelectObject(&FooterFont);
    //Format the footer
    line.Format(
        "ODBC Report \tPage %d \tVisual C++ DB Guide",
        pInfo->m_nCurPage);
    //Output the footer at the bottom using tabs
    pDC->TabbedTextOut(0, -1025, line, 2, FooterTabStops,
0);
}
```

The `OutputReport` function follows:

```
void CODBCReportView::OutputReport(CDC* pDC, CPrintInfo* pInfo)
{
    CString line;     //This is the print line
    TEXTMETRIC metrics;     //Font measurements
    int y = 0;        //Current y position on report
    CFont TitleFont;    //Font for Title
    CFont HeadingFont;    //Font for headings
    CFont DetailFont;    //Font for detail lines
    CFont FooterFont;    //Font for footer
    //Tab stops at 1 inch, 2.5 inches, and 6.5 inches
    int TabStops[] = {100, 275, 650};
    //Tab stops at 3.5 inches and 6.5 inches
    int FooterTabStops[] = {350, 650};
    if (!pInfo || pInfo->m_nCurPage == 1) {
        //Set the recordset at the beginning
        m_pSet->Requery();
    }
    //Bold font for Title
    TitleFont.CreateFont(44, 0, 0, 0, FW_BOLD, FALSE, FALSE, 0,
        ANSI_CHARSET, OUT_DEFAULT_PRECIS, CLIP_DEFAULT_PRECIS,
```

```
        DEFAULT_QUALITY, DEFAULT_PITCH | FF_ROMAN,
        "Times New Roman");
    //Bold and underlined font for headings
    HeadingFont.CreateFont(36, 0, 0, 0, FW_BOLD, FALSE, TRUE, 0,
        ANSI_CHARSET, OUT_DEFAULT_PRECIS, CLIP_DEFAULT_PRECIS,
        DEFAULT_QUALITY, DEFAULT_PITCH | FF_ROMAN,
        "Times New Roman");
    //Normal font for detail
    DetailFont.CreateFont(18, 0, 0, 0, FW_NORMAL, FALSE, FALSE, 0,
        ANSI_CHARSET, OUT_DEFAULT_PRECIS, CLIP_DEFAULT_PRECIS,
        DEFAULT_QUALITY, DEFAULT_PITCH | FF_ROMAN,
        "Times New Roman");
    //Small font for footer
    FooterFont.CreateFont(12, 0, 0, 0, FW_NORMAL, FALSE, FALSE, 0,
        ANSI_CHARSET, OUT_DEFAULT_PRECIS, CLIP_DEFAULT_PRECIS,
        DEFAULT_QUALITY, DEFAULT_PITCH | FF_ROMAN,
        "Times New Roman");
    //Capture default settings when setting the title font
    CFont* OldFont = (CFont*) pDC->SelectObject(&TitleFont);
    //Retrieve the heading font measurements
    pDC->GetTextMetrics(&metrics);
    //Compute the heading line height
    int LineHeight = metrics.tmHeight + metrics.tmExternalLeading;
    //Set Y to the line height.
    y -= LineHeight;
    pDC->TextOut(200, 0, "ODBC Student Report");
/*
    Y must be set to negative numbers because MM_LOENGLISH was
    used in the CODBCReportView::OnInitialUpdate funciton.
*/
    //Set the Heading font
    pDC->SelectObject(&HeadingFont);
    //Format the heading
    line.Format("%s\t%s\t%s\t%s","Dept","Instructor","Class",
"Student");
    //Output the heading at (0, y) using 3 tabs
    pDC->TabbedTextOut(0, y, line, 3, TabStops, 0);
    //Detect empty recordset
    if (m_pSet->IsBOF()) {
        return;
    }
    //Compute the detail line height
    LineHeight = metrics.tmHeight + metrics.tmExternalLeading;
    y -= LineHeight;    //Adjust y position
    //Set the detail font
```

```
pDC->SelectObject(&DetailFont);
//Retrieve detail font measurements
pDC->GetTextMetrics(&metrics);
//Compute the detail line height
LineHeight = metrics.tmHeight + metrics.tmExternalLeading;
//Scroll through the recordset
while (!m_pSet->IsEOF()) {
    if (pInfo && abs(y) > 1000) {
        pInfo->SetMaxPage(pInfo->m_nCurPage + 1);
        break;
    }
    //Format the detail line
    line.Format("%s\t%s\t%s\t%s %s",
        m_pSet->m_DepartmentCode,
        m_pSet->m_Name,
        m_pSet->m_Description,
        m_pSet->m_FirstName,
        m_pSet->m_LastName);
    //Output the print line at (0, y) using 3 tabs
    pDC->TabbedTextOut(0, y, line, 3, TabStops, 0);
    //Get the next recordset number
    y -= LineHeight;    //Adjust y position
    m_pSet->MoveNext();
}
if (pInfo) {
    //Set the footer font
    pDC->SelectObject(&FooterFont);
    //Format the footer
    line.Format(
        "ODBC Report \tPage %d \tVisual C++ DB Guide",
        pInfo->m_nCurPage);
    //Output the footer at the bottom using tabs
    pDC->TabbedTextOut(0, -1025, line, 2, FooterTabStops, 0);
}
//Restore default settings
pDC->SelectObject(OldFont);
}
```

When you're finished, your report should display all pages, not just one
(Figure 6-13).

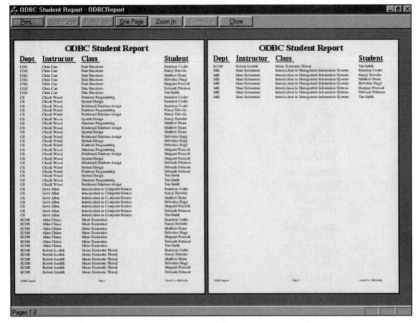

Figure 6-13: Most database reports are multipage reports.

Summary

This chapter delved into database reports. Although the database design and entry screens are necessary, the database report is the ultimate product of a database system that can be used to make decisions and guide the database user. To recap:

◆ Device contexts enable a Windows application to "talk" to devices, such as monitors and printers.

◆ A device can be set to display or print using a given font.

◆ The TEXTMETRIC structure can be used to return measurement information about a font, which is handy for keeping your place inside the device.

◆ The OnDraw function controls printing to the monitor.

◆ The OnPrint function, by default, calls the OnDraw function so that your printouts look almost identical to your display.

◆ You usually need to override the OnPrint function to add footers and multiple pages.

◆ The OnPrint function is called for each page rather than once per report.

Part III

OLE DB Programming

Chapter 7

Understanding OLE DB Structure

IN THIS CHAPTER

◆ Understanding OLE DB fundamentals

◆ Enumerating the OLE DB components

◆ Understanding COM (Component Object Model)

◆ Understanding C++ templates

◆ Understanding ADO access

◆ Understanding how OLE DB affects the Windows Registry

THIS CHAPTER DESCRIBES OLE DB in detail. Not only does this chapter go over some of the basic OLE DB concepts, but it also delves into some tangential topics, such as template use, COM, and how ADO and OLE DB relate to each other. This chapter also serves as a type of road map to the rest of this part of the book by using cross-references to point you to a more detailed discussion of some of the OLE DB topics introduced in this chapter.

Understanding the Importance of OLE DB

Traditional programs in languages written prior to Visual C++ 6.0 usually used ODBC for their database access. ODBC is a definition of how to access a database. Vendors would often write an ODBC driver to supplement their proprietary driver so programs could rely on the ODBC protocol to access their data.

For a description of Universal Data Access, see Chapter 1.

ODBC is still a viable technology that can be used for relational database access. However, ODBC falls short in two areas:

♦ ODBC is a small part of Microsoft's UDA (Universal Data Access). As such, ODBC is to be used for relational database access only. Previously, data access had been moving from text files to database files. Today, however, there are many data sources (e-mail, Word documents, text, directory structure, and Internet socket transmissions, to name a few) that are not relational data but require data access. OLE DB picks up where ODBC leaves off and supplies a tool in the OLE DB consumer/provider combination that can access these data sources.

♦ OLE DB providers use component technology (COM) that can be accessed from any program. While many tools can determine a table structure from ODBC, specialized access to specific data is not enabled. ODBC is not robust enough to enable such specialization. On the other hand, OLE DB makes it possible to have more variety in data access specialization because OLE DB providers can be written to accommodate specialized data access needs.

For more about ODBC, see the three chapters in Part II.

Using Component Technology: COM, DCOM, and ActiveX

There's been a lot of talk lately about component technology. Component technology enables precompiled modules to interact with each other dynamically. Unlike class libraries that enable you to share code, components used by your applications can be changed without recompiling each application. Component technology enables easy implementation of new functionality.

For any component technology to work, there must be standards that enable modules to query the component to see if new functionality exists. COM (Component Object Model) is a standard put forth by Microsoft that strictly defines how components should be written so that applications can use components. ActiveX is a further extension of COM that defines modules for easy cross-language use. DCOM (Distributed Component Object Model) is another extension of COM that takes into account objects that are distributed across machines, such as objects that can be run over the Internet.

COM really simplifies application development. For example, say you accessed a database OLE DB module that did not support database transactions. You could query your OLE DB provider, which is a COM module, to see if database transactions were supported and then act accordingly, depending on whether or not the support was present.

Understanding OLE DB Components

OLE DB components consist of a consumer that exists inside a database application and a provider that serves as a gateway between the consumer and the database, as shown in Figure 7-1.

Figure 7-1: OLE DB systems include an OLE DB consumer that exists inside an application and an OLE DB provider to access a database.

The OLE DB provider is a COM object that can be accessed from any application. The consumer makes calls to the provider to access the database.

Building a Rowset in OLE DB

Database access consists of three steps, or four steps if transactions are enabled:

1. Create and initialize a data source object, which is used to establish the connection from the application to a data source.

2. Establish a database session contained within the data source.

   a. Start a transaction for that session, if you want transaction support.

3. Define a database table or SQL command to use to form an OLE DB rowset.

The steps can be seen graphically in Figure 7-2.

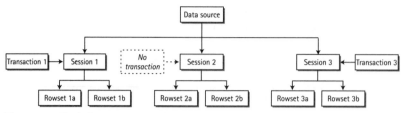

Figure 7-2: Each data source can be used to create several sessions, which can be used to create several rowsets.

As you can see in Figure 7-2, each data source can support many sessions, and each session can support many rowsets. In addition, each session may or may not support transactions, depending on provider capability and whether or not the consumer wants this support. In practice, however, a single data source is usually used to establish a single session that is used to establish a single rowset.

Using OLE DB Classes in the ATL

The easiest way to use OLE DB from C++ is to use the Active Template Library (ATL), which provides helpful classes for dealing with COM in general, and for dealing with OLE DB interfaces as well as some other specific COM interfaces. Table 7-1 shows the ATL classes that are used to deliver this support.

TABLE **7-1** ATL CLASSES USED FOR OLE DB

Component	ATL Class	Description
Data Source	CDataSource	The CDataSource class is used to create a data source object that provides a connection from the OLE DB consumer to the OLE DB provider. CDataSource is used to send properties such as user ID, password, and data source name to the provider. After properties are established, the CDataSource::Open method is called to open a connection to the database through the OLE DB provider.
Session	CSession	The session object represents a single conversation between a consumer and provider. It is somewhat similar to the ODBC HSTMT in that many simultaneous sessions can be active.

Component	ATL Class	Description
		The session object is the primary link to get to OLE DB functionality. In order to get to a command, transaction, or rowset object, you go through the session object.
Command	CCommand	The command object handles operations on data such as queries. It can handle parameterized or nonparameterized statements.
		The command object is also responsible for handling bindings for parameters and output columns. A binding is a structure that contains information about how a column, in a rowset, should be retrieved. It contains information such as ordinal, data type, length, status, and so on.
Rowset	CRowset	The rowset object represents the data from the data source. The object is responsible for the bindings of that data and any basic operations (update, fetch, movement, and so on) on the data. You always have a rowset object to contain and manipulate data.
Accessor	CAccessor	An accessor describes how data is stored in the OLE DB consumer. Accessors are used to define storage and to transfer data to and from the rowset. Accessors also control binding of consumer variables to the data returned by the provider.
Transaction	Not Applicable	The transaction object defines an atomic unit of work on a data source and determines how those units of work relate to each other.
		Although no actual class comprises a transaction, transactions can be established using the StartTransaction method on the ATL CSession object.

To obtain information on coding OLE DB rowsets, sessions, and data sources, see Chapter 9.

To learn how to code OLE DB Transactions, see Chapter 9.

Understanding Templates

ATL uses templates in many of their class definitions. Templates enable type independence of a variable used in a class or function. Because templates are relatively new to C++, this section explains how they work.

Templates are particularly handy when dealing with record structures that vary in size. For an example, consider the following CompareStuff class definition:

```
class CompareStuff {
    static int Max(int a, int b) {
        if (a < b)
            return a;
        return b;
    }
}
```

The preceding class Max function works only with integers. To make the function type independent, you would need to overload the function for every data type:

```
class CompareStuff {
    static int Max(int a, int b) {
        if (a < b)
            return a;
        return b;
    }
    static double Max(double a, double b) {
        if (a < b)
            return a;
        return b;
    }
    static CString Max(CString a, CString b) {
        if (a < b)
            return a;
        return b;
    }
}
//etc.
```

To get around this problem, many C++ developers used the #define directive to define a "global" process:

```
#define MAX(a,b) (a < b) ? a : b
```

However, the preceding code forces MAX(a, b) to be reserved for this function only. Whenever you type in MAX(a, b), the C++ precompiler automatically replaces your code with the conditional expressions. If you needed a MAX function, you had to be careful that you wanted a global replace of all occurrences with the definition in the #define directive.

With templates, you can make a class type independent without hurting the encapsulation needed in object-oriented languages such as C++. Templates are defined using the following syntax:

```
template <class arg>
class ClassName {
    FunctionName(arg parameter) {
//...
    }
};
//...
// Define the class
    Class<DataType> ClassInstance;
    ClassInstance.FunctionName(parameter);
```

In the preceding syntax, you can pass an argument that is of any data type or class. Templates enable you to replace a type at compile time with the appropriate type. For instance, the preceding Max function could be written with templates as follows:

```
template < class T >
class CompareStuff {
  public:
    static T Max(T a, T b) {
        if (a < b)
            return a;
        return b;

    }
};
```

Now to execute the Max function on, for example, CString types, you could simply write the following function:

```
CString cstrMax = CompareStuff<CString>::Max(cstr1, cstr2);
```

Conversely, you could also instantiate the CompareStuff class and not worry about the type anymore:

```
CompareStuff<CString> cs;
CString cstrMax = cs.Max(cstr1, cstr2);
```

This replaces the T argument in the Max function with the appropriate class at compile time:

```
static CString Max(CString a, CString b) {
    if (a < b)
        return a;
    return b;
}
```

As you can see, templates enable type-safe dynamic type casting so that parameter types can adjust depending on the needs of the calling program. In a similar vein, the CCommand declaration enables the department table layout to be sent to the CAccessor class as a data type:

```
class CDepartmentAccessor {
    char DepartmentCode [5];
    char Departmentname [51];
};

class Department : CCommand <CAccessor <CDepartmentAccessor> >
{
//...
```

Now your CAccessor template used in the Command template can use the CDepartmentAccessor class. This illustrates the power of C++ templates. Compare this process with MFC classes where you always have to derive your own recordset class from CRecordset. When you use CCommand and CAccessor, you need to create only a class definition that is specific to your own information (the CDepartmentAccessor class in which all your data columns are defined). Then you can use the template to get a CCommand class that contains your information.

Understanding the OLE DB Consumer Structure

OLE DB uses a series of classes that interact with each other. Figure 7-3 shows the consumer architecture for OLE DB.

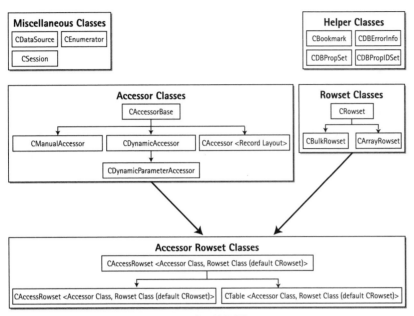

Figure 7-3: The consumer architecture for OLE DB.

Inside the ATL, OLE DB providers and consumers are written using templates. Templates deliver a type of type-independent functionality to their classes.

The types of classes and the OLE DB functionality they contain are the following:

◆ Accessor classes describe how the data is to be accessed. Using Accessor classes, you can automatically bind class variables to your database variables or control when and how to retrieve your variables.

For information on using different accessors and manually binding data, see Chapter 12.

◆ Rowset classes describe how information retrieved from the database is to be stored internally. Array rowsets enable array access to a rowset. Bulk rowsets enable a bulk of rows to be retrieved at once. Standard single-row rowsets are used for the majority of database access and are covered extensively throughout this part of the book.

For information on bulk rowsets and array rowsets, see Chapter 12.

♦ AccessorRowset classes combine the functionality defined in the accessor classes and the functionality defined in the rowset classes with a command or table that tells what rows to retrieve from the database. AccessorRowsets are used throughout this part of the book to form OLE DB rowsets.

♦ There are four helper classes contained in the OLE DB architecture:

■ The CBookmark class not only enables you to mark a particular row to later return to, but also enables you to retrieve row position in an OLE DB rowset.

To learn how to use the useful CBookmark class, see Chapter 11.

■ The CDBErrorInfo is useful for retrieving the errors that exist on the database.

To see the CDBErrorInfo class in action, refer to Chapter 10.

■ The CDBPropSet and CDBPropIDSet control the properties that can be set for the accessors, data sources, and sessions. These properties are all defined in Appendix C and are documented throughout the book.

For more information on properties, see Chapter 11.

♦ Three miscellaneous classes are contained in ATL's support for OLE DB. Although these classes don't fit nicely into any particular class category, two of these classes (CSession and CDataSource) are vital for OLE DB database access:

- The CDataSource class describes the provider that is used for database access. Before you can describe any standard rowset, you must first connect to a data source.

- The CSession class basically handles transaction support for a group of rowsets. There is usually only one CSession object per rowset, but you could have several rowsets all access the same CSession.

For more about the CSession class, see Chapters 9, 12, and 13.

- The CEnumerator class returns a rowset that describes all OLE DB provider data sources. This can be useful when trying to write a generic OLE DB routine.

For more about the CEnumerator class, see Chapter 12.

Understanding ADO's Position in OLE DB

When you discuss OLE DB, most programmers mention that the way to get to OLE DB data is through ADO consumers. With all other languages, and before Visual C++ 6.0, that used to be the case. ADO contains wrappers that help access OLE DB data sources in a way that is similar to the familiar ODBC or DAO formats. Figure 7-4 shows how an application goes through ADO to access information provided by an OLE DB provider.

Figure 7-4: ADO enables applications in other languages to access OLE DB information provided by an OLE DB provider.

When you write an OLE DB provider, all other languages, such as Java and Visual J++; Visual Basic, VBA, and VBScript; Visual Interdev; and many pre-Visual C++ 6.0 C++ compilers, use ADO as their standard method for accessing OLE DB providers.

Even in previous releases of Visual C++ or with other C++ compilers, a C++ ADO library was used to access OLE DB providers. Although it was possible to access OLE DB interfaces directly, it was extremely complicated, tedious, and difficult. Visual C++ 6.0 changed all of this. Now developers can easily access OLE DB directly without needing the additional overhead of an ADO layer between their program and their OLE DB consumer.

As you can see in this part of the book, the OLE DB wizards make it quite easy to access OLE DB data directly, and it no longer makes sense to develop new projects in C++ using ADO. However, there are still many legacy programs that use ADO, class libraries that were built based on ADO functionality, and some programmers who learned ADO or use it in other languages and feel quite comfortable programming with ADO. Microsoft does support ADO in C++, and Chapter 18 in this book is dedicated to ADO access inside Visual C++. However, for most of your OLE DB programming needs in Visual C++, you may find it easier to use the OLE DB routines that Visual C++ provides rather than "reinventing the wheel" by writing your own ADO routines that mimic the functionality already present in the wizards.

For more about ADO, see Chapter 18.

Summary

This chapter serves as a detailed introduction to OLE DB. To recap:

- OLE DB is a way to use the same routines to access any data source. While this data source is usually a database, it can be other sources too, such as e-mail or an Internet socket connection. In this way, OLE DB plays an important role in Microsoft's Universal Data Access (UDA).

- ATL's OLE DB access consists of several components described throughout this chapter. The most important are the CDatasource, the CSession, and the CRowset classes.

- Templates are a way to use type-independent functions. The ATL (Active Template Libraries) has many templates that make it easy to write OLE DB applications.

◆ ADO is used to access OLE DB providers from any language. ADO is the preferred method of database access in many languages, such as Visual Basic. Many pre–VC 6.0 database programs took advantage of ADO functionality.

◆ Although you can use ADO to access your OLE DB provider in Visual C++, Visual C++ 6.0 includes so much support for direct OLE DB access that you may want to reconsider using ADO inside a Visual C++ environment.

Chapter 8

Developing MFC OLE DB Consumers

IN THIS CHAPTER

◆ Using the MFC AppWizard to develop an OLE DB application

◆ Enabling transactions with OLE DB

◆ Joining tables with OLE DB

◆ Enabling and using the Update command for saving

◆ Creating OLE DB reports using the MFC AppWizard

THE MFC HAS BEEN GREAT for quickly developing applications, including ODBC database applications. Visual C++ 6.0 has added OLE DB to the MFC AppWizard so that you can use traditional development techniques to master this new database protocol.

TIP The MFC is great for quick, easy C++ development. The ATL (Active Template Library) Wizard delivers smaller, more portable applications but may be a little harder to use. In the next chapter, we delve into ATL applications and see how you can also easily develop OLE DB Windows applications with ATL.

Easy Development with an OLE DB Application

You can easily develop a scrolling and update database application using the following steps:

1. Define a new project using the MFC AppWizard for executables. Choose File → New from the Visual Studio menu, click the Projects tab, and click MFC AppWizard (exe). Call this project "OLEDBDepartmentMFC," as shown in Figure 8-1.

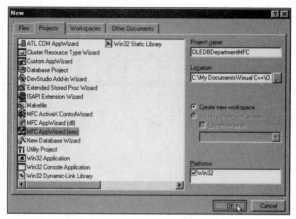

Figure 8-1: As with ODBC, you start developing a new project using the MFC AppWizard.

2. Using the MFC AppWizard, click the Single document radio button in Step 1 of 6, and then click the Next button.

3. In Step 2 of 6, choose Database View with File Support, and click the Data Source button as shown in Figure 8-2.

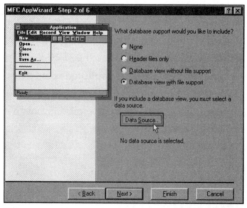

Figure 8-2: You need to choose some database support in order to enable OLE DB inside an application.

4. In the Database Options window, click Select OLE DB, and click the Select OLE DB Datasource button as shown in Figure 8-3.

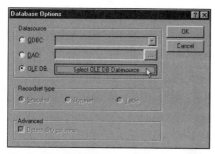

Figure 8-3: The Database Options window enables you to choose OLE DB as your database protocol.

5. Next, the Provider tab of the Data Link Properties window opens. Choose what type of database you will be using. In Figure 8-4, I selected the Microsoft Jet 3.51 OLE DB Provider to connect to an Access database. Click Next when you've picked an OLE DB database.

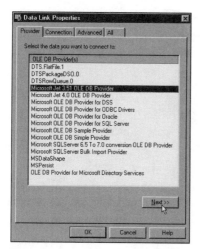

Figure 8-4: You need to select the type of database to connect to. I suggest avoiding the OLE DB ODBC driver and instead using the OLE DB driver specifically designed for your database, if possible.

TIP   You can use an OLE DB Provider for ODBC Drivers if you want to access an ODBC data source. However, if you have an OLE DB driver specifically for your database, it's probably a better idea to use it. Your database may enable features that are not supported through ODBC.

6. The Connection tab of the Data Link Properties window then opens. Here, enter any database-specific information needed to connect to your database. Access requires only the filename, user ID, and password, as shown in Figure 8-5.

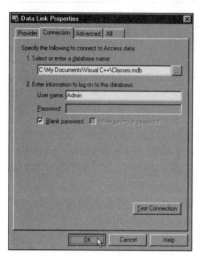

Figure 8-5: Database connection information is entered in the Connection tab of the Data Link Properties window.

7. You then return to the Database Options window shown earlier in Figure 8-3. Click OK to open the Select Database Tables window. Choose the development table (Department), and click OK, as shown in Figure 8-6.

8. In Step 3 of 6, choose None for compound document support, and click the ActiveX Controls checkbox. Then click the Next button. Deselect (click off) Printing and print preview in Step 4 of 6, and click the Next button. Accept the defaults in Step 5 of 6, and click the Next button.

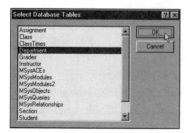

Figure 8-6: After you select your database, you must choose which table you want to access.

9. In Step 6 of 6, you should see the filenames shown in Figure 8-7. Notice that the base class for the view is COleDBRecordView. Just as with the CRecordView shown in Chapters 4 and 5, the COleDBRecordView is inherited from CFormView and enables scrolling as well as all the CFormView funtionality.

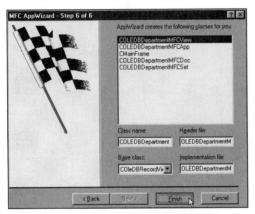

Figure 8-7: OLEDBDepartmentMFC filenames are automatically generated.

Figure 8-8 shows the options you selected to generate your MFC OLE DB application.

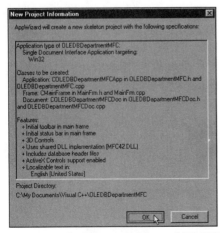

Figure 8-8: Options needed for an MFC OLE DB application

10. Next, you need to paint your dialog box. Because the Department table has two columns (DepartmentCode and DepartmentName), you need to define two window controls to contain them. The dialog box is shown in Figure 8-9. Don't forget to rename the edit boxes to IDC_DEPARTMENTCODE and IDC_DEPARTMENTNAME.

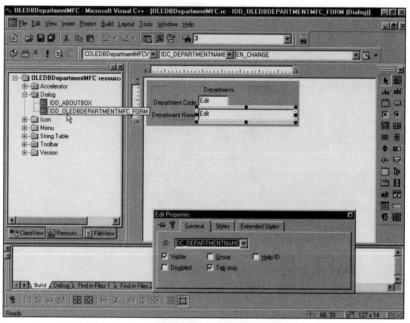

Figure 8-9: Dialog box for the OLEDBDepartmentMFC project

11. For the final step, you need to add variables to your DoDataExchange function inside your COLEDBDepartmentMFCView class in your OLEDBDepartmentMFCView.cpp program. With ODBC, you could use the Class Wizard to bind variables, but the Class Wizard does not support the COLEDBView class. The following nonshaded code shows the lines you need to add to the `COLEDBView::DoDataExchange` function to bind variables to your dialog boxes:

```
void COLEDBDepartmentMFCView::DoDataExchange(CDataExchange*
pDX)
{
  COleDBRecordView::DoDataExchange(pDX);
  //{{AFX_DATA_MAP(COLEDBDepartmentMFCView)
    // NOTE: the ClassWizard will add DDX and DDV calls here
  //}}AFX_DATA_MAP
```

```
DDX_Text(pDX, IDC_DEPARTMENTCODE, m_pSet->m_DepartmentCode,
5);
    DDV_MaxChars(pDX, m_pSet->m_DepartmentCode, 4);
    DDX_Text(pDX, IDC_DEPARTMENTNAME, m_pSet->m_DepartmentName,
51);
    DDV_MaxChars(pDX, m_pSet->m_DepartmentName, 50);
}
```

Notice that in the preceding DDX_Text command, you need to consider the null terminator in your field size parameter. If you don't, the MFC truncates a byte from your data.

When you're finished, you should see a working C++ OLE DB program that scrolls through table records and enables updates to the table (Figure 8-10). Here you have an example of a working OLE DB program that was automatically generated and required only four additional lines of code!

The project developed in this section can be found in the OLEDB DepartmentMFCa directory on the CD-ROM accompanying this book.

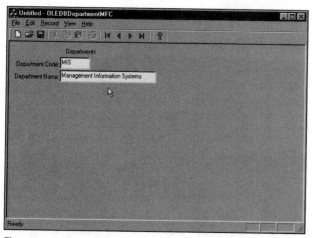

Figure 8-10: The MFC can generate a working Windows application in a few minutes.

In the foregoing example, all referential integrity (foreign keys) in Access were defined using Cascade delete. If normal Restrict referential integrity were used, the updates to the records would fail. This is because OLE DB tries to update every column in the rowset, not just the columns that have changed. Because columns that have foreign keys accessing them cannot be changed, the entire update fails. Note that this situation occurs only (as far as I can tell) with Microsoft Access. Other OLE DB database drivers that I've tested (such as SQL Server) don't seem to restrict updates in this manner. You should be aware of each database driver's foreign key restrictions with OLE DB (and test them) before deploying your OLE DB database application. It could not only affect your development but also may play a factor in which database to choose for your development efforts.

Using Adds, Deletes, and Queries in OLE DB

You probably want to add some functionality to the program shown in Figure 8-10 just as we did when we generated an ODBC MFC application in Chapter 5. Just as we did in that chapter, you need to add menu items that can handle inserts, deletes, and queries.

For more on ODBC MFC applications, see the section "Using Adds, Deletes, and Queries" in Chapter 5.

If you take the existing OLEDBDepartmentMFC project, you can easily make modifications that enable you to add, delete, and query inside your OLE DB application.

Making Menu and Toolbar Changes

In this example, you can use File → New to create a new department, and File → Open to open an existing department. You need to add a menu choice for deleting a record, which can be done under the Edit choice, as shown in Figure 8-11.

Next, you need to add a toolbar item to match the menu item. Paint the new icon in the resource painter, and choose the same ID as the menu delete option, as shown in Figure 8-12.

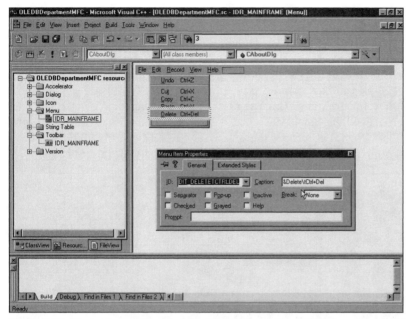

Figure 8-11: Menu changes have to be made to the existing OLEDBDepartmentMFC application to enable deletions from the database tables.

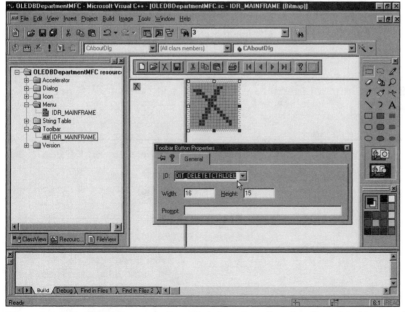

Figure 8-12: Toolbar changes can be added that share functionality with the menu items by using the same ID.

Using the Class Wizard

The Class Wizard can be used to automatically create event functions for you. When you choose View → ClassWizard from the Visual Studio menu, the MFC Class Wizard opens (Figure 8-13). All the function prototyping and function declarations are set up, and all you have to do is type in the C++ code to finish the function.

When you're finished, click OK. The Class Wizard automatically codes the view header file (OLEDBDepartmentMFCView.h) with the appropriate function prototypes. The Class Wizard also codes the source file (OLEDBDepartmentMFCView.cpp) with the appropriate empty function shells for each event you want to code.

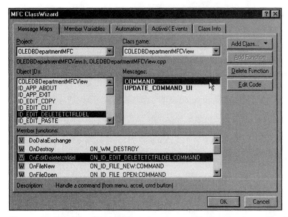

Figure 8-13: The Class Wizard can greatly improve productivity when you are developing MFC applications.

Table 8-1 lists the event functions you need to create and why. Use default Class Wizard names.

TABLE 8-1 CLASS WIZARD EVENTS NEEDED FOR OLEDBDepartmentMFCView

Object ID	Message	Description
COLEDBDepartmentMFCView	WM_DESTROY	This event is called whenever the window has been destroyed.
ID_EDIT_DELETECTRLDEL	COMMAND	This event is triggered when a new delete command has been entered.
ID_FILE_NEW	COMMAND	This event is triggered when a new department is requested.

Object ID	Message	Description
ID_FILE_OPEN	COMMAND	This event is triggered when the user wants to open a new department.
COLEDBDepartmentMFCView	OnMove	This event is triggered whenever a user clicks the first, next, last, or previous record. It *is not* triggered when a MoveFirst command is executed.

Saving Records

Before you add any functionality to your system, you need to add a function that can update the database from the window when called. To start, define a SaveRecord function prototype in the COLEDBDepartmentMFCView class in the OLEDBDepartmentMFCView.h file. While there, also define AddRecord and ResetRowSet function prototypes and the m_bAddingRecord Boolean variable for use later in this section:

```
class COLEDBDepartmentMFCView : public COleDBRecordView
{
protected: // create from serialization only
    COLEDBDepartmentMFCView();
    BOOL SaveRecord();
    void AddRecord();
    void ResetRowSet();
    BOOL m_bAddingRecord;
```

Next, write your SaveRecord function in the OLEDBDepartmentMFCView.cpp file. This function retrieves changes from the window using the UpdateData function. Then the SaveRecord function checks to see if a record is being added. If a record is in the middle of an add, the SaveRecord function uses the Insert function to insert the record into the database from the OLEDBDepartmentSet class variables. If no record is being added, the SetData function is used to update the database from the OLEDBDepartmentSet class variables:

```
BOOL COLEDBDepartmentMFCView::SaveRecord()
{
    if (!UpdateData(TRUE)) { //Save changes from the screen
        return FALSE;
    }
```

```
        if (m_bAddingRecord) {
            m_bAddingRecord = FALSE;
            if (FAILED(m_pSet->Insert())) {
                AfxMessageBox("Insert failed",
                    MB_ICONEXCLAMATION);
                m_pSet->MoveFirst();
                UpdateData(FALSE); // Show cleared values on window
                return FALSE;
            }
        }
        //Save changes from this accessor
        else if (FAILED(m_pSet->SetData(0))) {
            AfxMessageBox("Update via SetData failed",
                        MB_ICONEXCLAMATION);
            UpdateData(FALSE); // Show cleared values on window
            return FALSE;
        }
        return TRUE;
    }
```

The SaveRecord function is used to update the rowset, if needed, before the OnMove function, and to update the rowset, if needed, before the window is destroyed:

```
BOOL COLEDBDepartmentMFCView::OnMove(UINT nIDMoveCommand)
{
    SaveRecord();
    return COleDBRecordView::OnMove(nIDMoveCommand);
}
void COLEDBDepartmentMFCView::OnDestroy()
{
    SaveRecord();
    COleDBRecordView::OnDestroy();
}
```

Adding Records

Now your class needs to be set up to add new departments. First, in the COLEDBDepartmentMFCView constructor in the OLEDBDepartmentMFCView.cpp file, initialize the m_bAddingRecord Boolean class variable to FALSE:

```
COLEDBDepartmentMFCView::COLEDBDepartmentMFCView()
    : COleDBRecordView(COLEDBDepartmentMFCView::IDD)
```

```
{
  //{{AFX_DATA_INIT(COLEDBDepartmentMFCView)
  // NOTE: the ClassWizard will add member initialization here
  m_pSet = NULL;
  //}}AFX_DATA_INIT
  m_bAddingRecord = FALSE;
}
```

Next, rewrite some of your CDepartment class in your COLEDBDepartment MFCSet.h file by writing an inline ClearFields function:

```
class CDepartment
{
public:
    CDepartment()
    {
        ClearFields();
    }
    inline void ClearFields()
    {
        memset( (void*)this, 0, sizeof(*this) );
    }
    char m_DepartmentCode[5];
    char m_DepartmentName[51];
BEGIN_COLUMN_MAP(CDepartment)
        COLUMN_ENTRY_TYPE(1, DBTYPE_STR, m_DepartmentCode)
        COLUMN_ENTRY_TYPE(2, DBTYPE_STR, m_DepartmentName)
END_COLUMN_MAP()
};
```

By adding the preceding lines, instead of clearing fields in the constructor, you clear fields in a ClearFields function and then call that ClearFields function inside your constructor. The ClearFields function can then be added to a new AddRecord function in the OLEDBDepartmentMFCView.cpp file that clears the fields for adding and sets the m_bAddingRecord Boolean variable to TRUE.

```
void COLEDBDepartmentMFCView::AddRecord()
{
    m_bAddingRecord = TRUE;
    m_pSet->ClearFields();
    UpdateData(FALSE); // Show cleared values on window
}
```

Then, when the user chooses File → New from the program's menu or clicks the New icon, the OnFileNew function is triggered. You can call the SaveRecord function to save out the existing record, if needed, and then call the AddRecord function to set up your view to add a new record:

```
void COLEDBDepartmentMFCView::OnFileNew()
{
    SaveRecord();
    AddRecord();
}
```

When your program sets the m_bAddingRecord to TRUE, then the SaveRecord function inserts a new record the next time it is called.

Deleting Records

When the user clicks the Delete icon that was created earlier, or they click Edit, Delete, the OnEditDeletetctrldel function is called. This function performs the following tasks:

◆ Verifies to make sure that the user really wants to delete the current record:

```
if (AfxMessageBox(      //Be sure to verify your deletes
        "Are you sure you want to delete?",
        MB_YESNO)
    != IDYES) {
    return;
}
```

◆ Cancels the add if adding a record:

```
if (m_bAddingRecord) {
    //Just abort the add
    m_bAddingRecord = FALSE;
}
```

◆ If the user is not adding a record, the current record is deleted using the Delete function:

```
else if (FAILED(m_pSet->Delete())) {
    AfxMessageBox("Delete Failed:\n", MB_ICONEXCLAMATION);
}
```

◆ Finally, the ResetRowSet function, which is described next, is called to display the appropriate record:

```
ResetRowSet();
```

The additions to the OnEditDeletetctrldel function are seen in the unshaded area that follows:

```
void COLEDBDepartmentMFCView::OnEditDeletetctrldel()
{
    if (AfxMessageBox(      //Be sure to verify your deletes
            "Are you sure you want to delete?",
            MB_YESNO)
        != IDYES) {
        return;
    }
    //Delete record and test
    if (m_bAddingRecord) {
        //Just abort the add
        m_bAddingRecord = FALSE;
    }
    else if (FAILED(m_pSet->Delete())) {
        AfxMessageBox("Delete Failed:\n", MB_ICONEXCLAMATION);
    }
    ResetRowSet();
}
```

Next, the ResetRowSet function needs to be developed. The ResetRowSet function performs the following functions:

1. First it goes to the next record.

2. If there is no next record, it goes to the first record.

3. If no records can be found, a new record is added.

4. In any event, the UpdateData function is used to set the edit boxes on the dialog box to the values inside the COLEDBDepartmentMFCSet class.

The ResetRowSet function follows:

```
void COLEDBDepartmentMFCView::ResetRowSet()
{
    if (m_pSet->MoveNext() != S_OK) {     //Go to next record
        if (m_pSet->MoveFirst() != S_OK) {
            AfxMessageBox("No more records",
                MB_ICONEXCLAMATION);
            //No records, so set up an add record
            AddRecord();
        }
    }
```

```
        UpdateData(FALSE);     //Write changes to window
}
```

Querying Records

Sometimes queries use a field currently seen on the window, as was done previously with ODBC updates. Other times, a pop-up dialog box is used. For this query, a new dialog box was added to handle the query.

 To learn how ODBC queries specific records, see the section "Writing OnRecordQueryrecord" in Chapter 5.

MAKING A QUERY DIALOG BOX

In this example, I used a new dialog box that can be used for a query. To do this, perform the following steps:

1. Click the ResourceView tab in the Visual Studio Workspace.

2. Expand the OLEDBDepartmentMFC Resources so that the Dialog folder is showing.

3. Right-click the dialog to open a popup menu, and choose Insert Dialog. This inserts a new dialog box IDD_DIALOG1.

4. Right-click IDD_DIALOG1 to open the Dialog Properties dialog box. Type **IDD_FINDDEPARTMENT** in the ID textbox.

5. Lay out controls on the dialog as shown in Figure 8-14, and change the ID of the edit item to IDC_FINDDEPARTMENT.

The dialog box that was just created and shown in Figure 8-14 enables you to enter a new department and click either OK or Cancel.

By double-clicking a button in this dialog box, you can create a new class to contain the dialog. When the Adding a Class dialog box opens, choose Create a new class, and click OK, as seen in Figure 8-15.

Next, the New Class dialog box opens, as shown in Figure 8-16. Here, you enter the name of your new class (COpenDepartment), and the rest defaults for you.

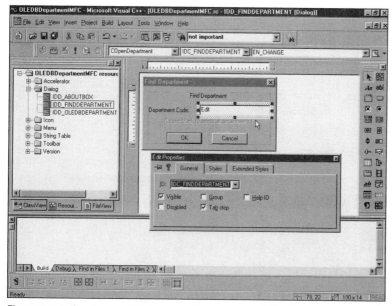

Figure 8-14: Queries are often done with a separate dialog box.

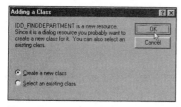

Figure 8-15: Double-clicking a button in a new dialog nables you to easily create a class for that dialog.

Figure 8-16: Double-clicking a button in a new dialog enables you to easily create a class for that dialog.

USING THE CLASS WIZARD FOR THE QUERY DIALOG BOX

In Figure 8-17, the Class Wizard Member Variable tab is used to bind the IDC_FIND DEPARTMENT edit control with a class variable named m_strDepartment.

Finally, you need to perform the following steps:

1. Define an m_strFilter CString variable in the COLEDBDepartmentMFCSet class in the OLEDBDepartmentMFCSet.h file:

```
class COLEDBDepartmentMFCSet : public
CCommand<CAccessor<CDepartment> >
{
public:
    CString m_strFilter;     //Define a filter
```

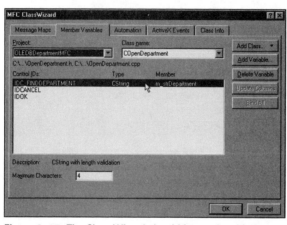

Figure 8-17: The Class Wizard should be used to bind new string variables to your dialog box textbox.

2. Add the m_strFilter to the SQL used to form a filter for the rowset in the COLEDBDepartmentMFCSet class in the OLEDBDepartmentMFCSet.h file:

```
hr = CCommand<CAccessor<CDepartment> >::Open(session,
 "SELECT * FROM Department" + m_strFilter, &propset);
```

3. Add a new include on the top of the OLEDBDepartmentMFCView.cpp file to access the new dialog box:

```
// OLEDBDepartmentMFCView.cpp : implementation of the
COLEDBDepartmentMFCView class
//

#include "stdafx.h"
#include "OLEDBDepartmentMFC.h"
```

```
#include "OLEDBDepartmentMFCSet.h"
#include "OLEDBDepartmentMFCDoc.h"
#include "OLEDBDepartmentMFCView.h"
#ifdef _DEBUG
#define new DEBUG_NEW
#undef THIS_FILE
static char THIS_FILE[] = __FILE__;
#endif
//Added by Chuck Wood for query dialog support
#include "OpenDepartment.h"
/////////////////////////////////////////////////////////
// COLEDBDepartmentMFCView
```

4. You need to code the OnFileOpen event function defined by the Class Wizard. Save the record by calling the SaveRecord function defined earlier:

```
SaveRecord();          //Save any changes first
```

5. Declare and open the modal Query Dialog Box:

```
COpenDepartment od;    //Query dialog box declaration
if (od.DoModal() == IDOK) {        //OK was clicked?
```

6. If OK was clicked, test the results of the COpenDepartment ::m_strDepartment variable to see if anything was entered, and form a filter string.

```
CString newFilter;     //Define a new filter
if (od.m_strDepartment > "") {      //Anything entered?
    //Fill the new filter with a WHERE clause
    newFilter = " WHERE DepartmentCode = '" +
od.m_strDepartment +"'";
}
else {
    //Empty out the filter if nothing entered
    newFilter = "";
}
```

7. If the strings are different, assign the new filter to the recordset filter, and requery the recordset. Display the results using the ResetRowSet function:

```
if (m_pSet->m_strFilter.CompareNoCase(newFilter)) {
    //Strings are different
    m_pSet->m_strFilter = newFilter;
    //Close and open to requery
    m_pSet->Close();
```

```
        m_pSet->Open();
        ResetRowSet();    //Display results
    }
```

Steps 4 through 7 are coded into the OnFileOpen function. The resulting OnFileOpen function should look like the following function. Added lines are not shaded:

```
void COLEDBDepartmentMFCView::OnFileOpen()
{
    COpenDepartment od;    //Query dialog box declaration
    SaveRecord();          //Save any changes first
    if (od.DoModal() == IDOK) {        //OK was clicked?
        CString newFilter;    //Define a new filter
        if (od.m_strDepartment > "") {    //Anything entered?
            //Fill the new filter with a WHERE clause
            newFilter =
                " WHERE Department.DepartmentCode = '" +
                od.m_strDepartment +"'";
        }
        else {
            //Empty out the filter if nothing entered
            newFilter = "";
        }
        if (m_pSet->m_strFilter.CompareNoCase(newFilter)) {
            //Strings are different
            m_pSet->m_strFilter = newFilter;
            //Close and open to requery
            m_pSet->Close();
            m_pSet->Open();
            ResetRowSet();    //Display results
        }
    }
}
```

When you're finished, your program, with the new query dialog box, should look like Figure 8-18.

This program can be found in the OLEDBDepartmentMFCb directory on your CD-ROM.

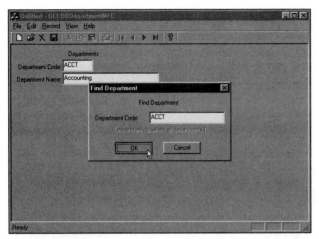

Figure 8-18: Dialog boxes used for queries can keep a program window from looking cluttered and give a professional feel to a program.

Joining Tables

You may wish to join tables inside an OLE DB MFC application so that related information can be retrieved from two tables simultaneously. The following steps show you how you can join two tables together inside an OLE DB MFC application.

1. Change your dialog box to reflect the additional information on the soon-to-be-joined table. In Figure 8-19, instructor information was added to the department information in the IDD_OLEDBDEPARTMENTMFC_FORM dialog box. Name the new edit boxes IDC_INSTRUCTORNAME, IDC_EMAIL, and IDC_NOTES.

2. You need to change the SQL used to create the rowset. You need to incorporate the joined table by using either an inner join or a WHERE clause. In the COLEDBDepartmentMFCSet class definition in OLEDBDepartmentMFCSet.h, change the line that defines the open SQL from:

```
hr = CCommand<CAccessor<CDepartment> >::Open(session,
    "SELECT * FROM Department" + m_strFilter,
    &propset);
```

to

```
hr = CCommand<CAccessor<CDepartment> >::Open(session,
    "SELECT Department.DepartmentCode,\
```

```
                Department.DepartmentName,\
                Instructor.Name,\
                Instructor.Email,\
                Instructor.Notes\
        FROM    Department INNER JOIN Instructor\
                ON    Department.DepartmentCode =\
                    Instructor.DepartmentCode" +
        m_strFilter, &propset);
```

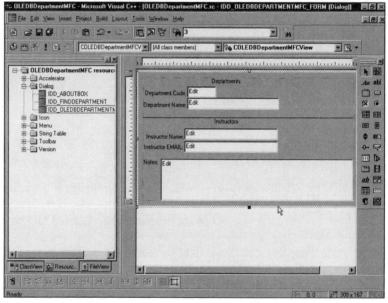

Figure 8-19: Information from the second joined table must be incorporated into the dialog box.

3. Next, you need to change the base storage class for your OLE DB Accessor. In the CDepartment class in the OLEDBDepartmentMFCSet.h file, you need to add class variables to contain the additional information, and you need to add new entries into the column map to make sure that the OLE DB driver knows to update the class variables with database column information. The following lines (those without gray shading) were added to the CDepartment class header:

```
class CDepartment
{
public:
    CDepartment()
    {
```

```
        ClearFields();
    };
    inline void ClearFields()
    {
        memset( (void*)this, 0, sizeof(*this) );
    };
    char m_DepartmentCode[5];
    char m_DepartmentName[51];
    char m_Name[51];
    char m_EMAIL[51];
    char m_Notes[1025];
BEGIN_COLUMN_MAP(CDepartment)
        COLUMN_ENTRY_TYPE(1, DBTYPE_STR, m_DepartmentCode)
        COLUMN_ENTRY_TYPE(2, DBTYPE_STR, m_DepartmentName)
        COLUMN_ENTRY_TYPE(3, DBTYPE_STR, m_Name)
        COLUMN_ENTRY_TYPE(4, DBTYPE_STR, m_EMAIL)
        COLUMN_ENTRY_TYPE(5, DBTYPE_STR, m_Notes)
END_COLUMN_MAP()
};
```

4. Finally, add the data exchange commands to the DoDataExchange
   function so that the new edit controls can transfer data to the rowset.
   In OLEDBDepartmentMFCView.cpp, the following lines (unshaded) were
   added to the DoDataExchange function:

```
void COLEDBDepartmentMFCView::DoDataExchange(CDataExchange*
pDX)
{
  COleDBRecordView::DoDataExchange(pDX);
  //{{AFX_DATA_MAP(COLEDBDepartmentMFCView)
     // NOTE: the ClassWizard will add DDX and DDV calls here
  //}}AFX_DATA_MAP
  DDX_Text(pDX, IDC_DEPARTMENTCODE, m_pSet->m_DepartmentCode,
5);
  DDV_MaxChars(pDX, m_pSet->m_DepartmentCode, 4);
  DDX_Text(pDX, IDC_DEPARTMENTNAME, m_pSet->m_DepartmentName,
51);
  DDV_MaxChars(pDX, m_pSet->m_DepartmentName, 50);
  DDX_Text(pDX, IDC_INSTRUCTORNAME, m_pSet->m_Name, 51);
  DDV_MaxChars(pDX, m_pSet->m_Name, 50);
  DDX_Text(pDX, IDC_EMAIL, m_pSet->m_EMAIL, 51);
  DDV_MaxChars(pDX, m_pSet->m_EMAIL, 50);
  DDX_Text(pDX, IDC_NOTES, m_pSet->m_Notes, 1025);
  DDV_MaxChars(pDX, m_pSet->m_Notes, 1024);
}
```

When you're finished with these four steps, your application should look like Figure 8-20. Unlike ODBC connections, OLE DB connections enable you to update any field (that is updatable). You therefore don't have as much of a need to define multiple rowsets as you did multiple ODBC recordsets in Chapter 5.

See Chapter 5 for more information on multiple ODBC recordsets.

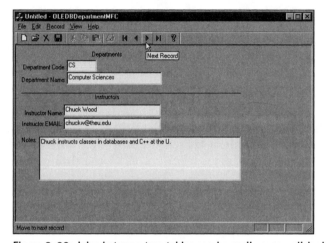

Figure 8-20: Joins between two tables can be easily accomplished with MFC and OLE DB.

This program can be found in the OLEDBDepartmentMFCd directory on the CD-ROM that accompanies this book.

Saving and Updating

ODBC database changes required the use of transactions to reverse the changes. OLE DB, on the other hand, supports delayed updates. This enables you to make updates to a rowset permanent in the database. Not only is this easier than using transactions, but it also is more stable (depending on the database) than using transactions for saving.

Delayed updates are a really neat feature of OLE DB, but providers *are not* required to implement them. In fact, some popular providers, such as the ODBC provider and the Microsoft Access (Jet) provider, have limited or no support for multiple updates. Test your provider to see if delayed update support is added. If not, use transactions instead.

Using delayed updates can be accomplished using the following simple steps:

1. First, you must set your rowset properties to enable delayed updates in your rowset constructor. In OLEDBDepartmentMFCSet.h, add the following property to your COLEDBDepartmentMFCView class definition, and make sure you are using a provider that supports delayed updates.

```
class COLEDBDepartmentMFCSet : public
CCommand<CAccessor<CDepartment> >
{
public:
    CString m_strFilter;      //Define a filter
    HRESULT Open()
    {
        CDataSource db;
        CSession    session;
        HRESULT     hr;

        CDBPropSet    dbinit(DBPROPSET_DBINIT);
//Don't use Access provider since it doesn't support
//updates very well.
        dbinit.AddProperty(
            DBPROP_AUTH_PERSIST_SENSITIVE_AUTHINFO, false);
        dbinit.AddProperty(DBPROP_AUTH_USERID, "sa");
        dbinit.AddProperty(DBPROP_AUTH_PASSWORD, "");
        dbinit.AddProperty(
            DBPROP_INIT_CATALOG,  "Classes");
        dbinit.AddProperty(
            DBPROP_INIT_DATASOURCE, "(local)");
        dbinit.AddProperty(DBPROP_INIT_LCID, (long)1033);
        dbinit.AddProperty(DBPROP_INIT_PROMPT, (short)4);
        hr = db.OpenWithServiceComponents(
            "SQLOLEDB.1", &dbinit);
        if (FAILED(hr))
            return hr;
```

```
        hr = session.Open(db);
        if (FAILED(hr))
            return hr;


        CDBPropSet    propset(DBPROPSET_ROWSET);
        propset.AddProperty(DBPROP_CANFETCHBACKWARDS, true);
        propset.AddProperty(DBPROP_IRowsetScroll, true);
        propset.AddProperty(DBPROP_IRowsetChange, true);
//2 properties Added by Chuck Wood to allow delayed updates
        propset.AddProperty(DBPROP_CANHOLDROWS, true);
        propset.AddProperty(DBPROP_IRowsetUpdate, true);
        propset.AddProperty(DBPROP_UPDATABILITY,
DBPROPVAL_UP_CHANGE | DBPROPVAL_UP_INSERT |
DBPROPVAL_UP_DELETE );
        hr = CCommand<CAccessor<CDepartment> >::Open(session,
            "SELECT Department.DepartmentCode,\
                    Department.DepartmentName,\
                    Instructor.Name,\
                    Instructor.Email,\
                    Instructor.Notes\
            FROM    Department INNER JOIN Instructor\
                    ON    Department.DepartmentCode =\
                        Instructor.DepartmentCode" +
            m_strFilter, &propset);
        if (FAILED(hr))
            return hr;


        return MoveNext();
    }
```

2. Add a Boolean variable to the CODBCDepartmentMFCView class
   definition in the ODBCDepartmentMFCView.h file to describe when
   changes are made:

```
class COLEDBDepartmentMFCView : public COleDBRecordView
{
protected: // create from serialization only
    COLEDBDepartmentMFCView();
    BOOL SaveRecord();
    void AddRecord();
    void ResetRowSet();
    BOOL m_bAddingRecord;
    BOOL m_bChangesMade;
    DECLARE_DYNCREATE(COLEDBDepartmentMFCView)
```

3. Initialize the newly created m_bChangesMade variable to FALSE in the COLEDBDepartmentMFCView constructor in the OLEDBDepartmentMFCView.cpp file to indicate that no changes have yet been made:

```
COLEDBDepartmentMFCView::COLEDBDepartmentMFCView()
  : COleDBRecordView(COLEDBDepartmentMFCView::IDD)
{
  //{{AFX_DATA_INIT(COLEDBDepartmentMFCView)
    // NOTE: the ClassWizard will add member initialization
here
  m_pSet = NULL;
  //}}AFX_DATA_INIT
  m_bAddingRecord = FALSE;
  m_bChangesMade = FALSE;
}
```

4. Use the Class Wizard to add the event functions shown in Table 8-2 to your COLEDBDepartmentMFCView class.

TABLE **8-2** EVENT FUNCTIONS NEEDED FOR DELAYED UPDATES

Object ID	Message	Description
IDC_DEPARTMENTCODE	EN_CHANGE	This event is triggered whenever a change is made to the department code.
IDC_DEPARTMENTNAME	EN_CHANGE	This event is triggered whenever a change is made to the department name.
IDC_EMAIL	EN_CHANGE	This event is triggered whenever a change is made to the instructor e-mail.
IDC_INSTRUCTORNAME	EN_CHANGE	This event is triggered whenever a change is made to the instructor name.
IDC_NOTES	EN_CHANGE	This event is triggered whenever a change is made to the instructor notes.
ID_FILE_SAVE	COMMAND	This event is triggered whenever the File → Save menu option is chosen or the corresponding toolbar button is clicked.

5. If you delete a record, set the m_bChangesMade **variable to** TRUE:

```
void COLEDBDepartmentMFCView::OnEditDeletetctrldel()
{
    if (AfxMessageBox(    //Be sure to verify your deletes
            "Are you sure you want to delete?",
            MB_YESNO)
        != IDYES) {
        return;
    }
    //Delete record and test
    if (m_bAddingRecord) {
        //Just abort the add
        m_bAddingRecord = FALSE;
    }
    else if (FAILED(m_pSet->Delete())) {  //Delete and test
        AfxMessageBox("Delete Failed:\n",
                      MB_ICONEXCLAMATION);
    }
    else {     //Set changes to true if Delete worked.
        m_bChangesMade = TRUE;
    }
    ResetRowSet();
}
```

6. Code all your OnChange... functions to set the m_bChangesMade **variable to** TRUE **when changes are made to any of your edit controls:**

```
void COLEDBDepartmentMFCView::OnChangeDepartmentcode()
{
    m_bChangesMade = TRUE;
}
void COLEDBDepartmentMFCView::OnChangeDepartmentname()
{
    m_bChangesMade = TRUE;
}
void COLEDBDepartmentMFCView::OnChangeEmail()
{
    m_bChangesMade = TRUE;
}
void COLEDBDepartmentMFCView::OnChangeInstructorname()
{
    m_bChangesMade = TRUE;
}
```

```
void COLEDBDepartmentMFCView::OnChangeNotes()
{
    m_bChangesMade = TRUE;
}
```

7. Code the `OnFileSave` function to enable a save when changes have been
   made:

```
void COLEDBDepartmentMFCView::OnFileSave()
{
    if (m_bChangesMade) {
        SaveRecord();
        m_bChangesMade = FALSE;
        if (FAILED(m_pSet->Update())) {   //Delete and test
            AfxMessageBox("Update failed in OnFileSave",
                MB_ICONEXCLAMATION);
        }
    }
}
```

8. Finally, code your OnDestroy function to ask the user if changes need to
   be saved if the user exits the program without first saving any changes
   made:

```
void COLEDBDepartmentMFCView::OnDestroy()
{
    if (m_bChangesMade) {
        //Yes was chosen. Save out record
        if (AfxMessageBox(
            "Do you want to save changes to the database?",
            MB_YESNO) == IDYES) {
            SaveRecord();
            OnFileSave();
        }
    }
    COleDBRecordView::OnDestroy();
}.
```

These changes enable your user to make changes, yet avoid saving them until
needed.

This program can be found in the OLEDBDepartmentMFCd directory on
the CD-ROM accompanying this book.

Developing OLE DB MFC Reports

In Chapter 6, you saw how to make an ODBC report. OLE DB reports developed in this chapter are similar to the reports developed in Chapter 6. In this section, a report is generated that shows the number of students that are taking each class.

Generating an OLE DB report can be accomplished in two parts. The first part involves using Visual C++ wizards to generate the program framework for reports. The second part involves inserting your own code to make the report operational.

Using Wizards to Generate a Reporting Framework

Use the following steps to create a WYSIWYG (What You See Is What You Get) report.

See the section "Generating Reports," in Chapter 6.

1. Use the MFC AppWizard to create a new project called OLEDBReportMFC (Figure 8-21).

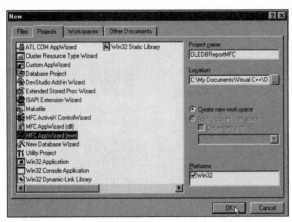

Figure 8-21: A new project is created to contain an OLE DB Report application.

2. Choose Single document in Step 1 of 6 in the MFC AppWizard, and click Next. Click Next to accept the rest of the defaults until Step 6 of 6. (Database support will be added later.)

3. In Step 6 of 6 in the MFC AppWizard, choose CScrollView as the base class (Figure 8-22). This enables your window to scroll if the report you generate takes up more than one window.

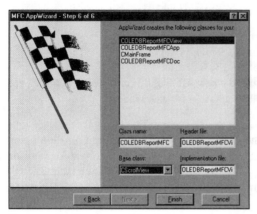

Figure 8-22: Usually use CScrollView as a base class when generating WYSIWYG reports.

4. When your MFC project is generated, you will have no database support. Choose Insert → New ATL object from the Visual Studio menu bar. This automatically adds an Active Template Library (ATL) module to your project.

The first time you add an ATL module to a project, a message box asks you if you want to add ATL support to your project. Usually you want to click Yes to this query, unless you accidentally chose a wrong menu option. Adding ATL support causes an IDL file to be created and added to your project. This IDL file enables your system to implement ActiveX.

5. After you choose to add a new ATL object, the ATL Object Wizard opens. This wizard enables you to choose between all ATL templates. Click the Data Access in the Category box, and choose Consumer in the Objects box as shown in Figure 8-23.

6. After you choose to add a OLE DB consumer for your project, the ATL Object Wizard Properties dialog box opens (Figure 8-24). Click the Select Datasource button.

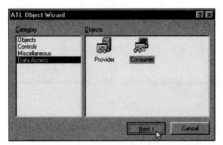

Figure 8-23: You need to add a new ATL OLE DB consumer to your MFC application to start accessing an OLE DB database for your report.

7. The Provider tab of the Data Link Properties dialog box then opens. Here, you choose which OLE DB data source you wish to use for your database connection. In Figure 8-25, an ODBC provider was chosen. The ODBC provider enables me to access any database through OLE DB that is currently accessible by ODBC.

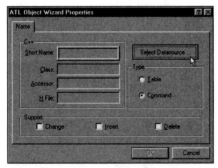

Figure 8-24: The ATL Object Wizard Properties dialog box opens whenever properties need to be set for an ATL object.

8. After you choose which driver you wish to use and click Next, the Connection tab of the Data Link Properties dialog box then opens. In Figure 8-26, the Classes database is chosen.

The Connection tab shown in Figure 8-26 differs from database to database depending on which connection information is needed for each database's OLE DB provider.

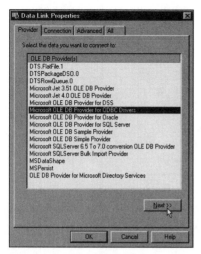

Figure 8-25: The Data Link Properties dialog box enables you to choose which OLE DB database driver you wish to use for your application.

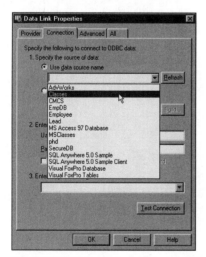

Figure 8-26: You must specify connection information after specifying which database to use.

9. Next, the Select Database Table dialog box opens (Figure 8-27). Here, you are expected to choose the table to be used for your report.

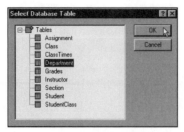

Figure 8-27: You need to choose a table to serve as a data source for your report.

 With multiple-table reports such as the one that we are creating in this section, it usually doesn't matter which table you choose because you will replace the table information with a customized SQL statement.

10. Now that you've chosen your data source, default names appear in the ATL Object Wizard Properties dialog box. These names can be changed. Figure 8-28 shows the names I used for this report.

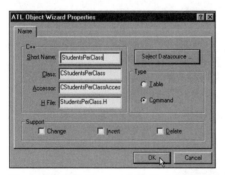

Figure 8-28: Names are defaulted in the ATL Object Wizard Properties dialog box, but you can override the defaults and use your own names, if you wish.

11. Now your project is generated. Get into the Class Wizard, and generate an OnPrint function for your view class, as shown in Figure 8-29.

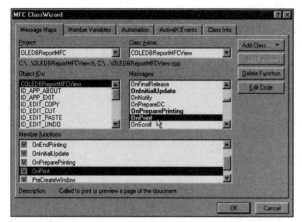

Figure 8-29: For most reports, the OnPrint event function must be generated.

Writing Code Needed to Generate a Report

Now you are ready to add the code needed to deliver a finished report. The rest of this section shows the kind of code needed for every MFC report. When creating reports in MFC, you only need to make code changes to the Accessor, the Document, and the View.

MAKING CHANGES TO THE ACCESSOR

Figure 8-30 shows the database relationships in the classes table. Because you need to generate a report that shows the number of students in each class, you then need to bring in the department and the class, and then you can indicate how many students are enrolled in each class by joining the Section and StudentClass tables.

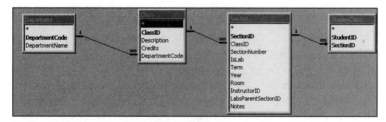

Figure 8-30: Reports often involve joining several tables.

Go to where you defined your new ATL class (StudentsPerClass.h), and change the Accessor to report the department name, the class description, and the number of students. First, change the variables that store the database columns:

```
class CStudentsPerClassAccessor
{
public:
    TCHAR m_DepartmentName[51];
    TCHAR m_Description[51];
    LONG m_NumberOfStudents;
```

Next, change the column map to reflect the changes you've just made to the class variables:

```
BEGIN_COLUMN_MAP(CStudentsPerClassAccessor)
    COLUMN_ENTRY(1, m_DepartmentName)
    COLUMN_ENTRY(2, m_Description)
    COLUMN_ENTRY(3, m_NumberOfStudents)
END_COLUMN_MAP()
```

Finally, start to code your SQL statement in the DEFINE_COMMAND macro. The DEFINE_COMMAND macro enables you to specify default SQL used for the Accessor. Using the DEFINE_COMMAND macro enables you to be more object-oriented than defining SQL later when you open your accessor.

In the following SQL, three tables (Department, Class, and Section) are joined together. StudentClass uses a left outer join so that classes can be counted even if no students have registered:

```
DEFINE_COMMAND(CStudentsPerClassAccessor, _T(" \
    SELECT \
        DepartmentName, \
        Description, \
        Count(StudentID) AS NumberOfStudents \
    FROM (Department \
        INNER JOIN (Class \
                INNER JOIN Section \
                    ON Class.ClassID = Section.ClassID) \
            ON Department.DepartmentCode \
                = Class.DepartmentCode) \
        LEFT JOIN StudentClass \
            ON Section.SectionID \
                = StudentClass.SectionID \
    GROUP BY DepartmentName, \
            Description \
"));
```

You can often generate complex SQL using a Query painter, such as the one found in Microsoft Access or the one found in Visual Studio used to paint views. These tools not only make it easy to generate complex SQL code, but they also help in developing bug-free SQL code.

MAKING CHANGES TO THE DOCUMENT

Because most MFC programs used documents and views, you should probably create an instance of the new Accessor in the Document header (OLEDBReport MFCDoc.h):

```
#include "StudentsPerClass.h"
class COLEDBReportMFCDoc : public CDocument
{
protected: // create from serialization only
    COLEDBReportMFCDoc();
    DECLARE_DYNCREATE(COLEDBReportMFCDoc)

// Attributes
public:
    CStudentsPerClass m_StudentsPerClass;
```

MAKING CHANGES TO THE VIEW

Most of your code changes and additions occur in your view class. Here, you need to make additions to the class definition, the OnDraw, OnInitialUpdate, and the OnPrint functions. You also need to create a new function to output the report. These additions are similar to those in Chapter 6.

See the section "Generating Reports" in Chapter 6.

MAKING CHANGES TO THE VIEW HEADER FILE   First, go into the view header file (OLEDBReportMFCView.h), add an #include statement, define an Accessor pointer, and declare a new function prototype to be used to output the report:

```
#include "StudentsPerClass.h"
class COLEDBReportMFCView : public CScrollView
{
```

```
protected: // create from serialization only
    COLEDBReportMFCView();
    void OutputReport(CDC* pDC, CPrintInfo* pInfo = NULL);
    DECLARE_DYNCREATE(COLEDBReportMFCView)
// Attributes
public:
    COLEDBReportMFCDoc* GetDocument();
    CStudentsPerClass* m_pSet;
```

MAKING CHANGES TO THE OnInitialUpdate FUNCTION   Changes made to the OnInitialUpdate function are almost identical to the changes made to the OnInitialUpdate function in Chapter 6. The only difference is that the Open function results are checked rather than an EOF flag.

See the section "Reports Using the OnDraw Function" in Chapter 6.

The OnInitialUpdate function is defined as follows:

```
void COLEDBReportMFCView::OnInitialUpdate()
{
    CScrollView::OnInitialUpdate();
    //Limit size to 8" x 20"
    CSize sizeTotal(800, 2000);
    //Because of MM_LOENGLISH, Sizes are in .01 of an inch
    SetScrollSizes(MM_LOENGLISH, sizeTotal);
    //Set the window title
    GetDocument()->SetTitle("OLE DB Students Per Class Report");
    //Set the m_pSet pointer to the m_dbSet recordset
    m_pSet = &GetDocument()->m_StudentsPerClass;
    //Open the recordset
    HRESULT hr = m_pSet->Open();
    if (hr != S_OK)
    {
        AfxMessageBox(_T("Row set failed to open."), MB_OK);
    }
}
```

If your Open statement fails, the most probable cause is bad SQL. If you can't open your Accessor, try a simple SQL command in place of your complex SQL command to see if it resolves the problem. If so, try reworking your SQL command so that your Accessor can open.

WRITING THE OutputReport FUNCTION   The OutputReport function in your view program (OLEDBReportMFCView.cpp) is almost identical to the OutputReport function defined in Chapter 6 for ODBC. The only changes made are that the title, tab stops, and columns have changed to reflect different data.

See the section "Building Reports Using the OnPrint Function" in Chapter 6.

The OutputReport function is defined as follows:

```
void COLEDBReportMFCView::OutputReport(CDC* pDC, CPrintInfo* pInfo)
{
    CString line;     //This is the print line
    TEXTMETRIC metrics;    //Font measurements
    int y = 0;          //Current y position on report
    CFont TitleFont;    //Font for Title
    CFont HeadingFont;     //Font for headings
    CFont DetailFont;    //Font for detail lines
    CFont FooterFont;    //Font for footer
    //Tab stops at 1 inch, 2.5 inches, and 6.5 inches
    int TabStops[] = {300, 650};
    //Tab stops at 3.5 inches and 6.5 inches
    int FooterTabStops[] = {350, 650};
    HRESULT m_hrMoveResult = S_OK;
    if (!pInfo || pInfo->m_nCurPage == 1) {
        //Set the recordset at the beginning
        m_hrMoveResult = m_pSet->MoveFirst();
    }
    //Bold font for Title
```

```
TitleFont.CreateFont(44, 0, 0, 0, FW_BOLD, FALSE, FALSE, 0,
    ANSI_CHARSET, OUT_DEFAULT_PRECIS, CLIP_DEFAULT_PRECIS,
    DEFAULT_QUALITY, DEFAULT_PITCH | FF_ROMAN,
    "Times New Roman");
//Bold and underlined font for headings
HeadingFont.CreateFont(36, 0, 0, 0, FW_BOLD, FALSE, TRUE, 0,
    ANSI_CHARSET, OUT_DEFAULT_PRECIS, CLIP_DEFAULT_PRECIS,
    DEFAULT_QUALITY, DEFAULT_PITCH | FF_ROMAN,
    "Times New Roman");
//Normal font for detail
DetailFont.CreateFont(18, 0, 0, 0, FW_NORMAL, FALSE, FALSE, 0,
    ANSI_CHARSET, OUT_DEFAULT_PRECIS, CLIP_DEFAULT_PRECIS,
    DEFAULT_QUALITY, DEFAULT_PITCH | FF_ROMAN,
    "Times New Roman");
//Small font for footer
FooterFont.CreateFont(12, 0, 0, 0, FW_NORMAL, FALSE, FALSE, 0,
    ANSI_CHARSET, OUT_DEFAULT_PRECIS, CLIP_DEFAULT_PRECIS,
    DEFAULT_QUALITY, DEFAULT_PITCH | FF_ROMAN,
    "Times New Roman");
//Capture default settings when setting the title font
CFont* OldFont = (CFont*) pDC->SelectObject(&TitleFont);
//Retrieve the heading font measurements
pDC->GetTextMetrics(&metrics);
//Compute the heading line height
int LineHeight = metrics.tmHeight + metrics.tmExternalLeading;
//Set Y to the line height.
y -= LineHeight;
pDC->TextOut(100, 0, "OLE DB Students Per Class Report");
/*
Y must be set to negative numbers because MM_LOENGLISH was
used in the CODBCReportView::OnInitialUpdate function.
*/
//Set the Heading font
pDC->SelectObject(&HeadingFont);
//Format the heading
line.Format("%s \t%s \t%s","Dept", "Class", "Students");
//Output the heading at (2, y) using 2 tabs
pDC->TabbedTextOut(2, y, line, 2, TabStops, 0);
//Compute the detail line height
LineHeight = metrics.tmHeight + metrics.tmExternalLeading;
y -= LineHeight;    //Adjust y position
```

```
//Set the detail font
pDC->SelectObject(&DetailFont);
//Retrieve detail font measurements
pDC->GetTextMetrics(&metrics);
//Compute the detail line height
LineHeight = metrics.tmHeight + metrics.tmExternalLeading;
//Scroll through the recordset
while (m_hrMoveResult == S_OK) {
    if (pInfo && abs(y) > 1000) {
        pInfo->SetMaxPage(pInfo->m_nCurPage + 1);
        break;
    }
    //Format the detail line
    line.Format("%s \t%s \t%d",
        m_pSet->m_DepartmentName,
        m_pSet->m_Description,
        m_pSet->m_NumberOfStudents);
    //Output the print line at (2, y) using 2 tab
    pDC->TabbedTextOut(2, y, line, 2, TabStops, 0);
    //Get the next recordset number
    y -= LineHeight;     //Adjust y position
    m_hrMoveResult = m_pSet->MoveNext();
}
if (pInfo) {
    //Set the footer font
    pDC->SelectObject(&FooterFont);
    //Format the footer
    line.Format(
        "OLE DB Report \tPage %d \tVisual C++ DB Guide",
        pInfo->m_nCurPage);
    //Output the footer at the bottom using tabs
    pDC->TabbedTextOut(1, -1025, line, 2, FooterTabStops, 0);
}
//Restore default settings
pDC->SelectObject(OldFont);
}
```

MAKING CHANGES TO THE OnDraw AND OnPrint FUNCTIONS Because all output to the device contexts of both the monitor and the printer are handled by the OutputReport function, the OnDraw and OnPrint functions simply need to call the OutputReport function.

```
void COLEDBReportMFCView::OnDraw(CDC* pDC)
{
    OutputReport(pDC);    //Display contents
}
void COLEDBReportMFCView::OnPrint(CDC* pDC, CPrintInfo* pInfo)
{
    OutputReport(pDC, pInfo);    //Display contents
}
```

Although they are shown contiguously here, the OnDraw and OnPrint functions appear in different locations inside your OLEDBReportMFCView.cpp program.

Viewing the Finished Report

Figure 8-31 shows how your finished report looks in the window. Headers and footers are inserted for possible multipage results, and Figure 8-32 shows how the report looks as a printout or in page preview.

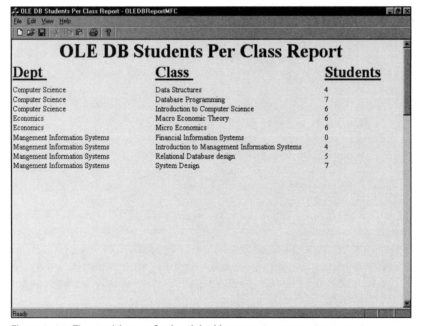

Figure 8-31: The resulting professional-looking report was easy to generate.

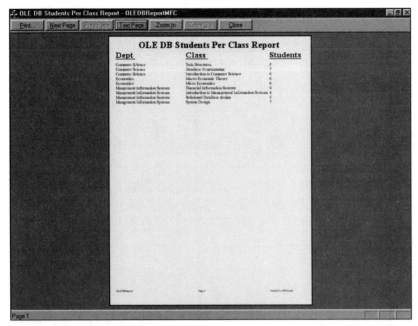

Figure 8–32: Not only can this report generate printouts and displays with the same code, but the printouts are appropriately formatted for headers and footers.

Summary

This chapter delves into easy OLE DB programming. You created add, change, and delete windows that showed data and enabled modifications. You also easily created reports with a technique that enables reports to be created in minutes using a combination of MFC and ATL. To recap:

♦ The MFC and Class Wizard are handy for quickly developing almost complete OLE DB applications.

♦ Joins are done through the Accessor using a WHERE SQL clause.

♦ The SetData function enables updates to the database in OLE DB.

♦ Instead of transactions, you can save using the CDBPropSet::AddProperty (DBPROP_IRowsetUpdate, true) function call and the CRowSet::Update function.

♦ Reports are accomplished much like ODBC reports, except that the Accessor must include SQL for the join required for the report.

Chapter 9

Developing ATL OLE DB Consumers

IN THIS CHAPTER

- ◆ Understanding the basics of ATL OLE DB applications
- ◆ Using the ATL wizards
- ◆ Using ATL controls and events
- ◆ Understanding database/dialog box integration
- ◆ Implementing transaction management with OLE DB

THE MFC MAKES IT EASY to develop a database application, either with ODBC or with OLE DB. However, the MFC includes a large amount of overhead with each application. Some applications may require a leaner implementation of database technology. This chapter describes how to use the AppWizard to generate Active Template Library (ATL) OLE DB applications.

Developing ATL OLE DB Applications

ATL applications are harder to develop than MFC applications. However, ATL applications tend to be smaller and maybe somewhat faster than MFC applications. This section gives you step-by-step instructions and shows how to easily develop an ATL application.

Using the ATL Wizards

Although ATL applications are not as easy to develop as MFC applications, Visual Studio does provide some help that enables a developer to quickly develop applications. ATL applications can be started using the ATL AppWizard and the ATL Object Wizard.

CREATING AN ATL APPLICATION WITH THE ATL APPWIZARD

The first step in creating a new ATL application is to generate a new ATL project. This can be accomplished by choosing File → New from the Visual Studio menu to open the New dialog box and choosing the Projects tab. In Figure 9-1, the ATL COM AppWizard is chosen, and the project name (OLEDBDepartmentATL) is entered.

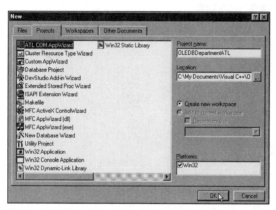

Figure 9-1: Visual Studio's ATL COM AppWizard enables you to easily create ATL applications.

When you click OK in the New dialog box, the ATL COM AppWizard dialog box opens. Unlike the MFC AppWizard, which usually consists of many steps, the only step in the ATL COM AppWizard is that you must choose which type of application you are developing. In Figure 9-2, Executable was chosen as the server type. This causes Visual C++ to create a Windows executable when it is finished running.

When you click Finish, the New Project Information dialog box opens. If you're following this example, the information in your New Project Information dialog box should look like the New Project Information dialog box shown in Figure 9-3.

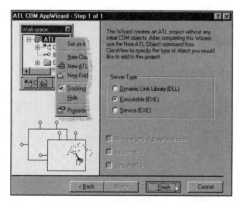

Figure 9-2: The ATL COM AppWizard consists of one step in which you choose your server type.

Figure 9-3: The New Project Information dialog box shows the options you chose while in the ATL COM AppWizard.

ADDING A CONSUMER WITH THE ATL OBJECT WIZARD

Now you are finished with the AppWizard, but at this point, you have only a shell of a program. The ATL COM AppWizard created some ATL objects for you to use in your application, but you need to add more ATL objects to make this program functional. Choose Insert → New ATL Object from the Visual Studio menu as shown in Figure 9-4.

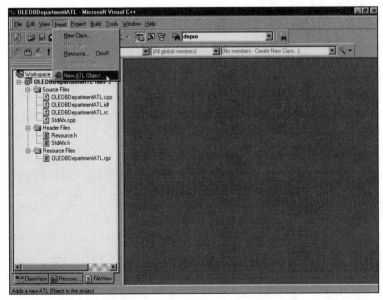

Figure 9-4: ATL objects need to be added to your program after you leave the ATL COM AppWizard.

The ATL Object Wizard should now open. Here, click Data Access, and choose Consumer as shown in Figure 9-5. Click Next.

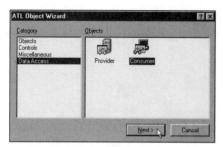

Figure 9-5: OLE DB consumers are just one of the ATL objects you can add using the ATL Object Wizard.

Next, the ATL Object Wizard Properties should open. You cannot enter any information in this window until you first choose a data source. Click the Select Datasource button as shown in Figure 9-6.

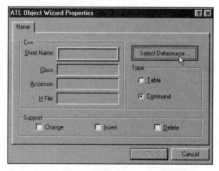

Figure 9-6: You can't enter any OLE DB consumer properties until you select an OLE DB consumer datasource.

After you click the Select Datasource button, the Data Link Properties dialog box should open. Here, you must choose an OLE DB provider. In Figure 9-7, the Microsoft Jet 3.51 provider was chosen so I could connect to my Access database. Click Next.

After you click Next, the Connection tab is selected in the Data Link Properties dialog box (Figure 9-8). Here, you choose what database you will be connecting to through your OLE DB provider. You can enter user ID and password information as well.

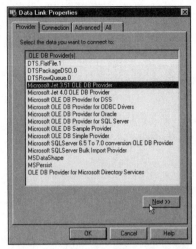

Figure 9-7: You must choose an OLE DB provider for your OLE DB consumer.

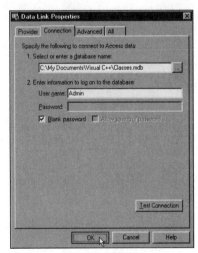

Figure 9-8: Database information, user information, and passwords are all entered in the Connection tab of the Data Link Properties dialog box.

After you choose your database, a table list opens. Here, you can choose the table you wish to use for your data source. In Figure 9-9, the Department table is chosen. After choosing which table to use as a data source, click OK.

When you click OK, the ATL Object Wizard Properties dialog box opens and shows default information about the new class that you are about to create (Figure 9-10). Be sure to check Change, Insert, and Delete if you want your users to be able to manipulate data in your table. When you're finished, click OK.

Figure 9-9: You must choose a table for your data source after selecting your database.

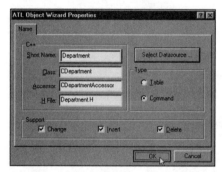

Figure 9-10: The ATL Object Wizard Properties dialog box is filled after you select a data source.

ADDING A DIALOG BOX WITH THE ATL OBJECT WIZARD

Next, you must create a dialog box. Like the consumer, a dialog box can be created using the ATL Object Wizard. Choose Insert → New ATL Object from the Visual Studio menu to open the ATL Object Wizard. Then choose Miscellaneous, click Dialog, and click Next as shown in Figure 9-11.

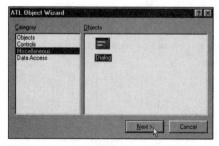

Figure 9-11: The ATL Object Wizard can also be used to create dialog boxes.

The ATL Object Wizard Properties dialog box then opens and enables you to type in the name of your class. In Figure 9-12, DBDialog is entered as the short name. This creates a CDBDialog class as well as DBDialog.cpp and DBDialog.h source files. Click OK when you've entered a short name.

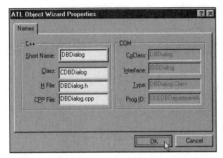

Figure 9-12: The ATL Object Wizard Properties dialog box is used to enter information needed to generate code to support your dialog box.

When you're finished, you should see the starting dialog box shown in Figure 9-13. You should also see in the Workspace window all your classes and header files added so far.

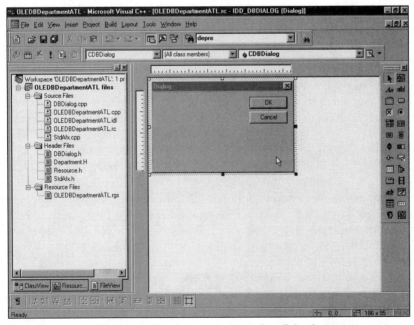

Figure 9-13: The ATL Object Wizard generates a starting dialog box.

Adding Controls and Events

From here, you can change the dialog box to fit your needs. In Figure 9-14, the dialog box is changed to enable entry into the Department table.

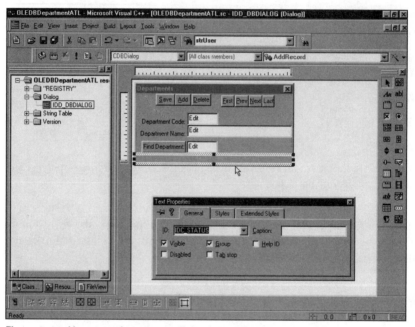

Figure 9-14: You must change your dialog box to fit your data entry needs.

After adding all the controls you need for your dialog box, you must add event code to handle any event that the user may invoke. Certain controls, such as static text, usually require no event. Others, such as command buttons, almost always require an event.

To add an event, double-click any control on the dialog box. This opens the New Windows Message and Event Handlers for class CDBDialog dialog box. In Figure 9-15, the IDC_SAVE command button is chosen, the BN_CLICKED Windows message is chosen, and the Add Handler button is clicked.

This automatically creates a function inside the header file for the dialog box. The Add Member Function dialog box opens (Figure 9-16) so you can supply the name of the function you want to handle this event. (In this example, the default names are always chosen.)

After you choose the function name, the New Windows Message and Event Handlers for class CDBDialog dialog box shows the event and gives the function associated with it (Figure 9-17). The dialog box header file (DBDialog.h) now contains a function prototype and the start of an inline function.

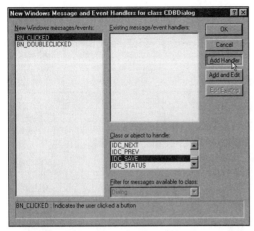

Figure 9-15: The New Windows Message and Event Handlers dialog box enables you to add events for your dialog box and the controls on your dialog box.

Figure 9-16: The Add Member Function dialog box enables you to choose the name of your event functions.

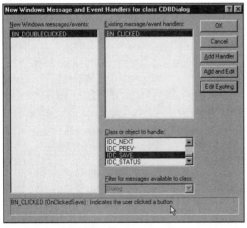

Figure 9-17: The New Windows Message and Event Handlers dialog box shows all the events defined for a dialog box.

Table 9-1 shows the controls added to the dialog box in Figure 9-14. Notice that a blank status line was also added to display warnings that aren't severe enough to require a dialog box. (For example, "No More Records" while scrolling should display a message but not a dialog box.)

TABLE 9-1 CONTROLS ON THE DBDIALOG DIALOG BOX

Control	Caption	ID	Event – Function	Description
Button	&Save	IDC_SAVE	BN_CLICKED / OnClickedSave	This function is called when the Save button is clicked.
Button	&Add	IDC_ADD	BN_CLICKED / OnClickedAdd	This function is called when the Add button is clicked.
Button	&Delete	IDC_DELETE	BN_CLICKED / OnClickedDelete	This function is called when the Delete button is clicked.
Button	Find Department	IDC_F INDDEPARTMENT	BN_CLICKED / OnClickedF indepartment	This function is called whenever the Find Department button is clicked.
Button	&First	IDC_FIRST	BN_CLICKED / OnClickedFirst	This function is called whenever the First button is clicked.
Button	&Prev	IDC_PREV	BN_CLICKED / OnClickedPrev	This function is called whenever the Prev button is clicked.
Button	&Next	IDC_NEXT	BN_CLICKED / OnClickedNext	This function is called whenever the Next button is clicked.
Button	&Last	IDC_LAST	BN_CLICKED / OnClickedLast	This function is called whenever the Last button is clicked.
Static Text		IDC_STATUS		No event is necessary for the static text message.

Adding Code

A framework has been set up for your OLE DB program. You must now add code to the framework in order for a functional program to be the result.

ADDING DIALOG BOX CODE

The first code you need is to add a dialog box instance to your main .cpp program. In OLEDBDepartmentATL.cpp, the ATL AppWizard has already generated needed code for a Windows executable. You need to make two changes to this program. First, add an #include statement for your dialog box:

```
// OLEDBDepartmentATL.cpp : Implementation of WinMain
// Note: Proxy/Stub Information
//    To build a separate proxy/stub DLL,
//    run nmake -f OLEDBDepartmentATLps.mk in the project directory.

#include "stdafx.h"
#include "resource.h"
#include <initguid.h>
#include "OLEDBDepartmentATL.h"

#include "OLEDBDepartmentATL_i.c"
//This include was added by Chuck Wood for dialog box support
#include "DBDialog.h"
```

Next, you need to replace the loop that waits for messages with a dialog box declaration inside the _tWinMain function. This is shown by the following unshaded lines:

```
extern "C" int WINAPI _tWinMain(HINSTANCE hInstance,
    HINSTANCE /*hPrevInstance*/, LPTSTR lpCmdLine, int /*nShowCmd*/)
{
    lpCmdLine = GetCommandLine(); //this line necessary for
_ATL_MIN_CRT

#if _WIN32_WINNT >= 0x0400 & defined(_ATL_FREE_THREADED)
    HRESULT hRes = CoInitializeEx(NULL, COINIT_MULTITHREADED);
#else
    HRESULT hRes = CoInitialize(NULL);
#endif
    _ASSERTE(SUCCEEDED(hRes));
    _Module.Init(ObjectMap, hInstance,
&LIBID_OLEDBDEPARTMENTATLLib);
    _Module.dwThreadID = GetCurrentThreadId();
```

```
    TCHAR szTokens[] = _T("-/");

    int nRet = 0;
    BOOL bRun = TRUE;
    LPCTSTR lpszToken = FindOneOf(lpCmdLine, szTokens);
    while (lpszToken != NULL)
    {
        if (lstrcmpi(lpszToken, _T("UnregServer"))==0)
        {

_Module.UpdateRegistryFromResource(IDR_OLEDBDepartmentATL, FALSE);
            nRet = _Module.UnregisterServer(TRUE);
            bRun = FALSE;
            break;
        }
        if (lstrcmpi(lpszToken, _T("RegServer"))==0)
        {

_Module.UpdateRegistryFromResource(IDR_OLEDBDepartmentATL, TRUE);
            nRet = _Module.RegisterServer(TRUE);
            bRun = FALSE;
            break;
        }
        lpszToken = FindOneOf(lpszToken, szTokens);
    }

    if (bRun)
    {
        _Module.StartMonitor();
#if _WIN32_WINNT >= 0x0400 & defined(_ATL_FREE_THREADED)
        hRes = _Module.RegisterClassObjects(CLSCTX_LOCAL_SERVER,
            REGCLS_MULTIPLEUSE | REGCLS_SUSPENDED);
        _ASSERTE(SUCCEEDED(hRes));
        hRes = CoResumeClassObjects();
#else
        hRes = _Module.RegisterClassObjects(CLSCTX_LOCAL_SERVER,
            REGCLS_MULTIPLEUSE);
#endif
        _ASSERTE(SUCCEEDED(hRes));

//Added by Chuck Wood to construct the dialog box
        CDBDialog newDialog;
        _Module.RevokeClassObjects();
```

```
        Sleep(dwPause); //wait for any threads to finish
    }

    _Module.Term();
    CoUninitialize();
    return nRet;
}
```

Next, you need to open the dialog box inside the CDBDialog constructor in the DBDialog.h source file. This can be done with the DoModal() method:

```
class CDBDialog :
    public CAxDialogImpl<CDBDialog>
{
public:
    CDBDialog()
    {
        //Added by Chuck Wood to open the dialog box
        DoModal();
    }
```

Finally, you need a way to open and close your program. The preferred way to handle this in an ATL application is to use the _Module.Lock in the OnInitDialog function as shown in the unshaded area that follows:

```
LRESULT OnInitDialog(UINT uMsg, WPARAM wParam, LPARAM lParam, BOOL&
bHandled)
{
    _Module.Lock();
    return 1;  // Let the system set the focus
}
```

Then add a _Module.Unlock in the OnCancel function as shown in the following unshaded area:

```
LRESULT OnCancel(WORD wNotifyCode, WORD wID, HWND hWndCtl, BOOL&
bHandled)
{
    EndDialog(wID);  //Close the dialog box
    _Module.Unlock();//End this program
    return 0;
}
```

Now your program should run. Granted, it won't do any database access yet, but the dialog box should pop up, as shown in Figure 9-18.

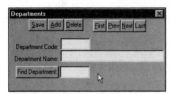

Figure 9-18: Not much code is needed to change an ATL program shell generated by the AppWizard to a working Windows program.

ADDING CODE TO THE OLE DB DEPARTMENT HEADER

The ATL Object Wizard created a fully functional OLE DB consumer class for the Department table. Usually, few or no additions need to be made to the generated consumer class for a working OLE DB program. However, in this case, some filter support and a WHERE clause need to be added.

First, add a constructor to allocate storage for a filter, which is shown in the following code. Because no filter is present at first, this can be an empty string.

```
class CDepartment : public CCommand<CAccessor<CDepartmentAccessor> >
{
public:

    //Constructor added by Chuck Wood
    CDepartment () {
        //Initialize 1 byte for SQL WHERE clause
        m_strFilter = new char[1];
        strcpy (m_strFilter, "");
    }
    //Destructor added by Chuck Wood
    ~CDepartment () {
        //Release resources
        delete m_strFilter;
    }
```

Next, you must apply the filter, if it exists, to the rowset. The OpenRowset function automatically opens the CCommand using the following syntax:

```
return CCommand<CAccessor<CDepartmentAccessor> >::Open(m_session,
NULL, &propset);
```

In the preceding code, the NULL is where the SQL command needed to generate the CCommand is supposed to go. A NULL in place of the SQL command indicates that the CCommand is to use the default Command, defined by using the DEFINE_COMMAND macro in the CDepartmentAccessor class:

```
DEFINE_COMMAND(CDepartmentAccessor, _T(" \
    SELECT \
        DepartmentCode, \
        DepartmentName  \
        FROM Department"))
```

You can retrieve the default SQL from a CCommand by using the GetDefaultCommand function. A new SQL command can then be formed that appends a WHERE clause to the default SQL. You then must replace the NULL in the Open function with the new SQL command that you just formed. This can be done with the following syntax:

```
HRESULT OpenRowset()
{
    // Set properties for open
    CDBPropSet    propset(DBPROPSET_ROWSET);
    propset.AddProperty(DBPROP_IRowsetChange, true);
    propset.AddProperty(DBPROP_UPDATABILITY, DBPROPVAL_UP_CHANGE |
DBPROPVAL_UP_INSERT | DBPROPVAL_UP_DELETE);

    //The rest of this function was added by Chuck Wood
    //Allow 512 bytes for the new SQL Command
    char newSQL[512];
    char *SQLCommand;
    GetDefaultCommand((const char **) &SQLCommand);
    strcpy(newSQL, SQLCommand);
    if (strlen(m_strFilter)) {
        strcat(newSQL, " WHERE ");
        strcat(newSQL, m_strFilter);
    }
    return CCommand<CAccessor<CDepartmentAccessor> >
            ::Open(m_session, newSQL, &propset);

}
char       *m_strFilter;
CSession    m_session;
```

Now, instead of using the default SQL command, a new SQL command is created that appends a WHERE clause, when needed, to the default SQL command. Notice also that the m_strFilter class variable must be defined. This can be done anywhere in the class but probably should be defined with the other class variable (m_session) for clarity.

ADDING FUNCTIONS TO THE DIALOG BOX

Before you start coding events, it's helpful to have some functionality built into the dialog box. In the dialog box header file (DBDialog.h), you need to define a Boolean flag showing that you're adding a record. In addition, you need to define a class variable for the OLE DB consumer:

```
CDepartment* m_pSet;
BOOL m_bAddingRecord;
```

You also need to define the following function prototypes:

♦ Messages need to be conveyed to the user. An error routine is needed to display error messages when appropriate, and a status routine is needed to display status messages, which aren't errors but rather information that the user must see:

```
void DisplayError(char *strMessage, HRESULT hr = S_OK, char
*strFunction = NULL);
void DisplayStatus(char *strMessage);
```

♦ A function to handle saves to the rowset:

```
HRESULT SaveDepartment();
```

♦ A function to handle movement within the CDepartment rowset, which would take a positional enum parameter to indicate where in the rowset you are to move:

```
enum {    FIRST = 0,
          LAST = 1,
          NEXT = 2,
          PREV = 3 };
void OnMove(int position);
```

♦ A function to clear the dialog box and start adding a record:

```
void AddRecord();
```

♦ A function to try to go to a record in the rowset:

```
void ResetRowSet();
```

◆ A function is needed that mimics the MFC capability to update the window from the database and update the database from the window:

```
void UpdateData(BOOL bSaveChangesToSet = TRUE);
```

These changes can be viewed in the CDBDialog class definition in the DBDialog.h header file:

```
class CDBDialog :
    public CAxDialogImpl<CDBDialog>
{
```

```
/*
    Protected variables and function prototypes added by
    Chuck Wood for Visual C++ Database Developer's Guide
*/
protected:
    CDepartment* m_pSet;
    BOOL m_bAddingRecord;
    enum {    FIRST = 0,
              LAST = 1,
              NEXT = 2,
              PREV = 3 };
    void DisplayError(char *strMessage, HRESULT hr = S_OK, char
*strFunction = NULL);
    void DisplayStatus(char *strMessage);
    HRESULT SaveDepartment();
    void OnMove(int position);
    void AddRecord();
    void ResetRowSet();
```

BEGINNING ERROR HANDLING   Most database programs need a way to display messages that do not use a message box to halt a program. Messages such as "Update Successful", "Last Record Reached", and "First Record Reached" should be displayed for informational purposes but should not require a response from the user.

The dialog box formed for CDBDialog contains a static text control named IDC_STATUS that is used solely for messages to the user. The DisplayStatus function places a message on this text area.

```
void CDBDialog::DisplayStatus(char *strMessage)
{
    SetDlgItemText(IDC_STATUS, strMessage);
}
```

For more serious errors, a message box should be displayed that requires a response from the user. For serious error handling, you can use the FAILED macro to test the HRESULT that is returned from most OLE DB function calls. A function containing error processing for the CDBDialog class follows:

```
void CDBDialog::DisplayError(char *strMessage, HRESULT hresult, char
*strFunction)
{
    //Allow 1 k for the error message
    char message[1024];
    strcpy(message, strMessage);
    if (strFunction) {      //Check for function equal to null
        //Function was passed, so see what function it was
        strcat(message, " in the ");
        strcat(message, strFunction);
        strcat(message, " function ");
    }
    if (FAILED(hresult)) {
        //Allow 512 bytes for HR message
        char holdmessage[512];
        sprintf(holdmessage, "\n\nHRESULT was %ld", hresult);
        strcat(message, holdmessage);
    }
    MessageBox(message, "An error has occurred");
}
```

Error handling is discussed in greater detail in the next chapter.

See "Examining the HRESULT" in Chapter 10.

See "Error Trapping and Recovery" in Chapter 10.

WRITING THE SaveDepartment FUNCTION   In OLE DB, two methods are key to updating existing data. The Insert function takes data from the Accessor and attempts to create a new record. The SetData function takes data from the Accessor and attempts to update the database with the new data. The SaveDepartment function that follows shows how records can be updated inside a function:

```
HRESULT CDBDialog::SaveDepartment()
{
    UpdateData(TRUE);     //Read from screen
    HRESULT hr;
    if (m_bAddingRecord) {
        hr = m_pSet->Insert();     //Insert New rew
    }
    else {
        hr = m_pSet->SetData();     //Update current row
    }
    if (FAILED(hr)) {
        DisplayError("Update Failed.", hr, "SaveDepartment");
    }
    else {
        m_bAddingRecord = FALSE;
    }
    return hr;
}
```

Notice how the results of the Insert and Update function calls are tested using the FAILED macro and the resulting error, if any, is displayed using the DisplayError function.

WRITING THE UpdateData FUNCTION   One of the most powerful functions in the MFC is the UpdateData function, which enables a programmer to easily update the window from the rowset or fill the rowset from window data. Unfortunately, as mentioned previously, the MFC carries a lot of overhead.

The following UpdateData function mimics the MFC UpdateData function and sends data either from the dialog box to a rowset or from a rowset to the dialog box:

```
void CDBDialog::UpdateData(BOOL bSaveChangesToSet)
{
    if (bSaveChangesToSet) {
        //Read From Screen
        GetDlgItemText(IDC_DEPARTMENTCODE,
            (char *) m_pSet->m_DepartmentCode, 5);
        GetDlgItemText(IDC_DEPARTMENTNAME,
```

```
        (char *) m_pSet->m_DepartmentName, 51);
}
else {
    //Write to Screen
    SetDlgItemText(IDC_DEPARTMENTCODE,
        (char *) m_pSet->m_DepartmentCode);
    SetDlgItemText(IDC_DEPARTMENTNAME,
        (char *) m_pSet->m_DepartmentName);
}
}
```

WRITING THE ADDRECORD FUNCTION   The `AddRecord` function is not used to
actually add a record. As seen previously, the `SaveDepartment` function is used
to add a record. The `AddRecord` function is used to clear the dialog box and set up
a new record to be added. This involves simply clearing the data from the rowset,
setting an adding record flag, and using the `UpdateData` function to display that
cleared record to the dialog box:

```
void CDBDialog::AddRecord()
{
    m_pSet->ClearRecord();
    m_bAddingRecord = TRUE;
    UpdateData(FALSE);      //Update the window
}
```

WRITING THE ONMOVE FUNCTION   One function should be written to handle all
movement within a rowset so those functions that need to be called before the current record pointer changes can reside in one place. Move functions should perform
the following operations:

1. Move functions should save any changes to the current record before the
   move takes place. The results of the save should be tested:

   ```
   if (FAILED(SaveDepartment())) {
       DisplayStatus("Save failed. No move is possible.");
       return;        //End if save did not work.
   }
   ```

2. Move functions should, initially, clear the status message at the bottom of
   the dialog window:

   ```
   DisplayStatus("");
   ```

3. Move functions should then move to the appropriate record:

   ```
   HRESULT hr;
   ```

```
switch (position) {
case (FIRST) :
    hr = m_pSet->MoveFirst();
    break;
case (NEXT) :
// and so on.
```

4. The results of the move should be tested. If an error occurs, either a message box should be displayed or a message should be sent to the status text area. Appropriate actions also should be taken. The following code shows this:

```
if (FAILED(hr)) {
    DisplayError("No records found. Adding new record");
    DisplayStatus("No records found.");
    AddRecord();
}
```

These steps can be viewed in the following OnMove function:

```
void CDBDialog::OnMove(int position)
{
    //This OnMove is not really an event, but
    //rather is called by other move functions
    if (FAILED(SaveDepartment())) {
        DisplayStatus("Save failed. No move is possible.");
        return;          //End if save did not work.
    }
    DisplayStatus("");
    HRESULT hr;
    switch (position) {
    case (FIRST) :
        hr = m_pSet->MoveFirst();
        break;
    case (NEXT) :
        hr = m_pSet->MoveNext();
        if (hr != S_OK) {      //EOF
            DisplayStatus("Last record reached.");
            hr = m_pSet->MoveLast();
        }
        break;
    case (LAST) :
        hr = m_pSet->MoveLast();
        break;
    case (PREV) :
```

```
        hr = m_pSet->MovePrev();
        if (hr != S_OK) {      //BOF
            DisplayStatus("First record reached.");
            hr = m_pSet->MoveFirst();
        }
        break;
    }
    if (FAILED(hr)) {
        DisplayError("No records found. Adding new record");
        DisplayStatus("No records found.");
        AddRecord();
    }
    UpdateData(FALSE);      //Update Screen
}
```

 This function mimics the MFC OnMove function. However, unlike the MFC, there is no ancestor OnMove function with ATL. Therefore, your code must handle all the move functionality instead of calling an ancestor.

WRITING THE ResetRowSet FUNCTION   The ResetRowSet function is simply used to try to go to a record, which is especially useful after a delete. First, a move to the next record is attempted with the MoveNext function. If that fails, a MoveFirst function is called to attempt to move to the first record in a rowset. Another failure indicates that the rowset is empty, and the AddRecord function is called to set up a new record. After all this is complete, a call to the UpdateData function is made to display the rowset in the dialog box.

```
void CDBDialog::ResetRowSet()
{
    if (m_pSet->MoveNext() != S_OK) {      //Go to next record
        if (m_pSet->MoveFirst() != S_OK) {
            MessageBox("No more records", "",
                MB_ICONEXCLAMATION);
            //No records, so set up an add record
            AddRecord();
        }
    }
    UpdateData(FALSE);      //Write changes to window
}
```

CODING THE DIALOG BOX EVENTS

All the supporting functionality for your dialog box has been written. Now you are
ready to add code to your events. The remainder of this section shows what code is
needed for the dialog events in your dialog header file (CDBDialog.h).

WRITING THE OnInitDialog EVENT In CDBDialog.h, you should see an
OnInitDialog function. This function is called when the dialog box is initialized.
You can add the following unshaded code to the OnInitDialog function to limit
the length of the dialog box textboxes, open the rowset, move to the first record,
and display the results in the dialog box:

```
LRESULT OnInitDialog(UINT uMsg, WPARAM wParam, LPARAM lParam, BOOL&
bHandled)
{
    _Module.Lock();
    SendMessage(GetDlgItem(IDC_DEPARTMENTCODE),
        EM_LIMITTEXT, (WPARAM)4, 0);
    SendMessage(GetDlgItem(IDC_DEPARTMENTNAME),
        EM_LIMITTEXT, (WPARAM)50, 0);
    SendMessage(GetDlgItem(IDC_FINDDEPARTMENTEDIT),
        EM_LIMITTEXT, (WPARAM)50, 0);
    HRESULT hr = m_pSet->Open();
    if (FAILED(hr)) {
        DisplayError("Open Rowset failed", hr, "OnInitDialog");
        exit(1);    //Better not start
    }
    //Start DB Transaction
    hr = m_pSet->m_session.StartTransaction();
    if (FAILED(hr)) {
        DisplayError("StartTransaction failed",
            hr, "OnInitDialog");
    }
    m_pSet->MoveFirst();
    UpdateData(FALSE);    //Write Values to Window
    return 1; // Let the system set the focus
}
```

WRITING THE OnClickedAdd EVENT The OnClickedAdd event is executed whenever the Add button is clicked. The event simply calls the SaveDepartment and
AddRecord functions described earlier in this chapter to save the current record
and set up the rowset to add an additional record. Changes to the OnClickedAdd

event from the function generated by the ATL Object Wizard are shown in the unshaded area that follows:

```
LRESULT OnClickedAdd(WORD wNotifyCode, WORD wID, HWND hWndCtl, BOOL&
bHandled)
{
    if (FAILED(SaveDepartment())) {
        return 0;
    }
    AddRecord();
    return 0;
}
```

WRITING THE OnClickedDelete EVENT The steps needed to code the OnClickedDelete event are similar to those needed to delete events discussed in other chapters:

1. Make sure that the user really wants to delete a record:

```
if (MessageBox(    //Be sure to verify your deletes
        "Are you sure you want to delete?", "",
        MB_YESNO)
    != IDYES) {
    return 0;
}
```

2. See if an add is in progress. If it is, simply cancel the add:

```
if (m_bAddingRecord) {
    //Just abort the add
    m_bAddingRecord = FALSE;
}
```

3. If an add is not in progress, delete the current record in the rowset, and test the results:

```
HRESULT hr = m_pSet->Delete();
if (FAILED(hr)) {    //Test Delete
    DisplayError("Delete Failed", hr, "OnClickedDelete");
}
```

4. Call the ResetRowSet function to move to an appropriate record in the database:

```
ResetRowSet();
```

All this can be seen in the following `OnClickedDelete` function that follows. Note that the changes to the function generated by the ATL Object Wizard are shown in the unshaded area:

```
LRESULT OnClickedDelete(WORD wNotifyCode, WORD wID, HWND hWndCtl,
BOOL& bHandled)
{
    if (MessageBox(     //Be sure to verify your deletes
            "Are you sure you want to delete?", "",
            MB_YESNO)
        != IDYES) {
        return 0;
    }
    //Delete record and test
    if (m_bAddingRecord) {
        //Just abort the add
        m_bAddingRecord = FALSE;
    }
    else {
        //Delete the current row in the rowset
        HRESULT hr = m_pSet->Delete();
        if (FAILED(hr)) {    //Test Delete
            DisplayError("Delete Failed",
                hr, "OnClickedDelete");
        }
    }
    ResetRowSet();
    return 0;
}
```

 Be sure you always check before actually performing a delete on a rowset. The user could have hit the Delete button accidentally or not really understood the intent of the Delete button.

WRITING THE OnClickedFindepartment EVENT The `OnClickedFindepartment` event is triggered when the user clicks the Find Department button. This method relies on the filter that was set up earlier in this chapter to restrict the rowset to those departments that were already set.

This function simply takes the string from the FindDepartmentEdit textbox and uses it to build a filter in the OLE DB CDepartment class:

```
LRESULT OnClickedFindepartment(WORD wNotifyCode, WORD wID, HWND
hWndCtl, BOOL& bHandled)
{
    char filterDepartment[5];
    if (FAILED(SaveDepartment())) {
        return 0;
    }
    GetDlgItemText(IDC_FINDDEPARTMENTEDIT,
        filterDepartment, 5);
    delete m_pSet->m_strFilter;
    m_pSet->m_strFilter = new char[25];
    strcpy (m_pSet->m_strFilter, "DepartmentCode = '");
    strcat (m_pSet->m_strFilter, filterDepartment);
    strcat (m_pSet->m_strFilter, "'");
    //Requery for new filter
    m_pSet->Close();
    m_pSet->OpenRowset();
    m_pSet->MoveFirst();
    UpdateData(FALSE);      //Update the window
    return 0;
}
```

As you can see by the preceding code listing, after the filter is built, the rowset is closed and then opened to reinitialize the rowset with the new filter. Then the first record is displayed.

WRITING THE MOVE EVENTS   Every move event moves the rowset pointer to a new row. Because all the move functionality is in the OnMove function, all move events call the OnMove function to perform their moves using the FIRST, LAST, NEXT, and PREV enum flags that were set up at the beginning of this chapter. The lines added to the move events are shown in the unshaded area that follows:

```
LRESULT OnClickedFirst(WORD wNotifyCode, WORD wID, HWND hWndCtl,
BOOL& bHandled)
{
    OnMove(FIRST);
    return 0;
}
```

```
LRESULT OnClickedLast(WORD wNotifyCode, WORD wID, HWND hWndCtl,
BOOL& bHandled)
{
    OnMove(LAST);
    return 0;
}
LRESULT OnClickedNext(WORD wNotifyCode, WORD wID, HWND hWndCtl,
BOOL& bHandled)
{
    OnMove(NEXT);
    return 0;
}
LRESULT OnClickedPrev(WORD wNotifyCode, WORD wID, HWND hWndCtl,
BOOL& bHandled)
{
    OnMove(PREV);
    return 0;
}
```

ADJUSTING THE OnCancel EVENT   Currently, the OnCancel event closes the dialog box whenever the Esc key is pressed or the close box is clicked. With database programming, you need to adjust the OnCancel event to save any data, if necessary, and to exit the program. Furthermore, if the save fails, the program should not exit. This functionality can be seen in the following OnCancel function:

```
LRESULT OnCancel(WORD wNotifyCode, WORD wID, HWND hWndCtl, BOOL&
bHandled)
{
    //Save the department if needed
    if (SUCCEEDED(SaveDepartment())) {
        EndDialog(wID);    //Close the dialog box
        _Module.Unlock();  //End this program
    }
    return 0;
}
```

Observing the Final Product

As you can see, without much work, you have developed a functional ATL OLE DB program that adds, deletes, changes, and browses through records. The output dialog box is shown in Figure 9-19.

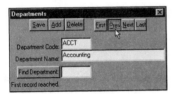

Figure 9-19: OLE DB database access is easily accomplished using ATL.

The example shown in Figure 9-19 does not yet include Save functionality. This is added in the next section.

The program listing for OLE DB is on the CD-ROM accompanying this book under OLEDBDepartmentATLa.

Saving and Transactions

Transactions were discussed in both Chapters 4 and 5. Transactions are a way to make "temporary" changes to a database. After these changes are made, you can make them permanent by "committing" them to the database, or you can erase them by "rolling back" the changes.

See Chapter 4, "Using ODBC Transactions."

See Chapter 4, "Testing Cursor Behavior with Transactions."

See Chapter 5, "Saving and Transactions."

As mentioned in a previous chapter, you could use the Update() method in conjunction with the DBPROP_IRowsetUpdate property to mimic temporary changes in an OLE DB rowset. You can also use transactions for the same purpose. The difference is that, with transactions, the database handles the temporary data. With the Update() method in conjunction with the DBPROP_IRowsetUpdate property, the OLE DB rowset handles all changes. Transactions are often more tested than the OLE DB interface. To find out which is better for saving, try both methods, and pick the one that functions best in your environment.

See Chapter 8, "Saving and Updating."

It's easy to set up your application with transaction support. Just complete the following steps:

1. Define a Boolean variable (m_bChangesMade) to indicate if changes were made:

```
class CDBDialog :
    public CAxDialogImpl<CDBDialog>
{
/*
    Protected variables and function prototypes added by
    Chuck Wood for Visual C++ Database Developer's Guide
*/
protected:
    CDepartment* m_pSet;
```

```
BOOL m_bAddingRecord;
BOOL m_bChangesMade;
enum {     FIRST = 0,
            LAST = 1,
            NEXT = 2,
            PREV = 3 };
```

2. Initialize m_bChangesMade to FALSE in the constructor:

```
CDBDialog()
{
//Added by Chuck Wood to open & initialize the dialog box
    m_pSet = new CDepartment();
    m_bChangesMade = FALSE;
    m_bAddingRecord = FALSE;
    DoModal();
}
```

3. Whenever a change is made, the m_bChangesMade variable needs to be set to TRUE. Double-click the Department Code and the Department Name fields in the dialog box, declare EN_CHANGE events for each textbox, and then add code to set m_bChangesMade to true when the fields have been changed:

```
LRESULT OnChangeDepartmentcode(WORD wNotifyCode, WORD wID,
HWND hWndCtl, BOOL& bHandled)
{
    m_bChangesMade = TRUE;
    return 0;
}
LRESULT OnChangeDepartmentname(WORD wNotifyCode, WORD wID,
HWND hWndCtl, BOOL& bHandled)
{
    m_bChangesMade = TRUE;
    return 0;
}
```

4. Start your transaction in the InitDialog function. This can be done by using the CSession::StartTransaction method. The unshaded code that follows shows the addition to the OnInitDialog method that was needed:

```
LRESULT OnInitDialog(UINT uMsg, WPARAM wParam, LPARAM lParam,
BOOL& bHandled)
{
    HRESULT hr = m_pSet->Open();
    if (FAILED(hr)) {
        DisplayError("Open Rowset failed", hr,
```

```
"OnInitDialog");
      exit(1);      //Better not start
   }
   //Start DB Transaction
   hr = m_pSet->m_session.StartTransaction();
   if (FAILED(hr)) {
      DisplayError("StartTransaction failed",
            hr, "OnInitDialog");
   }
   m_pSet->MoveFirst();
   UpdateData(FALSE);      //Write Values to Window
   return 1;  // Let the system set the focus
}
```

Transactions are controlled by the session, not by the rowset. You can have multiple rowsets open at one time, but all are affected by the same session variable.

5. Declare a function specifically designed for committing temporary changes to the database by performing the following steps:

   a. Declare a function prototype in your dialog box header file (CDBDialog.h):

```
class CDBDialog :
    public CAxDialogImpl<CDBDialog>
{
protected:
    HRESULT UpdateDepartment();
```

   b. Create a function that first saves out any existing data by using a call to the SaveDepartment function:

```
HRESULT CDBDialog::UpdateDepartment() {
    m_bChangesMade = FALSE;
    HRESULT hr = SaveDepartment();
    if (FAILED(hr)) {
        return hr;
    }
```

   c. Make changes permanent by issuing a commit:

```
hr = m_pSet->m_session.Commit();      //Make Changes
permanent
```

```
if (FAILED(hr)){
    DisplayError("Commit failed", hr, "UpdateDepartment");
}
```

d. A commit ends the transaction, so you must restart the transaction after every commit. Test the commit, and if the commit succeeds, restart the transaction with code that looks similar to this:

```
//Restart transaction
hr = m_pSet->m_session.StartTransaction();
if (FAILED(hr)){
    DisplayError("StartTransaction failed",
             hr, "UpdateDepartment");
}
```

The following is a function listing for this step:

```
HRESULT CDBDialog::UpdateDepartment() {
    m_bChangesMade = FALSE;
    HRESULT hr = SaveDepartment();
    if (FAILED(hr)) {
        return hr;
    }
    //Make Changes permanent
    hr = m_pSet->m_session.Commit();
    if (FAILED(hr)){
        DisplayError("Commit failed", hr,
                        "UpdateDepartment");
    }
    //Restart transaction
    hr = m_pSet->m_session.StartTransaction();
    if (FAILED(hr)){
        DisplayError("StartTransaction failed",
                 hr, "UpdateDepartment");
    }
    return hr;
}
```

6. Write the OnClickedSave event function. The only addition needed for this function is a call to the UpdateDepartment function written in step 5.

```
LRESULT OnClickedSave(WORD wNotifyCode, WORD wID, HWND
hWndCtl, BOOL& bHandled)
{
    UpdateDepartment();
    return 0;
}
```

7. Rewrite the OnCancel button to check for changes and to call the
   UpdateDepartment function if the user wants to save their functions.
   Because UpdateDepartment starts a transaction, you also want to issue a
   call to the Abort function, which rolls the transaction back:

```
LRESULT OnCancel(WORD wNotifyCode, WORD wID, HWND hWndCtl,
BOOL& bHandled)
{
    if (m_bChangesMade) {
        if (MessageBox(
            "Changes were made. Do you wish to save?",
            "Save Changes?", MB_YESNO) == IDYES) {
            UpdateDepartment();
        }
    }
    m_pSet->m_session.Abort();    //Rollback the transaction
    EndDialog(wID);       //Close the dialog box
    exit(0);              //End this program
    return 0;
}
```

That's all it takes to add transaction support to your OLE DB program.

Transactions can affect open rowsets differently from database to database.
Check with your DBA or your database documentation to see exactly how
starting and stopping transactions affects any open cursors.

The program listing for OLE DB is on the CD-ROM under OLEDB
DepartmentATLb.

Summary

In this chapter, you learned how to make a Windows application using ATL instead
of MFC. This can be important, especially because ATL applications tend to be
smaller and run more quickly than corresponding MFC applications. To recap:

◆ Wizards are the easiest way to develop ATL applications. You can use ATL wizards to create the ATL shell and to add OLE DB consumers and dialog boxes to your application.

◆ As with MFC, ATL applications are developed using controls that fire off events. These events can be coded inside the dialog box module.

◆ Transactions can be added using ATL. These transactions rely on the `StartTransaction`, the `Commit`, and the `Abort` functions to begin a transaction, commit a transaction, and roll back a transaction.

Chapter 10

Catching Errors

IN THIS CHAPTER

♦ Using FAILED and SUCCEEDED macros

♦ Examining the HRESULT

♦ Calling the database for error messages

♦ Retrieving the error code and SQLState from the database

ONE OF THE MOST COMPLEX difficulties when coding any database program is error checking. OLE DB is particularly complex in this regard. This chapter shows how you can check the results of an operation in one or more ways to really figure out what error has occurred.

 Examples of the code contained in this chapter can be found in the OLEDBErrorChecking.h file in the OLEDBErrorChecking directory on the CD-ROM that accompanies this book.

Error Trapping and Recovery

Error trapping is probably the most overlooked, yet one of the most necessary, components of database development. It's good to check the error codes *every time* you access your database. If an error occurs and you don't detect it, you may start issuing other commands to your database that would adversely affect the integrity of its data.

The following steps should be taken for *every* database operation:

1. Make the database function call.

2. Evaluate the success or failure of that call.

3. Take action if an error occurs.

By performing these steps, you can be more confident that your database program is functioning correctly, and you run less risk of corrupting the database or the database data.

 You should check for database errors after *every* database call. If you don't, you could have database errors that occur during runtime that, if left unchecked, could corrupt your database without notifying the user or developer.

Although it's a lot of work to check for database errors every time you call a database function, you can write functions or ancestor routines that can automatically or with little effort handle all your database problems. This chapter shows how several of those routines should look and how, with little effort, you can call these routines after your database call.

Examining the HRESULT

All OLE DB calls return an HRESULT variable. HRESULT is a long integer that contains an error return value. It is important to check the HRESULT of every OLE DB database routine. Visual C++ contains macros that can help determine if an error occurred. In addition, this section shows you how to check for a bad HRESULT code.

Using S_OK, FAILED, and SUCCEEDED

In previous chapters, you have already seen some OLE DB error checking. The following constructs can be used to detect errors:

- S_OK is an HRESULT constant that describes a zero return code. If anything causes your function to fail, S_OK is not true. The following code shows how S_OK can detect a failed function.

```
HRESULT hr = m_pSet->MoveNext();
if (hr != S_OK) {
    //Error handling goes here
}
```

- Sometimes a failed function is not necessarily an error. For instance, in the preceding example, the MoveNext function can fail because of a database bug, or it can fail simply if there are no more records to scroll through in a rowset. The FAILED macro ignores database warnings and is flagged only if a serious error has occurred.

The following code shows a combination of S_OK and FAILED processing:

```
HRESULT hr = m_pSet->MoveNext();
if (SUCCEEDED(hr)) {
    if (hr != S_OK) {      //EOF
        //Call a function to display a message in the status
line
        DisplayStatus("Last record reached.");
        hr = m_pSet->MoveLast();    //Move to last record
    }
}
//No move has been successful yet
if (FAILED(hr)) {
    //Add a new record, since no records were found
    AddRecord();
    //Display a error message
    DisplayError("No records found. Adding new record");
    //Clear the status area of the window
    DisplayStatus("No records found.");
}
```

◆ The SUCCEEDED macro is the exact opposite of the FAILED macro. The SUCCEEDED macro returns TRUE if no serious errors were issued during execution.

Often, the SUCCEEDED macro is used in an _ASSERTE (for debugging only) or the assert statement (during both debugging and runtime). The following line of code aborts the program if a database call fails when the -DEBUG is defined:

```
_ASSERTE(SUCCEEDED(hr));
```

Deciphering the HRESULT

The FAILED and SUCCEEDED macros are useful in determining that an error has occurred. However, when a database error occurs, you usually not only want to be able to detect the error, but you also want information about what error occurred.

UNDERSTANDING THE HRESULT

The HRESULT is a 32-bit (8 hex digits) code that is returned from all OLE DB calls. The bit layout is as follows:

◆ The 31st (last) bit contains a 1 for a severe error or a 0 for a nonsevere error. The FAILED and SUCCEEDED macros test this bit to see if an OLE DB call has succeeded or failed.

♦ The next four bits (28–30) are not often used. They are reserved for the NT facility codes that correspond to the second severity bit, the NT C code, and the mapped NT status variable.

♦ The 27th bit is used internally by Visual C++ to indicate that a status error is not an error code but rather a message ID used for a display string.

♦ The next 10 bits (bits 16–26) are used for a facility code that groups the errors into the facility where they occur. Bit 11 is used to indicate the system service responsible for the error.

♦ The final 16 bytes (bits 0–15) are used for an error code.

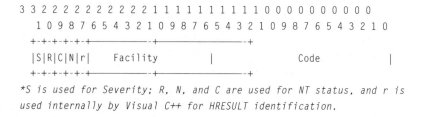

*S is used for Severity; R, N, and C are used for NT status, and r is used internally by Visual C++ for HRESULT identification.

Using the preceding code, you can decode any HRESULT. For example, a hex value of 0x80040E01 is returned if you try to put too many rows onto a rowset in C++. You can decode this using the following steps:

1. Decode the severity. The bit representation of 8 is 1000. Therefore, you know that you have a severe error, but that none of the NT facility codes were set.

2. Decode the facility. The three bytes following the 8 are 004, which translates into a bit representation of 000000000100. You can tell from this that the internal r code is set to zero, and the facility code is 4.

3. Decode the code. The last four bytes of the HRESULT are 0E01, or 3585 in decimal. These bytes represent the error code generated by the database.

It's much easier to use macros rather than bit masks to extract information from the HRESULT. Along with SUCCEEDED and FAILED, which test the severity, you can also use HRESULT_SEVERITY to return the severity, HRESULT_FACILITY to return the facility, and HRESULT_CODE to return the code. These three macros enable you to break down the error code you received from your OLE DB call.

DECODING THE HRESULT WITH A FUNCTION

Although it is possible to decipher the HRESULT code using bits, you probably would rather use a list of HRESULT error codes, which gives you a specific error for your database. The HRESULT code can be deciphered using the error codes found in the OLEDBERR.H header file and a switch statement.

Listing 10-1 shows a function that can be used to decipher error codes. The code is simple but long, due to the numerous HRESULT error codes that can be returned from an OLE DB driver.

 Because of its length, most of the code in Listing 10-1 has been deleted from this text. However, the code is present on the CD-ROM, and all HRESULT error codes that are used to develop this function can be found in Appendix A.

Listing 10-1: HRESULT Error Deciphering Function

```
//Added by Chuck Wood for HRESULT error support
#include <oledberr.h>

void CDepartment::GetHRESULTMessage(HRESULT hr)
{
    char msg[1024];
    strcpy(msg, "");
    sprintf(msg, "%s\n\nHRESULT was 0x%X", msg, hr);
    switch (hr) {
    case DB_E_ABORTLIMITREACHED :
        strcat(msg, "\n\nYour execution was aborted because a
resource limit has been reached. No results are returned when this
error occurs.");
        break;
    case DB_E_ALREADYINITIALIZED :
        strcat(msg, "\n\nYou tried to initialize a data source that
has already been initialized.");
        break;
    case DB_E_BADACCESSORFLAGS :
        strcat(msg, "\n\nInvalid accessor flags");
        break;
//    case DB_E_BADID :
//        DB_E_BADID is deprecated.
//        Use DB_E_BADTABLEID instead.
//        break;
    case DB_E_BADTABLEID :
        strcat(msg, "\n\nInvalid table ID");
        break;
//. . .
//The rest of the function follows this pattern using the
//error codes found in Appendix A
//. . .
#if(OLEDBVER >= 0x0250)
```

```
        //Errors if OLE DB version is greater than 2.5
        case DB_E_BADREGIONHANDLE :
            strcat(msg, "\n\nInvalid region handle");
            break;
        case DB_E_CANNOTFREE :
            strcat(msg, "\n\nOwnership of this tree has been given to
the provider. You cannot free the tree.");
            break;
        case DB_E_COSTLIMIT :
            strcat(msg, "\n\nUnable to find a query plan within the
given cost limit");
            break;
        case DB_E_GOALREJECTED :
            strcat(msg, "\n\nNo nonzero weights specified for any goals
supported, so goal was rejected; current goal was not changed.");
            break;
        case DB_E_INVALIDTRANSITION :
            strcat(msg, "\n\nA transition from ALL* to MOVE* or EXTEND*
was specified.");
            break;
        case DB_E_LIMITREJECTED :
            strcat(msg, "\n\nSome cost limits were rejected.");
            break;
        case DB_E_NONCONTIGUOUSRANGE :
            strcat(msg, "\n\nThe specified set of rows was not
contiguous to or overlapping the rows in the specified watch
region.");
            break;
        case DB_S_ERRORSINTREE :
            strcat(msg, "\n\nErrors found in validating tree.");
            break;
        case DB_S_GOALCHANGED :
            strcat(msg, "\n\nSpecified weight was not supported or
exceeded the supported limit and was set to 0 or the supported
limit.");
            break;
        case DB_S_TOOMANYCHANGES :
            strcat(msg, "\n\nThe provider was unable to keep track of
all the changes. You must refetch the data associated with the watch
region using another method.");
            break;
#endif    //OLEDBVER >= 0x0250
        default :
            strcat(msg, "\n\nHRESULT returned an unknown error.");
            break;
```

```
    }
    ::MessageBox(NULL, msg, "An error has occurred", MB_OK);
}
```

The FAILED macro used in conjunction with the GetHRESULTMessage function can access the functions listed so far in this chapter:

```
HRESULT hr = m_pSet->MoveNext();
if (FAILED(hresult)) {
    GetHRESULTMessage(hresult);
}
```

Listing 10-1 returns the error code shown in Figure 10-1.

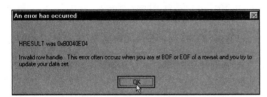

Figure 10-1: Error messages can be deciphered using the HRESULT return code.

For a description of HRESULT error codes, see Appendix A.

Retrieving Errors from the Database

Not only can you examine the database for OLE DB errors, but also most modern databases keep track of error messages and enable a program to access recent errors made on the database. This section shows you how to retrieve a single error or multiple errors from a database.

The GetErrorInfo Function and the IErrorInfo Interface

The HRESULT return value of the GetErrorInfo function contains either an S_OK value indicating that an error was retrieved, or an S_FALSE value indicating that no errors were retrieved. The two parameters of the GetErrorInfo function are the number of the error (starting with zero) and the pointer to an IErrorInfo class.

Windows is a multithreaded operating system. This means that Windows can run multiple programs at one time, each Windows program running on a specific "thread." When an error occurs in an OLE DB object, an internal call to a SetErrorInfo function is made. The SetErrorInfo function places an IErrorInfo error object containing error information on a queue that exists only for the logical thread. This message sits on the error queue of the thread, waiting for a call to a GetErrorInfo function to return the error object.

The IErrorInfo interface is a structure that enables you to retrieve error information directly from the database. You can retrieve an IErrorInfo interface variable by using the GetErrorInfo function:

```
IErrorInfo *pErrorInfo;
HRESULT hr = GetErrorInfo(0, &pErrorInfo);
```

Table 10-1 lists the functions available to the IErrorInfo class.

TABLE 10-1 IERRORINFO FUNCTIONS

Function	Description
GetDescription (BSTR *pbstrDescription)	Stores the description of the error in the pbstrDescription string.
GetGUID(GUID *pguid)	Stores the GUID of the interface that defined the error in the pguid variable.
GetHelpContext (DWORD *pdwHelpContext)	Stores the Help context ID for the error in the DWORD pointer.
GetHelpFile(BSTR *pbstrHelpFile)	Stores the path of the Help file that describes the error in the pbstrHelpFile string.
GetSource (BSTR *pbstrSource)	Stores the ProgID of the component that generated the error, such as "ODBC *driver-name*" in the pbstrSource string.
Release( )	Releases the error message from the thread error queue.

Of these functions, the GetDescription function is the most often used because the GetDescription function returns the error message of the error that occurred. The Release function is also used often because the error stays in the thread error queue until the thread ends or until a Release function is called.

IErrorInfo processing looks something like the following code:

```
char msg[1024];
IErrorInfo *pErrorInfo = NULL;
BSTR pErrorDesc = NULL;
if (SUCCEEDED(GetErrorInfo(0, &pErrorInfo))) {
    //Get the error description
    if (SUCCEEDED(pErrorInfo->GetDescription(&pErrorDesc))) {
        //Convert error description to single-width character
        sprintf(msg, "%s\n\n%S", msg, pErrorDesc);
        //Clean up
        SysFreeString(pErrorDesc);
    }
    else {
        strcat(msg, "Could not find the error description");
    }
    pErrorInfo->Release();
}
else {
    strcat(msg, "Could not retrieve error information");
}
::MessageBox(NULL, msg, "An error has occurred", MB_OK);
```

TIP The GetDescription function stores the error message in a BSTR string. A BSTR string uses a double-byte *Unicode* string representation rather than a single-byte ASCII string representation. Unicode is needed when programming internationally in languages such as Chinese, Japanese, and Korean.

ASCII can be used for most users in the United States and Europe, and most string functions inherited from C or C++ require the ASCII character set rather than the Unicode character set. I've found one of the easiest ways to convert from Unicode to ASCII is to use the sprintf function, which is used to create a formatted string. The %S (Capital S) format specifier type is used in Visual C++ to indicate a double-byte character string. The following code:

```
BSTR pErrorDescription;
char message[512];
sprintf(message, "%S", pErrorDescription);
```

can be used to convert a Unicode error message into an ASCII string.

To test this code, replace the data source property in your OLE DB consumer (Department.h) with a database that does not exist:

```
//Replaced the classes database with a database that was not there
dbinit.AddProperty(DBPROP_INIT_DATASOURCE,
    OLESTR("C:\\My Documents\\Visual C++\\NotThere.mdb"));
```

When you try to open your database, your error trapping routine displays the error message shown in Figure 10-2.

Figure 10-2: A single error message can result if an error occurs while connecting to the database.

The message shown in Figure 10-2 can be displayed using the following GetSingleError function:

```
static void GetSingleError()
{
    char msg[1024];
    strcpy (msg, "");
    IErrorInfo *pErrorInfo = NULL;
    BSTR pErrorDescription = NULL;
    if (SUCCEEDED(GetErrorInfo(0, &pErrorInfo))) {
        //Get the error description
        if (SUCCEEDED(pErrorInfo->GetDescription(
                            &pErrorDescription))) {
//Convert error description to single-width character
            sprintf(msg, "%s\n\n%S", msg, pErrorDescription);
            //Clean up
            SysFreeString(pErrorDescription);
        }
        else {
            strcat(msg,"Could not find the error description");
        }
        pErrorInfo->Release();
    }
    else {
        strcat(msg, "Could not retrieve error information");
    }
```

```
    ::MessageBox(NULL, msg, "An error has occurred", MB_OK);
}
```

Retrieving Multiple Errors

After a database error has been detected, you can receive multiple errors from a single database operation. For instance, say you wrote the following Department table trigger in MS SQL Server:

```
Create Trigger DELETEDEPARTMENT
On DEPARTMENT
For DELETE
As
DECLARE @count tinyint,
        @errors tinyint
SET @errors = 0
SELECT @count = COUNT(*)
FROM Instructor e INNER JOIN deleted d ON e.DepartmentCode =
d.DepartmentCode
IF (@count > 0)
BEGIN
    RAISERROR ('Instructor has related records so this department
cannot be deleted', 16, 1)
    SET @errors = @errors + 1
END
SELECT @count = COUNT(*)
FROM Class c INNER JOIN deleted d ON c.DepartmentCode =
d.DepartmentCode
IF (@count > 0)
BEGIN
    RAISERROR ('Class has related records so this department cannot
be deleted', 16, 1)
    SET @errors = @errors + 1
END
IF (@errors > 0)
    ROLLBACK TRANSACTION
```

With certain versions of SQL Server, you may need to replace the instances of SET in the preceding code with SELECT in order to get the stored procedure to compile.

The trigger in the preceding code checks for relationships between Department and Instructor and/or Class before enabling the deletion of the Department row. However, there is a possibility of a Department row's having both related Instructor rows and related Class rows. If this happens, you'll notice that the trigger generates two different errors.

If you only trap single errors or check the HRESULT, you simply get a message saying that errors occurred, as shown in Figure 10-3. This is because you have several error messages and need to check all of them. When multiple errors occur, you receive a message simply that errors have occurred.

Figure 10-3: If multiple errors occur after a database command, you simply receive an "Errors occurred" message if you retrieve a single database error.

Multiple errors can be retrieved from a database after the database connection has been established. To do so, you need to capture an IUnknown interface used for the OLE DB Command or Table COM module, and you need to use the CDBErrorInfo class.

The CDBErrorInfo class consists of functions you can use to retrieve database error information. The main function you will use is the GetErrorRecords function that returns information about the current error records. You can write an error routine using the following steps:

1. Define a CDBErrorInfo class variable, and use the IUnknown interface and the IID_ICommandPrepare constant variable to retrieve the number of database errors currently stored in the current database connection. This enables you to access OLE DB interface directly rather than through ATL:

```
CDBErrorInfo errInfo;
ULONG ulRecords = 0;
HRESULT hr =
    errInfo.GetErrorRecords(m_pSet->m_spCommand,
            IID_ICommandPrepare, &ulRecords);
```

2. Once you've retrieved the number of errors, you need to retrieve the user default LCID (Locale Identifier). This enables the provider to give the error message in the correct language for the user (if multiple languages are supported). (On single-user machines, the user default LCID is the same as

the system default LCID.) This can be done using the
GetUserDefaultLCID function:

```
LCID lcid = GetUserDefaultLCID();
```

3. Now you're ready to start scrolling through errors. Use a loop to scroll through the records:

```
for (ULONG loop = 0; loop < ulRecords; loop ++) {
```

4. Inside each loop, use the CDBErrorInfo.GetErrorInfo function (different from the global GetErrorInfo function) to retrieve each error into a IErrorInfo variable:

```
IErrorInfo *pErrorInfo;
hr = errInfo.GetErrorInfo(loop, lcid, &pErrorInfo);
```

5. After getting each error inside the loop, retrieve the error description using the GetDescription function and convert it to a string, as was done before:

```
BSTR pErrorDescription;
char holder[512];
pErrorInfo -> GetDescription(&pErrorDescription);
//Convert error description to single-width character
sprintf(holder, "\n\n%S", pErrorDescription);
```

The full function (GetDBErrors) follows:

```
void GetDBErrors(CComPtr<IUnknown> m_spUnk, char *msg)
{
    CDBErrorInfo errInfo;
    IErrorInfo *pErrorInfo = NULL;
    BSTR pErrorDescription = NULL;
    ULONG ulRecords = 0;
    HRESULT hr =
        errInfo.GetErrorRecords(m_spUnk,
            IID_ICommandPrepare, &ulRecords);
    if (FAILED(hr) || hr == S_FALSE || ulRecords == 0) {
        //The error info object could not be retrieved
        strcat(msg,
            "\n\nCould not retrieve an error info object.");
        strcat(msg, "\nTherefore, additional error \
information is not available.");
    }
    else {
      //Error info object was retrieved successfully
        LCID lcid = GetUserDefaultLCID();
```

```
        for (ULONG loop = 0; loop < ulRecords; loop ++) {
    //Get the error information from the source
            hr = errInfo.GetErrorInfo(loop,
                            lcid, &pErrorInfo);
            if (FAILED(hr)) {
                continue;
            }
    //Get the error description
            hr = pErrorInfo->GetDescription(&pErrorDescription);
    //Convert error description to single-width character
            sprintf(msg, "%s\n\n%S",
                msg, pErrorDescription);
    //Clean up
            SysFreeString(pErrorDescription);
            pErrorInfo->Release();
        }
    }
    ::MessageBox(NULL, msg,
        "An error has occurred", MB_OK);
}
```

To call the GetDBErrors function defined in the preceding code, simply pass it the m_spCommand variable and a string large enough to hold the messages:

```
GetDBErrors(m_pSet->m_spCommand, msg);
```

The function returns all the errors currently allocated to a database connection, as shown in Figure 10-4.

Figure 10-4: OLE DB enables the detection of multiple errors.

Checking the SQLState and Error Codes

In addition to proprietary error codes, most databases also support SQLState codes. SQLState is a five-character string defined by the ANSI SQL standard. The SQLState guideline defines prefixes for error conditions and some SQLStates for common errors. OLEDB supports SQLState codes as well as proprietary error codes.

To retrieve the error code and the SQLState code, perform the following steps:

1. Use the CDBErrorInfo.GetCustomErrorObject function to retrieve an ISQLErrorInfo interface for, in this case, the first error (error 0). The ISQLErrorInfo interface will be used to retrieve the error codes:

```
CDBErrorInfo errInfo;
errInfo.GetCustomErrorObject(0,
                             IID_ISQLErrorInfo,
                             (IUnknown**) &spSQLErrorInfo);
```

 CDBErrorInfo internally makes a call to the IErrorRecords interface. This interface is locked when CDBErrorInfo first calls it and cannot be called again. Consequently, you should never have more than one CDBErrorInfo class instantiated at one time.

2. After the ISQLErrorInfo interface has been retrieved, you can use the GetSQLInfo function to retrieve the error codes and the SQLState:

```
BSTR bstrSQLState = NULL;    //SQLState that's returned
LONG errorCode;              //SQL Code that's returned
//Retrieve the error code and SQLState
spSQLErrorInfo->GetSQLInfo(&bstrSQLState, &errorCode);
```

3. Next, convert the error codes to a message using the sprintf function and display the error message:

```
char msg[500];
//Form an error message
sprintf(msg,
        "\n\nSQLState is %S\nError code is %ld",
        bstrSQLState, errorCode);
::MessageBox(NULL, msg,
        "An error has occurred", MB_OK);
```

All in all, retrieving the error codes is a pretty simple procedure. The preceding three steps, with some additional error checking for successful error retrieval, can be viewed in the following GetSQLCodes function:

```
void CDBDialog::GetSQLCodes()
{
    char msg[1024];
    CDBErrorInfo errInfo;
```

```
          //COM Error Interface to retrieve error codes
          CComPtr<ISQLErrorInfo> spSQLErrorInfo;
   //Get error codes for the first error—Error 0
      if (SUCCEEDED(errInfo.GetCustomErrorObject(0,
                      IID_ISQLErrorInfo,
                      (IUnknown**) &spSQLErrorInfo))) {
          BSTR bstrSQLState = NULL;    //SQLState that's returned
          LONG errorCode;            //SQL Code that's returned
          char SQLState[100];     //Buffer for error message
      //Retrieve the error code and SQLState
          if (SUCCEEDED(spSQLErrorInfo->GetSQLInfo(
                  &bstrSQLState, &errorCode))) {
          //Form an error message
              sprintf(SQLState,
                      "\n\nSQLState is %S\nError code is %ld",
                      bstrSQLState, errorCode);
          //Concatenate the error message to the existing message
              strcat(msg, SQLState);
              SysFreeString(bstrSQLState); //Clean up
          }
          else {
              strcat(msg,
                  "\n\nCould not get SQL info.");
          }
      }
      else {      //Something went wrong
          strcat(msg,
                  "\n\nCould not get error or SQLState code.");
      }
      ::MessageBox(NULL, msg,
          "An error has occurred", MB_OK);
}
```

For a duplicate record in Microsoft Access, the GetSQLCodes function returns both an error code and an SQLState code as shown in Figure 10-5.

Figure 10-5: OLE DB can retrieve the proprietary SQL code and the SQLState code from an error message.

For a table that shows common SQLState codes and a method to debug
SQLState codes, see Appendix A.

Checking for Error Capability

The OLE DB standard supports database error messages, but it's not a requirement
for all OLE DB databases to provide error messages. You can check for database
error capabilities by using the QueryInterface method in conjunction with the
SUCCEEDED macro:

```
CComPtr<ISupportErrorInfo> spSupportErrorInfo;
if (SUCCEEDED(
    m_pSet->m_spCommand->QueryInterface(
            IID_ISupportErrorInfo,
            (void **) &spSupportErrorInfo))) {
    //Database supports error information
}
```

The preceding code checks to see if errors are supported and populates an
ISupportErrorInfo interface. The ISupportErrorInfo interface is important because
even though a database supports error information, it doesn't necessarily support
error messaging. Error messaging is part of extended error information. You can
use the `ISupportErrorInfo.InterfaceSupportsErrorInfo` function to test for
extended error messaging:

```
if (SUCCEEDED(pSupportErrorInfo->
        InterfaceSupportsErrorInfo(
            m_pSet->GetIID())))){
    //Extended error information is supported.
}
```

The following function returns a TRUE if database error messaging is supported
and a FALSE if it is not:

```
BOOL DBErrorsAreSupported(CComPtr<IUnknown> m_spUnk)
{
    CComPtr<ISupportErrorInfo> spSupportErrorInfo;
    if (SUCCEEDED(
        m_spUnk->QueryInterface(IID_ISupportErrorInfo,
        (void **) &spSupportErrorInfo))) {
        if (SUCCEEDED(
```

```
                    spSupportErrorInfo->InterfaceSupportsErrorInfo(
                                IID_ICommandPrepare))){
                    return TRUE;
            }
        }
    return FALSE;
}
```

Bringing It All Together

Single methods of error decoding fail at times. For instance, your program may not anticipate a new HRESULT code, or a database vendor may not have adequately defined an error message. It should be the goal of every developer to retrieve as much error information as possible when a runtime error occurs so debugging won't be so difficult. This can be accomplished by using a combination of error-capturing techniques so that you can retrieve as much information as possible when debugging your program.

Unfortunately, as shown by this chapter, error retrieval can be somewhat complicated. Error retrieval using OLE DB requires knowledge of Visual C++ as well as of COM, OLE DB, and the database itself. For enterprise development where several developers, each with different skill levels, are all developing using Visual C++, a standard set of error functions would make the development process much easier.

The following `DisplayAllErrors` function shows how you can call these functions that were written in this section when an error occurs:

```
void DisplayAllErrors(CComPtr<IUnknown> m_spUnk,
    char *msg = NULL,
    HRESULT hresult = S_OK,
    char *strFunction = NULL) {
    //Allow 1 k for the error message
    char message[1024];
    if (msg) {
        strcpy(message, msg);
    }
    else {
        strcpy(message, "");
    }
    if (strFunction) {      //Check for function equal to null
        //Function was passed, so see what function it was
        strcat(message, " in the ");
```

```
        strcat(message, strFunction);
        strcat(message, " function ");
    }
    if (FAILED(hresult)) {
        sprintf(message,
                "%s\n\nHRESULT was 0x%X",message, hresult);
        GetHRESULTMessage(hresult, message);
        strcat(message, holdmessage);
    }
    if (DBErrorsAreSupported()) {
        if (m_spUnk) {      //Connection has been successful
            GetMultipleErrors(message);
        }
        else {      //Connection has not yet been established
            GetSingleError(message);
        }
    }
    else {
        strcat(message,
            "/n/nUnable to retrieve database errors.");
    }
    //Finally, display the error message
    ::MessageBox(NULL, msg,
        "An error has occurred", MB_OK);
}
```

For simplicity, I used a 1K buffer [1024 bytes] to hold the error message. While this works for most error messages, you should make sure that your error buffering does not cause a memory overrun.

In each of the functions that displays an error (GetSingleError, Get Multiple-Errors, GetHRESULTMessage, and GetSQLCodes), perform the following steps:

1. Add a `msg` string pointer parameter to each display function. This will be used to build onto any existing error message.

2. Remove the `strcpy(msg, "");` command, because you want to build on an error message rather than initialize it.

3. Remove the `::MessageBox` command.

Now each function that used to *display* an error helps *build* an error instead. The message is displayed by the `DisplayError` function. A new `GetSingleError` function follows that adds to a `msg` string parameter:

```
void CDBDialog::GetSingleError(char *msg)
{
    IErrorInfo *pErrorInfo = NULL;
    BSTR pErrorDescription = NULL;
    HRESULT hr = GetErrorInfo(0, &pErrorInfo);
    if (FAILED(hr)) {
        strcat(msg, "Error not discernable from database");
    }
    else {
        //Get the error description
        pErrorInfo->GetDescription(&pErrorDescription);
    //Convert error description to single-width character
        char holder[512];
        sprintf(holder, "\n\n%S", pErrorDescription);
        //Concatenate error message
        strcat(msg, holder);
        //Concatenate error codes
        CDBErrorInfo c;
        GetSQLCodes(msg, &c);
        //Clean up
        SysFreeString(pErrorDescription);
        pErrorInfo->Release();
    }
}
```

By combining all the error routines into one routine, you make it easy to check for errors. For instance, look at the error processing required for the `SaveDepartment` function:

```
HRESULT CDBDialog::SaveDepartment()
{
    UpdateData(TRUE);     //Read from screen
    HRESULT hr;
    if (m_bAddingRecord) {
        hr = m_pSet->Insert();     //Insert New row
    }
    else {
        hr = m_pSet->SetData();     //Update current row
    }
    if (FAILED(hr)) {
        DisplayError("Update Failed", hr, "SaveDepartment");
```

```
    }
    else {
        m_bAddingRecord = FALSE;
    }
    return hr;
}
```

As you can see by the preceding code, the `DisplayError` function is called whenever an `Insert` or `SetData` function is called. However, as shown by the display in Figure 10-6, a wealth of information is provided when one attempts to add a duplicate key to the database.

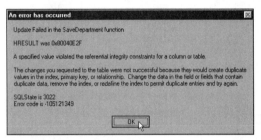

Figure 10-6: It should be the goal of every developer to display as much error information as possible when an error occurs.

 TIP Many developers put their error checking in as the last activity during development. I've tried writing code that way, and it's crazy. Try putting error detection code in your programs right away, and when — not if — a database error occurs, you'll be able to get an idea of your program bug right away rather than further down the road.

Summary

Error checking is one of the most important single activities a programmer can perform. Without error checking, programming errors can run unchecked, often causing bad relations with the user communit
y or even corrupting a database. This chapter provided a complete discussion of OLE DB error checking:

◆ Error trapping can be accomplished using the `S_OK` constant and the `FAILED` and `SUCCEEDED` macros.

◆ An HRESULT variable is returned for every SQL error. These HRESULT variables can be decoded using defined constants from the oledberr.h header file.

◆ You can retrieve error codes, SQLStates, and actual error messages from databases, if these databases support the ISupportErrorInfo interface.

◆ Error checking is best done throughout development, and it's easiest when some predefined error routines, such as the ones shown in this chapter, are already built.

Chapter 11

Managing Rowsets

IN THIS CHAPTER

- ◆ Using the CCommand and CTable classes
- ◆ Retrieving column name, type, and size from a rowset
- ◆ Using OLE DB bookmarks
- ◆ Understanding OLE DB properties
- ◆ Implementing OLE DB asynchronous access

SO FAR, WE'VE DISCUSSED how to implement OLE DB databases inside a Visual C++ project. The techniques discussed in previous chapters should meet almost all of your database needs. However, more control over the OLE DB rowset is required in a small percentage of development projects. This chapter delves into advanced features that can return column and row information. In addition, this chapter shows how to use OLE DB bookmarks to save positions and properties, and how to implement asynchronous database access.

This chapter uses MFC on occasion because MFC makes it easy to build a user interface for the examples.

Commands versus Tables

You create rowsets using an Accessor. These Accessors can be derived from either the CCommand or CTable structure. These two ATL structures are extremely similar. Both are inherited from the CAccessorRowset class. There are few differences between the two:

- ◆ The CTable class takes a table name as its argument when opening a rowset:

```
CTable<CAccessor<CRowDefinitionTableAccessor> table;
table.Open(m_session, _T("Department"), &propset);
```

♦ By contrast, the CCommand class takes an SQL command to open a rowset:

```
char sql[] =
"SELECT DepartmentCode, DepartmentName FROM Department";
CCommand<CAccessor<CRowDefinitionCommandAccessor> command;
command.Open(m_session, sql, &propset);
```

A CTable class should be used if every row and column from a view or a table is needed to populate a rowset. The CTable class uses less overhead and typically operates more efficiently than the CCommand class. However, the CCommand class is much more flexible and probably is used most of the time when doing OLE DB development.

An example of CTable is in the OLEDBMFCMisc directory on the CD-ROM that accompanies this book.

Using Bookmarks

With older record-handling interfaces, such as DAO, RDO, and ODBC, records were navigated using record number. However, when a record was deleted, it was no longer possible to navigate to that record. By using absolute record positions in a recordset, many programs were subject to errors at runtime. At this time, Microsoft recommended using *bookmarks* rather than absolute record positions to mark a record and to return to a record. A bookmark is a pointer that uniquely identifies a record. When you navigated through a recordset, because you couldn't always rely on the absolute position of a record, bookmarks were the only reliable way to keep track of the position of a record. However, bookmarks in ODBC and DAO are somewhat complicated to use.

OLE DB did away with absolute position support in their ATL OLE DB libraries. Bookmarks in OLE DB are extremely simple, yet strangely they are sparsely documented in the MSDN. This section delves into OLE DB bookmarks and describes when and how to use them.

Understanding OLE DB Bookmarks

Although most developers don't see it, every row that is returned contains one more column than is defined in the column map. Say you defined a column map in your OLE DB Accessor with two variables declared:

```
char Column1[50];
char Column2[50];
BEGIN_COLUMN_MAP(CRowDefinition)
    COLUMN_ENTRY_TYPE(1, DBTYPE_STR, Column1)
    COLUMN_ENTRY_TYPE(2, DBTYPE_STR, Column2)
END_COLUMN_MAP()
```

In actuality, three columns (columns 0–2) are returned to you. The zero column is the bookmark, as shown in Figure 11-1.

Bookmark	Column 1	Column 2

Figure 11-1: Bookmarks are returned with every row retrieved in an OLE DB database.

Unlike other database access techniques, every row in an OLE DB data source has a bookmark. To retrieve that row, all you need to do is assign that bookmark to a local CBookmark variable.

Setting Row Position with Bookmarks

It's relatively easy to use bookmarks in a database program. You just have to perform the following steps:

1. As mentioned previously, the bookmark is always the first column retrieved by OLE DB for each row. However, you have to declare a bookmark variable to hold your bookmark when you get a new row from your rowset. To do so, you must declare a CBookmark variable and add a BOOKMARK_ENTRY macro call in your column map in your Accessor:

```
class CRowDefinition
{
public:
    CRowDefinition()
    {
        memset( (void*)this, 0, sizeof(*this) );
    };
```

```
        // Added by Chuck Wood for bookmarks
        CBookmark<4> m_RowsetBookmark;
        char m_DepartmentCode[5];
        char m_DepartmentName[51];
BEGIN_COLUMN_MAP(CRowDefinition)
        // Added by Chuck Wood for bookmarks
        BOOKMARK_ENTRY(m_RowsetBookmark)
        COLUMN_ENTRY_TYPE(1, DBTYPE_STR, m_DepartmentCode)
        COLUMN_ENTRY_TYPE(2, DBTYPE_STR, m_DepartmentName)
END_COLUMN_MAP()
};
```

The CBookmark class is a template that takes the size of the bookmark (in number of bytes) as an argument. OLE DB for ODBC data sources uses 4 bytes for each bookmark. A declaration of CBookmark<4> declares a bookmark with 4 bytes to hold the bookmark data. If you use zero as an argument (CBookmark<0>), the bookmark is dynamically allocated, and its size adjusts as needed. If you're not using OLE DB for ODBC, you need to use zero as an argument or check with your OLE DB database to see the size returned for your bookmarks.

2. Before you open the rowset, you must tell the provider that you need to set the DBPROP_BOOKMARKS property to TRUE in your property set. Although space is reserved for a bookmark, the bookmark is not actually retrieved unless you specify the DBPROP_BOOKMARKS property:

```
class COLEDBMFCMiscSet : public
CTable<CAccessor<CRowDefinition>, CRowset >
{
public:
    ULONG m_lRecordInAccessor;
    HRESULT MoveNext();
    void DisplayColumnInfo();
    char *getType(DBTYPE wType, char* strType);
    HRESULT Open()
    {
        CDataSource db;
        CSession    session;
        HRESULT         hr;
```

```
        m_lRecordInAccessor = 0;
        CDBPropSet    dbinit(DBPROPSET_DBINIT);

dbinit.AddProperty(DBPROP_AUTH_PERSIST_SENSITIVE_AUTHINFO,
false);
        dbinit.AddProperty(DBPROP_INIT_DATASOURCE,
"Classes");
        dbinit.AddProperty(DBPROP_INIT_PROMPT, (short)4);
        dbinit.AddProperty(DBPROP_INIT_LCID, (long)1033);
        hr = db.OpenWithServiceComponents("MSDASQL.1",
&dbinit);
        if (FAILED(hr))
            return hr;

        hr = session.Open(db);
        if (FAILED(hr))
            return hr;

        CDBPropSet    propset(DBPROPSET_ROWSET);
        propset.AddProperty(DBPROP_CANFETCHBACKWARDS, true);
        propset.AddProperty(DBPROP_IRowsetScroll, true);
        propset.AddProperty(DBPROP_IRowsetChange, true);
        propset.AddProperty(DBPROP_UPDATABILITY,
DBPROPVAL_UP_CHANGE | DBPROPVAL_UP_INSERT |
DBPROPVAL_UP_DELETE );
//Added by Chuck Wood for bookmark support
        propset.AddProperty(DBPROP_BOOKMARKS, true);
        hr = CTable<CAccessor<CRowDefinition>, CRowset>::
Open(session, "Department", &propset);
        if (FAILED(hr))
            return hr;

        return MoveNext();
    }
};
```

3. To store the value of a row so you can retrieve it later, you need to define a bookmark variable in your class definition:

```
protected:
    CBookmark<4> m_ViewBookmark;
```

4. Now you can use that bookmark and the = operator to assign the rowset's bookmark to your class variable bookmark:

```
void COLEDBMFCMiscView::OnRecordSetbookmark()
```

```
    {
        //Assign the current row's bookmark to the
        //view bookmark
        m_ViewBookmark = m_pSet->m_RowsetBookmark;
    }
```

5. Now, whenever you want to return to your previously set bookmark, you can simply use the MoveToBookmark function:

```
void COLEDBMFCMiscView::OnRecordGotobookmark()
{
    //Go to the view bookmark and update the window
    m_pSet->MoveToBookmark(m_ViewBookmark);
    UpdateData(FALSE);
}
```

As you can see, with the help of the Active Template Library (ATL), bookmarks are not that difficult to use.

Getting Row Position with the GetApproximatePosition Function

Using bookmarks and the GetApproximatePosition function, you can retrieve the row-positioning information. Just perform the following steps:

1. Declare ULONG variables to hold the current row count and the total row count:

```
ULONG ulCurrentRow;
ULONG ulTotalRows;
```

2. Next, use the GetApproximatePosition function to determine the current position of the row and the total number of rows in the rowset:

```
m_pSet->GetApproximatePosition(&m_pSet->m_RowsetBookmark,
    &ulCurrentRow, &ulTotalRows);
```

This position is approximate because, if any deletes have occurred, the current row and the total rows returned may be invalid.

The `OnRecordDisplayposition` function that follows shows how you can display the current record position using bookmarks:

```
void COLEDBMFCMiscView::OnRecordDisplayposition()
{
    //Display the current record
    ULONG ulCurrentRow;
    ULONG ulTotalRows;
    char strDisplay[50];        //String to display

    m_pSet->GetApproximatePosition(
        &m_pSet->m_RowsetBookmark,
        &ulCurrentRow, &ulTotalRows);
    sprintf(strDisplay, "You are at row %d out of %d total rows",
        ulCurrentRow, ulTotalRows);
    MessageBox(strDisplay, "Column Information");
}
```

 Some versions of the MSDN are incorrect regarding the type of the first parameter to GetApproximatePosition [(`CBookmark   bm`)]. The actual parameter is the *address* of the bookmark [(`CBookmark &bm`)].

The results of the `OnRecordDisplayposition` function can be viewed in Figure 11-2.

Figure 11-2: Using bookmarks, you can display column information.

Getting a Rowset's Column Information

It's always best to use a predefined command to retrieve your information. However, in a fast-changing environment where tables and views change often, you might need to dynamically adjust your rowset to handle the new table or view schema definition.

The GetColumnInfo function can retrieve a rowset's column information. The GetColumnInfo function retrieves column information about the rowset and stores the number of columns, an array of the column names, and a DBCOLUMNINFO structure containing the column information. This function is a member of CAccessorRowset so it is available in your classes derived from CTable and CCommand, which in turn are derived from CAccessorRowset:

```
ULONG ulColumns;                //Number of columns
DBCOLUMNINFO *pColumnInfo;      //Arrow of column information
LPOLESTR pColumnNames;          //Array of column names
GetColumnInfo(&ulColumns,&pColumnInfo, &pColumnNames);
```

The DBCOLUMNINFO structure is defined as follows:

```
typedef struct tagDBCOLUMNINFO {
  LPOLESTR       pwszName;
  ITypeInfo*     pTypeInfo;
  ULONG          iOrdinal;
  DBCOLUMNFLAGS  dwFlags;
  ULONG          ulColumnSize;
  DBTYPE         wType;
  BYTE           bPrecision;
  BYTE           bScale;
  DBID           columnid;
} DBCOLUMNINFO;
```

In the DBCOLUMNINFO structure, you can retrieve information about the rowset you just retrieved.

Getting a Column Type

To retrieve a column data type, you need to use the wType structure variable. For example, if you wanted to test if the first column in your rowset was a string, you could use the following code:

```
ULONG ulColumns;                //Number of columns
DBCOLUMNINFO *pColumnInfo;      //Arrow of column information
LPOLESTR pColumnNames;          //Array of column names
GetColumnInfo(&ulColumns,&pColumnInfo, &pColumnNames);
if (pColumnInfo[1].wType == DBTYPE_STR)
    ::MessageBox(NULL, "Type is a string array",
                "Column 1 Information", MB_OK);
```

TIP The pTypeInfo variable is reserved for future use, and current OLE DB providers are not supposed to place any values in this.

The following sections describe how to write a function to detect the column type.

RETRIEVING AGGREGATE COLUMN TYPES

Most column types are standard. For instance, DBTYPE_BOOL is a Boolean variable, while DBTYPE_I4 is a four-byte integer. However, you need to be aware of three types that can cause compares to be malformed:

◆ DBTYPE_ARRAY returns a SAFEARRAY pointer to your data type.

◆ DBTYPE_BYREF returns a pointer to your variable.

◆ DBTYPE_VECTOR returns a DBVECTOR structure containing a vector of your variables.

To test for these aggregate rowsets, you need to logically OR the aggregate type with the standard type. For instance, if the first column of your rowset were a string array, the following code would display a message box describing that:

```
ULONG ulColumns;              //Number of columns
DBCOLUMNINFO *pColumnInfo;    //Arrow of column information
LPOLESTR pColumnNames;        //Array of column names
GetColumnInfo(&ulColumns,&pColumnInfo, &pColumnNames);
if (pColumnInfo[1].wType == DBTYPE_STR|DBTYPE_ARRAY)
    ::MessageBox(NULL, "Type is a string array",
                 "Column 1 Information", MB_OK);
```

WRITING A COLUMN TYPE FUNCTION

The following function tests for all possible DBTYPEs that can be returned by the GetColumnInfo function:

```
char *COLEDBMFCMiscSet::getType(DBTYPE wType, char *strType) {
    strcpy(strType, "");
    //Test for type without reference, array, or vector
    switch (wType& ~(DBTYPE_BYREF | DBTYPE_ARRAY | DBTYPE_VECTOR)){
        case DBTYPE_BOOL:
            strcpy(strType, "boolean ");
            break;
        case DBTYPE_BSTR:
            strcpy(strType, "wide-character string (BSTR)");
```

```
            break;
        case DBTYPE_BYTES:
            strcpy(strType, "byte array ");
            break;
        case DBTYPE_CY:
            strcpy(strType, "currency ");
            break;
        case DBTYPE_DATE:
            strcpy(strType, "date ");
            break;
        case DBTYPE_DBDATE:
            strcpy(strType, "DBDATE ");
            break;
        case DBTYPE_DBTIME:
            strcpy(strType, "DBTIME ");
            break;
        case DBTYPE_DBTIMESTAMP:
            strcpy(strType, "DBTIMESTAMP ");
            break;
        case DBTYPE_DECIMAL:
            strcpy(strType, "Decimal ");
            break;
        case DBTYPE_ERROR:
            strcpy(strType, "32-bit error code ");
            break;
        case DBTYPE_FILETIME:
            strcpy(strType,
            "FILETIME (100-nanoseconds since 1/1/1601 ");
            break;
        case DBTYPE_GUID:
            strcpy(strType,
                    "GUID (globally unique identifier)");
            break;
        case DBTYPE_HCHAPTER:
            strcpy(strType, "4-byte chapter ");
            break;
        case DBTYPE_I1:
            strcpy(strType, "one-byte signed integer ");
            break;
        case DBTYPE_I2:
            strcpy(strType, "2-byte integer ");
            break;
        case DBTYPE_I4:
            strcpy(strType, "4-byte integer ");
```

```
            break;
        case DBTYPE_I8:
            strcpy(strType, "eight byte signed integer ");
            break;
        case DBTYPE_IDISPATCH:
            strcpy(strType,
                    "OLE IDispatch interface pointer ");
            break;
        case DBTYPE_IUNKNOWN:
            strcpy(strType,
                    " OLE IUnknown interface pointer  ");
            break;
        case DBTYPE_NULL:
            strcpy(strType, "null ");
            break;
        case DBTYPE_NUMERIC:
            strcpy(strType, "numeric ");
            break;
        case DBTYPE_PROPVARIANT:
            strcpy(strType, "PROPVARIANT ");
            break;
        case DBTYPE_R4:
            strcpy(strType,
                    "single-precision floating point ");
            break;
        case DBTYPE_R8:
            strcpy(strType,
                    "double-precision floating point ");
            break;
        case DBTYPE_RESERVED:
            strcpy(strType, "reserved (unknown)");
            break;
        case DBTYPE_STR:
            strcpy(strType, "char * ");
            break;
        case DBTYPE_UDT:
            strcpy(strType, "user-defined data type ");
            break;
        case DBTYPE_UI1:
            strcpy(strType, "one-byte unsigned integer ");
            break;
        case DBTYPE_UI2:
            strcpy(strType, "two-byte unsigned integer ");
            break;
```

```
            case DBTYPE_UI4:
                strcpy(strType, "four byte unsigned integer ");
                break;
            case DBTYPE_UI8:
                strcpy(strType, "eight byte unsigned integer ");
                break;
            case DBTYPE_VARIANT:
                strcpy(strType, "VARIANT ");
                break;
            case DBTYPE_VARNUMERIC:
                strcpy(strType, "DB_VARNUMERIC ");
                break;
            case DBTYPE_WSTR:
                strcpy(strType, "unicode string (wchar_t)");
        } //End Switch
        if (wType & DBTYPE_ARRAY)
            strcat (strType, "SAFEARRAY pointer ");
        if (wType & DBTYPE_BYREF)
            strcat (strType, "(by reference)");
        if (wType & DBTYPE_VECTOR)
            strcat (strType, "DBVECTOR structure ");
        return strType;
}
```

In the preceding code, the standard data types are tested for with a switch command. A logical AND (&) is used to test for the aggregate data types. A string is built and returned that describes the data type.

An example of the getType function is the OLEDBMFCMisc directory in the OLEDBMFCMiscSet.cpp source file on the CD-ROM that accompanies this book.

Getting a Column Size and Precision

The DBCOLUMNINFO structure also contains the following information:

♦ Field size can be determined by using the ulColumnSize ULONG variable.

♦ Numeric values have a field precision where they report the number of decimals that they are precise to. The precision size is stored in a byte-sized DBCOLUMNINFO structure field called bPrecision.

◆ NUMERIC and DECIMAL types enable decimal scale to be specified. Decimal scale is the number of decimals you can have behind the decimal point. For instance, 3.14159265 has a precision of 9 and a scale of 8. The scale is stored in a byte-sized DBCOLUMNINFO structure field called bScale.

> When a field is not numeric, the DBCOLUMNINFO::bPrecision and DBCOLUMNINFO::bScale variables have high values stored in them. This is equivalent to 255, so if you want to see if bPrecision or bScale is not valid for the data type, test it to be not equal to 255.

Column names, data types (using the getType function previously written), sizes, precision, and scale are all reported using the following function:

```
void COLEDBMFCMiscSet::DisplayColumnInfo(){
    ULONG ulColumns;            //Number of columns
    DBCOLUMNINFO *pColumnInfo;  //Arrow of column information
    LPOLESTR pColumnNames;      //Array of column names
    char strDisplay[500];       //String to display

    GetColumnInfo(&ulColumns,&pColumnInfo, &pColumnNames);
    sprintf(strDisplay,
            "The number of columns is %d\n\n",
            ulColumns-1);
    strcat(strDisplay, "The columns are:");
    for (ULONG loop = 1; loop < ulColumns; loop++) {
        char mbstr[50];         //String for w_str conversion
        char strType[50];
        strcpy(mbstr, "");      //Initialize string
        if (pColumnInfo[loop].pwszName) {
            wcstombs(mbstr, pColumnInfo[loop].pwszName, 50);
        }
        sprintf(strDisplay, "%s\n  %d) %-30s %s [%d]",
            strDisplay, loop,
            mbstr,
            getType(pColumnInfo[loop].wType, strType),
            pColumnInfo[loop].ulColumnSize);
        if (pColumnInfo[loop].bPrecision != 255) {
            if (pColumnInfo[loop].bScale != 255) {
                sprintf (strDisplay, "%s(%d.%d)",
                    strDisplay,
                    pColumnInfo[loop].bPrecision,
```

```
                              pColumnInfo[loop].bScale);
            }
            else {
                sprintf (strDisplay, "%s(%d)",
                    strDisplay,
                    pColumnInfo[loop].bPrecision);
            }
        }
    }
    ::MessageBox(NULL, strDisplay, "Column Information", MB_OK);
}
```

As you remember from the previous section, the first column of a rowset is always reserved for bookmarks. As a result, you must subtract one from the column count that is retrieved to get an accurate column count:

```
sprintf(strDisplay,
            "The number of columns is %d\n\n",
            ulColumns - 1);
```

In addition, the zero column returned is the bookmark column, so your columns must start from 1 as opposed to the usual C++ 0:

```
for (ULONG loop = 1; loop < ulColumns; loop++) {
```

This function reports the columns of the rowset irrespective of which rowset is used. For example, say you opened a CTable rowset that selects records from the Department table with the following command:

```
hr = CTable<CAccessor<CRowDefinition>, CBulkRowset >::Open(session,
"Department", &propset);
```

In this example, two columns are reported using the DisplayColumnInfo function, as shown in Figure 11-3.

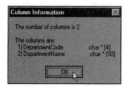

Figure 11-3: You can retrieve column information using the GetColumnInfo function.

Now say you opened a CTable rowset that selects records from the Grades table with the following command:

```
CTable<CAccessor<CRowDefinition> table;
hr = table.Open(session, "Grades", &propset);
```

In this example, five columns are reported using the DisplayColumnInfo function, as shown in Figure 11-4.

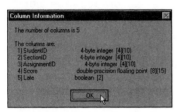

Figure 11-4: As the columns on a rowset change, the DisplayColumnInfo function adjusts to display new column information.

Using the GetColumnInfo function enables your program to automatically adjust to the current schema of your rowset. This can be extremely useful if the environment you're in involves frequent changes to the tables in use.

An example of the DisplayColumnInfo function is in the OLEDBMFCMisc directory in the OLEDBMFCMiscSet.cpp source file on the CD-ROM accompanying this book.

Getting the BLOBs

BLOBs (binary large objects) are data types supported by most databases. BLOBs are usually used in a corporate environment to contain large amounts of text, but BLOBs can also be used to contain elements that are unusually large in size, such as a picture.

BLOBs should not be used as traditional columns. Allocating storage for a BLOB takes a large amount of system resources. In addition, BLOBs may not need to be processed by every rowset function. This section shows the various ways of handling BLOBs and how they can be used.

Accessor Maps

Accessors are normally created using the BEGIN_COLUMN_MAP and END_COLUMN_MAP macros. These macros enable the MoveNext function to automatically retrieve data for all bound columns.

You can read a BLOB column in an Accessor by standard techniques. However, if BLOBs, such as huge comments or pictures, are viewed only occasionally by the user, you may want to separate BLOBs by using Accessor maps. Accessor maps enable you to set up multiple Accessors for a single rowset. You can define these Accessors to either automatically bind columns or to manually retrieve columns using the GetData function if the columns need to be retrieved only occasionally. That way, your database traffic is significantly reduced, and the database is used only by those people who need to see the BLOB data.

The following code example shows how to use multiple Accessors inside a single rowset:

```
class CStudent
{
public:
    CStudent()
    {
        memset( (void*)this, 0, sizeof(*this) );
    };
    char m_FirstName[31];
    char m_MidName[31];
    char m_LastName[31];
    char m_UserID[51];
    char m_Password[51];
    char m_Address[31];
    char m_City[51];
    char m_StateOrProvince[21];
    char m_PostalCode[21];
    char m_PhoneNumber[16];
    char m_EMAIL[51];
    char m_Major[51];
    char m_StudentSSN[31];
    char m_Comments[32000];     //BLOB data area
// output binding map
BEGIN_ACCESSOR_MAP(CArtists, 2)
    BEGIN_ACCESSOR(0, true)     //Automatically bind these columns
    COLUMN_ENTRY_TYPE(1, DBTYPE_STR, m_FirstName)
    COLUMN_ENTRY_TYPE(2, DBTYPE_STR, m_MidName)
    COLUMN_ENTRY_TYPE(3, DBTYPE_STR, m_LastName)
    COLUMN_ENTRY_TYPE(4, DBTYPE_STR, m_UserID)
    COLUMN_ENTRY_TYPE(5, DBTYPE_STR, m_Password)
    COLUMN_ENTRY_TYPE(6, DBTYPE_STR, m_Address)
```

```
   COLUMN_ENTRY_TYPE(7, DBTYPE_STR, m_City)
   COLUMN_ENTRY_TYPE(8, DBTYPE_STR, m_StateOrProvince)
   COLUMN_ENTRY_TYPE(9, DBTYPE_STR, m_PostalCode)
   COLUMN_ENTRY_TYPE(10, DBTYPE_STR, m_PhoneNumber)
   COLUMN_ENTRY_TYPE(11, DBTYPE_STR, m_EMAIL)
   COLUMN_ENTRY_TYPE(12, DBTYPE_STR, m_Major)
   COLUMN_ENTRY_TYPE(13, DBTYPE_STR, m_StudentSSN)
  END_ACCESSOR()
// Not an auto accessor. Don't Bind this column
  BEGIN_ACCESSOR(1, false)
   COLUMN_ENTRY_TYPE(14, DBTYPE_STR, m_Comments)
  END_ACCESSOR()
END_ACCESSOR_MAP()
};
```

In the preceding code, the COLUMN_MAP macros are replaced with ACCES-SOR_MAP macros for the entire set of Accessors and BEGIN_ACCESSOR_MAP macros to define each column in each Accessor. The preceding code defines two Accessors:

◆ Accessor 0 automatically binds its columns to the variables whenever a Move command is executed.

◆ Accessor 1 is used to define the Comments memo field. Accessor 1 does not pull in any data until a GetData function is executed. Using the GetData function, you specify the Accessor you want to retrieve:

```
m_pSet->GetData(1);   //Retrieve Accessor 1 data.
```

Because Accessor 1 does not automatically bind, the data from Accessor 1 is not retrieved until an actual GetData function is called.

Calling the GetData function when data already exists refreshes the rowset data and erases any changes to the rowset variables, so be sure you want to refresh the data before you make a GetData function call.

BLOB_ENTRY and the ISequentialStream Interface

Although multiple Accessors work well with BLOB data, you still have some ineffi-ciencies with multiple Accessors. When you use multiple Accessors, you need to allocate huge amounts of heap memory for every instance of your Accessor. Therefore, although using multiple Accessors is easy, for reusable Accessors, you should define a better way of BLOB manipulation.

Microsoft recommends using the ISequentialStream interface to handle BLOBs in OLE DB. Although the ISequentialStream interface is more efficient than using multiple Accessor maps, it is much more complex. ISequentialStream is a subset of the OLE IStream interface and provides forward-only reading and writing of data. The IStream interface inherits its Read and Write methods from ISequentialStream.

To tie a column to a ISequentialStream pointer, you should use the BLOB_ENTRY macro, not the COLUMN_ENTRY. The following Accessor defines 13 columns and one BLOB that can be bound to an ISequentialStream pointer called m_Comments:

```
class CStudent
{
public:
    CStudent()
    {
        memset( (void*)this, 0, sizeof(*this) );
    };
    char m_FirstName[31];
    char m_MidName[31];
    char m_LastName[31];
    char m_UserID[51];
    char m_Password[51];
    char m_Address[31];
    char m_City[51];
    char m_StateOrProvince[21];
    char m_PostalCode[21];
    char m_PhoneNumber[16];
    char m_EMAIL[51];
    char m_Major[51];
    char m_StudentSSN[31];
    ISequentialStream *m_Comments;
BEGIN_COLUMN_MAP(CStudent)
    COLUMN_ENTRY_TYPE(1, DBTYPE_STR, m_FirstName)
    COLUMN_ENTRY_TYPE(2, DBTYPE_STR, m_MidName)
    COLUMN_ENTRY_TYPE(3, DBTYPE_STR, m_LastName)
    COLUMN_ENTRY_TYPE(4, DBTYPE_STR, m_UserID)
    COLUMN_ENTRY_TYPE(5, DBTYPE_STR, m_Password)
    COLUMN_ENTRY_TYPE(6, DBTYPE_STR, m_Address)
    COLUMN_ENTRY_TYPE(7, DBTYPE_STR, m_City)
    COLUMN_ENTRY_TYPE(8, DBTYPE_STR, m_StateOrProvince)
    COLUMN_ENTRY_TYPE(9, DBTYPE_STR, m_PostalCode)
    COLUMN_ENTRY_TYPE(10, DBTYPE_STR, m_PhoneNumber)
    COLUMN_ENTRY_TYPE(11, DBTYPE_STR, m_EMAIL)
    COLUMN_ENTRY_TYPE(12, DBTYPE_STR, m_Major)
    COLUMN_ENTRY_TYPE(13, DBTYPE_STR, m_StudentSSN)
```

```
    BLOB_ENTRY(14, IID_ISequentialStream,
        STGM_READWRITE,
        m_Comments)
END_COLUMN_MAP()
```

The BLOB_ENTRY column has the following format:

```
BLOB_ENTRY(columnNumber, iid, STGM constant,
    ISequentialStream buffer)
```

In the BLOB entry in the preceding code, column 14 uses an ISequentialStream IID, and a read-write indicator to tie the BLOB to a sequential stream.

When you use an ISequentialStream pointer for BLOB retrieval, you don't actually retrieve a BLOB but rather a pointer that can access the BLOB's contents sequentially, in whatever size chunks are desired. BLOBs are read into and written from the area in strorage using the ISequentialStream::Read and ISequential Stream::Write methods.

The following methods can be used to read data into a multiline text area from a BLOB. First, you must capture each move so that your BLOB can be retrieved with the rest of your data. In the following code, the OnMove function has been overridden to call a local UpdateData function. This is necessary because CWnd::UpdataData is not a virtual function and therefore cannot be overridden directly:

```
BOOL COLEDBMFCBlobView::OnMove(UINT nIDMoveCommand)
{
    UpdateData(TRUE);
    BOOL returnValue =
        COleDBRecordView::OnMove(nIDMoveCommand);
    UpdateData(FALSE);
    return returnValue;
}
```

The UpdateData function must also be overwritten to bring in the BLOB for display:

```
BOOL COLEDBMFCBlobView::UpdateData(BOOL bSaveAndValidate) {
    //Use SteveMcQueen to get the BLOB
    CString SteveMcQueen = "";
    const int BUFFER_SIZE = 1000;    //Size of the buffer
    ULONG ulIOBytes;
    if (!bSaveAndValidate) {
        //Test to see if comments exist
        if (m_pSet->m_Comments) {
            char bBuffer[BUFFER_SIZE];    //Allocate buffer
            do {
                m_pSet->m_Comments->Read(
```

```
                    bBuffer, BUFFER_SIZE-1, &ulIOBytes);
                bBuffer[ulIOBytes] = 0; //Null terminate
                SteveMcQueen = SteveMcQueen + bBuffer;
            } while (ulIOBytes > 0);
        }
        SetDlgItemText(IDC_COMMENT, (LPCTSTR) SteveMcQueen);
    }
    //Update the normal, non-BLOB fields
    return CWnd::UpdateData(bSaveAndValidate);
}
```

In the preceding code, the following steps are performed:

1. A CString named SteveMcQueen is used to get a BLOB (Get it? Steve McQueen and the Blob? Hey, don't blame me! It was my editor's idea!):

   ```
   CString SteveMcQueen = "";
   ```

2. A buffer size of 1000 is declared:

   ```
   const int BUFFER_SIZE = 1000;     //Size of the buffer
   ```

3. The m_Comments pointer is checked to see if a pointer to data really exists:

   ```
   if (m_pSet->m_Comments) {
   ```

4. If a pointer really exists, a character buffer of BUFFER_SIZE is allocated:

   ```
   char bBuffer[BUFFER_SIZE];     //Allocate buffer
   ```

5. Then, in a loop, bytes are read into the buffer until the whole BLOB is transferred to the SteveMcQueen variable:

   ```
   hr = m_pSet->m_Comments->Read(
   do {
       m_pSet->m_Comments->Read(
           bBuffer, BUFFER_SIZE-1, &ulIOBytes);
       bBuffer[ulIOBytes] = 0; //Null terminate
       SteveMcQueen = SteveMcQueen + bBuffer;
   } while (ulIOBytes > 0);
   ```

6. Finally, the SteveMcQueen CString is transferred to a multiline text area:

   ```
   SetDlgItemText(IDC_COMMENT, (LPCTSTR) SteveMcQueen);
   ```

This code is used to display a huge amount of text. In Figure 11-5, the entire Magna Carta is displayed inside a comments area.

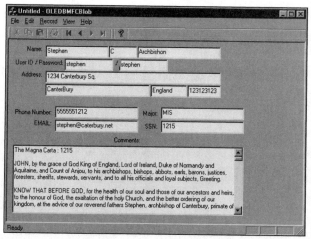

Figure 11-5: BLOBs can be used to handle large fields, such as an enormous piece of text (like this Magna Carta).

As you can see, BLOB processing using the ISequentialStream is somewhat more difficult than using multiple Accessors, but you get the benefit of smaller Accessors as well as the capability to handle an unknown number of bytes inside a BLOB.

ON THE CD

This code can be found on the CD-ROM in the OLEDBMFCBlob directory. The code also implements change detection and saving of BLOB data (in case the Magna Carta is ever updated).

Asynchronous Operations

Asynchronous code is code that can be executed at the same time as other code. Often an SQL procedure is fairly time consuming. By using asynchronous code, you can start to work on partial rowsets that are not yet built or even go on to other code while your rowset is being built.

XREF

See Appendix C for a list of all properties that you can use with OLE DB.

Using Properties

Properties have been used in the previous chapters, but no complete explanation of properties has been given so far. Although properties are specifically a COM feature and not necessarily an OLE DB feature, OLE DB relies on properties extensively.

A definition of property terms may be helpful to those who are not familiar with properties:

♦ A *property ID* is an integer that identifies a property within a GUID.

♦ A *property* is identified by a GUID and a property ID that identifies some aspect or behavior of a COM object, such as an OLE DB connection. Each property belongs to one or more property groups.

♦ A *property set* is the set of all properties that share the same GUID. Generally, a property set is a way of determining which provider defined the property. OLE DB predefines a number of property sets and the properties in them.

♦ A *property group* is a set of logically related properties that could apply to a particular COM object such as a rowset or a data source object. Property groups are identified by a DBPROPFLAGS value that is returned in the DBPROPINFO structure. OLE DB defines property groups. Providers cannot define provider-specific property groups.

Property sets and property groups can overlap. Consider the following CDBPropSet definition:

```
CDBPropSet    dbinit(DBPROPSET_DBINIT);
dbinit.AddProperty(DBPROP_INIT_DATASOURCE, "Classes");
CDBPropSet    propset(DBPROPSET_ROWSET);
propset.AddProperty(DBPROP_CANFETCHBACKWARDS, true);
```

In the preceding code, DBPROP_INIT_DATASOURCE and DBPROP_CANFETCHBACKWARDS are the properties that will be assigned values. DBPROPSET_DBINIT and DBPROPSET_ROWSET are the property sets that contain a set of related properties. All of these objects belong to the OLE DB property group.

Properties are needed to access any data source. They encapsulate functionality so that the programmer can declare properties without worrying about the functionality that underlies each property implementation.

Before now, we've confined our discussion to lazily populated rowsets, also called *lazy rowsets* or *nonasynchronous rowsets*. With lazy rowsets, the program may have access to the rowset before it is fully built, but if the program makes any OLE DB call that requires data that hasn't been loaded, the call does not return until the data is available. This means that the "laziness" of the rowset is invisible to the program using the rowset. With asynchronous rowsets, the rowset itself is fully initialized, but the rows are not populated with data. As the rows are populated, all interfaces and functions for the rowset become available and fully functional, even though the set of rows returned is not yet complete.

Asynchronous operations are a good example of property use where the provider supports asynchronous operations and the programmer need not be concerned with the actual implementation of asynchronous processing. To set a rowset to perform asynchronous data retrieval, set the DBPROPSET_ROWSET properties to either DBPROP-VAL_ASYNCH_SEQUENTIAL or DBPROPVAL_ASYNCH_RANDOM prior to opening the rowset:

```
CDBPropSet     propset(DBPROPSET_ROWSET);
propset.AddProperty(DBPROPVAL_ASYNCH_SEQUENTIAL,
        DBPROPVAL_ASYNCH_SEQUENTIAL);
```

When using asynchronous routines, any move (for example, MoveLast or MoveNext) that goes beyond the current rowset waits for the rowset to be filled in before continuing.

Summary

This chapter delves into some advanced OLE DB topics that may be of some use in your OLE DB projects. To recap:

♦ The CTable class is used to develop rowsets from simple queries. The CCommand class is used to develop more selective or complex queries. CTable has less overhead than CCommand.

♦ You can use bookmarks to retrieve row information and row position within a rowset.

♦ The GetColumnInformation function retrieves column name, type, and size information about all the columns in a rowset.

♦ Properties are used to provide encapsulated functionality to a data source so that the OLE DB consumer can control how a data source and rowsets are to be accessed.

♦ Asynchronous rowsets enable you to start a long query and continue your program while that query runs.

Chapter 12

Using Special Rowsets

IN THIS CHAPTER

- ◆ Using array rowsets
- ◆ Understanding bulk rowsets
- ◆ Implementing multiple result rowsets
- ◆ Using manual accessors
- ◆ Using enumerator rowsets

THERE ARE THREE TYPES of ATL rowsets. Simple rowsets are rowsets that return a single row per operation. Single rowsets have been covered elsewhere in this book. Bulk rowsets, covered in this chapter, return a bulk of rows at a time with every move operation. Array rowsets, also covered in this chapter, return an array of rows following each row operation. In addition to these types of rowsets, all rowsets can return multiple results, which require manual or dynamic accessors to retrieve. In this chapter, rowset types that differ from traditional rowsets are discussed.

Understanding Array Rowsets

Figure 12-1 shows how an array rowset compares to traditional rowsets.

As indicated by Figure 12-1, array rowsets can be accessed by array notation. However, they can also be accessed using traditional OLE DB `Move` calls. This enables array rowset consumers the versatility of usability no matter what the preference of the end programmer.

ON THE CD An array rowset example can be found in the OLEDBATLArrayRowset directory on the CD-ROM that accompanies this book.

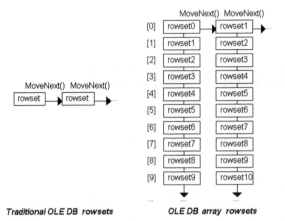

MoveNext() MoveNext()

Traditional OLE DB rowsets   OLE DB array rowsets

Figure 12-1: Array rowsets return an array of rows for each Move call.

To make and use an array rowset consumer, perform the following steps:

1. Generate a traditional ATL application complete with a Department table consumer and a dialog as described in Chapter 9 or an MFC OLE DB application as described in Chapter 8. ATL was used for this example.

2. Use the CArrayRowset class to form your CCommand rowset rather than the default CRowset class in your consumer header file (Department.h):

```
//Chuck Wood changed class definition
//to use an array rowset
class CDepartment :
    public CCommand<CAccessor<CDepartmentAccessor>,
CArrayRowset<CDepartmentAccessor> >
```

3. In the OpenRowset function (or the Open function if using MFC) in your consumer header file (Department.h), change the CCommand::Open function to use the proper ancestor:

```
HRESULT OpenRowset()
{
    // Set properties for open
    CDBPropSet    propset(DBPROPSET_ROWSET);
    propset.AddProperty(DBPROP_IRowsetChange, true);
    propset.AddProperty(DBPROP_UPDATABILITY,
        DBPROPVAL_UP_CHANGE | DBPROPVAL_UP_INSERT |
        DBPROPVAL_UP_DELETE);
//Changed by Chuck Wood to use proper ancestor
```

```
return CCommand<CAccessor<CDepartmentAccessor>,
    CArrayRowset<CDepartmentAccessor> >::
Open(m_session, NULL, &propset);
}
```

4. Now the changes to your consumer are complete. You can now use this rowset in the traditional fashion or to access rows using array notation. To use arrays rather than single records, you must make changes to your OnMove function, your UpdateData function and your dialog class definition. In the dialog class definition in your dialog header file (DeptDialog.h), you need to assign variables for the current record (starting with zero) and the maximum record (assigned to the number of rows less one):

```
class CDeptDialog :
    public CAxDialogImpl<CDeptDialog>
{
public:
    CDepartment* m_pSet;
    int m_nCurrentRow;
    int m_nMaxRows;
```

5. After you declare your class variables, you should initialize them in either the CDeptDialog constructor or in the InitDialog function in your dialog header file (DeptDialog.h). You also don't want to use any Move commands if you're going to use array access, so remove the MoveFirst function from the OnInitDialog function:

```
LRESULT OnInitDialog(UINT uMsg, WPARAM wParam, LPARAM lParam,
BOOL& bHandled)
{
    HRESULT hr = m_pSet->Open();
    if (FAILED(hr)) {
        OLEDBErrorChecking::DisplayHRRESULTMessage(hr,
"OnInitDialog");
        exit(1);    //Better not start
    }
//Added by Chuck Wood to set array bounds
    m_nCurrentRow = 0;
    m_nMaxRows = 8;
    UpdateData(FALSE);    //Write Values to Window
    return 1;  // Let the system set the focus
}
```

For ease of understanding and coding, I hard-coded the number of rows into the preceding code. This usually won't be acceptable, but you can count the number of rows in a rowset by using bookmarks, which is described in Chapter 11.

Array rowsets can be used identically to traditional rowsets. That means that you can use MoveFirst, MoveNext, and so on to navigate around the rowset rather than arrays. However, it usually is a bad idea to mix and match access methods. As shown in Figure 12-1, Move commands distort the array in an array rowset so that you may lose rows off your array rowset, and your array elements may not positionally correspond to the elements in your rowset.

6. Your menu options in both the ATL example and when using the MFC AppWizard all end up calling the OnMove function to handle navigation in the rowset. You must remove all Move commands from the OnMove function and instead concentrate on record positioning:

```
void CDeptDialog::OnMove(CPosition position)
{
    UpdateData(TRUE);      //Read from screen
    DisplayStatus("");
    switch (position) {
    case (FIRST) :
        m_nCurrentRow = 0;
        break;
    case (NEXT) :
        m_nCurrentRow++;
        if (m_nCurrentRow > m_nMaxRows) {      //EOF
            m_nCurrentRow = m_nMaxRows;
            DisplayStatus("Last record reached.");
        }
        break;
    case (LAST) :
        m_nCurrentRow = m_nMaxRows;
        break;
    case (PREV) :
        m_nCurrentRow--;
        if (m_nCurrentRow < 0) {      //BOF
            m_nCurrentRow = 0;
```

```
            DisplayStatus("First record reached.");
        }
        break;
    }
    UpdateData(FALSE);      //Update Screen
}
```

7. Similarly, you must change your UpdateData function to use array positions rather than GetData and SetData functions:

```
void CDeptDialog::UpdateData(BOOL bSaveChangesToSet)
{
    if (bSaveChangesToSet) {
        //Read From Screen
        GetDlgItemText(IDC_CODE,
            (char *)
m_pSet[0][m_nCurrentRow].m_DepartmentCode, 5);
        GetDlgItemText(IDC_NAME,
            (char *)
m_pSet[0][m_nCurrentRow].m_DepartmentName, 51);
    }
    else {
        //Write to Screen
        SetDlgItemText(IDC_CODE,
            (char *)
m_pSet[0][m_nCurrentRow].m_DepartmentCode);
        SetDlgItemText(IDC_NAME,
            (char *)
m_pSet[0][m_nCurrentRow].m_DepartmentName);
    }
}
```

Notice that instead of using an m_pSet pointer (m_pSet->), you use an m_pSet zero array element (m_pSet[0]). Most consumers in this book and in the Visual Studio wizards generate rowset pointers rather than rowset variables. When you use a rowset pointer with array rowsets, you must use the zero element of the array and treat the array rowset as a multidimensional array of size (1 x numberOfRows).

Now, when you scroll through the rows on a rowset, your code actually uses an array instead of database commands. One of the major benefits of array access is that there is only one call to the database provider for the open. Array access is typically faster than provider calls; hence array rowset processing can be much more efficient than traditional methods when scrolling through records in a rowset.

The first time you visit each record, array rowsets will be slower than normal rowsets because the array rowset is allocating enough memory to store a separate buffer (for example, CDepartmentAccessor object) for each row, rather than reusing the same object. However, if the rowset is not too large, and if your application jumps around a lot in the rowset and accesses the rows many times, it may be faster to use an array rowset because it avoids the additional calls to the OLE DB provider. You will need to experiment with the performance for your application. Additionally, array rowsets are best for read-only access, such as in reports. The traditional ways of saving data (for example, SetData) are used for single-record access only. If you want to perform updates to your data, then you should probably use either traditional methods (even with an Array rowset consumer) or bulk rowsets, which are described next.

Array rowset default limitation size is 10,000 rows. You can override this by passing a maximum number of rows to the constructor of your CArrayRowset. However, for large numbers of rows, array rowsets may not be appropriate because they store all the rowset data in virtual memory. For large rowsets you should use traditional OLE DB methods or bulk rowsets, which are described next.

Using Bulk Rowsets

Databases come with built-in protection that enables several operations:

◆ Multiuser support is enabled by semaphore processing, transaction support, and record locking.

◆ Reference checking supports referential integrity so that relationships are preserved in a database operation.

While these support operations are important for day-to-day multiuser activity, these commands take some time. If you're processing a single record, the time dedicated to these support operations is negligible. However, if you are updating, inserting, or selecting several hundred thousand records or more, referential integrity checking and multiuser support on each operation can add hours to your processing time. Bulk commands bypass these features to enable bulk operations to occur on a database. Bulk operations involve several rowset pointers returned by a single operation. A `MoveNext` command retrieves a bulk of rows, not a single row, as shown in Figure 12-2.

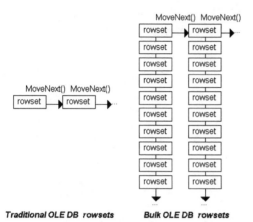

Figure 12-2: While traditional rowsets return only one row pointer at a time, bulk rowsets return several row pointers with one call.

Setting Up Bulk Mode

Setting up bulk mode using MFC classes requires only two changes to the `CCommand`. First, the `CCommand` ancestor uses a `CRowset` class in its template by default. You must add a `CBulkRowset` parameter so that `CCommand` uses `CBulkRowset` rather than the default `CRowset` during the class definition:

```
class COLEDBBBulkSet :
public CCommand<CAccessor<CRowDefinition>, CBulkRowset>
```

Second, you must change the `Open` call in your `Open` function to call the proper ancestor. Your new ancestor is not `CCommand<CAccessor<CRowDefinition>`, which uses a `CRowset` default, but rather `CCommand<CAccessor<CRowDefinition>, CBulkRowset>`.

```
{
public:

    HRESULT Open()
    {
        CDataSource db;
```

```
         CSession    session;
         HRESULT        hr;

         CDBPropSet    dbinit(DBPROPSET_DBINIT);
         dbinit.AddProperty(DBPROP_AUTH_PERSIST_SENSITIVE_AUTHINFO,
false);
         dbinit.AddProperty(DBPROP_INIT_DATASOURCE, "Classes");
         dbinit.AddProperty(DBPROP_INIT_PROMPT, (short)4);
         dbinit.AddProperty(DBPROP_INIT_LCID, (long)1033);

         hr = db.OpenWithServiceComponents("MSDASQL.1", &dbinit);
         if (FAILED(hr))
             return hr;

         hr = session.Open(db);
         if (FAILED(hr))
             return hr;

         CDBPropSet    propset(DBPROPSET_ROWSET);
         propset.AddProperty(DBPROP_CANFETCHBACKWARDS, true);
         propset.AddProperty(DBPROP_IRowsetScroll, true);
         propset.AddProperty(DBPROP_IRowsetChange, true);
         propset.AddProperty(DBPROP_UPDATABILITY, DBPROPVAL_UP_CHANGE
| DBPROPVAL_UP_INSERT | DBPROPVAL_UP_DELETE );

         hr = CCommand<CAccessor<CRowDefinition>, CBulkRowset
>::Open(session, "SELECT * FROM Department", &propset);
         if (FAILED(hr))
             return hr;

         return MoveNext();
     }
};
```

Using Bulk Commands and Attributes

Now your rowset is set up to handle bulk rows. However, standard bulk rowsets default to only ten records at a time. The SetRows function can increase or decrease the number of row handles retrieved by each call. If you call this function, it must be before the rowset is opened. The following command opens a Table BulkRowset and populates it with records from the Department table:

```
//Change the number of row pointers from 10 default to 3
SetRows(3);
hr = CTable<CAccessor<CRowDefinition>, CBulkRowset >::Open(session,
"Department", &propset);
```

Unlike array rowsets, bulk rowsets cannot function as traditional rowsets because they retrieve a bulk of records at a time. As a result, you need special attributes and methods to navigate through a bulk rowset. To achieve this functionality, bulk rowsets contain an additional set of attributes that contain information. Four are particularly important:

- The m_hRow variable is the OLE DB row handle (HROW) representing the current row.

- The m_phRow variable is a pointer to the array of OLE DB row handles (HROWs) returned from the bulk operation.

- The m_nCurrentRow variable is an ULONG that contains the number of the current row, starting at zero and going to 1, less than the value used in the SetRows function.

- The m_nCurrentRows variable is an ULONG that contains the number of row pointers returned by the last bulk operation.

These operations can be viewed in the following MoveNext function to scroll through the records in a bulk rowset:

```
HRESULT COLEDBMFCMiscSet::MoveNext(){
    if (m_nCurrentRow >= 0 && m_nCurrentRow+1 < m_nCurrentRows)
{
        // Get the data for the next row
        m_nCurrentRow++;
        m_hRow = m_phRow[m_nCurrentRow];
        return GetData();
    }
    return CTable<CAccessor<CRowDefinition>, CBulkRowset >
        ::MoveNext();
}
```

In the preceding code, the following steps are performed:

1. The MoveNext ancestor function is superseded in the descendent class.

```
HRESULT COLEDBMFCMiscSet::MoveNext(){
```

The problem with overriding the MoveNext method is that it is not declared as "virtual" in CRowset. This means that there is no polymorphism for this method. Hence, your new MoveNext is called only if the calling program uses a COLEDBMFCMiscSet* pointer type rather than a CRowset* pointer type.

2. The current row counter (m_nCurrentRow) is checked to see if it falls in a valid range between zero and 1, less than the number of row pointers in the bulk rowset (m_nCurrentRows):

```
if (m_nCurrentRow >= 0 && m_nCurrentRow+1 < m_nCurrentRows)
```

3. Then the current row counter (m_nCurrentRow) is incremented, and the current row pointer (m_hRow) is assigned to the appropriate row in the array of row pointers (m_phRow):

```
m_nCurrentRow++;
m_hRow = m_phRow[m_nCurrentRow];
```

4. Finally, a GetData function is used to retrieve the current record:

```
return GetData();
```

5. If there are no more records, the ancestor MoveNext function is called to retrieve a new bulk of rows:

```
return CTable<CAccessor<CRowDefinition>, CBulkRowset >
   ::MoveNext();
```

By using the preceding code, you have retrieved and processed a bulk of records from a database with only one call to the database. Any updates to the rowset are not performed except at the bulk level, enabling you to update this rowset in its entirety before trying to write all these records to the database.

 An example of a CBulkRowset is in the OLEDBMFCMisc CD on the CD-ROM that accompanies this book.

As mentioned previously, because the ATL Move functions are not virtual, there is no way to constantly override them unless the programmer is aware they are being overridden. The preceding code goes forward to the next bulk of records but does not function too well using other Move commands. If you want to make this work for all Move commands, such as `MovePrev`, try copying the entire function body of `COleDBRecordView::OnMove` into the `OnMove` of the view class, then changing the first line from this:

```
CRowset* pSet = OnGetRowset();
to this:
CBulkRowset* pSet = m_pSet;
so that all the method calls go to the bulk version.
```

Handling Multiple Result Rowsets

CCommand has three template arguments: an accessor class, a rowset class, and CNoMultipleResults (by default) or CMultipleResults. If you specify CMultiple-Results, the CCommand class supports the IMultipleResults interface and handles multiple results from a single query. While this is usually more trouble than it is worth, you should be aware of the technique in case a stored procedure returns multiple results or a programmer placed multiple SQL statements inside a rowset.

Some databases, such as Access, do not support multiple results from a single query. This is not necessarily a bad thing, but you should be aware that you can't try this example using Microsoft Access.

Assume you had the following stored procedure in an MS SQL Server database:

```
Create Procedure TestMultipleRowset
As
    SELECT * FROM DEPARTMENT
    SELECT RTRIM(FirstName)+' '+RTRIM(LastName) AS StudentName,
      EMAIL
     FROM STUDENT
```

As you can see by the preceding `TestMultipleRowset` procedure, multiple SELECT statements are inside a single procedure. When you execute this stored procedure, you will get multiple sets of results. If you try to use traditional rowsets to open the return value from this stored procedure, your program will GPF when you try to open the rowset.

Need I point out that you should *never* place multiple SELECT statements inside a single stored procedure, as is done in the TestMultipleRowset procedure? This section involves using existing stored procedures that may return multiple results. However, when possible, code two different stored procedures to handle two different SQL tasks. That way, your stored procedure are easy to implement using traditional programming techniques.

Figure 12-3 shows the internal structure of multiple rowsets. In traditional rowsets, a single set of columns that make up a rowset is retrieved. With multiple rowsets, more than one rowset that uses multiple columns is retrieved.

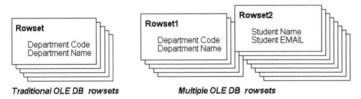

Traditional OLE DB rowsets   Multiple OLE DB rowsets

Figure 12-3: While traditional rowsets return only one rowset at a time, multiple rowsets enable you to use data sources that return several sets of rows at one time.

Setting Up Your MFC Project for Multiple Results

The following steps convert an MFC application to use multiple results from a single rowset. To handle multiple results, perform the following steps:

1. Declare a new MFC EXE project. In Figure 12-4, this project is called OLEDBMFCMultiple.

2. Now the MFC AppWizard opens. Choose Single Document, and click Next. Then choose Database View without File support, and click the Data Source button. Now the Database options open. Choose OLE DB, and click the Select OLE DB Datasource button.

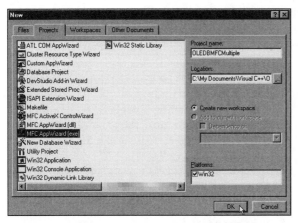

Figure 12-4: With a little extra coding, MFC OLE DB programs can handle multiple results.

3. Be sure you choose a database in the Data Link Properties window that supports multiple results. In Figure 12-5, Microsoft's OLE DB Provider for SQL Server was selected. Then enter all the variables needed for that database connection, and click OK to return to the Database Options window. Click OK again to open the Select Database Tables option. Select any table (because you'll end up replacing the table with a call to the stored procedure), and click OK. In this example, the DEPARTMENT table was chosen.

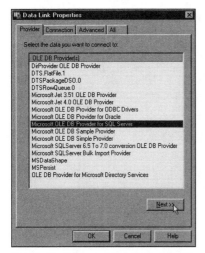

Figure 12-5: Be sure to select a database that supports multiple results.

4. Continue in the MFC AppWizard. Turn off Printing and print preview in step 4 of 6, and click Finish. Click OK when the New Project Information window opens. Your default MFC EXE project is now built. Your dialog box then appears with a TODO label. Delete the label, and build a dialog box that befits the return values of your stored procedure. The `TestMultipleRowset` procedure returns either DepartmentCode and DepartmentName from the DEPARTMENT table or StudentName and EMAIL from the STUDENT table. Because there are two columns, you need to define two columns on your dialog box, as shown in Figure 12-6.

Notice in Figure 12-6 that not only were edit boxes added (called IDC_COLUMN1 and IDC_COLUMN2), but also the text labels were named (IDC_STATIC1 and IDC_STATIC2). This is so you can change the column names to match the result set that you wish to display.

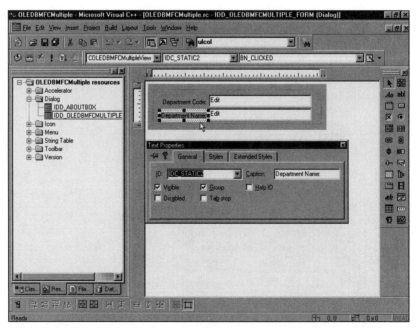

Figure 12-6: Your dialog box needs to reflect the return values of your stored procedure.

5. When dealing with multiple results, you need some event to occur that indicates that you should change to another rowset. In Figure 12-7, a Change Rowset option is added to the Records menu option to enable the user to switch between rowsets.

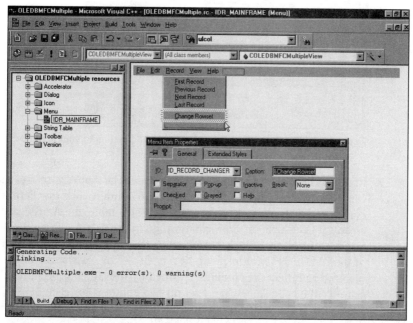

Figure 12-7: You need an event to occur, such as a menu choice, to indicate that you should change rowsets when you have multiple results.

6. Go into the Class Wizard (View → Class Wizard on your menu bar) to add an event for the new menu item to the COLEDBMFCMultipleView class, as shown in Figure 12-8.

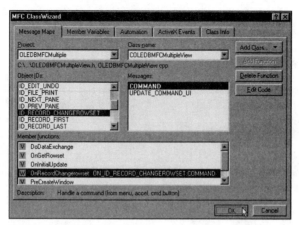

Figure 12-8: The Class Wizard can be used to add menus to your menu event.

7. Now you need to start changing some code. The AppWizard creates a class needed by the CAccessor template to contain your row definition. For instance, if you picked the DEPARTMENT table, the AppWizard creates a CDepartment class containing string variables to hold values retrieved from the DEPARTMENT table. (You can find this class at the top of the OLEDBMFCMultipleSet.h header file.) This class needs to be replaced to reflect the columns returned by the stored procedures. To simplify the code somewhat, I set up two columns for each SELECT statement in the stored procedure. You need to define an area to store the retrieval contents, as shown by the following code:

```
class CRowDefinition
{
public:
    CRowDefinition()
    {
        memset( (void*)this, 0, sizeof(*this) );
    };
    char    column1[62];
    char    column2[51];
};
```

In the preceding code, two columns are allocated that can handle the results of both SELECT statements.

If you use different data types or a different number of columns, you must dynamically allocate your variables based on the content of your recordset. You can see earlier in this chapter how to get a column count or column name from a SELECT statement.

8. Also in the OLEDBMFCMultipleSet.h header file, a CCommand (COLEDBMFCMultipleSet) is created. You need to declare your CCommand class to use a CMultipleResults instead of the default CNoMultiple Results. Also, because you are using multiple results, it's a good idea to use CManualAcccessor rather than a CAccessor so you can better control what is retrieved from the rowset:

```
class COLEDBMFCMultipleSet : public CCommand<CManualAccessor,
CRowset, CMultipleResults>
```

9. You need to add some variables to your CCommand class, and you need to write a constructor to initialize any variables. These changes are detailed in the following code:

```
class COLEDBMFCMultipleSet : public CCommand<CManualAccessor,
CRowset, CMultipleResults>
{
public:
    CRowDefinition m_Rows;      //Row Definition
    int m_iResultNumber;        //Current result
    char m_columnName1[17];     //Name of the first column
    char m_columnName2[17];     //Name of the second column
    COLEDBMFCMultipleSet(){ //Constructor
      m_iResultNumber = 0;  //Initialize the result number
    };
```

10. You need to make three changes to your Open function:

   a. You need to rename the function to another name (for example, OpenSession) so you can use the Open function to open a new rowset.

   b. You need to use the Create function to create a new SQL statement to execute your stored procedure:

   ```
   hr = Create(session, "EXEC TestMultipleRowset");
   ```

   c. You need to use the Prepare function to prepare your new statement to be executed one time and return the HRESULT to the calling function:

   ```
   return Prepare(1);
   ```

Create and Prepare are used to send an SQL statement to the database but not execute it. By using Create and Prepare, you can execute any statement by opening Accessor in the session where the statements are declared.

These changes can be seen in the OpenSession function that follows:

```
HRESULT OpenSession() {   //Used to be HRESULT Open()
    CDataSource db;
    HRESULT         hr;
    CDBPropSet      dbinit(DBPROPSET_DBINIT);
    dbinit.AddProperty(DBPROP_AUTH_PASSWORD, "");
    dbinit.AddProperty(
        DBPROP_AUTH_PERSIST_SENSITIVE_AUTHINFO, false);
    dbinit.AddProperty(DBPROP_AUTH_USERID, "sa");
    dbinit.AddProperty(DBPROP_INIT_CATALOG,  "Classes");
    dbinit.AddProperty(DBPROP_INIT_DATASOURCE, "(local)");
    dbinit.AddProperty(DBPROP_INIT_LCID, (long)1033);
    dbinit.AddProperty(DBPROP_INIT_PROMPT, (short)4);
    hr = db.OpenWithServiceComponents("SQLOLEDB.1", &dbinit);
    if (FAILED(hr))
        return hr;
    hr = session.Open(db);
    if (FAILED(hr))
        return hr;
//Create a new SQL statement
    hr = Create(session, "EXEC TestMultipleRowset");
    if (FAILED(hr))
        return hr;
//Prepare the statement to be executed once
    return Prepare(1);
//The rest of this functionality has been moved
//to the Open function
};
```

11. Don't forget to change the data exchange to use the new column names and the new static names:

```
void COLEDBMFCMultipleView::DoDataExchange(CDataExchange*
pDX)
{
    COleDBRecordView::DoDataExchange(pDX);
    //{{AFX_DATA_MAP(COLEDBMFCMultipleView)
        // NOTE: the ClassWizard will add DDX and DDV calls
```

here

```
    //}}AFX_DATA_MAP
    DDX_Text(pDX, IDC_COLUMN1, m_pSet->m_Rows.column1, 62);
    DDX_Text(pDX, IDC_COLUMN2, m_pSet->m_Rows.column2, 51);
    DDX_Text(pDX, IDC_STATIC1, m_pSet->m_columnName1, 17);
    DDX_Text(pDX, IDC_STATIC2, m_pSet->m_columnName2, 17);
}
```

12. You also need to add code to your `OnRecordChangerowset` function to close the existing rowset and open the new rowset. (The toggling between rowsets will be handled by the Open function you are writing in the next section.)

```
void COLEDBMFCMultipleView::OnRecordChangerowset()
{
    UpdateData(TRUE);     // Update from Window
    m_pSet->Close();      // Close the last rowset
    m_pSet->Open();       // Toggle to the new rowset
    UpdateData(FALSE);    // Update to Window
}
```

TIP Because you are using a manual accessor, you don't need to use a COL-UMN_MAP macro in OLEDBMfcMultipleSet.h. I suggest you delete it from your project to avoid extra work or confusion.

Writing a New Open Function

Now you must write an `Open` function that not only opens a rowset but also toggles between multiple rowsets. This can be done using the following steps:

1. Open the session if needed.

2. Open the rowset without automatically binding.

3. Choose which result set you want, and change the appropriate variables to reflect your choice.

4. Create an accessor, and bind the database columns to C++ class variables.

These steps are documented in this section. At the end of the section, the new `Open` function can be viewed in its entirety.

OPENING THE SESSION
Remember that View calls the `Open` function of the consumer to open the result set. You need to call the `OpenSession` function only once if it has not been called yet.

This can be done by testing a variable that is set in the Open function. If that variable has not yet been set, you can then call the OpenSession function to open the data source and session and prepare for open rowsets:

```
if (m_iResultNumber == 0) {
    hr = OpenSession();
    if (hr != S_OK)
        return hr;
}
```

The preceding code executes only once, before the m_iResultNumber is called. This way, the user of your new OLE DB consumer can use the standard Open and Close functions without worrying about the OLE DB session.

OPENING THE ROWSET

Ordinarily, you use the CCommand::Open function to automatically open a rowset and create a rowset accessor. However, when using a CManualAccessor, you probably don't want to do this. Open the CCommand rowset, but don't bind it:

```
hr = CCommand<CManualAccessor, CRowset, CMultipleResults>::
    Open(NULL, NULL, false);  //Don't bind
```

Later in this section, you manually bind your accessor to your CCommand rowset.

CHOOSING THE RESULT SET

Next, you need to decide which result set to use. In step 12 in the previous section, "Setting Up Your MFC Project for Multiple Results," I indicated that this project toggles between rowsets based on a menu selection. This means that every time you want to toggle between rowsets, you close the rowset and open it again. An internal class variable, m_iResultNumber, has been defined to control which rowset is currently being used. When you first open a rowset, the default for a multiple result rowset is to open the first result, but you can use the GetNextResult function to scroll through all the result sets:

```
if (m_iResultNumber == 1) {
    m_iResultNumber = 2;
//Get the next result set, but don't bind it.
    GetNextResult(NULL, false);
    strcpy(m_columnName1, "Student Name:");
    strcpy(m_columnName2, "Student EMAIL:");
}
else {
//First result set.  No extra code needed
    m_iResultNumber = 1;
```

```
    strcpy(m_columnName1, "Department Code:");
    strcpy(m_columnName2, "Department Name:");
}
```

CREATING THE ACCESSOR AND MANUALLY BINDING THE COLUMNS

The final step is to create an accessor that points to the row definition and bind the columns to that row. The CreateAccessor command can be used to indicate the size and address of the buffer needed to hold each row that is retrieved:

```
CreateAccessor(2, &m_Rows, sizeof(CRowDefinition));
```

You can use the AddBindEntry function to describe exactly which columns get bound to which variables in the accessor. In the following code, two columns are bound to two variables inside the CRowDefinition class:

```
AddBindEntry(1, DBTYPE_STR,
        sizeof(m_Rows.column1),
        &m_Rows.column1);
AddBindEntry(2, DBTYPE_STR,
        sizeof(m_Rows.column2),
        &m_Rows.column2);
```

When you're finished creating an accessor and adding bind entries for all your variables to the columns in the rowset, you use the Bind function to manually bind the variables:

```
Bind();
```

VIEWING THE FINISHED OPEN FUNCTION

The new Open Function can be viewed in its entirety in the following code:

```
HRESULT Open() {
//For the original Open function,
//view the OpenSession function
    HRESULT hr;
    if (m_iResultNumber == 0) {
        hr = OpenSession();
        if (hr != S_OK)
            return hr;
    }
//Open the rowset to get the information
//so we can then bind the columns
    hr = CCommand<CManualAccessor, CRowset, CMultipleResults>::
        Open(NULL, NULL, false);
```

```
if (hr != S_OK)
    return hr;
if (m_iResultNumber == 1) {
    m_iResultNumber = 2;
    GetNextResult(NULL, false);
    strcpy(m_columnName1, "Student Name:");
    strcpy(m_columnName2, "Student EMAIL:");
}
else {
    m_iResultNumber = 1;
    strcpy(m_columnName1, "Department Code:");
    strcpy(m_columnName2, "Department Name:");
}
CreateAccessor(2, &m_Rows, sizeof(CRowDefinition));
AddBindEntry(1, DBTYPE_STR,
        sizeof(m_Rows.column1),
        &m_Rows.column1);
AddBindEntry(2, DBTYPE_STR,
        sizeof(m_Rows.column2),
        &m_Rows.column2);
Bind();
return MoveNext();
}
```

Viewing the Finished Product

When you run this program, you can see that the window in Figure 12-9 opens and
displays the department code and department name.

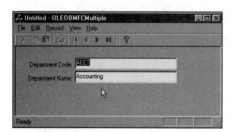

Figure 12-9: The opening window of the OLEDBMFCMultiple project.

However, when choosing Record → Change Rowset from the menu, you can see (in Figure 12-10) that the window changes (along with the labels) to give you a new window that reports on the student name and student e-mail.

Figure 12-10: Multiple rowsets enable you to handle data sources that return more than one row at a time.

Using Enumerator Rowsets

OLE DB enumerators are used to build a rowset that lists all the OLE DB providers available to a machine. Enumerators used to be quite complicated and difficult to use. However, enumerator support added by the ATL makes coding for enumerator support quite easy.

Did I mention that coding for enumerators with ATL was easy? It is ... *but* it simply is not documented. No sample programs exist, and the documentation on enumerators in the MSDN, at least in Visual 6.0a (which is the version I'm currently using) is very sparsely documented and somewhat incorrect. Don't worry though, because this section gives you everything you need to start programming with enumerators.

The OLE DB CEnumerator class is used in ATL to define an enumerator rowset. The CEnumerator class is derived from CAccessorRowset, and therefore it has most of the functionality of a traditional consumer.

Like any consumer, the CEnumerator rowset contains all the traditional read-only rowset functionality, such as MoveFirst, MoveNext, and so on. Also, like other consumers, the CEnumerator rowset contains five variables that you can use to retrieve information about your provider. These five variables are shown in Table 12-1.

TABLE 12-1 CENUMERATOR BOUND ROWSET VARIABLES

Rowset Variable	Definition	Description
m_szName	WCHAR [129]	This is the name of the provider.
m_szParseName	WCHAR [129]	This is the class ID of the provider.
m_szDescription	WCHAR [129]	This is the description of the provider. Usually, this is the name you see when you pick your provider from a list in Visual Studio.
m_nType	USHORT	The CEnumerator class lists all providers and enumerators. The m_nType field tells whether the entry in the rowset is a provider or an enumerator. The DBSOURCETYPE_DATASOURCE constant indicates that this entry is an OLE DB provider. The DBSOURCETYPE_ENUMERATOR constant indicates that this entry is an OLE DB consumer. Because a single module can serve as both a data source and as an enumerator, a single rowset may be listed twice with two different m_nType entries.
m_bIsParent	VARIANT_BOOL	Enumerators can be nested. This field indicates if this field is the highest enumerator or if this entry has a parent. This field is not often used.

The following steps can be used to open a dialog box and list all the OLE DB providers as well as any enumerators currently installed on your system:

1. Define an ATL project called OLEDBATLEnumerator. Click Executable so that the application can run, although in practice you could make a DLL to be called by everybody. Continue clicking Next or OK until you return to your Visual Studio environment.

2. Add a dialog box to your project by clicking Insert → New ATL Object. When the ATL Object Wizard opens, click the Miscellaneous Category and the Dialog control, and click Next, as shown in Figure 12-11. Type in **EnumDialog** in the short name in the ATL Object Wizard Properties dialog box that opens, and click OK.

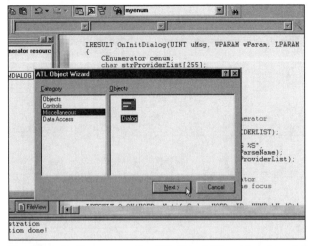

Figure 12-11: You can use the ATL Object Wizard to add a dialog box to your ATL application.

3. Add a listbox to your dialog box, and call it IDC_PROVIDERLIST. You can delete the Cancel button if you wish and move the OK button to the bottom of the dialog box. (See Figure 12-12 later in this section.)

4. Add an #include directive to your main file (OLEDBATLEnumerator.cpp) so that you can have dialog box support in your application.

```
#include "stdafx.h"
#include "resource.h"
#include <initguid.h>
#include "OLEDBATLEnumerator.h"

#include "OLEDBATLEnumerator_i.c"
//Added by Chuck Wood for dialog box support
#include "EnumDialog.h"

const DWORD dwTimeOut = 5000; // time for EXE to be idle
before shutting down
const DWORD dwPause = 1000; // time to wait for threads to
finish up

// Passed to CreateThread to monitor the shutdown event
static DWORD WINAPI MonitorProc(void* pv)
{
```

5. In your _tWinMain function (in OLEDBATLEnumerator), construct your dialog box. You can also delete the wait for a message because all messages in this application are handled by the dialog box:

```
extern "C" int WINAPI _tWinMain(HINSTANCE hInstance,
    HINSTANCE /*hPrevInstance*/, LPTSTR lpCmdLine, int
/*nShowCmd*/)
{
    lpCmdLine = GetCommandLine(); //this line necessary for
_ATL_MIN_CRT

#if _WIN32_WINNT >= 0x0400 & defined(_ATL_FREE_THREADED)
    HRESULT hRes = CoInitializeEx(NULL,
COINIT_MULTITHREADED);
#else
    HRESULT hRes = CoInitialize(NULL);
#endif
    _ASSERTE(SUCCEEDED(hRes));
    _Module.Init(ObjectMap, hInstance,
&LIBID_OLEDBATLENUMERATORLib);
    _Module.dwThreadID = GetCurrentThreadId();
    TCHAR szTokens[] = _T("-/");

    int nRet = 0;
    BOOL bRun = TRUE;
    LPCTSTR lpszToken = FindOneOf(lpCmdLine, szTokens);
    while (lpszToken != NULL)
    {
        if (lstrcmpi(lpszToken, _T("UnregServer"))==0)
        {

_Module.UpdateRegistryFromResource(IDR_OLEDBATLEnumerator,
FALSE);
            nRet = _Module.UnregisterServer(TRUE);
            bRun = FALSE;
            break;
        }
        if (lstrcmpi(lpszToken, _T("RegServer"))==0)
        {

_Module.UpdateRegistryFromResource(IDR_OLEDBATLEnumerator,
TRUE);
            nRet = _Module.RegisterServer(TRUE);
            bRun = FALSE;
            break;
```

```
            }
            lpszToken = FindOneOf(lpszToken, szTokens);
        }

        if (bRun)
        {
            _Module.StartMonitor();
#if _WIN32_WINNT >= 0x0400 & defined(_ATL_FREE_THREADED)
            hRes =
_Module.RegisterClassObjects(CLSCTX_LOCAL_SERVER,
                REGCLS_MULTIPLEUSE | REGCLS_SUSPENDED);
            _ASSERTE(SUCCEEDED(hRes));
            hRes = CoResumeClassObjects();
#else
            hRes =
_Module.RegisterClassObjects(CLSCTX_LOCAL_SERVER,
                REGCLS_MULTIPLEUSE);
#endif
            _ASSERTE(SUCCEEDED(hRes));
//Added by Chuck Wood to open the dialog box
            CEnumDialog c;
            _Module.RevokeClassObjects();
            Sleep(dwPause); //wait for any threads to finish
        }

        _Module.Term();
        CoUninitialize();
        return nRet;
}
```

6. Add a `DoModal` function in your dialog box constructor (in EnumDialog.h) so the dialog box automatically opens when instantiated in the _tWinMain function.

```
class CEnumDialog :
    public CAxDialogImpl<CEnumDialog>
{
public:
    CEnumDialog()
    {
        //Added by Chuck Wood to automatically go modal
        DoModal();
    }
```

7. Add two include statements in your dialog header (EnumDialog.h) — one for CEnumerator support, and one so you can use the ListBox_Addstring function in the next step:

```
// EnumDialog.h : Declaration of the CEnumDialog

#ifndef __ENUMDIALOG_H_
#define __ENUMDIALOG_H_

#include "resource.h"        // main symbols
#include <atlhost.h>
//Added by Chuck Wood — #include for CEnumerator support
#include <atldbcli.h>
//Added by Chuck Wood — #include for ListBox_AddString
support
#include <WindowsX.h>
/////////////////////////////////////////////////////////////
// CEnumDialog
class CEnumDialog :
    public CAxDialogImpl<CEnumDialog>
{
```

8. The final step is to code your OnInitDialog function in your dialog box header (EnumDialog.h) to handle the information in your enumerator. To scroll through your enumerator, you simply need to:

a. Declare your CEnumerator class.

b. Open your CEnumerator class the same way you open any rowset (for example, myEnum.Open( );).

c. Move to the first row with (you guessed it) the MoveFirst function.

d. Handle any CEnumerator variables that are shown in Table 12-1. Use MoveNext to scroll to the next row.

e. Close the rowset using (you guessed it again) the Close function.

These steps are shown in the OnInitDialog function that follows:

```
LRESULT OnInitDialog(UINT uMsg, WPARAM wParam, LPARAM lParam,
BOOL& bHandled)
{
//This function was written by Chuck Wood
//to show an enumerator
    CEnumerator cenum;      //Declare an enumerator
// String for building the list
    char strProviderList[255];
    cenum.Open();      //Open a class enumerator
```

```
//Go to the first provider in the rowset
    HRESULT hr = cenum.MoveFirst();
//Retrieve the list box control
    HWND hwndCtl = GetDlgItem(IDC_PROVIDERLIST);
//Go until the end of the rowset
    while (hr == S_OK) {
//Build a string with the name and parse name of the
//Enumerator
        sprintf(strProviderList, "%-60S %S",
            cenum.m_szName, cenum.m_szDescription);
//Use the ListBox_AddString function to add the string
//to the list box
        ListBox_AddString(hwndCtl, strProviderList);
//Get the next provider in the rowset
        hr = cenum.MoveNext();
    }
//Close your rowset
    cenum.Close();     //Close the enumerator
    return 1;  // Let the system set the focus
}
```

A list of providers and enumerators is then displayed in a listbox, as shown in Figure 12-12.

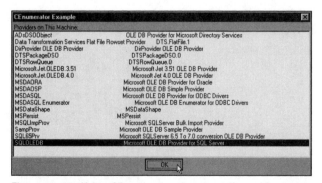

Figure 12-12: Using CEnumerator rowsets easily enables you to see which OLE DB providers are available.

The code for the CEnumerator class can be found in the EnumDialog directory on the CD-ROM that accompanies this book.

Summary

For most, if not all, of your database access, you can use traditional, simple rowsets. However, you should be aware of your options when using a consumer in case your development efforts can be improved or your finished product can be enhanced. To recap:

- ◆ Array rowsets can be used to retrieve an entire rowset and access it using array notation rather than using Move operations. This technique is best used for reports.

- ◆ Bulk rowsets enable you to retrieve and update records in bulk. This technique can be used to enhance access time when multiple updates are performed on several records.

- ◆ Multiple rowsets can be retrieved by an SQL statement separated by a semicolon or by a database stored procedure containing multiple SELECT statements. It is usually never a good idea to have a data source require multiple rowsets, but it's good to know the technique in case you need multiple accessors for data someone else provided.

- ◆ Multiple rowsets require a manual accessor or a dynamic accessor to function properly. Normal automatic accessors won't function because they can't handle the multiple results that are returned by the multiple rowset function.

- ◆ You won't be able to find good enumerator documentation in several versions of the MSDN, but it's not that hard to do, as shown in this chapter.

Chapter 13

Developing OLE DB Providers

IN THIS CHAPTER

- ◆ Understanding when and why providers should be created

- ◆ Using the Provider Wizard to generate an OLE DB provider

- ◆ Understanding the components of an OLE DB provider

- ◆ Changing an OLE DB provider to meet your needs

- ◆ Writing a consumer for your new provider

A PROVIDER IS A set of COM components that provide a gateway to some sort of data, usually a database. Because OLE DB providers are COM components, any OLE DB consumer or ADO program in any language (Visual Basic, Java, and so on) can access data from any OLE DB provider. Visual C++ 6 developers can use OLE DB templates to aid in creating an OLE DB provider that can be used from any OLE DB consumer.

Why Create a Provider?

Many developers think that creating a provider is great for those mega-corporations that sell databases and need to grant access to those databases. However, providers can ease the development burden in *any* multiuser environment. Microsoft currently is pushing the Universal Data Access technique that enables programmers to access data no matter what form that data is in: text, e-mail, directory structure, graphics, and so on. By creating a provider for those programs that you wish to access, you get some major benefits:

- ◆ You expose data to programmers in a way that is familiar to them and consistent across data storage types. This not only enables control for performance and security in one central location, but also makes it possible for a developer to give special access to programmers who typically don't have that type of access with that data format. For example, programmers can query an e-mail account for messages containing a certain text.

◆ You enable programmers to migrate their access from one form to another (for example, text files to database tables, one e-mail package to another, and so on) without major changes to all the programs that access those tables. By simply rewriting a provider or changing a provider, you can make all your programs change the way they access data with very little work.

◆ Using ADO, you can access data in almost any language, whether it be Visual Basic, PowerBuilder, Java, or other languages that support ActiveX controls. Your provider can serve to help all programmers at your site access your data in the same, consistent way.

Universal Data Access (UDA) is a vision put forth by Microsoft to simplify and standardize development. The Provider Wizard described in this chapter enables you to deliver UDA support without much effort.

See the section "Understanding Universal Data Access" in Chapter 1.

Understanding the Provider Structure

Providers have to enable consumers to have access to a data source, a session within that data source, a command within that session, a transaction that affects the session, or a rowset contained in either the session or the command. This is shown graphically in Figure 13-1.

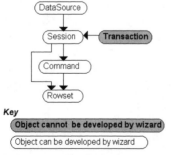

Figure 13-1: The OLE DB provider structure enables OLE DB consumers to access various parts of a data source.

For more information about the OLE DB structure and a definition of these terms, see Chapter 7.

Easily Generating an OLE DB Provider

Writing an OLE DB provider can be a tedious task. Fortunately, Visual C++ provides a wizard that enables you to easily create your own provider. The OLE DB Wizard is designed to generate an OLE DB directory structure provider that you can then change to suit your own needs. To access the wizard, perform the following five easy steps:

1. Create a new ATL COM project by clicking File → New and clicking the project tab. In previous chapters, you have always created .exe files with the ATL COM Wizard, but when you create providers, you need to create a .DLL. In Figure 13-2, I create a new ATL COM project called OLEDB DirProvider. Click OK, then accept all the defaults, and click Finish.

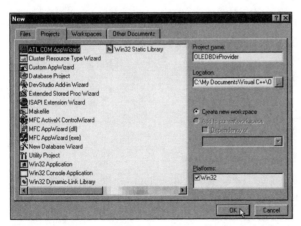

Figure 13-2: A new OLE DB provider can be created using an ATL COM project.

2. The ATL COM Wizard creates a minimal program shell so you can add ATL objects to your code. Click Insert → New ATL Object to add a new object to your provider, as shown in Figure 13-3.

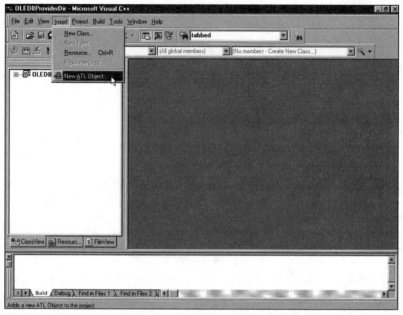

Figure 13-3: You add ATL objects to a project by clicking Insert → New ATL Object.

3. Now you should see the ATL Object Wizard. Choose the Data Access category, and click Provider, as shown in Figure 13-4. Then click Next.

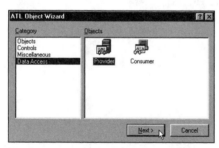

Figure 13-4: The ATL Object Wizard enables you to easily add a provider to your current application.

4. You should then see the ATL Object Wizard Properties window. Type in the name of your new OLE DB provider in the Short Name textbox. In Figure 13-5, I typed DirProvider to indicate that any consumer should choose DirProvider as their OLE DB provider if they want to use the provider I am now generating. The rest of the textboxes are filled in automatically as you type in the short name, but you can change them if you wish.

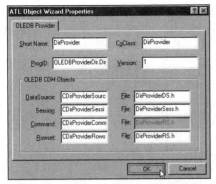

Figure 13-5: The ATL Object Wizard Properties window enables
you to name your new OLE DB provider.

Now you are finished. The OLE DB Provider Wizard has automatically written a
directory provider that provides directory information in a database format. You
now have a provider that takes the directory as the command name and returns the
following fields:

- Attributes of the file

- Long name of the file

- Short name of the file

- High size of the file

- Low size of the file

Inside the Provider

Before we go into altering the provider to suit your needs, you need a little understanding of the provider structure. This section describes the data source header
file, the session header file, the rowset header file, and the .cpp file.

Inside the Data Source

The data source is the original COM object the consumer deals with when using
your OLE DB provider. The data source is all contained in a header file
(DirProviderDS.h) that contains the class declaration, the Registry declaration, the
property set map, and the COM map.

THE CLASS DECLARATION
The data source class (CDirProviderSource) uses multiple inheritance, as shown
by the following code:

```
// CDataSource
class ATL_NO_VTABLE CDirProviderSource :
    public CComObjectRootEx<CComSingleThreadModel>,
    public CComCoClass<CDirProviderSource, &CLSID_DirProvider>,
    public IDBCreateSessionImpl<CDirProviderSource,
CDirProviderSession>,
    public IDBInitializeImpl<CDirProviderSource>,
    public IDBPropertiesImpl<CDirProviderSource>,
    public IPersistImpl<CDirProviderSource>,
    public IInternalConnectionImpl<CDirProviderSource>
```

The following base classes are used inside the CDirProviderSource class:

- ◆ The CComObjectRootEx class contains an implementation of the COM interface IUnknown, which is implemented by all COM objects. IUnknown provides access to other COM interfaces on the object and also handles reference counting.

- ◆ The CComCoClass class implements the necessary functionality for the object to be created externally by other COM applications. This is necessary for an OLE DB data source, because the first step done by a data source consumer is to create the data source object.

- ◆ The IDBInitializeImpl ATL class provides an implementation of the OLE DB interface IDBInitialize, which is mandatory on data source objects.

- ◆ The IDBPropertiesImpl ATL class provides an implementation of the IDBProperties interface, which is mandatory on data source objects.

- ◆ The IPersistImpl ATL class provides an implementation of the IPersist interface, which enables the data source object to be queried for its CLSID. The CLSID identifies the type of COM object.

- ◆ The InternalConnectionImpl ATL class provides an implementation of IInternalConnection, which is an internal ATL interface that keeps track of the number of sessions open on this data source.

By using multiple inheritance, the data source class can implement much of the technology already present in other classes.

THE REGISTRY DECLARATION

The Registry declaration is a single line of code that indicates that the provider needs to be placed inside the Registry:

```
DECLARE_REGISTRY_RESOURCEID(IDR_DIRPROVIDER)
```

After the provider is registered, it can be used by any consumer on the same machine.

THE PROPERTY SET MAP

The property set map lists the properties that are supported by your data source. The code generated by the ATL Wizard is as follows:

```
BEGIN_PROPSET_MAP(CDirProviderSource)
    BEGIN_PROPERTY_SET(DBPROPSET_DATASOURCEINFO)
        PROPERTY_INFO_ENTRY(ACTIVESESSIONS)
        PROPERTY_INFO_ENTRY(DATASOURCEREADONLY)
        PROPERTY_INFO_ENTRY(BYREFACCESSORS)
        PROPERTY_INFO_ENTRY(OUTPUTPARAMETERAVAILABILITY)
        PROPERTY_INFO_ENTRY(PROVIDEROLEDBVER)
        PROPERTY_INFO_ENTRY(DSOTHREADMODEL)
        PROPERTY_INFO_ENTRY(SUPPORTEDTXNISOLEVELS)
        PROPERTY_INFO_ENTRY(USERNAME)
    END_PROPERTY_SET(DBPROPSET_DATASOURCEINFO)
    BEGIN_PROPERTY_SET(DBPROPSET_DBINIT)
        PROPERTY_INFO_ENTRY(AUTH_PASSWORD)
        PROPERTY_INFO_ENTRY(AUTH_PERSIST_SENSITIVE_AUTHINFO)
        PROPERTY_INFO_ENTRY(AUTH_USERID)
        PROPERTY_INFO_ENTRY(INIT_DATASOURCE)
        PROPERTY_INFO_ENTRY(INIT_HWND)
        PROPERTY_INFO_ENTRY(INIT_LCID)
        PROPERTY_INFO_ENTRY(INIT_LOCATION)
        PROPERTY_INFO_ENTRY(INIT_MODE)
        PROPERTY_INFO_ENTRY(INIT_PROMPT)
        PROPERTY_INFO_ENTRY(INIT_PROVIDERSTRING)
        PROPERTY_INFO_ENTRY(INIT_TIMEOUT)
    END_PROPERTY_SET(DBPROPSET_DBINIT)
    CHAIN_PROPERTY_SET(CDirProviderCommand)
END_PROPSET_MAP()
```

The property map lists all of the properties supported by the provider. Each property is grouped inside a property set. By default, the data source has two property sets:

◆ The DBPROPSET_DATASOURCEINFO property set lists properties that affect the property data source.

◆ The DBPROPSET_DBINIT property set lists properties that are used at initialization.

The PROPERTY_SET macro creates a block that contains an array of properties. The provider uses the property map whenever the consumer calls the IDBProperties interface. You don't need to implement every property in the specification. If you do not want to support a property, you can remove it from the map. If you wish to support a property, just add it into the map using a PROPERTY_INFO_ENTRY macro. The property sets and properties are defined by OLE DB. For a list of the available properties, consult the OLE DB documentation.

THE COM MAP

The COM map is important because it controls what functionality is available to the consumer. The COM map for the DirProvider follows:

```
BEGIN_COM_MAP(CDirProviderSource)
    COM_INTERFACE_ENTRY(IDBCreateSession)
    COM_INTERFACE_ENTRY(IDBInitialize)
    COM_INTERFACE_ENTRY(IDBProperties)
    COM_INTERFACE_ENTRY(IPersist)
    COM_INTERFACE_ENTRY(IInternalConnection)
END_COM_MAP()
```

The consumer calls the QueryInterface method to determine what interfaces are supported by the provider. The COM_INTERFACE_ENTRY macro returns the appropriate interfaces to the QueryInterface method.

Inside the Session

The code needed for the session is inside a session header file. (In this case, that would be DirProviderSess.h.) Whereas an application should create only one data source object per application, each data source object can have several sessions. The main reason you might have multiple sessions per application is if you needed multiple transactions open at the same time. Because transactions are supported at the session level, each transaction would need a separate session.

 The Provider Wizard generates the data source, session, command, and rowset objects, but not transaction objects. A transaction object would entail saving out any old records and restoring them if there is a rollback.

If your OLE DB provider supports schema rowsets (and there's no reason why it wouldn't), the OLE DB specification requires that your provider support three schema rowset types:

◆ DBSCHEMA_COLUMNS provides column information.

◆ DBSCHEMA_PROVIDER_TYPES provides data type information.

◆ DBSCHEMA_TABLES provides table information.

Schema rowsets return *metadata* to the consumer without the consumer's having to execute a query or fetch data. The Provider wizard generates implementations for each of these schema rowset types and uses a schema map to tell which classes support which schemas:

```
BEGIN_SCHEMA_MAP(CDirProviderSession)
  SCHEMA_ENTRY(DBSCHEMA_TABLES,
      CDirProviderSessionTRSchemaRowset)
  SCHEMA_ENTRY(DBSCHEMA_COLUMNS,
      CDirProviderSessionColSchemaRowset)
  SCHEMA_ENTRY(DBSCHEMA_PROVIDER_TYPES,
      CDirProviderSessionPTSchemaRowset)
END_SCHEMA_MAP()
```

Each class contained in the schema map contains an execute function that is used to return an S_OK or an E_FAIL depending if the session supports the schema. The classes listed in the schema map are derived from `CRowsetImpl`, which is the easiest way to create a rowset class. The only method required is Execute, which initializes the rowset's array "m_rgRowData" to contain the data for all the rows. The ATL classes implement the other rowset methods.

 Schema rowsets are complicated. In the example in this section, the `DBSCHEMA_TABLES` rowset initializes itself to indicate that there is one table named "c:\curdir*.*" (where "c:\curdir" is the current directory). The `DBSCHEMA_COLUMNS` rowset initializes itself by actually opening a new rowset in the session and copying the column info from it.

Inside the Rowset

The rowset header file contains code needed to provide rowsets to the consumer. In the rowset header file (DirProviderRS.h), three classes are used to provide rowsets to the consumer:

♦ The CDirProviderWindowsFile class defines the data of a single row. In general terms, this class represents the type of data record that the provider wants to expose through OLE DB.

♦ The provider command class provides a COM map and a property set map used by the consumer to determine what COM interfaces are provided and what properties are supported.

♦ The provider rowset class actually defines the rowset object that the provider gives out to the consumer. Because CRowsetImpl is used as a base class, the only required method is the Execute method, which initializes the rowset contents.

This section describes the provider windows file and the provider rowset.

The provider command class, while important, is similar in structure to the data source and needs no further explanation. For explanations of a COM map or a property set map, see the section "Inside the Provider" earlier in this chapter.

THE PROVIDER WINDOWS FILE

The provider windows file is the default that contains the definition of one row of data. At first glance, it looks as if our providers file contains no data because it contains no variable definitions. However, the windows file automatically generated by the Provider Wizard is inherited from the WIN32_FIND_DATA structure:

```
class CDirProviderWindowsFile:
    public WIN32_FIND_DATA
```

This structure is a Windows system structure and contains file information:

```
typedef struct _WIN32_FIND_DATA { // wfd
    DWORD    dwFileAttributes;
    FILETIME ftCreationTime;
    FILETIME ftLastAccessTime;
    FILETIME ftLastWriteTime;
    DWORD    nFileSizeHigh;
    DWORD    nFileSizeLow;
    DWORD    dwReserved0;    DWORD    dwReserved1;
    TCHAR    cFileName[ MAX_PATH ];
    TCHAR    cAlternateFileName[ 14 ];
} WIN32_FIND_DATA;
```

A subset of these variables are defined inside the provider column map, which defines which variables are to be used for the rowset:

```
BEGIN_PROVIDER_COLUMN_MAP(CMoreJunkWindowsFile)
    PROVIDER_COLUMN_ENTRY("FileAttributes", 1, dwFileAttributes)
    PROVIDER_COLUMN_ENTRY("FileSizeHigh",   2, nFileSizeHigh)
    PROVIDER_COLUMN_ENTRY("FileSizeLow",    3, nFileSizeLow)
    PROVIDER_COLUMN_ENTRY("FileName",       4, cFileName)
    PROVIDER_COLUMN_ENTRY("AltFileName",    5, cAlternateFileName)
```

```
END_PROVIDER_COLUMN_MAP()
};
```

Now, whenever a consumer attaches to your provider, the consumer needs to declare five variables to contain the five columns defined by the column map.

THE PROVIDER ROWSET

The provider rowset contains the most important class function in the entire provider project. The Execute method inside the rowset class (CDirProviderRowset inside DirProviderRS.h) contains the code needed to populate your rowset with rows from your data source.

The class declaration of the rowset inherits from the CRowsetImpl template and uses the provider rowset, windows file, and command:

```
class CDirProviderRowset: public CRowsetImpl< CDirProviderRowset,
CDirProviderWindowsFile, CDirProviderCommand>
```

The Execute function retrieves the necessary information and adds it to the rowset using the CRowsetImpl::m_rgRowData.add method until the entire rowset is built:

```
HRESULT Execute(DBPARAMS * pParams, LONG* pcRowsAffected)
{
    USES_CONVERSION;
    BOOL bFound = FALSE;
    HANDLE hFile;
    LPTSTR  szDir = (m_strCommandText == _T("")) ? _T("*.*") :
OLE2T(m_strCommandText);
    CDirProviderWindowsFile wf;
    hFile = FindFirstFile(szDir, &wf);
    if (hFile == INVALID_HANDLE_VALUE)
        return DB_E_ERRORSINCOMMAND;
    LONG cFiles = 1;
    BOOL bMoreFiles = TRUE;
    while (bMoreFiles)
    {
        if (!m_rgRowData.Add(wf))
            return E_OUTOFMEMORY;
        bMoreFiles = FindNextFile(hFile, &wf);
        cFiles++;
    }
    FindClose(hFile);
    if (pcRowsAffected != NULL)
```

```
            *pcRowsAffected = cFiles;
        return S_OK;
    }
};
```

Adding Code to the Provider

The provider you generated provides directory information through the OLE DB interface. In this section, that code is changed slightly so that you can see the changes that will probably occur when you write your own provider.

Although the directory structure provided by the new provider is useful, perhaps a new specification is called for:

- ◆ The attributes returned are in a bit mask and will be changed to include one of the following characters:

    - ■ "D" is used for directories.

    - ■ "R" is used for read-only files.

    - ■ "S" is used for system files.

    - ■ "A" is used for archived files.

    - ■ "H" is used for hidden files.

    - ■ "T" is used for temporary files.

    For example, if a file were a directory and were hidden, the attributes listed would be "DH", or if a file were a read-only, hidden system file that had been archived, the attributes would be "RSAH".

- ◆ The file size is returned, rather than the low file size and the high file size.

- ◆ The short filename (8.3 format) and the long filename are both returned.

This section describes how to make these changes.

Rowset Changes

The first changes are made to the rowset. Remember how the windows file was inherited from `WIN32_FIND_DATA` in the `CDirProviderWindowsFile` in the DirProviderRS.h header file? This inheritance is almost always removed for any provider. In its place are the actual variables you need present in your provider:

```
class CDirProviderWindowsFile
{
public:
```

```
TCHAR      cFileName[ MAX_PATH ];
TCHAR      cShortFileName[ 14 ];
DWORD      nFileSize;
TCHAR      strFileAttributes[7];
BEGIN_PROVIDER_COLUMN_MAP(CDirProviderWindowsFile)
    PROVIDER_COLUMN_ENTRY("FileName",       1, cFileName)
    PROVIDER_COLUMN_ENTRY("AltFileName",    2, cShortFileName)
    PROVIDER_COLUMN_ENTRY("FileSize",       3, nFileSize)
    PROVIDER_COLUMN_ENTRY("FileAttributes", 4, strFileAttributes)
END_PROVIDER_COLUMN_MAP()
};
```

As you can see, the code for the CDirProviderWindowsFile class is substantially different from the code generated by the ATL Object Wizard. Next you need to change your execute method to populate the code you need:

```
HRESULT Execute(DBPARAMS * pParams, LONG* pcRowsAffected)
{
    USES_CONVERSION;
    BOOL bFound = FALSE;
    HANDLE hFile;
    LPTSTR  szDir = (m_strCommandText == _T("")) ? _T("*.*") :
OLE2T(m_strCommandText);
    CDirProviderWindowsFile wf;
    WIN32_FIND_DATA fileInfo;
    hFile = FindFirstFile(szDir, &fileInfo);
    if (hFile == INVALID_HANDLE_VALUE)
    return DB_E_ERRORSINCOMMAND;
    LONG cFiles = 1;
    BOOL bMoreFiles = TRUE;
    while (bMoreFiles)
    {
        wf.nFileSize = fileInfo.nFileSizeLow;
        strcpy(wf.cFileName, fileInfo.cFileName);
        strcpy(wf.cShortFileName, fileInfo.cAlternateFileName);
        strcpy (wf.strFileAttributes, "");
        if (fileInfo.dwFileAttributes & FILE_ATTRIBUTE_DIRECTORY) {
            strcat(wf.strFileAttributes, "D");
        }
        if (fileInfo.dwFileAttributes &  FILE_ATTRIBUTE_READONLY) {
            strcat(wf.strFileAttributes, "R");
        }
        if (fileInfo.dwFileAttributes & FILE_ATTRIBUTE_SYSTEM) {
            strcat(wf.strFileAttributes, "S");
        }
```

```
    if (fileInfo.dwFileAttributes & FILE_ATTRIBUTE_ARCHIVE) {
        strcat(wf.strFileAttributes, "A");
    }
    if (fileInfo.dwFileAttributes & FILE_ATTRIBUTE_HIDDEN) {
        strcat(wf.strFileAttributes, "H");
    }
    if (fileInfo.dwFileAttributes & FILE_ATTRIBUTE_TEMPORARY) {
        strcat(wf.strFileAttributes, "T");
    }
    if (!m_rgRowData.Add(wf))
        return E_OUTOFMEMORY;
    bMoreFiles = FindNextFile(hFile, &fileInfo);
    cFiles++;
}
FindClose(hFile);
if (pcRowsAffected != NULL)
    *pcRowsAffected = cFiles;
return S_OK;
}
```

As you can see by the changes in the code, although we are providing similar functionality to the default functionality written by the Provider Wizard, some substantial changes were needed to the class definition and to the CDirProviderWindowsFile ::Execute method to effect these changes.

Session Changes

You're not finished making changes. The session that is generated by the Provider Wizard relies on the fact that the CDirProviderWindowsFile class is inherited from the WIN32_FIND_DATA structure.

TIP   As a general rule, you never want your classes to be needlessly dependent on other classes. The Provider Wizard breaks this important rule by using CDirProviderWindowsFile instead of WIN32_FIND_DATA when querying data, even though there is no need for the additional functionality that class provides. As soon as CDirProviderWindowsFile is changed, the session will no longer work.

All declarations of CDirProviderWindowsFile are replaced by declarations using the WIN32_FIND_DATA structure in the following code. This needs to happen in two functions:

◆ In the `CDirProviderSessionTRSchemaRowset::Execute` method:

```
class CDirProviderSessionTRSchemaRowset :
    public CRowsetImpl< CDirProviderSessionTRSchemaRowset,
CTABLESRow, CDirProviderSession>
{
public:
    HRESULT Execute(LONG* pcRowsAffected, ULONG, const
VARIANT*)
    {
        USES_CONVERSION;
        //Changed session to not rely on rowset
//        CDirProviderWindowsFile wf;
        WIN32_FIND_DATA wf;
        CTABLESRow trData;
        lstrcpyW(trData.m_szType, OLESTR("TABLE"));
        lstrcpyW(trData.m_szDesc, OLESTR(
                "The Directory Table"));
        HANDLE hFile = INVALID_HANDLE_VALUE;
        TCHAR szDir[MAX_PATH + 1];
        DWORD cbCurDir = GetCurrentDirectory(MAX_PATH,
szDir);
        lstrcat(szDir, _T("\\*.*"));
        hFile = FindFirstFile(szDir, &wf);
        if (hFile == INVALID_HANDLE_VALUE)
            return E_FAIL; // User doesn't have a c:\ drive
        FindClose(hFile);
        lstrcpynW(trData.m_szTable, T2OLE(szDir),
SIZEOF_MEMBER(CTABLESRow, m_szTable));
        if (!m_rgRowData.Add(trData))
            return E_OUTOFMEMORY;
        *pcRowsAffected = 1;
        return S_OK;
    }
};
```

◆ In the `CDirProviderSessionColSchemaRowset::Execute` method:

```
class CDirProviderSessionColSchemaRowset :
    public CRowsetImpl< CDirProviderSessionColSchemaRowset,
CCOLUMNSRow, CDirProviderSession>
{
public:
    HRESULT Execute(LONG* pcRowsAffected, ULONG, const
VARIANT*)
    {
```

```
        USES_CONVERSION;
        //Changed session to not rely on rowset
//      CDirProviderWindowsFile wf;
        WIN32_FIND_DATA wf;
        HANDLE hFile = INVALID_HANDLE_VALUE;
        TCHAR szDir[MAX_PATH + 1];
        DWORD cbCurDir = GetCurrentDirectory(MAX_PATH,
szDir);
        lstrcat(szDir, _T("\\*.*"));
        hFile = FindFirstFile(szDir, &wf);
        if (hFile == INVALID_HANDLE_VALUE)
            return E_FAIL; // User doesn't have a c:\ drive
        FindClose(hFile);// szDir has got the tablename
        DBID dbid;
        memset(&dbid, 0, sizeof(DBID));
        dbid.uName.pwszName = T2OLE(szDir);
        dbid.eKind = DBKIND_NAME;
        return InitFromRowset < _RowsetArrayType >
(m_rgRowData, &dbid, NULL, m_spUnkSite, pcRowsAffected);
    }
};
```

The preceding code checks to see if a rowset can be formed. You will need to make more drastic changes for most session validation checks that don't return directory information.

Now you're finished altering the provider to provide the information that you want to provide. In the next section, a consumer is developed that shows how to access your provider.

In the next chapter, you see how other providers are developed as we access a text file using OLE DB.

On the CD-ROM that accompanies this book, the project name for this example is in the OLEDBDirProvider directory.

Writing an OLE DB Consumer for the New Provider

Now an MFC OLE DB consumer is quickly developed to access the new provider. Perform the following steps:

1. You'll need to create a new MFC project using the MFC AppWizard. Click File → New, click the Projects tab, choose MFC AppWizard (exe), and type in your project name. In Figure 13-6, the name of the project chosen was OLEDBDirConsumer.

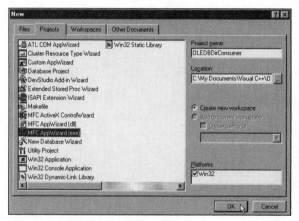

Figure 13-6: You can use the MFC to create new applications that access your new OLE DB provider.

2. In the MFC AppWizard Step 1, choose Single Document, and click the Next button. In the MFC AppWizard Step 2 of 6, choose Database view without file support, as shown in Figure 13-7, and click the Data Source button.

3. The Database Options window should then be open. Choose OLE DB, and click the Select OLE DB Datasource button, as shown in Figure 13-8.

4. The Data Link Properties window should then open. Notice in Figure 13-9 how the new OLE DB provider (DIRProvider OLE DB Provider) is listed in the listbox. Choose the new OLE DB provider (DIRProvider OLE DB Provider), and click OK.

Figure 13-7: You need to choose database view in the MFC
AppWizard to get database support.

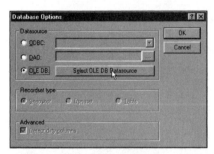

Figure 13-8: You need to choose an OLE DB datasource to
build a consumer for your new provider.

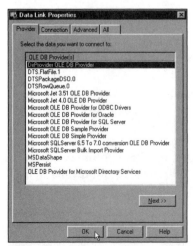

Figure 13-9: Your new provider should be listed in the
Data Link Properties window.

5. You are returned to the Database Options window. Click OK to close the window. The Select Database Tables window is then displayed. You should see a pathname at the top of your list. If no table was defined, you should see a blank line. Click it to highlight it, as shown in Figure 13-10. Then click OK.

Figure 13-10: You need to "choose" the blank line in the Select Database Tables listbox to continue building your OLE DB project.

6. You then return to the MFC AppWizard, Step 2 of 6 window. Click Next twice, turn off the printing and print preview choice, and click Finish. Then click OK when the New Project Information dialog box appears.

7. Make your dialog box look similar to the dialog box shown in Figure 13-11.

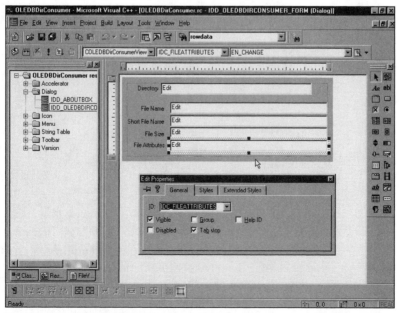

Figure 13-11: For the DirProvider consumer, be sure to make textboxes for every variable returned by the provider.

8. In your rowset header file (OLEDBDirConsumer.h), the CMy class contains the variables needed to communicate with the provider. Change your variable names in the CMy class to fit the variables returned by the provider. In the code that follows, the column names returned by the provider are left commented out so you can see a comparison of the old names and the new names:

```
class CMy
{
public:
    CMy()
    {
        memset( (void*)this, 0, sizeof(*this) );
    };
/*  Old Structure
    char m_column0[261];
    char m_column1[15];
    unsigned int m_column2;
    char m_column3[8];
*/
    char m_strFileName[261];
    char m_strShortFileName[15];
    unsigned int m_nFileSize;
    char m_strFileAttributes[8];


BEGIN_COLUMN_MAP(CMy)
/* Old map
    COLUMN_ENTRY_TYPE(1, DBTYPE_STR, m_column0)
    COLUMN_ENTRY_TYPE(2, DBTYPE_STR, m_column1)
    COLUMN_ENTRY_TYPE(3, DBTYPE_UI4, m_column2)
    COLUMN_ENTRY_TYPE(4, DBTYPE_STR, m_column3)
*/
    COLUMN_ENTRY_TYPE(1, DBTYPE_STR, m_strFileName)
    COLUMN_ENTRY_TYPE(2, DBTYPE_STR, m_strShortFileName)
    COLUMN_ENTRY_TYPE(3, DBTYPE_UI4, m_nFileSize)
    COLUMN_ENTRY_TYPE(4, DBTYPE_STR, m_strFileAttributes)
END_COLUMN_MAP()
};
```

9. The rowset class declaration (COLEDBDirConsumerSet in OLEDBDir Consumer.h) needs routines that initialize the current directory and enable you to change the directory to reinitialize the rowset. Add a CString variable that can hold the directory, and write SetDir and GetDir functions to set or return the current directory:

```
class COLEDBDirConsumerSet : public CCommand<CAccessor<CMy> >
{
```

```
protected:
    CString m_strDirectory;
public:
    COLEDBDirConsumerSet() {
        //Initialize directory
        m_strDirectory = _T("C:\\*.*");
    }
    void SetDir(CString dirName) {
        //Reset Directory
        if (dirName != GetDir()) {
            Close();
            m_strDirectory = dirName;
            Open();
        }
    }
    CString GetDir() {
        return m_strDirectory;
    }
```

10. Because there is no update property for the provider, you don't need to set the update property in your consumer in your Open function in OLEDBDirConsumer.h. Additionally, you should use the m_strDirectory variable to pass to the CCommand.Open function:

```
HRESULT Open()
{
    CDataSource db;
    CSession    session;
    HRESULT        hr;

    CDBPropSet    dbinit(DBPROPSET_DBINIT);
    dbinit.AddProperty(DBPROP_AUTH_PASSWORD, "");

dbinit.AddProperty(DBPROP_AUTH_PERSIST_SENSITIVE_AUTHINFO,
false);
    dbinit.AddProperty(DBPROP_AUTH_USERID, "");
    dbinit.AddProperty(DBPROP_INIT_DATASOURCE, "");
    dbinit.AddProperty(DBPROP_INIT_LCID, (long)0);
    dbinit.AddProperty(DBPROP_INIT_LOCATION, "");
    dbinit.AddProperty(DBPROP_INIT_MODE, (long)0);
    dbinit.AddProperty(DBPROP_INIT_PROMPT, (short)2);
    dbinit.AddProperty(DBPROP_INIT_PROVIDERSTRING, "");
    dbinit.AddProperty(DBPROP_INIT_TIMEOUT, (long)0);

    hr =
db.OpenWithServiceComponents("OLEDBDirProvider.DirProvider.1"
```

```
, &dbinit);
    if (FAILED(hr))
        return hr;
    hr = session.Open(db);
    if (FAILED(hr))
        return hr;

    CDBPropSet      propset(DBPROPSET_ROWSET);
    propset.AddProperty(DBPROP_CANFETCHBACKWARDS, true);
    propset.AddProperty(DBPROP_IRowsetScroll, true);
    propset.AddProperty(DBPROP_IRowsetChange, true);
//    propset.AddProperty(DBPROP_UPDATABILITY,
//DBPROPVAL_UP_CHANGE | DBPROPVAL_UP_INSERT |
//DBPROPVAL_UP_DELETE );
    hr = CCommand<CAccessor<CMy> >::Open(session,
m_strDirectory, &propset);
    if (FAILED(hr))
        return hr;

    return MoveNext();
}
```

11. You need a variable that can hold the directory structure in your view program. In the Class Wizard (View → Class Wizard), tie a variable to your directory textbox (IDC_DIRECTORY), as shown in Figure 13-12.

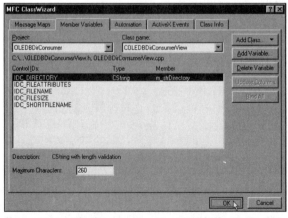

Figure 13-12: The directory is not a database variable and needs a string tied to it.

12. In the Class Wizard, you need to capture the EN_KILLFOCUS event for the directory textbox, as shown in Figure 13-13. This enables you to detect any changes made to the directory textbox. When the directory changes, you need to reinitialize your rowset.

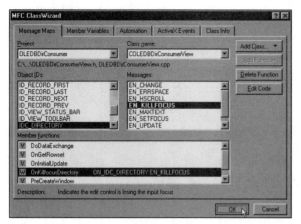

Figure 13-13: The EN_KILLFOCUS triggers every time focus leaves the directory textbox and enables you to check for changes.

13. Add your dynamic data exchange functions for your variables inside your DoDataExchange function in your COLEDBDirConsumerView class in the OLEDBDirConsumerView.cpp source file:

```
void COLEDBDirConsumerView::DoDataExchange(CDataExchange*
pDX)
{
    COleDBRecordView::DoDataExchange(pDX);
    //{{AFX_DATA_MAP(COLEDBDirConsumerView)
    DDX_Text(pDX, IDC_DIRECTORY, m_strDirectory);
    DDV_MaxChars(pDX, m_strDirectory, 260);
    //}}AFX_DATA_MAP
//Added by Chuck Wood to link OLE DB Variables to text boxes
    DDX_Text(pDX, IDC_FILEATTRIBUTES, m_pSet->
m_strFileAttributes, 7);
    DDX_Text(pDX, IDC_FILESIZE, m_pSet->m_nFileSize);
    DDX_Text(pDX, IDC_FILENAME, m_pSet->m_strFileName, 260);
    DDX_Text(pDX, IDC_SHORTFILENAME, m_pSet->
m_strShortFileName, 14);
}
```

14. Be sure to initialize your directory variable with your default directory in the OnInitialUpdate function in your COLEDBDirConsumerView class in the OLEDBDirConsumerView.cpp source file:

```
void COLEDBDirConsumerView::OnInitialUpdate()
{
    m_pSet = &GetDocument()->m_oLEDBDirConsumerSet;
    {
        CWaitCursor wait;
```

```
        HRESULT hr = m_pSet->Open();
        if (hr != S_OK)
        {
            AfxMessageBox(_T("Record set failed to open."),
MB_OK);
            m_bOnFirstRecord = TRUE;
            m_bOnLastRecord = TRUE;
        }
    }
    //Added by Chuck Wood to initialize the directory
    m_strDirectory = m_pSet->GetDir();
    COleDBRecordView::OnInitialUpdate();
}
```

15. Finally, your Class Wizard created an `OnKillfocusDirectory` function
    in the `COLEDBDirConsumerView` class in the **OLEDBDirConsumerView.cpp**
    source file. Code needs to be added that sets the directory every time focus
    leaves the textbox. This can be done using the `COLEDBDirConsumerSet`
    `::SetDir` function written in step 9. The `UpdateData` function can be
    used to take data to and from the dialog box:

```
void COLEDBDirConsumerView::OnKillfocusDirectory()
{
    UpdateData(TRUE);
    m_pSet->SetDir(m_strDirectory);
    UpdateData(FALSE);
}
```

Now you have a working consumer for your new producer. Figure 13-14 shows
how the producer can automatically scroll through directory entries.

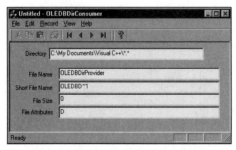

Figure 13-14: Your new OLE DB provider can provide directory
information in a database format.

It really is better to complete your OLE DB provider before using it in a consumer program. If you work on both at the same time, you are likely to write consumer code that does not quite fit the provider's new structure. This leads to database errors that are extremely difficult to track down.

Be sure to build your OLEDBDirProvider project, if you have not done so already. This is not really a step for developing your consumer, but your consumer won't work unless Visual C++ has registered your provider.

As shown in this section, developers need to know only one access method in order to access both database and nondatabase data. In addition, this provider works with any OLE DB consumer or any ADO program written in any language. Microsoft's push for Universal Data Access can reduce the learning curve for program development.

If you want to see some more providers, check out the next chapter, where we discuss text file providers and e-mail providers.

On the CD-ROM accompanying this book, the project name for this example is in the OLEDBDirConsumer directory.

Summary

Provider development is not just for database developers. Providers can enable any developer to simplify access to nonrelational data. To recap:

◆ Providers are a way to enable Universal Data Access for nonrelational data.

◆ The Provider Wizard makes provider development a breeze.

- ◆ The Execute function inside the rowset in a provider always needs to be changed to build the rowset the way you want.

- ◆ The session also needs to be changed to meet individual specifications.

- ◆ Once written, an OLE DB provider enables consumers and ADO programs to access your data in any language.

Part IV

Special Database Topics

Chapter 14

Developing Web-Based Databases

IN THIS CHAPTER

- ◆ Understanding Dynamic HTML

- ◆ Building a DHTML project

- ◆ Building a DHTML ActiveX OLE DB project

- ◆ Understanding Active Server Pages and client versus server programs

MANY WEB PAGES USED TO CONSIST of raw text and perhaps some Java-enabled program that caused an object to spin around on the page. However, in today's competitive environment, companies are insisting that their Web pages provide specific information, take orders, and respond to user inquiries using a database. This chapter shows you how to build an ActiveX control that retrieves database information and how to place that control on a Web page. This ActiveX control is hosted in an HTML Active Server Page (asp) and uses Dynamic HTML (DHTML) to create an HTML-based display for the ActiveX control. This chapter concludes by showing the difference between client computing and server computing. It describes how to make an Active Server Page so that the Web user doesn't need to load any additional software, doesn't need a specific Web browser, and doesn't need to have direct access to the database to run a database program.

 This chapter goes heavily into HTML, especially into HTML forms and HTML tables. Many C++ developers can follow HTML pretty closely, but if HTML is a mystery to you, I suggest purchasing an introductory HTML book and concentrating on HTML tables and HTML forms before reading this chapter. In addition, while this chapter covers *some* Dynamic HTML, the main thrust of this chapter (and this book) is adding database access to your Web page. You may want to invest in a C++ book that covers Dynamic HTML in more detail if you want to find out more that you can do with Dynamic HTML.

Understanding Dynamic HTML

When Microsoft came out with Internet Explorer 4.0, they introduced the concept of Dynamic HTML. Dynamic HTML (DHTML) is a revolutionary HTML object model that enables developers to manipulate HTML interactively based on events, such as button clicks or form entries. You can use Active Template Libraries (ATL) to create a project that contains Dynamic HTML capability in a Web browser or other container. OLE DB can send information to a Web page through DHTML, as shown in Figure 14-1.

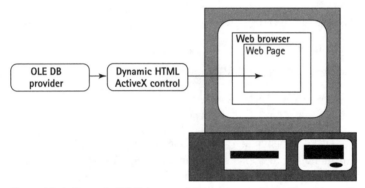

Figure 14-1: Dynamic HTML is one of the best ways ActiveX enables active database content inside a Web page.

Because it uses standard ATL libraries, you can tie HTML to OLE DB inside an ActiveX control to give your programs interaction capability that is simply not available with standard Web pages. In addition, you can develop DHTML ActiveX OLE DB projects inside your Visual Studio environment using standard Visual C++.

Understanding ActiveX with HTML

ActiveX controls are components that can be used with most Windows development environments, and they also can be inserted on an HTML Web page (if the browser is Microsoft Internet Explorer or by using a plug-in). Using Dynamic HTML and an ActiveX control, you can actually write HTML code to the client's browser from your server. Internet Explorer 3.x and later support embedding ActiveX controls on a Web page. This addition to standard HTML enables Web pages to share the advanced, sophisticated modules available in other Windows environments.

To embed an ActiveX control on a Web page, you need to use the <OBJECT> tag. In the tag, you need to specify the ID of the control and the CLASSID of the control that is contained in your Registry. You probably also need to increase the default width and height so your program can run:

```
<HTML><HEAD>

<TITLE>Dynamic HTML Example</TITLE>
</HEAD>
<BODY>
<OBJECT
ID="DHTMLControl"
WIDTH=640
HEIGHT=480
CLASSID="CLSID:E40A11EE-AA4B-11D2-9949-C4CF5F772B46">
</OBJECT>

</BODY></HTML>
```

Fortunately, C++ generates the class ID inside the Windows Registry using ATL's registration code inside your Registry resource in the (.rc) file of your Windows project. You can find your class ID inside your IDL file in your Visual C++ project:

```
[
    uuid(E40A11EE-AA4B-11D2-9949-C4CF5F772B46),
    helpstring("DHTMLControl Class")
]
```

As a result, not only can you easily develop an ActiveX control, but it automatically runs on your machine when you are finished building your project.

Building a DHTML Project

This section gives a step-by-step description of using the ATL Object Wizard to build a Dynamic HTML project. This section also explains the parts of the code that were developed. To build a DHTML project, perform the following steps:

1. Click File → New to open the New dialog box. Click the Projects tab, and click ATL COM AppWizard. Enter a project name (DHTMLGrades in this example), and click OK, as shown in Figure 14-2.

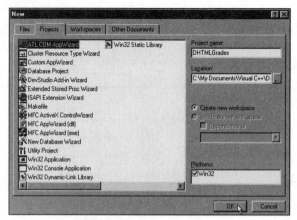

Figure 14-2: The ATL COM AppWizard can be used to create ActiveX DHTML projects.

2. When the ATL COM AppWizard appears, click the Finish button, and click
OK when the New Project Information dialog box appears. The ATL COM
AppWizard then generates code needed for a Visual C++ DLL using the
ATL library. When this is done, click Insert → New ATL Object to open
the ATL Object Wizard, as shown in Figure 14-3.

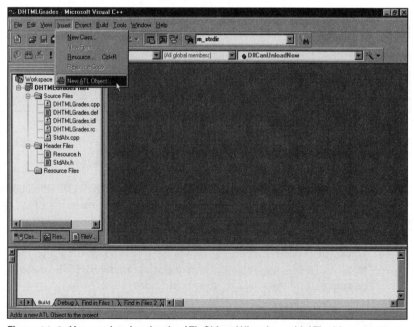

Figure 14-3: You need to invoke the ATL Object Wizard to add ATL objects to your
ATL project.

3. When the ATL Object Wizard opens, click the Controls category, and choose the HTML Control object, as shown in Figure 14-4.

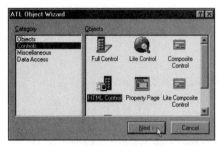

Figure 14–4: DHTML controls use HTML objects generated from the ATL Object Wizard.

4. The ATL Object Wizard Properties dialog box then opens. Type in the short name of your new DHTML control. The rest of the textboxes automatically fill in with default values based on the short name for the control, as shown in Figure 14-5.

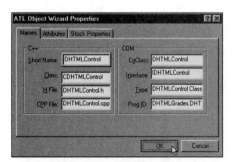

Figure 14–5: The ATL Object Wizard generates classes, .cpp source files, and .h header files based on the short name you use for your ActiveX control.

5. Finally, press F7 to build your project.

Now a working DHMTL project is created. This project uses three buttons that change the color of the HTML background.

Running the DHTML Project

To run the DHTML project you just created, you need to find the HTML file that contains the ActiveX module you created. In this case, the name of the generated HTML file is DHTMLControl.htm, and the code listing is as follows:

```
<HTML>
<HEAD>
<TITLE>ATL 3.0 test page for object DHTMLControl</TITLE>
</HEAD>
<BODY>
<OBJECT ID="DHTMLControl"
CLASSID="CLSID:E40A11EE-AA4B-11D2-9949-C4CF5F772B46">
</OBJECT>
</BODY>
</HTML>
```

As you can see by this code, the HTML contains only an `<OBJECT>` tag that is used to call the DHTML .dll that you just created. When you run this HTML code in Internet Explorer, you end up executing the DHTML code that you just created, as shown by Figure 14-6.

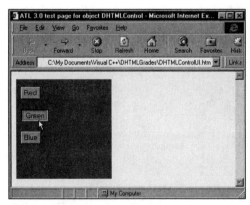

Figure 14–6: You can use Internet Explorer to run and test your new DHTML ActiveX control.

Notice, however, that the code you execute affects only the object within the HTML screen. In Figure 14-6, the background color of the HTML document was changed because of the ActiveX control on the page, but *only the background of the ActiveX control was affected*. To affect an entire HTML page, you should use the LENGTH and WIDTH operators inside the <OBJECT> tag to expand the ActiveX control to the whole window *and* not include any other HTML that can display text in your program. This really shouldn't be too difficult because you can code any required HTML directly into the ActiveX control.

Behind DHTML

To use dynamic HTML to design a project, you need to understand at least four different components of the DHTML project. These components are:

◆ The internal HTML that is used to display your code, which is different from the generated HTML that was previously discussed

◆ The OnCreate function that is executed when the ActiveX control is created

◆ The IDL file used to create an ActiveX/COM module

◆ The STDMETHOD macro and the events it captures

The rest of this section describes these components.

THE USER INTERFACE HTML VERSUS THE ACTIVEX HTML

The HTML used to run and test your ActiveX project (hereafter referred to as the "ActiveX HTML") is different from the user interface HTML that is used to format the document inside your Internet Explorer browser.

When you first generate your project, the user interface HTML is created for you. The following program is a listing of the DHTMLControlUI.htm that is created by the ATL Object Wizard:

```
DHTMLControlUI.htm
<HTML>
<BODY id=theBody>
<BUTTON onclick='window.external.OnClick(theBody,
"red");'>Red</BUTTON>
<BR>
<BR>
<BUTTON onclick='window.external.OnClick(theBody,
"green");'>Green</BUTTON>
```

```
<BR>
<BR>
<BUTTON onclick='window.external.OnClick(theBody,
"blue");'>Blue</BUTTON>
</BODY>
</HTML>
```

As you can see by the preceding HTML code, the HTML that gets executed by the ActiveX control consists of three buttons (labeled "Red", "Green", and "Blue") that process the OnClick event and pass the <BODY> identifier and a string containing the appropriate color.

You probably will want to drastically change your HTML code to fit your project. This involves replacing the preceding HTML code with HTML code that is more specific to your needs. (This is covered later in this chapter.)

THE STDMETHOD MACRO AND THE IDL

The Interface Definition Language (IDL) is a standard language for specifying the interface for remote procedure calls. Microsoft creates an IDL file for you that contains the functions that can be accessed from other applications. These functions often correspond to events that occur in another application.

The user interface HTML contains calls to a OnClick function that corresponds to the click event of the three buttons that change color. The OnClick function, then, must be defined in the IDL file:

```
The OnClick definition in the DHTMLControl.idl source file
interface IDHTMLControlUI : IDispatch
{
    // Example method that will be called by the HTML
    HRESULT OnClick(    [in]IDispatch* pdispBody,
[in]VARIANT varColor);
};
```

In the preceding OnClick method, two parameters are received. The first contains a pointer to the HTML body definition, and the second defines a VARIANT that contains a string containing the new background color.

Each method defined in the IDL should have a STDMETHOD call in the control's header file. In DHTMLControl.h, the user interface HTML calls the OnClick method when a user clicks a button:

```
The OnClick method in DHTMLControl.h
STDMETHOD(OnClick)(IDispatch* pdispBody, VARIANT varColor)
{
    CComQIPtr<IHTMLBodyElement> spBody(pdispBody);
    if (spBody != NULL)
```

```
        spBody->put_bgColor(varColor);
    return S_OK;
}
```

In the preceding code, a new background color is set for the <BODY> tag when a button is clicked. You have to change the methods that are defined both in the IDL file and in the control's header file when you modify your DHTML to suit your needs.

THE ONCREATE FUNCTION

The following OnCreate function is executed when your ActiveX control is first instantiated:

```
The OnCreate method in DHTMLControl.h
LRESULT OnCreate(UINT /*uMsg*/, WPARAM /*wParam*/, LPARAM
/*lParam*/, BOOL& /*bHandled*/)
{
    CAxWindow wnd(m_hWnd);
    HRESULT hr = wnd.CreateControl(IDH_DHTMLCONTROL);
    if (SUCCEEDED(hr))
        hr =
wnd.SetExternalDISPATCH(static_cast<IDHTMLControlUI*>(this));
    if (SUCCEEDED(hr))
        hr = wnd.QueryControl(IID_IWebBrowser2,
(void**)&m_spBrowser);
    return SUCCEEDED(hr) ? 0 : -1;
}
```

If you need to do any initialization, you probably should do it during the OnCreate function. However, most likely you won't need to change the OnCreate function but rather just need to define the user interface HTML and the events that are called.

Building a DHTML ActiveX OLE DB Project

Now that you've gone over a little of DHTML, you are prepared to add database support to your Web page. Say you wanted a Web page that enabled students to enter a user ID and a password and pull up their grades for all their classes, as shown in Figure 14-7.

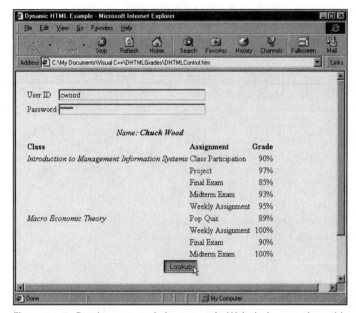

Figure 14-7: Database access is important in Web designs, such as this grade reporter.

A student enters their username and password to pull up their grades. Of course, you wouldn't want any student seeing any grades other than their own. In this section, we show you how to quickly build a Web page that enables these features.

Adding an OLE DB Consumer to Your DHTML Project

The following steps show how you can easily add OLE DB support to your ActiveX module.

1. First, create a view or query with the fields you want to display. The following SQL works in Oracle, Sybase, or MS SQL Server to create a view named "Lookup" to look up the scores for all the assignments of a student:

```
CREATE VIEW Lookup AS
SELECT UserID,
       Password,
       FirstName + ' ' + LastName AS Name,
       Class.Description AS Description,
       Assignment.Description AS Assignment,
       Grades.Score
  FROM Student,
       Grades,
```

```
          Assignment,
          Section,
          Class
  WHERE Student.StudentID = Grades.StudentID
    AND Assignment.AssignmentID = Grades.AssignmentID
    AND Assignment.SectionID = Grades.SectionID
    AND Section.SectionID = Assignment.SectionID
    AND Class.ClassID = Section.ClassID
```

The Access query painter can also be used to create a Lookup query that functions identically to a Lookup view. The Lookup query is shown in Figure 14-8.

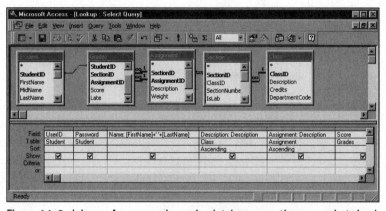

Figure 14-8: Joins or Access queries make database reporting somewhat simpler.

TIP You should use joins (or queries in Access) whenever making complex database reports. Joins enable you to view and debug SQL before executing it inside a program.

2. After you develop a join or query, you should insert a new ATL object. Click Insert → New ATL Object to open the ATL Object Wizard. Choose the Data Access Category, and choose Consumer, as shown in Figure 14-9.

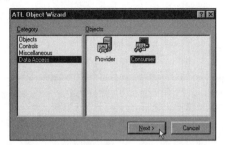

Figure 14-9: Use the ATL Object Wizard to add an OLE DB consumer to your
ATL project.

3. The ATL Object Wizard Properties dialog box opens next. Click the Select
   Datasource button to choose the OLE DB data source needed for your ATL
   object, as shown in Figure 14-10.

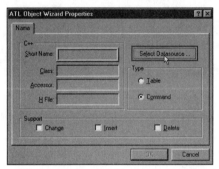

Figure 14-10: You need to select an OLE DB datasource to complete adding an
OLE DB consumer to your project.

4. The Data Link Properties window opens next. Here, you can choose any
   OLE DB database provider that you want to use to connect to your
   database. For this example, I used an OLE DB consumer that mimicked
   an ODBC driver, as shown in Figure 14-11.

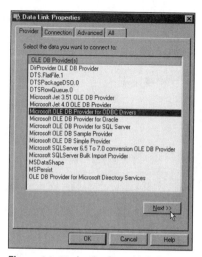

Figure 14-11: In the Data Link Properties window, you first need to select your OLE DB provider.

5. Next, provide the connection information in your Data Link Properties window. In Figure 14-12, I chose the Classes database to use as a database source for this example.

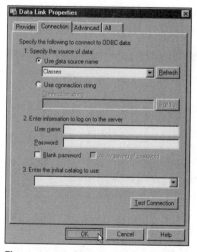

Figure 14-12: Next in the Data Link Properties window, you need to select the database to access your OLE DB consumer.

6. Now the Select Database Table dialog box opens. Here, you choose the table or tables you wish to access. Notice in Figure 14-13 that the Lookup query that was defined in the Access database is also listed at the bottom of the list.

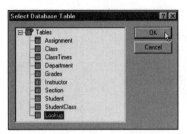

Figure 14-13: Views (or Access queries) are visible within the Select Database Table dialog box.

7. When you return to the ATL Object Wizard Properties dialog box, you can see that the Short Name, Class, Accessor, and header file are all filled in for you (as shown in Figure 14-14). You don't need any update capabilities, so you can simply click OK at this point to create your OLE DB consumer object for your DHTML project.

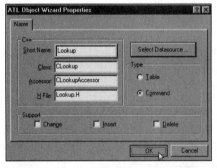

Figure 14-14: The ATL Object Wizard Properties window is filled in with defaults that reflect your database table, view, or in this case, query choice.

Now you are finished adding an OLE DB consumer to your project that accesses the Lookup view that you created in the first step. However, you still need to add some code to enable the DHTML to access your new OLE DB consumer.

Changing the DHTML to Use the Consumer

So far, you have used Visual C++ wizards only to create DHTML and OLE DB consumer objects for you. Some coding changes have to be made to these default objects to be integrated and to provide class information. You need to make the code changes described in the following steps:

1. Web-based ActiveX controls default to 100 pixels by 200 pixels on an Internet Explorer Web page. You probably want to change your ActiveX HTML page (DHTMLControl.htm) to enlarge the size of the ActiveX control using the WIDTH and LENGTH options and to add a new title to your HTML Web page:

```
The new DHTMLControl.htm
<HTML><HEAD>
<TITLE>Dynamic HTML Example</TITLE>
</HEAD>
<BODY><OBJECT ID="DHTMLControl"
WIDTH=640 HEIGHT=480
CLASSID="CLSID:E40A11EE-AA4B-11D2-9949-C4CF5F772B46">
</OBJECT></BODY></HTML>
```

2. As described earlier, you want to have a Web page that accepts a user ID and password and then displays the name, classes, and grades for that student. You need to change the user interface HTML (DHTMLControlUI.htm) to reflect the functionality. This HTML can be typed in by clicking the ResourceView tab in the Workspace window, double-clicking the HTML folder under the DHTMLGrades resources folder, and double-clicking the IDH_DHTMLCONTROL entry. Code similar to the following HTML code can be used for this:

```
The new DHTMLControlUI.htm
<HTML>
<BODY>
<FORM id=theForm>
<TABLE length="80%">
<TR><TD>User ID<TD><Input type="text" size=40 name="UserID">
<TR><TD>Password<TD><Input type="password" size=40
name="Password">
</TABLE>
</FORM>
<TABLE length="80%" id=theTable>
</Table>
```

```
<CENTER><BUTTON
onclick='window.external.Lookup(theForm, theTable);'>
Lookup
</BUTTON></CENTER>
</BODY>
</HTML>
```

The preceding HTML has three main sections. The first is an HTML form with an ID of "theForm" that enables data entry from the user. Here, the user enters their user ID and password. The second is an empty HTML table with an ID of "theTable". This HTML table builds the results of the database query that reports the grades. The third section contains a button that calls a Lookup function and passes the input form ID (theForm) and the table ID (theTable) to eventually contain the grade output. After you've built your DHTML project again by clicking F7 in the Visual Studio environment and using Internet Explorer to run DHTMLControl.htm, the Web page generated by the preceding HTML code will look similar to the Web page shown in Figure 14-15.

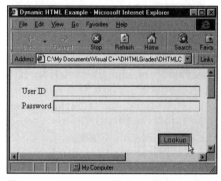

Figure 14–15: Initial HTML page in the DHTMLGrades project.

3. Change the IDL source file (DHTMLControl.idl), and replace the OnClick function definition with a Lookup function definition that defines the variables that are passed from the user interface:

```
The OnClick definition in the DHTMLControl.idl source file
interface IDHTMLControlUI : IDispatch
{

    //Added by Chuck Wood
    HRESULT Lookup([in]IDispatch* pdispForm,
                   [in]IDispatch* pdispTable);
};
```

Don't bother making any changes to the main header file in your project. (In this case, that file would be DHTMLGrades.h.) Although the DHTMLGrades.h header file contains information on what is passed to an ActiveX control from an HTML file, it is always generated from the IDL, so any changes you make to the file are overwritten at build time anyway.

4. Next, in your HTML control header file (DHTMLControl.h), replace the STDMETHOD(OnClick) function with a STDMETHOD(Lookup) to be called when the Lookup button is pressed on the HTML page. Here, the form IDispatch is converted to an IHTMLFormElement, and the table IDispatch is converted to an IHTMLElement.

```
public:
    STDMETHOD(Lookup)(
        IDispatch* pdispForm,
        IDispatch* pdispTable)
    {
//Added by Chuck Wood
        CComQIPtr<IHTMLFormElement> spForm(pdispForm);
        CComQIPtr<IHTMLElement>
                spTableElement(pdispTable);

        if (!spForm || !spTableElement) {
            return E_FAIL;
        }
        else {
            fillGrades(spForm, spTableElement);
        }
        return S_OK;
    }
```

At the top of the Lookup function, IHTMLFormElement and IHTMLElement variables were declared to hold the address of the HTML form and the HTML table. The IHTMLFormElement and IHTMLElement classes are both COM interfaces from Microsoft's Dynamic HTML object model. These interfaces are used to control the document being displayed in an HTML window or the response displayed in an ASP window.

The Lookup function is called every time the Lookup button is clicked on the HTML user interface page. The fillGrades function is developed in the last two steps to display the student's grades on the HTML user interface page.

5. Next, change your Accessor to retrieve only the variables you need. Because the userID and the password are used for retrieval criteria only, you do not need to declare them inside the Accessor. You need to delete their entries in the column map, renumber your column entries (1 through 4), change your SELECT statement so you are selecting only four variables, and finally delete any unused variables from the CLookupAccessor class declaration:

```
class CLookupAccessor
{
public:
    TCHAR m_Name[62]; //Reduce size.  1024 is not necessary.
    TCHAR m_Description[51];
    TCHAR m_Assignment[51];
    double m_Score;

BEGIN_COLUMN_MAP(CLookupAccessor)
    COLUMN_ENTRY(1, m_Name)
    COLUMN_ENTRY(2, m_Description)
    COLUMN_ENTRY(3, m_Assignment)
    COLUMN_ENTRY(4, m_Score)
END_COLUMN_MAP()

DEFINE_COMMAND(CLookupAccessor, _T(" \
    SELECT \
        Name, \
        Description, \
        Assignment, \
        Score  \
    FROM Lookup"))
```

With a generated Accessor, the Visual C++ Wizard is often unable to determine the maximum size of strings when the strings are contained in an expression in a view. As a result, the ATL Object Wizard tries to define a default size for the string. This default size is often wrong. (For instance, on one computer, the default size returned was 1024, whereas on another computer the size returned was 31.) Because the name is a combination of two thirty-character names plus a space in the middle, the maximum value for the m_Name field in the Lookup query is 62 (61 + 1 for a null terminator). Be sure to change that in your program so you don't use as many resources.

6. In your Command class (the CLookup class in the Lookup.h header file),
   declare a findUser function that loads UserID and Password class variables
   (declared in the next step). Overload this function to also use BSTR
   variables, which seem to be used often in DHTML functions:

```
class CLookup : public CCommand<CAccessor<CLookupAccessor> >
{
public:
    HRESULT findUser(char *userID, char *password) {
        if (strlen(userID) > 50 || strlen(password) > 50) {
            ::MessageBox(NULL,
                "User name or password is too long",
                "Could not find user", MB_OK);
            return -1;
        }
        strcpy(m_strUser, userID);
        strcpy(m_strPassword, password);
        return Open();
    }
    HRESULT findUser(BSTR uid, BSTR pwd)
    {
        char userID[51];
        char password[51];
        sprintf(userID, "%S", uid);
        sprintf(password, "%S", pwd);
        return findUser(userID, password);
    }
```

7. At the bottom of your Command class definition (the CLookup class in the
   Lookup.h header file), declare two strings to hold the user and password
   declarations. These are used to hold the user ID and password variables
   stored in the last step.

```
    CSession    m_session;
    char        m_strUser[50];
    char        m_strPassword[50];
};
#endif // __LOOKUP_H_
```

8. You need to completely rewrite your OpenRowset function in the CLookup
   class in the Lookup.h header file. You need to add a where clause that
   retrieves only the current user ID and password from the database:

```
HRESULT OpenRowset()
{
    //The rest of this function was added by Chuck Wood
```

```
        //Allow 512 bytes for the new SQL Command
        char newSQL[512];
        char *SQLCommand;
        GetDefaultCommand((const char **) &SQLCommand);
        strcpy(newSQL, SQLCommand);    //Get the default SQL
        strcat(newSQL, " WHERE UserID = '"); //Add the filter
        strcat(newSQL, m_strUser);
        strcat(newSQL, "' AND Password = '");
        strcat(newSQL, m_strPassword);
        strcat(newSQL, "'");
//Message box for debugging
//    ::MessageBox(NULL, newSQL, "Lookup.h", MB_OK);
        return CCommand<CAccessor<CLookupAccessor>::
Open(m_session, newSQL);
}
```

When building new SQL from the default SQL, most programmers benefit from displaying the SQL before executing it, using a message box. SQL errors are often difficult to debug, but they often are the result of a missed quote or space that can be easily seen inside a message box. When you are sure the SQL is fully functional, you can delete the message box or comment it out as was done in the preceding SQL.

9. In the final step before you write the fillGrades function to tie your consumer to your user interface HTML, you need to add an #include statement to your DHTMLControl.h header file:

```
// DHTMLControl.h : Declaration of the CDHTMLControl

#ifndef __DHTMLCONTROL_H_
#define __DHTMLCONTROL_H_

#include "resource.h"        // main symbols
#include <atlctl.h>
//Added by Chuck Wood for database support
#include "lookup.h"
```

The project defined in this section is not really sufficient to handle security in an HTML Web page because the user could just query the database for all the passwords. However, if you converted this code to an Active Server Page simply by renaming the extension from .htm or .html to .asp, your Microsoft IIS server would convert all this code to HTML and run all queries from the server side, not the client side, which would help your security situation quite a lot by not informing the client exactly how your HTML is populated and by controlling security from a centralized location.

Tying the Consumer to the HTML

The final step of making a database-enabled Web page is to write a function that can tie the user interface HTML to the OLE DB consumer. As mentioned previously, this function is called fillGrades and can perform the following tasks:

♦ Query the database for the user ID and password.

♦ If a valid password is found, a new instance of the consumer is created, and the database view or access query are opened.

♦ A new HTML table is developed that replaces the existing empty table in the user interface HTML. This new HTML table contains the grades of all the assignments taken by the user.

Do the following steps to write this function:

1. Add a fillGrades function prototype to your DHTMLControl.h header file:

```
// Handler prototypes:
//   LRESULT MessageHandler(UINT uMsg, WPARAM wParam, LPARAM
lParam, BOOL& bHandled);
//   LRESULT CommandHandler(WORD wNotifyCode, WORD wID, HWND
hWndCtl, BOOL& bHandled);
//   LRESULT NotifyHandler(int idCtrl, LPNMHDR pnmh, BOOL&
bHandled);

// IViewObjectEx
   DECLARE_VIEW_STATUS(0)

//fillGrades prototype Added by Chuck Wood
protected:
   void fillGrades(CComQIPtr<IHTMLFormElement> &spForm,
```

```
CComQIPtr<IHTMLElement> &spTableElement);
```

```
// IDHTMLControl
public:

// IDHTMLControlUI
public:
    STDMETHOD(Lookup)(
```

2. Declare your `fillGrades` function:

```
void CDHTMLControl::fillGrades(
    CComQIPtr<IHTMLFormElement> &spForm,
    CComQIPtr<IHTMLElement> &spTableElement) {
```

3. Now you must write the `fillGrades` function. Inside the `fillGrades` function, the first thing you need to do is retrieve your user ID and password from what the user entered in the textboxes on the HTML screen. You can retrieve a textbox by sending the name of the textbox in a Variant string to the IFormElement.item function. A pointer to a IDispatch will be returned containing the name of the textbox:

```
CComVariant vZero(0); // Variant set to zero
CComVariant vColumnName;
CComPtr<IDispatch> spUserDisp;
CComQIPtr<IHTMLInputTextElement> spUserBox;
HRESULT hr = spForm->item(vColumnName = "UserID", vZero,
&spUserDisp);
```

4. You can use the `CComQIPtr<IHTMLInputTextElement>` constructor and the `QueryInterface` method to construct a textbox control from the IDispatch pointer:

```
//Form an IHTMLInputTextElement for
//the user ID from the text box pointer
CComQIPtr<IHTMLInputTextElement> spUserBox;
HRESULT hr = spUserDisp->QueryInterface(&spUserBox);
```

5. You can retrieve a BSTR containing the contents of the textbox by using the `IHTMLInputTextElement::get_value` command:

```
HRESULT hr = spUserBox->get_value(&strUser);
```

6. Repeat steps 3 through 5 for the password.

7. Construct a new OLE DB `CLookup` consumer, and use the `findUser` function written earlier in the chapter to open the OLE DB rowset with the proper variables. After the rowset is open, move to the first record:

```
//Construct a new OLE DB Consumer
CLookup *pSet = new CLookup();
//Open a new rowset for the new user
if (SUCCEEDED(pSet->findUser(user, password))) {
//If the find user works, find the first record
    hr = pSet->MoveFirst();
```

8. Build a new HTML <TABLE>. First, create a new table command, and then scroll through the rowset to go through each OLE DB row and place the contents of each table into a row on the HTML table. If the class changes, be sure to add a new class description to the first cell on the row. Otherwise, leave the first cell on each row empty:

```
char strHTML[1500];     //String to hold the new HTML
char description[51]; //Current Class Description
//Start new HTML table
strcpy(strHTML, "<TABLE length=\"80%\" id=theTable>\n");
//Initialize Class Description
strcpy (description, "");
do {
//Start new row and a new cell
    strcat(strHTML, "<TR><TD>");
//If new class, display it
    if (strcmp(description, pSet->m_Description)){
//New description
        strcpy (description, pSet->m_Description);
        strcat(strHTML, "<EM>");
        strcat(strHTML, description);
        strcat(strHTML, "</EM>");
    }
//Add the assignment cell and the score cell
    sprintf(strHTML,
    "%s<TD>%s<TD ALIGN=RIGHT>%2.0f%%\n",
    strHTML, pSet->m_Assignment, pSet->m_Score);
//Continue loop if there are more records to process
} while (pSet->MoveNext() == S_OK);
```

9. Add the ending table tag to the HTML string you are building:

```
//End new table
strcat(strHTML, "</TABLE>");
```

10. Use the `ITHMLElement::put_outerHTML` command to replace the current
    table with the new table:

```
//Now  put the new HTML onto the web page
CComBSTR html = strHTML;
spTableElement->put_outerHTML(html.copy());
```

The spTableElement variable is of type `IHTMLElement`, not of `IHTML`
`Table`. The reason is that working with tables involves several different
IHTML types (`IHTMLTable`, `IHTMLTableRow`, `IHTMLTableColumn`, `IHTML`
`TableSection`, and `IHTMLTableCell`). Working with so many different
HTML COM elements can be time consuming and difficult, and your program
will run a little slower when you're done. Instead, this program uses a standard HTML element and the `ITHMLElement::put_outerHTML` method to
replace the entire HTML text with new HTML text. The new code is easier to
write, easier to follow, easier to debug, and faster at execution time.

It often saves time when sending a lot of HTML to a DHTML object if you display the HTML object before you print it out.

```
//Messagebox containing the HTML you're getting,
//for debugging
    ::MessageBox(NULL, strHTML, "DHTMLGrades", MB_OK);
```

This results in a message box that displays the HTML you are about to write
out, as seen in Figure 14-16. When you're done, you can comment out the
message box or delete it.

Figure 14-16: During debugging, it's a good idea to display the HTML code you are
about to implement.

11. Clean up if the rowset worked or display an error if it didn't:

```
//Clean up or report errors
if (hr == S_OK)
    pSet->Close();      //Close the current row set
else                        //Some database option failed
    ::MessageBox(NULL, "Could not open rowset",
"DHTMLGrades", MB_OK);
```

 It's a good idea if you open and close the database connection every time the user needs access to the Web page. You can't rely on the user's staying connected to your Web page while Web browsing.

These steps can be viewed in the fillGrades function shown below:

```
///////////////////////////////////////////////////////////////////
// CDHTMLControl
void CDHTMLControl::fillGrades(
        CComQIPtr<IHTMLFormElement> &spForm,
        CComQIPtr<IHTMLElement> &spTableElement) {
    HRESULT hr;
    char strHTML[1500];    //String to hold the new HTML
    char description[51]; //Current Class Description
//Variants that contain zero and the current column name
    CComVariant vZero(0); // Variant set to zero
    CComVariant vColumnName;

//Start new HTML table
    strcpy(strHTML, "<TABLE length=\"80%\" id=theTable>\n");

//Get the UserID
    CComBSTR strUser;  //Will contain the user ID value
    CComPtr<IDispatch> spUserDisp;
    CComQIPtr<IHTMLInputTextElement> spUserBox;
    hr = spForm->item(vColumnName = "UserID", vZero, &spUserDisp);
    if (SUCCEEDED(hr)) {
        hr = spUserDisp->QueryInterface(&spUserBox);
    }
    if (SUCCEEDED(hr)) {
        hr = spUserBox->get_value(&strUser);
    }
//Get the password
```

```
    CComBSTR strPassword;  //Will contain the password value
    CComPtr<IDispatch> spPasswordDisp;
    CComQIPtr<IHTMLInputTextElement> spPasswordBox;
    if (SUCCEEDED(hr)) {
        hr = spForm->item(vColumnName = "Password", vZero,
&spPasswordDisp);
    }
    if (SUCCEEDED(hr)) {
        hr = spPasswordDisp->QueryInterface(&spPasswordBox);
    }
    if (SUCCEEDED(hr)) {
        hr = spPasswordBox->get_value(&strPassword);
    }
//Continue if everything worked.
    if (SUCCEEDED(hr))
    {
        CLookup *pSet = new CLookup();
        if (SUCCEEDED(pSet->findUser(strUser, strPassword)) &&
            SUCCEEDED(pSet->MoveFirst()))
        {
    //If everything is still OK, continue forming HTML
    //First add a table title (<CAPTION>) containing the name
            strcat(strHTML, "<CAPTION><EM>Name: <STRONG>");
            strcat(strHTML, pSet->m_Name);
            strcat(strHTML, "</STRONG></EM></CAPTION>\n");
        //Next add CLASS, ASSIGNMENT, and GRADE column headings
            strcat(strHTML,
          "<TR><TH ALIGN=LEFT><STRONG>Class</STRONG>\n");
            strcat(strHTML,
          "<TH ALIGN=LEFT><STRONG>Assignment</STRONG>");
            strcat(strHTML,
          "<TH ALIGN=RIGHT><STRONG>Grade</STRONG>\n");
            //Initialize Class Description
            strcpy (description, "");
            do {
    //Start new row and a new cell
                strcat(strHTML, "<TR><TD>");
    //If new class, display it
                if (strcmp(description, pSet->m_Description)){
    //New description
                    strcpy (description, pSet->m_Description);
                    strcat(strHTML, "<EM>");
                    strcat(strHTML, description);
                    strcat(strHTML, "</EM>");
```

```
                        }
//Add the assignment cell and the score cell
                sprintf(strHTML,
            "%s<TD>%s<TD ALIGN=RIGHT>%2.0f%%\n",
            strHTML, pSet->m_Assignment,pSet->m_Score);
//Continue loop if there are more records to process
        } while (pSet->MoveNext() == S_OK);
        }
//End new table
    strcat(strHTML, "</TABLE>");
//Messagebox containing the HTML you're getting, for debugging
//    ::MessageBox(NULL, strHTML, "DHTMLGrades", MB_OK);
//Now  put the new HTML onto the web page
    CComBSTR html = strHTML;
    spTableElement->put_outerHTML(html.Copy());
//Clean up or report errors
    if (hr == S_OK)
        pSet->Close();     //Close the current row set
    else                          //Some database option failed
        ::MessageBox(NULL, "Could not open rowset",
            "DHTMLGrades", MB_OK);
    }
}
```

Server versus Client Programs

Now you've seen how Dynamic HTML can be useful when you're trying to deliver Web pages that respond to user requests and provide data from a database. However, the code we have written here is an HTML Web page and therefore is executed on the client's Web machine. There are several consequences of running this program at the client site:

◆ The client must have a Web browser capable of Dynamic HTML, usually Internet Explorer 4.0 or later.

◆ The client must have the ActiveX control installed on their machine.

◆ The client must be running Windows 95 or NT 4.0 or later.

◆ The client must have access to the OLE DB data source.

Continued

Server versus Client Programs *(Continued)*

If any of these conditions is not met, the client machine cannot run your program. Clearly, a server-side program would be easier to maintain. A client-side DHTML program runs all programs on the client machine and uses the server machine only as a database server. This is shown graphically in the accompanying figure.

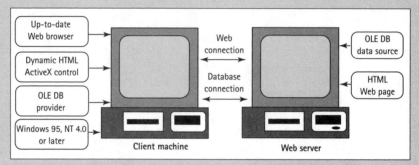

With Dynamic HTML pages, you are expecting a lot from the client machine.

You're asking a lot for all users to install the ActiveX control from the Web, use the newest version of Internet Explorer and not use competing products, and even change their operating system. However, the database access is a thorny issue, because it is often hard or even impossible for client machines to have access to your Web data source. This setup is usually viable only on an intranet with internal company access where machine setup can be controlled.

For general Web access, you probably need some other type of access. Although server gateways, such as CGI or ISAPI, enable you to access a Web database from a client site. However, probably the easiest way to access server information from a client site is to use VBSCRIPT on an Active Server Page (ASP) and use Microsoft IIS (Internet Information Server) as your Internet provider software. With Active Server Pages (ASPs), you send only HTML that can be interpreted by almost any system, regardless of that client's setup.

If you use a newer HTML tag, the client's browser must support that tag. For instance, the <TABLE> tag is available in HTML 2.0 and later. This version of HTML was supported by Netscape 2.0 and later and Internet Explorer 1.0 and later.

The code generated in this chapter can be found in the DHTMLGrades directory on the CD-ROM accompanying this book.

Summary

Web development is a necessary component for most developers in today's technical environment. Without database support for your Web page, your Web pages are little more than electronic billboards that aren't of much use or interest to your customers. To recap:

◆ Dynamic HTML can be used to alter the content of a Web page.

◆ OLE DB providers can be added to a Dynamic HTML Web page rather easily.

Chapter 15

Database Access to Non-Relational Information

IN THIS CHAPTER

◆ Developing an in-depth understanding of Universal Data Access

◆ Reading fixed-format text files as OLE DB databases

◆ Reading e-mail files with a MAPI OLE DB provider

ONE OF Universal Data Access' (UDA's) promises is the capability to access any data using the same consumer interface. In this chapter, you get to see UDA in action. In Chapter 13, you learned how to create an OLE DB provider by giving OLE DB access the list of files in a directory on your hard drive. This chapter delves into more practical uses of UDA by showing how both text files and e-mail data can be accessed using OLE DB. Along the way, you should develop a real appreciation for UDA because, once coded, UDA standardizes all data access rather than just access to relational data.

For information on how to create a provider, see Chapter 13.

Revisiting Universal Data Access

Chapter 1 discussed Universal Data Access and how OLE DB can be used to deliver access to data from a myriad of data sources. There are three main benefits that UDA delivers using OLE DB:

◆ First, OLE DB providers standardize all data access. The commands you use to view and update data in a database are the same commands that you can use to update information in an OLE DB data source. Figure 15-1 shows how OLE DB developers can write new providers that an application developer can access without much training or communication. With an appropriately named provider, the application developer often simply sees the provider on the list of available OLE DB providers and begins immediate use.

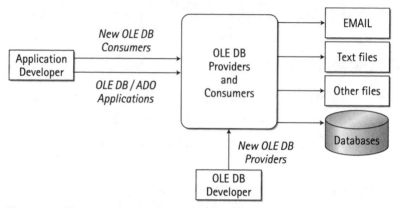

Figure 15-1: New OLE DB providers can be accessed with standard OLE DB or ADO techniques, thereby enhancing reuse and making development easier.

◆ Second, OLE DB hides complexity. For instance, in this chapter, access to MAPI files through the Windows MAPI interface is discussed. MAPI access is pretty technical, but only one developer needs to understand the access. Others can use any providers or consumers that are developed without needing to understand the underlying data access.

◆ Finally, OLE DB enhances reuse. Code that can be reused is often not reused because it takes too long for developers to (a) learn that the functionality exists and (b) learn how to integrate that functionality into their program. With standard access to OLE DB providers, any code developed can automatically be listed as a data source *and* can automatically have an understandable interface. OLE DB is a way to ensure that your code is reused so that your corporation doesn't have every developer "reinvent the wheel" by writing code similar to code already written by other developers.

For more on UDA, see Chapter 1.

Reading Text with OLE DB

Databases are usually preferred for easy access to corporate data. However, many corporations and many applications still use text files either as input and output to and from a program, or as one of the only available export types. This is especially true in COBOL environments where fixed-width text files are easy to create and use.

For many database programmers, text files are a huge headache. With fixed-width files, you need to know the exact format for each file, which can be a problem unless you are using an OLE DB provider that is designed to read the file for you. This section shows how an OLE DB provider can be written and accessed by a consumer for text file access using OLE DB calls.

Creating the Text File You Need for This Project

You can create the text file from your Access database included on the CD-ROM by completing the following steps:

1. Make a query that contains the fields you want. In the accompanying figure, I show the six tables needed to make my query. This query exists on the Access database that comes with the CD.

2. Open the query to display the fields. Then click File → Save As/Export from your File menu as shown in the figure.

3. The Save As dialog box then opens. Click To an External File or Database, and click OK as shown in the figure.

Continued

Creating the Text File You Need for This Project
(Continued)

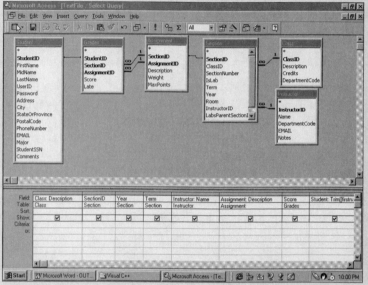

Query the fields you want in your text file.

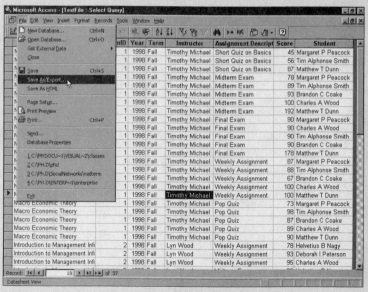

To start saving your file, you must first display the query.

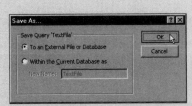

The Save As dialog box enables you to specify where you want to save the contents of your query.

4. Next the Save Query 'TextFile' As dialog box opens, as shown in the next figure. Here, navigate to the directory where you want your text file, type in your filename, choose Text Files as your file type, and click OK.

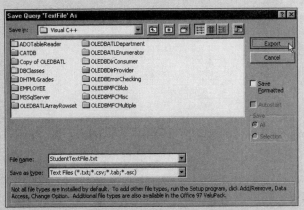

The Save Query 'TextFile' As dialog box enables you to specify the file type, filename, and location of your new text file.

5. The Export Text Wizard then opens. Choose Fixed Width as the format, and click the Advanced button as shown in the next figure.

Continued

Creating the Text File You Need for This Project
(Continued)

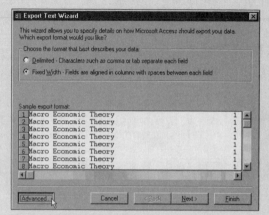

The Export Text Wizard enables you to specify characteristics about your text file.

6. Finally, specify the width using the Export Specification window, as shown in the next figure. This window is important for two reasons. First, it gives you control over your text file output format. Second, it serves as a valuable resource on the text layout. When you're done, click Finish.

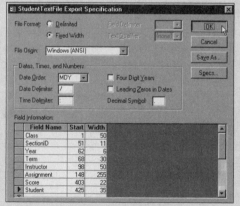

The Export Specification window can be used to control the output of your output file.

When your Export Specification is finished, as shown in the final figure in the sidebar, be sure you do a print screen, paste it to Word, and print it out so you have the layout for your text file while you write your provider. You'll be glad you did.

If you don't want to go through the hassle of creating this file, use the copy of the StudentTextFile.txt that you can find on the CD-ROM accompanying this book.

Writing a Text Provider

To create a provider, you must perform the following steps:

1. Create a new project using the ATL COM AppWizard, as shown in Figure 15-2. This project should be a DLL so that it can be easily accessed as a COM object.

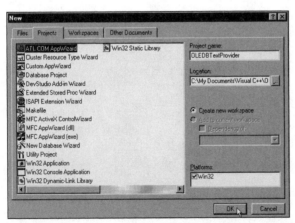

Figure 15-2: Use the ATL COM AppWizard to create a new OLE DB provider.

2. Next, click Insert → Insert ATL Object to open the ATL Object Wizard. Click the Data Access category, and choose the provider object as shown in Figure 15-3.

3. The ATL Object Wizard Properties dialog box then opens. Type in the short name of your provider (for example, OLEDBTextProvider). The other fields are filled in automatically, although you can change these fields if you wish (see Figure 15-4). When you're finished, click OK.

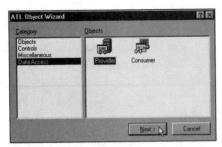

Figure 15-3: A new OLE DB provider can be created using the ATL Object Wizard.

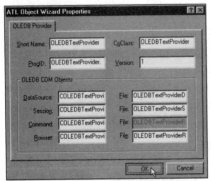

Figure 15-4: The provider name and the files and COM objects associated with the provider can be entered using the ATL Object Wizard Properties dialog box.

4. Build your project by pressing F7. Your program should compile, build the Registry entries, and enable you to partially build your project or compile a single module while working on your provider.

Now you have built the default provider described in Chapter 13. However, this provider requires many changes to the rowset and to the session before becoming a text file provider.

The provider project used in this section can be found in the OLEDBText Provider directory on the CD-ROM accompanying this book.

MAKING ROWSET CHANGES

The logic for establishing a rowset is contained in the OLEDBTextProviderRS.h header file. The default provider written here returns the directory structure. You can make changes here to turn the directory provider into a text file provider.

File IO C++ Access Commands

To access a text file, you need to use C++ file I/O functions. The functions are prototyped in the <stdio.h> header file. The three file I/O functions needed for this project are defined in Table 15-1:

TABLE 15-1 FILE IO C++ COMMANDS

File IO Command	Description
`char *fgets (char *buffer, int size, FILE *stream)`	The `fgets` function retrieves an entire line from the file stream until the newline character (`'\n'`) is hit. The newline character is appended on the end of the line if it is encountered. A null terminator is always appended on the end of the buffer used in the `fgets` function. A pointer to the buffer is returned. If the `fgets` reached the end of the stream or failed, a NULL is returned.
`FILE *fopen( const char *filename,const char *mode )`	The `fopen` function creates a file stream based on a filename provided by the developer. You can specify the access mode you wish as well. Valid values are read only (`"r"`), read-write (`"r+"`), output (`"w"`), output-read (`"w+"`), append (`"a"`), and append read (`"a+"`). The output modes (`"w"` and `"w+"`) erase any file that currently exists before opening a new file.
`int fclose( FILE *stream );`	The `fclose` function closes a file stream and deallocates any resources in use by the file stream. It returns a zero if the function worked.

To change your rowset provider, you need to perform the following changes to your rowset header file (OLEDBTextProviderRS.h):

1. Add an #include <stdio.h> directive at the top of your file. This directive gives you access to C++'s file IO functions:

```
// OLEDBTextProviderRS.h : Declaration of the
COLEDBTextProviderRowset
#ifndef __COLEDBTextProviderRowset_H_
#define __COLEDBTextProviderRowset_H_
#include "resource.h"        // main symbols
// Added by Chuck Wood for text file support
#include <stdio.h>
```

2. You should do a complete rewrite of the rowset layout class. In this class, you don't inherit from WIN32_FIND_DATA, and you have different variables you want to pass. Based on the text file layout, the following CTextFile should be declared, changing the name from COLEDBTextProviderWindowsFile to CTextFile:

```
//Remove inheritance from class
class CTextFile
{
public:
    TCHAR strClass[51];
    TCHAR strSectionID[12];
    TCHAR strYear[7];
    TCHAR strTerm[31];
    TCHAR strInstructor[51];
    TCHAR strAssignment[256];
    TCHAR strScore[23];
    TCHAR strStudent[36];
BEGIN_PROVIDER_COLUMN_MAP(CTextFile)
    PROVIDER_COLUMN_ENTRY_STR("Class", 1, strClass)
    PROVIDER_COLUMN_ENTRY_STR("SectionID", 2, strSectionID)
    PROVIDER_COLUMN_ENTRY_STR("Year", 3, strYear)
    PROVIDER_COLUMN_ENTRY_STR("Term", 4, strTerm)
    PROVIDER_COLUMN_ENTRY_STR("Instructor", 5, strInstructor)
    PROVIDER_COLUMN_ENTRY_STR("Assignment", 6, strAssignment)
    PROVIDER_COLUMN_ENTRY_STR("Score", 7, strScore)
    PROVIDER_COLUMN_ENTRY_STR("Student", 8, strStudent)
END_PROVIDER_COLUMN_MAP()
};
```

3. You need to change the GetColumnInfo method to call the
   `CTextFile::GetColumnInfo` function:

```
static ATLCOLUMNINFO* GetColumnInfo(
    COLEDBTextProviderCommand* pv, ULONG* pcInfo)
{
    return CTextFile::GetColumnInfo(pv, pcInfo);
}
```

4. You also need to change the class declaration of your rowset to use
   `CTextFile` in the `CRowsetImpl` template:

```
class COLEDBTextProviderRowset :
        public CRowsetImpl< COLEDBTextProviderRowset,
            CTextFile, COLEDBTextProviderCommand>
{
```

5. The rest of the changes in this section affect the
   `COLEDBTextProviderRowset` class. Write a function that can return a
   filename so you don't need to retype the filename every time you use it,
   and the filename can be changed from a single location:

```
class COLEDBTextProviderRowset : public CRowsetImpl<
COLEDBTextProviderRowset, CTextFile,
COLEDBTextProviderCommand>
{
public:
    static char* GetFileName() {
        //Change this file name
        //if you want to use a different one
        return
        "C:\\My Documents\\Visual C++\\StudentTextFile.txt";
    }
```

> Be sure to change this pathname to wherever the file is actually located.
> Otherwise, you will get an error when your consumer tries to access
> this provider.

6. In fixed-length text files, most of your columns have spaces or newline
   characters. Be sure to write a function that can remove them, or all your
   developers need to write their own "trim" functions:

```
static void StrTrim(char *instring) {
    static char strBlank[] = " \n";      // chars to strip
```

```
        // remove trailing spaces or newlines
        for (char *pchEnd = instring + strlen(instring);
                pchEnd != instring && strchr(
                    strBlank, *(pchEnd - 1)) != NULL;
                *--pchEnd = '\0');
        // remove leading spaces or newlines
        char *pchStart = &instring[strspn(instring, strBlank)];
        memmove(instring, pchStart,
                sizeof(char) * (pchEnd - pchStart + 1));
    }
```

7. When you read in a row of text, you need to copy a portion of that row to a column. The following `ColumnCopy` function takes a string, which is an entire row or part of a row, and copies a given length to a column. The column is trimmed using the `StrTrim` function written in the last step.

```
class COLEDBTextProviderRowset : public CRowsetImpl<
COLEDBTextProviderRowset, CTextFile,
COLEDBTextProviderCommand>
{
private:
    void ColumnCopy(char* row, char* column, int length) {
        column[length] = 0;        //Null Terminate
        StrTrim(column);           //Trim for users
    }
public:
```

8. Finally, you must completely rewrite the `COLEDBTextProviderRowset::Execute` function to open the text file, scroll through the file row by row until the end of file (EOF), and close the file. Each row must be "dissected" into individual columns, each column must be copied to the CTextFile class, and each CTextFile class entry must be added to the rowset using the m_rgRowData.Add function:

```
HRESULT Execute(DBPARAMS * pParams, LONG* pcRowsAffected)
{
    CTextFile tf;
    FILE *fp;           //Text file pointer
    char row[500];      //row buffer;
    *pcRowsAffected = 0;
    fp = fopen(
        GetFileName(),
        "r+");           //Open for reading and writing
    if (fp == NULL) {
        return DB_E_INVALID;
    }
```

```
while (fgets(row, 500, fp)) {     //Go until EOF
    ColumnCopy(row, tf.strClass, 50);
    ColumnCopy(row+50, tf.strSectionID, 11);
    ColumnCopy(row+61, tf.strYear, 6);
    ColumnCopy(row+67, tf.strTerm, 30);
    ColumnCopy(row+97, tf.strInstructor, 50);
    ColumnCopy(row+147, tf.strAssignment, 255);
    ColumnCopy(row+402, tf.strScore, 22);
    ColumnCopy(row+424, tf.strStudent, 35);
    if (!m_rgRowData.Add(tf))
        return E_OUTOFMEMORY;
    *pcRowsAffected++;
}
fclose(fp);
return S_OK;
}
```

Now your rowset is ready for action. However, you still need to make session changes before you can use the provider. Session changes are discussed in the next section.

MAKING SCHEMA ROWSET CHANGES IN THE SESSION CLASSES

Schema rowsets are rowsets that describe your tables and files for the consumer. Consumers often want to query the schema rowset rather than the traditional rowset to determine exactly what columns and fields are available. There are three types of schema rowsets:

◆ Table schema rowsets are rowsets that describe the tables that can be accessed by a provider.

◆ Column schema rowsets are rowsets that describe the columns and attributes defined by a provider.

◆ Provider type schema rowsets are rowsets that contain the data types supplied by the provider and a description for each one.

You need to make changes to your session header file (OLEDBTextProviderSess.h) to change these schema rowsets. These changes affect the Execute functions in the table row schema and in the column schema.

There are four Execute functions inside your provider:

- The rowset class (`COLEDBTextProviderRowset` in the OLEDBTextProvider S.h header file) contains an `Execute` function that builds a rowset.

- The table schema rowset class (`COLEDBTextProviderSessionTRSchema Rowset` in the OLEDBTextProviderSess.h header file) contains an `Execute` function that defines the tables accessed by a provider.

- The column schema rowset class (`COLEDBTextProviderSessionCol SchemaRowset` in the OLEDBTextProviderSess.h header file) contains an `Execute` function that defines the columns in a table.

- The provider type schema rowset class (`COLEDBTextProviderSessionPT SchemaRowset` in the OLEDBTextProviderSess.h header file) contains an `Execute` function that defines the data types that the provider defines.

Be sure not to confuse these Execute functions when you make your changes.

 With most providers, such as the ones written in this book, standard OLE DB data types are used, so there is no need to modify the provider type schema rowset.

IMPLEMENTING TABLE ROWSET SCHEMA CHANGES   The ATL Object Wizard creates a session that relies on a rowset inherited from the WIN32_FIND_DATA structure. Because we no longer inherit from that structure, the session needs to be changed.

The session can be used to check for the existence of your text file using logic similar to the logic that checks for the existence of your current directory in the default provider. The following changes can be made to your `COLEDBTextProvider SessionTRSchemaRowset::Execute` function in your session header file (OLEDBText ProviderSess.h):

```
class COLEDBTextProviderSessionTRSchemaRowset :
    public CRowsetImpl< COLEDBTextProviderSessionTRSchemaRowset,
CTABLESRow, COLEDBTextProviderSession>
{
public:
    HRESULT Execute(LONG* pcRowsAffected, ULONG, const VARIANT*)
    {
        USES_CONVERSION;
        CTABLESRow trData;
        lstrcpyW(trData.m_szType, OLESTR("TABLE"));
/* ************************* */
```

```
    //Error if file does not exist
    WIN32_FIND_DATA wf;
    HANDLE fileHandle;
    fileHandle = FindFirstFile(
        COLEDBTextProviderRowset::GetFileName(),
        &wf);
    if (fileHandle == INVALID_HANDLE_VALUE)
        return E_FAIL; // The file does not exist
    FindClose(fileHandle);
    lstrcpyW(trData.m_szDesc,
        T2OLE(COLEDBTextProviderRowset::GetFileName()));
    lstrcpyW(trData.m_szTable, T2OLE("Text File"));
/* ************************** */
    if (!m_rgRowData.Add(trData))
        return E_OUTOFMEMORY;
    *pcRowsAffected = 1;
    return S_OK;
    }
};
```

IMPLEMENTING COLUMN SCHEMA ROWSET CHANGES Column schema rowsets are used to enable users to detect your columns and their attributes. The column schema rowset in this provider is built by the COLEDBTextProvider SessionColSchemaRowset class.

You need to change your Column Schema rowset, which can be done by rewriting the Execute function inside the COLEDBTextProvider Session ColSchema Rowset class in your session header file (OLEDBTextProvider Sess.h):

```
class COLEDBTextProviderSessionColSchemaRowset :
    public CRowsetImpl< COLEDBTextProviderSessionColSchemaRowset,
CCOLUMNSRow, COLEDBTextProviderSession>
{
public:
    HRESULT Execute(LONG* pcRowsAffected, ULONG, const VARIANT*)
    {
        USES_CONVERSION;
        //******
        static const struct { char *szName; int maxLength; }
        rgcolumns[] =
            {{"Class", 50},
             {"SectionID", 11},
             {"Year", 6},
             {"Term", 30},
             {"Instructor", 50},
```

```
                    {"Assignment", 255},
                    {"Score", 22},
                    {"Student", 35}};

        const int NUMBERCOLUMNS = sizeof(rgcolumns) /
                                    sizeof(rgcolumns[0]);
        WIN32_FIND_DATA wf;
        HANDLE fileHandle;
        //Error if file does not exist
        fileHandle = FindFirstFile(
            COLEDBTextProviderRowset::GetFileName(),
            &wf);
        if (fileHandle == INVALID_HANDLE_VALUE)
            return E_FAIL; // The file does not exist
        FindClose(fileHandle);

        // Fill out all the CCOLUMNSRow records
        for (int column=0; column<NUMBERCOLUMNS; column++) {
            CCOLUMNSRow crColumnInfo;

            lstrcpyW(crColumnInfo.m_szTableName,
                T2OLE(COLEDBTextProviderRowset::GetFileName()));
            crColumnInfo.m_ulOrdinalPosition = column+1;
            crColumnInfo.m_bIsNullable = VARIANT_FALSE;
            crColumnInfo.m_bColumnHasDefault = VARIANT_FALSE;
            crColumnInfo.m_ulColumnFlags = 0;
            crColumnInfo.m_nDataType = DBTYPE_STR;

            lstrcpyW(crColumnInfo.m_szColumnName,
                    T2OLE(rgcolumns[column].szName));
            lstrcpyW(crColumnInfo.m_szDescription,
                    T2OLE(rgcolumns[column].szName));
            crColumnInfo.m_ulCharMaxLength =
                    rgcolumns[column].maxLength;

            // Declare new schema row
            m_rgRowData.Add(crColumnInfo);
        }
        *pcRowsAffected = NUMBERCOLUMNS;  // for the four columns
        //******
        return S_OK;
    }
};
```

Now your provider is complete. To use it, you must press F7 to build the provider and register it for use.

Writing a Text Consumer

After you build the provider, any consumer can access it. In this example, a new MFC OLE DB consumer is created to access the text file provider that you just finished. Do the following steps to write this consumer:

1. Click File → New to open the New dialog box. As shown in Figure 15-5, choose MFC AppWizard (exe), type in the name of your project (OLEDBTextConsumer), and click OK.

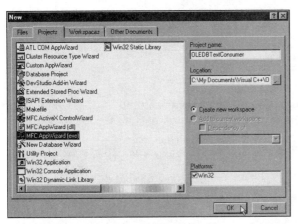

Figure 15-5: You can use an MFC application to access your new text file provider.

2. Choose Single Document in Step 1, and in Step 2 of 6, choose Database view without file support, and click the Data Source button. This opens the Database Options window. Choose the OLE DB radio button, and click the Select OLE DB Datasource button.

3. Now the Data Link Properties window opens. Choose the OLEDBTextProvider OLE DB Provider for your OLE DB provider, as shown in Figure 15-6.

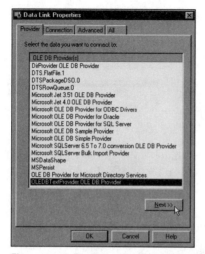

Figure 15-6: The Data Link Properties window enables you to choose which provider you want to access with your consumer.

4. Click the Next button and then the OK button to close the Data Link Properties window and the OK button to close the Database Options window after choosing your provider. The Select Database Tables window opens next. Click the first line to indicate no table, and click OK.

5. Continue through the MFC AppWizard until you're finished. When you're done, a dialog box opens. You must build a dialog box that contains all the fields you will access. You need the following textboxes defined for this project:

- IDC_CLASS is used for the class field.

- IDC_SECTION is used for the section ID.

- IDC_YEAR is used for the year string.

- IDC_TERM is used for the term.

- IDC_INSTRUCTOR is used for the instructor.

- IDC_ASSIGNMENT is used for the assignment.

- IDC_SCORE will be used for the score.

- IDC_STUDENT is used for the student name.

Figure 15-7 shows how the completed dialog box looks.

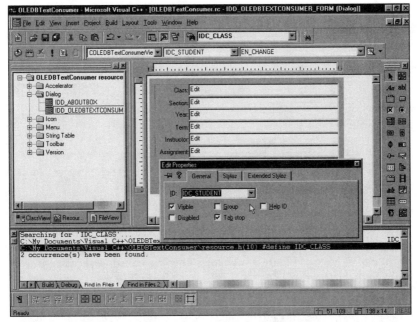

Figure 15-7: The dialog box layout for the OLEDBTextConsumer project

6. Finally, add your fields to your data exchange:

```
void COLEDBTextConsumerView::DoDataExchange(CDataExchange*
pDX)
{
    COleDBRecordView::DoDataExchange(pDX);
    //{{AFX_DATA_MAP(COLEDBTextConsumerView)
        // NOTE: the ClassWizard will add DDX and DDV calls
here
    //}}AFX_DATA_MAP
    //Added by Chuck Wood for data transfer
    DDX_Text(pDX, IDC_CLASS, m_pSet->m_strClass, 51);
    DDX_Text(pDX, IDC_SECTION, m_pSet->m_strSectionID, 12);
    DDX_Text(pDX, IDC_YEAR, m_pSet->m_strYear, 7);
    DDX_Text(pDX, IDC_TERM, m_pSet->m_strTerm, 31);
    DDX_Text(pDX, IDC_INSTRUCTOR, m_pSet->m_strInstructor,
51);
    DDX_Text(pDX, IDC_ASSIGNMENT, m_pSet->m_strAssignment,
256);
    DDX_Text(pDX, IDC_SCORE, m_pSet->m_strScore, 23);
    DDX_Text(pDX, IDC_STUDENT, m_pSet->m_strStudent, 36);
    DDV_MaxChars(pDX, m_pSet->m_strClass, 51);
```

```
DDV_MaxChars(pDX, m_pSet->m_strSectionID, 12);
DDV_MaxChars(pDX, m_pSet->m_strYear, 7);
DDV_MaxChars(pDX, m_pSet->m_strTerm, 31);
DDV_MaxChars(pDX, m_pSet->m_strInstructor, 51);
DDV_MaxChars(pDX, m_pSet->m_strAssignment, 256);
DDV_MaxChars(pDX, m_pSet->m_strScore, 23);
DDV_MaxChars(pDX, m_pSet->m_strStudent, 36);
}
```

You cannot use the Class Wizard to add OLE DB fields to your data exchange. You must type these in yourself.

There you have it. Figure 15-8 shows how the consumer accesses the text file as if it were a database.

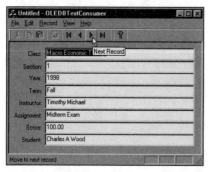

Figure 15-8: Here's how the finished OLEDBTextConsumer looks now that it accesses the OLEDBTextProvider.

As you can see, actually developing a consumer to access your provider is not too difficult. In addition, you are able to take advantage of OLE DB features (for example, scrolling backward, familiar interface, MFC AppWizard support) that you would not be able to easily implement with standard file access techniques. Although a text file was used here, spreadsheet access, comma-delimited files, or proprietary file formats from various software packages could also be used.

The provider project used in this section can be found in the OLEDBText Consumer directory on the CD-ROM accompanying this book.

Reading E-mail with OLE DB

Now we move on to the more complicated task of reading e-mail. Way back in the Windows 3.0 days, Microsoft provided a standard routine interface called MAPI (Messaging Application Programming Interface) that enabled C programs to access e-mail. Although technology has moved on to C++, MAPI is still pretty archaic and requires an understanding of older technology to which many current C++ programmers have never been exposed.

This section shows how a complicated procedure, once incorporated in a provider, can be easily used by everyone – even those who have no understanding of the complicated procedure.

Understanding MAPI

Simple MAPI is a set of structures and functions that can be used to add e-mail capability to C, C++, or Visual Basic applications. The simple MAPI functions are available in C and C++ and Visual Basic versions. Table 15-2 describes some of the simple MAPI functions used in this section.

TABLE 15-2 SIMPLE MAPI FUNCTIONS

MAPI Function	Description
ULONG FAR PASCAL MAPIFindNext(LHANDLE lhSession, ULONG ulUIParam, LPTSTR lpszMessageType, LPTSTR lpszSeedMessageID, FLAGS flFlags, ULONG ulReserved, LPTSTR lpszMessageID)	Returns the identifier of the first or next e-mail message. The session is the session established by the MAPILogon function. The ulUIParam is the handle of the parent window and is usually zero, indicating an application modal window if one is needed (which it usually isn't). The seed message ID and the message ID are usually the same variable. The seed message ID tells where to start the find, and the message ID returned is the start of the next record.

Continued

TABLE 15-2 SIMPLE MAPI FUNCTIONS *(Continued)*

ULONG FAR PASCAL MAPILogoff (LHANDLE lhSession, ULONG ulUIParam, FLAGS flFlags, ULONG ulReserved)	Ends an e-mail session. Usually all that's required for the parameters is the session. Zeros are used for the rest of the parameters.
ULONG FAR PASCAL MAPILogon(ULONG ulUIParam, LPTSTR lpszProfileName LPTSTR lpszPassword FLAGS flFlags, ULONG ulReserved, LPLHANDLE lplhSession)	Starts a session that enables e-mail access. Usually when you write a provider, you leave the profile name and the password null. The session is returned from this function and is used in all other MAPI functions.
ULONG FAR PASCAL MAPIReadMail(LHANDLE lhSession, ULONG ulUIParam LPTSTR lpszMessageID, FLAGS flFlags, ULONG ulReserved, lpMapiMessage FAR * lppMessage)	Reads an e-mail message. It uses the session retrieved from the logon and the message ID retrieved from the FindNext. The lpMapiMessage is a structure that contains information about the message, including the author, date, time, and content.

So far, these functions seem pretty complicated simply because of the number of parameters needed to access each one. Microsoft does not provide library (.lib) files for linking to the Simple MAPI APIs. Instead, you need to define all the MAPI APIs you use as function pointers. Your DLL initialize those function pointers by calling Win32 APIs to load MAPI32.dll and find out its entry point addresses. To use the MAPI functions, you need to perform the following steps:

1. Include MAPI.H in your source file. MAPI.H contains definitions for all of the functions, return value constants, and data types:

```
#include <mapi.h>
```

2. You probably want to define MAPI functions using type definitions:

```
typedef ULONG (FAR PASCAL *pMAPILOGON)(HWND, LPSTR, LPSTR,
FLAGS, ULONG, LPLHANDLE);
```

3. Next, declare your functions. If you are using a header file for your declarations (which you probably are), you need to define the functions *only once* throughout the whole project and then define the functions as extern in the rest of the project. This can be done with a #define directive and an #ifdef directive. First, in the main source program (some .cpp file), define MAIN before you include the MAPI header file you're creating:

```
#define MAIN
#include "MAPIProviderRS.h"
```

Then, in your header file (MAPIProviderRS.h), you need to define your MAPI function using the typedef in step 2:

```
#ifdef MAIN
pMAPILOGON pfnMAPILogon;
#else
extern pMAPILOGON pfnMAPILogon;
#endif
```

4. As weird as this sounds, you really haven't defined your function yet. Because the function is part of a DLL, you need to load the DLL and then allocate the MAPI function to your function pointer using the GetProcAddress function:

```
HMODULE hLibrary = LoadLibrary("MAPI32.dll");
pfnMAPILogon =
(pMAPILOGON)GetProcAddress(hLibrary,"MAPILogon");
```

Pretty complicated, right? Now try explaining this to the 70 (or however many) programmers who work in your corporation. Fortunately, OLE DB enables you to mask the complexity so that all your 70 programmers need to know is that they can use an OLE DB MAPI provider to access their e-mail.

Developing MAPI Rowset Support

You can use the following steps to create a MAPI provider:

1. Define a provider as shown in steps 1 through 4 in the section "Writing a Text Provider," earlier in this chapter. Use the ATL Com AppWizard, and name your project OLEDBMail as shown in Figure 15-9.

   Also, use "MAPIProvider" as your short name in the ATL Object Wizard Properties dialog box (Figure 15-10).

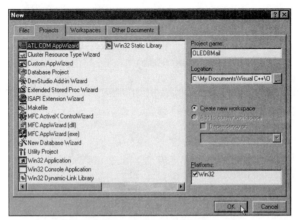

Figure 15-9: Once more, use the ATL to define your provider.

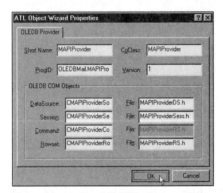

Figure 15-10: Use MAPIProvider as your provider name.

2. Add an `#include <mapi.h>` statement to your rowset header file
   (MAPIProviderRS.h):

```
// MAPIProviderRS.h : Declaration of the CMAPIProviderRowset
#ifndef __CMAPIProviderRowset_H_
#define __CMAPIProviderRowset_H_
#include "resource.h"          // main symbols
//Added by Chuck Wood — #include mapi.h for MAPI support
#include <mapi.h>
```

3. Underneath the `#include <mapi.h>` statement, add typedefs for the
   function pointer to be used for MAPI functions:

```
//Added by Chuck Wood — Now for a bunch of early '90s C
//stuff.  No object-oriented here!
typedef ULONG (FAR PASCAL *pMAPILOGON)(HWND, LPSTR, LPSTR,
```

```
FLAGS, ULONG, LPLHANDLE);
typedef ULONG (FAR PASCAL *pMAPILOGOFF)(LHANDLE, HWND,
FLAGS,ULONG);
typedef ULONG (FAR PASCAL *pMAPIFINDNEXT)(LHANDLE, HWND,
LPSTR, LPSTR, FLAGS, ULONG, LPSTR);
typedef ULONG (FAR PASCAL *pMAPIREADMAIL)(LHANDLE, HWND,
LPSTR, FLAGS, ULONG, lpMapiMessage FAR *);
```

4. Underneath the `typedef` statements, create function pointers for each of
   the MAPI functions you'll be using:

```
#ifdef MAIN

pMAPILOGON pfnMAPILogon;
pMAPILOGOFF pfnMAPILogoff;
pMAPIFINDNEXT pfnMAPIFindNext;
pMAPIREADMAIL pfnMAPIReadMail;

#else

extern pMAPILOGON pfnMAPILogon;
extern pMAPILOGOFF pfnMAPILogoff;
extern pMAPIFINDNEXT pfnMAPIFindNext;
extern pMAPIREADMAIL pfnMAPIReadMail;

#endif
```

5. In your rowset source file (MAPIProviderRS.cpp), define MAIN before
   including your rowset header file (MAPIProviderRS.h):

```
// Implementation of the CMAPIProviderCommand
#include "stdafx.h"
#include "OLEDBMail.h"
//Added by Chuck Wood
//This is to ensure that only one set of non-extern mapi
//functions are declared.
#define MAIN
#include "MAPIProviderRS.h"
```

In the rowset header file (MAPIProviderRS.h), replace the class used for
the directory information with the `CMAPILayout` class that follows:

```
class CMAPILayout
{
public:
    char m_strAuthor[50];
```

```
char m_strSubject[256];
char m_strDate[20];
char m_strBody[1024];

BEGIN_PROVIDER_COLUMN_MAP(CMAPILayout)
    PROVIDER_COLUMN_ENTRY("Author", 1, m_strAuthor)
    PROVIDER_COLUMN_ENTRY("Subject", 2, m_strSubject)
    PROVIDER_COLUMN_ENTRY("Date", 3, m_strDate)
    PROVIDER_COLUMN_ENTRY("Body", 4, m_strBody)
END_PROVIDER_COLUMN_MAP()
};
```

Any mail application requires more than a maximum of a single kilobyte buffer. For ease of understanding, a fixed buffer was used, but providers also support streams as data values.

7. You have to change "CMAPIProviderWindowsFile" to "CMAPILayout" in the GetColumnInfo column in the rowset header file (MAPIProviderRS.h):

```
static ATLCOLUMNINFO* GetColumnInfo(
        CMAPIProviderCommand* pv, ULONG* pcInfo)
{
    return CMAPILayout::GetColumnInfo(pv,pcInfo);
}
```

8. You also have to change "CMAPIProviderWindowsFile" to "CMAPILayout" in the rowset base class definition and in places in MAPIProviderRS.h:

```
class CMAPIProviderRowset :
        public CRowsetImpl< CMAPIProviderRowset,
            CMAPILayout, CMAPIProviderCommand>
```

9. You need to replace all of the Execute functions in your rowset header file (MAPIProviderRS.h). This is pretty complicated, so in this step, I'm going to build the Execute function one step at a time.

a. First, declare your variables to hold the MAPI session handle, the e-mail message, and a CMAPILayout instance (CMAPILayout was defined in the last step):

```
class CMAPIProviderRowset : public CRowsetImpl<
CMAPIProviderRowset, CMAPILayout, CMAPIProviderCommand>
{
```

```
public:
    HRESULT Execute(DBPARAMS * pParams, LONG*
pcRowsAffected)
    {
        USES_CONVERSION;
        LHANDLE hMAPISession;
        CMAPILayout ml;
        lpMapiMessage lppMessage;
```

b. Now, load the MAPI .dll file (MAPI32.dll), and allocate the function pointers to it:

```
HRESULT Execute(DBPARAMS * pParams, LONG* pcRowsAffected)
{
    USES_CONVERSION;
    LHANDLE hMAPISession;
    CMAPILayout ml;
    lpMapiMessage lppMessage;
HMODULE hLibrary = LoadLibrary("MAPI32.dll");
if (hLibrary < (HANDLE)32)
    return DB_E_INVALID;
//Now to allocate the functions witht the
//right function address ********************************
pfnMAPILogon =
(pMAPILOGON)GetProcAddress(hLibrary,"MAPILogon");
if (!pfnMAPILogon)
    return DB_E_INVALID;
pfnMAPILogoff =
(pMAPILOGOFF)GetProcAddress(hLibrary,"MAPILogoff");
if (!pfnMAPILogoff)
    return DB_E_INVALID;
pfnMAPIFindNext=
(pMAPIFINDNEXT)GetProcAddress(hLibrary,"MAPIFindNext");
if (!pfnMAPIFindNext)
    return DB_E_INVALID;
pfnMAPIReadMail=
(pMAPIREADMAIL)GetProcAddress(hLibrary,"MAPIReadMail");
if (!pfnMAPIReadMail)
    return DB_E_INVALID;
```

c. Next, use the function pointers to log on. Don't forget to check the results:

```
if (((*pfnMAPILogon)(0, NULL, NULL,
            MAPI_NEW_SESSION | MAPI_LOGON_UI, OL,
            &hMAPISession))
```

```
                          != SUCCESS_SUCCESS)
           return DB_E_INVALID;
```

d. Initialize your CMAPILayout layout variables and a message ID string that is used to keep track of your position in the e-mail message queue:

```
char lpszMessageID[512];
strcpy (lpszMessageID, "");          //Start at first message
//Null terminate my strings for later
ml.m_strAuthor[49] = 0;
ml.m_strSubject[255] = 0;
ml.m_strDate[19] = 0;
ml.m_strBody[1023] = 0;
```

e. Use your pointer for the MAPIFindNext function to loop through the e-mail to build your rowset. In each loop, read the mail pointed to by the MAPI pointer, and fill the fields in your CMAPILayout layout variables:

```
while ((*pfnMAPIFindNext)(    hMAPISession, 0, NULL,
                    lpszMessageID,
                    MAPI_LONG_MSGID, 0,
                    lpszMessageID)
      == SUCCESS_SUCCESS) {
    (*pfnMAPIReadMail)(    hMAPISession, 0,
                    lpszMessageID,
                    MAPI_PEEK, 0,
                    &lppMessage);
    strncpy(ml.m_strAuthor,
        lppMessage->lpOriginator->lpszName, 49);
    strncpy(ml.m_strSubject,
        lppMessage->lpszSubject,255);
    strncpy(ml.m_strDate,
        lppMessage->lpszDateReceived, 19);
    strncpy(ml.m_strBody,
        lppMessage->lpszNoteText, 1023);
    if (!m_rgRowData.Add(ml))
        return E_OUTOFMEMORY;
    *pcRowsAffected++;
}
```

f. Finally, log off, and free your DLL because you are finished building your rowset.

```
(*pfnMAPILogoff)(hMAPISession, 0, 0, 0);
FreeLibrary(hLibrary);    //Close Mail Library
return S_OK;
```

This entire Execute function is in the rowset header file (MAPIProviderRS.h) in the OLEDBMail directory on the CD-ROM accompanying this book.

The MAPI provider used in this section can be found in the OLEDBMail directory on the CD-ROM that accompanies this book.

Developing MAPI Session Support

You still need to change your schema rowsets in your session. This can be done with the following steps:

1. Change the Execute function in the
   `CMAPIProviderSessionTRSchemaRowset` class in the session header file
   (MAPIProviderSession.h). Delete any code about checking drive C:, and
   add the appropriate table name:

```
class CMAPIProviderSessionTRSchemaRowset :
    public CRowsetImpl< CMAPIProviderSessionTRSchemaRowset,
CTABLESRow, CMAPIProviderSession>
{
public:
    HRESULT Execute(LONG* pcRowsAffected, ULONG, const
VARIANT*)
    {
        USES_CONVERSION;
        CTABLESRow trData;
        lstrcpyW(trData.m_szType, OLESTR("TABLE"));
        lstrcpyW(trData.m_szDesc, OLESTR("The Mail Table"));
        lstrcpynW(trData.m_szTable,
            T2OLE("Mail"),
            SIZEOF_MEMBER(CTABLESRow, m_szTable));
        if (!m_rgRowData.Add(trData))
            return E_OUTOFMEMORY;
        *pcRowsAffected = 1;
        return S_OK;
    }
};
```

2. Change the column schema to reflect the four columns that we are providing for our e-mail access (author, subject, date, and body):

```
class CMAPIProviderSessionColSchemaRowset :
    public CRowsetImpl< CMAPIProviderSessionColSchemaRowset,
CCOLUMNSRow, CMAPIProviderSession>
{
public:
    HRESULT Execute(LONG* pcRowsAffected, ULONG, const
VARIANT*)
    {
//******
        static const struct { char *szName; int maxLength; }
        rgcolumns[] =
            {{"Author", 50},
             {"Subject", 256},
             {"Date", 20},
             {"Body", 1024}};

        const int NUMBERCOLUMNS = sizeof(rgcolumns) /
                                  sizeof(rgcolumns[0]);
        WIN32_FIND_DATA wf;
        HANDLE fileHandle;
        //Error if file does not exist
        fileHandle = FindFirstFile(
            COLEDBTextProviderRowset::GetFileName(),
            &wf);
        if (fileHandle == INVALID_HANDLE_VALUE)
            return E_FAIL; // The file does not exist
        FindClose(fileHandle);

        // Fill out all the CCOLUMNSRow records
        for (int column=0; column<NUMBERCOLUMNS; column++) {
            CCOLUMNSRow crColumnInfo;

            lstrcpyW(crColumnInfo.m_szTableName,
                T2OLE(
                COLEDBTextProviderRowset::GetFileName()));
            crColumnInfo.m_ulOrdinalPosition = column+1;
            crColumnInfo.m_bIsNullable = VARIANT_FALSE;
            crColumnInfo.m_bColumnHasDefault = VARIANT_FALSE;
            crColumnInfo.m_ulColumnFlags = 0;
            crColumnInfo.m_nDataType = DBTYPE_STR;
```

```
        lstrcpyW(crColumnInfo.m_szColumnName,
                T2OLE(rgcolumns[column].szName));
        lstrcpyW(crColumnInfo.m_szDescription,
                T2OLE(rgcolumns[column].szName));
        crColumnInfo.m_ulCharMaxLength =
                rgcolumns[column].maxLength;

        // Declare new schema row
        m_rgRowData.Add(crColumnInfo);
    }
    *pcRowsAffected = NUMBERCOLUMNS;
    //******
    return S_OK;
    }
};
```

Writing the MAPI Consumer

For the final section in this chapter, an MFC MAPI consumer is written to access the MAPI provider:

1. First, define a MAPI consumer using the MFC AppWizard, as shown in Figure 15-11.

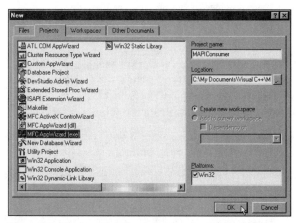

Figure 15–11: As with other providers, a standard MFC program is used to access the MAPI provider.

2. In Step 1, click Single Document, and click Next. In Step 2, click Database view without file support, and click the Data Source button. This opens the Database Options dialog box. Choose the OLE DB radio button, and click the Select OLE DB Datasource button. This opens the Data Link Properties window shown in Figure 15-12. If you have successfully built your MAPI provider, here you should see the MAPIProvider listed as one of the choices.

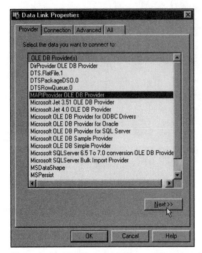

Figure 15-12: Your MAPI provider should be listed as one of the provider choices.

3. Click the Next button and then the OK button to close the Data Link Properties window and the OK button to close the Database Options window after choosing your provider. The Select Database Tables window opens next. Click the first line to indicate the table, and click OK.

4. Continue through the MFC AppWizard until you're finished. When you're finished, a dialog box opens. You must build a dialog box that contains all the fields you want to access. You need the following textboxes defined for this project:

- IDC_SENDER is used for the author/sender field.

- IDC_SUBJECT is used for the subject field.

- IDC_DATE is used for the date field.

- IDC_MESSAGE is used for the message/body field.

Figure 15-13 shows how the completed dialog box looks

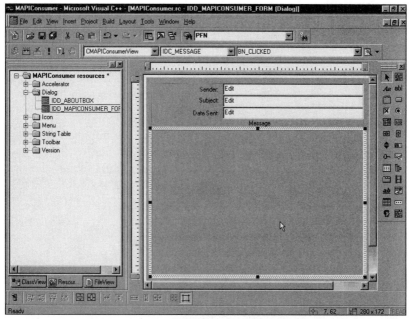

Figure 15-13: The dialog box layout for the MAPIConsumer project

5. Finally, add the fields to your data exchange:

```
void CMAPIConsumerView::DoDataExchange(CDataExchange*
iew::DoDataExchange(pDX);
    //{{AFX_DATA_MAP(CMAPIConsumerView)
// NOTE: the ClassWizard will add DDX and DDV calls here
    //}}AFX_DATA_MAP
    //Added by Chuck Wood for data exchange support
    DDX_Text(pDX, IDC_SENDER, m_pSet->m_Author, 50);
    DDX_Text(pDX, IDC_SUBJECT, m_pSet->m_Subject, 256);
    DDX_Text(pDX, IDC_DATE, m_pSet->m_Date, 20);
    DDX_Text(pDX, IDC_MESSAGE, m_pSet->m_Body, 1024);
    DDV_MaxChars(pDX, m_pSet->m_Author, 50);
    DDV_MaxChars(pDX, m_pSet->m_Subject, 256);
    DDV_MaxChars(pDX, m_pSet->m_Date, 20);
    DDV_MaxChars(pDX, m_pSet->m_Body, 1024);
}
```

Now you're finished. When you run your provider, you are asked to logon to your e-mail service, as shown in Figure 15-14. This is a result of the MAPILogon function that was coded by the provider.

Figure 15-14: The MAPI provider forces a logon – just more complexity hidden from the user.

When you log on, your consumer retrieves all the information from the MAPI provider without the need for any MAPI commands and enables your consumer application to display this information. This shows how the provider can handle complexity and hide it from the myriad other developers needing the same access. Figure 15-15 shows the complete project.

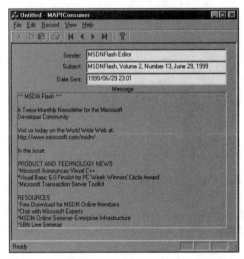

Figure 15-15: Finally, e-mail access is available at a fraction of the complexity.

The MAPI consumer used in this section can be found in the MAPIConsumer directory on the CD-ROM that accompanies this book.

Summary

This chapter shows how to connect to nonrelational sources using a provider, which is particularly important for UDA. To recap:

- ◆ UDA uses OLE DB to enable access to data that is not in relational format.

- ◆ OLE DB can access text files and give them some added functionality, such as scrolling.

- ◆ OLE DB can be used to hide complex access operations from the developer. In this chapter, a MAPI provider was written that can be used by several developers. These developers don't need to understand MAPI access to get to e-mail data.

Chapter 16

Deploying Your Visual C++ Database Applications

IN THIS CHAPTER

◆ Understanding release types

◆ Understanding how to deploy MFC applications

◆ Understanding how to deploy ATL applications

◆ Distributing programs with database support

WHEN YOU'RE FINISHED PROGRAMMING, you need to deploy your application. Although this has nothing to do with development, here's a short chapter that describes exactly what is needed to send your application to your users.

Understanding Release Targets

A *release* is the final project you deliver after compiles. A release can be a debug release for debugging, or a minimum release for efficient execution. If you click the Build→Configurations menu option, you see a list of current configurations for your release, as shown in Figure 16-1.

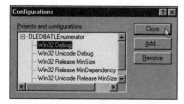

Figure 16-1: The Configurations window enables you to specify which configuration you want to release to your users.

Currently, when you compile during development, you default to the debug release. This release is used for development. The executable contains debug information that Visual Studio uses to help you debug and step through code.

When you release your final project, you probably don't want to release a large executable that contains debug information. Instead, you probably want to release a minimal version that contains no debug information and is optimized for execution. To change your release type, you need to click Build → Set Active Configuration. This opens the Set Active Project Configuration window as seen in Figure 16-2.

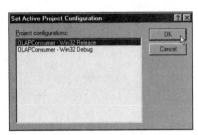

Figure 16-2: The Set Active Project Configuration window.

There are many differences between release configurations and debug configurations:

◆ Debug configurations enable debugging. Release configurations have disabled debugging. You can run the release configuration under the debugger, but it is not likely to be useful because you won't be able to see any of your variables or source code.

◆ MFC programs use diagnostic macros that help detect coding or logic errors in your project. Debug configurations enable these macros. Release configurations disable these macros.

◆ Debug configurations and release configurations use different libraries for linking. The release configuration libraries are smaller and more efficient.

◆ Finally, debug configuration programs are never optimized, which enables a faster compile. Release configurations are optimized for speed so that your release configuration actually runs faster than your debug configuration.

Deploying MFC Applications

When you deploy your MFC applications, you just need to include your executable (.EXE). You also need to be sure that the client machine has an MFC .DLL file (for example, MFC42.DLL) in the Windows System folder so that MFC calls can be processed.

 If you choose Use MFC in a static library under the General tab in the Project Settings dialog, then the MFC .DLL file is not required on the client, but your executable is larger.

Deploying ATL Applications

ATL applications give the developer a lot more distribution options as shown by the Set Active Project Configuration window in Figure 16-3.

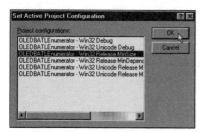

Figure 16-3: The Set Active Project Configuration window shows more distribution options when deploying ATL applications.

Table 16-1 shows the release options and their differences.

TABLE 16-1 RELEASE OPTIONS FOR ATL PROJECTS

Release Type	Description
Win32 Release MinSize	The MinSize release tries to make the smallest release possible. The MinSize release enables the minimum possible executable size. The MinSize release requires that the ATL.DLL file be installed in the Windows System directory.
Win32 Release MinDependency	The MinDependency release is identical to the MinSize release, except that the ATL.DLL file is not required. ATL functionality is built right into the executable.
Win32 Unicode Release MinSize	This is the same as the MinSize release, except Unicode support is added. Unicode enables international language support, even with character-based languages such as Chinese, Japanese, and Korean.
Win32 Unicode Release MinDependency	This is the same as the MinDependency release, except Unicode support is added.

 You also need to register all ATL controls in the system Registry.

Deploying Web DHTML Applications

To deploy your Web application, you need to follow three steps:

◆ Set up database permissions for all your users inside the database.

◆ Set up database connections on all the machines that you'll be using.

◆ Deploy just as you would with ATL. However, you need the HTML along with your executable.

Establishing Database Support

After your programs are deployed, you need to establish database support. You should consider the following when adding support for your database on a client machine:

◆ OLE DB and ADO require that OLE DB and ADO COM files be installed on the client machine. If you are distributing OLE DB or ADO programs, you need to retrieve the "Microsoft Data Access Components" from Microsoft's Web site (www.microsoft.com/data/oledb) to add to your installation procedures.

◆ ODBC and OLE DB for ODBC requires that an ODBC entry is set up for every database. You can accomplish this in three ways:

■ Include instructions for ODBC setup.

■ Programmatically add the Registry entries yourself.

■ Use a file DSN file rather than a user or system DSN. This ODBC file DSN should be in the same directory as your application.

Need I say that no distribution technique works well in every environment? Try to find a representative sample of your client machines, and test the installation procedure on each one to see if your program installs and runs correctly. You'll be glad you did.

Summary

After the coding is over, you still need to distribute your application to your users. This chapter gives a brief overview of what is needed to test your application. To recap:

◆ Release targets are different than debug targets. Release targets are geared for execution speed, not debugging and development.

◆ MFC applications and ATL applications have different release requirements. Be sure you review the release requirements before releasing your product.

◆ Web deployment requires you set up a database connection to the Web site and deploy the HTML along with the application. This deployment works best with intranets.

◆ Don't forget to test your application release.

Chapter 17

Developing OLAP OLE DB Consumers

IN THIS CHAPTER

- ◆ Understanding basic OLAP concepts

- ◆ Viewing OLAP languages

- ◆ Performing OLAP programming with OLE DB

OLAP (ONLINE ANALYTICAL PROCESSING) is a way of storing data on a database that enables multidimensional access rather than simple relational access. OLAP is a budding technology that is just now being supported by major vendors. It's conceivable that OLAP may replace traditional relational databases for many developers, and database vendors and developers alike are carefully scrutinizing the technology used in OLAP. OLE DB for OLAP is a set of objects and interfaces that extends OLE DB to provide access to multidimensional data sources. This chapter explains OLAP, shows how OLAP is defined on a MS SQL Server database, and shows how OLE DB can be used to access OLAP data sources.

Understanding OLAP

Before you begin to access OLAP, you should understand some basic concepts. This section describes and defines terms that are associated with OLAP.

Using Cubes and Multidimensional Schemas

The concept of OLAP deals with multidimensional storage of data. Traditional database tables have, really, only one dimension of data, called the *column*. You select all the columns you need from the database and process each column one at a time.

OLAP stores data in a multidimensional format. For example, employers often want to know how well a student did in all their classes in a given department (for example, "What was your GPA in your computer science classes?") and how well they did each of the four years ("Did your GPA go up your senior year, or did you quit trying and coast on your GPA?"). For our Classes database on the CD-ROM, this query would be difficult. You would have to average the grades per class, then average the grades per year, and then average the grades per department and department and student. Relational access is fine, but it starts to become difficult when you want to retrieve relational data across several dimensions.

OLAP enables you to access data in a multidimensional manner. As shown in Figure 17-1, data could be stored along Student, Class, and Department *axes*. These three axes make a *cube*. Then simply by specifying those three axes, the user could retrieve the data. Although it requires a different way of thinking, OLAP may be the way to go for future database access.

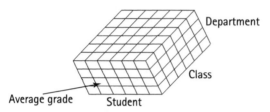

Figure 17-1: Database access in OLAP is based on a cube, not a table.

Unlike in standard geometry, cubes can be a cross section of any number of dimensions (not just three). The data points of interest are the points in this cross section, and each such point is uniquely identified by a set of coordinates. Each coordinate consists of the cross section of each dimension. For example, the cube in Figure 17-1 is a cube with three dimensions: Department, Class, and Student. Its points of interest are the average grade, which is a cross section between those three dimensions.

The Benefits of OLAP

OLAP can provide many benefits not found in traditional databases:

◆ OLAP *preaggregates* its cubes. If data is often sought in aggregate form, preaggregation of frequently queried data enables a very fast response time to *ad hoc* queries.

◆ OLAP enables the formation of an intuitive multidimensional data model. In many cases, this data model is easier to manipulate when one is selecting, navigating, and exploring the data.

◆ OLAP is a powerful tool for creating new views of data based upon a rich array of *ad hoc* calculation functions.

◆ OLAP enables easier management of security, optimization, and facilities to make the most out of your database system based upon your user needs.

Inserts, Updates, and Deletes with OLAP Cubes

When you store data in an OLAP data source, you not only have different ways of querying the database, but you also need to have a different idea of data updates:

- OLAP cells are not always atomic. This means that each cell might contain an aggregate value (sum or average) of other cells. As a result, updates to cells may be problematic. Some databases enable you to update every column that contributes to a cell, while others don't. Check with your OLAP database vendor to see what access is enabled.

- Inserts and deletes make no sense in OLAP. Rather, each cell is defined as empty or full. When you delete a cell, you don't get rid of the cell as you do when you delete a row in a relational database. Instead, you have no value in a cell, or you place a value in a cell.

Definitions

Following is a list of definitions for OLAP. Although some of these terms may seem a little ambiguous at this point, they will be used in context as the chapter progresses.

- A *cube* is the central metadata object recognized by OLAP. Cubes in OLAP are analogous to tables in traditional relational tables. As discussed previously, a cube is a cross section of several *dimensions*.

- A *dimension* in a cube in a variable or component that makes up one of the cross sections of the cube. For instance, there are three dimensions in the cube shown in Figure 17-1: Department, Class, and Student.

- Dimensions consist of *levels* contained in a *hierarchy*. For instance, students could be classified into undergraduate and graduate levels. In addition, each dimension may have more than one hierarchy. For instance, the Department dimension could have a hierarchy containing two levels: Department and Instructor. The Department dimension could also, in the same database, have a different hierarchy that could contain two other levels: Department and Class. A level in one hierarchy is not necessarily contained in another hierarchy. For instance, a class does not need to be taught by an instructor in the department, and not every instructor necessarily teaches a class.

- A *schema* is a set of cubes. Schemas are used when you want to treat a series of cubes identically, as with security.

- All the schemas together make up a *catalog*.

♦ A *measure* is the number at the cross section of the dimensions. A measure can simply be the value in a column, or it can be an aggregate function, such as a sum, a count, or an average.

♦ A *member* is an instance or a sublevel of the dimension. For example, say you had six students in your database; three graduate students (Tom, Dick, and Harry) and three undergraduates (Larry, Moe, and Curly). (Before you start wondering, I'm not trying to make any kind of statement with the names.) The members of Student would be {[All Students], Grads, Undergrads, Tom, Dick, Harry, Larry, Moe, Curley}. The members of the graduate level would be {[All Grads], Tom, Dick, Harry}, and the members of the undergraduate level would be {[All Undergrads], Larry Moe, Curly}.

♦ A Microsoft *MDX*, or *multidimensional expression,* is a command for accessing data on a Microsoft OLAP database. Microsoft's MDX statements for OLAP databases are analogous to SQL statements for relational databases.

♦ *Oracle Express* is a definition of commands for accessing data on an Oracle OLAP database. Oracle Express statements for Oracle OLAP databases are analogous to SQL statements for relational databases.

♦ Cubes and *virtual cubes* hold the same relationship as tables and views. The database schema defines a cube. A virtual cube is created by the combination of several other cubes. Just as with tables and views, virtual cubes are not as efficient as cubes.

♦ *ROLAP*, or *Relational OLAP*, is a relational DBMS (database management system) that stores information in tables but has such information available in a cube layout. Such database can use either standard SQL or MDX.

♦ *MOLAP*, or *Multidimensional OLAP* is a database that is designed to store its information in cube format. MOLAP is the opposite of ROLAP.

♦ An *axis dimension* is a dimension that contains multiple members. In Figure 17-2, Class and Department are axis dimensions because they contain more than one row.

♦ By contrast, a *slicer dimension* is when a single member is returned from a query. In Figure 17-2, Curly is a slicer dimension because only one member of the student is displayed.

♦ A *tuple* is a conditional expression in the WHERE clause of an MDX statement that creates a slicer dimension.

GPA for Curly ← Slicer dimension (student)

Axis dimensions → Department; ↓ Year

Year	Computer Science	MIS	Math	English
1996	3.4	3.6	3.0	2.0
1997	3.2	3.5		2.0
1998	2.9	3.1		
1999	2.1	2.9		

Figure 17-2: Slicer dimensions restrict the information selected.

Using OLAP Syntax

Now we start coding. Microsoft MDX statements, or multidimensional expression statements, are analogous to SQL. MDX is the language used to query a Microsoft OLAP database. Some of the statements that follow are SQL, and some are MDX. I tell you which one is which as I go along.

A typical MDX query takes the following form:

```
SELECT <axis_specification> [, <axis_specification>...]
FROM <cube_specification>
WHERE <slicer_specification>
```

Oracle Express syntax is somewhat different. Oracle syntax is as follows:

```
LIMIT <slicer-specification> [LIMIT <axis_specification>...]
REPORT DOWN <axis_specification>
```

Herein lies one of the problems with OLAP. The current syntax differs from OLAP database to OLAP database. As a result, unlike SQL, OLAP code is not transferable. As academia tries to develop a standard and corporations jockey for market control, this situation may change, but currently, coding for OLAP is different for every database. You should check with your specific database vendor to see if OLAP is supported, and the syntax required to access OLAP.

Querying an OLAP Cube

Say you want to make a report for a single student that lists the department, year, and average grade. An example of the summary data for this report is shown in Figure 17-3.

Average scores for Charles A Wood by year and department		
Department Code	Year	Average Score
CS	1997	89
ECON	1998	94
MIS	1997	92
MIS	1998	92

Figure 17-3: Your users may often require a cross-section summary report.

Based on our Classes database, the SQL SELECT statement required to perform this query is somewhat complicated:

```
SQL query
SELECT FirstName + ' ' + MidName + ' ' + LastName AS Student,
        Department.DepartmentCode AS DepartmentCode,
        Year,
        FLOOR(Avg(Grades.Score)) AS AverageScore
FROM Department,
     Class,
     Section,
     Student,
     Grades
WHERE Student.StudentID = Grades.StudentID
  AND Section.SectionID = Grades.SectionID
  AND Class.ClassID = Section.ClassID
  AND Department.DepartmentCode = Class.DepartmentCode
  AND Grades.StudentID = 1
GROUP BY Department.DepartmentCode,
         Section.Year,
         FirstName + ' ' + MidName + ' ' + LastName
```

However, OLAP queries aren't as complicated. Assuming you had a cube set up with average score by year, student, and section, the Microsoft MDX or Oracle Express statements are not quite as complicated. The following code shows the Microsoft MDX statements needed to perform the same query:

```
MDX OLAP query
SELECT NON EMPTY Section.MEMBERS DIMENSION PROPERTIES
        Section.Department, Section.Year ON ROWS,
NON EMPTY CROSSJOIN(AverageScore) ON COLUMNS
FROM GradesCube
WHERE ('Charles A. Wood')
```

With Oracle Express, the query would look somewhat different:

```
Oracle Express OLAP query
LIMIT student TO 'Charles A. Wood'
LIMIT section BASED ON Year
REPORT DOWN Section.Department, Section.Year
```

As you can see, the Microsoft MDX query is much simpler than the equivalent SQL code, and the Oracle Express query is simpler than both other queries. This is because much of the setup costs associated with the query are defined in a cube ahead of time. When the same queries are used often, OLAP not only makes coding easier, but also optimizes the cube for quick access. Queries that used to take quite long can be shortened considerably when the data is placed in a cube.

Programming for OLAP

OLAP is relatively new. Its inexperience in the market is shown by the lack of standards and support that it currently receives. However, vendors such as Microsoft and Oracle are rushing to provide support to developers for new OLAP offerings from their respective companies.

There are currently three ways to add OLAP support to your OLE DB provider:

◆ One of the easiest ways is to find or write an OLAP provider that handles the OLAP functionality for you.

◆ Another easy way to get OLAP functionality is to use the Microsoft PivotTable Service. This is an OLAP implementation that runs in the same process as your data consumer and can create an OLAP cube using data from some other OLE DB provider.

◆ Finally, you can use the new dataset object incorporated by the emerging OLE DB for OLAP standard, which is difficult because an ATL class has not yet wrapped the dataset object. Although this technique is more difficult and more restrictive, you can retrieve axis and slicer dimensions, cell properties, and other OLAP-specific information.

OLE DB for OLAP Consumer Programming

The first and easiest way to add OLAP support to your OLE DB provider is to get a provider that supports OLAP and send the commands to the provider, forming a standard recordset. Such providers are currently in development. The code that follows shows the consumer using this technique:

```
class CDepartment
{
public:
    CDepartment()
    {
        memset( (void*)this, 0, sizeof(*this) );
    };

    char m_Student[51];
    char m_DepartmentCode[5];
    int m_Year;
    int m_Average;


BEGIN_COLUMN_MAP(CDepartment)
        COLUMN_ENTRY_TYPE(1, DBTYPE_STR, m_Student)
        COLUMN_ENTRY_TYPE(2, DBTYPE_STR, m_DepartmentCode)
        COLUMN_ENTRY_TYPE(3, DBTYPE_I2, m_Year)
        COLUMN_ENTRY_TYPE(4, DBTYPE_I2, m_Average)
END_COLUMN_MAP()

};

class COLAPConsumerSet : public CCommand<CAccessor<CDepartment> >
{
public:

    HRESULT Open()
    {
        CDataSource db;
        CSession     session;
        HRESULT         hr;

        CDBPropSet     dbinit(DBPROPSET_DBINIT);
        dbinit.AddProperty(DBPROP_AUTH_PERSIST_SENSITIVE_AUTHINFO,
false);
        dbinit.AddProperty(DBPROP_INIT_DATASOURCE, "Classes");
        dbinit.AddProperty(DBPROP_INIT_PROMPT, (short)4);
        dbinit.AddProperty(DBPROP_INIT_LCID, (long)1033);

        hr = db.OpenWithServiceComponents("OracleExpressProvider.1",
&dbinit);
            if (FAILED(hr))
                return hr;
```

```
    hr = session.Open(db);
    if (FAILED(hr))
        return hr;

    CDBPropSet     propset(DBPROPSET_ROWSET);
    propset.AddProperty(DBPROP_CANFETCHBACKWARDS, true);
    propset.AddProperty(DBPROP_IRowsetScroll, true);
    char *oracleExpressSyntax = "\
            LIMIT student TO 'Charles A. Wood' \
            LIMIT section BASED ON Year \
    REPORT DOWN Section.Department, Section.Year";
    hr = CCommand<CAccessor<CDepartment> >::Open(
        session, oracleExpressSyntax, &propset);
    if (FAILED(hr))
        return hr;

    return MoveNext();
    }

};
```

In this code, Oracle Express syntax is passed directly to the provider. This technique works well with ROLAP databases that support both OLAP and relational queries, because ROLAP databases can be easily set up for OLAP access through existing OLE DB architecture.

OLE DB for OLAP Programming Constructs

The only new object created for OLE DB for OLAP is the dataset object. This object provides an abstraction for a multidimensional result set. It has interfaces and methods on it that perform the following functions:

◆ Give the number of axes and the contents of each axis

◆ Describe the number, data type, and so on of cell properties

◆ Retrieve cell property values

◆ Retrieve an interface on the command object that created the dataset object

Microsoft has attempted to reuse as much OLE DB infrastructure as possible, making the OLAP for OLE DB familiar to the user. OLE DB for OLAP uses the Dataset object to capture cube data.

OLE DB for OLAP currently does not enable any updates to the OLAP data. OLE DB for OLAP is a query tool only. Update capabilities are expected in version 2.0. However, if a OLAP dataset object has defined the IMDRangeRowset interface, it can give out a rowset containing a relational view of all the data items in a slice of the cube. This rowset is updateable and currently is the only way to update OLAP data.

The dataset functions are not currently defined in any ATL class. However, an IMDDataset COM interface uses dataset functions that contain or use the following constructs:

♦ The MDAXISINFO structure is used to hold information that has been retrieved using the GetAxisInfo method. In addition, the FreeAxisInfo method also uses this structure to free any axis information already retrieved. The definition for the MDAXISINFO structure is as follows:

```
struct tag MDAXISINFO {
    ULONG cbSize;
    ULONG iAxis;
    ULONG cDimensions;
    ULONG cCoordinates;
    ULONG __RPC_FAR *rgcColumns;
    LPOLESTR __RPC_FAR *rgpwszDimensionNames;
} MDAXISINFO;
```

♦ The GetAxisRowset method retrieves a rowset containing information about an OLAP axis based on properties set by the user:

```
virtual HRESULT STDMETHODCALLTYPE GetAxisRowset(
    /* [in] */ IUnknown __RPC_FAR *pUnkOuter,
    /* [in] */ ULONG iAxis,
    /* [in] */ REFIID riid,
    /* [in] */ ULONG cPropertySets,
    /* [size_is][out][in] */ DBPROPSET __RPC_FAR
rgPropertySets[ ],
    /* [iid_is][out] */ IUnknown __RPC_FAR *__RPC_FAR
*ppRowset) = 0;
```

♦ The GetAxisInfo retrieves information about a particular axis and stores it in a MDAXISINFO structure:

```
virtual HRESULT STDMETHODCALLTYPE GetAxisInfo(
    /* [out][in] */ ULONG __RPC_FAR *pcAxes,
    /* [size_is][size_is][out] */ MDAXISINFO __RPC_FAR
*__RPC_FAR *prgAxisInfo) = 0;
```

◆ The FreeAxisInfo frees an axis based on information in the MDAXISINFO structure:

```
virtual HRESULT STDMETHODCALLTYPE FreeAxisInfo(
    /* [in] */ ULONG cAxes,
    /* [size_is][in] */ MDAXISINFO __RPC_FAR *rgAxisInfo) = 0;
```

◆ The GetCellData method retrieves cell information based on an accessor and cell location specifications:

```
virtual HRESULT STDMETHODCALLTYPE GetCellData(
    /* [in] */ HACCESSOR hAccessor,
    /* [in] */ ULONG ulStartCell,
    /* [in] */ ULONG ulEndCell,
    /* [out] */ void __RPC_FAR *pData) = 0;
```

◆ The GetSpecification method is used to maintain a relationship between the dataset object and the command object that created it:

```
virtual HRESULT STDMETHODCALLTYPE GetSpecification(
    /* [in] */ REFIID riid,
    /* [iid_is][out] */ IUnknown __RPC_FAR *__RPC_FAR
*ppSpecification) = 0;
```

Summary

OLAP is in its infancy. However, the technology has the potential to replace relational databases much as relational databases replaced hierarchial databases in the 1970s and 1980s. To recap:

◆ OLAP is based on a *cube*, which is a multidimensional construct containing several axes.

◆ Data is retrieved in OLAP by *slicing* the cube for certain information. This *slice* is called a *slicer* axis.

◆ Traditional SQL is not used by OLAP. Microsoft's MDX and Oracle's Oracle Express are two languages that support OLAP. While Oracle Express seems to be more concise and is easier for the beginner to learn, MDX is closer to traditional SQL and may be easier for current database developers to pick up.

◆ Traditional OLE DB techniques may be best for coding OLAP calls. This involves passing the appropriate OLAP language call (MDX, Oracle Express, or whatever you're using) to the CCommand object. This technique forms a standard rowset based on OLAP data.

◆ The dataset COM object can be used to retrieve specific information about an OLAP data source. This COM object is difficult to use. Look for an ATL equivalent in future versions of Visual C++.

Chapter 18

Developing with ADO

IN THIS CHAPTER

◆ Understanding the ADO architecture

◆ Using ADO connections

◆ Using ADO recordsets

◆ Understanding ADO fields

◆ Running SQL statements inside ADO

◆ Writing a fully featured ADO program

ADO (ACTIVEX DATA OBJECTS) is used for all non-Visual C++ OLE DB access. ADO is a database programming model that enables OLE DB access from multiple languages, such as Visual Basic, Java, and VBScript. ADO is used extensively before the current version (version 6.0) of Visual C++ when the developers had no OLE DB tools with which to develop. A lot of ADO class libraries and ADO legacy programs are currently in use. This chapter delves into the internal structure of ADO and shows how to make ADO work for you.

Delving into the ADO Programming Model

ADO is used as an OLE DB generic consumer. ADO wraps much of the functionality of OLE DB and enables developers in all languages to have access to a myriad of data sources, as shown in Figure 18-1.

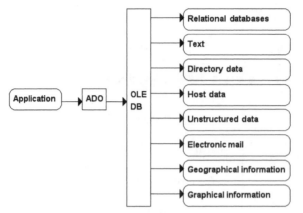

Figure 18-1: As a consumer, ADO gives C++ and non-C++ programmers the same access to OLE DB that C++ programmers enjoy through traditional OLE DB consumers.

Much ADO About Nothing in Visual C++?

There are two really good reasons why a Visual C++ developer would choose *not* to develop in ADO:

◆ Although OLE DB is complex, it's really easy to develop OLE DB consumer applications because the wizards write a lot of the complex code for you. It's not so easy to develop ADO applications because the Visual C++ environment does not have any wizards to write your ADO client code for you, so you have to write all the code yourself.

◆ To top off the previous point, OLE DB consumers are more efficient than ADO programs. ADO is itself an OLE DB consumer that is not optimized for your specific database access. So not only are OLE DB consumers more easily developed, they're also more efficient.

The preceding two reasons are why such little attention is given to raw ADO in this book. For the most part, you should avoid ADO for new Visual C++ applications and use OLE DB consumers instead.

That being said, there are still some reasons why you won't be able to avoid coding ADO applications:

◆ Job standards or class libraries may be written for ADO applications but not for OLE DB consumers. To take advantage of some existing code, you may be forced to accept ADO as your database access library.

◆ Some providers are not as kind to the developer as others. For example, the provider I wrote in Chapter 17 does not enable backward scrolling. ADO serves as a wrapper for providers and provides additional functionality (such as backward scrolling) that may not be provided for in other OLE DB providers.

◆ You may have legacy systems that are written in ADO. Before Visual C++ 6.0, ADO made a lot more sense because it was an easy way to access OLE DB providers. These older systems may be complicated and may need maintenance, but you may not want to rewrite them immediately just because a new technology was introduced.

◆ Finally, other development environments, such as Visual J++ and Visual Basic, use ADO as their means to ADO access. If you or your fellow developers have become extremely comfortable using ADO, you may develop applications faster by ADO techniques than by OLE DB consumer techniques. That being said, OLE DB and ADO use similar commands. If ADO familiarity is the only thing keeping you from OLE DB consumer development, I suggest you take a look at OLE DB consumer development and see if you can pick it up. You may be surprised how easy it is once you already know ADO.

For the people who need to code in ADO, this chapter describes ADO access and architecture.

ADO programming involves making calls to the ADO class library. The ADO library is set up in a hierarchical fashion so that you can "drill down" through the database to find the data you want. Figure 18-2 shows how ADO is configured.

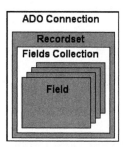

Figure 18-2: The ADO interface consists of three major categories: connections, recordsets, and fields.

Following is a description of each ADO construct:

◆ Each ADO Connection object uses a data source name, a user ID, and a password to establish a connection to a database.

◆ Each ADO recordset is formed by executing some SQL that returns a database cursor containing data rows. These rows can be retrieved as well as updated through the ADO recordset.

◆ Each recordset contains a Fields collection that, in turn, contains several Field objects. These Field objects contain information about database fields that have been retrieved including data type, length, and stored value.

What About the ADO Errors Object?

ADO also contains an Errors container that contains individual Error objects. The Errors container encapsulates the error handling previously discussed in Chapter 10. Because HR codes are returned for each error routine, and you can query the database directly with the OLEDBError header file, C++ programmers need not access the ADO Errors object. The ADO Errors object is primarily for use by non-C++ programmers who don't have access to the routines available in Visual C++.

To find out more about OLE DB error handling (which works identically for ADO), see Chapter 10.

Understanding ADO Connections

Before you access an ADO database, you must first establish a connection to the database. This is done through an ADOConnection interface. To create a connection, declare a pointer to the ADOConnection interface, and use the CoCreateInstance method to set up the connection in memory:

```
CComPtr<ADOConnection> m_ADOConn;
CoCreateInstance(CLSID_CADOConnection, NULL,
    CLSCTX_INPROC_SERVER, IID_IADOConnection,
    (LPVOID *)&m_ADOConn);
```

In the preceding statement, the CLSCTX_INPROC_SERVER variable directs the ADO connection object to run in a DLL in your process, rather than an .exe in a separate process or even on a different machine. The three connection locations you can have are listed in Table 18-1, although CLSCTX_INPROC_SERVER is used most often.

TABLE 18-1 ADO CONNECTION LOCATIONS

Cursor Constant	Description
CLSCTX_INPROC_SERVER	The ADO connection object runs in a DLL in your process.
CLSCTX_INPROC_CLIENT	The ADO connection object runs in an .exe in a separate process.
CLSCTX_INPROC_NONE	Use the default connection location.

Once you have allocated your ADO connection, you can use it to connect to the database. You need to specify BSTR variables that contain the database name, user ID, password, and cursor type for all future cursors. This can be shown in the following code:

```
//Use the connection to open a link to database
CComBSTR bstrODBCDatabase = "classes";
CComBSTR bstrUserId = "cwood";
CComBSTR bstrPassword = "mypassword";
m_ADOConn->Open(
        bstrODBCDatabase,
        bstrUserId,
        bstrPassword,
        adOpenUnspecified);
```

You have not yet defined the cursor type used for the recordsets. Table 18-2 shows all the cursors that you can define when connecting through ADO.

TABLE 18-2 CURSOR TYPES

Cursor Type Property	Description
adOpenUnspecified	This indicates an unspecified value for the cursor type. With this cursor type, the OLE DB provider is queried to see what cursor access is enabled. This is the most common cursor type.
adOpenForwardOnly	This cursor type indicates that cursors formed with this connection enable forward-only access, and changes made by other users are not visible after the connection is established. This cursor type is great for reports.

Continued

TABLE **18-2 CURSOR TYPES** (*Continued*)

Cursor Type Property	Description
adOpenKeyset	A keyset cursor type indicates that all movement is enabled, but new records added by other users won't be visible to the program after the connection is established. Changes to existing records and deleted records are visible after the connection is established.
adOpenDynamic	A dynamic cursor forces all additions, changes, and deletions by other users to be visible, and all types of movement through the recordset are enabled.
adOpenStatic	A static cursor enables all types of movement, but no changes made by other users are visible after the connection is established.

Understanding ADO Recordsets

Once you have established an ADO connection, you can create an ADO recordset that contains the results of an SQL SELECT statement. To create an ADO recordset, you must first allocate it using the CoCreateInstance method, just as you did with the ADO connection:

```
//Allocate a new ADORecordset variable
    CComPtr<ADORecordset> m_pSet;
    CoCreateInstance(CLSID_CADORecordset, NULL,
        CLSCTX_INPROC_SERVER, IID_IADORecordset,
        (LPVOID *)&m_pSet);
```

Just as with the connection, you can determine where each recordset cursor is to be stored. They are usually stored at the database server level. Once you have allocated an ADO recordset, you can open the recordset with an Open function. The ADORecordset.Open function uses the following syntax:

```
HRESULT Open(
        VARIANT Source,
        VARIANT ActiveConnection,
        CursorTypeEnum CursorType,
        LockTypeEnum LockType,
        LONG Options /*CommandTypeEnum*/)
```

Table 18-3 defines the parameters of the `ADORecordset.Open` function.

TABLE **18-3** ADORECORDSET.OPEN PARAMETERS

Parameter	Description
source	The source parameter is a VARIANT that contains the source string. Usually this is an SQL string, but it can also be other sources depending on the CommandTypeEnum options.
ActiveConnection	This is the connection you have already opened. This can also be an ODBC connection string if you want to bypass creating a connection object and have ADO worry about the connection object for you.
CursorType	This is a cursor type variable that has already been described in Table 18-2.
LockType	This is the type of database lock you wish to employ. Locks are covered later in this section.
Options	This is the option whose valid values are listed in the CommandTypeEnum enum in ADOINT.h header file. These options affect how ADO interprets your source statement. Options are covered later in this section.

Following is an example of how to open a recordset. A keyset cursor, an optimistic lock, and a command text option were used:

```
//Form an SQL statement from the table
    CComBSTR bstrSQL = "SELECT * FROM Department";
//Allocate a new ADORecordset variable
    CoCreateInstance(CLSID_CADORecordset, NULL,
        CLSCTX_INPROC_SERVER, IID_IADORecordset,
        (LPVOID *)&m_pSet);
//Open the newly formed recordset with the SQL
//and the connection
    HRESULT hr = m_pSet->Open(
        CComVariant(bstrSQL),
        CComVariant(m_ADOConn),
        adOpenKeyset, adLockOptimistic, adCmdText);
```

The Many Ways to Open a Recordset

Because of its use with other languages, ADO has enabled optional parameters. These optional parameters must always be provided because of Visual C++ type safety. However, you can still implement other functionality to open a recordset.

For instance, instead of passing a source string and a connection to an Open statement, you can specify the source string and connection ahead of time. The connection can be specified by using the `ADORecordset::putref_ActiveConnection` method and passing an active connection as a parameter:

```
m_pSet->putref_ActiveConnection(m_ADOConn);
```

The source string can be assigned to a recordset by using the `ADORecordset.put_Source` method:

```
CComBSTR bstrSQL = "SELECT * FROM Department";
m_pSet->put_Source(bstrSQL);
```

You can then define a `VARIANT` that is assigned to a `VT_ERROR` type with a `DISP_E_PARAMNOTFOUND` assigned to the `VARIANT.scode` variable. Passing this `VARIANT` tells the ADO function to use existing variable definitions:

```
VARIANT vNULL;
vNULL.vt = VT_ERROR;
vNULL.scode = DISP_E_PARAMNOTFOUND;
```

When you finally open your recordset, you can issue an open without any additional code:

```
m_pSet->Open(vNULL, vNULL,
    adOpenKeyset, adLockOptimistic, adCmdText);
```

Such techniques can result in less code, especially if you are constantly reusing a recordset and don't want to reset the source or connection every time you open the recordset.

UNDERSTANDING ADORECORDSET LOCKING
There can be four different values for the LockType parameter used when opening a recordset, as shown in Table 18-4.

IMPLEMENTING ADORECORDSET OPTIONS
Options affect how ADO interprets your source statement. Valid options are listed in Table 18-5.

TABLE 18-4 ADO RECORDSET LOCK TYPES

Lock Type	Description
adLockReadOnly	The current record is read-only. Therefore, the application never locks a database page.
adLockPessimistic	Pessimistic locking is used. Pessimistic locking ensures database integrity at the highest level by locking a database page every time a record is edited or an AddNew function is called to add a new record. While pessimistic locking ensures integrity, it does so at a performance cost because only one application can update an entire *page*, not just one record, at a time.
adLockOptimistic	Optimistic locking is used. Optimistic locking enables a page to become locked only during the actual update command. Optimistic locking keeps locks established for the shortest period of time and therefore is more often used than any other locking mechanism.
adLockBatchOptimistic	Batch optimistic locking is used when performing bulk operations on a database. It is a very unsafe form of record locking but is often used when some application needs to process through many records, especially during a low- or no-database use period. Batch optimistic locking saves much time during large update and insert processes but is very risky to use in a multiuser environment.

TABLE 18-5 ADORECORDSET AND EXECUTE OPTIONS

Option Name	Description
adCmdUnspecified	The type of command is unspecified. The OLE DB provider tries to interpret the source without guidance from the developer.
adCmdUnknown	The type of command is unknown. While an option was passed, it is not an option that the OLE DB provider understands. The OLE DB provider tries to interpret the source without guidance from the developer.
adCmdText	The type of command is an SQL statement.
adCmdTable	The type of command is a table name.
adCmdStoredProc	The type of command is a stored procedure to be executed.

These options are also used in the Execute statement found later in this chapter.

USING ADORECORDSET METHODS

There are many methods that you can call from the Recordset object. These methods are listed in the adoint.h header file that comes with Visual C++. Some methods you may find particularly useful. These methods are listed in Table 18-6.

TABLE **18-6 ADORECORDSET METHODS**

Method	Description
AddNew(VARIANT Fields, VARIANT Values)	Adds a new record to the recordset. The record is not added to the database until an Update is called.
CancelUpdate();	This cancels any pending update or any pending AddNew.
Close()	This function closes the recordset.
Delete(AffectEnum);	This method deletes records from the recordset. Most often, the adAffectCurrent AffectEnum variable is used, although you can also use adAffectGroup and adAffectAll.
get_BOF(*VARIANT_BOOL);	This method determines if you are at the beginning of the recordset and stores the value in a VARIANT_BOOL variable.
get_EditMode(*EditModeEnum);	This method returns the edit mode of the recordset. Valid return values are adEditNone, adEditInProgress, adEditAdd, and adEditDelete. This is most often used with adEditAdd to see if an AddNew method has been called, but the Update method that terminates the AddNew method has not yet been called.
get_EOF(*VARIANT_BOOL);	This method determines if you are at the end of the recordset and stores the value in a VARIANT_BOOL variable.
get_Fields(*ADOFields)	This method returns the fields associated with a recordset and stores the value in an ADOFields variable.

Method	Description
Move(int position);	This method moves the recordset pointer to a specific record.
MoveFirst();	This method moves the recordset pointer to first record.
MoveLast();	This method moves the recordset pointer to last record.
MoveNext();	This method moves the recordset pointer to next record.
MovePrevious();	This method moves the recordset pointer to previous record.
Open(VARIANT, VARIANT, CursorTypeEnum, LockTypeEnum,LONG Options)	This method opens the recordset.
Update(VARIANT Fields, VARIANT Values);	This method updates the recordset.

Examples of all these methods are shown throughout this chapter, with the exception of the Move method, which is self-explanatory.

Understanding ADO Fields

After you retrieve the recordset, you need to retrieve and set the values within the recordset. This is done through a three-step process:

1. Retrieve the ADOFields container from the ADO recordset:

```
CComPtr<ADOFields> pFields;    //Fields Container
HRESULT hr = m_pSet->get_Fields(&pFields);
```

2. Get each field contained in the ADOFields container and store it in an ADOField variable:

```
CComPtr<ADOField> pField;
pFields->get_Item(CComVariant(0), &pField);
```

3. Now you are ready to view and manipulate information inside the field. You can retrieve the value in each ADO field and store it in a VARIANT or CComVariant:

```
CComVariant varValue;
hr = pField->get_Value(&varValue);
```

Or, conversely, put a new value in each ADO field:

```
CComVariant varValue;
hr = pField->put_Value(varValue);
```

Using these techniques, you can retrieve information from fields and update information inside fields. Table 18-7 shows other methods you may need to use, especially when you're not sure about which field you are retrieving.

TABLE **18-7 FIELD METHODS AND PROPERTIES**

Field Method	Return Value
AppendChunk(VARIANT)	Gets a BLOB from the field
GetChunk(*VARIANT)	Retrieves a BLOB from the field
get_Name(*BSTR)	A string containing the name of the field
get_DefinedSize(*long)	A long integer containing the size of the field
get_Type(*DataTypeEnum)	An enum that defines the field's data type
get_Attributes(long *FieldAttributeEnum)	A long integer that describes all the field's attributes

 TIP You can consult the ADO documentation for the complete list of properties and methods. The MSDN topic titled "ADO Object Model" is particularly useful. It contains a clickable graph of the entire object model.

USING FIELD DATA TYPES

As shown in Table 18-7, the ADOField.get_Type method returns the data type of a field:

```
CComPtr<ADOFields> pFields;    //Fields Container
CComPtr<ADOField> pField;    //Individual Field
DataTypeEnum dte;

m_pSet->get_Fields(&pFields);
//Get the first field
```

```
pFields->get_Item(CComVariant(0), &pField);
pField->get_Type(&dte);
```

The `DataTypeEnum` variable is an enum that contains the data type. It can take one of the values listed in Table 18-8.

TABLE 18-8 FIELD DATA TYPES

DataTypeEnum Value	Description
adBigInt	Big integer fields contain an 8-byte signed integer. Big integer fields can be placed inside long variables.
adBinary	Binary fields can be placed in byte arrays. Don't confuse with adChar, which is a string.
adBoolean	Boolean fields can be placed in a Boolean variable.
adBSTR	Big string fields can be placed in BSTR fields.
adChar	Character fields can be placed in character arrays or strings.
adCurrency	Several databases, such as Access, support a currency data type. Currency fields can be placed inside double variables.
adDate	A date field is a timestamp that is stored as a double. The whole part is the number of days since December 30, 1899, and the fractional part is the fraction of a day.
adDBDate	An adDBDATE value is a date field whose value is stored in a YYYYMMDD format.
adDBTime	An adDBTIME value is a time field whose value is stored in a HHMMSS format.
adDBTimeStamp	An adDBTIMESTAMP value is a timestamp field whose value is stored in a YYYYMMDDHHMMSSFFFFFF format.
adDecimal	Decimal fields can be stored inside double variables.
adDouble	Double fields can be stored inside double variables.
adEmpty	Empty fields contain null values.
adError	Error fields are used to store database errors. Most databases don't have these, and you probably don't need to trap for these field types.

Continued

TABLE **18-8** FIELD DATA TYPES *(Continued)*

DataTypeEnum Value	Description
adGUID	A GUID field contains OLE information. Only Microsoft databases contain these fields, and you probably don't need to worry about them inside your application.
adIDispatch	An IDISPATCH interface is used for an OLE IDispatch COM interface and probably isn't used.
adInteger	An INTEGER field is a 4-byte signed integer and can be placed inside an INT field.
adIUnknown	An adIUnknown interface is used to indicate an OLE unspecified interface and probably isn't used often.
adLongVarBinary	Long VarBinary fields can be placed in byte arrays.
adLongVarChar	Long Varchar fields can be placed in character arrays.
adLongVarWChar	Long VarWChar fields can be placed in WCHAR character arrays.
adNumeric	Numeric fields can be stored inside double variables.
adSingle	Single fields can be stored inside float variables.
adSmallInt	A small integer is a 2-byte signed integer. It can be placed in a short integer.
adTinyInt	A tiny integer is a 1-byte signed integer. It can be placed in a byte variable or character variable.
adUnsignedBigInt	An unsigned big integer can be stored inside an unsigned long variable.
adUnsignedInt	An unsigned integer can be stored inside an unsigned int variable.
adUnsignedSmallInt	An unsigned small integer can be stored inside an unsigned short variable.
adUnsignedTinyInt	An unsigned tiny int is a 1-byte unsigned integer. It can be placed in an unsigned character variable.
adUserDefined	Some databases enable the user to define unique field data types. There is no way to trap for these inside a program unless you know exactly how to handle each user-defined data type.
adVarBinary	VarBinary fields can be placed in byte arrays.

DataTypeEnum Value	Description
adVarChar	VarChar fields can be placed in character arrays.
adVariant	Microsoft databases support variants. A variant is a Microsoft data type construct that enables any data type to be placed inside it. Variant types can be placed inside a VARIANT object.
adVarWChar	VarWChar fields can be placed in WCHAR character arrays.
adWChar	WChar fields can be placed in WCHAR character arrays.

USING FIELD ATTRIBUTES

Field attributes are probably the most nonintuitive part of ADO. Although a long integer is returned, that long integer is a logically ANDed combination of the attributes in the FieldAttributeEnum enum. Table 18-9 shows the ADO field attributes.

TABLE **18-9** ADO FIELD ATTRIBUTES

FieldAttributeEnum Field Attribute	Description
adFldCacheDeferred	Indicates that the provider caches field values; subsequent reads are done from the cache.
adFldFixed	Indicates that the field contains fixed-length data.
adFldIsNullable	Indicates that the field accepts null values.
adFldLong	Indicates that the field is a long binary field. Also indicates that you can use the AppendChunk and GetChunk methods.
adFldMayBeNull	Indicates that you can read null values from the field.
adFldMayDefer	Indicates that the field is deferred — that is, the field values are not retrieved from the data source with the whole record, but only when you explicitly access them.
adFldRowID	Indicates that the field contains a persistent row identifier that cannot be written to and has no meaningful value except to identify the row (such as a record number, unique identifier, and so forth).

Continued

TABLE **18-9** ADO FIELD ATTRIBUTES *(Continued)*

FieldAttributeEnum Field Attribute	Description
adFldRowVersion	Indicates that the field contains some kind of timestamp or date stamp used to track updates.
adFldUnknown Updatable	Indicates that the provider cannot determine if you can write to the field.
adFldUpdatable	Indicates that you can write to the field. This attribute is handy for testing autoincrement fields.

The integer returned by the get_Attributes method is the sum of all the attributes listed in Table 18-9. Each sum represents a unique combination of attributes. The best way to test for an attribute is to retrieve the attribute with the get_Attributes method and then logically bitwise AND that field with the attribute you want to test. A zero value of the bitwise AND operation indicates that the attribute is not present on the field. For instance, the following code tests if a field is updatable:

```
/*
Use UPDATEABLE bitwise anded with attributes to determine if you can
update a column, or if you cannot. (for example, an autoincrement
field cannot be updated.)
*/
CComPtr<ADOFields> pFields = NULL; //Fields Container
CComPtr<ADOField> pField = NULL;          //Individual Field

m_pSet->get_Fields(&pFields);
//Get the first field
pFields->get_Item(CComVariant(0), &pField);
long FieldAttributes;
pField->get_Attributes(&FieldAttributes);
long m_lIsUpdatable = adFldUpdatable & FieldAttributes;
if (m_lIsUpdatable == 0) {
    // This field is not updatable.
    //It's probably autoincrement.
```

Using SQL Commands in ADO

Along with recordsets, ADO enables you to run SQL directly against a connection. This is handy if you just need a simple SQL statement to be run and don't need to worry about forming a recordset. The format for the `ADOConnection::Execute` statement used to run SQL is as follows:

```
ADOConnection.Execute( BSTR CommandText,
                       VARIANT *RecordsAffected,
                       long Options,
                       ADORecordset *ppiRset)
```

In the preceding code:

◆ The CommandText parameter is a BSTR containing an SQL statement.

◆ The RecordsAffected parameter is an optional VARIANT pointer that returns the number of rows affected by the statement.

◆ The Options parameter contains any additional options you wish while running your command.

◆ The ppiRset parameter is an optional ADORecordset in case rows were returned from your command.

The following SQL function can be written, which takes advantage of the ADOConnection.Execute method:

```
void CADODialog::ExecuteSQL(char *SQL) {
    CComBSTR bstrSQL = SQL;
    //Execute an SQL string
    HRESULT hr = m_ADOConn->Execute(
        bstrSQL,               //SQL Source statement
        NULL,                  //VARIANT records Affected
        adOptionUnspecified,   //Options—Usually leave unspecified
        NULL);                 //ADORecordset results;
    if (FAILED(hr)) {
        //Error handling goes here
    }
}
```

To call this function, you can simply pass it an SQL string:

```
ExecuteSQL( "UPDATE Student \
            SET FirstName = 'Charles' \
            WHERE StudentID = 1");
```

Although I don't reference it in the program, I kept the ExecuteSQL function in the ADOTableReader project on the CD-ROM accompanying this book so you can see how it works or make calls to it after you establish a database connection.

Building an ADO Application

Using what you've learned so far in this chapter, you are ready to build an ADO application that queries, updates, and deletes records. This section is divided into two subsections:

- ◆ Graphical shell building where a dialog box and menu structure are formed using the Visual C++ tools that come with Visual Studio

- ◆ Coding takes the shell that was developed in the first section and adds C++ code so that the new program uses ADO to access database information and display it on the window

Building the Program Shell with Visual C++ ATL Tools

This section deals with using the ATL COM AppWizard and the Insert Resource window to build a working functional program shell where ADO can be added. The following simple steps can be used to create a program shell:

1. Create a new ATL project. Use the ATL COM AppWizard, as shown in Figure 18-3. This project is called ADOTableReader. Make it an executable so that you can run it when you're finished building it.

2. When you return to Visual Studio, you need to create a dialog box. Click New ATL Object, as shown in Figure 18-4, to invoke the ATL Object Wizard.

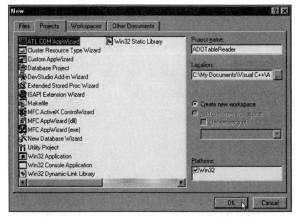

Figure 18-3: You can use ATL projects to effectively build ADO applications.

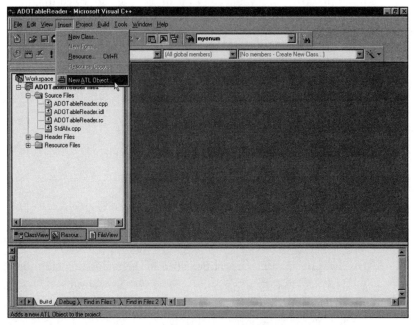

Figure 18-4: A dialog can be used by invoking the ATL Object Wizard.

3. In the ATL Object Wizard, click the Miscellaneous category, and choose the Dialog object, as shown in Figure 18-5.

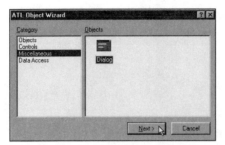

Figure 18-5: ATL dialog boxes can be found in the Miscellaneous category.

4. After you click Next, the ATL Object Wizard Properties window opens. Enter the ADO short name, and the other fields are filled in automatically. For this project, a short name of ADODialog was given, as shown in Figure 18-6.

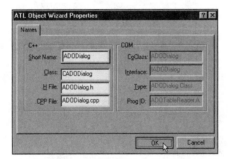

Figure 18-6: You must enter filenames and class names for your dialog box.

5. For this project, a menu will be added to the dialog box, so right-click the top of the Resources tree view in your Project window, and choose Insert, as shown in Figure 18-7.

6. When the Insert Resource window opens (Figure 18-8), click Menu, and click the New button to add a new menu to your resource.

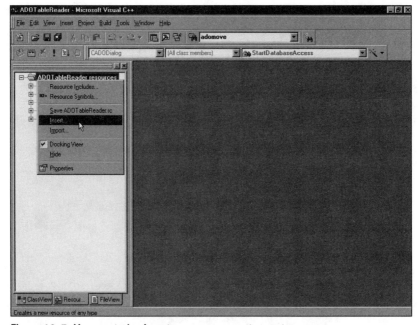

Figure 18-7: You must also insert a new resource to create a menu.

Figure 18-8: Menus can be added using the Insert Resource window.

7. In your menu, you need to add enough items to enable proper window functioning. Assuming that we are saving as changes are made, you still need buttons for moving, inserting, and deleting records. Figure 18-9 shows the menu that is to be used with the finished product.

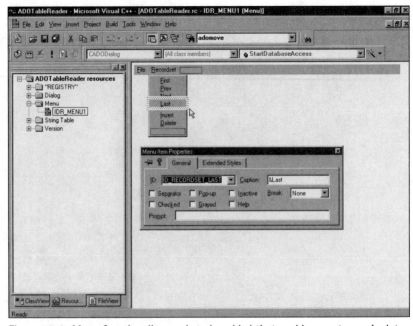

Figure 18-9: Menu functionality needs to be added that enables you to manipulate your recordset.

Table 18-10 lists all the menu options you'll need for this project. Note that there isn't an update or a save option because they are handled automatically.

TABLE **18-10** MENU OPTIONS FOR THE ADOTABLEREADER PROJECT

Menu Option	ID	Description
File → Exit	IDCANCEL	Closes the system down.
Recordset → First	ID_RECORDSET_FIRST	Positions the recordset pointer to the first record in a recordset.
Recordset → Prev	ID_RECORDSET_PREV	Positions the recordset pointer to the previous record in a recordset.
Recordset → Next	ID_RECORDSET_NEXT	Positions the recordset pointer to the next record in a recordset.

Menu Option	ID	Description
Recordset → Last	ID_RECORDSET_LAST	Positions the recordset pointer to the last record in a recordset.
Recordset → Insert	ID_RECORDSET_INSERT	Inserts a new record at the end of the recordset and into the database.
Recordset → Delete	ID_RECORDSET_DELETE	Deletes the current record from the recordset and from the database.

8. On your dialog box, you need buttons for record navigation and manipulation that mimic the menu options. You also need text fields to accept information. Finally, you need an empty static text line at the bottom of your dialog box to display messages. Table 18-11 lists the controls needed for your dialog box in the ADOTableReader project.

TABLE 18-11 DIALOG BOX CONTROLS FOR THE ADOTABLEREADER PROJECT

Control	Control ID	Description
First Button	ID_RECORDSET_FIRST	Positions the recordset pointer to the first record in a recordset. Because this button shares an ID with the menu item, both the menu item and the button are handled identically by the Visual C++ program.
Prev Button	ID_RECORDSET_PREV	Positions the recordset pointer to the previous record in a recordset. Because this button shares an ID with the menu item, both the menu item and the button are handled identically by the Visual C++ program.
Next Button	ID_RECORDSET_NEXT	Positions the recordset pointer to the next record in a recordset. Because this button shares an ID with the menu item, both the menu item and the button are handled identically by the Visual C++ program.

Continued

TABLE 18-11 DIALOG BOX CONTROLS FOR THE ADOTABLEREADER PROJECT
           (Continued)

Control	Control ID	Description
Last Button	ID_RECORDSET_LAST	Positions the recordset pointer to the last record in a recordset. Because this button shares an ID with the menu item, both the menu item and the button are handled identically by the Visual C++ program.
Insert Button	ID_RECORDSET_INSERT	Inserts a new record at the end of the recordset and into the database. Because this button shares an ID with the menu item, both the menu item and the button are handled identically by the Visual C++ program.
Delete Button	ID_RECORDSET_DELETE	Deletes the current record from the recordset and from the database. Because this button shares an ID with the menu item, both the menu item and the button are handled identically by the Visual C++ program.
Code Text Box	IDC_CODE	Used to contain the DepartmentCode field from the database. Users can update this field by typing a new value into this textbox.
Name Text Box	IDC_NAME	Used to contain the DepartmentName field from the database. Users can update this field by typing a new value into this textbox.
Status Text	IDC_STATUS	This is an empty "invisible" text field that appears at the bottom of your dialog box. Status messages (for example, "Last Record Reached" are displayed here.)

When you've finished designing your dialog box, you need to tie the menu to the dialog box. The layout for this dialog box and its properties is shown in Figure 18-10.

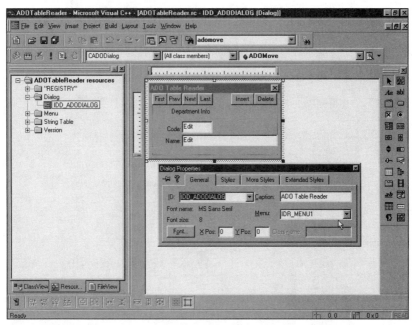

Figure 18-10: The dialog box needs to have the menu associated with it.

9. Add an Include to your main C++ program (ADOTableReader.cpp) that includes functionality for your new dialog box:

```
#include "stdafx.h"
#include "resource.h"
#include <initguid.h>
#include "ADOTableReader.h"

#include "ADOTableReader_i.c"
//Added by Chuck Wood for dialog support
#include "ADODialog.h"
```

10. In the same main C++ program (ADOTableReader.cpp), in the _tWinMain function, add a constructor for your dialog box so that control of the program is passed to the dialog box. Because you're not adding any other features outside of the dialog box, you can also delete or comment out waiting for a message:

```
extern "C" int WINAPI _tWinMain(HINSTANCE hInstance,
```

```
    HINSTANCE /*hPrevInstance*/, LPTSTR lpCmdLine, int
/*nShowCmd*/)
{
    lpCmdLine = GetCommandLine(); //this line necessary for
_ATL_MIN_CRT

#if _WIN32_WINNT >= 0x0400 & defined(_ATL_FREE_THREADED)
    HRESULT hRes = CoInitializeEx(NULL,
COINIT_MULTITHREADED);
#else
    HRESULT hRes = CoInitialize(NULL);
#endif
    _ASSERTE(SUCCEEDED(hRes));
    _Module.Init(ObjectMap, hInstance,
&LIBID_ADOTABLEREADERLib);
    _Module.dwThreadID = GetCurrentThreadId();
    TCHAR szTokens[] = _T("-/");

    int nRet = 0;
    BOOL bRun = TRUE;
    LPCTSTR lpszToken = FindOneOf(lpCmdLine, szTokens);
    while (lpszToken != NULL)
    {
        if (lstrcmpi(lpszToken, _T("UnregServer"))==0)
        {

_Module.UpdateRegistryFromResource(IDR_ADOTableReader,
FALSE);
            nRet = _Module.UnregisterServer(TRUE);
            bRun = FALSE;
            break;
        }
        if (lstrcmpi(lpszToken, _T("RegServer"))==0)
        {

_Module.UpdateRegistryFromResource(IDR_ADOTableReader, TRUE);
            nRet = _Module.RegisterServer(TRUE);
            bRun = FALSE;
            break;
        }
        lpszToken = FindOneOf(lpszToken, szTokens);
    }

    if (bRun)
```

```
    {
        _Module.StartMonitor();
#if _WIN32_WINNT >= 0x0400 & defined(_ATL_FREE_THREADED)
        hRes =
_Module.RegisterClassObjects(CLSCTX_LOCAL_SERVER,
            REGCLS_MULTIPLEUSE | REGCLS_SUSPENDED);
        _ASSERTE(SUCCEEDED(hRes));
        hRes = CoResumeClassObjects();
#else
        hRes =
_Module.RegisterClassObjects(CLSCTX_LOCAL_SERVER,
            REGCLS_MULTIPLEUSE);
#endif
        _ASSERTE(SUCCEEDED(hRes));
        //Added by Chuck Wood to start the dialog box
        CADODialog adod;
//The message waiting is not needed anymore
//          MSG msg;
//          while (GetMessage(&msg, 0, 0, 0))
//              DispatchMessage(&msg);
        _Module.RevokeClassObjects();
        Sleep(dwPause); //wait for any threads to finish
    }

    _Module.Term();
    CoUninitialize();
    return nRet;
}
```

11. Now you can start coding your dialog box. In the dialog box header
    (ADODialog.h), you need to add a DoModal statement to the constructor:

```
CADODialog()
{
    DoModal();              //Open this dialog box
}
```

Your program can now run with the dialog box opening. Try compiling it
and running it right now, and correct any errors you may find.

Now the easy part is over. Notice that no ADO functionality has yet been added
to the system. This is because Visual C++ graphical tools don't handle ADO, and
you must code your ADO calls yourself. The next section describes the code you
need to add to complete your ADO application.

VARIANT Conversion Functions

Before you start using ADO, you should be used to dealing with VARIANT structures. ADO uses the VARIANT structure extensively. The VARIANT structure is important because it enables a single parameter to be of any type. However, VARIANT structures are extremely hard to deal with. It always helps me to add functionality that automatically converts a value to a VARIANT for processing. String, integer, and IDispatch conversion are usually enough, although you can code any VARIANT conversion functions to suit your needs. In addition, you need a VARIANT function that returns a "null" VARIANT so the ADO functions know that you decided not to pass a VARIANT value.

Microsoft has provided a CComVariant structure that can handle a lot of your VARIANT conversion needs. You can use CComVariant for any parameter that requires a VARIANT, and it's easier to use. For instance, CComVariant(2) would assign a 2 to a CComVariant, while CComVariant("DepartmentCode") would assign a "DepartmentCode" string to the CComVariant. By using CComVariant, you can make VARIANT access much simpler than by using the raw VARIANT data type.

Making an ADO Application

This section contains step-by-step instructions for adding the ADO Visual C++ code needed to tie a database to the dialog box that was created in the last section.

The following steps can be used to add the code and finish the ADO program:

1. In your dialog box header file (ADODialog.h), you need to include ADO support. You need the <adoid.h> and the <adoint.h> header files included with Visual C++. For error processing, why not include the header file created in Chapter 10 ("..\OLEDBErrorChecking\OLEDBError Checking.h")?

```
// ADODialog.h : Declaration of the CADODialog
#ifndef __ADODIALOG_H_
#define __ADODIALOG_H_
#include "resource.h"        // main symbols
#include <atlhost.h>
//The next two were added by Chuck Wood for ADO Support
#include <adoid.h>  // ADO header file
#include <adoint.h> // ADO header file
//Added by Chuck Wood for OLE DB Error support
#include "..\OLEDBErrorChecking\OLEDBErrorChecking.h"
```

2. Add fields for the connection variable, the recordset, and the database fields to the dialog header (ADODialog.h). Also include one variant that can be set to an empty value for ADO calls that use a default. Finally, include variables for the database name, table name, user ID, and password:

```
class CADODialog :
    public CAxDialogImpl<CADODialog>
{
private :
    //Database Fields
    char m_DepartmentCode[5];
    char m_DepartmentName[51];
    //ADO Connection and Recordset variables
    //ADO Connection and Recordset variables
    CComPtr<ADOConnection> m_ADOConn;
    CComPtr<ADORecordset> m_pSet;
    //Variant for null VARIANT parameters
    VARIANT m_varNoVariant;
    //Name of database fields
    char *m_strODBCDatabase; //Database Name
    char *m_strUserID;       //User ID
    char *m_strPassword;     //Password
    char *m_strDBTable;      //Table for data source
```

3. Next, you need to enter function prototypes in the dialog header (ADODialog.h) for the following functionality:

   - You need a function to display status messages on the dialog box:

     ```
     //Show a status message on the dialog box
     void DisplayStatus(char *strMessage);
     //Take data to and from the dialog box
     ```

   - You need an `UpdateData` function (equivalent to the MFC `UpdateData` function) to put data to and from the dialog box. You also need similar functionality to take data to and from the database fields and to save changes made to the database:

     ```
     void UpdateData(BOOL bSaveChangesToSet = TRUE);
     //Take data from database fields
     HRESULT GetFields();
     //Take data to database fields
     HRESULT SetFields();
     HRESULT SaveChanges();              //Save Changes
     ```

■ You need functions for opening and closing the database connection and the recordset:

```
HRESULT OpenConnection(); //Connect
HRESULT OpenRecordset();  //Form Recordset
void CloseConnection();   //End Connection
void CloseRecordset();    //End Recordset
```

■ You need a function for moving around in the recordset. You also need an Enum that contains the valid values for the move function:

```
//enum for ADOMove function
enum ADOMoveEnum {FIRST, PREV, NEXT, LAST, SAME};
//Move recordset pointer around
void ADOMove(ADOMoveEnum p, BOOL SaveFirst = TRUE);
```

4. Now you need to start coding the functions that you defined in your dialog header file (ADODialog.h). First, you must initialize any class variables in your ADODialog constructor:

```
CADODialog()
{
    //Initialize a variant for inserting and updating
    m_varNoVariant.vt = VT_ERROR;
    m_varNoVariant.scode = DISP_E_PARAMNOTFOUND;
    //Set up your ADO database access
    m_strODBCDatabase = strdup("Classes");
    m_strUserID = strdup("");
    m_strPassword = strdup("");
    m_strDBTable = strdup("Department");
    m_ADOConn = NULL;     //Initialize connection
    m_pSet = NULL;        //Initialize recordset
    DoModal();            //Open this dialog box
}
```

5. Next, you must write a function to open your connection to your database in your dialog source file (ADODialog.cpp). This function involves assigning character strings to BSTR strings, allocating the ADOConnection by using the CoCreateInstance function, and then using the allocated connection, along with the database name, user ID, and password, to establish a link to the database:

```
HRESULT CADODialog::OpenConnection() {
    CComBSTR bstrODBCDatabase = m_strODBCDatabase;
    CComBSTR bstrUserId = m_strUserID;
    CComBSTR bstrPassword = m_strPassword;
```

```
//Create new connection
CoCreateInstance(CLSID_CADOConnection, NULL,
    CLSCTX_INPROC_SERVER, IID_IADOConnection,
    (LPVOID *)&m_ADOConn);
//Use the connection to open a link to database
HRESULT hr = m_ADOConn->Open(
    bstrODBCDatabase,
    bstrUserId,
    bstrPassword,
    adOpenUnspecified);
if (FAILED(hr)) {
    COLEDBErrorChecking::DisplaySingleError(hr,
        "OpenConnection");
    m_ADOConn = NULL;
}
return hr;
}
```

6. I always make it a habit to immediately write the code to close a connection once opening it. If the connection succeeded, the following function closes the connection:

```
void CADODialog::CloseConnection() {
    if (m_ADOConn != NULL) {
        //Close the connection
        m_ADOConn->Close();
        m_ADOConn = NULL;
    }
}
```

7. Next, you need a function to open your recordset. This function builds a BSTR string containing an SQL statement derived from the m_strDBTable class variable, allocates the ADORecordset by using the CoCreate Instance function, and then opens the recordset with the appropriate options. If everything works, this function positions the recordset on the first record by making a call to the ADOMove function discussed later in this section:

```
HRESULT CADODialog::OpenRecordset() {
//Form an SQL statement from the table
CComBSTR bstrSQL = "SELECT * FROM ";
bstrSQL += m_strDBTable;
//Allocate a new ADORecordset variable
CoCreateInstance(CLSID_CADORecordset, NULL,
        CLSCTX_INPROC_SERVER, IID_IADORecordset,
        (LPVOID *)&m_pSet);
```

```
//Open the newly formed recordset with the SQL
//and the connection
HRESULT hr = m_pSet->Open(
        CComVariant(bstrSQL),
        CComVariant(m_ADOConn),
        adOpenKeyset, adLockOptimistic, adCmdText);
if (FAILED(hr)) {
        COLEDBErrorChecking::DisplaySingleError(hr,
                "OpenRecordset");
        m_pSet = NULL;
}
else {
        //Everything worked.  Move to the first record.
        ADOMove(FIRST, FALSE);
}
return hr;
}
```

8. Next, you need a function to close the recordset if it was successfully opened and to release all resources:

```
void CADODialog::CloseRecordset() {
    if (m_pSet != NULL ) {
        //Close recordset
        m_pSet->Close();
        m_pSet = NULL;
    }
}
```

9. Now, you need to connect to your database and recordset using the OnInitDialog function already generated by the ATL Object Wizard in your dialog header file (ADODialog.h). Here, add calls to connect to the database and the recordset:

```
LRESULT OnInitDialog(UINT uMsg, WPARAM wParam, LPARAM lParam,
BOOL& bHandled)
{
    DisplayStatus("Opening Connection.  Please Wait.");
    //Open a connection
    if (SUCCEEDED(OpenConnection())) {
        DisplayStatus(
            "Now Opening RecordSet.  Please wait.");
        //Open a Recordset
        if (SUCCEEDED(OpenRecordset())) {
            DisplayStatus("");
        }
```

```
    }
    return 1;   // Let the system set the focus
}
```

10. In your dialog box header file (ADODialog.h), code the destructor to call the close routines written in steps 6 and 8 and to deallocate the strings allocated in step 4:

```
~CADODialog()
{
    CloseRecordset();     //Close the crecord set
    CloseConnection();    //Close a connection
    delete m_strODBCDatabase;    //Clean up strings
    delete m_strUserID;
    delete m_strPassword;
    delete m_strDBTable;
}
```

11. Code a display status function in your dialog source file (ADODialog.cpp) to display messages in the IDC_STATUS text field on your dialog box. This helps communicate with your user without the need for a pop-up message box:

```
void CADODialog::DisplayStatus(char *strMessage)
{
    //Send a message to the status line in the dialog box
    SetDlgItemText(IDC_STATUS, strMessage);
}
```

12. Next, you must write a function to get the fields from the ADO recordset. This involves three steps:

    a. Getting the ADO fields container from the ADO recordset:

    ```
    HRESULT hr = m_pSet->get_Fields(&pFields);
    ```

    b. Getting each ADO field from the ADO fields container:

    ```
    hr = pFields->get_Item(CComVariant(0), &pField);
    ```

    c. Getting the value of the ADO field and storing it in a VARIANT:

    ```
    CComVariant varValue;
    hr = pField->get_Value(&varValue);
    ```

    These steps can be seen in the GetFields function that follows (found in ADODialog.h). Error checking and BSTR processing to copy the value of the field into the class variables are added:

```
HRESULT CADODialog::GetFields() {
    CComPtr<ADOFields> pFields = NULL;    //Fields Container
```

```
        CComPtr<ADOField> pDeptCode = NULL;      //Individual Field
        CComPtr<ADOField> pDeptName = NULL;      //Individual Field
        CComVariant varValue; // Variant set to zero
    //Get all the fields in the Fields container
        HRESULT hr = m_pSet->get_Fields(&pFields);
        if (FAILED(hr)) return hr;
    //Get the DepartmentCode Field (Field 0)
        hr = pFields->get_Item(CComVariant(0), &pDeptCode);
        if (FAILED(hr)) return hr;
    //Get the value of the DepartmentCode field
        hr = pDeptCode->get_Value(&varValue);
        if (FAILED(hr)) return hr;
    //Assign Variant to Department Code
        sprintf(m_DepartmentCode, "%S", varValue.bstrVal);
    //Get the DepartmentName Field (Field 1)
        hr = pFields->get_Item(CComVariant(1), &pDeptName);
        if (FAILED(hr)) return hr;
    //Get the value of the DepartmentName field
        hr = pDeptName->get_Value(&varValue);
        if (FAILED(hr)) return hr;
    //Assign Variant to Department Name
        sprintf(m_DepartmentName, "%S", varValue.bstrVal);
        return hr;
    }
```

13. You need to write a function to take the data from the class variables and display it in the dialog box fields. This can be done using the UpdateData function.

```
void CADODialog::UpdateData(BOOL bSaveChangesToSet) {
    HRESULT hr;
    //Write to Screen
    //Take data from database fields
    hr = GetFields();
    if (FAILED(hr)) {
        COLEDBErrorChecking::DisplaySingleError(hr,
            "OnMove GetFields");
        DisplayStatus("No records found.");
    }
    SetDlgItemText(IDC_CODE, m_DepartmentCode);
    SetDlgItemText(IDC_NAME, m_DepartmentName);
}
```

This `UpdateData` function so far displays only the information to the dialog box. In the next section, more code is added to the UpdateData function to take data to and from the dialog box.

14. Now you need to write the `ADOMove` function to enable the user to scroll around the ADO recordset. The `ADOMove` function is analogous to the `OnMove` function found in MFC database programs:

```
void CADODialog::ADOMove(ADOMoveEnum position, BOOL
SaveFirst) {
    //This function is called by other move functions
    HRESULT hr;
    VARIANT_BOOL vb;
    DisplayStatus("");
    switch (position) {
        case (FIRST) :     //first record
            hr = m_pSet->MoveFirst();
            break;
        case (NEXT) :     //next record
            hr = m_pSet->MoveNext();
            m_pSet->get_EOF(&vb);
            if (vb) {
                //EOF.  No more records
                DisplayStatus("Last record reached.");
                hr = m_pSet->MoveLast();
            }
            break;
        case (LAST) :     //last record
            hr = m_pSet->MoveLast();
            break;
        case (PREV) :     //previous record
            hr = m_pSet->MovePrevious();
            m_pSet->get_BOF(&vb);
            if (vb) {
                //BOF.  No previous records
                DisplayStatus("First record reached.");
                hr = m_pSet->MoveFirst();
            }
            break;
    }
    if (FAILED(hr)) {
        COLEDBErrorChecking::DisplaySingleError(hr,
```

```
                         "OnMove Move");
                   DisplayStatus("No records found.");
                   return;
               }
               UpdateData(FALSE);     //Update Screen
           }
```

15. Now you must capture the events from the dialog box. Because inserts and deletes are done in the next section, you need to worry only about the recordset navigation commands. Code the message map in the dialog header (ADODialog.h) to handle the additional functionality:

```
BEGIN_MSG_MAP(CADODialog)
    MESSAGE_HANDLER(WM_INITDIALOG, OnInitDialog)
    COMMAND_ID_HANDLER(IDCANCEL, OnCancel)
    COMMAND_ID_HANDLER(ID_RECORDSET_FIRST, OnMoveFirst)
    COMMAND_ID_HANDLER(ID_RECORDSET_LAST, OnMoveLast)
    COMMAND_ID_HANDLER(ID_RECORDSET_PREV, OnMovePrev)
    COMMAND_ID_HANDLER(ID_RECORDSET_NEXT, OnMoveNext)
END_MSG_MAP()
```

16. Finally, you must write your OnMove functions (in ADODialog.h) to call the `ADOMove` function with the appropriate parameter whenever their menu event is triggered:

```
LRESULT OnMoveFirst(WORD wNotifyCode, WORD wID, HWND hWndCtl,
BOOL& bHandled)
{
    ADOMove(FIRST);     //Move to first record
    return 0;
}
LRESULT OnMoveNext(WORD wNotifyCode, WORD wID, HWND hWndCtl,
BOOL& bHandled)
{
    ADOMove(NEXT);     //Move to next record
    return 0;
}
LRESULT OnMovePrev(WORD wNotifyCode, WORD wID, HWND hWndCtl,
BOOL& bHandled)
{
    ADOMove(PREV);     //Move to previous record
    return 0;
}
LRESULT OnMoveLast(WORD wNotifyCode, WORD wID, HWND hWndCtl,
BOOL& bHandled)
{
```

```
ADOMove(LAST);      //Move to last record
return 0;
}
```

Now you have a working program that can scroll through your ADO recordset. In the next section, update, insert, and delete capability are added to make this program fully functional.

Updating Your Database with ADO Code

In the last section, you wrote an ADO program that queried the database and displayed rows from a database table. In this section, code is added that enables you to update, delete, and insert new rows in your database using the ADO recordset.

ADDING CODE TO UPDATE RECORDS

As with MFC programs, this program is designed to update automatically. To perform this goal, you need to accomplish four tasks:

◆ You need to be able to set the fields in the database with any new values.

◆ You need to be able to pull data from the dialog box and move it to the ADO fields.

◆ You need to issue an update command to update the database with the new values.

◆ You need to check before each move to make sure that any updates are recorded.

These four tasks can be accomplished with the following steps:

1. Write a SetFields function that updates the ADO recordset fields. This involves three steps:

   a. Getting the ADO fields container from the ADO recordset:

   ```
   HRESULT hr = m_pSet->get_Fields(&pFields);
   ```

   b. Get each field contained in the fields container:

   ```
   hr = pFields->get_Item(CComVariant(0), &pField);
   ```

   c. Putting a new value in each ADO field:

   ```
   hr = pField->put_Value(CComVariant(m_DepartmentCode));
   ```

   These three steps can be seen in the SetFields function that follows (found in ADODialog.cpp). Error checking is added:

```
HRESULT CADODialog::SetFields() {
```

```
                CComPtr<ADOFields> pFields = NULL;
                CComPtr<ADOField> pDeptCode = NULL;     //Individual Field
                CComPtr<ADOField> pDeptName = NULL;     //Individual Field

        //Get all the fields
            HRESULT hr = m_pSet->get_Fields(&pFields);
            if (FAILED(hr)) return hr;
        //Get the DepartmentCode Field (Field 0)
            hr = pFields->get_Item(CComVariant(0), &pDeptCode);
            if (FAILED(hr)) return hr;
        //Set the value of the DepartmentCode field
            hr = pDeptCode ->
        put_Value(CComVariant(m_DepartmentCode));
            if (FAILED(hr)) return hr;

        //Get the DepartmentName Field (Field 1)
            hr = pFields->get_Item(CComVariant(1), &pDeptName);
            if (FAILED(hr)) return hr;
        //Set the value of the DepartmentName field
            return pDeptName ->
        put_Value(CComVariant(m_DepartmentName));
        }
```

2. Alter the UpdateData function to read values from the dialog box as well as write values to the dialog box:

```
void CADODialog::UpdateData(BOOL bSaveChangesToSet) {
    HRESULT hr;

    if (bSaveChangesToSet) {
        //Read From Screen
        GetDlgItemText(IDC_CODE, m_DepartmentCode, 5);
        GetDlgItemText(IDC_NAME, m_DepartmentName, 51);
        //Place data in database fields
        hr = SetFields();
        if (FAILED(hr)) {
            COLEDBErrorChecking::DisplaySingleError(hr,
                "SaveDepartment SetFields");
        }
    }
    else {
        //Write to Screen
        //Take data from database fields
        hr = GetFields();
        if (FAILED(hr)) {
```

```
        COLEDBErrorChecking::DisplaySingleError(hr,
            "OnMove GetFields");
        DisplayStatus("No records found.");
    }
    SetDlgItemText(IDC_CODE, m_DepartmentCode);
    SetDlgItemText(IDC_NAME, m_DepartmentName);
}
```

3. Write a function to update the database from any changes made to the
   ADO fields. The SaveChanges function that follows uses the Update
   function to ensure that any changes made are written to the database:

```
HRESULT CADODialog::SaveChanges() {
    UpdateData(TRUE);    //Read from screen
    //Update database from fields
    HRESULT hr = m_pSet->Update(m_varNoVariant,
            m_varNoVariant);
    if (FAILED(hr)) {
        COLEDBErrorChecking::DisplaySingleError(hr,
            "SaveDepartment Update");
    }
    return hr;
}
```

4. Next, change the OnCancel function to try to save any changes made
   before exiting the program. That way, changes made to the current
   recordset will be recorded:

```
LRESULT OnCancel(WORD wNotifyCode, WORD wID, HWND hWndCtl,
BOOL& bHandled)
{
    SaveChanges();
    EndDialog(wID);    //End Program
    return 0;
}
```

5. Finally, change the ADOMove function to save out every time the user
   moves off the current record:

```
void CADODialog::ADOMove(ADOMoveEnum position, BOOL
SaveFirst) {
    //This function is called by other move functions
    HRESULT hr;
    VARIANT_BOOL vb;
    if (SaveFirst) {
```

```
//Don't save deleted records or on your first time through
      hr = SaveChanges();    //Save changes
      if (FAILED(hr)) {
          DisplayStatus(
"Save failed.  Can't move off this record.");
          return;         //End if save did not work.
      }
   }
   DisplayStatus("");
   switch (position) {
      case (FIRST) :    //first record
          hr = m_pSet->MoveFirst();
          break;
      case (NEXT) :     //next record
          hr = m_pSet->MoveNext();
          m_pSet->get_EOF(&vb);
          if (vb) {
              //EOF.  No more records
              DisplayStatus("Last record reached.");
              hr = m_pSet->MoveLast();
          }
          break;
      case (LAST) :     //last record
          hr = m_pSet->MoveLast();
          break;
      case (PREV) :     //previous record
          hr = m_pSet->MovePrevious();
          m_pSet->get_BOF(&vb);
          if (vb) {
              //BOF.  No previous records
              DisplayStatus("First record reached.");
              hr = m_pSet->MoveFirst();
          }
          break;
   }
   if (FAILED(hr)) {
      COLEDBErrorChecking::DisplaySingleError(hr,
          "OnMove Move");
      DisplayStatus("No records found.");
      return;
   }
   UpdateData(FALSE);    //Update Screen
}
```

The `SaveFirst` parameter passed to the `ADOMove` function is used to determine whether or not to save first. In certain cases, such as when first initializing the ADO recordset or when deleting the current record and moving to the next record, you won't want to save before the move. The `SaveFirst` parameter defaults to `TRUE`.

Now your application can record any updates made by the user. If you wish, you can compile the project right now and try it out.

ADDING CODE TO INSERT RECORDS

Now you need to write code that enables you to insert records when the user clicks the Insert button or the Recordset → Insert menu option. First, change your message map in your dialog header file to capture any insert command from the user:

```
BEGIN_MSG_MAP(CADODialog)
    MESSAGE_HANDLER(WM_INITDIALOG, OnInitDialog)
    COMMAND_ID_HANDLER(IDCANCEL, OnCancel)
    COMMAND_ID_HANDLER(ID_RECORDSET_FIRST, OnMoveFirst)
    COMMAND_ID_HANDLER(ID_RECORDSET_LAST, OnMoveLast)
    COMMAND_ID_HANDLER(ID_RECORDSET_PREV, OnMovePrev)
    COMMAND_ID_HANDLER(ID_RECORDSET_NEXT, OnMoveNext)
    COMMAND_ID_HANDLER(ID_RECORDSET_INSERT, OnInsert)
END_MSG_MAP()
```

Now you must write your `OnInsert` function. The `OnInsert` function must perform three steps:

1. You most save the current record. This can be done with an ADOMove to the same record, which really doesn't move the recordset pointer but takes advantage of the ADOMove functionality to save:

   ```
   ADOMove(SAME);          //Don't move, just do the updating
   ```

2. Place the recordset in AddNew mode. When you invoke AddNew mode, you automatically add a record to the recordset. Because you can use the current fields container to do the add, you can default the VARIANT parameters in the `AddNew` function to "blank" VARIANT structures stored in the `m_varNoVariant` class variable:

   ```
   HRESULT hr = m_pSet->AddNew(m_varNoVariant, m_varNoVariant);
   ```

3. You've not added a blank row on your recordset, but you also need to blank out your fields on your dialog box:

   ```
   SetDlgItemText(IDC_CODE, "");
   SetDlgItemText(IDC_NAME, "");
   ```

This code can be viewed in the `OnInsert` function (found in ADODialog.h) that follows:

```
LRESULT OnInsert(WORD wNotifyCode, WORD wID, HWND hWndCtl, BOOL&
bHandled)
{
    ADOMove(SAME);          //Don't move, just do the updating
    //Place the recordset in addnew mode
    HRESULT hr = m_pSet->AddNew(m_varNoVariant, m_varNoVariant);
    if (FAILED(hr)) {
        COLEDBErrorChecking::DisplaySingleError(hr,
            "Can't set addnew mode");
        DisplayStatus("Cannot add.");
        return 0;
    }
    //Clear Record
    SetDlgItemText(IDC_CODE, "");
    SetDlgItemText(IDC_NAME, "");
    return 0;
}
```

Now your application can insert new records into the database. If you wish, you can compile the project right now and try it out.

ADDING CODE TO DELETE RECORDS

In the final steps for this project, you need to write an OnDelete function that deletes the current record from the rowset. You need to add a command handler to your message map in your dialog header (ADODialog.h) for your OnDelete function just as you did for the OnInsert function:

```
BEGIN_MSG_MAP(CADODialog)
    MESSAGE_HANDLER(WM_INITDIALOG, OnInitDialog)
    COMMAND_ID_HANDLER(IDCANCEL, OnCancel)
    COMMAND_ID_HANDLER(ID_RECORDSET_FIRST, OnMoveFirst)
    COMMAND_ID_HANDLER(ID_RECORDSET_LAST, OnMoveLast)
    COMMAND_ID_HANDLER(ID_RECORDSET_PREV, OnMovePrev)
    COMMAND_ID_HANDLER(ID_RECORDSET_NEXT, OnMoveNext)
    COMMAND_ID_HANDLER(ID_RECORDSET_INSERT, OnInsert)
    COMMAND_ID_HANDLER(ID_RECORDSET_DELETE, OnDelete)
END_MSG_MAP()
```

Now you must write your `OnDelete` Function. The `OnDelete` function must perform three steps:

1. Use a message box to ask if the user really wants to delete. You don't want to go ahead with a delete just because of an accidental mouse click.

2. Check the edit mode status to see if a record is being added. If so, just abort the add using the CancelUpdate function and return:

```
HRESULT hr = m_pSet->get_EditMode(&eme);
if (eme == adEditAdd) {      //In add mode?
    //Just abort the add
    m_pSet->CancelUpdate();
    ADOMove(NEXT);
    DisplayStatus("Add aborted");
    return 0;
}
```

3. If the user really wants the add and is not in the middle of an add, go ahead, and issue the delete to the recordset:

```
hr = m_pSet->Delete(adAffectCurrent);
```

These steps can be viewed in the OnDelete function that follows:

```
LRESULT OnDelete(WORD wNotifyCode, WORD wID, HWND hWndCtl, BOOL&
bHandled)
{
    if (MessageBox(       //Be sure to verify your deletes
            "Are you sure you want to delete?",
            "Delete this record?",
            MB_YESNO)
        != IDYES) {
        DisplayStatus("Delete aborted");
        return 0;
    }
    //Delete record and test
    EditModeEnum eme;      //Edit Mode variable
    //Get Edit Mode to test for currently adding
    HRESULT hr = m_pSet->get_EditMode(&eme);
    if (FAILED(hr)) {
        COLEDBErrorChecking::DisplaySingleError(hr,
            "OnDelete get_EditMode");
        DisplayStatus(
            "Cannot determine edit mode. Delete aborted");
        return 0;
    }
    if (eme == adEditAdd) {      //In add mode?
        //Just abort the add
```

```
      m_pSet->CancelUpdate();
      ADOMove(NEXT);
      DisplayStatus("Add aborted");
      return 0;
   }
   //Ready to delete current record
   hr = m_pSet->Delete(adAffectCurrent);
   if (FAILED(hr)) {
      COLEDBErrorChecking::DisplaySingleError(hr,
         "OnDelete Delete");
      DisplayStatus("Delete had failed.");
      return 0;
   }
   ADOMove(NEXT, FALSE);      //Reposition record
   return 0;
}
```

Viewing the Final Project

Now you have a working ADO database project. All in all, it really isn't that hard to code ADO programs, which explains ADO's popularity in such languages as VBScript. But because of Visual C++ wizard support, ADO is not as easy or efficient as coding your own OLE DB consumer. Figure 18-11 shows the final project.

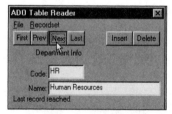

Figure 18-11: ADO/ATL projects are not that hard to create, but it's easier to program and more efficient to code your own OLE DB consumers.

 This application can be viewed or copied from the CD-ROM in the ADOTableReader project.

Summary

This chapter covers database development using ADO inside Visual C++. To recap:

- ADO is used almost exclusively for database access in other languages such as Visual J++, VB Script, and Visual Basic. However, in Visual C++, you should probably be writing OLE DB consumers rather than ADO programmers. It's easier, and the consumers are more efficient.

- ADO architecture consists primarily of connections, recordsets, and fields.

- Traditional OLE DB error handling works with ADO. It probably should be used when in Visual C++ rather than the ADO error collections, which merely encapsulate the error processing.

Chapter 19

Developing DAO Applications

IN THIS CHAPTER

◆ Understanding the DAO structure

◆ Viewing the relationships between DAO objects

◆ Implementing database security with DAO

◆ Using DAO workspaces

◆ Using the MFC with DAO in single table and joined table applications

◆ Writing reports with DAO and MFC

THIS CHAPTER DISCUSSES Data Access Objects. You'll find that DAO development is remarkably similar to ODBC development, reducing the learning curve for both technologies. Out of all the database technologies covered in this book (DAO, ODBC, and OLE DB), DAO is the most lightly covered, because DAO has been largely supplanted in Visual C++ by both ODBC and OLE DB and really shouldn't be used for new application development. However, DAO is still used in both legacy systems and in some shops that are using some older packages and want to support only DAO.

 DAO is a mature technology that is well supported in existing Visual C++ books and in the Visual C++ documentation. However, it seems clear that ODBC is the best-supported current method of programming, and OLE DB is what Microsoft envisions for the future. Consequently, you should give a lot of thought before starting any new development in DAO, and instead use ODBC or OLE DB. This chapter is designed to give you a background in DAO in case you are supporting legacy systems that use DAO, or if your place of work forces the DAO standard and has not updated yet.

Understanding DAO's Internal Structure

The DAO database engine uses the Jet database engine for data access, so books or documentation on the Jet database engine might help you when programming DAO.

 Code examples are given for DAO throughout this chapter, but the tables in this section delve into the entire DAO structure and may make it easier to code DAO programs when you cannot find an exact example of the DAO functionality that you wish to use.

The DAO object model is made of several objects, as shown in Table 19-1 and Figure 19-1.

TABLE **19-1 DAO OBJECTS**

DAO Object	Description
Engine	The database engine is needed to access a database. Only one engine can be running on a machine at any given time. There is no equivalent "CDAOEngine" class, but a COM Engine object is automatically created when you create a DAO workspace, database, or recordset. You can use CDaoWorkspace functions to perform database engine functions, as seen by the CDaoWorkspace functions listed in Table 19-2.
Errors	If DAO database errors occur after an engine is started, they are stored in the engine's errors component. There is no class for Errors constructor. Using MFC, errors can be detected by catching a `CDaoException`.
Error	A single error stored in the Errors collection. There is no "CDaoError" class that you can create to contain error information, but you can return the error number and description by using a try...catch block to catch a CDaoException. There is a function called CDaoException.GetErrorInfo that returns a CDaoError structure.

DAO Object	Description
Workspaces	Workspaces enable several transactions to run at the same time in the same program. Workspaces are also used to control database security. Although workspaces are not needed to access a database, a default workspace is started when the database engine is started. Any commands that access the database also access this workspace. The Workspaces collection class is not encapsulated inside the MFC, but you can call `CDaoWorkspace.GetWorkspaceCount` to return the number of workspaces currently opened by the database engine, and you can use `CDaoWorkspace.GetWorkspaceInfo` to return information about the workspaces.
Workspace	A Workspace enables you to use transactions and user security. Workspaces are contained in the `CWorkspace` class found later in this section.
Databases	Every database that is opened or created in a workspace is contained in the Databases class. While the Databases container class is not specifically encapsulated by the MFC, you can call `CDaoWorkspace.GetDatabaseCount` to return the number of databases currently opened by the current workspace, and you can use `CDaoWorkspace.GetDatabaseInfo` to return information about each database.
Database	The `CDaoDatabase` class is used to access tables and fields in your DAO database. The `CDaoDatabase` class is discussed later in this chapter.
Users, User, Groups, and Group	The Groups and Users collection and the User and Group collection are used for managing security. MFC does not support these routines, but you can manage security by passing SQL to set up a user or group. See more about users and groups in the section "Using CDaoWorkspace."

This section discusses how to use the Workspace, Exception and Database objects from C++. Instead of describing the definitions of these COM objects directly, I discuss the MFC classes that provide easy access to these objects in C++.

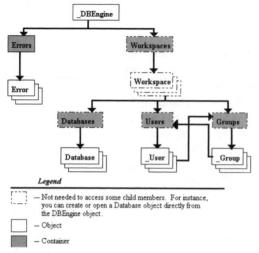

Figure 19-1: The DAO engine hierarchy shows the many components of a DAO database engine.

Using CDaoWorkspace

The CDaoWorkspace class is used to access database engine functions, other work-spaces started within the same database engine, and multiple databases stored using the same workspace. The CDaoWorkspace class is used extensively when using transactions in your application. Table 19-2 lists the functions of the CDaoWorkspace class.

TABLE **19-2 CDAOWORKSPACE FUNCTIONS**

Function	Description
Append	Appends a new workspace to the database engine's Workspaces collection.
BeginTrans	Begins a new transaction.
CDaoWorkspace	Constructs a workspace object. After the CDaoWorkspace constructor is called, you also need to call the CDaoWorkspace. Create or the CDaoWorkspace.Open function to populate the workspace.
Close	Closes the workspace and all of the objects it contains. *Pending transactions are rolled back* so you must call the CDaoWorkspace.CommitTrans function if you want changes made during a transaction to be committed.

Function	Description
CommitTrans	Completes the current transaction and saves the changes.
CompactDatabase	Compacts or duplicates a database.
Create	Creates a new DAO workspace object after the CDaoWorkspace constructor is called.
GetDatabaseCount	Returns the number of DAO database objects in the workspace's Databases collection.
GetDatabaseInfo	Returns information about a specified DAO database defined by an index in the workspace's Databases collection.
GetIniPath	Gets the location of the Microsoft Jet database engine's initialization settings from the Windows Registry.
GetIsolateODBCTrans	Returns the isolation level of an ODBC data source that is connected to via DAO. The isolation level is a value that indicates whether multiple transactions that involve the same ODBC data source are isolated via forced multiple connections to the data source.
GetLoginTimeout	Returns the number of seconds allotted for the user to log in to an ODBC data source that is connected to via DAO.
GetName	Returns the user-defined name for the workspace object.
GetUserName	Returns the workspace owner specified when the workspace was created.
GetVersion	Returns the version of the database engine associated with the workspace.
GetWorkspaceCount	Returns a count of the DAO workspace objects in the database engine's Workspaces collection.
GetWorkspaceInfo	Returns information about a specified DAO workspace defined by an index in the database engine's Workspaces collection.
Idle	Call this function to enable the database engine to perform background tasks.
IsOpen	Returns a zero if the workspace is closed.

Continued

TABLE **19-2 CDAOWORKSPACE FUNCTIONS** *(Continued)*

Function	Description
Open	Opens a workspace object associated with DAO's default workspace after a CDaoWorkspace object has been constructed.
RepairDatabase	Attempts to repair a damaged database.
Rollback	Ends the current transaction and does not save the changes.
SetDefaultPassword	Sets the password that the database engine uses when a workspace object is created without a specific password.
SetDefaultUser	Sets the user name that the database engine uses when a workspace object is created without a specific username.
SetIniPath	Sets the location of the Microsoft Jet database engine's initialization settings in the Windows Registry.
SetIsolateODBCTrans	Sets the isolation level of an ODBC data source that is connected to via DAO. The isolation level is a value that indicates whether multiple transactions that involve the same ODBC data source are isolated via forced multiple connections to the data source.
SetLoginTimeout	Sets the number of seconds before an error occurs when the user attempts to log in to an ODBC data source.

Implementing DAO Security

Along with the functions listed in Table 19-2, workspaces are also used to control for security. Although no MFC classes wrap security functions, you can control DAO security by calling the DAO COM methods directly. To establish DAO security, you need to point to a system database. The Jet database engine requires that a system database be set up to handle security.

 TIP To create or manage security accounts in a system database, use the *MS Access Workgroup Administrator* that comes with Microsoft Access.

To point to a systems database, perform the following six steps:

1. Define a `COleVariant` that can contain the filename of the system database using the `varSystemDB` function:

```
// Set the system database
COleVariant sysDB("C:\\mydir\\myengine.mdw", VT_BSTRT);
```

2. Although it's probably not necessary when in a MFC DAO application, you may need to initialize the database engine MFC library routines using the `AfxDaoInit` function. If DAO is already initialized, the `AfxDaoInit` function simply returns:

```
// Initialize DAO for MFC
   AfxDaoInit( );
```

3. You can retrieve the database engine using the `AfxDaoGetEngine` function. Be sure to make sure that a null isn't returned:

```
DAODBEngine* pDBEngine = AfxDaoGetEngine( );
ASSERT(pDBEngine);
```

4. Use the `put_SystemDB` method to place the string containing the system database into the system database property of the database engine:

```
// Call put_SystemDB method to set the system database
DAO_CHECK(pDBEngine->put_SystemDB( sysDB.bstrVal));
```

 Use the DAO_CHECK macro when you make non–MFC DAO database calls. The DAO_CHECK macro automatically checks your non–MFC DAO database calls and makes sure that they are returned with a valid code. Internally, DAO_CHECK is used by all MFC DAO calls, so you get the same error handling that you get when using straight MFC.

---

5. Now that you've pointed to the right systems database, you must assign the default username and password so that when the user connects, instead of using "Admin", the user uses their own user name. First declare user and password variants:

```
COleVariant user("userName", VT_BSTRT);
COleVariant password("Password", VT_BSTRT);
```

6. Your final step is to place the username and password into the database engine properties so that when a connection is made, the password is used to connect:

```
// Set default user and password:
DAO_CHECK(pDBEngine->put_DefaultUser(user.bstrVal));
DAO_CHECK(pDBEngine->put_DefaultPassword(password.bstrVal));
```

These six steps enable you to access DAO security. As you can see, because there are no DAO MFC wrappers for security, security for a Jet database can be extremely complicated.

Using CDaoException

Most exception handling in DAO consists of using a try . . . catch block and the GetErrorMessage function to retrieve any error message that may have occurred during execution. Consider the following error processing block:

```
try {
    m_pSet->Delete();      //Delete record
}
catch(CDaoException* e1) {     //Failed
    TCHAR message[200];
    TCHAR display[255];
    e1->GetErrorMessage(message, 200);
    strcpy (display, "Delete Failed:\n");
    strcat (display, message);
    AfxMessageBox( display, MB_ICONEXCLAMATION);
    m_pSet->MoveFirst();     //We lost our place.
    e1->Delete();          //Delete Error Message
    UpdateData(FALSE);     //Update dialog box fields
    return;
}
```

In the preceding code, an error is caught, the error message is retrieved, and appropriate action is taken based on the error. At the end of the error processing, the Delete function is used to deallocate all memory storage based on the error.

The error trapping algorithm described previously is usually sufficient for all DAO errors. However, the CDaoException class has many class variables and functions that can increase the knowledge you have about your error. These class variables and functions are described in Table 19-3.

TABLE 19-3 CDAOEXCEPTION CLASS VARIABLES AND FUNCTIONS

Class Variables or Function	Description
CDaoException	Constructs a CDaoException object.
Delete	Releases resources used to store the error information.
GetErrorCount	Returns the number of errors in the database engine's Errors collection.
GetErrorInfo	Returns a CDaoError structure containing error information about a particular Error object denoted by an index in the Errors collection.
GetErrorMessage	Returns an error string describing the error routine.
m_nAfxDaoError	Contains an extended error code for any error in the MFC DAO classes.
m_pErrorInfo	A pointer to a CDaoErrorInfo object that contains information about one DAO error object.

Using CDaoDatabase

The CDaoDatabase class itself is used to access a Jet database. Help files on the CDaoDatabase class are quite extensive, but the help files don't really bring the information all together so that you can easily tell how objects are joined. This section describes DAO functions and shows you how the DAO database object relates to other DAO objects. Table 19-4 lists the functions available within the CDaoDatabase object. Some of these functions will be discussed in detail later in the chapter.

TABLE 19-4 CDAODATABASE VARIABLES AND FUNCTIONS

Class Variables or Function	Description
CanTransact	Returns zero if the database does not support transactions.
CanUpdate	Returns zero if the CDaoDatabase object is read-only.
CDaoDatabase	This is the CDaoDatabase constructor. You must still call the Open or Create function to connect to a database.

Continued

TABLE **19-4 CDAODATABASE VARIABLES AND FUNCTIONS** *(Continued)*

Class Variables or Function	Description
Close	Closes the database connection.
Create	Creates a database object and opens a connection to the new database via the CDaoDatabase object.
CreateRelation	Defines a new relation among the tables in a database.
DeleteQueryDef	Deletes a QueryDef object saved in the database's QueryDefs collection.
DeleteRelation	Deletes an existing relation between tables in the database.
DeleteTableDef	Deletes the table data and the table definition from the database.
Execute	Executes an SQL statement or query. Calling Execute for a query that returns results throws an exception.
GetConnect	Returns the ODBC connect string (if applicable) used to connect the CDaoDatabase object to a database.
GetName	Returns the database name currently in use.
GetQueryDefCount	Returns the number of queries defined for the database.
GetQueryDefInfo	Retrieves information about a specified query defined in the database and stores it in a CDaoQueryDefInfo class object.
GetQueryTimeout	Returns the number of seconds after which a database query operation times out.
GetRecordsAffected	Returns the number of records affected by the last update, edit, or add operation or by a call to the Execute function.
GetRelationCount	Returns the number of relations defined between tables in the database.
GetRelationInfo	Retrieves information about a specified relation defined between tables in the database and stores it in a CDaoRelationInfo class variable.
GetTableDefCount	Returns the number of tables defined in the database.
GetTableDefInfo	Retrieves information about a specified table in the database and stores it in a CDaoTableDefInfo class variable.

Class Variables or Function	Description
GetVersion	Returns the version of the database engine associated with the database.
IsOpen	Returns zero if the CDaoDatabase object is not currently connected to a database.
m_pDAODatabase	Contains a pointer to the underlying DAO database object.
m_pWorkspace	Contains a pointer to the CDaoWorkspace object that contains the database and defines its transaction space.
Open	Connects to a database.
SetQueryTimeout	Sets the number of seconds after which ODBC database query operations time out.

CDaoDatabase is the MFC class containing the functionality to open a database using DAO calls. CDaoDatabase deals with several classes of underlying DAO objects, because the DAO object model is not organized quite the same way as MFC's DAO classes. It is useful to understand the hierarchy of DAO objects, which is shown in Figure 19-2, and which is made up of the classes shown in Table 19-5.

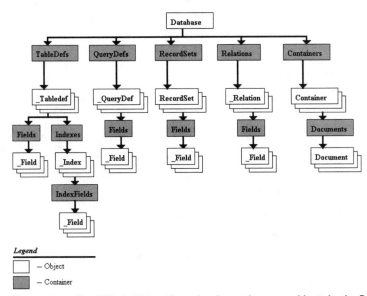

Figure 19-2: The DAO database hierarchy shows the many objects in the DAO object model.

TABLE 19-5 DAO DATABASE COMPONENTS

Database Component	Description
TableDefs	The TableDefs collection object lists all the _TableDefs in a database.
_TableDef	The _TableDef object corresponds to a database table. Using the _TableDef object, you can list all the fields or indexes for a table and retrieve table information, such as table name.
Fields	The Fields collection object lists all the fields for a component. The components that have fields are _TableDef, _QueryDef, Recordset, Relation, and Index. Using the Fields object, you can list, add, or delete any field in these components.
_Field	The _Field object is a field contained in an _TableDef, _QueryDef, Recordset, Relation, or Index. You can use the _Field object to define a new field or to retrieve information about an existing field.
Indexes	The Indexes collection object contains all the indexes used in a table.
_Index	The _Index object lists a single index used in a table.
IndexFields	The IndexFields collection object lists all the fields for an index. The use of Variants is necessary with the IndexFields class. Indexes are discussed later in this chapter.
QueryDefs	The QueryDefs collection object contains all the QueryDefs used in a database.
_QueryDef	The _QueryDef object is a single _QueryDef. QueryDefs are used to define stored procedures inside a DAO database.
Recordsets	The Recordsets collection object contains all the Recordsets currently defined in a database.
Recordset	The Recordset object enables the programmer to view or update information in the database.
Relations	The Relations collection object contains all the relations in a database.
_Relation	The _Relation object defines the relationship or referential integrity between two tables.

Database Component	Description
Containers	The Containers collection object lists all the Container objects for a database.
Container	The Container object is a Microsoft Access–specific object that stores macros, reports, and so on. Most of the time, the Container object is of little use to the Visual C++ developer.
Documents	The Documents collection object lists all the Document objects for a database.
Document	The Document object stores all the Microsoft Access predefined forms. Forms are a handy way to set security inside the Microsoft Access package but are usually of little use to the Visual C++ developer.

Developing DAO Applications with MFC

While you can and will use the DAO functions to write your DAO application, you probably will rely heavily on the MFC AppWizard when doing DAO development. As with ODBC, the easiest way to make a DAO application is through the MFC AppWizard.

 In Visual C++, DAO applications are remarkably similar to ODBC applications. In this chapter, you see much of the same techniques used in Chapter 5.

To develop an application that scrolls through a table and enables you to update any record takes only 14 easy steps:

1. Click File → New to open the New dialog box, and click the Projects tab, as shown in Figure 19-3. Next, click MFC AppWizard (exe), type in the Project name (DAODepartment), and click OK.

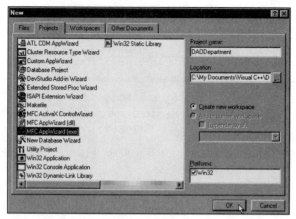

Figure 19-3: The MFC AppWizard is the easiest way to make DAO applications.

2. The MFC AppWizard - Step 1 of 6 dialog box now opens. Click Single Document and Document/View architecture support. Then click Next.

3. In the MFC AppWizard - Step 2 of 6 dialog box, click Database View with File Support, and click the Data Source button, as shown in Figure 19-4.

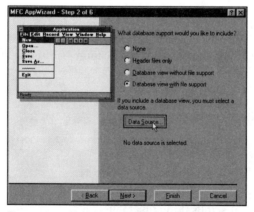

Figure 19-4: You must choose a data source for your DAO application.

4. In the Database Options dialog box, choose DAO, Dynaset, and check Detect dirty columns. Click the ellipses (. . .) to choose your data source, as shown in Figure 19-5.

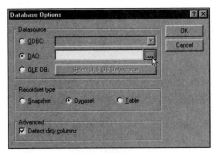

Figure 19-5: The Database Options dialog box enables you to enter data source and connection information.

Dirty Columns

Unlike other database products, DAO gives you the option of whether or not to detect *dirty columns*. Dirty columns occur when two people are trying to change the same row in a database. Observe the accompanying figure. Here, Person A pulls up a database record, and then goes to lunch. Person B pulls up the same database record while Person A is at lunch and updates it. Person A then returns from lunch and tries to update the same record. If you have your database set to Detect dirty columns, then Person A cannot update the database record without re-retrieving it first.

Dirty column detection is vital in a multiuser environment. Otherwise, one person (in this case, Person A) could overwrite another person's (in this case, Person B) changes *without either person knowing it*. Other database APIs supported by Visual C++ (ODBC and OLE DB) have locking mechanisms that can detect dirty columns without specifically programming for it, as you need to do in DAO.

Detecting dirty columns is one way DAO deals with concurrent users.

5. Next, you should select the database that you want to use with your DAO program. This database is usually an Access .mdb file. In Figure 19-6, Classes.mdb is chosen as the database file.

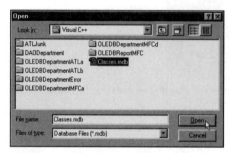

Figure 19–6: DAO's Jet database engine uses Access files as data sources.

6. The Database Options dialog box then reopens as before (Figure 19-5) except that the DAO data source is shown in the DAO textbox. Click OK, and the Select Database Tables dialog box opens and lists all the tables available for that database (Figure 19-7). Choose the table you wish to use (Department), and click OK.

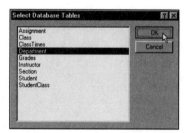

Figure 19–7: The Select Database Tables dialog box enables you to choose which table you want to use as your data source for your application.

7. After choosing which table you wish to use, you return to the MFC AppWizard - Step 2 of 6 dialog box in the MFC AppWizard. Here, you see that the DAO data source you have selected is displayed beneath the Data Source button (Figure 19-8).

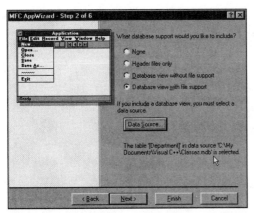

Figure 19-8: As with ODBC and OLE DB, data sources are displayed in Step 2 of 6 in the MFC AppWizard.

8. The MFC AppWizard - Step 3 of 6 dialog box opens. Accept all the defaults, and click Next. The MFC AppWizard - Step 4 of 6 dialog box then opens. Deselect (turn off) printing and print preview, and click Next. The MFC AppWizard - Step 5 of 6 dialog box then opens. Accept all the defaults, and click Next. The MFC AppWizard - Step 6 of 6 dialog box opens. Here, you can change the program names of the C++ classes that are generated for you. Usually you accept all the defaults and click Finish. Finally, you should see the New Project Information message box appear. As with ODBC, these options reflect the options you have chosen throughout the MFC AppWizard. Click OK, and your Visual C++ environment should return. Your Visual C++ environment should look like the environment shown in Figure 19-9.

9. Next, delete the TODO message on the dialog box. Then add any fields you need to contain your database fields. In Figure 19-10, two edit boxes were added to contain the two columns in the department table. Then the properties were opened, and the edit box names were changed to IDC_DEPARTMENTCODE and IDC_DEPARTMENTNAME.

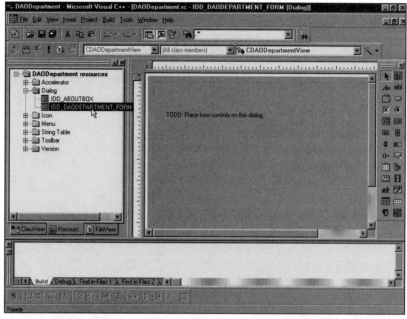

Figure 19-9: The MFC AppWizard helps generate the shell of an MFC application.

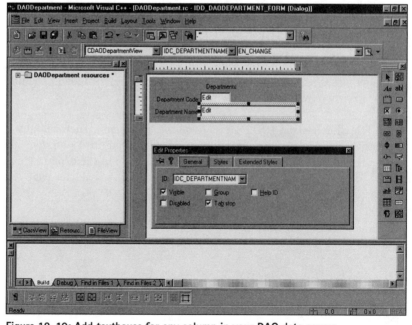

Figure 19-10: Add textboxes for any column in your DAO data source.

10. Pull up the MFC Class Wizard by clicking View → ClassWizard. Click the Member Variables tab. In Figure 19-11, you can see the names of the control IDs that you just added to your dialog box. Choose a variable (IDC_DEPARTMENTCODE), and click the Add Variable button.

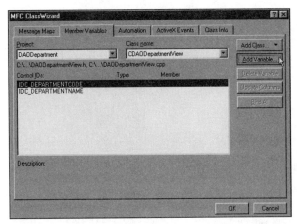

Figure 19-11: Each control ID must be associated with a database variable.

11. For each control listed in the Member Variables tab of the MFC Class Wizard, choose which database column is to be bound to which window control. After you click the Add Variable button, shown in Figure 19-11, the Add Member Variable dialog box opens. In Figure 19-12, the m_DepartmentCode variable contained in the m_pSet CRecordset variable is joined to the IDC_DEPARTMENTCODE window control.

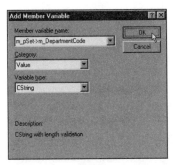

Figure 19-12: The Add Member Variable dialog box enables you to join database variables to window controls.

12. When you're finished, you should see your CRecordset variables listed next to the appropriate window control, as shown in Figure 19-13. Click OK.

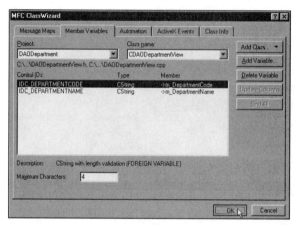

Figure 19-13: The MFC Class Wizard shows the database variables that are tied to your window control variables.

13. Choose Build → Execute from the menu, or click Ctrl+F5. This builds and runs your DAO program.

Just as with ODBC, it's easy to develop a fully functional MFC database application using the MFC Wizard, as shown in Figure 19-14. This application enables scrolling through records and updating.

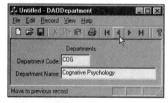

Figure 19-14: The MFC AppWizard makes creating DAO applications simple.

The code for the version of DAODepartment can be found in the DAODepartmentA directory on the CD-ROM that accompanies this book.

Using Adds, Deletes, and Queries

The DAODepartment example in the previous section enabled scrolling through records as well as updates. In this section, you learn how to easily add add, delete, and query functionality inside an MFC DAO application using five simple steps:

1. Expand Menu in the Resources tab, and open the IDR_MAINFRAME menu. Add the menu items listed in Table 19-6 to the Record menu item.

TABLE **19-6** ADDITIONAL DAODEPARTMENT MENU ITEMS

Text	ID	Prompt
&Delete Record	ID_RECORD_DELETERECORD	Delete this record.
&Query Record	ID_RECORD_QUERYRECORD	Find a department code.

Figure 19-15 shows how the menu should look when you're finished.

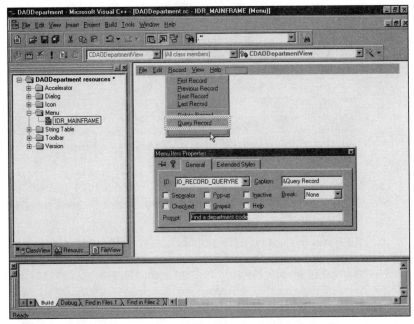

Figure 19-15: New menu items are needed for more DAO functionality.

Chapter 5 creates toolbar items for menu items.

2. Edit your dialog box to include an edit box used for querying. The query box in Figure 19-16 includes an edit box named IDC_FINDCODE to contain the new department number that is used to query the database.

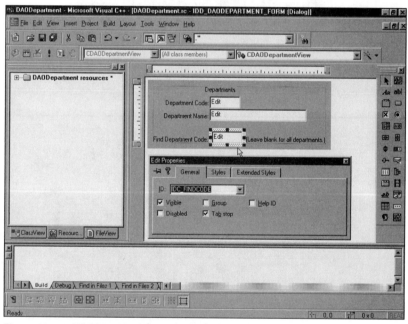

Figure 19-16: DAODepartment needs an edit box for querying.

3. Now use the Class Wizard to bind a new variable (m_FindDeptCode) to your new control (IDC_FINDCODE). When you're finished, your member variables should look like Figure 19-17.

4. While still in the Class Wizard, click the Message Maps tab, and add an OnMove function to the CDAODepartmentView class. Also add COMMAND functions for ID_FILE_NEW, ID_RECORD_DELETERECORD, and ID_RECORD_QUERYRECORD. Also add an UPDATE_COMMAND_UI function for ID_RECORD_DELETERECORD so that you can disable delete functionality if you don't have a record. Figure 19-18 shows how your Class Wizard should look after you complete this step.

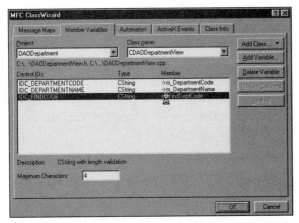

Figure 19-17: You need to bind a variable to an edit box for your query.

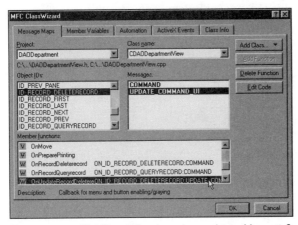

Figure 19-18: The Class Wizard can be used to add event functions to your controls.

5. Now it's time to finally write some Visual C++ code. To complete this program, you need to write five functions: `OnMove`, `OnFileNew`, `OnRecordDeleterecord`, `OnUpdateRecordDeleterecord`, and `OnRecordQueryrecord`.

WRITING ONFILENEW

You need an `OnFileNew` function to add new records to your table. To write the `OnFileNew` function in your CDaoRecordView descendent class, you need to complete the following steps:

1. Update any program variables that currently need updating from the dialog box by using the `UpdateData` function, setting Edit mode if needed, and issuing an Update command:

```
UpdateData(TRUE);      //Get data from dialog box
if (m_pSet->GetEditMode() != dbEditAdd) {
    //Not currently adding a record
    m_pSet->Edit();      //Set for edit mode
}
m_pSet->Update();      //Update data if needed
```

2. Move to the last field using the MoveLast function. This ensures that you're not on the first record when you add:

```
m_pSet->MoveLast();      //Get off record 1
```

3. Clear the fields in the dialog window by setting them to NULL:

```
m_pSet->SetFieldNull(NULL);      //Clear all fields
```

4. Place the recordset in AddNew mode:

```
m_pSet->AddNew();      //Set database in AddNew mode
```

5. Use the UpdateData function to display the cleared fields in dialog box:

```
UpdateData(FALSE);      //Update dialog box fields
```

These steps can be seen in the following OnFileNew function:

```
void CDAODepartmentView::OnFileNew()
{
    if (!m_pSet->IsBOF()
            && !m_pSet->IsDeleted()
            && !m_pSet->IsEOF()) {
        //On a valid record
        UpdateData(TRUE);      //Get data from dialog box
        if (m_pSet->GetEditMode() != dbEditAdd) {
            //Not currently adding a record
            m_pSet->Edit();      //Set for edit mode
        }
        m_pSet->Update();      //Update data if needed
        m_pSet->MoveLast();      //Get off record 1
    }
    m_pSet->SetFieldNull(NULL);      //Clear all fields
    m_pSet->AddNew();      //Set database in AddNew mode
    UpdateData(FALSE);      //Update dialog box fields
}
```

WRITING ONMOVE
By default, the OnMove function updates the existing record before completing its move by placing the recordset in Edit mode and calling the Update function.

However, because you are now enabling adds to the recordset, you need to override this action so you can add any new records that need to be added. This can be done by making the following additions to the OnMove function:

```
BOOL CDAODepartmentView::OnMove(UINT nIDMoveCommand)
{
    if (m_pSet->GetEditMode() == dbEditAdd) {
        //Currently adding a record
        //So update the record before the move
        UpdateData(TRUE);    //Get data from dialog box
        m_pSet->Update();    //Update data if needed
        m_pSet->MoveLast();    //Go to the added record
    }
    //Continue with normal processing
    return CDaoRecordView::OnMove(nIDMoveCommand);
}
```

WRITING ONRECORDDELETERECORD

While adding a record takes the greatest understanding of MFC and ODBC, deleting a record requires the most handling and error checking. While the Delete function itself is relatively straightforward, there are other considerations whenever a record is deleted:

◆ You need to make sure that the user really wants to delete the record. This is usually done with a message box asking if the user really wants the record deleted:

```
if (AfxMessageBox(    //Be sure to verify your deletes
        "Are you sure you want to delete?",
        MB_YESNO)
!= IDYES) {
return;
}
```

◆ You have to make sure that the record really exists. If the user tries to delete a new record before adding it, then you merely cancel the add rather than delete a record:

```
if (m_pSet->GetEditMode() == dbEditAdd) {
//Currently adding so don't delete, just cancel add.
m_pSet->CancelUpdate();
m_pSet->MovePrev();
return;
}
```

◆ You have to catch any errors that may occur during a delete. The CDaoRecordset::Delete function throws a CDBException if a database error occurs during the delete:

```
try {
m_pSet->Delete();      //Delete record
}
catch(CDaoException* e1) {   //Failed
TCHAR message[200];
TCHAR display[255];
e1->GetErrorMessage(message, 200);
strcpy (display, "Delete Failed:\n");
strcat (display, message);
AfxMessageBox( display, MB_ICONEXCLAMATION);
m_pSet->MoveFirst(); //We lost our place.
e1->Delete();          //Delete Error Message
UpdateData(FALSE);     //Update dialog box fields
return;
}
```

◆ After a successful delete, you need to reposition the recordset so the user can still view records. If the last record is deleted, you should probably go to either the previous record or the first record. Otherwise, you should probably reposition the recordset to the next record:

```
m_pSet->MoveNext();                     //Go to next record
if (m_pSet->IsDeleted()) {   //Was there a next record?
m_pSet->MoveFirst(); //Deleted last record
}
```

◆ Finally, if you have deleted the last record, you probably need to set the fields up to add a new record because there are no records to display. This involves closing and opening the recordset to position the pointer off the deleted record and then calling the OnRecordAddrecord function written in the last section to set up a new record:

```
try {
    m_pSet->MoveNext();                 //Go to next record
    if (!m_pSet->IsBOF()
                && !m_pSet->IsDeleted()
                && !m_pSet->IsEOF()) {
        //Was there a next record?
        m_pSet->MoveFirst();    //Deleted last record
    }
    if (!m_pSet->IsBOF()
                && !m_pSet->IsDeleted()
                && !m_pSet->IsEOF()) {
```

```
            //Can't find a record
            AfxThrowDaoException();
        }
        UpdateData(FALSE);      //Update dialog box fields
    }
    catch(CDaoException* e2) {      //No records exist
        AfxMessageBox("No more records",
            MB_ICONEXCLAMATION);
        e2->Delete();            //Delete Error Message
        //Close and Open to get rid of the Deleted record
        m_pSet->Close();
        m_pSet->Open();
        //No records, so set up an add record
        OnFileNew();
    }
```

The code you need to add to the CODBCDepartmentView::OnRecordDeleterecord
function is as follows:

```
void CDAODepartmentView::OnRecordDeleterecord()
{
    if (AfxMessageBox(      //Be sure to verify your deletes
            "Are you sure you want to delete?",
            MB_YESNO)
        != IDYES) {
        return;
    }
    if (m_pSet->GetEditMode() == dbEditAdd) {
    //Currently adding so don't delete, just cancel add.
        m_pSet->CancelUpdate();
        m_pSet->MovePrev();
        return;
    }
    try {
        m_pSet->Delete();      //Delete record
    }
    catch(CDaoException* e1) {      //Failed
        TCHAR message[200];
        TCHAR display[255];
        e1->GetErrorMessage(message, 200);
        strcpy (display, "Delete Failed:\n");
        strcat (display, message);
        AfxMessageBox( display, MB_ICONEXCLAMATION);
        m_pSet->MoveFirst();      //We lost our place.
```

```
        e1->Delete();          //Delete Error Message
        UpdateData(FALSE);     //Update dialog box fields
        return;
    }
    try {
        m_pSet->MoveNext();    //Go to next record
//Is there a next record?
        if (m_pSet->IsBOF()
                || m_pSet->IsDeleted()
                || m_pSet->IsEOF()) {
            m_pSet->MoveFirst();    //Deleted last record
        }
        if (m_pSet->IsBOF()
                || m_pSet->IsDeleted()
                || m_pSet->IsEOF()) { //Can't find a record
            AfxThrowDaoException();
        }
        UpdateData(FALSE);     //Update dialog box fields
    }
    catch(CDaoException* e2) {    //No records exist
        AfxMessageBox("No more records",
            MB_ICONEXCLAMATION);
        e2->Delete();          //Delete Error Message
        //Close and Open to get rid of the Deleted record
        m_pSet->Close();
        m_pSet->Open();
        //No records, so set up an add record
        OnFileNew();
    }
}
```

WRITING OnUpdateRecordDeleteRecord

The OnUpdateRecordDeleterecord function is used to disable ("gray out") the Delete Record menu item and any corresponding toolbar item if a delete does not make sense. Here, you test using the IsBOF, IsEOF, and IsDeleted functions to see if there's a current record. If so, you enable the Delete functionality. Adding an Enable function call to the OnUpdateRecordDeleterecord function can do this:

```
void CODBCDepartmentView::OnUpdateRecordDeleterecord(CCmdUI* pCmdUI)
{
    //Disable delete functionality if no record is found
    pCmdUI->Enable(          //Enable delete if there's a record
```

```
!m_pSet->IsBOF() &&
!m_pSet->IsDeleted() &&
!m_pSet->IsEOF());
}
```

WRITING OnRecordQueryRecord

To add a query, you need to assign a value to the CRecordset::m_pSet->m_str
Filter variable. The can be done with the following steps:

1. If you are in the middle of updating or adding a new record, you need to
   issue an Edit (unless you are adding a record and have already issued an
   AddNew):

```
UpdateData(TRUE);     //Get data from dialog box
if (m_pSet->GetEditMode() == dbEditAdd) {
//Not currently adding, so set to update
m_pSet->Edit();
}
m_pSet->Update();     //Update data if needed
```

2. Check the bound filter variable defined in the Writing
   OnRecordQueryrecord section earlier in this chapter. If there is a value in
   the field, form an SQL WHERE clause (without the WHERE) and assign it to a
   string variable:

```
CString newFilter = "";     //Default is no filter
if (m_FindDeptCode != "") {
    //Setup new filter
    newFilter = "DepartmentCode = '" + m_FindDeptCode + "'";
}
```

3. Check to see if you need to apply the new filter. You need to apply the
   filter if it is different from the last filter used to perform the recordset
   query. The last filter is stored in the CRecordset::m_strFilter variable.
   If you reassign the filter, you must call the Requery function to apply the
   new filter:

```
if (newFilter != m_pSet->m_strFilter) {
    //Filter has changed
    m_pSet->m_strFilter = newFilter;     //Assign new filter
    try {
        m_pSet->Requery();                 //Requery
    }
    catch(CDaoException* e1)     {
        AfxMessageBox("Requery has failed");
```

```
                    m_pSet->m_strFilter = "";            //Try to get back
                    m_pSet->Requery();                   //Requery again
                    e1->Delete();            //Delete Error Message
                }
            //Continue processing
            }
```

4. Finally, test to see if the new recordset has any records, and move to the first record if possible. If not, display a message saying there are no records, and issue an Add by calling the OnRecordAddrecord function to clear the fields:

```
try {
//Go to the first record of the new filtered recordset
    m_pSet->MoveFirst();
}
catch(CDaoException* e2)    {
    //Move failed because there are no records
    AfxMessageBox("No records were found",
                MB_ICONEXCLAMATION );
    e2->Delete();            //Delete Error Message
    //No records, so set up an add record
    OnFileNew();
}
```

Put the code in the OnRecordQueryrecord function. The following code can be written to accomplish the preceding tasks:

```
void CDAODepartmentView::OnRecordQueryrecord()
{
    CString newFilter = "";      //Default is no filter
    UpdateData(TRUE);      //Get data from dialog box
    if (m_pSet->GetEditMode() != dbEditAdd) {
        //Not currently adding, so set to update
        m_pSet->Edit();
    }
    m_pSet->Update();      //Update data if needed
    if (m_FindDeptCode != "") {
        //Setup new filter
        newFilter = "DepartmentCode = '"
                + m_FindDeptCode + "'";
    }
    if (newFilter != m_pSet->m_strFilter) {
        //Filter has changed
        m_pSet->m_strFilter = newFilter;      //Assign new filter
```

```
    try {
        m_pSet->Requery();                  //Requery
    }
    catch(CDaoException* e1)    {
        AfxMessageBox("Requery has failed");
        m_pSet->m_strFilter = "";           //Try to get back
        m_pSet->Requery();                  //Requery again
        e1->Delete();           //Delete Error Message
    }
    try {
    //Go to the first record of the new filtered recordset
        m_pSet->MoveFirst();
    }
    catch(CDaoException* e2)    {
        //Move failed because there are no records
        AfxMessageBox("No records were found",
                MB_ICONEXCLAMATION );
        e2->Delete();           //Delete Error Message
        //No records, so set up an add record
        OnFileNew();
    }
    }
    UpdateData(FALSE);      //Update dialog box fields
}
```

When you're finished, your application should look similar to the application shown in Figure 19-19.

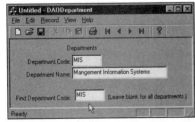

Figure 19-19: As in ODBC, coding a few DAO functions can quickly generate a full-featured application.

The code for the version of DAODepartment can be found in the DAO DepartmentB directory on the CD-ROM accompanying this book.

Saving and Transactions Using DAO Workspaces

If you remember the DAO structure that was discussed at the beginning of this chapter, you remember that the database engine contains one or more workspaces. These workspaces contain one or more database objects that, in turn, contain one or more recordset objects. The MFC's main DAO variable, m_pSet, is a DAO recordset. However, the m_pSet variable contains a CDaoRecordset.m_pDatabase variable that points to a CDatabase object. Each CDatabase object, in turn, contains a CDatabase.m_pWorkspace variable that points to a CDaoWorkspace object. By using a chain of pointers, you can execute workspace commands by starting with your m_pSet variable. For instance, the following command:

```
m_pSet->m_pDatabase->m_pWorkspace->BeginTrans();
```

begins a transaction for the m_pSet variable through the m_pWorkspace variable. This section describes how to use DAO transactions to add save/reject change functionality to your DAO application. Using transactions to save can be accomplished with five easy steps.

1. Use the existing DAODepartment project. Go into the Class Wizard, and add the functions shown in Table 19-7.

TABLE 19-7 NEW EVENTS FOR ADDING TRANSACTION SUPPORT TO CDAODepartmentView

Function Name	Object ID	Message
OnFileSave	ID_FILE_SAVE	COMMAND
OnUpdateFileSave	ID_FILE_SAVE	UPDATE_COMMAND_UI
OnDestroy	CODBCDepartmentView	WM_DESTROY
OnChangeDepartmentcode	IDC_DEPARTMENTCODE	EN_CHANGE
OnChangeDepartmentname	IDC_DEPARTMENTNAME	EN_CHANGE

2. You need to write a SaveData function that saves the data to the database by using the Update command. First, put the SaveData function prototype in the DAODepartmentView.h header file:

```
// Operations
public:
    void SaveData();
```

3. Next, write the SaveData function you just declared. Place it in the DAODepartmentView.cpp source file:

```
void CDAODepartmentView::SaveData()
{
    if (m_pSet->GetEditMode() != dbEditAdd) {
        //Currently not adding a record, so set edit mode
        m_pSet->Edit();
    }
    UpdateData(TRUE);    //Get data from dialog box
    m_pSet->Update();    //Update data if needed
}
```

4. Now, replace the OnMove function save functionality with a call to the new SaveData function. This eliminates some duplicate code in your program:

```
BOOL CDAODepartmentView::OnMove(UINT nIDMoveCommand)
{
    SaveData();
    return CDaoRecordView::OnMove(nIDMoveCommand);
}
```

5. Next, declare a Boolean variable to indicate that changes have been made to your recordset:

```
protected: // create from serialization only
    BOOL m_bChangesMade;
```

6. Initialize this in your constructor:

```
CDAODepartmentView::CDAODepartmentView()
    : CDaoRecordView(CDAODepartmentView::IDD)
{
    //{{AFX_DATA_INIT(CDAODepartmentView)
    m_pSet = NULL;
    m_FindDeptCode = _T("");
    //}}AFX_DATA_INIT
    m_bChangesMade = FALSE;
}
```

7. Now make sure that every time you change a field, you make sure that your Boolean variable is set to `true`:

```
void CDAODepartmentView::OnChangeDepartmentcode()
{
    m_bChangesMade = TRUE;
}
void CDAODepartmentView::OnChangeDepartmentname()
{
    m_bChangesMade = TRUE;
}
```

8. Now it's time to start using your transactions. First, start a transaction in the `OnInitialUpdate` function by first checking to see if the database supports transactions, and then, if it does, close the recordset, start the transaction, and reopen the recordset:

```
void CDAODepartmentView::OnInitialUpdate()
{
    m_pSet = &GetDocument()->m_dAODepartmentSet;
    CDaoRecordView::OnInitialUpdate();
    GetParentFrame()->RecalcLayout();
    ResizeParentToFit();
    if (m_pSet->m_pDatabase->CanTransact()) {
        m_pSet->Close();     //Close to start transaction
        m_pSet->m_pDatabase->m_pWorkspace->BeginTrans();
        m_pSet->Open();      //Open after starting transaction
    }
}
```

9. Write the OnFileSave function to commit changes after saving the current record:

```
void CDAODepartmentView::OnFileSave()
{
    SaveData();
    if (m_pSet->m_pDatabase->CanTransact()
            && m_bChangesMade) {
        m_pSet->m_pDatabase->m_pWorkspace->CommitTrans();
        m_pSet->m_pDatabase->m_pWorkspace->BeginTrans();
    }
    m_bChangesMade = FALSE;
}
```

10. Next, add to the Class Wizard–generated `OnUpdateFileSave` function to enable updates only if changes have been made and transactions are enabled:

```
void CDAODepartmentView::OnUpdateFileSave(CCmdUI* pCmdUI)
{
    //Enable save if records have been changed
    pCmdUI->Enable(m_bChangesMade &&
        m_pSet->m_pDatabase->CanTransact());
}
```

11. Finally, add to the Class Wizard–generated `OnDestroy` function to make sure that the user can't exit without saving any changed records:

```
void CDAODepartmentView::OnDestroy()
{
//Check for changed fields and transaction ability
    if (m_pSet->m_pDatabase->CanTransact()
            && m_bChangesMade) {
        if (AfxMessageBox (
    "Records have been changed.  Do you want to save?",
                MB_YESNO) == IDYES) {
            SaveData();
            OnFileSave();
        }
    }
    //Roll back last transaction
    m_pSet->m_pDatabase->m_pWorkspace->Rollback();
    CDaoRecordView::OnDestroy();
}
```

Transactions are discussed in detail in Chapter 5. You may want to look at the "Access, Transactions, and `CRecordset`" sidebar for more information about transactions.

When you're finished, you have transaction support within your DAO program. Save is now enabled, and every time the user exits without saving, your DAO application will ask the user if the changes made are to be saved.

The code for the version of DAODepartment can be found in the DAO DepartmentC directory on the CD-ROM that accompanies this book.

Implementing DAO Joins

You may need to bring in more than one table for display. For instance, say you wanted to see and update Instructor records as you scrolled through each department. The simplest way to achieve this is through a table join. DAO development using table joins with the MFC Application Wizard is almost identical to development with a single table. Perform the following seven simple steps:

1. Use the MFC Application Wizard. In the Step 2 of 6 dialog box, choose Single document. In the Step 3 of 6 dialog box, choose Database view without file support. Then click the Data Source button.

2. In the Database Options dialog box, choose DAO, and click the ellipses (. . .) to choose a data source. After you've chosen a data source, choose Dynaset and Detect dirty columns, and click OK.

3. When the Select Database Tables dialog box opens, choose two or more tables to be joined together. In Figure 19-20, the Department table and the Instructor table are chosen for the join.

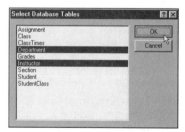

Figure 19-20: You can choose multiple database tables to use for your data source.

4. Continue with the MFC AppWizard until you are finished with the wizard. Be sure to leave the printing turned on (by default) this time because we want to print the report.

5. Add all the controls you need for both database tables, as shown in Figure 19-21.

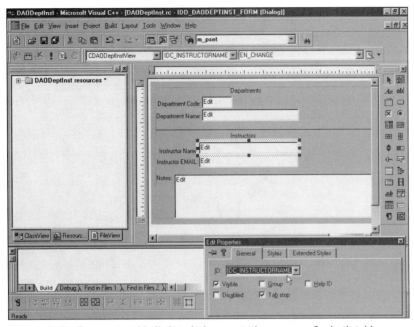

Figure 19-21: Be sure to add all the window controls necessary for both tables in a join.

6. Use the Class Wizard to bind database fields to your edit boxes, as shown in Figure 19-22.

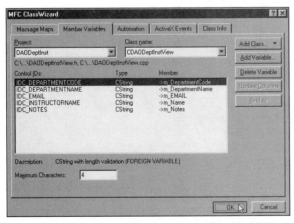

Figure 19-22: The Class Wizard can be used to bind DAO database fields to your dialog box.

7. Add just one line of code to the recordset class constructor that tells how the database filter is to perform the join:

```
CDAODeptInstSet::CDAODeptInstSet(CDaoDatabase* pdb)
    : CDaoRecordset(pdb)
{
    //{{AFX_FIELD_INIT(CDAODeptInstSet)
    m_DepartmentCode = _T("");
    m_DepartmentName = _T("");
    m_InstructorID = 0;
    m_Name = _T("");
    m_DepartmentCode2 = _T("");
    m_EMAIL = _T("");
    m_Notes = _T("");
    m_nFields = 7;
    //}}AFX_FIELD_INIT
    m_nDefaultType = dbOpenDynaset;
    m_strFilter =
"Instructor.DepartmentCode = Department.DepartmentCode";
}
```

When you're finished, you can see the results of a join as shown in Figure 19-23.

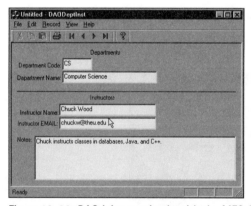

Figure 19-23: DAO joins are simple with the MFC AppWizard.

The code for this DAODeptInst example can be found in the DAODeptInstA directory on the CD-ROM accompanying this book.

Writing DAO Reports

Database programs, of course, often need reporting capability. DAO reports are similar to ODBC reports.

Chapter 6 delves into reports for ODBC programs. Many reporting constructs carry over to reports for both DAO and OLE DB. If you need further understanding of reports, consult that chapter. This chapter simply goes through the steps to create a DAO report.

This section delves into creating a simple DAO report using the following simple steps:

1. Use the `DAODeptInst` program that you've already built in the previous section.

2. Declare the `OnPrint` message in the Class Wizard using CDAODepartmentView as your class name.

3. Set your scroll size in your `OnInitialUpdate` function to your preferred size. I like `MM_LOENGLISH` the best because the measurement units are in inches and the position on the page is in positive numbers, not negative numbers as is the default. However, you can pick any scroll size you wish.

```
void CDAODeptInstView::OnInitialUpdate()
{
    m_pSet = &GetDocument()->m_dAODeptInstSet;
    CDaoRecordView::OnInitialUpdate();
    GetParentFrame()->RecalcLayout();
    ResizeParentToFit();
    //Limit size to 8" x 20"
    CSize sizeTotal(800, 2000);
    //Because of MM_LOENGLISH, Sizes are in .01 of an inch
    SetScrollSizes(MM_LOENGLISH, sizeTotal);
}
```

4. Go into your OnPrint method, and code your report. This report is almost identical to the report shown in Chapter 6, so if you have questions about this code, consult that text.

```
void CDAODeptInstView::OnPrint(CDC* pDC, CPrintInfo* pInfo)
{
    CString line;    //This is the print line
```

```
TEXTMETRIC metrics;      //Font measurements
int y = 0;          //Current y position on report
CFont TitleFont;     //Font for Title
CFont HeadingFont;      //Font for headings
CFont DetailFont;      //Font for detail lines
CFont FooterFont;      //Font for footer
//Tab stops at 1 inch, 2.5 inches, and 6 inches
int TabStops[] = {250, 600};
//Tab stops at 3.5 inches and 6.5 inches
int FooterTabStops[] = {350, 650};
//Limit size to 8" x 20"
CSize sizeTotal(800, 2000);
//Because of MM_LOENGLISH, Sizes are in .01 of an inch
SetScrollSizes(MM_LOENGLISH, sizeTotal);
if (!pInfo || pInfo->m_nCurPage == 1) {
    //Set the recordset at the beginning
    m_pSet->Requery();
    //Detect empty recordset
    if (m_pSet->IsBOF()) {
        return;
    }
}
//Bold font for Title
TitleFont.CreateFont(44, 0, 0, 0, FW_BOLD, FALSE, FALSE,
    0,ANSI_CHARSET, OUT_DEFAULT_PRECIS,
    CLIP_DEFAULT_PRECIS, DEFAULT_QUALITY,
    DEFAULT_PITCH | FF_ROMAN, "Times New Roman");
//Bold and underlined font for headings
HeadingFont.CreateFont(36, 0, 0, 0, FW_BOLD, FALSE, TRUE,
    0, ANSI_CHARSET, OUT_DEFAULT_PRECIS,
    CLIP_DEFAULT_PRECIS, DEFAULT_QUALITY,
    DEFAULT_PITCH | FF_ROMAN, "Times New Roman");
//Normal font for detail
DetailFont.CreateFont(18, 0, 0, 0, FW_NORMAL, FALSE,
    FALSE, 0, ANSI_CHARSET, OUT_DEFAULT_PRECIS,
    CLIP_DEFAULT_PRECIS, DEFAULT_QUALITY,
    DEFAULT_PITCH | FF_ROMAN, "Times New Roman");
//Small font for footer
FooterFont.CreateFont(12, 0, 0, 0, FW_NORMAL, FALSE,
    FALSE, 0, ANSI_CHARSET, OUT_DEFAULT_PRECIS,
    CLIP_DEFAULT_PRECIS, DEFAULT_QUALITY,
    DEFAULT_PITCH | FF_ROMAN, "Times New Roman");
//Capture default settings when setting the title font
CFont* OldFont = (CFont*) pDC->SelectObject(&TitleFont);
```

```
    //Retrieve the heading font measurements
    pDC->GetTextMetrics(&metrics);
    //Compute the heading line height
    int LineHeight = metrics.tmHeight +
metrics.tmExternalLeading;
    //Set Y to the line height.
    y -= LineHeight;
    pDC->TextOut(200, 0, "DAO Student Report");
/*
 Y must be set to negative numbers because MM_LOENGLISH was
used
*/
    //Set the Heading font
    pDC->SelectObject(&HeadingFont);
    //Format the heading
    line.Format("%s \t%s \t%s ","Dept Code", "Department",
"Instructor");
    //Output the heading at (0, y) using 3 tabs
    pDC->TabbedTextOut(0, y, line, 2, TabStops, 0);
    //Compute the detail line height
    LineHeight = metrics.tmHeight +
metrics.tmExternalLeading;
    y -= LineHeight;      //Adjust y position
    //Set the detail font
    pDC->SelectObject(&DetailFont);
    //Retrieve detail font measurements
    pDC->GetTextMetrics(&metrics);
    //Compute the detail line height
    LineHeight = metrics.tmHeight +
metrics.tmExternalLeading;
    //Scroll through the recordset
    while (!m_pSet->IsEOF()) {
        if (pInfo && abs(y) > 1000) {
            pInfo->SetMaxPage(pInfo->m_nCurPage + 1);
            break;
        }
        //Format the detail line
        line.Format("%s \t%s \t%s",
            m_pSet->m_DepartmentCode,
            m_pSet->m_DepartmentName,
            m_pSet->m_Name);
        //Output the print line at (0, y) using 3 tabs
        pDC->TabbedTextOut(0, y, line, 2, TabStops, 0);
        //Get the next recordset number
```

```
            y -= LineHeight;      //Adjust y position
            m_pSet->MoveNext();
        }
        if (pInfo) {
            //Set the footer font
            pDC->SelectObject(&FooterFont);
            //Format the footer
            line.Format(
                "DAO Report \tPage %d \tVisual C++ DB Guide",
                pInfo->m_nCurPage);
            //Output the footer at the bottom using tabs
            pDC->TabbedTextOut(0, -1025, line, 2, FooterTabStops,
0);
        }
        //Restore default settings
        pDC->SelectObject(OldFont);
}
```

This code now enables printing and print preview functionality. Figure 19-24 shows the print preview generated by this application.

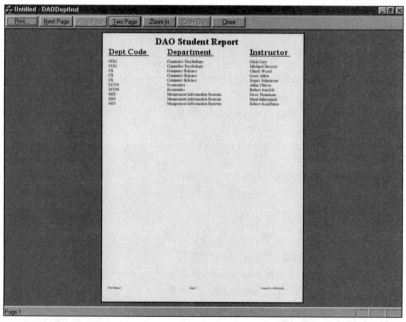

Figure 19-24: DAO reports can be generated by using the Class Wizard and adding code to two functions.

The code for this DAODeptInst example can be found in the DAODeptInstB directory on the CD-ROM accompanying this book.

Summary

DAO is one of the most developed database access environments available. The help files in MSDN are extensive, and the functionality is more complete than that of several competing database access methodologies. However, DAO is specific to the Jet database engine that is used with Microsoft Access and Microsoft FoxPro. With an emphasis on open standards, ODBC and OLE DB have eclipsed DAO as the premier way to develop database applications. Still, there are DAO legacy systems and shops that still require DAO development, so DAO cannot be completely ignored. To recap:

◆ When doing new development, try to move to ODBC or OLE DB. It's what the rest of the industry is moving toward.

◆ DAO development inside MFC is much like that of ODBC, although the internal structure is somewhat different.

◆ Reporting in DAO is almost identical to that in ODBC.

◆ DAO database transactions are handled through the `CDaoWorkspace` object, although you can use the `CDaoDatabase.CanTransact` function to see if transactions are enabled with databases.

Appendix A

Database Error Codes

Error handling is important for any database manipulation. This appendix describes the OLE DB HRESULT error codes that are returned from OLE DB calls, and the SQL-STATE codes that can be retrieved from a database with either ODBC or OLE DB calls.

OLE DB HRESULT Error Codes

Most OLE DB functions return an HRESULT error code. You can use the defined variables in Table A-1 to test your HRESULT variables when an error occurs. The #define statements for these errors can be found in the OLEDBERR.H header file.

TABLE A-1 OLE DB HRESULT ERROR CODES

OLE DB HRESULT Error Code	Description
DB_E_ABORTLIMITREACHED	Your execution was aborted because a resource limit has been reached. No results are returned when this error occurs.
DB_E_ALREADYINITIALIZED	You tried to initialize a data source that has already been initialized.
DB_E_BADACCESSORFLAGS	Invalid accessor flags.
DB_E_BADACCESSORHANDLE	Invalid accessor handle.
DB_E_BADACCESSORTYPE	The specified accessor was not a parameter accessor.
DB_E_BADBINDINFO	Invalid binding information.
DB_E_BADBOOKMARK	Invalid bookmark.
DB_E_BADCHAPTER	Invalid chapter.
DB_E_BADCOLUMNID	Invalid column ID.
DB_E_BADCOMPAREOP	The comparison operator was invalid.

Continued

TABLE **A-1 OLE DB HRESULT ERROR CODES** *(Continued)*

OLE DB HRESULT Error Code	Description
DB_E_BADCONVERTFLAG	Invalid conversion flag.
DB_E_BADCOPY	Errors were detected during a copy.
DB_E_BADDYNAMICERRORID	The supplied DynamicErrorID was invalid.
DB_E_BADHRESULT	The supplied HRESULT was invalid.
DB_E_BADID	DB_E_BADID is deprecated. Use DB_E_BADTABLEID instead.
DB_E_BADLOCKMODE	Invalid lock mode.
DB_E_BADLOOKUPID	Invalid LookupID.
DB_E_BADORDINAL	The specified column number does not exist.
DB_E_BADPARAMETERNAME	The given parameter name is not recognized.
DB_E_BADPRECISION	A specified precision is invalid.
DB_E_BADPROPERTYVALUE	The value of a property is invalid.
DB_E_BADRATIO	Invalid ratio.
DB_E_BADRECORDNUM	The specified record number is invalid.
DB_E_BADREGIONHANDLE	Invalid region handle.
DB_E_BADROWHANDLE	Invalid row handle. This error often occurs when you are at BOF or EOF of a rowset and you try to update your data set.
DB_E_BADSCALE	A specified scale was invalid.
DB_E_BADSOURCEHANDLE	Invalid source handle.
DB_E_BADSTARTPOSITION	The rows offset specified would position you before the beginning or past the end of the rowset.
DB_E_BADSTATUSVALUE	The specified status flag was neither DBCOLUMNSTATUS_OK nor DBCOLUMNSTATUS_ISNULL.
DB_E_BADSTORAGEFLAG	One of the specified storage flags was not supported.
DB_E_BADSTORAGEFLAGS	Invalid storage flags.

OLE DB HRESULT Error Code	Description
DB_E_BADTABLEID	Invalid table ID.
DB_E_BADTYPE	A specified type was invalid.
DB_E_BADTYPENAME	The given type name was unrecognized.
DB_E_BADVALUES	Invalid value.
DB_E_BOOKMARKSKIPPED	Although the bookmark was validly formed, no row could be found to match it.
DB_E_BYREFACCESSORNOTSUPPORTED	By reference accessors are not supported by this provider.
DB_E_CANCELED	The change was canceled during notification; no columns are changed.
DB_E_CANNOTFREE	Ownership of this tree has been given to the provider. You cannot free the tree.
DB_E_CANNOTRESTART	The rowset was built over a live data feed and cannot be restarted.
DB_E_CANTCANCEL	The executing command cannot be canceled.
DB_E_CANTCONVERTVALUE	A literal value in the command could not be converted to the correct type due to a reason other than data overflow.
DB_E_CANTFETCHBACKWARDS	The rowset does not support backward scrolling.
DB_E_CANTFILTER	The requested filter could not be opened.
DB_E_CANTORDER	The requested order could not be opened.
DB_E_CANTSCROLLBACKWARDS	The rowset cannot scroll backwards.
DB_E_CANTTRANSLATE	Cannot represent the current tree as text.
DB_E_CHAPTERNOTRELEASED	The rowset was single-chaptered and the chapter was not released when a new chapter formation is attempted.
DB_E_CONCURRENCYVIOLATION	The rowset was using optimistic concurrency and the value of a column has been changed since it was last read.

Continued

TABLE **A-1 OLE DB HRESULT ERROR CODES** *(Continued)*

OLE DB HRESULT Error Code	Description
DB_E_COSTLIMIT	Unable to find a query plan within the given cost limit.
DB_E_DATAOVERFLOW	A literal value in the command overflowed the range of the type of the associated column.
DB_E_DELETEDROW	The row that is referred to has been deleted.
DB_E_DIALECTNOTSUPPORTED	The provider does not support the specified dialect.
DB_E_DUPLICATECOLUMNID	A column ID was occurred more than once in the specification.
DB_E_DUPLICATEDATASOURCE	A new data source is trying to be formed when a data source with that specified name already exists.
DB_E_DUPLICATEINDEXID	The specified index already exists.
DB_E_DUPLICATETABLEID	The specified table already exists.
DB_E_ERRORSINCOMMAND	The command contained one or more errors.
DB_E_ERRORSOCCURRED	Errors occurred. This message is thrown when an error occurs that is not captured by one of the other error messages.
DB_E_GOALREJECTED	No nonzero weights specified for any goals supported, so goal was rejected; current goal was not changed.
DB_E_INDEXINUSE	The specified index was in use.
DB_E_INTEGRITYVIOLATION	A specified value violated the referential integrity constraints for a column or table.
DB_E_INVALID	The rowset was not chaptered.
DB_E_INVALIDTRANSITION	A transition from ALL* to MOVE* or EXTEND* was specified.
DB_E_LIMITREJECTED	Some cost limits were rejected.
DB_E_MAXPENDCHANGESEXCEEDED	The number of rows with pending changes has exceeded the set limit.

OLE DB HRESULT Error Code	Description
DB_E_MULTIPLESTATEMENTS	The provider does not support multi-statement commands.
DB_E_MULTIPLESTORAGE	Multiple storage objects can not be open simultaneously.
DB_E_NEWLYINSERTED	The provider is unable to determine identity for newly inserted rows.
DB_E_NOAGGREGATION	A non-NULL controlling IUnknown was specified and the object being created does not support aggregation.
DB_E_NOCOMMAND	No command has been set for the command object.
DB_E_NOINDEX	The specified index does not exist.
DB_E_NOLOCALE	The specified locale ID was not supported.
DB_E_NONCONTIGUOUSRANGE	The specified set of rows was not contiguous to or overlapping the rows in the specified watch region.
DB_E_NOQUERY	Information was requested for a query, and the query was not set.
DB_E_NOTABLE	The specified table does not exist.
DB_E_NOTAREFERENCECOLUMN	Specified column does not contain bookmarks or chapters.
DB_E_NOTASUBREGION	The specified region is not a proper subregion of the region identified by the given watch region handle.
DB_E_NOTFOUND	No key matching the described characteristics could be found within the current range.
DB_E_NOTPREPARED	The command was not prepared.
DB_E_NOTREENTRANT	Provider called a method from IRowsetNotify in the consumer and the method has not yet returned.
DB_E_NOTSUPPORTED	The provider does not support this method.

Continued

TABLE **A-1** **OLE DB HRESULT ERROR CODES** *(Continued)*

OLE DB HRESULT Error Code	Description
DB_E_NULLACCESSORNOTSUPPORTED	Null accessors are not supported by this provider.
DB_E_OBJECTOPEN	An object was open.
DB_E_PARAMNOTOPTIONAL	No value given for one or more required parameters.
DB_E_PARAMUNAVAILABLE	The provider cannot derive parameter info and SetParameterInfo has not been called.
DB_E_PENDINGCHANGES	There are pending changes on a row with a reference count of zero.
DB_E_PENDINGINSERT	Unable to get visible data for a newly-inserted row that has not yet been updated.
DB_E_READONLYACCESSOR	Unable to write with a read-only accessor.
DB_E_ROWLIMITEXCEEDED	Creating another row would have exceeded the total number of active rows supported by the rowset.
DB_E_ROWSETINCOMMAND	Cannot clone a command object whose command tree contains a rowset or rowsets.
DB_E_ROWSNOTRELEASED	All HROWs must be released before new ones can be obtained.
DB_E_SCHEMAVIOLATION	Given values violate the database schema.
DB_E_TABLEINUSE	The specified table was in use.
DB_E_UNSUPPORTEDCONVERSION	Requested conversion is not supported.
DB_E_WRITEONLYACCESSOR	The given accessor was write-only.
DB_S_ASYNCHRONOUS	The operation is being processed asynchronously.
DB_S_BADROWHANDLE	Invalid row handle. This error often occurs when you are at BOF or EOF of a rowset and you try to update your data set.
DB_S_BOOKMARKSKIPPED	Skipped bookmark for deleted or non-member row.

OLE DB HRESULT Error Code	Description
DB_S_BUFFERFULL	Variable data buffer full. Increase system memory, commit open transactions, free more system memory, or declare larger buffers in your database setup.
DB_S_CANTRELEASE	Server cannot release or downgrade a lock until the end of the transaction.
DB_S_COLUMNSCHANGED	In order to reposition to the start of the rowset, the provider had to reexecute the query; either the order of the columns changed or columns were added to or removed from the rowset.
DB_S_COLUMNTYPEMISMATCH	One or more column types are incompatible. Conversion errors will occur during copying.
DB_S_COMMANDREEXECUTED	The provider re-executed the command.
DB_S_DELETEDROW	A given HROW referred to a hard-deleted row.
DB_S_DIALECTIGNORED	Input dialect was ignored and text was returned in different dialect.
DB_S_ENDOFROWSET	Reached start or end of rowset or chapter.
DB_S_ERRORSINTREE	Errors found in validating tree.
DB_S_ERRORSOCCURRED	Errors occurred.
DB_S_ERRORSRETURNED	The method had some errors; errors have been returned in the error array.
DB_S_GOALCHANGED	Specified weight was not supported or exceeded the supported limit and was set to 0 or the supported limit.
DB_S_LOCKUPGRADED	A lock was upgraded from the value specified.
DB_S_MULTIPLECHANGES	Updating this row caused more than one row to be updated in the data source.
DB_S_NONEXTROWSET	There are no more rowsets.
DB_S_NORESULT	There are no more results.
DB_S_PARAMUNAVAILABLE	A specified parameter was invalid.

Continued

Tᴀʙʟᴇ **A-1 OLE DB HRESULT ERROR CODES** *(Continued)*

OLE DB HRESULT Error Code	Description
DB_S_PROPERTIESCHANGED	One or more properties were changed as allowed by provider.
DB_S_ROWLIMITEXCEEDED	Fetching requested number of rows would have exceeded total number of active rows supported by the rowset.
DB_S_STOPLIMITREACHED	Execution stopped because a resource limit has been reached. Results obtained so far have been returned but execution cannot be resumed.
DB_S_TOOMANYCHANGES	The provider was unable to keep track of all the changes. You must refetch the data associated with the watch region using another method.
DB_S_TYPEINFOOVERRIDDEN	Caller has overridden parameter type information.
DB_S_UNWANTEDOPERATION	Consumer is uninterested in receiving further notification calls for this reason.
DB_S_UNWANTEDPHASE	Consumer is uninterested in receiving further notification calls for this phase.
DB_S_UNWANTEDREASON	Consumer is uninterested in receiving further notification calls for this reason.
DB_SEC_E_AUTH_FAILED	Authentication failed.
DB_SEC_E_PERMISSIONDENIED	Permission denied.
MD_E_BADCOORDINATE	Bad coordinate for the OLAP dataset.
MD_E_BADTUPLE	Bad tuple for the OLAP dataset
MD_E_INVALIDAXIS	The given axis is not valid for this OLAP dataset.
MD_E_INVALIDCELLRANGE	One or more of the given cell ordinals is invalid for this OLAP dataset.

SQL State Errors

The ANSI SQL '92 standard has defined SQLSTATE errors that all databases must return. Although most databases have their own error codes, most also can return an SQLSTATE code as well. With ODBC, the SQLGetDiagRec and SQLGetDiagField functions return SQLSTATE values that can be used for debugging. The SQLSTATE return string consists of a 5-character code. The first two characters of this code indicate the state of the error:

- ◆ Codes that begin with "00" indicate that a successful operation has completed.

- ◆ Codes that begin with "01" indicate a warning. In other words, an operation has successfully completed, but there was some minor error or unusual condition.

- ◆ Codes that begin with "07" indicate a variable or parameter problem, with type, access, or availability.

- ◆ Codes that begin with "08" indicate a connection problem.

- ◆ Codes that begin with "21" indicate a list problem. Probably an INSERT was issued that did not match the table.

- ◆ Codes that begin with "22" indicate that something was wrong with the data provided in an SQL statement. (i.e. Division by zero, string too long, number too large for field type, etc.)

- ◆ Codes that begin with "25" indicate that a transaction is being ended when it should not be. This usually occurs when a transaction is ended before a COMMIT or ROLLBACK command has been issued.

- ◆ Codes that begin with "28" indicate a user authorization error.

- ◆ Codes that begin with "34" indicate an invalid cursor name.

- ◆ Codes that begin with "3C" indicate a duplicate cursor name.

- ◆ Codes that begin with "3D" indicate an invalid catalog name.

- ◆ Codes that begin with "3F" indicate an invalid schema name.

- ◆ Codes that begin with "40" indicate a database integrity error.

- ◆ Codes that begin with "42" indicate an SQL syntax error.

- ◆ Codes that begin with "44" indicate a check option violation.

- ◆ Codes that begin with "HY" indicate a serious database engine error.

- ◆ Codes that begin with "IM" indicate an implementation warning or error, rather than a database error.

- ◆ Class values other than "01," except for the class "IM," indicate an error and are accompanied by a return code of SQL_ERROR. The class "IM" is specific to warnings and errors that derive from the implementation of the database engine itself. The subclass value "000" in any class indicates that there is no subclass for that SQLSTATE. The assignment of class and subclass values is defined by SQL92.

Note Although successful execution of a function is normally indicated by a return value of SQL_SUCCESS, the SQLSTATE 00000 also indicates success. Table A-2 shows the SQLSTATE error codes.

TABLE **A-2 SQLSTATE ERROR CODES**

SQLSTATE	Error
00000	No error
01000	General warning
01001	Cursor operation conflict
01002	Disconnect error
01003	NULL value eliminated in set function
01004	String data, right truncated
01006	Privilege not revoked
01007	Privilege not granted
01S00	Invalid connection string attribute
01S01	Error in row
01S02	Option value changed
01S06	Attempt to fetch before the result set returned the first rowset
01S07	Fractional truncation
01S08	Error saving File DSN
01S09	Invalid keyword
07001	Wrong number of parameters

SQLSTATE	Error
07002	COUNT field incorrect
07005	Prepared statement not a cursor-specification
07006	Restricted data type attribute violation
07009	Invalid descriptor index
07S01	Invalid use of default parameter
08001	Client unable to establish connection
08002	Connection name in use
08003	Connection does not exist
08004	Server rejected the connection
08007	Connection failure during transaction
08S01	Communication link failure
21S01	Insert value list does not match column list
21S02	Degree of derived table does not match column list
22001	String data, right truncated
22002	Indicator variable required but not supplied
22003	Numeric value out of range
22007	Invalid datetime format
22008	Datetime field overflow
22012	Division by zero
22015	Interval field overflow
22018	Invalid character value for cast specification
22019	Invalid escape character
22025	Invalid escape sequence
22026	String data, length mismatch
23000	Integrity constraint violation
24000	Invalid cursor state

Continued

TABLE **A-2 SQLSTATE ERROR CODES** *(Continued)*

SQLSTATE	Error
25000	Invalid transaction state
25S01	Transaction state
25S02	Transaction is still active
25S03	Transaction is rolled back
28000	Invalid authorization specification
34000	Invalid cursor name
3C000	Duplicate cursor name
3D000	Invalid catalog name
3F000	Invalid schema name
40001	Serialization failure
40002	Integrity constraint violation
40003	Statement completion unknown
42000	Syntax error or access violation
42S01	Base table or view already exists
42S02	Base table or view not found
42S11	Index already exists
42S12	Index not found
42S21	Column already exists
42S22	Column not found
44000	WITH CHECK OPTION violation
HY000	General error
HY001	Memory allocation error
HY003	Invalid application buffer type
HY004	Invalid SQL data type
HY007	Associated statement is not prepared
HY008	Operation canceled

SQLSTATE	Error
HY009	Invalid use of null pointer
HY010	Function sequence error
HY011	Attribute cannot be set now
HY012	Invalid transaction operation code
HY013	Memory management error
HY014	Limit on the number of handles exceeded
HY015	No cursor name available
HY016	Cannot modify an implementation row descriptor
HY017	Invalid use of an automatically allocated descriptor handle
HY018	Server declined cancel request
HY019	Non-character and non-binary data sent in pieces
HY020	Attempt to concatenate a null value
HY021	Inconsistent descriptor information
HY024	Invalid attribute value
HY090	Invalid string or buffer length
HY091	Invalid descriptor field identifier
HY092	Invalid attribute/option identifier
HY095	Function type out of range
HY096	Invalid information type
HY097	Column type out of range
HY098	Scope type out of range
HY099	Nullable type out of range
HY100	Uniqueness option type out of range
HY101	Accuracy option type out of range
HY103	Invalid retrieval code
HY104	Invalid precision or scale value

Continued

TABLE **A-2 SQLSTATE ERROR CODES** *(Continued)*

SQLSTATE	Error
HY105	Invalid parameter type
HY106	Fetch type out of range
HY107	Row value out of range
HY109	Invalid cursor position
HY110	Invalid driver completion
HY111	Invalid bookmark value
HYC00	Optional feature not implemented
HYT00	Timeout expired
HYT01	Connection timeout expired
IM001	Driver does not support this function
IM002	Data source name not found and no default driver specified
IM003	Specified driver could not be loaded
IM004	Driver's SQLAllocHandle on SQL_HANDLE_ENV failed
IM005	Driver's SQLAllocHandle on SQL_HANDLE_DBC failed
IM006	Driver's SQLSetConnectAttr failed
IM007	No data source or driver specified; dialog prohibited
IM008	Dialog failed
IM009	Unable to load translation DLL
IM010	Data source name too long
IM011	Driver name too long
IM012	DRIVER keyword syntax error
IM013	Trace file error
IM014	Invalid name of File DSN
IM015	Corrupt file data source

ADO Error Codes

The ADOINT.H header file contains ADO errors that can occur. These error are listed in Table A-3.

TABLE A-3 ADO ERROR CODES

Constant name	Number	Description
adErrInvalidArgument	3001	The application is using arguments that are of the wrong type, are out of acceptable range, or are in conflict with one another.
adErrNoCurrentRecord	3021	The current record pointer cannot be found. Either BOF or EOF is TRUE, or the current record has been deleted.
adErrIllegalOperation	3219	The operation requested by the application is not allowed.
adErrInTransaction	3246	Your program attempted a close of a Connection object while in the middle of a transaction.
adErrFeatureNotAvailable	3251	The provider does not support the operation requested by the application.
adErrItemNotFound	3265	You requested a specific item from a collection. This item was not found.
adErrObjectInCollection	3367	You tried to append an object to a collection when that object is already in the collection.
adErrObjectNotSet	3420	The object referenced by the application no longer points to a valid object.
adErrDataConversion	3421	An operation was attempted using the wrong data type.
adErrObjectClosed	3704	You requested an operation on a closed object.

TABLE **A-3 ADO ERROR CODES** *(Continued)*

Constant name	Number	Description
adErrObjectOpen	3705	The operation requested by the application is not allowed if the object is open.
adErrProviderNotFound	3706	ADO could not find the specified provider.
adErrBoundToCommand	3707	The application cannot change the Active-Connection property of a Recordset object with a Command object as its source.
adErrInvalidParamInfo	3708	You have improperly defined a Parameter object.
adErrInvalidConnection	3709	You requested an operation when you weren't connected to the database.
adErrNotReentrant	3710	The OLE DB Provider called a method from IRowsetNotify in the consumer and the method has not yet returned.
adErrStillExecuting	3711	An operation was called while the provider was still executing the last instruction.
adErrOperationCancelled	3712	The provider canceled an operation during notification. No columns are changed.
adErrStillConnecting	3713	An operation was attempted before the connection to the data source was completed.
adErrNotExecuting	3714	The cancel command cannot be executed because the command that was the application was attempting to cancel has finished executing.
adErrUnsafeOperation	3715	The provider has determined that this operation is unsafe to perform. The operation is canceled.

Appendix B

The ODBC API

Sometimes, you may find yourself needing to access the ODBC API directly instead of through the MFC. This appendix is designed to help you navigate through the ODBC API.

ODBC API Return Codes

Table B-1 describes the possible return codes that can result from an ODBC API call.

TABLE **B-1** ODBC API RETURN CODES

Return Code	Description
SQL_SUCCESS	Function completed successfully.
SQL_SUCCESS_WITH_INFO	Function completed successfully, but there was some informational warning that may have been issued. Additional information can be obtained by calling SQLError.
SQL_NO_DATA_FOUND	There was no syntax error, but a Recordset fetch retrieved no rows.
SQL_ERROR	Function failed. Additional information can be obtained by calling SQLError.
SQL_INVALID_HANDLE	Function failed because of an invalid environment handle, connection handle, or statement handle. This error indicates a programming error rather than a database error, and therefore no additional information is available from SQLError.
SQL_STILL_EXECUTING	A function that was started asynchronously is still executing. This message is somewhat obsolete since MFC uses only synchronous processing.
SQL_NEED_DATA	Parameter information is needed.

ODBC API Functions

Table B-2 lists the functions contained in the ODBC API.

TABLE **B-2** ODBC API FUNCTIONS

ODBC API Function	Description

`SQLRETURN SQLAllocHandle(`
`SQLSMALLINT HandleType,`
`SQLHANDLE InputHandle,`
`SQLHANDLE *OutputHandlePtr );`
	Obtains an environment, connection, statement, or descriptor handle:
	The input handle in whose context the new handle is to be allocated. If HandleType is SQL_HANDLE_ENV, InputHandle is SQL_NULL_HANDLE. If HandleType is SQL_HANDLE_DBC, InputHandle must be an environment handle, and if HandleType is SQL_HANDLE_STMT or SQL_HANDLE_DESC, InputHandle must be a connection handle.
	
	The OutputHandlePtr is a pointer to a buffer in which to return the handle to the newly allocated data structure. After calling SQLAllocHandle, you need to call SQLFreeHandle on the handles you get back from SQLAllocHandle to free allocated memory.
	
	Possible return values are SQL_SUCCESS, SQL_SUCCESS_WITH_INFO, SQL_INVALID_HANDLE, or SQL_ERROR.

`SQLBindCol`	Assigns storage for a result column and specifies the data type.
`SQLBindParameter`	Assigns storage for a parameter in an SQL statement.

ODBC API Function	Description
SQLRETURN SQLBrowseConnect(SQLHDBC ConnectionHandle, SQLCHAR *InConnectionString, SQLSMALLINT StringLength1, SQLCHAR *OutConnectionString, SQLSMALLINT BufferLength, SQLSMALLINT *StringLength2Ptr);	Returns successive levels of connection attributes and valid attribute values. When a value has been specified for each connection attribute, connects to the data source. Valid parameters are: **ConnectionHandle** is the connection handle defined in the SQLAllocHandle function; **InConnectionString** is the ODBC connection string to use for the connection; **StringLength1** is the length of the InConnectionString; **OutConnectionString** is a pointer to a buffer for the completed connection string. Upon successful connection to the target data source, this buffer contains the completed connection string. Applications should allocate at least 1,024 bytes for this buffer; **BufferLength** is length of the OutConnectionString; **StringLength2Ptr** is the pointer to a buffer in which to return the total number of characters (excluding the null-termination character) available.

Possible return values are SQL_SUCCESS, SQL_SUCCESS_WITH_INFO, SQL_NEED_DATA, SQL_ERROR, or SQL_INVALID_HANDLE. |
SQLBulkOperations	Performs bulk insertions and bulk bookmark operations, including update, delete, and fetch by bookmark.
SQLCancel	Cancels an SQL statement.
SQLCloseCursor	Closes a cursor that has been opened on a statement handle.
SQLColAttribute	Describes attributes of a column in the result set.
SQLColumnPrivileges	Returns a list of columns and associated privileges for one or more tables.

Continued

TABLE **B–2 ODBC API FUNCTIONS** *(Continued)*

ODBC API Function	Description
SQLColumns	Returns the list of column names in specified tables.
SQLRETURN SQLConnect(SQLHDBC ConnectionHandle, SQLCHAR *ServerName, SQLSMALLINT NameLength1, SQLCHAR *UserName, SQLSMALLINT NameLength2, SQLCHAR *Authentication, SQLSMALLINT NameLength3);	Connects to a specific driver by data source name, user ID, and password. The following variables are required: **ConnectionHandle** is the connection handle defined in the SQLAllocHandle function; **ServerName** is the ODBC data source name; **NameLength1** is the length of the ServerName; **UserName** is the user ID; **NameLength2** is the length of the UserName; **Authentication** is the authentification string. This is typically a password; **NameLength3** is the length of the Authenticaiton. Possible return values are SQL_SUCCESS, SQL_SUCCESS_WITH_INFO, SQL_ERROR, or SQL_INVALID_HANDLE.
SQLRETURN SQLDataSources(SQLHENV EnvironmentHandle, SQLUSMALLINT Direction, SQLCHAR *ServerName, SQLSMALLINT BufferLength1, SQLSMALLINT *NameLength1Ptr, SQLCHAR *Description, SQLSMALLINT BufferLength2, SQLSMALLINT *NameLength2Ptr);	Returns the list of available data sources. Valid parameters are: **EnvironmentHandle** is the environment handle defined in the SQLAllocHandle function; **Direction** is Determines which data source the Driver Manager returns information on. Valid values are SQL_FETCH_NEXT (to fetch the next data source name in the list), SQL_FETCH_FIRST (to fetch from the beginning of the list), SQL_FETCH_FIRST_USER (to fetch the first user DSN), or SQL_FETCH_FIRST_SYSTEM (to fetch the first system DSN); **ServerName** is the ODBC data source name; **BufferLength1** is the length of the ServerName; **NameLength1Ptr** is a pointer that points to bytes available in ServerName; **Description** is a pointer to a buffer in which to return the description of the driver associated with the data source; **BufferLength2** is the length of the description; **NameLength2Ptr** is a pointer that points to bytes available in the Description. Possible return values are SQL_SUCCESS, SQL_SUCCESS_WITH_INFO, SQL_NO_DATA, SQL_ERROR, or SQL_INVALID_HANDLE.

ODBC API Function	Description
SQLDescribeCol	Describes a column in the result set.
SQLDescribeParam	Returns the description for a specific parameter in a statement.
SQLDisconnect	Closes the connection.
SQLRETURN SQLDriverConnect(SQLHDBC ConnectionHandle, SQLHWND WindowHandle, SQLCHAR *InConnectionString, SQLSMALLINT StringLength1, SQLCHAR *OutConnectionString, SQLSMALLINTBufferLength, SQLSMALLINT *StringLength2Ptr, SQLUSMALLINT DriverCompletion);	Connects to a specific driver by connection string or requests that the Driver Manager and driver display connection dialog boxes for the user. The following variables are required: **ConnectionHandle** is the connection handle defined in the SQLAllocHandle function; **WindowHandle** is the handle of the parent window, if applicable, or a null pointer if not; **InConnectionString** is the ODBC connection string to use for the connection; **StringLength1** is the length of the InConnectionString; **OutConnectionString** is a pointer to a buffer for the completed connection string. Upon successful connection to the target data source, this buffer contains the completed connection string. Applications should allocate at least 1,024 bytes for this buffer; **BufferLength** is length of the OutConnectionString; **StringLength2Ptr** is the pointer to a buffer in which to return the total number of characters (excluding the null-termination character) available to return in; **DriverCompletion** is a flag that indicates whether the Driver Manager or driver must prompt for more connection information. Valid values for DriverCompletion are SQL_DRIVER_PROMPT, SQL_DRIVER_COMPLETE, SQL_DRIVER_COMPLETE_REQUIRED, or SQL_DRIVER_NOPROMPT.

Possible return values are SQL_SUCCESS, SQL_SUCCESS_WITH_INFO, SQL_NO_DATA, SQL_ERROR, or SQL_INVALID_HANDLE. |

Continued

TABLE **B-2 ODBC API FUNCTIONS** *(Continued)*

ODBC API Function	Description
SQLRETURN SQLDrivers(SQLHENV EnvironmentHandle, SQLUSMALLINT Direction, SQLCHAR *DriverDescription, SQLSMALLINT BufferLength1, SQLSMALLINT *DescriptionLengthPtr, SQLCHAR *DriverAttributes, SQLSMALLINT BufferLength2, SQLSMALLINT *AttributesLengthPtr);	Returns the list of installed drivers and their attribute keywords. The following parameters are required: **EnvironmentHandle** is the environment handle defined in the SQLAllocHandle function; **Direction** is Determines which data source the Driver Manager returns information on. Valid values are SQL_FETCH_NEXT (to fetch the next data source name in the list) or SQL_FETCH_FIRST (to fetch from the beginning of the list); **Driver Description** is a pointer to a buffer in which to return the description of the driver; **BufferLength1** is the length of the DriverDescription; **Description LengthPtr** is a pointer which contains the total number of bytes available to return in *Driver Description; **DriverAttributes** is a pointer to a buffer in which to return the list of driver attribute value pairs; **BufferLength2** is the length of the DriverAttributes buffer; **AttributesLengthPtr** is a pointer to a buffer which contains the total number of bytes available to return in *DriverAttributes.

Possible return values are SQL_SUCCESS, SQL_SUCCESS_WITH_INFO, SQL_NO_DATA, SQL_ERROR, or SQL_INVALID_HANDLE. |
SQLEndTran	Commits or rolls back a transaction.
SQLExecDirect	Executes a statement.
SQLExecute	Executes a prepared statement.
SQLFetch	Returns multiple result rows.
SQLFetchScroll	Returns scrollable result rows.
SQLForeignKeys	Returns a list of column names that make up foreign keys, if they exist for a specified table.
SQLFreeHandle	Releases an environment, connection, statement, or descriptor handle.
SQLFreeStmt	Ends statement processing, discards pending results, and, optionally, frees all resources associated with the statement handle.

ODBC API Function	Description
SQLGetCursorName	Returns the cursor name associated with a statement handle.
SQLGetData	Returns part or all of one column of one row of a result set (useful for long data values).
SQLGetDescField	Returns the value of a single descriptor field.
SQLGetDescRec	Returns the values of multiple descriptor fields.
SQLGetDiagField	Returns additional diagnostic information (a single field of the diagnostic data structure).
SQLGetDiagRec	Returns additional diagnostic information (multiple fields of the diagnostic data structure).
SQLGetEnvAttr	Returns the value of an environment attribute.
SQLRETURN SQLGetFunctions(SQLHDBCConnectionHandle, SQLUSMALLINTFunctionId, SQLUSMALLINT *SupportedPtr);	Returns supported driver functions. Parameters are: **ConnectionHandle** is the connection handle defined in the SQLAllocHandle function; **FunctionId** is a #define value that identifies the ODBC function of interest. Function IDs are available for viewing in the MSDN help; **SupportedPtr** is an SQLUSMALLINT variable that points to a SQL_TRUE or SQL_FALSE value if the specified function is supported.
SQLRETURN SQLGetInfo(SQLHDBC ConnectionHandle, SQLUSMALLINT InfoType, SQLPOINTER InfoValuePtr, SQLSMALLINT BufferLength, SQLSMALLINT *StringLengthPtr);	Returns information about a specific driver and data source. Parameters are: **ConnectionHandle** is the connection handle defined in the SQLAlloc Handle function; **InfoType** is the type of information. There are many types that are defined in the MSDN that came with Visual C++; **InfoValue Ptr** is a pointer to a buffer in which to return the information; **BufferLength** is length of the InfoValue Ptr; **StringLengthPtr** is the pointer to a buffer in which to return the total number of characters available to return in the InfoValuePtr buffer. Possible return values are SQL_SUCCESS, SQL_SUCCESS_WITH_INFO, SQL_ERROR, or SQL_INVALID_HANDLE.
SQLGetStmtAttr	Returns the value of a statement attribute.

Continued

TABLE **B-2** **ODBC API FUNCTIONS** *(Continued)*

ODBC API Function	Description
SQLRETURN SQLGetTypeInfo(SQLHSTMT StatementHandle, SQLSMALLINT DataType);	Returns information about supported data types. Parameters are: **StatementHandle** is the statement handle defined in the SQLAllocHandle function; **DataType** is a valid ODBC data type. These can be found in MSDN Help.
SQLMoreResults	Determines whether there are more result sets available and, if so, initializes processing for the next result set.
SQLNativeSql	Returns the text of an SQL statement as translated by the driver.
SQLNumParams	Returns the number of parameters in a statement.
SQLNumResultCols	Returns the number of columns in the result set.
SQLParamData	Used in conjunction with SQLPutData to supply parameter data at execution time. (Useful for long data values.)
SQLPrepare	Prepares an SQL statement for later execution.
SQLPrimaryKeys	Returns the list of column names that make up the primary key for a table.
SQLProcedureColumns	Returns the list of input and output parameters, as well as the columns that make up the result set for the specified procedures.
SQLProcedures	Returns the list of procedure names stored in a specific data source.
SQLPutData	Sends part or all of a data value for a parameter. (Useful for long data values.)
SQLRowCount	Returns the number of rows affected by an insert, update, or delete request.
SQLSetConnectAttr	Sets a connection attribute.
SQLGetConnectAttr	Returns the value of a connection attribute.
SQLSetCursorName	Specifies a cursor name.
SQLSetDescField	Sets a single descriptor field.
SQLSetDescRec	Sets multiple descriptor fields.

ODBC API Function	Description
SQLSetEnvAttr	Sets an environment attribute.
SQLSetPos	Positions a cursor within a fetched block of data, and allows an application to refresh data in the rowset, or update or delete data in the result set.
SQLSetScrollOptions	Sets options that control cursor behavior.
SQLSetStmtAttr	Sets a statement attribute.
SQLSpecialColumns	Returns information about the optimal set of columns that uniquely identifies a row in a specified table, or the columns that are automatically updated when any value in the row is updated by a transaction.
SQLStatistics	Returns statistics about a single table and the list of indexes associated with the table.
SQLTablePrivileges	Returns a list of tables and the privileges associated with each table.
SQLTables	Returns the list of table names stored in a specific data source.

ODBC 2.x Deprecated Functions

With the introduction of ODBC 3.0, several ODBC 2.x functions were deprecated (made obsolete). Table B-3 lists the functions that were deprecated, and the corresponding 3.x function that performs the same task. If there is any confusion, consult the MSDN help files to find out about these ODBC 3.x functions.

TABLE B-3 ODBC 2.X DEPRECATED FUNCTIONS

ODBC 2.x function	ODBC 3.x function
SQLAllocConnect	SQLAllocHandle
SQLAllocEnv	SQLAllocHandle

Continued

TABLE **B-3 ODBC 2.X DEPRECATED FUNCTIONS** *(Continued)*

ODBC 2.x function	ODBC 3.x function
SQLAllocStmt	SQLAllocHandle
SQLBindParam	SQLBindParameter
SQLColAttributes	SQLColAttribute
SQLError	SQLGetDiagRec
SQLFreeConnect	SQLFreeHandle
SQLFreeEnv	SQLFreeHandle
SQLFreeStmt	SQLFreeHandle
SQLGetConnectOption	SQLGetConnectAttr
SQLGetStmtOption	SQLGetStmtAttr
SQLParamOptions	SQLSetStmtAttr
SQLSetConnectOption	SQLSetConnectAttr
SQLSetParam	SQLBindParameter
SQLSetScrollOption	SQLSetStmtAttr
SQLSetStmtOption	SQLSetStmtAttr
SQLTransact	SQLEndTran

Appendix C

OLE DB Properties

OLE DB supports a myriad of properties. Some important properties are shown throughout this book, but a comprehensive list of OLE DB properties are listed in this appendix.

DBPROPSET_COLUMN Properties

DBPROPSET_COLUMN properties set or return information about a column. Table C-1 lists DBPROPSET_COLUMN properties.

TABLE C-1 DBPROPSET_COLUMN PROPERTIES

Property ID	Description
DBPROP_COL_AUTOINCREMENT	TRUE or FALSE indicating whether the values of the column are autoincrementing.
DBPROP_COL_DEFAULT	A VARIANT specifying the default value for an object (usually for setting defaults for a domain or column).
DBPROP_COL_DESCRIPTION	A string specifying a human-readable description of the specified column.
DBPROP_COL_FIXEDLENGTH	If the value of this property is TRUE, the column is fixed length and *ulColumnSize* in the DBCOLUMNDESC structure contains the fixed-length value. If the value of this property is FALSE or is not specified, the column is variable length and *ulColumnSize* represents the maximum size of the column.
DBPROP_COL_NULLABLE	TRUE or FALSE indicating whether a column can contain a NULL value.
DBPROP_COL_PRIMARYKEY	TRUE or FALSE indicating whether the column is part of the primary key.

Continued   605

TABLE C-1 DBPROPSET_COLUMN PROPERTIES *(Continued)*

Property ID	Description
DBPROP_COL_UNIQUE	TRUE or FALSE indicating whether values of the column must be unique in the table.
DBPROP_COLUMNLCID	The locale ID of the column.

DBPROPSET_DATASOURCEINFO Properties

DBPROPSET_DATASOURCEINFO properties set or return information about all data sources supported by this provider. Table C-2 lists DBPROPSET_DATASOURCEINFO properties.

TABLE C-2 DBPROPSET_DATASOURCEINFO PROPERTIES

Property ID	Description
DBPROP_ACTIVESESSIONS	The maximum number of sessions that can exist at the same time. If this property is set to zero, there is no limit on the number of sessions that can exist at one time.
DBPROP_ALTERCOLUMN	A bitmask describing which portions of the DBCOLUMNDESC structure can be used in a call to IAlterTable::AlterColumn. A combination of one or more of the following: DBCOLUMNDESCFLAG_TYPENAME DBCOLUMNDESCFLAG_ITYPEINFO DBCOLUMNDESCFLAG_PROPERTIES DBCOLUMNDESCFLAG_CLSID DBCOLUMNDESCFLAG_COLSIZE DBCOLUMNDESCFLAG_DBCID DBCOLUMNDESCFLAG_WTYPE DBCOLUMNDESCFLAG_PRECISION DBCOLUMNDESCFLAG_SCALE

Property ID	Description
DBPROP_ASYNCTXNABORT	TRUE or FALSE indicating whether transactions can be aborted asynchronously.
DBPROP_ASYNCTXNCOMMIT	TRUE or FALSE indicating whether transactions can be committed asynchronously.
DBPROP_BYREFACCESSORS	TRUE or FALSE indicating whether the provider supports the DBACCESSOR_PASSBYREF flag in IAccessor::CreateAccessor. This applies to both row and parameter accessors.
DBPROP_CATALOGLOCATION	The position of the catalog name in a qualified table name in a text command. It can be one of the following: DBPROPVAL_CL_START – The catalog name is at the start of the fully qualified name. DBPROPVAL_CL_END – The catalog name is at the end of the fully qualified name.
DBPROP_CATALOGTERM	The name the data source uses for a catalog; for example, "catalog", "database", or "directory". This is used for building user interfaces.
DBPROP_CATALOGUSAGE	This contains a bitmask specifying how catalog names can be used in text commands. A combination of zero or more of the following: DBPROPVAL_CU_DML_STATEMENTS – Catalog names are supported in all Data Manipulation Language statements. DBPROPVAL_CU_TABLE_DEFINITION – Catalog names are supported in all table definition statements. DBPROPVAL_CU_INDEX_DEFINITION – Catalog names are supported in all index definition statements. DBPROPVAL_CU_PRIVILEGE_DEFINITION – Catalog names are supported in all privilege definition statements.
DBPROP_COLUMNDEFINITION	A bitmask defining the valid clauses for the definition of a column. A combination of zero or more of the following:

Continued

TABLE **C-2 DBPROPSET_COLUMN PROPERTIES** *(Continued)*

Property ID	Description
	DBPROPVAL_CD_NOTNULL – Columns can be created non-nullable.
DBPROP_CONCATNULLBEHAVIOR	How the data source handles the concatenation of NULL-valued character data type columns with non–NULL-valued character data type columns. It can be one of the following:
	DBPROPVAL_CB_NULL – The result is NULL valued.
	DBPROPVAL_CB_NON_NULL – The result is the concatenation of the non–NULL-valued column or columns.
DBPROP_CONNECTIONSTATUS	The status of the current connection. It can be one of the following:
	DBPROPVAL_CS_UNINITIALIZED – The DSO is in an uninitialized state.
	DBPROPVAL_CS_INITIALIZED – The DSO is in an initialized state and able to communicate with the data store.
	DBPROPVAL_CS_COMMUNICATIONFAILURE – The DSO is unable to communicate with the data store.
	Some providers may have to silently spawn multiple connections to the database in order to support multiple concurrent Commands, Sessions, and Rowsets, according to DBPROP_MULTIPLE CONNECTIONS. For such providers, DBPROP_CONNECTIONSTATUS refers to the status of the primary connection, which was created when the user called Initialize.
DBPROP_DATASOURCENAME	The name of the data source. This might be used during the connection process.
DBPROP_DATASOURCEREADONLY	TRUE or FALSE indicating whether the data source is read-only.
DBPROP_DBMSNAME	The name of the product accessed by the provider.

Property ID	Description
DBPROP_DBMSVER	The version of the product accessed by the provider. The version is of the form ##.##.####, where the first two digits are the major version, the next two digits are the minor version, and the last four digits are the release version.
DBPROP_DSOTHREADMODEL	This contains a bitmask specifying the threading models supported by the data source object. A combination of one or more of the following: DBPROPVAL_RT_FREETHREAD DBPROPVAL_RT_APTMTTHREAD DBPROPVAL_RT_SINGLETHREAD
DBPROP_GROUPBY	The relationship between the columns in a GROUP BY clause and the nonaggregated columns in the select list. It can be one of the following:
	DBPROPVAL_GB_EQUALS_SELECT – The GROUP BY clause must contain all nonaggregated columns in the select list. It cannot contain any other columns. For example, SELECT DEPT, MAX(SALARY) FROM EMPLOYEE GROUP BY DEPT.
	DBPROPVAL_GB_COLLATE – A COLLATE clause can be specified at the end of each grouping column.
	DBPROPVAL_GB_CONTAINS_SELECT – The GROUP BY clause must contain all nonaggregated columns in the select list. It can contain columns that are not in the select list. For example, SELECT DEPT, MAX(SALARY) FROM EMPLOYEE GROUP BY DEPT, AGE.
	DBPROPVAL_GB_NO_RELATION – The columns in the GROUP BY clause and the select list are not related. The meaning of nongrouped, nonaggregated columns in the select list is data source–dependent. For example, SELECT DEPT, SALARY FROM EMPLOYEE GROUP BY DEPT, AGE.
DBPROP_HETEROGENEOUSTABLES	This contains a bitmask specifying whether the provider can join tables from different catalogs or providers. A combination of zero or more of the following:

Continued

TABLE **C-2 DBPROPSET_COLUMN PROPERTIES** *(Continued)*

Property ID	Description
	DBPROPVAL_HT_DIFFERENT_CATALOGS DBPROPVAL_HT_DIFFERENT_PROVIDERS
DBPROP_IDENTIFIERCASE	How identifiers treat case. It can be one of the following: DBPROPVAL_IC_UPPER — Identifiers in SQL are case insensitive and are stored in uppercase in system catalog. DBPROPVAL_IC_LOWER — Identifiers in SQL are case insensitive and are stored in lowercase in system catalog. DBPROPVAL_IC_SENSITIVE — Identifiers in SQL are case sensitive and are stored in mixed case in system catalog. DBPROPVAL_IC_MIXED — Identifiers in SQL are case insensitive and are stored in mixed case in system catalog.
DBPROP_MAXINDEXSIZE	The maximum number of bytes allowed in the combined columns of an index. If there is no specified limit or the limit is unknown, this value is set to zero.
DBPROP_MAXOPENCHAPTERS	The maximum number of chapters that can be open at any time. If a chapter must be released before a new chapter can be opened, this value is one; if the provider does not support chapters, this value is zero.
DBPROP_MAXORSINFILTER	The maximum number of disjunct conditions that can be supported in a view filter. Multiple conditions of a view filter are joined in a logical OR.
DBPROP_MAXROWSIZE	The maximum length of a single row in a table. If there is no specified limit or the limit is unknown, this value is set to zero.
DBPROP_MAXROWSIZEINCLUDESBLOB	TRUE or FALSE indicating whether the maximum row size returned for the DBPROP_MAXROWSIZE property includes the length of all BLOB data.

Property ID	Description
DBPROP_MAXSORTCOLUMNS	The maximum number of columns that can be supported in a View Sort. If there is no specified limit or the limit is unknown, this value is set to zero.
DBPROP_MAXTABLESINSELECT	The maximum number of tables allowed in the FROM clause of a SELECT statement. If there is no specified limit or the limit is unknown, this value is set to zero.
DBPROP_MULTIPLEPARAMSETS	TRUE or FALSE indicating whether the provider supports multiple parameter sets. Providers that support parameters support this property. Providers that do not support parameters do not support this property.
DBPROP_MULTIPLERESULTS	This contains a bitmask specifying whether the provider supports multiple results objects and what restrictions it places on these objects. A combination of zero or more of the following: DBPROPVAL_MR_SUPPORTED – The provider supports multiple results objects. DBPROPVAL_MR_CONCURRENT – More than one rowset created by the same multiple results object can exist concurrently. If this bit is not set, the consumer must release the current rowset before calling IMultipleResults::GetResult to get the next result. If multiple results objects are not supported, DBPROPVAL_MR_NOTSUPPORTED is returned.
DBPROP_MULTIPLE STORAGEOBJECTS	TRUE or FALSE indicating whether the provider supports multiple, open storage objects at the same time.
DBPROP_MULTITABLEUPDATE	TRUE or FALSE indicating whether the provider can update rowsets derived from multiple tables.
DBPROP_NULLCOLLATION	This property indicates where NULLs are sorted in a list. It can be one of the following: DBPROPVAL_NC_END – NULLs are sorted at the end of the list, regardless of the sort order.

Continued

TABLE C-2 **DBPROPSET_COLUMN PROPERTIES** *(Continued)*

Property ID	Description
	DBPROPVAL_NC_LOW – NULLs are sorted at the low end of the list.
	DBPROPVAL_NC_START – NULLs are sorted at the start of the list, regardless of the sort order.
DBPROP_OLEOBJECTS	This contains a bitmask specifying the ways in which the provider supports access to BLOBs and OLE objects stored in columns. A combination of zero or more of the following:
	DBPROPVAL_OO_BLOB – The provider supports access to BLOBs as structured storage objects. A consumer determines what interfaces are supported through DBPROP_STRUCTUREDSTORAGE.
	DBPROPVAL_OO_IPERSIST – The provider supports access to OLE objects through IPersistStream, IPersistStreamInit, or IPersistStorage.
DBPROP_ORDERBYCOLUMN SINSELECT	TRUE or FALSE indicating whether columns in an ORDER BY clause must be in the select list.
DBPROP_OUTPUTPARAME TERAVAILABILITY	The time at which output parameter values become available. It can be one of the following:
	DBPROPVAL_OA_NOTSUPPORTED – Output parameters are not supported.
	DBPROPVAL_OA_ATEXECUTE – Output parameter data is available immediately after ICommand::Execute returns.
	DBPROPVAL_OA_ATROWRELEASE – If a command returns a single result that is a rowset, output parameter data is available at the time the rowset is completely released. If a command returns multiple results, output parameter data is available when IMultipleResults::GetResult returns DB_S_NORESULT or the multiple results object is completely released, whichever occurs first. Before the output parameter data is available, the consumer's bound memory is in an indeterminate state.

Property ID	Description
DBPROP_PERSISTENTIDTYPE	An integer specifying the type of DBID that the provider uses when persisting DBIDs for tables, indexes, and columns. This is generally the type of DBID that the provider considers to be the most permanent under schema changes and physical data reorganizations. It can be one of the following: DBPROPVAL_PT_NAME DBPROPVAL_PT_PROPID DBPROPVAL_PT_GUID DBPROPVAL_PT_GUID_NAME DBPROPVAL_PT_GUID_PROPID DBPROPVAL_PT_PGUID_NAME DBPROPVAL_PT_PGUID_PROPID
DBPROP_PREPAREABORTBEHAVIOR	How aborting a transaction affects prepared commands. It can be one of the following:
	DBPROPVAL_CB_DELETE – Aborting a transaction deletes prepared commands. The application must reprepare commands before executing them.
	DBPROPAL_CB_PRESERVE – Aborting a transaction preserves prepared commands. The application can re-execute commands without repreparing them.
DBPROP_PREPARECOMMITBEHAVIOR	How committing a transaction affects prepared commands. It can be one of the following:
	DBPROPVAL_CB_DELETE – Committing a transaction deletes prepared commands. The application must reprepare commands before executing them.
	DBPROPAL_CB_PRESERVE – Committing a transaction preserves prepared commands. The application can re-execute commands without repreparing them.
DBPROP_PROCEDURETERM	A character string with the data source vendor's name for a procedure.
DBPROP_PROVIDERFRIENDLYNAME	The friendly name of the provider.
DBPROP_PROVIDERNAME	The filename of the provider.

Continued

TABLE **C-1 DBPROPSET_COLUMN PROPERTIES** *(Continued)*

Property ID	Description
DBPROP_PROVIDEROLEDBVER	The version of OLE DB supported by the provider. The version is of the form ##.##, where the first two digits are the major version and the next two digits are the minor version.
DBPROP_PROVIDERVER	The version of the provider. The version is of the form ##.##.####, where the first two digits are the major version, the next two digits are the minor version, and the last four digits are the release version. The provider can append a description of the provider.
DBPROP_QUOTEDIDENTIFIERCASE	How quoted identifiers treat case. It can be one of the following:
	DBPROPVAL_IC_UPPER – Quoted identifiers in SQL are case insensitive and are stored in uppercase in system catalog.
	DBPROPVAL_IC_LOWER – Quoted identifiers in SQL are case insensitive and are stored in lowercase in system catalog.
	DBPROPVAL_IC_SENSITIVE – Quoted identifiers in SQL are case sensitive and are stored in mixed case in system catalog.
	DBPROPVAL_IC_MIXED – Quoted identifiers in SQL are case insensitive and are stored in mixed case in system catalog.
DBPROP_ROWSETCONVERSIONSON COMMAND	TRUE or FALSE indicating whether callers to IConvertType::CanConvert can inquire on a command about conversions supported on rowsets generated by the command, or only about conversions supported by the command.
DBPROP_SCHEMATERM	The name the data source uses for a schema.
DBPROP_SCHEMAUSAGE	This contains a bitmask specifying how schema names can be used in text commands. A combination of zero or more of the following:

Property ID	Description
	DBPROPVAL_SU_DML_STATEMENTS — Schema names are supported in all Data Manipulation Language statements.
	DBPROPVAL_SU_TABLE_DEFINITION — Schema names are supported in all table definition statements.
	DBPROPVAL_SU_INDEX_DEFINITION — Schema names are supported in all index definition statements.
	DBPROPVAL_SU_PRIVILEGE_DEFINITION — Schema names are supported in all privilege definition statements.
DBPROP_SORTONINDEX	TRUE or FALSE indicating whether the provider supports SetSortOrder only for columns contained in an index.
DBPROP_SQLSUPPORT	This contains a bitmask specifying the level of support for SQL. A combination of zero or more of the following:
	DBPROPVAL_SQL_NONE — SQL is not supported.\ DBPROPVAL_SQL_ODBC_MINIMUM DBPROPVAL_SQL_ODBC_CORE DBPROPVAL_SQL_ODBC_EXTENDED — These levels correspond to the levels of SQL conformance defined in ODBC version 2.5. These levels are cumulative. That is, if the provider supports one level, it also sets the bits for all lower levels. For example, if the provider sets the DBPROPVAL_SQL_ODBC_CORE bit, it also sets the DBPROPVAL_SQL_ODBC_ MINIMUM bit.
	DBPROPVAL_SQL_ESCAPECLAUSES — The provider supports the ODBC escape clause syntax. DBPROPVAL_SQL_ANSI92_ENTRY DBPROPVAL_SQL_FIPS_TRANSITIONAL DBPROPVAL_SQL_ANSI92_INTERMEDIATE DBPROPVAL_SQL_ANSI92_FULL — These levels correspond to the levels in ANSI SQL92. These levels are cumulative. That is, if the provider supports one level, it also sets the bits for all lower levels.

Continued

TABLE **C-2 DBPROPSET_COLUMN PROPERTIES** *(Continued)*

Property ID	Description
	DBPROPVAL_SQL_ANS189_IEF–The provider supports the ANS189 Integrity Enhancement Facility
	DBPROPVAL_SQL_SUBMINIMUM – The provider supports the DBGUID_SQL dialect and parses the command text according to SQL rules, but does not support either the minimum ODBC level nor the ANSI SQL92 Entry level. This level is not accumulative; providers that support at least the minimal ODBC Level or ANSI SQL92 Entry Level do not set this bit. OLE DB consumers can determine whether or not the provider supports the DBGUID_SQL dialect by verifying that the DBPROPVAL_SQL_NONE bit is not set.
DBPROP_STRUCTUREDSTORAGE	This contains a bitmask specifying what interfaces the rowset supports on storage objects. If a provider can support any of these interfaces it is also required to support ISequentialStream. A combination of zero or more of the following: DBPROPVAL_SS_ISEQUENTIALSTREAM DBPROPVAL_SS_ISTREAM DBPROPVAL_SS_ISTORAGE DBPROPVAL_SS_ILOCKBYTES
DBPROP_SUBQUERIES	This contains a bitmask specifying the predicates in text commands that support subqueries. A combination of zero or more of the following: DBPROPVAL_SQ_CORRELATEDSUBQUERIES DBPROPVAL_SQ_COMPARISON DBPROPVAL_SQ_EXISTS DBPROPVAL_SQ_IN DBPROPVAL_SQ_QUANTIFIED
	The DBPROPVAL_SQ_CORRELATEDSUBQUERIES bit indicates that all predicates that support subqueries support correlated subqueries.
DBPROP_SUPPORTEDTXNDDL	Whether Data Definition Language (DDL) statements are supported in transactions. It can be one of the following:

Property ID	Description
	DBPROPVAL_TC_NONE – Transactions are not supported.
	DBPROPVAL_TC_DML – Transactions can only contain Data Manipulation Language (DML) statements. DDL statements within a transaction cause an error.
	DBPROPVAL_TC_DDL_COMMIT – Transactions can only contain DML statements. DDL statements within a transaction cause the transaction to be committed.
	DBPROPVAL_TC_DDL_IGNORE – Transactions can only contain DML statements. DDL statements within a transaction are ignored.
	DBPROPVAL_TC_ALL – Transactions can contain DDL and DML statements in any order.
DBPROP_SUPPORTEDTXNISOLEVELS	This contains a bitmask specifying the supported transaction isolation levels. A combination of zero or more of the following: DBPROPVAL_TI_CHAOS DBPROPVAL_TI_READUNCOMMITTED DBPROPVAL_TI_BROWSE DBPROPVAL_TI_CURSORSTABILITY DBPROPVAL_TI_READCOMMITTED DBPROPVAL_TI_REPEATABLEREAD DBPROPVAL_TI_SERIALIZABLE DBPROPVAL_TI_ISOLATED
DBPROP_SUPPORTEDTXNISORETAIN	This contains a bitmask specifying the supported transaction isolation retention levels. A combination of zero or more of the following:
	DBPROPVAL_TR_COMMIT_DC – The transaction may either preserve or dispose of isolation context across a retaining commit.
	DBPROPVAL_TR_COMMIT – The transaction preserves its isolation context (that is, it preserves its locks, if that is how isolation is implemented) across a retaining commit.

Continued

TABLE **C-2 DBPROPSET_COLUMN PROPERTIES** *(Continued)*

Property ID	Description
	DBPROPVAL_TR_COMMIT_NO — The transaction is explicitly not to preserve isolation across a retaining commit.
	DBPROPVAL_TR_ABORT_DC — The transaction may either preserve or dispose of isolation context across a retaining abort.
	DBPROPVAL_TR_ABORT — The transaction preserves its isolation context across a retaining abort.
	DBPROPVAL_TR_ABORT_NO — The transaction is explicitly not to preserve isolation across a retaining abort.
	DBPROPVAL_TR_DONTCARE — The transaction may preserve or dispose of isolation context across a retaining commit or abort. This is the default.
	DBPROPVAL_TR_BOTH — Isolation is preserved across both a retaining commit and a retaining abort.
	DBPROPVAL_TR_NONE — Isolation is explicitly not to be retained across either a retaining commit or abort.
	DBPROPVAL_TR_OPTIMISTIC — Optimistic concurrency control is to be used. If DBPROPVAL_TR_OPTIMISTIC is specified, then whatever isolation technology is in place (such as locking), it must be the case that other transactions' ability to make changes to the data and resources manipulated by this transaction is not in any way affected by the data read or updated by this transaction. That is, optimistic control is to be used for all data in the transaction.
DBPROP_TABLETERM	The name the data source uses for a table.
DBPROP_USERNAME	A character string with the name used in a particular database, which can be different than a login name.

DBPROPSET_DATASOURCE

DBPROPSET_DATASOURCE properties set or return information about a specific data source. Table C-3 lists DBPROPSET_DATASOURCE properties.

TABLE C-3 DBPROPSET_DATASOURCE PROPERTIES

Property ID	Description
DBPROP_CURRENTCATALOG	The name of the current catalog.
DBPROP_MULTIPLE CONNECTIONS	Some providers may have to spawn multiple connections to the database in order to support multiple concurrent Commands, Sessions, and Rowsets. Such providers may expose DBPROP_MULTIPLECONNECTIONS in order to let the consumer disable making additional connections under the covers. Providers that can support multiple concurrent Commands, Sessions, and Rowsets without spawning multiple connections do not support this property.
	TRUE indicates that the provider silently creates additional connections as required in order to support concurrent Command, Session, and Rowset objects. FALSE indicates the provider returns DB_E_OBJECTOPEN if a method would require spawning an additional connection to the database.
DBPROP_RESETDATASOURCE	This contains a bitmask specifying the data source state to be reset. A combination of zero or more of the following:
	DBPROPVAL_RD_RESETALL — The provider should reset all states associated with the data source, such that the DSO appears as if it were newly initialized, with the exception that any open object is not released.
	DBPROP_RESETDATASOURCE is generally used by a consumer in order to reuse an existing data source object without paying the cost of uninitializing and reinitializing the DSO.
DBPROP_SERVERNAME	The name of the server.

DBPROPSET_INDEX Properties

DBPROPSET_INDEX properties set or return information about a specific index on a table inside a data source. Table C-4 lists DBPROPSET_INDEX properties.

TABLE **C-4 DBPROPSET_INDEX PROPERTIES**

Property ID	Description
DBPROP_INDEX_AUTOUPDATE	TRUE indicates that the index is maintained automatically when changes are made to the corresponding base table. FALSE indicates that the consumer must maintain the index through explicit calls to IRowsetChange.
DBPROP_INDEX_CLUSTERED	TRUE or FALSE indicating whether an index is clustered.
DBPROP_INDEX_FILLFACTOR	For a B+-tree index, this property represents the storage utilization factor of page nodes during the creation of the index. The value is an integer from 1 to 100 representing the percentage of use of an index node. For a linear hash index, this property represents the storage utilization of the entire hash structure (the ratio of the used area to the total allocated area) before a file structure expansion occurs.
DBPROP_INDEX_INITIALSIZE	The total number of bytes allocated to this structure at creation time.
DBPROP_INDEX_NULLCOLLATION	How NULLs are collated in the index. It can be one of the following:
	DBPROPVAL_NC_END — NULLs are collated at the end of the list, regardless of the collation order.
	DBPROPVAL_NC_START — NULLs are collated at the start of the list, regardless of the collation order.
	DBPROPVAL_NC_HIGH — NULLs are collated at the high end of the list.
	DBPROPVAL_NC_LOW — NULLs are collated at the low end of the list.

Property ID	Description
DBPROP_INDEX_NULLS	Whether NULL keys are allowed. It can be one of the following values:
	DBPROPVAL_IN_DISALLOWNULL – The index does not allow entries where the key columns are NULL. If the consumer attempts to insert an index entry with a NULL key, then the provider returns an error.
	DBPROPVAL_IN_IGNORENULL – The index does not insert entries containing NULL keys. If the consumer attempts to insert an index entry with a NULL key, then the provider ignores that entry and no error code is returned.
	DBPROPVAL_IN_IGNOREANYNULL – The index does not insert entries where some column key has a NULL value. For an index having a multi-column search key, if the consumer inserts an index entry with NULL value in some column of the search key, then the provider ignores that entry and no error code is returned.
DBPROP_INDEX_PRIMARYKEY	Whether the index represents the primary key on the table.
DBPROP_INDEX_SORTBOOKMARKS	TRUE or FALSE indicating whether the index sorts repeated keys by bookmark.
DBPROP_INDEX_TEMPINDEX	TRUE or FALSE indicating whether the index is temporary.
DBPROP_INDEX_TYPE	The type of the index. It can be one of the following:
	DBPROPVAL_IT_BTREE – The index is a B+-tree.
	DBPROPVAL_IT_HASH – The index is a hash file using linear or extensible hashing.
	DBPROPVAL_IT_CONTENT – The index is a content index.
	DBPROPVAL_IT_OTHER – The index is some other type of index.

Continued

TABLE **C-4 DBPROPSET_INDEX PROPERTIES** *(Continued)*

Property ID	Description
DBPROP_INDEX_UNIQUE	TRUE or FALSE indicating whether index keys must be unique.

DBPROPSET_DBINIT Properties

DBPROPSET_DBINIT properties set or return information about initialization procedures needed to connect to a data source. Table C-5 lists DBPROPSET_DBINIT properties.

TABLE **C-5 DBPROPSET_DBINIT PROPERTIES**

Property ID	Description
DBPROP_AUTH_CACHE_AUTHINFO	TRUE or FALSE indicating whether the data source object or enumerator is allowed to cache sensitive authentication information such as a password in an internal cache.
DBPROP_AUTH_ENCRYPT_PASSWORD	TRUE or FALSE indicating whether the consumer requires that the password be sent to the data source or enumerator in an encrypted form. This property specifies a stronger form of masking than DBPROP_AUTH_MASKPASSWORD because it uses cryptographic techniques.
DBPROP_AUTH_INTEGRATED	A string containing the name of the authentication service used by the server to identify the user using the identity provided by an authentication domain.
DBPROP_AUTH_MASK_PASSWORD	TRUE or FALSE indicating whether the consumer requires that the password be sent to the data source or enumerator in a masked form.

Property ID	Description
DBPROP_AUTH_PASSWORD	The password to be used when connecting to the data source or enumerator. When the value of this property is retrieved with IDBProperties::GetProperties, the provider might return a mask such as "*******" or an empty string instead of the actual password.
DBPROP_AUTH_PERSIST_ENCRYPTED	TRUE or FALSE indicating whether the consumer requires that the data source object persist sensitive authentication information such as a password in encrypted form.
DBPROP_AUTH_PERSIST_SENSITIVE_AUTHINFO	TRUE or FALSE indicating whether the data source object is allowed to persist sensitive authentication information such as a password along with other authentication information.
DBPROP_AUTH_USERID	The user ID to be used when connecting to the data source or enumerator.
DBPROP_INIT_ASYNCH	This contains a bitmask specifying the asynchronous processing performed on the data source. A combination of zero or more of the following:
	DBPROPVAL_ASYNCH_INITIALIZE: IDBInitialize::Initialize returns immediately, but the actual initialization of the data source is done asynchronously. The data source behaves as an unititialized data source prior to completing the initialization process, except that any call to IDBInitialize returns E_UNEXPECTED.
	If no bits are set (the default), IDBInitialize::Initialize does not return until the data source is completely initialized.

Continued

TABLE **C–5 DBPROPSET_DBINIT PROPERTIES** *(Continued)*

Property ID	Description
DBPROP_INIT_CATALOG	The name of the initial, or default, catalog to use when connecting to the data source. If the provider supports changing the catalog for an initialized data source, the consumer can specify a different catalog name through the DBPROP_CURRENCATALOG property in the DBPROPSET_DATASOURCE property set after initialization.
DBPROP_INIT_DATASOURCE	The name of the database or enumerator to connect to. DBPROP_INIT_DATASOURCE is used to identify the data source to connect to, for instance a relational database server or a local file. If the provider uses two-part naming to identify the data source, then the data source name is qualified with the location specified in DBPROP_INIT_DATASOURCE.
DBPROP_INIT_HWND	The window handle to be used if the data source object or enumerator needs to prompt for additional information.
DBPROP_INIT_ IMPERSONATION_LEVEL	The level of impersonation that the server is allowed to use when impersonating the client. This property applies only to network connections other than Remote Procedure Call (RPC) connections; these impersonation levels are similar to those provided by RPC. The values of this property correspond directly to the levels of impersonation that can be specified for authenticated RPC connections, but can be applied to connections other than authenticated RPC. It can be one of the following: DB_IMP_LEVEL_ANONYMOUS – The client is anonymous to the server. The server process cannot obtain identification information about the client and cannot impersonate the client. DB_IMP_LEVEL_IDENTIFY – The server can obtain the client's identity. The server can impersonate the client for ACL checking but cannot access system objects as the client.

Property ID	Description
	DB_IMP_LEVEL_IMPERSONATE — The server process can impersonate the client's security context while acting on behalf of the client. This information is obtained when the connection is established, not on every call.
	DB_IMP_LEVEL_DELEGATE — The process can impersonate the client's security context while acting on behalf of the client. The server process can also make outgoing calls to other servers while acting on behalf of the client.
DBPROP_INIT_LCID	The locale ID of preference for the consumer. Consumers specify the LCID at initialization. This provides a method for the server to determine the consumer's LCID of choice in cases where it can use this information. This property does not guarantee that all text returned to the consumer will be translated according to the LCID.
	Providers may wish to set the *dwOptions* of the DBPROP structure for this property to DBPROPOPTIONS_OPTIONAL.
DBPROP_INIT_LOCATION	The location of the data source or enumerator to connect to. Typically, this will be a server name. DBPROP_INIT_LOCATION is used as the first part of a two-part name to qualify the data source specified in the DBPROP_INIT_DATASOURCE property. For example, if the data source is defined on a different machine, this might be the machine name on which to look for the data source definition. This is typically not used if the provider can identify the data source using a single name, such as the name of an RDBMS server, that the consumer can use to identify the data source directly.
DBPROP_INIT_MODE	This contains a bitmask specifying access permissions. A combination of zero or more of the following: DB_MODE_READ — Read-only. DB_MODE_WRITE — Write-only.

Continued

TABLE **C-5 DBPROPSET_DBINIT PROPERTIES** *(Continued)*

Property ID	Description
	DB_MODE_READWRITE–Read/w
	DB_MODE_SHARE_DENY_READ — Prevents others from opening in read mode.
	DB_MODE_SHARE_DENY_WRITE — Prevents others from opening in write mode.
	DB_MODE_SHARE_EXCLUSIVE — Prevents others from opening in read/write mode (DB_MODE_SHARE_DENY_READ | DB_MODE_SHARE_DENY_WRITE).
	DB_MODE_SHARE_DENY_NONE — Neither read nor write access can be denied to others.
DBPROP_INIT_OLEDBSERVICES	This contains a bitmask specifying OLE DB services to enable. A combination of zero or more of the following:
	DBPROPVAL_OS_RESOURCEPOOLING — Resources should be pooled.
	DBPROPVAL_OS_TXNENLISTMENT — Sessions in an MTS environment should automatically be enlisted in a global transaction where required (implies DBPROPVAL_OS_RESOURCEPOOLING).
	DBPROPVAL_OS_ENABLEALL (default) — All services should be invoked. By default, all services are enabled and invoked as requested. Individual services can be deselected by specifying the bitwise-OR of DBPROPVAL_OS_ENABLEALL along with the bitwise complement of any services to be deselected. For example, DBPROPVAL_OS_ ENABLEALL | ~DBPROPVAL_OS_TXNENLISTMENT enables all services except automatic transaction enlistment in an MTS environment.
DBPROP_INIT_PROMPT	This contains one of the following values indicating how to prompt the user during initialization:

Property ID	Description
	DBPROMPT_PROMPT — Always prompt the user for initialization information.
	DBPROMPT_COMPLETE — Prompt the user only if more information is needed.
	DBPROMPT_COMPLETEREQUIRED — Prompt the user only if more information is needed. Do not allow the user to enter optional information.
	DBPROMPT_NOPROMPT — Do not prompt the user.
DBPROP_INIT_PROTECTION_LEVEL	The level of protection of data sent between client and server. This property applies only to network connections other than RPC connections; these protection levels are similar to those provided by RPC. The values of this property correspond directly to the levels of protection that can be specified for authenticated RPC connections, but can be applied to connections other than authenticated RPC. It can be one of the following:
	DB_PROT_LEVEL_NONE — Performs no authentication of data sent to the server.
	DB_PROT_LEVEL_CONNECT — Authenticates only when the client establishes the connection with the server.
	DB_PROT_LEVEL_CALL — Authenticates the source of the data at the beginning of each request from the client to the server.
	DB_PROT_LEVEL_PKT — Authenticates that all data received is from the client.
	DB_PROT_LEVEL_PKT_INTEGRITY — Authenticates that all data received is from the client and that it has not been changed in transit.
	DB_PROT_LEVEL_PKT_PRIVACY — Authenticates that all data received is from the client, that it has not been changed in transit, and protects the privacy of the data by encrypting it.

Continued

TABLE **C-5 DBPROPSET_DBINIT PROPERTIES** *(Continued)*

Property ID	Description
DBPROP_INIT_PROVIDERSTRING	A string containing provider-specific, extended connection information. Use of this property implies that the consumer knows how this string will be interpreted and used by the provider. Consumers should use this property only for provider-specific connection information that cannot be explicitly described through the property mechanism.
DBPROP_INIT_TIMEOUT	The amount of time (in seconds) to wait for initialization to complete. For maximum user concurrency and component interoperability, providers for whom initialization is a potentially lengthy operation, such as connection across a network, are strongly encouraged to support this property.

DBPROP_ROWSET Properties

DBPROP_ ROWSET properties set or return information about a rowset. Table C-6 lists DBPROP_ROWSET properties.

TABLE **C-6 DBPROP_ROWSET PROPERTIES**

Property ID	Description
DBPROP_ABORTPRESERVE	TRUE or FALSE indicating whether, after aborting a transaction, the rowset remains active. That is, it is possible to fetch new rows, update, delete, and insert rows, and so on.
DBPROP_ACCESSORDER	The order in which columns must be accessed on the rowset. It can be one of the following values: DBPROPVAL_AO_RANDOM — Columns can be accessed in any order.

Property ID	Description
	DBPROPVAL_AO_SEQUENTIALSTORAGEOBJECTS — Columns bound as storage objects can only be accessed in sequential order as determined by the column ordinal. Further, storage objects from one row must be retrieved before calling GetData on any columns in any subsequent row. Calling GetData on a column bound as a storage object returns DBSTATUS_E_UNAVAILABLE for any columns bound as storage objects if (a) columns beyond the column bound as a storage object are specified in the accessor, (b) columns beyond the column bound as a storage object have been accessed in a previous call to GetData for that row, (c) GetData has been called for any columns on a row returned after the specified row, or (d) providers that never impose restrictions on column access ordering return DBPROPSTATUS_S_OK when this value is set. However, they upgrade the property to DBPROPVAL_AO_RANDOM such that calling GetProperty continues to return DBPROPVAL_AO_RANDOM for this property. BPROPVAL_AO_SEQUENTIAL — All columns must be accessed in sequential order determined by the column ordinal. Further, all columns from one row must be retrieved before calling GetData on any columns in any subsequent row. Calling GetData returns DBSTATUS_E_UNAVAILABLE for three different conditions. First, the column is bound as a storage object and columns beyond it are specified in the accessor. Second, columns beyond the bound column have been accessed in a previous call to GetData for that row. Finally, GetData has been called for any columns on a row returned after the specified row.
DBPROP_APPENDONLY	A rowset opened with this property set to TRUE will be initially empty. If the rowset was obtained by IOpenRowset::OpenRowset, this is equivalent to positioning the start of the rowset at the end of the table; if it was obtained by executing a command, it is equivalent to placing the start of the rowset at the end of the command's results. A rowset opened with DBPROP_APPENDONLY set to TRUE will be populated only by those rows inserted in it.

Continued

TABLE **C-6 DBPROP_ROWSET PROPERTIES** *(Continued)*

Property ID	Description
	Setting DBPROP_APPENDONLY to TRUE also requires that DBPROP_IROWSETCHANGE and DBPROP_OWNINSERT are set to TRUE, DBPROP_OTHERINSERT is set to FALSE, and DBPROP_UPDATABILITY has the flag DBPROPVAL_UP_INSERT set.
DBPROP_BLOCKINGSTORAGE-OBJECTS	TRUE or FALSE indicating whether instantiated storage objects might prevent the use of other methods on the rowset.
DBPROP_BOOKMARKINFO	This contains a bitmask with the value of zero or of DBPROPVAL_BI_CROSSROWSET, which indicates that bookmark values returned by this rowset are valid across rowsets with the same metadata. If not set, bookmark values are specific to this rowset and are not guaranteed to return the same values in other rowsets, even those resulting from the same specification.
DBPROP_BOOKMARKS	TRUE or FALSE indicating whether the rowset supports bookmarks. If bookmarks are supported, column 0 is the bookmark for the rows. If FALSE, the rowset is sequential and the values of the DBPROP_LITERALBOOKMARKS and DBPROP_ORDEREDBOOKMARKS properties are ignored.
	The value of this property is automatically set to TRUE if the value of DBPROP_IRowsetLocate, DBPROP_LITERALBOOKMARKS, or DBPROP_ORDEREDBOOKMARKS is set to TRUE.
DBPROP_BOOKMARKSKIPPED	TRUE or FALSE indicating whether the rowset allows IRowsetLocate::GetRowsAt, IRowsetScroll::GetApproximatePosition, or IRowsetFind::FindNextRow if a bookmark row was deleted, is a row to which the consumer does not have access rights, or is no longer a member of the rowset.

Property ID	Description
DBPROP_BOOKMARKTYPE	The bookmark type supported by the rowset. It can be either DBPROPVAL_BMK_NUMERIC or DBPROPVAL_BMK_KEY.
	DBPROPVAL_BMK_NUMERIC indicates that the bookmark type is numeric. Numeric bookmarks are based upon a row property that is not dependent on the values of the row's columns. For instance, they can be based on the absolute position of the row within a rowset, or on a row ID that the storage engine assigned to a tuple at its creation. Modifying the row's columns does not change the validity of numeric bookmarks.
	DBPROPVAL_BMK_KEY indicates that the bookmark type is key. Key bookmarks are based on the values of one or more of the row's columns and these values form a unique key for each row.
DBPROP_CACHEDEFERRED	TRUE or FALSE indicating whether the provider caches the value of a deferred column when the consumer first gets a value from that column.
	Consumers should set the value of this property to TRUE rather sparingly, because it might require substantial memory use in the provider. Such use might limit the number of rows that can be held at one time. Setting the value of this property to TRUE automatically sets the value of the DBPROP_DEFERRED property to TRUE.
DBPROP_CANFETCHBACKWARDS	TRUE or FALSE indicating whether the rowset can fetch backward. If TRUE, *cRows* in IRowset::GetNextRows, IRowsetLocate::GetRowsAt, and IRowsetScroll::GetRowsAtRatio can be negative. When it is negative, these methods fetch rows backward from the specified row.
DBPROP_CANHOLDROWS	TRUE or FALSE indicating whether the rowset allows the consumer to retrieve more rows or change the next fetch position while holding previously fetched rows with pending changes.

Continued

TABLE **C-6 DBPROP_ROWSET PROPERTIES** *(Continued)*

Property ID	Description
DBPROP_CANSCROLLBACKWARDS	TRUE or FALSE indicating whether the rowset can scroll backward. If TRUE, the *lRowsOffset* parameter in the IRowset::GetNextRows or IRowsetLocate::GetRowsAt functions can be negative.
	If the rowset supports IRowsetLocate, then the value of this property is TRUE, because this method supports backward scrolling by definition.
DBPROP_CHANGEINSERTEDROWS	TRUE or FALSE indicating whether the consumer can call IRowsetChange::DeleteRows or IRowsetChange::SetData for newly inserted rows.
	A newly inserted row is a row for which the insertion has been transmitted to the data source. This should not be confused with a pending insert row which has not yet been transmitted to the database. Pending rows may have other properties depending on the provider.
DBPROP_COLUMNRESTRICT	TRUE or FALSE indicating whether access rights are restricted on a column-by-column basis. If the rowset exposes IRowsetChange, IRowsetChange::SetData cannot be called for at least one column. A provider must not execute a query that would specify a column for which the consumer has no read access rights.
DBPROP_COMMANDTIMEOUT	Contains the number of seconds before a command times out. A value of 0 indicates an infinite timeout.
DBPROP_COMMITPRESERVE	TRUE or FALSE indicating whether, after committing a transaction, the rowset remains active. That is, it is possible to fetch new rows, update, delete, and insert rows, and so on. If FALSE, after committing a transaction, the only operations allowed on a rowset are to release row and accessor handles and to release the rowset.

Property ID	Description
DBPROP_DEFERRED	TRUE or FALSE indicating whether the data in the column is not fetched until an accessor is used on the column. If FALSE, the data in the column is fetched when the row containing it is fetched.
	The value of this property is automatically set to TRUE if the value of the DBPROP_CACHEDEFERRED property is set to TRUE.
DBPROP_DELAYSTORAGEOBJECTS	TRUE or FALSE indicating whether, in delayed update mode, storage objects are also used in delayed update mode. Setting this to TRUE has three consequences *only if the rowset is in immediate update mode*. First, changes to the object are not transmitted to the data source until IRowsetUpdate::Update is called. Second, IRowsetUpdate::Undo undoes any pending changes. Finally, IRowsetUpdate::GetOriginalData retrieves the original value of the object.
DBPROP_FILTERCOMPAREOPS	This contains a bitmask describing the comparison operations supported by IViewFilter for a particular column. If no column is specified, this is the full set of comparison operators that may be supported:
	DBPROPVAL_CO_EQUALITY — Provider supports the following comparison operators: DBCOMPAREOPS_LT DBCOMPAREOPS_LE DBCOMPAREOPS_EQ DBCOMPAREOPS_GE DBCOMPAREOPS_GT DBCOMPAREOPS_NE
	DBPROPVAL_CO_STRING — Provider supports the DBCOMPAREOPS_BEGINSWITH.
	DBPROPVAL_CO_CONTAINS — Provider supports DBCOMPAREOPS_CONTAINS and DBCOMPAREOPS_NOTCONTAINS.
	DBPROPVAL_CO_BEGINSWITH — Provider supports DBCOMPAREOPS_BEGINSWITH and DBCOMPAREOPS_NOTBEGINSWITH.

Continued

TABLE **C-6 DBPROP_ROWSET PROPERTIES** *(Continued)*

Property ID	Description
	DBPROPVAL_CO_CASESENSITIVE — Provider supports the DBCOMPAREOPS_CASESENSITIVE modifier.
	DBPROPVAL_CO_CASEINSENSITIVE — Provider supports the DBCOMPAREOPS_CASEINSENSITIVE modifier.
	Providers supports DBPROPVAL_CO_CASESENSITIVE, or DBPROPVAL_CO_CASEINSENSITIVE, or both.
DBPROP_FINDCOMPAREOPS	A bitmask describing the comparison operations supported by IRowsetFind for a particular column. If no column is specified, this is the full set of comparison operators that may be supported:
	DBPROPVAL_CO_EQUALITY — Provider supports the following comparison operators: DBCOMPAREOPS_LT DBCOMPAREOPS_LE DBCOMPAREOPS_EQ DBCOMPAREOPS_GE DBCOMPAREOPS_GT DBCOMPAREOPS_NE
	DBPROPVAL_CO_STRING — Provider supports the following comparison operators: DBCOMPAREOPS_BEGINSWITH
	DBPROPVAL_CO_CONTAINS — Provider supports the following comparison operators: DBCOMPAREOPS_CONTAINS DBCOMPAREOPS_NOTCONTAINS
	DBPROPVAL_CO_BEGINSWITH — Provider supports the following comparison operators: DBCOMPAREOPS_BEGINSWITH DBCOMPAREOPS_NOTBEGINSWITH
	DBPROPVAL_CO_CASESENSITIVE — Provider supports the DBCOMPAREOPS_CASESENSITIVE modifier.
	DBPROPVAL_CO_CASEINSENSITIVE — Provider supports the DBCOMPAREOPS_CASEINSENSITIVE modifier.

Property ID	Description
	All providers that support IRowsetFind must support DBPROPVAL_CO_EQUALITY and DBPROPVAL_CO_STRING.
	Providers may support one, or the other, or both of DBPROPVAL_CO_CASESENSITIVE and DBPROPVAL_CO_CASEINSENSITIVE.
DBPROP_IACCESSOR DBPROP_ICHAPTEREDROWSET DBPROP_ICOLUMNSINFO DBPROP_ICOLUMNSROWSET DBPROP_ICONNECTIONPOINT CONTAINER DBPROP_ICONVERTTYPE DBPROP_IDBASYNCHSTATUS DBPROP_IMULTIPLERESULTS DBPROP_IROWSET DBPROP_IROWSETCHANGE DBPROP_IROWSETFIND DBPROP_IROWSETIDENTITY DBPROP_IROWSETINDEX DBPROP_IROWSETINFO DBPROP_IROWSETLOCATE DBPROP_IROWSETREFRESH DBPROP_IROWSETSCROLL DBPROP_IROWSETUPDATE DBPROP_IROWSETVIEW DBPROP_ISUPPORTERRORINFO	If the value of any of these properties is set to TRUE, the rowset supports the specified interface. Providers that support an interface must support the property associated with that interface with a value of TRUE. These properties are primarily used to request interfaces through ICommandProperties:: SetProperties. The values of the DBPROP_IRowset, DBPROP_I Accessor, DBPROP_IColumnsInfo, DBPROP_IConvert Type, and DBPROP_IRowsetInfo properties are read-only and are always TRUE. They cannot be set to FALSE. If the consumer does not set the value of any of these properties to true, the resulting rowset supports IRowset, IAccessor, IColumnsInfo, IConvertType, and IRowsetInfo. Setting DBPROP_IRowsetLocate to TRUE implicitly causes the created rowset to support bookmarks and IRowsetInfo::GetProperties will return TRUE for the property DBPROP_BOOKMARKS. Setting DBPROP_IRowsetUpdate to TRUE automatically sets DBPROP_IRowsetChange to TRUE.
DBPROP_ILOCKBYTES DBPROP_ISEQUENTIALSTREAM DBPROP_ISTORAGE DBPROP_ISTREAM	If the value of this property is set to TRUE, then the rowset is capable of manipulating the contents of columns as a storage object supporting the specified interface. The provider reports its ability to enable this property on a per-column basis by setting the flag DBPROPFLAGS_COLUMNOK. A provider that does not have the ability to turn the property on/off on a per-column basis, does not set

Continued

TABLE C-6 DBPROP_ROWSET PROPERTIES *(Continued)*

Property ID	Description
	DBPROPFLAGS_COLUMNOK. Regardless of whether the property is supported in the rowset as a whole or on a per-column basis, the ability to manipulate a column value as a storage object depends on whether the provider supports the coercion from the column's native type (BLOB or non-BLOB) to the particular storage interface.
DBPROP_IMMOBILEROWS	If this is TRUE, the rowset will not reorder inserted or updated rows. Rows inserted using the IRowsetChange::InsertRow function will appear at the end of the rowset. If FALSE and the rowset is ordered, then inserted rows and updated rows (where one or more of the columns in the ordering criteria are updated) obey the ordering criteria of the rowset. If the rowset is not ordered, then inserted rows are not guaranteed to appear in a determinate position, and the position of updated rows is not changed.
DBPROP_LITERALBOOKMARKS	TRUE or FALSE indicating whether bookmarks can be compared literally. That is, they can be compared as a sequence of bytes. Furthermore, if the bookmarks are ordered (as specified by the DBPROP_ORDERED BOOKMARKS property), the bytes are guaranteed to be ordered so that an arithmetic comparison as their scalar type yields the same result as a call to IRowsetLocate::Compare. Setting the value of this property to TRUE automatically sets the value of DBPROP_BOOKMARKS to TRUE.
DBPROP_LITERALIDENTITY	TRUE or FALSE indicating whether the consumer can perform a binary comparison of two row handles to determine whether they point to the same row. FALSE indicates that the consumer must call IRowsetIdentity::IsSameRow to determine whether two row handles point to the same row.
DBPROP_LOCKMODE	The level of locking peformed by the rowset. It can be one of the following:

Property ID	Description
	DBPROPVAL_LM_NONE — The provider is not required to lock rows at any time to ensure successful updates. Updates may fail when sent to the server for reasons of concurrency (for example, if someone else has updated the row).
	DBPROPVAL_LM_SINGLEROW — The provider uses the minimum level of locking necessary to ensure that changes successfully written to a single row returned by the most recent fetch will not fail due to a concurrency violation if Update is called before any additional rows are retrieved. Typically this means that the provider takes a lock on the row when SetData is first called on the row, but the provider may lock the row as early as when it is read in order to guarantee that calling Update will succeed.
	Lock Mode and Isolation Level are closely related, but distinct. A consumer's isolation level specifies the isolation of that consumer from changes made by other users to the underlying data. Lock mode defines when underlying data is locked in order to ensure updates succeed. The provider may use locking in order to enforce higher levels of isolation, in which case a higher level of locking may occur than required to enforce the specified lock mode. Lock mode specifies the minimum level of locking.
DBPROP_MAXOPENROWS	The maximum number of rows that can be active at the same time. This limit does not reflect resource limitations such as RAM, but does apply if the rowset implementation uses some strategy that results in a limit. If there is no limit, the value of this property is zero. The provider is free to support a greater number of active rows than the maximum specified by the consumer. In this case, the provider will return its actual maximum number of active rows instead of the value specified by the consumer.

Continued

TABLE **C-6 DBPROP_ROWSET PROPERTIES** *(Continued)*

Property ID	Description
DBPROP_MAXPENDINGROWS	The maximum number of rows that can have pending changes at the same time. This limit does not reflect resource limitations such as Random Access Memory (RAM), but does apply if the rowset implementation uses some strategy that results in a limit. If there is no limit, this value is zero. The provider is free to support a greater number of pending rows than the maximum specified by the consumer. In this case, the provider will return its actual maximum number of pending rows instead of the value specified by the consumer.
DBPROP_MAXROWS	The maximum number of rows that can be returned in a rowset. If there is no limit, this value is zero. If the provider supports setting DBPROP_MAXROWS the provider must ensure that the rowset never contains more than the specified number of rows.
DBPROP_MAYWRITECOLUMN	TRUE or FALSE indicating whether a particular column is writable or not. This property can be set implicitly through the command used to create the rowset. For example, if the rowset is created by the SQL statement SELECT A, B FROM MyTable FOR UPDATE OF A, then this property is TRUE for column A and FALSE for column B.
DBPROP_MEMORYUSAGE	This property estimates the amount of memory that can be used by the rowset. If it is 0, the rowset can use unlimited memory. If it is between 1 and 99 inclusive, the rowset can use the specified percentage of total available virtual memory (physical and page file). If it is greater than or equal to 100, the rowset can use up to the specified number of kilobytes of memory.
DBPROP_NOTIFICATION GRANULARITY	This function describes how the OLE DB notifies occur. It can be one of the following values: DBPROPVAL_NT_SINGLEROW — For methods that operate on multiple rows, the provider calls IRowsetNotify::OnRowChange separately for each phase for each row. A cancellation affects a single row; it does not affect the other rows, and notifications are still sent for these rows.

Property ID	Description
	DBPROPVAL_NT_MULTIPLEROWS – For methods that operate on multiple rows, then for each phase, the provider calls OnRowChange once for all rows that succeed and once for all rows that fail. This separation can occur at each phase where a change can fail. For example, if IRowsetChange::DeleteRows deletes some rows and fails to delete others during the Preliminary Work phase, it calls OnRowChange twice: once with DBEVENTPHASE_SYNCHAFTER and the array of handles of rows that it deleted, and once with DBEVENTPHASE_FAILEDTODO and the array of handles of rows it failed to delete. A cancellation affects all rows with handles that were passed to OnRowChange.
	DBPROP_NOTIFICATIONGRANULARITY does not affect how providers return notifications about events that affect columns or the entire rowset.
DBPROP_NOTIFICATIONPHASES	This contains a bitmask specifying the notification phases supported by the provider. A combination of two or more of the following: DBPROPVAL_NP_OKTODO DBPROPVAL_NP_ABOUTTODO DBPROPVAL_NP_SYNCHAFTER DBPROPVAL_NP_FAILEDTODO DBPROPVAL_NP_DIDEVENT
	The DBPROPVAL_NP_FAILEDTODO and DBPROPVAL_NP_DIDEVENT bits must be returned by all providers that support notifications.
DBPROP_NOTIFYCOLUMNSET DBPROP_NOTIFYROWDELETE DBPROP_NOTIFYROW FIRSTCHANGE DBPROP_NOTIFYROWINSERT DBPROP_NOTIFYROWRESYNCH DBPROP_NOTIFYROWSETRELEASE DBPROP_NOTIFYROWSETFETCH- POSITIONCHANGE DBPROP_NOTIFYROWUNDOCHANGE	These properties contain a bitmask specifying whether the notification phase is cancelable. A combination of zero or more of the following: DBPROPVAL_NP_OKTODO DBPROPVAL_NP_ABOUTTODO DBPROPVAL_NP_SYNCHAFTER

Continued

TABLE **C-6 DBPROP_ROWSET PROPERTIES** *(Continued)*

Property ID	Description
DBPROP_NOTIFYROWUNDODELETE DBPROP_NOTIFYROWUNDOINSERT DBPROP_NOTIFYROWUPDATE	
DBPROP_ORDEREDBOOKMARKS	TRUE or FALSE indicating whether bookmarks can be compared to determine the relative position of their associated rows in the rowset. Setting the value of this property to TRUE automatically sets the value of DBPROP_BOOKMARKS to TRUE.
	Whether bookmarks can be compared byte-by-byte or must be compared with IRowsetLocate::Compare depends on the value of the DBPROP_LITERALBOOKMARKS property.
DBPROP_OTHERINSERT	TRUE or FALSE indicating whether the rowset can see rows inserted by someone other than a consumer of the rowset. That is, if someone other than a consumer of the rowset inserts a row, any consumer of the rowset can see that row the next time it fetches a set of rows containing it. This includes rows inserted by other parties in the same transaction, as well as rows inserted by parties outside the transaction.
	The transaction isolation level does not affect the ability of the rowset to see rows inserted by other parties in the same transaction, such as other rowsets in the same session. However, it does restrict the ability of the rowset to see rows inserted by parties outside the transaction.
	For programmers accustomed to the cursor model in ODBC, the DBPROP_OTHERUPDATEDELETE and DBPROP_OTHERINSERT properties correspond to ODBC cursors as follows: Static cursor: DBPROP_OTHERINSERT = FALSE DBPROP_OTHERUPDATEDELETE = FALSE

Property ID	Description
	Keyset-driven cursor: DBPROP_OTHERINSERT = FALSE DBPROP_OTHERUPDATEDELETE = TRUE Dynamic cursor: DBPROP_OTHERINSERT = TRUE DBPROP_OTHERUPDATEDELETE = TRUE
	Furthermore, the DBPROP_OWNUPDATEDELETE and DBPROP_OWNINSERT properties correspond to the values returned by the SQL_STATIC_SENSITIVITY information type in SQLGetInfo in ODBC.
DBPROP_OTHERUPDATEDELETE	TRUE or FALSE indicating whether the rowset can see updates and deletes made by someone other than a consumer of the rowset. That is, suppose someone other than a consumer of the rowset updates the data underlying a row or deletes the row. If the row is released completely, any consumer of the rowset will see that change the next time it fetches the row. This includes updates and deletes made by other parties in the same transaction, as well as updates and deletes made by parties outside the transaction. The transaction isolation level does not affect the ability of the rowset to see updates or deletes made by other parties in the same transaction, such as other rowsets in the same session. However, it does restrict the ability of the rowset to see updates or deletes made by parties outside the transaction.
DBPROP_OWNINSERT	TRUE or FALSE indicating whether the rowset can see its own inserts. That is, if a consumer of a rowset inserts a row, any consumer of the rowset can see that row the next time it fetches a set of rows containing it.

Continued

TABLE **C-6 DBPROP_ROWSET PROPERTIES** *(Continued)*

Property ID	Description
DBPROP_OWNUPDATEDELETE	TRUE or FALSE indicating whether the rowset can see its own updates and deletes. That is, suppose a consumer of the rowset updates or deletes a row. If the row is released completely, any consumer of the rowset will see the update or delete the next time it fetches that row.
	This ability is independent of the transaction isolation level because all consumers of the rowset share the same transaction.
DBPROP_QUICKRESTART	TRUE or FALSE indicating whether the IRowset::RestartPosition function is relatively quick to execute. In particular, it does not reexecute the command that created the rowset. FALSE indicates that the RestartPosition function is expensive to execute and requires reexecuting the command that created the rowset.
	Although the value of this property can be set to TRUE, the provider is not required to honor it. The reason for this is that the provider does not know what the command is at the time the property is set; in particular, the consumer can set this property and then change the command text. However, the provider can fail this property if it is never able to quickly restart the next fetch position. Thus, if a consumer successfully sets this property, it must still check this flag on the rowset to determine if the next fetch position can be quickly set.
DBPROP_REENTRANTEVENTS	TRUE or FALSE indicating whether the provider supports reentrancy during callbacks to the IRowsetNotify interface. The provider might not support reentrancy on all rowset methods. These methods return DB_E_NOTREENTRANT.
	Regardless of this flag, all providers must support IRowset::GetData and IRowset::ReleaseRows calls during notifications, so long as the columns being accessed do not include deferred columns.

Property ID	Description
DBPROP_REMOVEDELETED	TRUE or FALSE indicating whether the provider removes rows it detects as having been deleted from the rowset. That is, fetching a block of rows that formerly included a deleted row does not return a handle to that row.
	Which rows the rowset detects as having been deleted is determined by the DBPROP_OWNUPDATEDELETE and DBPROP_OTHERUPDATEDELETE properties; whether the rowset removes these rows is determined by this property.
	This property is independent of the transaction isolation level. While the transaction isolation level in some cases determines whether the rowset can detect a row as having been deleted, it has no effect on whether or not the rowset removes that row.
	For programmers accustomed to the cursor model in ODBC, the value of this property is always TRUE for rowsets implemented through dynamic cursors; that is, dynamic cursors always remove deleted rows. Whether static and keyset-driven cursors remove deleted rows depends on the value of this property.
DBPROP_REPORTMULTIPLE CHANGES	TRUE or FALSE indicating whether an update or delete can affect multiple rows and the provider can detect that multiple rows have been updated or deleted. This happens when a provider cannot uniquely identify a row. For example, the provider might use the values of all the columns in the row to identify the row; if these columns do not include a unique key, an update or delete might affect more than one row.
DBPROP_RETURNPENDING INSERTS	TRUE or FALSE indicating whether the functions that fetch rows, such as IRowset::GetNextRows, can return pending insert rows; that is, rows that have been inserted in delayed update mode but for which IRowsetUpdate::Update has not yet been called.

Continued

TABLE **C-6 DBPROP_ROWSET PROPERTIES** *(Continued)*

Property ID	Description
DBPROP_ROW_BULKOPS	A bitmask describing optimizations that a provider may take for updates to the rowset. These optimizations are usually used for things like bulk loading of a table. The following values can be specified, and are usually set as OPTIONAL properties because they are hints to the provider. Additional bits may be defined in the future; providers should be prepared to handle new bits in this bitmask by ignoring them if the property is set as optional, or returning an error if the property is set as required.
	DBPROPVAL_BO_NOLOG – The provider is not required to log inserts or changes to the rowset.
	DBPROPVAL_BO_NOINDEXUPDATE – The provider is not required to update indexes based on inserts or changes to the rowset. Any indexes need to be re-created following changes made through the rowset.
	DBPROPVAL_BO_REFINTEGRITY – Referential Integrity constraints do not need to be checked or enforced for changes made through the rowset.
DBPROP_ROWRESTRICT	TRUE or FALSE indicating whether access rights are restricted on a row-by-row basis. If the rowset supports IRowsetChange, IRowsetChange::SetData can be called for some but not all rows if this is set to TRUE. A rowset must never count or return a handle for a row for which the consumer does not have read access rights.
DBPROP_ROWSET_ASYNCH	This contains a bitmask specifying the asynchronous processing performed on the rowset. A combination of zero or more of the following:
	DBPROPVAL_ASNYCH_INITIALIZE: The rowset is initialized asynchronously. The method requesting the rowset returns immediately, but attempting to call any interface other than IConnectionPointContainer to obtain the IID_IDBAsynchNotify connection point may fail and the full set of interfaces may not be available on the rowset until asynchronous initialization has completed.

Property ID	Description
	DBPROPVAL_ASNYCH_SEQUENTIALPOPULATION: The rowset is sequentially asynchronously populated; requests for rows may return DB_S_ENDOFROWSET before the end of the rowset is actually reached. Asynchronously populated rows are always added to the end of the rowset.
	DBPROPVAL_ASNYCH_RANDOMPOPULATION: The rowset is randomly asynchronously populated; requests for rows may return DB_S_ENDOFROWSET before the end of the rowset is actually reached. Asynchronously populated rows may be inserted anywhere in the rowset.
	The consumer may set both DBPROPVAL_ASNYCH_SEQUENTIALPOPULATION and DBPROPVAL_ASNYCH_RANDOMPOPULATION bits to request that the rowset be asynchronously populated either sequentially or randomly. The consumer is prepared for asynchronous notifications in OnRowChange as well as from IDBAsynchStatus. Only one property is returned by the rowset; if the rowset is asynchronously populated it returns either DBPROPVAL_ASNYCH_RANDOM or DBPROPVAL_ASNYCH_SEQUENTIAL.
	If no bits are set (the default) the rowset is initialized and populated synchronously. All requested interfaces are available when the method requesting the rowset returns and requesting rows block until the requested number of *hRows* are obtained or the end of the rowset is reached.
	DBPROPVAL_ASYNCH_BACKGROUNDPOPULATION: The rowset is to be populated asynchronously in the background. The rowset supports IDBAsynchStatus in order to get information about the population of the rowset or abort background population, and may support the connection point for IDBAsynchNotify to give status of the background population. DBPROPVAL_ASYNCH_BACKGROUNDPOPULATION is implied by

Continued

TABLE C-6 DBPROP_ROWSET PROPERTIES *(Continued)*

Property ID	Description
	DBPROPVAL_ASYNCH_SEQUENTIALPOPLUATION and DBPROPVAL_ASYNCH_RANDOMPOPULATION, however, if DBPROPVAL_ASYNCH_SEQUENTIALPOPLUATION or DBPROPVAL_ASYNCH_RANDOMPOPLUATION are not also set, the rowset appears to the consumer as if it were being populated synchronously in that requesting rows will always block until the requested number of hRows are obtained or the end of the rowset is reached.
	DBPROPVAL_ASYNCH_PREPOPULATE: The consumer prefers to optimize for retrieving all data when the rowset is materialized. This is a hint to the provider to fetch all of the data up-front. DBPROPVAL_ASYNCH_PREPOPULATE is only a hint to the provider, the provider should never fail opening the rowset based on the setting of this flag, and need not return it to the consumer, even if the rowset is prepopulated.
	DBPROPVAL_ASYNCH_POPULATEONDEMAND: The consumer prefers to optimize for getting each individual request for data returned as quickly as possible. This is a hint to the provider to populate the rowset as the data is fetched. DBPROPVAL_ASYNCH_POPULATEONDEMAND is only a hint to the provider, the provider should never fail opening the rowset based on the setting of this flag, and need not return it to the consumer, even if the rowset is populated on demand.
	Since DBPROPVAL_ASYNCH_PREPOPULATE and DBPROPVAL_ANSYCH_POPULATEONDEMAND are just hints to the provider, if the consumer sets one or both of these properties in addition to the asychronous population properties DBPROPVAL_ASYNCH_SEQUENTIALPOPULATION or DBPROPVAL_ASYNCH_RANDOMPOPULATION, then

Property ID	Description
	the provider should attempt to populate asynchronously according to DBPROPVAL_ASYNCH_SEQUENTIALPOPULATION and DBPROPVAL_ASYNCH_RANDOMPOPULATION. If the asynchronous population specified by DBPROPVAL_ASYNCH_SEQUENTIALPOPULATION or DBPROPVAL_ASYNCH_RANDOMPOPULATION can not be supported, the provider should fail if DBPROPOPTIONS_REQUIRED was specified for the property, or attempt to populate synchronously according to DBPROPVAL_ASYNCH_PREPOPULATE or DBPROPVAL_ASYNCH_POPULATEONDEMAND if the property was set with DBPROPOPTIONS_OPTIONAL.
DBPROP_ROWTHREADMODEL	This contains a bitmask specifying the threading models supported by the rowset. A combination of one or more of the following: DBPROPVAL_RT_FREETHREAD DBPROPVAL_RT_APTMTTHREAD DBPROPVAL_RT_SINGLETHREAD
DBPROP_SERVERCURSOR	TRUE or FALSE indicating whether the cursor underlying the rowset (if any) must be materialized on the server.
	If the value of this property is not set to TRUE with ICommandProperties::SetProperties, it is up to the provider to decide where to materialize the cursor.
	By checking the value of this property, the consumer can determine where the cursor materialized on the rowset.
DBPROP_SERVERDATAONINSERT	TRUE or FALSE indicating whether the provider retrieves server values for newly inserted rows. At the time an insert is transmitted to the server (when InsertRow is called in immediate mode, or when Update is called for an inserted row in deferred update mode), the provider retrieves data from the server to update the local row cache.

Continued

TABLE **C-6 DBPROP_ROWSET PROPERTIES** *(Continued)*

Property ID	Description
	Consumers should be aware that setting DBPROP_SERVERDATAONINSERT is potentially expensive, and may not be supported for certain types of rowsets.
DBPROP_STRONGIDENTITY	TRUE or FALSE indicating whether the handles of newly inserted rows can be compared as specified by DBPROP_LITERALIDENTITY.
	A newly inserted row is defined as a row for which an insertion has been transmitted to the data source, as opposed to a pending insert row.
DBPROP_TRANSACTEDOBJECT	TRUE or FALSE indicating whether any object created on the specified column is transacted. That is, data made visible to the data source through the object can be committed with ITransaction::Commit or aborted with ITransaction::Abort.
DBPROP_UNIQUEROWS	TRUE or FALSE indicating whether each row is uniquely identified by its column values.
	If this property is set to TRUE when opening the rowset, the provider adds additional columns, if necessary, in order to ensure that each row is uniquely identified by its values. These additional columns appear at the end of the rowset, have a DBID of type DBKIND_GUID_PROPID, DBKIND_PGUID_PROPID, DBKIND_GUID_NAME, or DBKIND_PGUID_NAME, and the guid (or pguid) element is (or points to) DBCOL_SPECIALCOL. These columns are typically not displayed to the user, but are used by components such as update services to uniquely identify a row.
	The provider may, but is not required to, duplicate existing columns in the rowset in order to make sure key columns are included.
	If this property is set to TRUE, and the provider supports the optional IColumnsRowset metadata column DBCOLUMN_KEYCOLUMN, then the set of

Property ID	Description
	columns which uniquely identify the row have a value of TRUE in the DBCOLUMN_KEYCOLUMN column returned by IColumnsRowset. This may be a subset of the columns in the row, or all of the columns if the provider cannot determine a proper subset that uniquely identifies the row. If this property is not TRUE, then DBCOLUMN_KEYCOLUMN may or may not be set to TRUE for key columns, but there is no guarantee that the set of columns that are flagged with this value are sufficient in order to uniquely identify the row.
DBPROP_UPDATABILITY	TThis contains a bitmask specifying the supported methods on IRowsetChange. A combination of zero or more of the following:
	DBPROPVAL_UP_CHANGE—SetData is supported.
	DBPROPVAL_UP_DELETE—DeleteRows is supported.
	DBPROPVAL_UP_INSERT—InsertRow is supported.
	DBPROP_UPDATABILITY should be used in conjunction with DBPROP_IRowsetChange. If DBPROP_IRowsetChange is TRUE and DBPROP_UPDATABILITY is not set, then it is provider-specific what methods are supported on IRowsetChange.
	If DBPROP_UPDATABILITY is specified, then the provider must not support any methods whose bits are not set.

Other Property Sets

Three other property sets may be of use to you:

◆ DBPROPSET_SESSION contains the DBPROP_SESS_AUTOCOMMITISOLEVELS property which contains a bitmask specifying the transaction isolation level while in auto-commit mode. The values that can be set in this bitmask are the same as those that can be set for DBPROP_SUPPORTEDTXNISOLEVELS.

- ◆ DBPROPSET_TABLE contains the DBPROP_TBL_TEMPTABLE that indicates how to handle temporary tables. If DBPROP_TBL_TEMPTABLE is set to TRUE, temporary tables are destroyed when the session is released. If DBPROP_TBL_TEMPTABLE is set to FALSE, temporary tables are created permanently.

- ◆ DBPROPSET_VIEW contains the following properties:

  - ■ DBPROP_IVIEWCHAPTER

  - ■ DBPROP_IVIEWFILTER

  - ■ DBPROP_IVIEWROWSET

  - ■ DBPROP_IVIEWSORT

  - ■ DBPROP_IACCESSOR

  - ■ DBPROP_ICOLUMNSINFO

  - ■ DBPROP_ISUPPORTERRORINFO

- ◆ DBPROPSET_VIEW should be set before creating a view for all methods returning a Rowset or View object.

Appendix D

What's on the CD-ROM?

The CD-ROM that comes with this book contains a searchable, electronic version of this book, along with a number of tools that can help you develop, test, and deploy your applications. Table D-1 describes the tools that you can find on the CD-ROM. Some of these tools have uses beyond strict Visual C++ development.

TABLE D-1 CD-ROM CONTENTS

Item or Package	Description
This Book	The entire text of *OLE DB and ODBC Developer's Guide* is on the CD-ROM in PDF format, which enables you to quickly search through the book's content.
Adobe Acrobat Reader 4.0	This utility from Adobe lets you read and print electronic documents saved as .PDF files. It also enables you to read this book.
Source Code examples, text files, and Access database from the book	Every program in any listing in the book is also on the CD in the folder named "CD Code". (Note that programs are each in their own direc-tory and listed by program name.) Also included is the Microsoft Access database.
WinZip 7.0, shareware version	Veteran Visual C++ programmers know how large compiled code can be, especially when using precompiled header files. This version of WinZip is the ultimate in file compression, and lets you develop with less fear of running out of disk space.
WS_FTP trial version	WS_FTP is a file transfer protocol that you can use to load data from your hard drive to a remote Web server. For those of you who've struggled with Windows FTP program, WS_FTP is a must-have.

Index

Symbols and Numbers

continued

continued

continued

IDG Books Worldwide, Inc.
End-User License Agreement

READ THIS. You should carefully read these terms and conditions before opening the software packet(s) included with this book ("Book"). This is a license agreement ("Agreement") between you and IDG Books Worldwide, Inc. ("IDGB"). By opening the accompanying software packet(s), you acknowledge that you have read and accept the following terms and conditions. If you do not agree and do not want to be bound by such terms and conditions, promptly return the Book and the unopened software packet(s) to the place you obtained them for a full refund.

1. **License Grant**. IDGB grants to you (either an individual or entity) a nonexclusive license to use one copy of the enclosed software program(s) (collectively, the "Software") solely for your own personal or business purposes on a single computer (whether a standard computer or a workstation component of a multiuser network). The Software is in use on a computer when it is loaded into temporary memory (RAM) or installed into permanent memory (hard disk, CD-ROM, or other storage device). IDGB reserves all rights not expressly granted herein.

2. **Ownership**. IDGB is the owner of all right, title, and interest, including copyright, in and to the compilation of the Software recorded on the disk(s) or CD-ROM ("Software Media"). Copyright to the individual programs recorded on the Software Media is owned by the author or other authorized copyright owner of each program. Ownership of the Software and all proprietary rights relating thereto remain with IDGB and its licensers.

3. **Restrictions On Use and Transfer**.

   (a) You may only (i) make one copy of the Software for backup or archival purposes, or (ii) transfer the Software to a single hard disk, provided that you keep the original for backup or archival purposes. You may not (i) rent or lease the Software, (ii) copy or reproduce the Software through a LAN or other network system or through any computer subscriber system or bulletin-board system, or (iii) modify, adapt, or create derivative works based on the Software.

   (b) You may not reverse engineer, decompile, or disassemble the Software. You may transfer the Software and user documentation on a permanent basis, provided that the transferee agrees to accept the terms and conditions of this Agreement and you retain no copies. If the Software is an update or has been updated, any transfer must include the most recent update and all prior versions.

4. **Restrictions on Use of Individual Programs**. You must follow the individual requirements and restrictions detailed for each individual program in Appendix D of this Book. These limitations are also contained in the individual license agreements recorded on the Software Media. These limitations may include a requirement that after using the program for a specified period of time, the user must pay a registration fee or discontinue use. By opening the Software packet(s), you will be agreeing to abide by the licenses and restrictions for these individual programs that are detailed in Appendix D and on the Software Media. None of the material on this Software Media or listed in this Book may ever be redistributed, in original or modified form, for commercial purposes.

5. Limited Warranty.

(a) IDGB warrants that the Software and Software Media are free from defects in materials and workmanship under normal use for a period of sixty (60) days from the date of purchase of this Book. If IDGB receives notification within the warranty period of defects in materials or workmanship, IDGB will replace the defective Software Media.

(b) IDGB AND THE AUTHOR OF THE BOOK DISCLAIM ALL OTHER WARRANTIES, EXPRESS OR IMPLIED, INCLUDING WITHOUT LIMITATION IMPLIED WARRANTIES OF MERCHANTABILITY AND FITNESS FOR A PARTICULAR PURPOSE, WITH RESPECT TO THE SOFTWARE, THE PROGRAMS, THE SOURCE CODE CONTAINED THEREIN, AND/OR THE TECHNIQUES DESCRIBED IN THIS BOOK. IDGB DOES NOT WARRANT THAT THE FUNCTIONS CONTAINED IN THE SOFTWARE WILL MEET YOUR REQUIREMENTS OR THAT THE OPERATION OF THE SOFTWARE WILL BE ERROR FREE.

(c) This limited warranty gives you specific legal rights, and you may have other rights that vary from jurisdiction to jurisdiction.

6. Remedies.

(a) IDGB's entire liability and your exclusive remedy for defects in materials and workmanship shall be limited to replacement of the Software Media, which may be returned to IDGB with a copy of your receipt at the following address: Software Media Fulfillment Department, Attn.: *OLE DB and ODBC Developer's Guide*, IDG Books Worldwide, Inc., 7260 Shadeland Station, Ste. 100, Indianapolis, IN 46256, or call 1-800-762-2974. Please allow three to four weeks for delivery. This Limited Warranty is void if failure of the Software Media has resulted from accident, abuse, or misapplication. Any replacement Software Media will be warranted for the remainder of the original warranty period or thirty (30) days, whichever is longer.

(b) In no event shall IDGB or the author be liable for any damages whatsoever (including without limitation damages for loss of business profits, business interruption, loss of business information, or any other pecuniary loss) arising from the use of or inability to use the Book or the Software, even if IDGB has been advised of the possibility of such damages.

(c) Because some jurisdictions do not allow the exclusion or limitation of liability for consequential or incidental damages, the above limitation or exclusion may not apply to you.

7. U.S. Government Restricted Rights. Use, duplication, or disclosure of the Software by the U.S. Government is subject to restrictions stated in paragraph (c)(1)(ii) of the Rights in Technical Data and Computer Software clause of DFARS 252.227-7013, and in subparagraphs (a) through (d) of the Commercial Computer – Restricted Rights clause at FAR 52.227-19, and in similar clauses in the NASA FAR supplement, when applicable.

8. General. This Agreement constitutes the entire understanding of the parties and revokes and supersedes all prior agreements, oral or written, between them and may not be modified or amended except in a writing signed by both parties hereto that specifically refers to this Agreement. This Agreement shall take precedence over any other documents that may be in conflict herewith. If any one or more provisions contained in this Agreement are held by any court or tribunal to be invalid, illegal, or otherwise unenforceable, each and every other provision shall remain in full force and effect.

my2cents.idgbooks.com

Register This Book — And Win!

Visit **http://my2cents.idgbooks.com** to register this book and we'll automatically enter you in our fantastic monthly prize giveaway. It's also your opportunity to give us feedback: let us know what you thought of this book and how you would like to see other topics covered.

Discover IDG Books Online!

The IDG Books Online Web site is your online resource for tackling technology — at home and at the office. Frequently updated, the IDG Books Online Web site features exclusive software, insider information, online books, and live events!

10 Productive & Career-Enhancing Things You Can Do at www.idgbooks.com

- Nab source code for your own programming projects.

- Download software.

- Read Web exclusives: special articles and book excerpts by IDG Books Worldwide authors.

- Take advantage of resources to help you advance your career as a Novell or Microsoft professional.

- Buy IDG Books Worldwide titles or find a convenient bookstore that carries them.

- Register your book and win a prize.

- Chat live online with authors.

- Sign up for regular e-mail updates about our latest books.

- Suggest a book you'd like to read or write.

- Give us your 2¢ about our books and about our Web site.

You say you're not on the Web yet? It's easy to get started with IDG Books' *Discover the Internet*, available at local retailers everywhere.

CD-ROM Installation Instructions

THE CD-ROM that accompanies this book is divided into several directories that contain source code examples, text files, a Microsoft Access database, a PDF version of this book, and other tools and utilities.

To use the source code examples, simply copy them from the CD-ROM to your hard drive. Note that all CD-ROM files are read-only. When you copy a file from the CD-ROM to your hard drive, it retains its read-only attribute. To change this attribute after copying a file, right-click the filename or icon and select Properties from the shortcut menu. In the Properties dialog box, click the General tab and remove the checkmark from the Read-only checkbox.

Internet Explorer 5.0, Adobe Acrobat Reader (used for viewing the PDF files), WinZip, and WS_FTP each have their own folder with installers and instructions.